Leadville T.

C000108311

History of the Leadville Trail 100 Mile Running Race

Written by
Marge Hickman and Steve Siguaw

Photo Credits

Front Cover –
- Hope Pass looking north toward Twin Lakes in the distance and Turquoise Lake in the far distance; Sarah Hoover

Back Cover –
- Jim Butera; Race photo; provided by Sheila Butera
- Prayer flags on top of Hope Pass; Sarah Hoover
- Background: Sunset looking west from Dominica, Caribbean; Steve Siguaw
- *"Into the mountains I run to lose my mind and find my soul."* by Steve Siguaw

Inside –
- Marge Hickman; Justin Talbot
- Jim Butera; Race photo; provided by Sheila Butera
- Last Ass trophy; David Strong
- Rockport shoes; David Strong
- Leadville Trail 100 course map; Google Maps
- All other photos; Steve Siguaw

Contents

Foreword
By Frank Shorter

In 1987 I leapt at the chance to do the NBC Sports television color commentary for the Leadville Trail 100 Running Race. I wanted to experience this relatively new sport of ultra distance running, literally, out on the racecourse and not from inside a production studio. There were some connections for me: Jim Butera had worked for me at my Cherry Creek, Colorado running specialty store in the early 1980's. Skip Hamilton, an eventual four time winner of the event had been an investor in these same stores, but I had never seen him perform in what turned out to be his true athletic calling. I wanted to gain some insight into the allure that was drawing a special group of superior runners so far beyond the marathon distance.

However, I had one minor personal training problem: the race would take approximately 20-35 hours from mass start to last finisher. How would I get in my daily training of 17-20 miles per day? No days off for me back then. I decided to run parts of the race route and have our camera truck pick me up at certain aid stations along the way. I was most excited and nervous about the chance to run a ten mile leg from the 50 mile half way point back towards the finish up and over 12,600 foot high Hope Pass.

It turned out that at the top of the pass, Skip Hamilton would stop to do an interview with me that was filmed from a helicopter overhead. I ran down the pass with Skip, arrived at the Twin Lakes Aid station and waited for my crew. Skip ran on. A while later, a runner came in, ate, drank and proceeded to fall asleep on a cot. Welcome to ultra running.

As I continued to jump off our truck and run, off and on, over the remaining sixty miles, I would meet up with several of the top runners. A creeping fatigue was obvious in their voices, even though they always seemed to sound aerobic when they talked, no gasping for breath. Then, something happened. I was running side by side and talking with someone who seemed just fine. Suddenly, he stopped talking and I looked back over my shoulder to see him on his knees on the side of the road. I suddenly realized that it takes a special mind set to do this. One's motivation switch can involuntarily turn off in a split second.

I thought of this again at the finish when I realized I had run a total of thirty miles while out on the course. These people were running more than three times that. This modest sum, by comparison, has remained the most I have ever run in a 24-hour period.

Genetics do play a role: Skip Hamilton's son Simi is a three time Olympic cross country skier, but, I also feel these super long endurance events attract a certain mental toughness that is much more essential to success than it is in Olympic endurance events. Ann Trason is both physically and mentally gifted and is simply fun to watch towards the end of a 100-mile race. She has her own brand of "Mental momentum."

And then, there is Matt Carpenter, who still holds the Leadville course record. As a competitor you want to get to the point where your opposition is more focused on you than they are on their own training plans and racing strategies. Matt achieved this in both trail running and ultra distance running.

In my view, the mental predispositions, levels of hard training and willingness to simply find out how high and far you can go have not changed over time, but the talent pool is getting larger and training expertise evolving as more and more athletes from outside the United States travel to the high Rocky Mountains to take part in the Leadville Trail 100 running race.

Of all the endurance sports I have covered for television and attended personally over the years, I have never witnessed a stronger sense of mutual admiration and respect between the male and female athletes. It's called equality. It's no surprise that Marge Hickman and Steve Siguaw have written this historic book. Between them they have run and finished the race 32 times and Marge is a past women's champion of the race.

I encourage the reader to now move along with me through this book into the 21st Century and up to this point in time to appreciate the true history of this race, that is now a tradition.

Foreword
By Marshall Ulrich

In August 1988 I entered the Sixth Street Gym in downtown Leadville, Colorado to attend my first Leadville Trail 100 run pre-race briefing. I sat down, mesmerized by the energy in the room generated by the athletes that had gathered to hear more about what we all signed up for. A rough and tumble gentleman stepped up to the microphone and startled me when he bellowed out, "You're better than you think you are, you can do more than you think you can."

I had just witnessed co-race director Ken Chlouber in all his glory. Standing next to him was Merilee Maupin, who was the quieter co-race director but, I would learn, was always steadfast, focused, and smiling.

I knew very little about running hundred milers, but was ready to create my own story at the race. Little did I know that, over the next twenty years and thirteen finishes, I would learn more about myself not only through my experiences but, more importantly, by acquiring knowledge of the Leadville Trail 100 and listening to the stories of others.

As the miles rolled beneath my feet, I learned about Leadville itself. Each time I visited the city I envision colorful ghosts from the past roaming the streets: Baby Doe Tabor, Doc Holiday, and "The Unsinkable" Molly Brown – as well as numerous miners, gunfighters, businessmen, swindlers, and hearty women – all shaped the city's history.

In 1983 it was Jim Butera's spark of creativity that created the Leadville Trail 100, which would go on to carve its own unique part of the Leadville story. Jim directed the race for two years before Ken and Merilee took over the race and became its heart and soul.

As with most mining towns, Leadville went through boom and bust cycles since the city's founding in 1859 with gold, silver, and molybdenum mining. It was one of these busts, the closing of the molybdenum mine in the early 1980s that inspired Ken and Merilee to use the race to breathe life into the failing economy.

Every runner who has ever toed the line at the Leadville Trail 100 is a part of history, including Marge Hickman, who helped Jim Butera at the 1983 race, was the woman's champion in 1985, and has more finishes (fourteen) than any other woman.

I remember seeing Marge on the trail many times, always smiling and shouting words of encouragement to everyone. Marge remains committed to the race and its colorful history. Impressively she is running again in 2020 at the age of 70; I'm not a bit surprised.

Similarly, Steve Siguaw was at that first race in 1983, as one of the runners, and freely admits that the race transformed and shaped his entire outlook on life. With an astounding eighteen finishes, I believe him. Back when we were both younger and faster, Steve and I would hop scotch, taking turns leading one another while exchanging stories and trail wisdom. I can't say that I got any smarter, but Steve has always had "the smarts" and is the statistician and record keeper for the race.

Stories of some of the runners may have been distorted over the years. Take the Tarahumara Indians, Tom Sobal writes about training with them and offers insights into their psyche, and the 1994 "battle" with Ann Trason. Make no mistake, Ann is no "witch," and her finish time of 18:06, placing her second overall that year, is *still* the women's course record.

Some stories may have been needlessly embellished; something I never understood as, trust me, just finishing a hundred-mile race is an accomplishment that doesn't need to be over hyped.

What's not hype is Matt Carpenter VO_2max of 90.2 (the average for athletes is 60-84), which helped him shatter the previous record by more than ninety minutes when he finished with a time of 15:42:59 in 2005.

It's impossible to overstate the accomplishments of Bill Finkbeiner, who has thirty *consecutive* Leadville Trail 100 finishes, especially since there are only four other men that have finished twenty or more times. Marge's fourteen finishes tops the women, with only two other women having ten or more finishes. They're all extraordinary athletes, but struggle and suffer just like the middle-and-back-of-pack runners.

This book attempts to tell the true stories of the Leadville Trail 100 and its people; stories that don't need to be exaggerated, just told.

The Leadville Trail 100 has grown up and evolved around people who know how to struggle, survive, and persevere; just like the miners and pioneers of the town of Leadville itself.

Every story is a great one. Ready, get set: to read a book that will entertain and astonish, make you gasp and laugh, and may even compel you to cry. The Leadville 100 is a book to inspire, a tribute to those who created and support the race, and all of the athletes who have toed the start line at over 10,000 feet to *Race Across the Sky*.

Preface

"So let me introduce to you, the one and only..."
– The Beatles, Sgt. Pepper's Lonely Hearts Club Band

Jim Butera: The genius, originator and creator of the Leadville Trail 100.

Through the mists of time, true facts can sometimes become distorted or conveniently misconstrued. As Douglas Adams wrote, "It is an important and popular fact that things are not always what they seem." (*Hitch Hikers Guide to the Galaxy*)

"What?"

"But I thought..."

"Well everybody knows that..."

"Jim Butera, who's he?"

As is sometimes the case, there are not many who remember. The most relevant and best example of that expression is the famous and first granddaddy 100-mile ultra race of them all, the Western States 100 Mile Endurance Run.

The race that inspired the Leadville Trail 100, at least in the mind of Jim Butera, was the Western States 100 mile running race. Western States, as it is commonly called, was founded in 1955 as a 100-mile horse race. Yet on July 30, 1972, seven runners, ultrarunners/soldiers crossed that famous finish line in just over forty-four hours to become the first runners to ever finish the Western States 100-mile race.[1]

However, historians of the Western States 100 mile running race seem to have forgotten, or dismissed those first seven runners from race history. Today, the first finisher of Western States is recognized as Gordy Ainsleigh, finishing the race in 1974, fully two years after the first runners lurched across that legendary finish line in Auburn, California.[1]

Facts are facts. Yet sometimes history is "explained" by putting facts aside and using folklore, memory lapses or omissions to remember or exaggerate true origins, as seems to be the case even with the venerable Western States 100 mile running race history.

The first Leadville Trail 100 was conceived, created, managed and executed by Jim Butera.

'So let us introduce to you,
The race you've known for all these years:
The Leadville Trail 100'

(With apologies to The Beatles)

References

Preface:

1   Western States 100 on Foot: The Forgotten First Finishers;
    By Davy Crockett and Phil Lowry; 2018
    (http://www.crockettclan.org/ultras/forgotten-finishers.pdf)

Introduction

Leadville, Colorado; a legendary name that conjures up images of mountain men, prospectors, miners, gunslingers and all sorts of famous (and infamous) people from Doc Holiday, Baby Doe Tabor, Texas Jack Omohundro, Poker Alice, Meyer Guggenheim and even the Unsinkable Molly Brown who are all part of the lore for a city in the clouds built on a mountain of silver at a lofty altitude of 10,152 feet and founded in 1859.

Leadville, the highest incorporated city in the United States, was one of the most lawless towns in the west at one time, but it also had an air of sophistication by inviting opera singers, entertainers and notables such as Oscar Wilde to the famous Tabor-opera house to perform during its heyday in the late 1800's.

Leadville sits astride the majestic Colorado Rocky Mountains, born during two episodes of tectonic activity, when dinosaurs roamed throughout Colorado and North America, making Leadville the epicenter for gold and silver prospectors from around the world during its peak during the 1880's. Dramatic economic booms and busts characterized the small town of Leadville that once boasted a population of over 20,000.

A prospector, Charles Senter, discovered and claimed an outcropping of molybdenite veins in 1879 during the Leadville silver boom. The discovery of molybdenite (moly), a mineral used to strengthen steel, would propel Leadville into the world spotlight, making Leadville the largest supplier of moly in the world during World War II when strengthened steel was a necessary commodity. The first shipments of moly from Climax Molybdenum Mine ("Climax") started in 1915. Climax was the largest supplier of moly in the world for many years, supplying three quarters of the world's moly.

Leadville's *Climax Mine* was the last molybdenum mine to close in 1983. The closure of the mine caused hardships for many and a huge unemployment rate for the town; another of the bust cycles the small town of Leadville continually experienced.

Down the road and at the foot of Hoosier Pass is another boom and bust ghost town named Alma.

Leadville did not want to become another ghost town, as so many similar mining towns had met that dreaded fate. Being a strong, tough and resilient community of miners and strong women, Leadville residents knew they could survive another bust, but how?

This book will describe how one man, Jim Butera, created a spectacular 100-mile trail race in 1983 and saved the town of Leadville from certain economic demise.

Then there is the heart and soul of the Leadville Trail 100; Ken Chlouber and Merilee Maupin who took the reins of the race two years later, molding, shaping and perfecting the Leadville Trail 100 into the iconic and affectionately known *"Race Across The Sky"*[1] that runners aspire to run, race and complete as the epitome of an ultra endurance event.

At the corner of West 6th Street and Harrison Avenue in downtown Leadville, Colorado sits an iconic building. Originally built in 1880, the structure partially burned in 1942 before being removed and replaced in 1955 with what exists today, the Lake County Courthouse marking the finish line for the famous Leadville Trail 100.

In 1983 there were 44 starters compared with over 750 entrants for the race in 2018. The biggest 100-mile race in North America during 2018 was the Leadville Trail 100. Second place was the Javelina 100 in Fountain Hills, AZ and in third place was Western States, followed by the Vermont 100 in fourth place.[2]

That lofty number one ranking for the Leadville Trail 100, the premier 100-mile ultramarathon to test every runner's abilities and absolute personal limits, explains how a race can save a town like Leadville from certain oblivion.

This book contains much more than cold finishing numbers, statistics and VO_2max attributes, although there will be lots of that. Primarily one will read about the runners who made the Leadville Trail 100 what it is today by having contributed stories, recollections and insights drawn from legendary encounters on the high altitude trail.

You will read previously unpublished stories that destroy myths and untruths about Jim Butera who started the Leadville Trail 100, peruse detailed descriptions for every year's race, find out how champions trained and tactics used before and during the race, determine your chances of entering and finishing this grueling event and how the race changed and evolved over the past thirty-seven years, learn how the Tarahumara Indian runners became world famous because of the race, understand Divine Madness Ultra Club (or cult) including their rituals, training methods and tactics, discover race controversies, cheating, how ordinary runners trained and raced among the clouds, high altitude physiology, find detailed course descriptions, absorb how not to be killed during the race, discover untold stories about the Tarahumara, racing with Ann Trason as well as Ann's story of racing the Tarahumara, along with many detailed blood and guts reflections from out on the course.

Advice and stories from Frank Shorter, Ann Trason, Marshall Ulrich, Tom Sobal, the two authors and many others are contained within these pages to appeal to every level of runner from champions to back-of-the-pack runners.

Then there are the remarkable accounts of race creator Jim Butera, who personified the true being of an ultrarunner and whose history is written by those of us who knew him: his friends, competitors, confidants and even Jim's wife Sheila.

Settle down into a comfortable chair while opening your mind to learn how reality and previously untold stories destroy myths and untruths about the Leadville Trail 100, along with thirty-seven years of amazing race history, great antidotes and maybe a twinge or two of nostalgia in reliving glory days from the past.

References

Introduction:

1. The name *"Race Across The Sky"* was first used to help promote and describe the Leadville Trail 100 after Ken and Merilee took over race management in 1985. The affectionate name "Race Across The Sky" denoted only the running race, nothing more. In recent years, that same name was used as the title for a movie about the 2009 Leadville Trail 100 Mile Mountain Bike Race; A novel (fiction) was also published using that same name, written by Derek Sherman in 2013, even though that book was not about the Leadville Trail 100.
2. UIltrarunning Magazine, February 2019

Dedication

Book Dedication

This book is dedicated to those ultrarunners who have run and raced in the Leadville Trail 100. This also includes everyone from weekend warriors, runners of elite status and all the way to professional athletes who call themselves ultrarunners.

The authors wish to recognize those special, unique and forever remembered ultrarunners who have passed and left us with incredible memories, stories, encouragement, inspiration and the desire to keep going forward, to continue reaching our dreams and goals in any and all things we want to accomplish in our lives.

Most importantly, this book is written as a tribute and in recognition of the man with the dream, vision, passion and a love for ultrarunning, Jim Butera, who brought the Leadville Trail 100 to a waiting world in 1983.

We have written this historical and factual book in our own words, from our hearts and depths of our souls to bring truthful memories, stories and recollections to other ultrarunners who have shared many years of camaraderie and friendships that we will always treasure and cherish.

Personal Dedications

Marge's Dedication

Love and gratitude to my husband Michael who has been my crew, pacer and greatest supporter of my ultrarunning. Also to Sheila Butera, my dear and special friend. Stan Arnold, 87, who was my long-time Denver neighbor who I ran with every morning at 4:30 a.m. who passed January 30, 2019.

Sam and Debby Samuelson who were like parents to me, and Sam crewed for me for years as well as during 1989 when I did the Grand Slam. My brother Ed, many ultrarunning friends, personal friends, past and present, who offered support and feedback, giving me valuable insight, advice, stories and encouragement to write this book.

Since I didn't have ultra-friends back when I started running, I had a hard time finding pacers and crew, so I searched in Leadville to find some; anybody. I met Ann Peniston who lived and worked in Leadville in the early 80's (and still lives there today) and who put me in touch with her friend Warren Glick who was a true "mountain man." My first two Leadville 100's in '84 and '85 were paced by Warren, with homemade brownies from Ann who also showed up along the course to crew and cheer me on. In 1985, the year I won, my friends Harold Strong paced me hard on the return over Hope Pass to May Queen and K'Lani Johnson paced me in from May Queen to the finish. Many thanks to Linda Lee, Linda Bolmer, Martha Boon, Melissa Sobal, Michelle Torres and Doug Nash for pacing me and making me laugh, as well as to all who have helped me along the way. An extra special thanks to my long-time friend Steve Siguaw for wanting to be a part of this great journey along with his amazing, exceptional contributions to this effort; a dream come true for us.

Steve's Dedication

For Maria, Zach and my pacers: Maria who is my wife and ever-present crewmember at the Leadville Trail 100. Maria has seen the best of times and the worst of times while helping me at the race, especially at midnight as I struggle to reach the May Queen Aid station at mile 87 in the cold and dark. For Zach, my son and pacer for me at Leadville since he was 7 years old. I could not have been successful at the Leadville Trail 100 without their fantastic help. Then there are the numerous pacers I have had throughout the many years during the race. I sincerely thank them all: Jim Astle, Dr. Ray Blum, Dan Bowers, Debbie Carlson, Tim Carlson, John Crawford, my Divine Madness female pacer (whose name I never got), Pennie Hobert, Christie McGuire, Doug Newton, Kurt Nickels, Jim Singletary, Brendan Slevin, Paul Slevin, Smokin' Joe, Bob Volzer, Jack White and Lori White. Finally, a huge thank you to Marge Hickman for reminding me that running is not all about statistics, split times, VO$_2$max, entry fees and equipment. The personal and "touchy-feely" aspects of the Leadville Trail 100 are just as important, if not more so, when writing a complete history of the race.

About the Authors

Marge Hickman is a Pittsburgh, Pennsylvania native raised in the Penn Hills. I went from a bashful, shy chubby young woman to being the champion of four major 100-mile races and broke course records across the country (Leadville Trail 100, Mohican Trail, Kettle Moraine and Umstead Trail 100).

I am a fourteen-time finisher of the Leadville Trail 100, a four-time big buckle achiever, holding the record for most finishes by a woman and was women's champion in 1985. My personal best finish time is 23:40:44. My ultrarunning dreams and passions were born on August 27, 1983 as I watched the first Leadville Trail 100 unfold while helping director and race creator Jim Butera orchestrate the first grueling event.

Approaching nearly forty years of athletic disappointments and accomplishments, here's some of my notable performances: Class "A" racquetball player, triathlete (winning and being the only woman entered in the Estes Park Alpine Classic Triathlon, 8th overall, 27 starters, 11 finishers; Mt. Elbert Ascent Snowshoe Challenge, 15 miles round trip to summit of Mt. Elbert (14,433 feet), 1st place Master, 6th woman, time of 6:17; multi-time champion marathoner (Boulder, Aspen, Steamboat, Leadville, Crested Butte (twice) and numerous time ultrarunner finisher since 1984; way too many to remember and list them all.

I don't know what might be next on my list of challenges; maybe a mountain biker, skydiving, paddle boarding or something less physically hard like "giving back" to the sport I love. However, I am entered in the 2019 Silver Rush 50 and the Leadville Trail 100...oh my. But I've also been told that, "Women are allowed to change their minds."

Reflecting on and reading over my years of racing resume, here are some of my accomplishments:

- Personal Best Marathon: 2:56 (1984 Olympic trials marathon qualifier, St. Patrick's Day Shamrock Marathon, Virginia Beach, VA)

- <u>Personal Best 50</u>: 7:08 (GNC 50 Mile Challenge, Pittsburgh, PA)
- <u>Personal Best 100</u>: 20:15 (Mohican Trail 100, Loudenville, Ohio)
- <u>Personal Best 24-Hour Track Run</u>: 110.5 miles, 1st woman, 4th overall and course record at The Bowl of Tears 24 Hour Track Run in Denver

Marge Hickman

<u>Course Records</u>:
1984 – 7:10: 1st woman, 4th overall, A.E. Packer 50 Mile Endurance Run, Denver
1985 – 26:57:50 1st place woman, Leadville Trail 100
1995 – 20:15: 1st place woman and 1st Master, 6th overall, Mohican Trail 100

1997 – 22:19: 3rd woman, 11th overall, Arkansas Traveler 100
1998 – 21:12: 1st place woman, 11th overall, Kettle Moraine 100
1998 – 20:10: 2nd place woman, 16th overall, Rocky Raccoon 100
1998 – 20:17: 1st place woman, 7th overall, Umstead 100
1989 – First Colorado woman and one of four women to become the first ever to complete the Grand Slam of Ultrarunning (Western States, Vermont, Leadville and Wasatch). Chosen and named Colorado Sportswoman of the Year in the running category three times and was inducted into the Colorado Hall of Fame. Also, a fourth recognition and win for *Perseverance* running and finishing the Leadville and Fairplay Burro races.

In summary, any ultra that I enter in 2019 and forward, I am probably guaranteed to win or place in my age group because I'm sometimes the only one entered in the "OLD" age group but I still feel so young and frisky.

Steve **Siguaw** is an ultrarunner, sailor and geophysicist who has written for Ultrarunning Magazine, Caribbean Compass Magazine and Colorado Serenity Magazine, having published numerous professional geophysical papers as well. Additionally, Steve is the author of *"Voyage Into Hell",* a book about a deadly Somali pirate attack in the Indian Ocean during Steve's journey around the world with his wife Maria on their sailboat.

Steve ran the inaugural Leadville Trail 100 in 1983 and received his first dreaded DNF (did not finish), a technical term meaning failure to finish, during that race at mile sixty. The Leadville Trail 100 transformed and shaped Steve's entire outlook on life.

Steve is an eighteen-time finisher of the Leadville Trail 100, a seven-time big buckle achiever with a best finishing place of 12th overall and a personal best finish time of 22:41:17. Steve is also the statistician for the race, having kept records and race results beginning with the first year, 1983.

Steve's other running highlights include:
- State of Colorado Master's 100k champion in 1994,
- Multi-day racer as well as finishing the first edition of the 310-mile "Race Across Colorado"

- Woodland Park 12-Hour high altitude track race; two-time champion
- Chatfield 50-Mile Ultra Race; race champion
- Raced numerous international marathons and ultras in Europe, South America and the South Pacific

Steve spends his summers running high altitude mountain trails near his Colorado home. Winters are spent onboard his sailboat named *"Aspen"* with his wife Maria, looking for white sandy beaches and chasing vivid rainbows while running trails on tropical islands scattered across the warm Caribbean Sea.

Steve Siguaw

Part 1

A Legendary 100-Mile Trail Race

"Choose the path with the most heart in order to be at your best."

– Modified from Carlos Castaneda, "The Teachings of Don Juan: A Yaqui Way of Knowledge." Jim Butera's favorite saying.

Chapter 1

Flash of Brilliance

The Leadville Trail 100 began, long ago, during the fall of 1982 in the mind of Jim Butera, an ultrarunner whose roots were firmly planted in Colorado.

Winter in Colorado comes early every year. By late September snow begins to cover the high peaks and trails of nature's majestic Rocky Mountains.

It was September of 1982; Jim Butera was working at Frank Shorter Fitness Wear running store in the heart of Denver at Cherry Creek, an eclectic collection of shops and stores scattered throughout an upscale neighborhood. Frank Shorter Fitness Wear was THE place to find race information and talk running with the great staff, especially since it was only about 10 minutes distance from many offices located in downtown Denver.

Steve's story:
"The first time I met and talked with Jim Butera was during my lunch hour. I remember Jim being very talkative as I perused the latest shoe offerings displayed on one entire wall of Frank Shorter's store. Jim casually walked up and asked me what kind of distances I ran. I proudly said "ultras.""

Jim lamented the fact that there were no 100 mile trail races in Colorado at the time and said he was working on putting something together for the following summer – the summer of 1983.

Jim had already founded and was directing a 50-mile race called the Alfred E. Packer 50. The Alfred E. Packer 50 was already legendary, at least in the Rocky Mountain region. In 1982 the race was ranked as the fifteenth largest Ultra race in the United States.[3]

I ran the Alfred E. Packer that year, on March 28, 1982, and managed to break the much sought-after seven-hour barrier for the first time (6:57:16), grabbing fifth place out of fifty-five finishers. The race was held at Chatfield Reservoir, south of Denver and it was a very windy day, as I recall.

One of Colorado's fastest ultrarunners (if not THE fastest), John Ravling, won the accurate and well run race with a time of 5:43:19, at an altitude of 5,502 feet. John Ravling's effort ranked him at position number twenty in the official U.S. 1982 list for the 50-mile distance.

Also on that prestigious list was an ultra runner named Jim Butera, ranked #376 according to Nick Marshall's "1982 Ultradistance Summary." Coming in at #1083 for the 50-mile distance in 1982 was none other than an ultrarunner named Ken Chlouber.[3]

Since I had only run 50 miles when I first met Jim, a 100-mile race seemed like something from the far reaches of the galaxy to me, I secretly thought to myself. However, I didn't want to seem like a lightweight runner in Jim's eyes; it was a classic ego thing, as most competitive runners are well aware. Remember, 1982 was during the early heady days of ultrarunning with very few 50-mile runners, and even fewer 100-mile ultra distance runners.

Jim was totally non-judgmental when talking about ultrarunning with runners at Frank Shorter's store. Jim said he thought a 100-mile trail race from Aspen, Colorado to Vail, Colorado would be a great race and he was trying to get both towns interested in the idea. Jim also believed during the first year of his proposed race, runners would run from Aspen to Vail. Then the following year the course would be reversed, with athletes racing from Vail to Aspen.

The one-way race sounded so fascinating, appealing and well thought-out, I said to myself when I left the store and back to my job in downtown Denver.

Jim was always an upbeat, jovial ultrarunning ambassador to everyone he met. Before I left the store on that fateful September day, Jim offered me an application for a new group he was forming called the Colorado Ultra Club. The attractive flyer had a logo on the front and an application form inside.

Two weeks after first meeting Jim, I again stopped by Frank Shorter Fitness Wear and luckily Jim was working that day. Jim said he was having a hard time convincing either Aspen or Vail to support, as well as host a 100-mile race between the two towns. Jim was complaining about how aloof and cold the town leaders of Aspen and Vail reacted toward his proposed race."

Aspen had a certain aura about it, a western type flavor that might appeal and attract a larger field of ultrarunners, Jim believed. The problem was that Aspen had become an upscale town, even back in the early 1980's. Gone were the rough and tumble mining town days. Instead, famous musicians, Hollywood movie stars and extreme amounts of wealth had changed the old mining town into an ultimate play area for the wealthy.

Some notable characters living and playing in Aspen during the 1980's included: Glen Frye of the rock group The Eagles, Jimmy Buffett and the gonzo writer Hunter Thompson. Then there were movie stars, trust fund kids as well as jet setters with a lot of money who called Aspen home.

Vail, Jim's other choice for the race, had become well known as an upscale ski area. Yet Vail had also changed from a former mining town because of a famous resident and past United States president, Gerald R. Ford who called Vail his home. Once again, Vail was another forlorn mining town that had grown up and changed dramatically.

It was October 1982 when Jim finally decided on the course for his 100-mile running race. His first choice of Aspen and Vail hosting the race were eliminated. Instead, Jim came up with an alternative venue for his race and it was another historic Colorado mining town. The race would start and end in Leadville, Colorado and it would probably be the most difficult ultrarunning race on the planet.[4]

Once Jim found a home for his race, over eight months of paperwork, organization and physical effort were required before the actual race started at 5:00 am on August 27, 1983. Unlike Western States 100, this race would not have a horse race associated with it.[2]

Jim determined the length the Leadville 100-mile route using a calibrated wheel to accurately measure the running course. GPS didn't exist during these early days so Jim had to physically run and walk the entire course while pushing a bicycle wheel equipped with a counter ahead of him on the trail.

Bouncing the wheel into the air didn't help with accuracy so this was a very time consuming process with reams of paperwork to fill out, ensuring a precise measurement of the course.

Early in the race planning, Jim recognized he needed support from the town of Leadville and Lake County, not to mention the U.S. Forest Service for his race.

He needed aid station volunteers, course marshals, medical staff and police cooperation to put on such a logistical nightmare covering thirty hours of racing on the trails in and around Leadville. Jim also needed physical locations for aid stations all along the course that could be accessed by the runners.

Jim contacted the Lake County Commissioners in Leadville, Colorado. He met with the county commissioners and one commissioner in particular named Ken Chlouber who was also a local miner at the Climax Molybdenum mine, located high atop Fremont Pass at an elevation of 11,318 feet. Ken was an ultrarunner, a burro racer and since he lived and worked near Leadville, familiar with many trails throughout the area.

The town of Leadville was in the midst of a severe depression due to the local mining industry collapse. The main employer, the Climax Molybdenum Mine, had severe layoffs for the majority of the workforce. Many of the former employees from the Climax Mine lived in Leadville. The town of Leadville was suffering and needed more sources of revenue since they lost their main employer. It was hard times back in the 80's, not only in Leadville but also in the state of Colorado and many of the Rocky Mountain States.

The Lake County Commissioners recognized that an endurance race might add much needed income to the local coffers. Jim was directed to meet with the High Altitude Sports Fitness Council who embraced Jim's idea of holding a 100-mile race in Leadville and became a sponsor and part of a legion of volunteers supporting the race.

Fundraising for the event was always at the forefront of Jim's efforts. Nearly every Colorado Ultra Club newsletter asked for volunteers as well as donations to pay expenses for the race.[5,6,7]

Sponsorship for the first Leadville Trail 100 consisted of:
1. Colorado Ultra Club
2. Frank Shorter Fitness Wear
3. Action Sportography
4. Rocky Mountain Road Runners
5. Nike
6. Aspen Home Mortgage

Putting on the Leadville Trail 100 was an enormous undertaking, as Jim described in the October 1983 (Summer Edition) Colorado Ultra Club newsletter:

"I spent every weekend, for the two months leading up to the race in Leadville. After the race I had to send pictures and a story to Ultrarunning within a week. It took me two weeks to recover from that one."[7]

To answer any questions about who was responsible for the first Leadville Trail 100 in 1983, here is the list:

- Jim Butera – Race Director [1,4,7,9,10,11]
- Merilee (Maupin) O'Neal – Operating 'Lady of the Lake' Aid Station[8]
- Ken Chlouber – County of Lake Commissioner; Race entrant[10]

In the midst of winter, 1982-1983, a welcome glimmer of spring arrived in the form of the first Colorado Ultra Club newsletter from Jim on February 14, 1983.[5]

In Colorado, runners constantly dream of long solitary runs in the mountains and this one page missive by Jim buoyed many runner's hopes for an early spring and melting snow on the high mountain trails. The Colorado Ultra Club newsletter that was received from Jim provided some basic tips for long runs over three hours, advice on the best trail packs for running, a club singlet and Jim's experience about finishing a 25-mile run with Kay Moore in the mountains west of Laporte, Colorado.

During the winter of 1982-1983 there were four Colorado Ultra Club meetings. Club officers were elected from those in attendance at the first meeting. Jim Butera was voted president and elected unanimously, of course.

The May 17, 1983 Colorado Ultra Club meeting notes, written by Jim, requested "volunteers for the 100 miler in Leadville" and also a schedule of tough trail runs for Ultra Club members to prepare for the 100 mile race.[6]

Jim Butera was an accomplished ultrarunner. He finished the Western States 100 race four times. His best time would be in 1984 with a time of 22:11 (Sixty-fifth place out of 250 runners).

Jim was always incredibly active creating and founding other ultra races. He established a 24-hour track race in Aurora, Colorado. The first race was held on September 24, 1983 and appropriately named, the "Bowl of Tears." And it was a true bowl of tears, as I (Steve) recall after running eighty-two and a half miles in twenty-four hours, around and around and around a quarter mile oval track with fifteen truly demented ultra runners. Jim's races were epic challenges.

Jim finished his ultimate creation, the Leadville Trail 100 race, one time. It was 1985 when Jim toed that high altitude starting line in Leadville and raced to fifth place overall with a time of 23:38:48.

Jim was also a very good mountain bike racer. He entered and finished the Leadville Trail 100 Mile MTB race the second year it was held, in 1995, and finished with a time of 11:16:09 at the age of forty-seven.

Bull riding was another of Jim's passions. He began riding calves at age 8, before graduating to bulls. He rodeoed for a couple of years before retiring from the circuit at the age of twenty-one.

Never one to let his past life lie dormant, Jim became the 1999 Canadian Senior Pro Finals Rodeo Bull Riding Champion at the age of fifty.[12]

Jim was always seeking another challenge, no matter what the sport may be. As only Jim could say, "As long as there is a course and a clock, I'll continue to compete."

Whatever happened to Jim Butera?

Jim moved to California in search of work during the mid-1980's but still kept his ties to Colorado.

Returning to the Rocky Mountains after retiring from his career with the fire department in San Francisco, CA during 1998, Jim built a house in the mountains near Winter Park, Colorado and married again, this time to Sheila Butera.

Always active in the ultrarunning community, Jim founded yet another trail 24-hour trail race in 2007. The race was held on dirt trails above Boulder, Colorado and was popular among local ultrarunners.

Jim died in Colorado on October 23, 2012 at the age of sixty-four. Jim died not from running, as ultrarunners sometimes expect or hope. Instead, early onset Alzheimer's took a toll on Jim's creative mind and well-being.

Neither of us will ever forget seeing Jim's picture and a much too brief paragraph in the August 2013 issue of Ultrarunning magazine:

"Died. Jim Butera, 64. The Wilds have lost one of their greatest friends. Jim Butera, ultrarunner, bull rider, mountain bike racer, adventurer, father, husband, and devoted friend, died of medical complications in Golden, Colorado."[13]

Jim Butera

References

Chapter 1: Flash of Brilliance

1   The Herald Democrat; 100 Mile Ultra Race Highlights, August 29, 1983

2   Western States 100 on Foot: The Forgotten First Finishers; By Davy Crockett and Phil Lowry; 2018 (http://www.crockettclan.org/ultras/forgotten-finishers.pdf)

3   1982 Ultradistance Summary by Nick Marshall, 1982 U.S. 50-Mile Rankings, page 90.

4   Colorado Sports Monthly. Interview with Jim Butera and article about the first race, written by Steve Voynick, September 1983.

5   Colorado Ultra Club Newsletter, February 14, 1983

6   Colorado Ultra Club Newsletter, Meeting Notes, May 17, 1983

7   Colorado Ultra Club Newsletter, Summer Edition, October 1983

8   The Herald Democrat; Thursday, August 25, 1983

9   Colorado Ultra Club Newsletter; Leadville Trail 100 Report from Cloud City; Race Info Sheet; August 1983

10 Board of County Commissioners, Lake County, Leadville, Colorado; Letter dated May 8, 1984

11 Podcast; Ultra Stories – Season 1 Episode 9: The True Story of How the Leadville 100 Run Was Founded; "Sherpa John Lacroix, January 9, 2018 (http://humanpotentialrunning.com/podcasts/ultra-stories-season-1-episode-9-the-true-story-of-how-the-leadville-100-run-was-founded/)

12 Medicine Hat News, October 18, 1999

13 Ultrarunning Magazine, page 75, by Boisseree, Kirk, August 2013

Chapter 2

And So It Began

Jim Butera was always dreaming about his next adventure. Whether it was running amongst his favorite mountains in Colorado or competing in a 100-mile ultra race in California, Jim was always full of energy and constantly driven for the next great chapter in his life.

Jim's semi-Afro hair and long dark beard suited him well in those early days of ultrarunning in Colorado. Jim looked like a mountain man who could get great things done. With Jim's spark of genius combined with his running endurance a legendary race was born in the Rocky Mountains of Colorado.

At the beginning of August 1983, after most but not all of the snow had melted from his proposed Leadville Trail 100 Mile Race, Jim was high atop Hope Pass wheeling the course for an accurate measurement.

Hope Pass is the epitome of the Leadville Trail 100. High and always windy and wild, Hope Pass is the highest point on Jim's 100-mile course at an altitude of 12,600 feet.

Jim was not going to run the 100-mile Leadville race that first year because directing the race had become his full-time job. Yet Jim wanted the race to be an example of what extreme running events could be like and imitated by those who followed his path.

According to the local Leadville newspaper, by Thursday, August 23, 1983 nearly sixty runners signed up for the first Leadville Trail 100 Mile Race.[1]

The 1983 race packet for the first Leadville Trail 100 consisted of a white envelope with vital information written on the outside: Your name, race number, sex (M or F) and a comment; all hand written by Jim Butera since he was the race director.

The entry fee for the race was $50.00.

Steve's envelope contained this information: #34, M, with Jim's comment, *"I hope you know that you are my Dark horse. Good luck. J"*

Race instructions in the packet were typed on a doubled-sided piece of paper with specific dates, meeting times and most importantly, cut-off times and mile points.[1]

Jim instructions clearly stated, "Important; There will not be anyone allowed to run the race who does not attend ALL of the meetings, NO exceptions."[2]

August 26, 1983,   9 am, Medical check-in at the
                   hospital
                   11:30 am, Trail briefing at the
                   Lake County Gym
                   3:00 pm until 4:00 pm, Supply
                   bag drop

August 27, 1983, 5 am, Start, need I say more

August 28, 1983, 11:00 am, Finish. Must reach finish at the Court
                   House to be eligible for buckle
                   5 pm, Awards and Banquet. Elks
                   Club.

During the medical examination at Lake County Hospital on Friday, the day before the race began, Dr. John Perna the race's chief medical director declared that "someone may die in this race", due to the extreme altitude and course difficulty the runners were facing.[3]

Every individual's weight, pulse and blood pressure was taken at the medical check. These values along with the runner's name and race number were hand written on a plastic band that was placed around each runner's wrist. This was the runner's official race band.

A few runners even gave a sample of their blood to help with a research study about running at altitude. Great, I thought to myself, who would give up their much-needed blood at a high altitude race for an experimental study? Geeze.

The results of the blood study were never published, as far as we know.

Following the medical exam there was a course briefing at the Lake County gym.

Jim went over what would be at the various aid stations in terms of food and drink. He explained the medical checks and that we needed to listen to any instructions the medical people gave us.

Jim concisely described the course over the first 50 miles. Then he explained once we arrived at Winfield to, "just turn around and run the same route back to town."

The pre-race briefing was a pretty low-key event, without fanfare, but with a lot of nervous runners eyeing each other.

Twelve hours later, ultrarunning history would be made as a rifle was pointed into the sky.

Original Leadville Trail 100 Race Route

37

References

Chapter 2: And So It Began

1 The Herald Democrat; Thursday, August 25, 1983
2 Colorado Ultra Club Newsletter; Leadville Trail 100 Report
   from Cloud City; Race Info Sheet; August 1983
3 Friday, August 26,1983. Dr. John Perna during the medical
   examination at Lake County Hospital.

Chapter 3

First Leadville Trail 100 Mile Running Race (by Steve)

The majestic Rocky Mountain night sky was ablaze with starlight when a local fur-clad mountain man raised a black powder rifle to his shoulder at the corner of Sixth and Harrison Avenue in downtown Leadville, Colorado.[2] Forty-four runners toed the starting line for the first Leadville Trail 100.[8]

A deafening blast tore through the historic mining streets and over the heads of the assembled runners, sending them into the nighttime shadows. It was 5:00 am on Saturday, August 27th, 1983 when the first Leadville Trail 100 mile trail race began.

The assembled groups of family and a few friends, maybe a total of thirty people, cheered loudly in the cold and crisp early morning air. The neon sign along Leadville's main street constantly flashed the number 37° to the departing runners, giving a subtle reminder of hardships that lay ahead on the trails.

As the noise from the rifle blast reverberated on the distant peaks before slowly fading away, runners ran together like a slow moving stream, away from city lights and toward dark and silent mountains looming in the distance.

Barely 100 yards away from the starting line, every runner was silent. Only the sound of quick soft footsteps could be heard as darkness engulfed a moving wave of runners. The enormity of what lay ahead weighed heavily on everyone's mind – 100 miles of high altitude and rocky trails were to be run before anyone hoped to see the finish line.

Only smart and more experienced 100-mile runners started out slowly, while other highly trained marathon and fifty-mile runners with no extreme long distance racing experience went out fast. Too fast, they would realize later.

Those participating in the first race included these runners:

- Skip Hamilton – Aspen, Colorado; exercise physiologist and member of the U.S. Cross-Country Ski Team. [6,7]
- Don Starbuck – Pine, Colorado; geophysicist and ultrarunner
- Andy Lapkass – Denver, Colorado; student, mountaineer and marathon runner
- John Lapkass – Denver, Colorado; ultrarunner
- Reb Wickersham – Woodland Park, Colorado; ultrarunner and former stock car race champion
- Brent Weigner – Cheyenne, Wyoming; ultrarunner and founder/race director of the Rocky Mountain 50 Mile Run
- Cliff Davies – Ontario, Canada; ultrarunner and mountain climber
- Arthur Schwartz – Aspen, Colorado; physician and ultrarunner
- Harry Dupree – Enid, Oklahoma; banker and ultrarunner
- Al Binder – Evergreen, Colorado; accountant and ultrarunner
- Ken Chlouber – Leadville, Colorado; miner, County Commissioner, burro racer and ultrarunner
- O.R. Peterson – Vail, Colorado; ultrarunner
- Gary Cross – Boulder, Colorado; youngest entrant at age 22, ultrarunner
- Barry Mink – Aspen, Colorado; physician and ultrarunner
- Dick Webster – Leadville, Colorado; physician and ultrarunner
- Benston Strider – Chicago, Illinois; ultrarunner
- Mark Lisak – Cheyenne, Wyoming; law enforcement and ultrarunner
- Rolly Portelance – Canadian; ultrarunner
- Steve Siguaw – Conifer, Colorado; geophysicist and ultrarunner
- Carol LaPlant – Berkley, California; attorney, champion ultrarunner, only female entrant

Jim Butera was not an entrant in the race. Jim said directing the race was a full-time job and did not want anything to go wrong. Jim wanted to ensure the Leadville race was successful and become an enduring annual event.

The first hill of the race comes quickly, at only a quarter mile from the start. 10,200 feet of altitude at Leadville is felt immediately with the faster runners sucking rarified air into their lungs as if they were in a full sprint.

It was too early to go into oxygen deprivation but that is exactly what runners were doing with the fast pace. Common sense is not something many runners are blessed with. Instead, half the field of racers ran as if high altitude and lack of oxygen didn't exist.

It might have been black spots dancing before our eyes before many runners realized the initial quickness wasn't really a good idea at only mile one into a 100-mile race.

At the one-mile mark, during this first race, runners passed by an eerie sight on the left side of the paved road out of town.

Leadville's cemetery and graveyard markers seemed to beckon us in, to relax and rest for a while. Now that was an eerie image, to say the least, especially with black spots clouding our vision as we ran by.

The initial Leadville Trail 100 race route was markedly different from what runners see today. The race starting line has not changed; it is still at 6th and Harrison Street in the center of town, right next to Leadville's County Court House.

In 1983, as now, runners run down 6th Street, up the first oxygen sucking hill and then cruise on a slight downhill to the end of the road.

That first year we turned right at the end of the road, instead of left (as the current route does), and proceeded down the paved road all the way to Turquoise Lake.

Arriving at Turquoise Lake we made a right turn, still on pavement, running further on the paved road and toward Lady of the Lake Campground.

In this first race, Jim gave little in the way of directions or rules for race crews. Common sense determined where a racer's crew would stop along the route.

My crew consisted of Maria, my wife, who drove to our pre-arranged stopping points along the route to give me water and ERG [9] (developed by Bill Gookin; Electrolyte replacement with glucose) or anything else she might have for me if I asked. Obviously if she was not able to drive to an aid station she didn't meet me. I was on my own between aid stations.

Lady of the Lake Campground on Turquoise Lake was the first official aid station, eight miles into the race. I remember the aid station being dimly lit and very cold as our first stop near Turquoise Lake. A handful of hardy volunteers handed out water, ERG and a few snacks to runners (pretzels, bananas, orange slices and saltine crackers). Support crews gathered at Lady of the Lake aid station to further assist, encourage and provide hope for their runner.

At Lady of the Lake aid station, race times for each runner were written and broadcast via citizen band radio (CB) to race headquarters in the Lake County Courthouse in downtown Leadville, Colorado.

Communications were a big problem during the race, as they still are today, even with cell phones. One week before this first race, the Leadville CB Club disbanded causing huge problems for race communications. Luckily, the Climax Mine and U.S. Forest Service stepped up and furnished radios to various aid stations. There would also be telephones available at the Inn of the Black Wolf in Twin Lakes, Fish Hatchery and a local garage that would be used for calling into race headquarters with race reports.[3]

Pat Butera, Jim Butera's wife at the time, established and set up race headquarters in the Lake County Courthouse. Pat stayed awake the entire race, taking care of communications, answering telephones and keeping a record of every runner and the runner's position along the course. Pat remained on duty the entire race, well over thirty hours, maintaining and receiving essential and crucial racer information.[4]

My running split at Lady of the Lake aid station was 2:22 elapsed time and I was in eighteenth place overall. That equates to running 10:15 minutes per mile this early in the race. Compare that with the two leaders, Don Starbuck and Skip Hamilton who both had 1:59 minute running splits to this same point, running at 9:20 minutes per mile.

No one spent much time at Lady of the Lake aid station. After all, we were still in race mode and everyone wanted to get moving, fast. Runners quickly exited the aid station, continuing to Lady of the Lake picnic area and then Tabor Boat Ramp, just a quarter mile ahead – adjacent to a dirt trail around Turquoise Lake.

Some runners started the race with lightweight running jackets because of the cool temperatures in the pre-dawn morning. Running tights were rare in these early ultra days. Instead runners only wore nylon running pants if it was really cold but we certainly didn't need pants this day since it was a balmy 37 degrees at Turquoise Lake.

Since the majority of the runners who entered this first 100-mile race at Leadville were marathon and fifty-mile runners, everyone simply ran in running shorts and long sleeve t-shirts while only a few runners wore an additional nylon windbreaker against the chilly pre-dawn rarified air.

Regarding race packs; nearly all runners wore a waist pack to carry water bottles, extra clothes and snacks. My pack weighed eight pounds. The heavy pack helped at medical checkpoints by providing additional weight while standing on the scale. Volunteers doing medical check sometimes forgot to ask runners to remove their packs, luckily.

From Lady of the Lake aid station runners ran on the rocky Turquoise Lake Trail along the water's edge for five miles to May Queen Campground at the far end of Turquoise Lake.

There was no May Queen aid station during this inaugural race. Who needed another aid station since we had just passed through an aid station at eight miles, or so Jim thought?

The next aid station was located at mile twenty-one, about three more hours of running, up and over 11,200-foot Sugarloaf Pass to get there. It all seemed entirely normal for us at this time.

Running through May Queen Campground there was a water faucet near the Campground restroom, if one needed water before heading up Sugarloaf Pass trail and to the infamous Power Line Trail.

Out of May Queen Campground, a short half-mile stretch of the main Turquoise Lake paved road led runners to another rocky trail in the forest, if you could find the correct route.

After crossing a raging stream, there were three trails to choose from and only a few of the leading runners knew which was the correct route over Sugarloaf Pass.

It seems some nasty people removed Jim's race markings prior to the race. Myself and five other runners chose a right fork toward a better defined trail and ran for three to four minutes before hearing shouts from another group of runners, also searching for the correct trail. The other group of runners found race markings on their trail.

My group of six runners backtracked to the correct trail and ran off in pursuit of other racers ahead, already on their way to the Hagerman Pass dirt road.

Once on the correct route this two-mile stretch of trail is flat to downhill until it crosses a bridge. Over the bridge, the trail relentlessly climbs upward until coming to an abrupt end at the Hagerman Pass gravel road. This one-mile climb toward Hagerman Pass road enables a runner to achieve their maximum heart rate once they crest the final stretch of trail and onto a dirt road.

We crossed the gravel road onto what is now the Colorado Trail. A new day's dawn broke around us, revealing Turquoise Lake far below as runners ran steadily and quietly while admiring expansive mountain vistas in the distance.

The climb to Sugarloaf Pass was steep and unrelenting, with tiny frigid snowmelt streams crossing our path. Most runners unwittingly ran this part of the trail to the top of Sugarloaf Pass. After all, this was a race so why walk? That racing attitude would ultimately haunt many runners later during the race.

The Colorado Trail crosses a rutted and rough jeep road at the top of Sugarloaf Pass. Runners crested the Colorado Trail and turned left onto this jeep road/Power Line Trail. The top of Sugarloaf Pass is easily identified by tall, massive, buzzing power lines stretching into the distance, east and west.

At the top of Sugarloaf Pass it was surreal hearing and even smelling electricity zapping along these giant power lines, as we ran under them. The trail suddenly became easy and flat, leading in the direction toward a rising sun.

Very few runners in the race had run the course before race day. Most runners had no idea what lay ahead or what was around the next corner.

In the case of Sugarloaf Pass, a mere quarter of a mile over the pass and runners were flying forever downward, reaching normal 10K race pace as the trail teased us to try and outrace each other. It was just another costly mistake in a 100-mile race.

Lower sections of the Power Line Trail became unbelievably steep and rutted. This was mining territory and only a Caterpillar D-4 machine was expected to be on this thing called a trail.

Most runners negotiated deep ruts, loose rocks and gravel along the power lines without injury before tearing down the lowest part of the trail and onto a section of pavement leading toward Fish Hatchery aid station and medical check a mere two miles away.

Asphalt was our friend when we got off the Power Line Trail. Everyone's legs needed a break from the rocky and rutted trail.

Once onto pavement there were three or four people waiting to cheer runners on their way. This was welcome encouragement after spending nearly three hours alone with nature.

It was still early in the race at 10:00 am when our ragged little group of runners reached Fish Hatchery aid station and medical check. The aid station was located at Leadville National Fish Hatchery, part of the U.S. Fish and Wildlife Service. The fragrance of fish was very obvious as runners made their way toward waiting volunteers.

Weight scales were set up to evaluate each runner. Runners were quickly weighed, our race wristbands checked for critical information like weight, race number and name before the friendly medical staff sent us on our way to the food table.

Food table? What a concept, I thought to myself.

I expected the aid station at Fish Hatchery to be like the one at Lady of the Lake where we were offered drinks and light snacks but little else. Well, I was mistaken.

Jim Butera had experience running the Western States 100 mile race so he knew how to keep ultra runners happy and full of energy.

At Fish Hatchery aid station there were several long tables filled with pretzels, bananas, oranges, apples, saltine crackers, Graham crackers, candy bars, M&M's, fudge sticks, bread and jelly sandwiches, peanut butter sandwiches, chicken noodle soup, chicken sandwiches and even lunch meat sandwiches. Drinks were water, coke (fizzed and de-fizzed), Kool Aid (grape and cherry) and ERG, of course. It was a feast for the senses and our slightly tired bodies.

Aid station volunteers could not do enough for the runners. They were enthusiastic, supportive and just fun to be around as new friends scurried to fetch whatever we wanted from expansive tables of food and drink. Without aid station support and volunteers, the race would not be the same, as all runners are well aware.

Remember, Fish Hatchery aid station was only at mile twenty-one and we had a long way to go before seeing the finish line. The leader at this point was Skip Hamilton with a split time of 3:12 and three minutes ahead of second place Don Starbuck. Third place was already twenty-five minutes behind the leader Skip Hamilton. My running split was 4:21 elapsed time and I was in twenty-second place, having lost four places between Lady of the Lake aid station and Fish Hatchery aid station.

Halfmoon aid station was seven miles down a long dusty washboard dirt road from Fish Hatchery. The first mile out of Fish Hatchery is on pavement before turning right onto that nasty road. Cars and trucks passed runners, throwing clouds of dust into the sky and threatening to choke out whatever air was left in our straining lungs.

Seeing crew vehicles parked on the dirt road gave everyone an indication of which runner was behind you (if you recognized the vehicle) or maybe even seeing a runner stopping to get aid from their support vehicle. These observations made for a competitive mindset, at least for a brief time, while trying to stay ahead of a runner behind you or pass one stopped on the side of the road.

Skip Hamilton was still leading the race by three minutes over Don Starbuck at the Halfmoon aid station. Skip's split at Halfmoon was 4:08. My running split at Halfmoon aid station was 5:43 in twentieth place overall.

Once past Halfmoon aid station we found great trail running again. The next trail section began just two miles past the aid station. This section of trail is the main route to climb Mount Elbert, the highest 14,000-foot peak in Colorado at 14,433 feet and a very popular hiking trail. Day hikers gave us the right of way as we ran past, encouraging us and wishing us well on our long journey.

The racecourse diverged from the Mount Elbert trail after thirty minutes of strenuous uphill running. It was warm and sunny at this point and the race seemed to have taken on a life of its own for all runners. No racer had dropped out of the race, yet. There were still forty-four runners somewhere in the vastness of Colorado's majestic mountain peaks.

Once the racecourse split from the Mount Elbert hiking trail, stretches of old logging roads thick with mud and elk prints challenged runners. Willows, creek crossings and even broad meadows added to the beauty of the course. If only we could appreciate our surroundings as we tried to conserve energy and strength in our legs.

It drizzled lightly on this section of the course but the moisture was not significant enough to cause any problems.

Toward the end of this trail, significant large beaver ponds were skirted before crossing a large stream adjacent to a parking area at the end of a dirt road. The parking area was built at the south end of the Mount Elbert hiking trail.

Luckily Jim's trail markings were still in place, directing runners to take a faded trail on the side of the dirt road. After a hundred yards and clear of the hiker's parking area, this trail suddenly became very well defined.

Even luckier for runners, this trail was mostly downhill with only occasional rolling ups and downs, all the way to Twin Lakes where the next aid station and medical checkpoint were waiting.

Once again, competitiveness took hold with runners running at 10K race pace, flying around bends in the trail while grabbing an occasional aspen tree to avoid careening off the trail.

At the end of this section of trail we crested a short hill, adjacent to an open gate. Fifty feet below and down a scrub covered hill (with no discernable path) was the Twin Lakes Fire Station – our destination at the Twin Lakes Aid Station and medical checkpoint.

It was warm by Leadville standards now, probably 68-degrees at this lower altitude of 9,200 feet. All runners were dreading the weight scale at this point of the race.

Maria met me before I went inside the tall Fire Station doors and handed me two full water bottles. I immediately put the bottles into my pack before stepping up and onto the scale.

The medical volunteer adjusted manual weights on the scale, looked at my race wristband and proclaimed I had lost ONE pound.

Then the volunteer smiled and asked me a question, "What is your name?"

Ok, I've just run thirty-seven miles, in the wilderness, with only nature, footprints of elk, bear scat and an occasional deer to keep me company. I've not seen another runner for quite a while, I'm hungry, dehydrated, tired, my legs are screaming with pain, the room is appearing hazy from my brain's lack of oxygen and I had to grab the front of the scale to maintain my balance. "What is my name?" I asked in surprise.

Suddenly my eyes opened wide as I immediately focused, knowing this was a trick question. I slurred the words, "Steve Siguaw."

There was a pause as the medical person looked at my wristband again. The next words out of the volunteer's mouth were, "Thanks. You can continue your race."

Three runners dropped out at Twin Lakes. One or two other runners were told to hydrate before continuing. I guess I was one of the lucky ones, with thoughts of running up Hope Pass as my reward for passing the physical.

The leader was still Skip Hamilton with a split of 5:30 elapsed time at Twin Lakes. Don Starbuck was hanging on to second place but losing ground to Skip by twenty minutes. My split time at the Twin Lakes aid station was 7:46, good enough to be in fifteenth place now. I was passing a few runners and that was surprising to me.

Maria, my crew, was standing beside me when I was on the scale for the medical check. As I walked out of the aid station area, she wished me good luck running to Parry Peak Campground, three miles west along the main road to Aspen. She warned me there was a lot of traffic on the road and to be careful.

Running uphill on the shoulder of the black asphalt pavement to Parry Peak Campground, cars, trucks and motorcycles whizzed by in their excitement to get over Independence Pass and find the affluent town of Aspen.

There were two runners ahead of me on the road and another three behind me. Everyone's pace was markedly slower than I would have thought, even my own pace. With the relatively easy uphill grade, no one seemed to be catching anyone.

It was a long forty minutes of slow running to Parry Peak Campground. Maria met me near the Campground entrance where she would have refilled my water bottles except I hadn't drunk anything yet, since leaving Twin Lakes. I was suffering now, with water and ERG being the furthest things from my thoughts.

Maria said she would see me at Winfield and left me alone with my race.

The racecourse went entirely through Parry Peak Campground before passing a closed steel gate arm.

Once around the gate it was a short downhill run on a jeep trail, high above raging Lake Creek. The deafening sound of whitewater thirty feet below drowned out any thoughts or possible conversation with two runners directly ahead of me.

Within a quarter of a mile there were more markings indicating the start of a trail section taking us away from thundering Lake Creek and through a small beaver pond before going around a very large beaver pond. Once past the large pond our trail climbed a steep rock section, steep enough that everyone hung onto trees for support.

Once on top of the nearly vertical section of rock, the trail rolled back east, toward Twin Lakes with extremely runnable but challenging trail sections due to bare granite rock surfaces in many places.

Quickly descending from the rolling smooth granite, the trail became flat as runners traversed beautiful flower strewn meadows with piles of bear scat and scared trees showing us the way forward.

Luckily there were no bears. Instead, two runners ahead of me, Brent Weigner and Mark Lisak, both from Wyoming, yelled *SNAKE* as they ran rather quickly across a dry creek bed.

By the time I got to the dry creek the snake was gone, or at least I didn't notice it.

Several creek beds on this trail section were filled with water, so primitive log bridges were used to cross them.

I rushed toward a final deep creek bed, flowing silently with icy water and negotiated a slippery log bridge to the other side. In front of me were more ribbons marking a quick right turn onto the long and steep trail up to Hope Pass at 12,600 feet.

This is an aside about crossing those slippery log bridges as well as stream crossings in general during the race. In these early ultrarunning days there were no hiking poles (or running poles or whatever you want to call them). We never thought about anything like that to help us since we were runners and didn't carry anything that would slow us down. Besides, poles are not running equipment.

Now for the first controversy during the race; during the 1983 Leadville Trail 100 a runner named Bentson Strider decided to run with a long stick he found along the trail while climbing toward Sugarloaf Pass. It seemed Strider used such a stick previously during other long running races.

Jim Butera saw Strider using his newfound stick during this early part of the race and emphatically talked to Strider about NOT using the stick as an aid. Jim didn't want anyone in his race using a stick because of safety concerns for other runners on the narrow steep trails.

Jim repeatedly admonished Strider about carrying his stick whenever he saw Strider on the course, but Strider continued to disregard Jim's instructions.

Jim was so upset with Strider carrying his stick that Jim threatened to disqualify Strider from the race when he saw him again with his stick at Twin Lakes aid station, mile sixty-three.

Lucky for Jim, Strider eventually missed the time cutoff at Halfmoon aid station coming back towards Leadville at mile seventy-two so Jim didn't have to disqualify Strider from his race for using a stick.

Because of Strider, in subsequent Leadville Trail 100 years, race instructions specifically forbid walking sticks, hiking poles, etc. during the race because of safety concerns for other runners.

However, use of hiking poles was eventually officially allowed in the race beginning in 1995, even though many runners disapproved changing the rule to allow them.

But that was not the end of the Strider story, as you will read later in this chapter.

Ribbons that marked the start of the steep climb to the top of Hope Pass remained in place during the race because very few people used the Hope Pass trail during these early years. That was very lucky for the runners.

The trail up to Hope Pass is an unrelenting brutally steep climb. Stream crossings, wet marsh areas, abandoned old mining cabins and even a grave marked with a weathered wooden cross were just some of the challenges and sights before reaching timberline at 11,500 feet.

There are only two places to get lost on this section of the course as we ran the trail below Hope Pass. But if common sense was used and Jim's ribbons were still in place, it was easy to negotiate the correct route, at least in daylight.

Timberline is easily recognized, not only because trees are basically missing but also because views of Hope Pass and adjacent 13,000-foot Mount Hope pop into view, both rising high above a majestic open alpine meadow.

One runner, Reb Wickersham (Reb or "The Rebel" as he was famously known), said his legs were so painful when he reached the meadow he decided to sit in a cold snow-fed stream to refresh himself. Reb didn't finish the race that first year.

Another runner on his initial approach to Hope Pass became hypothermic and had to turn around before the top of the pass and slowly make his way back to Parry Peak and warmer temperatures.

The trail crossed a high alpine meadow (where the Hopeless Aid Station would eventually be established in future editions of the race) onto tundra where the real climb up to Hope Pass began.

Sloping, slippery rocky scree, late season snowfields and a primitive deeply rutted trail from melting snow led runners into the thinnest air of the race.

There was no running now. Runners had managed a very slow walk/run up to tree line (Timberline) during the race. It was still a race to most entrants. But once runners traversed the alpine meadow it was impossible to run, let alone walk for that matter.

It was on this steepest part of the climb toward Hope Pass when Steve saw the race leader, Skip Hamilton, running toward him. Skip was running down from his second crossing of Hope Pass.

I greeted Skip with the usual "way to go" and "you're looking good" comments a lot of runners use with each other. I had no idea what Skip said to me as we passed. My only focus was getting to the top of Hope Pass, off the mountain and running to the next aid station and check point of Winfield at fifty miles.

Rarified air along with a steep, rocky and difficult trail took a mighty toll on every runner's pace.

It took me two and a half hours to climb from the base of the Hope Pass trail to the top of Hope Pass this race day. My mind and body were battered when I saw a final wooden stick marking the pinnacle for the pass at 12,600 feet.

There was no time to rest at the top of Hope Pass. Crucial minutes had been wasted during the climb and Jim's race cut-off times were very real and threatening at this point in the race.

Reaching the top of Hope Pass, I tried coaxing my aching legs to function in running mode again, something that was not easy at first. I sipped water and drank ERG, hoping that would help my running pace to quicken. Drinking must have worked because I found running was faster down Hope Pass except for rocky scree sections littering the trail.

The south side of Hope Pass had a trail but it was indistinct in many places. This was the 1980's and not many hikers ventured far off main trails in the Colorado Rockies. Yet there was the semblance of a trail, washed out or covered with scree in many places, but still a recognizable trail.

Once timberline was reached on the south side of Hope Pass, the trail became well established and easy to follow. Just keep running downhill, I told myself. Views of the beckoning pine tree covered valley far below were simply incredible and yet so far away.

After nearly an hour of painful running I reached the bottom of the Hope Pass trail and onto a dirt road leading to the ghost town of Winfield, half way point and 50-mile turn around for the race at an elevation of 10,200 feet. Only a little over two miles to go, I thought to myself. Then there will be Maria, friends and an aid station for comfort and much needed mental and physical support.

Winfield, an abandoned ghost town that once was a thriving mining town with a population of 1,500 in 1881, lay deep in the Sawatch Range of the Colorado Rockies. At its prime, Winfield featured three saloons, a post office, two hotels, a mill, church and school. Yet today Winfield signified the turnaround for a 100-mile trail race that I was desperately trying to finish.

Slowly walking up the remaining relentless, dirty, dusty and rough road into Winfield, I first saw smoke from the aid station's cooking fires in the distance.

My running was gone as I was forced to walk towards drifting smoke. Large canvas medical tents appeared, strung and tied together while merged into a single tiny canvas town. I had finally arrived at Winfield.

Maria rushed up to me and said I was running slow and needed to pick up the pace on the way back.

"On the way back?" I thought to myself. "Back over that monster of a mountain?" "Back into a cold and approaching darkness that is waiting out there on the trail?"

Those scary thoughts raced through my mind as Maria led me to the dreaded medical scales.

I grasped the scale again, steadying myself, while trying to stand upright to be weighed by friendly medical people. Dr. Perna, the medical director was there, along with a nurse and other volunteers.

I remember somebody saying my weight was 139 pounds, pulse was 98 and blood pressure was 128/98. I must have passed the physical since no one told me the race was finished, at least at this point. Yes, they asked my name again and for some odd reason that was easy to remember this time.

Maria led me to a cold gray metal folding chair where I sat down for the first time in 50-miles of running. My brother-in-law, Jim, and two friends from work had come up to witness the race spectacle and cheer me on.

Unbeknownst to me, all my friends including my brother-in-law told Maria not to say anything negative as I sat in the chair eating. Everyone was telling me how great I was doing in the race.

I thought it rather odd that Maria had very little to say as I was given a banana, hot soup and a bread and jelly sandwich while trying to regain my strength at the aid station.

My total time refueling at the Winfield aid station was less than twenty minutes before Maria said it was time for me to leave.

Twelve runners dropped out of the race at the Winfield 50-mile turnaround, including Don Starbuck, one of the early leaders during the race. Now there were only twenty-nine runners remaining in the race with Skip Hamilton having an insurmountable lead over any other runner.

Skip Hamilton's elapsed time at Winfield was 8:26 at the 50-mile point. Compare that time with my running split at Winfield of 12:54, good enough for me to be in thirteenth place overall.

Leaving the Winfield aid station was not dramatic or agonizing. My crew was cheering me onward so I just kind of walked away and began jogging down the two-mile dirt road back to the Hope Pass trailhead.

It was 6:00 pm now and I had beaten the Winfield cutoff by over an hour. In the back of my fuzzy mind I knew it would be dark somewhere near the top of Hope Pass. Luckily Maria had put a flashlight in my waist pack.

Most runners carried flashlights during the race instead of using headlamps. A hand-held light was much more common in these early days at Leadville because they were far more reliable and convenient.

Maria drove past me as I slowly ran on the long dusty road to the trailhead. She rolled her window down and yelled at me to pick up the pace. Maria is always encouraging during rough patches, I remember thinking.

I ran the entire way to the Hope Pass trailhead, thanks to Maria's advice, before starting my desperate grind up toward Hope Pass again.

Halfway up the trail to Hope Pass my stomach began cramping and wouldn't quit hurting. I drank water and ERG during the climb but nothing seemed to help calm my pain.

Catching Bentson Strider going up the climb was very uplifting for my spirits. I had actually passed a runner at this stage of the race. But Strider soon passed me back, before the top of the pass.

The upper Hope Pass switchbacks along with the talus slopes were taking their toll on every runner's weary legs. Being alone at this stage of the race didn't help a positive mental attitude either.

It was 8:00 pm when I reached the top of Hope Pass and it was dark. Jim Butera had scheduled the race around a time of a full moon but there was no sign of a moon just yet. Nothing lit up the path and darkness engulfed everything, including all signs of a trail.

I retrieved my flashlight from the pack and its blaze of light was heart-warming. Running and stumbling down the rocky and rutted trail from the pass to the broad meadow below was very tricky at night. Any fall would have been painful or worse, so I ran slowly and stayed focused.

The alpine meadow that was so beautiful on the initial first approach to Hope Pass during daylight was now completely changed. The marshy area seemed larger than before but more importantly there was no trail to be seen in the night.

Shining my light into the darkness I found it impossible to find any trace of a trail. There were no ribbons, markings or dirt patches indicating where I should run. Frigid air from the surrounding high peaks began funneling down the valley, through the meadow and toward Twin Lakes, causing temperatures to drop dramatically.

I put on every piece of clothing from my pack and was still uncomfortable and shivering. Mostly I was irritated and frustrated not being able to find any trail.

Thirty minutes passed as I walked down, back up and around the marshy meadow searching for any sign of a trail. Then I saw a green flicker in the distance as my light swung incessantly. It must be a florescent ribbon, I hoped.

Yes, it was a ribbon and I had found the elusive trail.

No sooner had I stepped on the long lost trail than a voice in the distance, high atop a rocky ridge yelled *"Hello."*

It took me several seconds before I comprehended it was a runner. I yelled back, *"Hello"* and several shouts from the ridge were returned. There were now two voices yelling at me as the runners screamed back.

Finally one voice was distant but clear and I heard these words, *"Where is the bloody trail?"*

I yelled back, *"I am standing on the bloody trail."*

The voice yelled, *"Don't move and we will come to you."*

Oh joy, I thought to myself. Even though I found the trail and can start running again, I had to help these guys who are lost.

It seemed like an eternity, but after half an hour I heard voices getting much closer and sparks of light could be seen from two flashlights.

A joyful reunion took place in the cold air of the alpine meadow as two runners ran toward my bright light. Cliff Davies and Rolly Portelance, both Canadian runners, said they had been lost for over an hour, stranded high on a ridge above the meadow. Luckily they heard my shout and knew there was a chance to find the trail without being rescued by a search party, they explained.

Without waiting, all three of us took off down the newfound trail back toward Parry Peak Campground.

Cliff and Rolly were running better than me so they were soon out of sight. I then came running up behind the lone female entrant in the race, Carol LaPlant, who was walking down the trail. With Carol was a race crew, sweeping the trail and looking for wayward runners in the dark.

I joined the group and together we walked and jogged all the way to Parry Peak Campground.

Waiting at the iron gate blocking the Parry Peak road was Maria and my brother-in-law along with several other race crews.

Maria hugged me in the cold night air and said I had to hurry if I wanted to make the 11:30 pm cut-off at Twin Lakes, three miles away. The time was 11:21 pm.

Hmmm, nine minutes to run three miles. I didn't think so. My race was over. This was my first DNF of my running career. If only I hadn't got lost, I thought to myself. Maybe, just maybe things might have been different.

Carol LaPlant missed the Twin Lakes cut-off, as did Cliff Davies and Rolly Portelance.

Waiting with Maria at Parry Peak Campground's iron gate was Debbie Dupree, Harry Dupree's wife. Debbie tearfully asked if I had seen Harry, one of the runners in the race? Harry had come from Oklahoma to run this race and was a strong and capable ultrarunner. Debbie was also an excellent runner and knew if Harry was this far back in the race, things were not looking good for him.

Debbie was sick with worry and even more so now that the trail sweeper crew had arrived, without Harry.

I told Debbie no, I hadn't seen Harry. That didn't help her spirits at all. Luckily Harry showed up less than an hour later, safe but tired and cold.

Eight runners failed to make the Twin Lakes cut-off or simply decided sixty-three miles was far enough for them this day.

As I walked stiffly with Maria to her waiting car, so many thoughts flashed through my exhausted brain:

If only I had eaten more,

If only I had run smarter,

If only I had longer training runs,

If only I had more warm clothes,

If only…

Maria drove me to the Twin Lakes aid station and medical check. Obviously the cut-off time had passed. The first medical person to greet me said I was out of the race. The words stung like a bee, even though I knew the race was finished for me.

The volunteer had me get on the weigh scale and checked my vitals before symbolically cutting the race band off my pathetic wrist, DNF.

Skip Hamilton's time into Twin Lakes aid station was 11:23 elapsed time or 4:23 pm in the late afternoon. Late afternoon, I loved hearing his time but could not comprehend running that fast. At least Skip got back over Hope Pass without getting lost.

In second place was a runner named John Lapkass with his brother Andy Lapkass right behind him, both several hours behind Skip. The race was still very much alive, as twenty-one runners left Twin Lakes aid station without missing the cut-off.

The night sky was clear as billions of stars along with a nearly full rising moon illuminated the trail for those left running. Temperatures also stayed around the 40-degree range for the remainder of the race.

Halfmoon aid station was another depressing stop for any remaining runners. Six runners didn't make the cut-off at Halfmoon, including Strider with his running stick.

Jim Butera was at Halfmoon when Strider arrived, after missing the cut-off time. Strider refused to let medical volunteers cut his race wristband off. Even though the race cut-off time was well past, Strider simply refused to relinquish his wristband and walked out of the aid station, much to the amazement of Jim and other volunteers.

Fifteen official runners made their way in the dark of night toward the Fish Hatchery aid station and medical check.

Skip was still well in front and leading the race by a huge margin. Skip's elapsed time at Halfmoon aid station was 13:25 and there was still plenty of daylight remaining. John and Andy Lapkass were cruising in second and third place.

Fish Hatchery aid station and medical check is a difficult place to stop. It is a dark, cold place with the nearby monster Power Line Trail climbing up to Sugarloaf Pass laughing at the approaching runners.

Skip arrived in the Fish Hatchery aid station at 7:32 pm. It was just getting dark for him with an elapsed time of 14:32. Second and third place wasn't changing as John and Andy trailed Skip by over four hours.

Powerful high-tension wires over the heads of any remaining racers were buzzing and sparking in the black Leadville sky as runners made their way upward toward Sugarloaf Pass. The moon was helping light the way for those still able to walk and jog the brutal trail to the top of the pass.

Once over Sugarloaf Pass it was all downhill and flat, or at least on paper it was, all the way to Lady of the Lake aid station.

Downhill is a relative term for this section of the course. Rocks jump out to grab an unsuspecting runner, tripping and pulling them off the trail without warning. Fatigue is extreme at this point of the race with every miss-step on the rugged trail warning a runner to wake up and run more carefully.

At Lady of the Lake aid station there were ten runners remaining in the race. Skip Hamilton was maintaining his insurmountable lead after arriving at 11:14 pm. His elapsed time was 18:14 and Skip might, just might be able to finish the race under twenty hours.

Skip Hamilton left Lady of the Lake aid station, ran uphill to the paved road and continued running past the Turquoise Lake Dam and onto the home stretch toward Leadville.

There is a relentless hill leading from near the base of the Turquoise Lake Dam all the way past Leadville High School, located less than one mile from the race finish line.

Remember the cemetery all racers passed on their way out of Leadville when everyone was full of energy? Now Skip passed that same cemetery at ninety-nine miles into the race and even he was reaching for any strength remaining to finish the race and avoid being planted in the cemetery.

A short distance past the cemetery, bending south on McWerthy Drive toward the high school, runners turned left onto 6th Street, still running uphill past Leadville High School.

This is the part of the course that will forever be etched in every Leadville Trail 100 finisher's brain.

Racers continued running uphill on 6th Street, past a long row of houses with a few scattered spectators standing on the curb, yelling and cheering at every runner passing by.

This long uphill stretch reaches a crest and briefly flattens out, enabling runners to finally focus on the elusive finish line they sought during all those long difficult hours on the trail.

It isn't far to the finish line now and legs miraculously begin working while running downhill. There is no reason to walk at this point in the race, unless death is near.

Now is the time for the Leadville Trail 100 finish line sprint, or whatever you want to call a lurching stride the final 100 yards.

The first person to ever see the Leadville Trail 100 finish line was Skip Hamilton. It was 1:11:18 am on Sunday, August 28, 1983 when Skip Hamilton became the first champion of the Leadville Trail 100 and crossed that legendary finish line. Skip's elapsed time was 20:11:18 with a course record, obviously.

Nearly five hours after Skip Hamilton finished the race, John Lapkass crossed the finish line in second place with an elapsed time of 25:10:18. Andy Lapkass captured third place in a time of 25:16:23.

There were ten finishers in the first Leadville Trail 100. In order of finishing, the *Magnificent Ten* were:

1. Skip Hamilton, 20:11:18
2. John Lapkass, 25:10:18
3. Andy Lapkass, 25:16:23

4. Mark Lisak, 26:24:13
5. Arthur Schwartz; 27:23:16
6. Dick Webster, 27:25:42
7. Gary Cross, 27:36:23
8. Al Binder, 27:56:26
9. Barry Mink, 28:39:21
10. Brent Weigner, 29:31:24

Ten finishers out of 44 starters in the first Leadville Trail 100 meant there was a finishing rate of 23%.

No one finished the race who did not live at altitude. In other words, no flatlanders finished the race.

The awards ceremony was held the same day as the finish, Sunday, at the Elks Club in Leadville, Colorado.

Luckily, Jim Butera convinced Nike to help pay for the awards. Skip Hamilton, the race champion, received a championship trophy consisting of a miniature ore cart on a timber base, filled with actual ore from the Climax mine and decorated with an engraved plaque.

The lone female entrant, Carol LaPlant, was out of the race at the Twin Lakes aid station coming back to Leadville, at mile sixty-three. Carol was presented with an award of a gold bracelet with a delicate heart charm to recognize her for her *"heart."*

Jim Butera presented Leadville booster Ken Chlouber with a special award at the ceremony. The award was for Ken's offer to Jim: to have the town of Leadville help put on the race.[7]

Ken Chlouber then presented Jim Butera with an engraving, placed on a large slab of molybdenum.[7]

All Leadville Trail 100 finishers received an engraved belt buckle that Jim helped design with an artist who also drew the Colorado Lottery logo.

Nearly every ultrarunning event has some kind of controversy. The Leadville Trail 100 had its share during this inaugural event as well.

Remember Bentson Strider with his running stick?

As you may recall, Jim Butera told Strider not to endanger other runners by using a stick during the race. Then Strider missed the time cut-off at Halfmoon aid station and was disqualified but refused to surrender his wristband indicating he was removed from the race.

Strider continued running, even though he was officially disqualified from the race. I watched Strider jog across the finish line before the race cut-off time of thirty hours and congratulated him, without knowing Strider had been disqualified from the race by missing the Halfmoon cut-off time.

Instead of being happy with his finish, Strider immediately complained about his disqualification and how he still finished the race under thirty hours.

Strider showed up at the awards ceremony on Sunday and talked with Jim. Strider tried to convince Jim he should be awarded a finisher belt buckle. Strider's reasoning was that he continued running and eventually did finish the race, even though he missed a cut-off time at the Halfmoon aid station.

Jim had time to think about Strider's conversation as the awards ceremony began.

Near the end of the awards ceremony, Strider's wife got up and gave an impassioned speech about Strider finishing the race and how her husband should receive a finisher belt buckle.

Unfortunately, Strider's wife didn't stop her speech at that point but instead continued talking and saying disparaging things about Jim Butera and the race rules.

When Strider initially appealed to Jim before the awards ceremony, Jim secretly decided to give Strider a finisher belt buckle. But that initial thought of an award for Strider was before Strider's wife's made her disapproving remarks about Jim and his race.

After hearing Strider's wife's remarks and criticism, Jim quietly and discretely slipped the extra finisher belt buckle back into his pocket and Strider never received a finisher's award. According to the local newspaper, "Strider was not given a belt buckle which left him with a dissatisfied attitude."[4]

That was just one of the controversies during the race.

Another very serious accusation was made against the race champion, Skip Hamilton, concerning shortcutting the trail during the race.

It seemed while running the initial power line section of the course, race leader Don Starbuck suddenly found he was in second place without being passed on the dirt road part of the course. Behind Starbuck at this point in the race was Skip Hamilton running in second place.

Don said he saw Skip run straight over the top of two hills on this downhill section of the race course instead of taking the clearly marked dirt road going around the two hills, thereby short cutting the race course and placing Skip in first place and ahead of Don.

The two hills in question had a faint path running straight down where the power lines were constructed. Jim had marked the racecourse for runners to take the dirt road instead of the more direct path and never marked the shorter, power line construction path as part of the racecourse.

Don talked at length with Jim about Skip cutting the trail and taking the shorter, unofficial path down the power line route.

Don dropped out of the race at Winfield and did not finish the race. Since Don would not be able to contest the final race results, this gave Jim an opportunity not to confront Skip with Don's accusations, luckily.

However, the next year when the Leadville Trail 100 was run, Jim announced at the trail briefing prior to the race that shortcutting the course at any point and not following the marked race course was not allowed and any runner shortcutting would be disqualified.

One last controversy during the first race concerned the removal of race markings by unknown individuals prior to and during the race.

Jim was very distressed about people getting lost because race markings were removed or taken down. Yet Jim was powerless to control that kind of behavior so Jim merely decided to mark the course as best he could, check course markings more often and use better designed course markings on sections of the course that were run during darkness.

Jim patterned the Leadville Trail 100 course from his experience and knowledge of the Western States 100 mile race. The Western States race started at 5:00 am so Jim assumed that same starting time would work at Leadville and give racers enough time to run over the hardest part of the course, Hope Pass, in daylight.

Starting the Leadville race at 5:00 am didn't work, as evidenced by darkness overtaking runners before or at the top of Hope Pass during the run. Jim wisely decided to move the starting time to 4:00 am for the 1984 Leadville Trail 100 and all subsequent races.

Finisher Buckle; 1983 & 1984

References

Chapter 3: The First Leadville Trail 100-Mile Running Race

1 The Herald Democrat; Thursday, August 25, 1983
2 Frontier Magazine; Steve Voynick, August 1984
3 The Herald Democrat; Friday, August 26, 1983
4 The Herald Democrat; Monday, August 29, 1983
5 Colorado Sports Monthly; The First Leadville Trail 100-Miler, Steve Voynick, September 1983
6 Snow Country Magazine; Drink Fluids Often In Winter, Skip Hamilton, Page 31, Jan-Feb 1991.
7 The Herald Democrat; 100 Mile Ultra Race Highlights, August 29, 1983
8 This number of original starters has been reported as 43, 44, 45 and even 46 runners. However, Jim Butera's published race report in Ultrarunning Magazine, October 1983, Colorado Ultra Club newsletters and race instructions for the second race in 1984 clearly state the number of starters was forty-four.

It seems the number forty-five came from a comment Jim made at the finish line to a reporter, during the first 1983 race. Jim said there were forty-four starters, **including** one woman. The reporter mistakenly thought Jim said there were forty-four starters **and** one woman. So the reporter increased the number of starters from forty-four to forty-five. Hence the incorrect and erroneous number of starters carried by many press reports was forty-five.

This book, "*Leadville Trail 100; History of The Leadville Trail 100 Mile Running Race*" will use the correct number of original starters as forty-four.
9 Bill Gookin formulated and developed "Gookinaid ERG" in the 1970's. ERG was the first electrolyte replacement drink. Bill Gookin died at the age of 86 in February 2019. "Times of San Diego", February 1, 2019.

Chapter 4

Reflections on The First Leadville Trail 100-Mile Running Race

The 1983 Leadville Trail 100 went into the history books as the highest 100-mile ultramarathon in the country. Never before had a race been run or had runners finish an ultramarathon at the altitudes encountered around Leadville, Colorado while running a distance of 100 miles.

Yet most importantly, no one died during the race as predicted by Dr. John Perna.

Here is what final finisher, Brent Weigner, had to say about the first Leadville Trail 100:

"During 1983 I ran thirty-two races. The week before Leadville, Mark Lisak and I ran the Wyoming State Fair 10K in the morning and up and down Laramie Peak in the afternoon. My quads were sore all week until the start of the Leadville Trail 100.

Mark and I were sitting in the Golden Burro Restaurant having breakfast when the race started. Since we were just a few minutes late, we were running in 43rd and 44th place.

Our plan was to walk a little every 20-30 minutes and never run up or down steep hills. We had moved from last place to 22nd and 23rd place at the 50-mile turnaround.

Throughout the race, Mark and I had to split up and find the correct trail because several trail ribbons had been removed. We would run different directions at a trail junction to find the correct trail and then yell back to each other. I don't remember how many wrong turns we experienced but there were enough.

We always kept moving and did not stay long at the aid stations or checkpoints. I probably walked about half the course. It turned out my fast walking strategy every 20-30 minutes, mixed with running, was successful.

Out of the 44 starters in the Leadville Trail 100, I was the last official 10th place finisher with a time of 29:31:25.

My friend Mark Lisak placed 4th overall (21:41:37) and put three hours on me the second time down Hope Pass because I took it easy in order to be ready to race hard the following weekend. We were very experienced trail runners and helped each other. Both of us were familiar with running at altitude."

(Authors Note: Brent has been racing marathons and all other races for fifty-one years. In 2018, at age 69, he raced forty-six races and placed first, twenty-four times in various divisions. Brent is the current World Record Holder for number of marathons and number of foreign country marathons completed. To date, Brent has run marathons in 177 countries for a total of 347 total marathons and ultras, and still counting.)

Arthur Schwartz was a finisher in the first Leadville Trail 100. This is Arthur's story:

"Another local physician and friend of mine was Barry Mink. Barry was also a runner who finished the Western States 100. Barry said, "Do you know about the Leadville Trail 100?"

I said, "no." Since Leadville was just around the corner from Aspen and the Leadville race was approaching, we both decided to keep our local racing streak going and entered the first running of the Leadville Trail 100.

"Barry was a good athlete", but he lacked restraint by going out too fast and then couldn't hold the pace to the finish line.

Barry did manage to finish in 28:39:22 that first year but in second to last place as I predicted. I was also successful in my first try with a time of 27:23:16 for fifth place. This was the first of many more finishes for me but Barry's one and only finish at Leadville."

Sheila Butera, Jim Butera's widow wrote:

"This particular race was dear to Jim since he put so much heart and soul into the original mapping out of the trails and was there from the beginning. He never dreamed that this would end up being one of the largest and most well known races in our country. He loved exploring new territory and finding the best place for the course, and relished knowing others would enjoy it as well."

This first Leadville Trail 100 opened the door for an explosion of extreme ultra events never seen before in the history of ultrarunning.

Careers would be created, lives changed forever and even the massive shoe industry would benefit significantly from the events that unfolded in a small backwater-mining town in the heart of the Colorado Rocky Mountains.

In addition, as we all know today, that nearly forgotten mining town of Leadville, Colorado survived the bust economy of 1983 because of the Leadville Trail 100 and has become a world famous mecca for extreme high altitude endurance events.

It hasn't been done yet and may never happen but a memorial to Jim Butera should be a prominent landmark along the Leadville Trail 100 course honoring what Jim accomplished on that August weekend in 1983.

Chapter 5

The First Women Finishers (1984; The Second Race)

Since many runners became lost during the first Leadville Trail 100 Mile race, Jim Butera decided those running needed to familiarize themselves with the course prior to the race itself. So for this second edition of the Leadville Trail 100, a Course Orientation event would be held one month before the actual event.[1]

A course orientation would be held over two days, July 21st and 22nd, 1984. Runners would receive water during the two days of running (nothing else except water.). Runners were responsible for the remainder of any aid they needed.

The first day of course orientation would begin at the race starting line and end before Halfmoon aid station. The second day of training would continue from just before Halfmoon aid station and proceed all the way to Winfield, the 50-mile mark and end of the training run.

For this second edition of the Leadville Trail 100, Jim Butera refined and perfected the event into nearly the final form runners still see today.[2]

The race start was moved to 4:00 am so that runners would be over the highest point on the racecourse, Hope Pass at 12,600 feet, during daylight hours. Jim had modeled his race after the Western States 100 mile running race but that didn't work well for the difficult Leadville Trail 100 course, as was apparent during the first 1983 edition of the race.

New for the 1984 race, Jim allowed pacers to accompany a runner. Pacers could be used from mile fifty, the Winfield turnaround, to the finish. Only one pacer was permitted during any part of the course but a runner could have as many pacers as they liked.

Whistles were given to all runners for use in case they became lost. That was a novel idea since many runners couldn't find the correct trail the previous year.

Another important addition for this year's race was a water station located at Timberline on the north side of Hope Pass. Jim thought this would be the highest aid station ever created for a 100-mile race.

Crews for the race were given additional instructions about where to park, where they would be permitted to drive, and areas prohibited to motor vehicles. The road to the Halfmoon aid station was no longer accessible to motor vehicles. No parking or crewing was allowed along the dirty dusty road to Windfield.

Remember the controversy during the first race regarding possible shortcutting of the course? As Jim promised to Don Starbuck following last year's race, this problem would be addressed and rectified.

During this year's race briefing, the day before the race, Jim spoke about how the course was marked with ribbons, glow sticks and signs. Jim went on to tell everyone that no shortcutting of the course was allowed and that all trail markings must be followed. Any runner shortcutting or not following the marked course would be disqualified. Jim's race instructions would hopefully alleviate any problems with shortcutting during the race.

However, this year there would be another new controversy and one that is pertinent throughout sports competitions even today: the use of supplemental oxygen. That debate will be addressed as it occurred, later in this chapter.

For this second race in 1984, Jim Butera remained the race director. [1,2,5]

Others involved for the 1984 race included: [1,2]

- Merilee O'Neal – Coordinator
- Doctor Perna – Medical
- Jean and Scott Bauer – Assistant Medical
- Bill and Jeffra Brown – Rescue & Timers
- Corky Watts – Consultant
- Ken Chlouber – Head PR

There were no other changes to the race or the racecourse.

1984 was the first year to see any female runners finish the race. The previous year, 1983, only one woman ran the race, Carol LaPlant, but she failed to get past the Twin Lakes aid station at mile sixty-three while missing the cut off time.

This year seven women entered the Leadville Trail 100[3]:

- Marge (Hickman) Adelman (Colorado)
- Debbie Deupree (Oklahoma)
- Teri Gerber (California)
- Kay Moore (Colorado)
- Laurel Myers (Colorado)
- Josafina Pabalan (California)
- Claudia Berryman Shafer (Alaska)

The women's competition was fierce, to say the least.

Kay Moore[4] (100 mile best of 17:44) was the first place woman running past the Halfmoon aid station at mile twenty-eight. However, Kay became lost on the trail high above the next aid station at Twin Lakes. Kay ran nearly two miles further after missing a critical trail junction before arriving at Twin Lakes, now in third place.

Since Kay was lost out on the trails, first into the Twin Lakes aid station was Teri Gerber (1984 Western States 100 mile finisher in 21:58) followed by Debbie Deupree (second place in Virginia's 1984 Old Dominion 100 in 25:19). Six female runners arrived at the Twin Lakes aid station, mile thirty-seven, within six minutes of each other with the seventh female runner further back.

Weighed, fueled and encouraged by a small crowd at the aid station, six women exited Twin Lakes with only Laurel Myers dropping out of the race at the Twin Lakes aid station. They were headed toward the steep climb toward Hope Pass, the highest point on the course at an altitude of 12,600 feet.

The First woman over Hope Pass and into the Winfield aid station at mile fifty was Teri Gerber, but her lead was short lived.

Debbie Deupree passed Teri Gerber to take over the lead as the women returned over Hope Pass, racing each other toward the finish line at Leadville.

Debbie and Teri continued their epic women's race until the Halfmoon aid station at mile seventy-two.

Halfmoon aid station at mile seventy-two is always a pitiful, agonizing, depressing place during the race. It is dark, cold and there are still twenty-eight miles left in the race, including the brutal climb up the Power Line Trail to Sugarloaf Pass.

Debbie Deupree became nauseous and was totally exhausted, dragging herself into the Halfmoon aid station. Teri Gerber was no better off. Teri was hypothermic and shivering as she slept in a friend's car near the aid station.

Teri's boyfriend, Jim Pellon who dropped out of the race by Winfield, found Teri in the car just as she was waking up. Teri told Jim she was determined to finish the race for the flatlanders, if nothing else.[5]

Debbie Deupree dropped out of the race at the Halfmoon aid station, unable to continue. This turn of events propelled Teri Gerber into the lead for the women's race.

Teri was still slightly hypothermic as she stumbled out of Halfmoon and continued her death march into Leadville, with her boyfriend Jim Pellon at her side. Teri mistakenly thought she was still in pursuit of Debbie, not knowing Debbie had dropped out at Halfmoon.

Teri Gerber became the first woman's champion of the Leadville Trail 100, finishing with a time of 28:17 and good enough for tenth place overall. Less than one hour behind Teri at the finish line was Marge (Adelman) Hickman, finishing as the second and final woman with a time of 29:13 in seventeenth place overall.

Marge crossed the finish line with the ankle injury she suffered only thirteen miles into the race. Running eighty-seven miles with her injury, Marge was asked at the finish line why she continued when aid station personnel tried to persuade her to quit. Marge typically replied, *"I wanted to finish the race."*[6]

The woman's race was much more competitive than the men's race.

The men's race featured Skip Hamilton, well in front the entire race and running the flatlanders into the ground once again. There had never been a runner finish the course that lived below 5,000 feet, hence the affectionate name 'flatlander' for those low altitude runners.

Yet at the end of the race there were actually seven flatlanders who finished the race. The first flatlander ever to finish the Leadville Trail 100 was Peter Gagarin from Massachusetts, the founder and editor of Ultrarunning Magazine.

The hotbed for ultrarunners from the far west, California, had twelve entrants, many with very fast 100-mile times. Only three of that strong contingent of runners from California struggled across the finish line. One of those finishers was none other than Bill Finkbeiner who would go on to finish a total of **thirty** Leadville Trail 100 races in the event's history.

Flatlanders had proven they could finish a race at Leadville's high altitude, even though their slow times reflected a definite lack of oxygen and lower VO_2 levels.

Finishers in the second Leadville Trail 100, in order of finishing:

1. Skip Hamilton – 18:43:50; Two-time champion now
2. Andy Lapkass – 23:45:44
3. O.R. Petersen – 25:07:49
4. Peter Gagarin – 25:42:18; Founder and co-editor of Ultrarunning magazine [7] and first "flatlander"
5. Harlan (Bud) Martin – 25:57:50
6. Arthur Schwartz – 27:27:54
7. Bill Finkbeiner – 28:00:38; First Californian finisher
8. Reb Wickersham – 28:00:59
9. Harry Deupree – 28:08:54; Husband of Debbie Deupree
10. Teri Gerber – 28:17:41; First woman's champion and first woman finisher
11. Jim Feistner – 28:29:41
12. Cliff Davies – 28:52:11; First Canadian finisher
13. Mark Humphrey – 28:52:11
14. Ken Chlouber – 28:55:29
15. Steve Siguaw – 28:59:22
16. Tommie Jackson – 29:01:40
17. Marge Adelman – 29:13:13; Second woman finisher
18. Wayne Baughman – 29:28:29
19. Dennis Christopherson – 29:35:02
20. Bob Willison – 29:36:51

There were a total of twenty finishers in the second Leadville Trail 100 Mile race, out of fifty-one starters (a 39% finishing success rate).

Jim Butera greeted me at the finish line, as he watched Steve complete his first 100-mile race. Jim, smiling and laughing in the bright morning sun, asked me if completing the race didn't *"feel like putting one's finger into an electrical socket?"*

The second Leadville Trail 100 had two women finish the race for the first time in race history: Teri Gerber and Marge Hickman.

Here is the race report from Marge:

"My first 100 miler at altitude; 10,200 feet, pitch black darkness with only street lights and a bright spot light to show me the way; it was cold with the temperature being in the low to mid thirty degrees.

I was shivering with my stomach in a twisted knot and feeling like I was going to throw up at any minute; I was as nervous as I've ever been. My knees would not stop quivering uncontrollably as I asked myself "why?"

I had met and knew that Teri Gerber was a seasoned ultrarunner from California who had completed Western States. I figured my chances of staying with her were slim to none, but you never know what may happen during thirty hours of running.

Nearing the end of the Turquoise Lake Trail and maneuvering swiftly over many large rocks and tree roots I suddenly tripped.

Oh no. One of the large roots jumped up from the ground catching the toe of my shoe. As I yelped, screamed and stumbled over the roots one foot after the other, I landed in a face plant, stunned. I clearly remember lying on the ground wondering if I could get up.

Slowly, with bloody hands, face, knees and a turned ankle, I managed to get to my feet. I wasn't even to May Queen Campground at the thirteen-mile mark yet.

I was in shock and disbelief that this could happen to me. I limped my way out of the Campground and things didn't look good. I was devastated but knew there was no way I was going to quit, no matter what. I had no time to waste so it was onward to the next aid station at Fish Hatchery.

Even at this early point of the race, my ankle was swelling and the medical team at Fish Hatchery wanted to wrap it. It was too early for me to stop for medical care, so I kept going, feeling good, and positive without much pain.

I ran out of the Fish Hatchery aid station and onto the asphalt road toward the dirt road leading to Halfmoon aid station. Continuing out of that aid station and toward the Mt. Elbert trailhead I was trying to stay focused on the race.

This stretch of the course was uneventful due to the short asphalt stretch and then dusty dirt road until reaching the long, steep, rocky switch backs of the Mt. Elbert trail section up and over into Twin Lakes at mile thirty-six.

By the time I reached Twin Lakes, my ankle had swollen to about the size of a small orange. This time the medical person suggested that I have my ankle wrapped. Feeling good and having enough time cushion for the cutoffs, I decided to listen to their suggestion.

Exiting the Twin Lakes aid station I quickly hit the asphalt for three miles up and through Perry Peak Campground to the trailhead and toward the high point of the race, Hope Pass.

This grueling, steep, rocky four-mile trail to the top of Hope Pass (12,600 feet) is very challenging and can be extremely demoralizing. The Hope Pass trail is where one can lose it mentally and feel defeated. Every runner has to begin "digging deep", staying strong and positive, with one step at a time.

Once reaching the crux of Hope Pass, runners catch their breath, take in the spectacular views and hopefully enjoy the fast descent down the steep scree and rock fields on the backside of Hope Pass and into the Winfield aid station at fifty miles. Hooray.

Runners are thrilled and invigorated to make it to this checkpoint. Halfway, and now all we have to do is turn-around and retrace our steps back to Leadville. Easier said than done.

I know my ankle is starting to throb due to more swelling, as the bandage was too tight causing even more pain. At this point, my crew person decided to take off the bandage, which felt much better and relieved some of the pain.

But now my ankle was the size of an orange…yikes, yet I had to keep moving. I've run halfway and on the way back home to the barn, so to speak.

Also, knowing that there are only four women left in the race I must keep moving as long as I haven't broken anything and can still run.

I race out of Winfield and reverse my steps but with a pacer (Warren Glick) who can now carry some of my gear, food, jacket, flashlight, etc. This is a huge relief and great to have a friend run or power walk with me back up and over Hope Pass back to Twin Lakes. Yet this is a difficult, shorter and steeper climb back up to the top of Hope Pass for the last time.

Time is turning to dusk when I arrive back at Twin Lakes aid station. I eat, go to the bathroom, put on warmer clothes and prepare for the probable all night long journey back to town.

My ankle continues to swell as well as my other ankle now. This is not good.

After Twin Lakes I tried to avoid aid stations so they wouldn't give me "the hook." Jim Butera was following my run like a hawk the entire time too.

I believe my determination and desire to desperately want to finish this once in a lifetime challenge was what helped me not feel the pain. I also wanted to be the first Colorado woman to finish the Leadville Trail 100.

From Twin Lakes back to and down toward the dirt Halfmoon Road was a grind. The trail winds up long switchbacks, passes beaver ponds and crosses wooden bridges over streams before reaching the aid station at Halfmoon Campground.

By this time, dusk has turned to total darkness and flashlights are aglow and on high beam. I'm really feeling the pain in my orange-sized ankle now and my pace has diminished to a walk/slow run pace. However, I hear along the way from a runner's crew or pacer that one of the women had dropped way back at the Twin Lakes aid station.

I'm concerned, but also know that there are only three of us women left in the race. Being the only Colorado woman runner and the other woman from California, I knew I just had to keep moving and digging deeper than ever before in my life. I wanted this and was going to get it if I had to crawl to the finish line.

Reaching the next aid station at Fish Hatchery I was moving slow and shuffling. The crisp, cold night air was bone chilling with no time to warm up except for sipping some hot chocolate and hot Ramen noodle soup.

My crew learned that Debbie Deupree had dropped from the race and told me this at Fish Hachery. I had no idea what time it was or where I was as far as cut-off times; that was my pacer's job. I didn't want to know what time it was. I just wanted to finish in under the 30-hour cut-off.

Although my pacer kept pushing me to run, he never said I was too close to the aid station cut-off time. That was good.

From Fish Hatchery to the bottom of power lines is three-miles on asphalt which feels like running on concrete. Then trekking up the Power Line Trail is the last major climb, but a dandy one with five false summits that seemed to just keep going and going, under crackling power lines, until reaching the top.

On a full moon night you can get dizzy from gazing at the sky and all the stars twinkling overhead. This is a spiritual and encouraging moment in the race, at least for me. Knowing at this point that I'm almost there, tears fill my eyes with gratitude and the ability to attempt and hopefully finish this huge goal and challenge. Onward and forward.

Depending upon how much fuel, grit and determination is left in your tank, one can run from the top of Power Line Trail down to May Queen Campground. That is why you shouldn't go out too fast from the start because you want to be able to run the second-half downhill stretches.

Cruising/shuffling down Power Line Trail feels fantastic knowing that from May Queen there is only thirteen miles more to go. From May Queen in, the trail around Turquoise Lake seems long, hilly even though it is just roly-poly. I'm mostly walking now, cold, exhausted and my ankles are huge making it hard for me to even walk.

The last miles climb steadily upward on pavement, past the graveyard toward the high school.

But, knowing I had time to spare and believing I would finish, I was stunned and "out there somewhere" as tears began to flow as I hobbled up the last hill, seeing the finish line in the distance and trying to run across the finish line at 6th and Harrison.

I have asked myself the question "why" every year since 1984.

My 1984 finish time was 29:13:13, second woman behind Teri Gerber. I tried chasing Teri down the entire race and would occasionally hear reports of how far ahead of me she was.

At one point on the return, in-bound, I was told that Teri had gotten in a vehicle to warm up and rest for a while. Wow, was this my lucky opportunity to try and pick up my pace to see if I could possibly catch up to her or maybe even pass her…?

I was encouraged, but how much did I had left in the tank to try and overtake her. Apparently there was not enough, even though I had significantly closed the gap.

And, all this happened because I met Jim Butera who sold me my first pair of trail running shoes and who inspired and encouraged me to 'just try it.' "

So what about that supplemental oxygen debate?

Charles Savage was reported clutching an oxygen mask to his wan face at the sixty-three mile aid station of Twin Lakes.[8] Charles Savage was a California runner who dropped out at the Twin Lake aid station so any oxygen use issue had no affect on the final race outcome.

Several runners observed racers at the 50-mile Winfield aid station taking supplemental oxygen from the volunteer medical personnel.

In 2017, after the Giro d'Italia bicycle race, Chris Froome used an inhaler containing salbutamol. Salbutamol opens the airways in the lungs to help breathing, similar to what oxygen can do for a runner at the altitude of the Leadville Trail 100.

In the case of Chris Froome, salbutamol is a banned substance above a certain threshold for cyclists suffering from asthma since salbutamol would give athletes an unfair advantage over other competitors. Chris Froome was cleared of any wrongdoing, according to the World Anti-Doping Agency (WADA) rules just prior to the July 2018 Tour de France race.

Remember, Chris Froome is a four-time Tour de France champion so there was a lot of publicity about his alleged performance enhancement.

Ultrarunners at the Leadville Trail 100 Mile race are not under the same microscope as professional cyclists. Ultrarunners just run, or at least that had been the case up until the 1984 Leadville Trail 100.

Was taking supplemental oxygen at an aid station during the Leadville Trail 100 Mile race a controversy or just something to be ignored?

The supplemental oxygen issue was not addressed at the 1984 Leadville Trail 100 Mile awards ceremony. There were no disqualifications, no finger pointing and no mention of any problems at the aid stations with using supplemental oxygen.

However, to jump ahead to the 1985 Leadville Trail 100, the issue of a runner using supplemental oxygen at an aid station was discussed during the pre-race briefing.

The decision made by race management, after a discussion by runners present at the 1985 pre-race briefing concerning supplemental oxygen, was that oxygen would continue to be available at certain aid stations. Oxygen was necessary for any medical emergencies that may arise, according to race management.

Runners were told NOT TO EXPECT access to supplemental oxygen at the aid stations but there would be no ban on using oxygen during the race.

References

Chapter 5: The First Women Finishers (1984; The Second Race)

1 Colorado Ultra Club; Leadville Trail 100 Course Orientation letter, June 1984
2 Colorado Ultra Club; Second Annual Leadville Trail 100 Entrant Information Sheet
3 Leadville Trail 100 Time/Entrant list – 1984
4 Ultrarunning Magazine; Cover and pages 36 & 43, January-February 1985
5 *"Long Day At Leadville";* Article by Lee Green; Outside Magazine, December 1984
6 Boulder Daily Camera newspaper; Page 9E, September 1, 1984
7 Ultrarunning Magazine; Pages 6-7 by Peter Gagarin, October 1984
8 *"Long Day At Leadville";* Article by Lee Green; Outside Magazine, Page 78, December 1984

Chapter 6

"Ch-ch-ch-ch-changes" in 1985

(David Bowie; lyrics from the song "Changes")

Jim Butera's January 1985 Colorado Ultra Club Newsletter defined the future for the Leadville Trail 100:

"Starting in 1985 the Leadville race will be taken care of by the people in Leadville. Ken Chlouber and Merilee O'Neal will head up the effort there. I'll still be on the board."[1]

Merilee O'Neal became race director and Ken Chlouber was race management.

Merilee O'Neal (n/k/a Maupin) was a travel agent in Leadville. Merilee had been a race volunteer and Jim Butera's assistant for the Leadville Trail 100 since the beginning in 1983.

Merilee excelled at organization and had great rapport with local officials and volunteers in Leadville and throughout Lake County. Merilee was also a burro racer and runner.

Ken Chlouber was a Lake County Commissioner, burro racer and ultrarunner. Ken worked at the Climax Molybdenum Mine as a crusher operator after arriving in Leadville from Oklahoma in 1976. Ken is married to Pat Chlouber who became a prominent local and national educator.

The 1985 Leadville Trail 100 still had the trademark Jim Butera aura: low key, tough ultrarunners dueling against each other and trying to survive in the rarified air high above Leadville, Colorado.

There would be something new at the 1985 Leadville Trail 100. Free Wheelin' Films of Aspen was persuaded by ESPN to make a documentary of the Leadville Trail 100 and the film company quickly become a sponsor.

The Leadville Trail 100 was always run on a shoestring budget, as was previously pointed out. Yet now there was a glimmer of hope the race might, just might grow larger in the coming years if it was marketed correctly.

Ken and Merilee had a vision to grow the race, help the town with more tourist income and include some income for them, of course.

Budweiser Light beer was recruited to become the major sponsor for the 1985 Leadville Trail 100 Mile race. Racers loved having beer available at the aid stations throughout the course. Yet few runners, except maybe Don Starbuck, took advantage of the refreshment during the race.

Race management began the tradition of welcoming all runners to the race by including them as part of the "Leadville family." Anyone who started the race or finished the race would be included in this exclusive 'family' from this race forward. Everyone felt welcome and slightly less nervous knowing they were not alone in attempting a 100-mile race at these extreme altitudes.

The 1985 race was also growing in size. There were seventy-two starters in 1985 including seven women (yes, that still makes the number of starters seventy-two). Eighty runners entered the race but eight failed to show up to the start.

Among the women running were Marge Adelman, second place the previous year and Carol LaPlant who crashed and burned during the first year of the race in 1983. Also returning from last year's race were Kay Moore and Debbie Deupree, both trying to avenge their dreaded DNF's in 1984.

The men's race featured two-time champion Skip Hamilton once again. However, California was well represented at this edition of the race by an incredibly strong group of ultrarunners.

Jim Howard, Western States 100 mile champion in 1983 (16:07), Ben Dewell a 1983 sixth place Western States finisher in 18:12, Mark Brotherton who finished the 1985 Western States race in fourth place (17:14) and 1984 Leadville Trail 100 finisher Bill Finkbeiner who was also a Western States 100 mile finisher with an excellent time in 1984 of 19:37 representing the talented flatlander group.

It looked as if flatlanders were throwing everything they had at the high altitude trained Leadville Trail 100 champion, Skip Hamilton.

One notable new entrant in the 1985 Leadville Trail 100 Mile race was race creator, Jim Butera.

Relieved of his race director duties for the Leadville race beginning in 1985, Jim had running credentials to challenge the best flatlanders, along with Skip.

Unfortunately, Skip Hamilton dropped out of the race at Winfield due to leg cramps, after getting massaged for 20 minutes and taking IV fluids provided by his physician father. Skip had also been suffering from a heel injury that limited his training during the summer.

This year's race finished with a new men's champion: Jim Howard from Foresthill, CA. Not only did Jim Howard win the third annual Leadville Trail 100, he also won the Western States 100 mile race earlier in June, becoming the first man to win both races.

Jim Howard's finish time did not break Skip Hamilton's 1984 record but was still fast enough to beat the second-place runner by more than three hours.

Before Skip retired from the race at the half way point, Howard and Hamilton dueled it out for 50 miles.

With Skip out of the race, Howard had his own problems. He was suffering from stomach cramps that threw him off from setting a record pace.

Approaching the Fish Hatchery aid station on the return, in-bound, Jim was seen by many and recorded by ESPN (Free Wheel'n Films) on all-fours heaving his guts out against a bridge over a small stream. Thereafter, Jim's pace slowed as he was having to run/walk all the way to the finish line.

Howard's winning time of 19:15:57 was over 30 minutes slower than Skip's 1984 course record. Second place was Ben Dewell 22:35:43 with Rolly Portelance running 23:03:35 for third place.

Rounding out the top five finishers was Andy Lapkass running 23:12:43 for fourth place and none-other than Jim Butera finishing in fifth place with a time of 23:38:48.

Local Leadville runners Jim Feistner and Ken Chlouber finished in 27:16:36 and 28:28:44, respectively.

Marge Hickman of Denver won the women's title and placed 11th overall in a course record time of 26:57:50. Finishing in second place was Lynne Whittenberg of Denver with a time of 29:4607. Only two women finished the race again this year.

The youngest finisher was Andy Lapkass (27), and the oldest finisher was Ed Williams (56).

Forty-five runners were forced to drop out. This attrition rate was reportedly due to problems with the rocky trail and steepness of the 12,600-foot Hope Pass that had to be crossed twice during the race. The other issue was the warm temperature of the day, even on top of Hope Pass. Nighttime temperatures were not too cold, but the moon had set early making some runners get off course and become lost for periods of time.[3]

Marge's championship race report:

"This year was an exciting year for me as I hoped to better my time from last year (1984) and maybe even win the women's division. I trained harder than ever before and put every ounce of energy into my long runs; running mountain hill repeats; racing for training; doing two-a-day runs along with a weekly track speed workout; and running 100+ mile weeks.

It all paid off and my dreams came true with an amazing race for me, as I became the first Colorado woman finisher, new course record holder and capturing the overall women's championship title.

I was hooked and knew I had a long future in ultrarunning; thirty-four years and still going strong."

Marge's strategy during the race:

"Anxiously waiting for the shotgun to go off and then the count down; 10, 9, 8, 7, 6, 5, 4, 3, 2, 1…the explosion of the shotgun echoing in the air with 72 runners hooting and hollering as we crossed the starting line of the third annual Leadville Trail 100.

The race, a long 30-hour adventure through the Rocky Mountains, began as runners asked themselves…why? Or at least I always ask myself that question. What have I gotten myself into? Can I do this? Have I trained enough? What if I fall again like I did last year? What if I miss a trail marker and get off the course? And so many other unknown questions.

These were questions racing through my mind in the cold darkness of the early morning. Besides asking myself all of those questions, I also asked myself if I had a chance to win or just place in the women's division. There were only five women entered this year, Carol LaPlant, Kay Moore, Debbie Deupree Lynne Whittenberg and myself.

I wondered if I had trained hard enough to possibly win.

My adrenalin and competitive juices started flowing making my heart pound harder and louder, which made me all the more nervous right from the start.

Still trying to calm my emotions, nerves, stomach and quivering knees, I ran the rocky, tree-rooted trail around Turquoise Lake.

Beams of light from the string of runners' flashlights made for magnificent, colorful reflections of white, pink and blue pastel streams and bolts of light across Turquoise Lake.

Progressing still nervously along the Turquoise Lake Trail, I passed the Tabor Boat Ramp where some crew congregate to spur their runner on.

I stopped here for a quick potty break. And, to this day, I still stop just beyond the Boat Ramp for a pit stop. Pausing here always seems to let me catch my breath as I try to relax. Yet it was the peaking of a gorgeous sunrise toward the end of Turquoise Lake that helped settle my nerves.

As the sun rose over the lake, my upset stomach calmed and my nervousness subsided, finally. I focused on running loose while monitoring how my body felt. I was feeling good, sipped some water, turned my flashlight off, and was on my way.

This is one of my greatest accomplishments finishing and winning the Leadville Trail 100, in 26:57:50, 11th place overall and first Colorado woman finisher. Wow, I did it. I couldn't believe it, I won." Marge Hickman

Reb Wickersham, age 51, was pulled from the race at the half way point of Winfield with severe chest pain. Reb was first taken to St. Vincent Hospital in Leadville where he was diagnosed with a blood clot from phlebitis in his leg that had broken loose and lodged in his lung. Reb was rushed to a Colorado Springs hospital and listed in stable condition.[3]

Reb, aka the Rebel, received the award, **Last Ass Over the Pass**, at the pre-race meeting before the start of the next 1986 race. It seems Reb underwent surgery three weeks before the 1985 race for his phlebitis and knew of the potential for blood clots. Yet Reb had signed up for the Leadville Trail 100 and nothing was going to keep him away, Reb told the authors. The award of **Last Ass Over the Pass** is a bronze trophy of the backside of a burro, of course. To this day, Reb still treasures his award.

"Last Ass Over The Pass" Award

References

Chapter 6: *"Ch-ch-ch-ch-changes"* in 1985

1   Colorado Ultra Club; January Newsletter, January 1985
2   Ultrarunning Magazine; Pages 6-9, October 1983
3   The Herald Democrat, Monday, August 26, 1985

Chapter 7

The Rest of the 80's

1986

The 4th annual Leadville Trail 100 was held on August 23-24, 1986.

During this fourth edition of the race in 1986, Printer Boy Camp Ground near Turquoise Lake became the first aid station. This location change for the aid station was made primarily because of complaints due to excessive noise by those camping near the Tabor Boat Ramp. It seemed runners and their crews made a lot of noise in those wee hours of the morning, disturbing slumbering campers.

This year was also the first time pacers were allowed for runners over sixty years of age for the entire race. However, this rule change only lasted a few years before it was realized sixty-year-old ultrarunners didn't really need any special treatment.

MAX energy replacement drink became the official drink for the race. Barry Mink, one of the original finishers in the 1983 Leadville Trail 100 and a physician, developed the drink to help ultrarunners with electrolyte replenishment in the dry high altitudes encountered during the race.

1986 was the first year the awards ceremony was moved to the 6th Street Gym. A crowd of 450 persons attending the awards ceremony necessitated a change from the rather small and previously used Elks Club to the larger gym venue.

It was during the 1986 Leadville Trail 100 trail briefing that Ken Chlouber first used the expression:

"You're better than you think you are and you can do more than you think you can."

That memorable phrase by Ken has enabled runners to endure countless hours of suffering on the Leadville Trail 100 course.

Skip Hamilton won his 3rd championship with a time of 19:26:09 by defeating Chuck Jones who was the Western States 100 mile champion in 1986. Chuck finished in second place, over an hour behind Skip in a time of 20:48:37.

The women's race featured returning champion Marge Hickman. Marge failed in her attempt to win a second Leadville Trail 100 by finishing behind champion Maureen Garty.

Maureen ran a course record time of 22:45:01 and placed 5th overall. Marge ran 2 hours and 20 minutes faster (24:37:53) than her course record from the previous year in her runner up position to Maureen.

There were only two women who finished the race in 1986: Maureen and Marge.

Micah True (aka Caballo Blanco) finished his first of three finishes at the Leadville Trail 100 in a time of 25:23:56.

Steve and Micah: "I remember racing Micah as we were coming back down Hope Pass, near the beaver ponds before Parry Peak Campground. Micah had a slight lead over me as he ran with his female pacer who was talking loudly to Micah somewhere ahead of me.

Coming around a bend in the narrow trail I saw Micah sitting on a rock ledge adjacent to the beaver pond, taking his running shoe off and lamenting that he wasn't feeling well.

His pacer was not happy and was telling Micah to get going again. It seems we all have our moments of despair on the trail.

Micah finished the race with a time of 25:23:56."

Besides one hundred entrants, ninety-three starters and forty-five finishers for a finishing percentage of 48%, there was at least one notable entrant in the race: Essie Garrett.

Marge writing about Essie:
"A special, unique and one-of-a-kind woman, Essie Garrett was an ultrarunner from Denver who died on April 1, 2014 at age 74.

Essie was known across Colorado for her big, warm and generous heart and love of running. Essie was easily recognized with her knee-length dreadlocks and sunny persevering smile.

She grew up in Riesel, Texas, joined the Army when she was sixteen, and served for three years before moving to Denver. Essie became a follower of Sri Chinmoy, the Indian spiritual master who believed enlightenment could be achieved through disciplined athletics, including long-distance running and swimming.

Essie was a solidly built woman with an inquisitive gaze and a deliberate way of speaking. She taught refrigeration mechanics at the Emily Griffith Opportunity School in Denver for more than two decades. Most of her students were male who were initially surprised to find their instructor was a female, and even more surprised at her self-assured competence with electronics.

Essie often ran from her longtime home in north Park Hill (Denver) to the school's downtown campus with her dreads tied in a ponytail that bounced along with her on her back.

Essie was always coming up with new ideas for fundraising. She led a walking group at lunchtime and she could always be seen running through many different sections of Denver. Almost always, she was in training for a goal.

First, it was the Leadville Trail 100, the brutal 100-mile race that initially defeated her when she was caught in a massive thunderstorm that included rain, hail and intense lightning strikes while she climbed Hope Pass.

Essie retreated from the thunderstorm, became lost but simply slept under a tree overnight before wandering into Parry Peak Campground in the early morning hours. [1]

Essie was never one to let adversity deter her. Instead she channeled those experiences into her training and goals. Essie decided she needed to become faster in order to beat the stringent time cut-offs for the Leadville Trail 100.

In 1988, Essie achieved her goal of finishing the Leadville Trail 100 with a time of 29:53:08. There was not a dry eye among those of us watching Essie gently cross the finish line in the bright morning light of a new and glorious day at 6th and Harrison in downtown Leadville.

As Essie became stronger, she started running for causes, including multiple-sclerosis research that she hoped would help a close friend diagnosed with the disease. Essie also ran for the Denver Rescue Mission, Cops & Kids, Emily Griffith Foundation, Children's Hospital Colorado, the Colorado Aids Project and many others.

In 1991, Essie began a Thanksgiving tradition of raising money for the homeless by running laps around the Colorado Capital building for 48 hours, stopping occasionally to refuel at the temporary soup kitchen she set up for her supporters.

Essie knew about real, true hunger. Essie would say, "Don't you ever say you're starving," as she scolded friends who casually used the phrase as they were sitting down to eat. "An appetite is not the same thing as starving."[3]

I clearly remember Essie doing the traditional Thanksgiving Fundraiser run around the Colorado Capitol building because I was there to enjoy the day with her and the many other people and runners who wanted to support her and the cause.

I recall running laps with her around the Denver Capitol building from mid-morning to late afternoon so that I could eat my Thanksgiving dinner when I returned home. I didn't want to be or say I was "starving," but wanted to have a big "appetite."

It was great running around the Capital building because I saw running friends who were also out running laps with wonderful camaraderie and gratefulness for Essie and her tireless fundraising for Colorado charities.

On January 10, 2005, Essie handed the Martin Luther King Jr. torch off to Governor Bill Owens that kicked off the year's celebrations in the city for that special day. The torch traveled to different locations around the state before returning to Denver.

From 1981 to 2012, Essie ran more than 25,000 miles and raised more than $1 million for charity. In 1993, she was inducted into the Sportswomen of Colorado Hall of Fame.

Essie retired in 2010 and moved into an apartment building designed for aging Denver Public Schools employees and retirees. She then joined residents in campaigning to improve conditions in the antiquated apartment building.

Unfortunately and sadly Essie's body was found emaciated in her apartment after a friend had been calling her and Essie never returned the phone calls. Essie never married and had no known survivors.

News of Essie's passing shocked Colorado and she will forever be remembered as a true friend and awesome person in all respects. In today's world we could use more people like Essie. You are missed Essie."

1987 (The Big Time)

The Leadville Trail 100 hit the big time this year. NBC's SportsWorld filmed the race with none other than gold medal Olympic champion Frank Shorter doing commentary along with NBC broadcaster Greg Lewis. Frank Shorter also paced Skip Hamilton back over Hope Pass during the race.

Some notable events for the 1987 race:

- Budweiser Light beer continued as the main sponsor with AT&T and Audi Automobiles also becoming major sponsors
- There was a new race packet design with Al Binder, original race finisher, proudly featured on the cover
- Ken Chlouber became the Colorado State Representative from District 61
- May Queen Campground became the first and last official aid station for the race, replacing Printer Boy Campground
- Entry fee was $100
- There were no complimentary entries for any runners, according to race management
- First year the name "Hopeless Aid Station" was officially used for the Hope Pass aid station
- Medical exam was moved to the 6th street gym, along with the trail briefing and awards ceremony
- The racecourse was still on pavement to Lady of the Lake and Tabor boat Ramp before getting on the Turquoise Lake Trail
- Californian race entrants were called the "Sierra Express" by John Demorest; (Ultrarunning Oct 1987, p 6)
- Frank Shorter presented special awards at the awards banquet
- The first time Ken Chlouber was called "race originator" (Ultrarunning Magazine, Oct 1987, p. 7)

As the initial shotgun blast rattled windows in the cold morning air in downtown Leadville starting the race at 4:00 am, the rain began.

Many runners would know this edition of the Leadville Trail 100 as the 'hypothermic' 100-mile race. The moniker was due to constant rain and snow falling throughout the weekend.

Marge remembers: "running down the Boulevard near the four mile point, where the dirt road turns right and parallels the railroad tracks to the asphalt. A man passed me on the inside of the turn, tripping me and causing me to fall flat into the mud. I was not happy but there was not much else to do other than cuss and keep going. At Winfield I got a sponge bath and changed clothes for the return trip home. I was wet, cold and miserable this year."

Skip Hamilton was once again running the race. He joined 192 other starters (193 total starters) in pursuit of the coveted championship ore cart trophy and big belt buckle.

Among the runners challenging Skip were former Leadville champion Jim Howard, Jim King (three-time Western States champion) and Steve Warshawer (second at Western States).

For the women, Randi Bromka and Kathy D'Onofrio (Western States champion) showed up in a highly contested race.

Front running in this edition of the race was intense, as was evidenced by the depth of talent for both men and women.

Steve remembers: "seeing Frank Shorter loping to the top of Hope Pass in front of a walking Skip Hamilton as I neared the top of the pass during my outbound ascent. Frank was pacing Skip Hamilton from the turnaround point at Winfield.

I asked Frank (we were on a first name basis of course, rather than **THE** Frank Shorter, gold medal Olympic champion that he truly is). Anyway, I asked Frank if Skip had run any of the trail up Hope Pass. Frank laughed and said, *"not a step."* That made me feel a little better in my oxygen deprived state at this point in the race."

Arthur Schwartz also remembers seeing Frank Shorter, but closer to the Winfield turnaround since Arthur was faster than Steve, as usual.

Arthur recalls: "Frank was running with another runner at the time, flying down the trail when Frank appeared ahead and just in front of a walking Skip Hamilton. Arthur asked, *"Aren't you Frank Shorter?"* Frank said, *'I used to be.'* " Frank must have been feeling the effects of the altitude.

Skip Hamilton would go on to win his fourth and final Leadville Trail 100 Mile race championship. Skip defeated the best of the best ultrarunners to achieve his lofty champion status.

Skip's elapsed time was 18:44:55, less than 10 minutes ahead of second place Steve Warshawer in 18:54:05. Third place was Dennis "The Animal" Herr in 21:04:12. Rounding out the top five was Martyn Greaves from England in fourth place in a time of 21:09:26 and Joe Hayes in fifth place with a time of 22:23:28.

What happened to the "Sierra Express" from California? Jim Howard was back in 14th place in 23:15:47 and Jim King was 18th with a time of 23:40:22.

Skip Hamilton was 42 years old for the race and Steve Warshawer was 29 years old. It seems that youth was poised to challenge the old guard for future races.

On the women's side, Randi Bromka took the women's championship honors in 24:12:57. A "Sierra Express" challenger, Kathy D'Onofrio was second with a time of 25:07:25. Third place woman was Bobbie Dixon of Montana with a time of 27:28:54.

Randi Bromka describes her training and championship race:

"When I began running in April of 1984 it was simply to create a healthier life for myself. A long-time smoker, it was an epiphany that caused me to pull on some paint-stained K-Mart sneakers and take off running. From one mile on the first day to three on the third, my newfound enthusiasm took off. Within one year I ran my first marathon at The Avenue of the Giants. Quite surprised to have qualified for Boston, that was my second marathon in April of 1986.

By the spring of 1987, with six marathons completed, I found myself looking for a way to "up the ante." I could either go faster or farther. After a couple of truly ugly sessions at the track I decided that longer was more likely than faster.

Living in Aspen, I didn't personally know very many people who had run marathons but I did know several who had run in the new race over the hill called the Leadville Trail 100. Crazy as it sounds, that seemed to be the logical progression for me: 5k, 10k, Marathon, 100 Miles. Being completely self-coached, I had to figure it out.

Creating a plan for myself, I started to do my longer runs ten days apart. This seemed to give my body the time it needed to be really ready for the next big effort. Increasing the distance of long runs gradually from 26 to 35 to 40 miles went well and my body was holding up.

I was lucky to have a job that allowed me a lot of time to train and a boss who was so supportive he paid my $100 entry fee to the Leadville Trail 100.

Living in Aspen allowed for easy access to the LT100 course and using typewritten course directions a friend had given me, I ran many, many miles on those trails.

In late June I ran a solo 50-mile training run around the Roaring Fork Valley, using gas stations and convenience stores as my aid stations.

In July, just five weeks before the Leadville Trail 100, I found out about an unsupported 50-mile race near Vail being run a couple of days later.

As my local running friends were all gearing up for a popular race in Snowmass, there was no one to tap for help at the low-key 50-mile race in Vail. So, I headed off to Vail in my minivan with a cooler of MAX sports drink in bike bottles and small peanut butter & jelly sandwiches.

After driving the course and identifying the 10, 20, 30 and 40 mile splits, I went back to the finish line where I slept in my van.

In the morning, I worked my way to the start line, stopping at pre-identified spots stashing my bottles and snacks in the bushes.

Expecting it to be a hot day, I'd frozen the bottles and topped them with MAX, anticipating they would melt by the time I reached them. But because of the cold, the later accessed bottles actually had larger amounts of frozen drinks in them.

The Vail Valley 50, organized by Trishul and Kaaren Cherns, attracted 21 racers, 20 men and me.

Weather that day didn't get as hot as expected and we ran into a strong headwind all day as we worked our way from Vail to Gypsum.

One by one, I passed the guys on the road, chatting happily about this being my first ultra. Having no experience other than my pressure-free training run weeks before, there were no expectations about what time I might run. When I won the race in 7:02 (1st place overall.) it was a great surprise to me and the other runners as well.

I was convinced my training program was working and the Leadville Trail 100 was the biggest test of all.

With a terrific crew consisting of my then-husband Barry, dear friends Lisa, Warren and Annie, I headed over Independence Pass to tackle the Race Across The Sky.

It rained for about 20 of the 24+ hours I was on the course. The trough-like trails were ankle deep in flowing water. Barry and Lisa dashed from one crew access point to another with my rain-soaked socks on the dashboard heater, trying so hard to have a dry pair of socks to offer up at the next aid station.

It's the little things you remember.

Like the sudden frenetic activity and noise at the aid stations - welcome, but jarring after the peace of the trail; like picking wild strawberries and sharing them with Greg Runson, the first person to convince me to set foot on a trail; like the life-giving potato soup at the Halfmoon aid station on the way back; seeing and hearing the May Queen aid station WAY before you get to it; sitting in Norma D'Onofrio's car on Hagerman Pass - with the heat BLASTING; someone bringing a sweater up the trail.

Scott Demaree heard I was hypothermic and had his pacer turn around and run back with the heavy wool sweater that saved me.

We weren't competitors out there - we were a stretched-out team of cheerleaders - each pulling for the others to do their best on that day.

Warmed by the wool sweater and the heaters at May Queen, Warren (my pacer) and I slowly made our way along the lake as the constellation Orion rose into the sky.

And then it was done, 100 miles in 24:12:57.

Three years and four months after I quit smoking and ran one mile, I had won the Leadville Trail 100.

It took a crew, a village, and well-organized race team to get me to that finish line. Having set out on such an individual endeavor it was a heart-filling realization that my race was full with so many others who cared."

Trishul Cherns, a Sri Chimnoy follower and organizer of the Vail 50-mile race Randi mentioned, finished the race just ahead of Ken Chlouber in 28:25:57 to Ken's time of 28:26:20. Ken managed to finish the race just ahead of Christine Gibbons (28:30:03), who you will hear more about later in this book when Christine becomes the women's champion.

There were 86 finishers of the 1987 Leadville Trail 100, despite the dreadful weather conditions. The number of finishers represented a finishing rate of 44.6%.

1988

Marshall Ulrich, who was to become without a doubt, the premier endurance athlete of our time, had this to say about his first Leadville Trail 100 finish:

"I had been running for less than ten years – including marathons, mountain ascents, a 50-miler, and a 24-hour race – when I read an article in Runners World where Dr. George Sheehan was talking about the Western States 100.

What's this? People run a hundred miles? I must give this a try. So, I signed up for the 1988 Western States 100 mile endurance race, and was able to finish in just over 22:30.

While my marathon times weren't bad (they also weren't great), I had discovered that I could keep a pretty steady pace for a hundred miles. A couple of days later, I started poking around and to my delight found that there was a hundred mile race right in my Colorado backyard: the Leadville Trail 100. I signed up and was able to finish in just under 23 hours (22:58:14). I was pleased, especially since the two races were only eight weeks apart. I was hooked."

For the first time in race history, the number of entrants in the Leadville Trail 100 was limited. The limitation as to number of runners permitted on the course was due to U.S. Forest Service regulations governing trail usage in National Forests, or so it appeared. Therefore, entries in the 1988 race were accepted on a first-come-first-served basis by race management.

There was another remarkable course change for the race: runners would no longer run on pavement to the Tabor boat Ramp and the beginning of the Turquoise Lake Trail. Instead, the course now used the start of the Turquoise Lake Trail at the Dam, following the trail for eight miles, from the Dam all the way to May Queen Campground.

This course change was a welcome relief in order to get runners away from vehicle traffic and onto a trail earlier in the race, as opposed to previous editions of the race.

The downside to the racecourse change was more congestion earlier in the race. Since the wide paved road was eliminated early in the race, more runners were forced to run on a narrow trail sooner rather than later.

The benefits of this new congestion were: better pictures for the photographers at the lake and a slowing of runners during the early stages of the race, helping racers conserve glycogen stores to be used during later stages of the race.

As usual, there were some interesting events during the 1988 race:

Essie Garrett finished her first Leadville Trail 100 in a time of 29:53:08, just ahead of the last place finisher Mark Macy who ran a time of 29:54:13.

Tim Tweitmeyer of Western States 100 mile race fame finished the race in 20:19:59 in 4th place overall.

Legendary Ann Trason showed up at the starting line for her first Leadville Trail 100 and finished in 21:40:26 as first woman, women's champion and setting a new course record. Second place woman, Christine Gibbons, ran a significantly improved time of 23:25:05 when compared with her 1987 debut time of 28:30:03. Third place was the previous years' champion Randi Bromka in a time of 26:28:09 but she was not able to repeat as two-time champion.

What happened with the men's race? Race history was made once again.

Two great runners dueled back and forth for nearly 100 miles. Rick Spady and Steve Warshawer battled back and forth with each runner taking the lead before the other runner overtook him. This exchange of the lead took place time after time during the entire race. Finally, with the finish line in downtown Leadville nearly in sight, the two runners agreed to tie.

Tie???

Ultrarunners are unlike few other runners. We race a clock, we race each other, and we race through pain, suffering and utter exhaustion. Camaraderie is a proud trademark of a true ultrarunner. We admire our adversaries even as we race them into the ground, trying to out distance them.

Yet on this day in 1988, two front-running ultrarunners decided they had battled long enough and decided not to sprint for the championship, trying to beat the other runner.

Rick Spady and Steve Warshawer crossed the Leadville Trail 100 finish line hand in hand, finishing with an identical time of 18:04:03; a championship tie.

For the next edition of the Leadville Trail 100 in 1989, Ken Chlouber declared at the trail briefing, 'finishing place, in the case of a tie, would be awarded to the oldest runner first', or words to that effect.

Further back in the pack and going for his sixth finish was Arthur Schwartz, an original 1983 finisher.

Arthur had been racing his friend, Odin Christensen. Odin managed to pass Arthur before the final May Queen aid station and was running well in front of Arthur. Entering the May Queen aid station, Arthur saw Odin lying on a stretcher, barely able to move.

Arthur simply said something to further confuse Odin, as he ran out of the aid station and regained his lead over Odin.

Giving Arthur a chance to run ahead, Odin came back to life, slid off the stretcher and proceeded to pass Arthur before the finish line, beating him by seven minutes.

It just goes to show you, never count a Leadville Trail 100 ultrarunner out of the race, no matter how dead they appear at the May Queen aid station.

1989

Marshall Ulrich provides his comments about the race:

"Every hundred-mile race is difficult; in particular the ones in the mountains, on trails, at high altitude, and with substantial altitude gain (and loss). But I wanted to prove that the human body was not only capable of finishing these ultra-distances, but could run them fairly quickly, and recover faster than most folks thought possible.

It's hard to imagine today, with over 170 hundred-mile races just in the U.S., but in 1988 there were only five trail 100's. Tom Green and Denny Hagele had finished all five in 1986 and 1988, respectively. A sixth race, Vermont, was added in 1989, so the six races were: Old Dominion, Western States, Vermont, Leadville Trail 100, Wasatch Front, and Angeles Crest.

Gordon Hardman and I set out to complete the challenge in 1989. After the first two, I discovered that my recovery was better than I had imagined, so I ran the last four aggressively. By doing this, I was able to finish top ten in five of the races, including sixth place at Leadville with a time of 21:20:21.

Gordon also finished all six races, although had slower finish times (my cumulative time was 128:52). Still, we proved that it was possible, and The Last Great Race was born. Of course, records are made to be broken; in 2003 Joe Kulak set the bar much higher with his time of 114:24 for 'The Last Great Race.' "

Highlights for the 1989 Leadville Trail 100 included:
- The entry fee for the race was $100
- There was a limit of 275 runners set by the San Isabel National Forest service
- Runners were still accepted on a first-come-first-served basis
- Oldsmobile became a title sponsor and offered a free, one year lease of an automobile for a 1989 Leadville Trail 100 finisher, based on a lottery drawing
- 257 runners started the race
- 140 runners finished the race
- The finishing percentage increased to 54%
- Reb Wickersham (the Rebel) decided there were too many "Sierra Express" runners and dropped out of the race

There were no ties among either the men or women first place finishers this year.

Sean Crom won the men's race in a time of 18:56:40, ahead of second place Mark Brotherton who ran 19:24:51, followed by Dick Brainard in third place with a time of 20:02:47.

For the women, Kathy D'Onofrio-Wood finally got her championship ore cart trophy by running an excellent time of 20:50:41, good for 5th place overall, and even ahead of the strong runner Marshall Ulrich who ran 21:20:21.

Christine Gibbons was the second place woman in 22:11:39 while Randi Bromka was definitely in the hunt for another championship by finishing as third woman in a time of 23:02:56. Marge Hickman finished as the last place woman (14th female) with a time of 29:52:39. Marge's slow (for her) time was because she was running the Grand Slam of Ultrarunning this year.

References

Chapter 7: The Rest of the 80's

1   The Herald Democrat, Friday, August 22, 1986
2   Ultrarunning Magazine; Pages 6-9, October 1983
3   Denver Post, by Claire Martin, April 4, 2014

Part 2

Historic Races

"It is hard to fail, but it is worse never to have tried to succeed."
– Theodore Roosevelt

Chapter 8

Tarahumara – The Raramuri

Ultra legends came to the Leadville Trail 100: The Tarahumara Indians of Mexico (Tarahumara). Some of the stories about them are true and others; well you know how things are sometimes exaggerated.

Tarahumara call themselves Raramuri, meaning "the footrunners."[2] In this book we will retain the name Tarahumara to avoid any confusion. These fleet-footed Tarahumara runners came to run the Leadville Trail 100 for the first time in 1992.

The Tarahumara have been in international competition before. Not these specific Tarahumara who came to Leadville but their forefathers.

In 1928, two Tarahumara runners represented Mexico and ran in the Amsterdam Olympic marathon. The Tarahumara didn't have much success in the Olympic marathon, other than finishing the race. The two runners claimed at the finish line the race was too short.

Tarahumara runners again represented Mexico at the 1968 Mexico City Olympics in the marathon. The results were the same for those runners: the race was too short but they finished, deep down in the pack of international marathoners.

Patrocinio Lopez and Richard Fisher came up with an idea in 1992 for the Tarahumara to run an ultra distance race in the Colorado Rockies.[1]

The Leadville Trail 100 is at altitude, something the Tarahumara liked since it was similar to their homeland.[2] Most importantly, the Leadville Trail 100 was much longer than a marathon, something they needed since their running skills were suited to multi-day running as well as long distances in the rugged Copper Canyon area of northern Mexico.

Richard Fisher was familiar with the Leadville Trail 100 because of Kitty Williams, his girlfriend. Kitty Williams was an ultrarunner who finished the Leadville Trail 100 twice, in 1987 and 1990.

Kitty's father was none-other than Ed Williams, thirteen time Leadville Trail 100 finisher and oldest finisher of the event (age 70) until 2013 when his age record was eclipsed by an older runner (Hans-Dieter Weisshaar; age 73). Kitty was obviously familiar with the Leadville Trail 100 having run with her Dad and finishing the race herself.

Kitty met Richard Fisher and they became a couple. The two of them, along with Patrocinio Lopez, brought a team of five Tarahumara runners to the 1992 Leadville Trail 100 as part of Fisher's "Wilderness Expeditions", a non-profit organization.[3]

Tarahumara runners have competitions in their native canyons with teams kicking and chasing wooden balls during multi-day events in a race type environment. The competition usually lasts until all but one team have either dropped out or conceded the race. The races usually last for several days and nights, until the carnage is complete. Endurance for a Tarahumara runner is their trademark and the Leadville Trail 100 would surely test them in that regard.

Five Tarahumara runners stood at the starting line for the 1992 Leadville Trail 100. The five Tarahumara racers were traditionally dressed in loin clothes, brightly colored shirts and leather thong sandals.

At the first aid station, May Queen Campground, five Tarahumara runners were leading the race. The Tarahumara continued leading the race until the Halfmoon aid station at thirty miles. Yet once past Halfmoon aid station all the Tarahumara runners dropped out of the race.

Many reasons were given for the poor Tarahumara performance: unfamiliarity with the race course, inability to take food and liquids from strangers, quality of the aid station food (the food available was not in their usual diet), bad pizza before the race and western-style clothing and equipment that was alien to them.

The Tarahumara runners and coaches went back to Copper Canyon in Mexico and regrouped. The Tarahumara decided to return and run the 1993 Leadville Trail 100 to demonstrate, beyond a doubt, their superior running abilities.

A new team was then chosen consisting of two previous members from the 1992 effort along with four new Tarahumara runners, for a total of six racers. Patrocinio Lopez would be the cabicero (Team leader). Richard Fisher and Kitty Williams accompanied the team as before, providing logistical support and coaching.

Once the new team arrived in Leadville, Colorado, members of the ultrarunning community were recruited to serve as crew for the team.*

Training runs with crewmembers covered the actual course prior to race day and the Tarahumara were able to practice using aid station foods as well as some western clothing.

Flashlights were also given the Tarahumara runners for a practice run. Those lights created quite a spectacle with Tarahumara runners instinctively pointing the flashlights up toward the night sky like a torch. The Tarahumara runners were familiar using torches during their nighttime runs but had never seen or used an electric flashlight. Luckily the technique of pointing the flashlight at the ground was mastered during these training runs.

The Tarahumara runners spent a lot of time making one additional and important piece of equipment for the race. This remarkable piece of footwear inspired a multi-**billion** dollar industry when it caught on as the next fringe fad in the United States and elsewhere for runners: The Tarahumara Huarache sandal.[4]

In making their Huarache sandals, the Tarahumara made a trip to the local Leadville landfill in search of discarded tires. The Tarahumara believed they had found a vast treasure trove when coming upon hundreds of discarded tires, many still with intact tread, at the Leadville landfill.

New sandals were fashioned by the six runners to use during the race. Additional tread material was sliced and taken for the long trip back to Copper Canyon for their families. Riches like these discarded tires simply were not available in their homeland.

* See Tom and Melissa Sobal's report below

Having previewed the course, adjusted to the aid station food and found local crewmembers and pacers for the race, the Tarahumara were better prepared for the Leadville Trail 100 than their previous attempt.

The team members (and ages) of the 1993 Tarahumara Leadville Trail 100 team were:

- Antonio Palma, 28
- Felipe Torres, 22
- Manuel Luna, 30
- Cerrildo Chacarito, 38
- Victoriano Churro, 55
- Benjamin Nava, 21

August 21, 1993 marked a turning point in ultrarunning history. Six Tarahumara runners started the Leadville Trail 100 when Merilee Maupin fired the gun at 4:00 am, sending 290 racers onto the racecourse.

Those of us running with the Tarahumara at Leadville witnessed a remarkable journey. Since the Tarahumara runners started slowly in the back of the pack, we could watch them during the race as they sped by.

Steve remembers: "trying to keep pace with three Tarahumara runners ascending Hope Pass on the way to Winfield. The Tarahumara's sandals were throwing rocks into the air as they negotiated the narrow trail toward tree line.

No, the Tarahumara did not run barefoot, contrary to popular belief. They wore homemade Huarache sandals along with colorful shirts that hung down to mid-thigh. It was impressive watching three Tarahumara pass me with what seemed like minimal effort.

Trying to keep up with them wasn't possible. The three Tarahumara runners crested Hope Pass in front of me where they didn't even pause before hurtling themselves down the trail toward Winfield at breakneck speed.

By the time I arrived at Winfield the three Tarahumara runners were twenty minutes ahead of my time. Twenty minutes ahead and I was trying to run fast downhill."

At the Winfield turnaround, fifty miles into the race, Victoriano had moved up to twentieth place overall, with Cerrildo and Manuel on his heels.

The real Leadville Trail 100 race begins at the Winfield turnaround. Sure the first fifty miles of the race are brutal but once a runner turns around, things become deadly serious. There is little joy as runners attack Hope Pass for a second time in the race. But for Tarahumara racers it was time to pick up the pace.

Arriving back at Twin Lakes aid station, Manuel was in fifth place overall with two of his team member right behind him.

Food at this point for the Tarahumara consisted of pinole, a corn meal type substance as the primary part of their diet.

Pacers were keeping the Tarahumara runners on track. By Halfmoon aid station, Manuel had moved into second place overall with Victoriano running slightly behind him. On the climb over Sugarloaf Pass, Victoriano led Manuel, as he became the new leader of the race with fifteen miles to go.

Watching Victoriano fly around the trail adjacent to Turquoise Lake must have been an incredible sight, but none of the runners could watch since we were so far behind him.

Vicoriano Churro crossed the Leadville Trail 100 finish line in 20:02:33, becoming the race champion for 1993 at the age of fifty-five years old. In second place was Cerrildo Chacarito in 20:43:06. Manuel Luna had faded to fifth place overall with a time of 21:26:09 because he broke his Huarache sandal during the final section of the race and had to make repairs. The final two Tarahumara finishers were Antonio Palma (26:40:19) and Benjamin Nava (27:45:49).

Five Tarahumara team members finished the 1993 Leadville Trail 100. One member of the team failed to finish; Felipe Torres dropped out of the race at mile ninety-three due to his new Huaraches causing blisters by not being broken in properly before the race.

History had been made not only in the Leadville Trail 100 but in the ultrarunning world as well with these Tarahumara runners.

Tom and Melissa Sobal's explanation of why they have the 1993 Tarahumara championship ore cart trophy:

"In 1993, a group of Tarahumara was brought to Leadville to run the Leadville Trail 100.

The Raramuri are a group of indigenous people from the Copper Canyon area of Mexico. They are known for their running ability and ultra-distance length runs that are a traditional part of their culture.

Leadville residents Melissa and Tom Sobal hosted these runners and their small support team in their cabin. As serious runners (Melissa has completed nearly 100 ultramarathons, including four Leadville Trail 100 finishes, while Tom has been inducted into the Colorado Running Hall of Fame) the Sobals thought it would be interesting to host this group. The Sobals had hosted many previous Leadville runners including Dennis "The Animal" Herr, Jim O'Brien and others in their home, and remembered all the runners that had previously hosted them while traveling.

The Sobals were living in a rustic cabin three miles outside of Leadville at the time. It was almost a mile away from the nearest neighbor, and offered seclusion and privacy that suited typical Tarahumara temperament. This was important for the culture-shocked runners, most of who had never been outside of their primitive home areas before. There was easy access to the cabin off a paved county road, and it had bunk bed space for sixteen.

The Raramuri stayed over a week with the Sobals. Communication was an issue. This group of runners was older, very traditional and only a few of them understood some Spanish. No one knew much of their native language.

The group spent most of their time sitting around. The Sobals did not heat the cabin in the summer, and it was poorly insulated. With temperatures below 40 degrees each night, mornings were cool. The Tarahumara spent a good part of every morning outside sitting on rocks to warm up in the sun, similar to lizards. Sometimes they would linger on the rocks outside well into the afternoon, changing locations to avoid tree shadows as the sun moved across the sky.

These runners spent the entire time in Leadville wearing their traditional skirt type attire with bare legs and feet. No long pants, no socks, no real shoes. The only time any of the runners wore anything over their bare legs was when Melissa offered to let them use some of her colorful running tights. The two youngest runners briefly tried a few pairs on, giggling all the time.

The group spent much of their time carving pairs of Huarache sandals from old tires they pulled from the Leadville dump. They seemed delighted with the opportunity to create many extra pairs of Huaraches using numerous different tire tread patterns and styles. One can imagine that tires discarded in Leadville were not as threadbare as their choices in Mexico. Rubber shavings are still visible in front of the cabin over fifteen years later.

They ate a simple diet primarily consisting of beans, corn, rice and tortillas. They were offered many different other foods, which they occasionally tasted but primarily declined to eat.

The Sobals initially became alarmed when they began to see corn in the poop of their dog Rosebud. They thought their dog was being given or was stealing uneaten food from the trash. After monitoring bathroom use in the cabin, the mystery was solved. The Tarahumara preferred using the surrounding woods instead of indoor facilities and the dog was snacking on the piles.

Unlike the average runner who spent days in Leadville running over numerous sections of the course, the Raramuri only ran a couple times during their stay before the race. They seemed to do so reluctantly. Tom and Melissa went out running every morning, but the Tarahumara sat on rocks in the sun.

Melissa did one point-to-point run with them over Sugarloaf Pass one night. They had to be taught to aim flashlights at the ground, instead of holding them over their heads pointing skyward like torches.

Melissa remembers how competitive they seemed to be, especially since she was woman. Every time she found herself leading the group, numerous Tarahumara would speed up to pass her.

Tom was only able to coax them out for one run. Tom was a champion burro racer, and they joined him and his champion burro Maynard for a 6½-mile run. It was evident that the Tarahumara were intrigued by the strength and speed of a burro running. Most burros in Copper Canyon struggle to eke out a poor existence foraging for themselves, and only run when necessary. Tom heard more banter from the Raramuri during this run with Maynard than he heard all week.

Being competitive, wanting to further impress the Raramuri with Maynard's ability, and as a test to find out if these guys could actually run, Tom gradually upped the pace during a long uphill. The Tarahumara stopped talking, but no one fell off the back.

Then someone farted, and everyone started laughing. Short sentences were blurted out, followed by more laughter. Tom laughed along too, even though he could not understand the jokes being told. He knew that their universal group response to the sound of passed gas while maintaining a strong pace uphill meant that they were runners, and could really run.

Another clue to their running ability came a few days before the race. As a licensed Massage Therapist, Melissa offered everyone in the group a therapeutic tune-up massage. This was accepted by most of the group only because Melissa was a woman, and she was described as a "touch doctor." Melissa found their bodies to be thin, sinewy but muscular running bodies.

Every one of the runners enjoyed their massage except the oldest, quietest and most traditional of the bunch: 55-year-old Victoriano Churro. He declined the offer for a massage, and instead spent the time looking at pictures in an old Cosmopolitan magazine.

Not much was expected of this new group of seven runners in 1993, as all of the Tarahumara who started the race in the previous year, 1992, dropped out.

Melissa was running the race this year (1993), and Tom paced her from Winfield to Halfmoon until she dropped out with stomach problems. Upon returning to the cabin in the middle of the night, they found a few of the Raramuri also there.

At first, Melissa and Tom believed this meant that the Raramuri had also dropped out of the race. Disappointment turned to shock when it was revealed the Tarahumara runners claimed 3 of the top 5 places overall in the race. Only one of their group did not finish, dropping out at ninety-five miles due to foot pain.

Victoriano, the 55 year old, won. He remains the oldest person to win the Leadville Trail 100.

As a reward the next day, it was communicated to the group that they could have anything they wanted to eat. Instead of more rice and beans, they dragged a member of the support team out behind the cabin and had him lift the lid to the propane tank.

Under it was an almost fully eaten rotisserie chicken. Apparently, the team member was tired of the normal Tarahumara diet, and bought the chicken as a personal treat. The Raramuri noticed this secret special food, and soon everyone had his own rotisserie chicken from the store for dinner.

As they were about to board vehicles to begin the long trip back to Copper Canyon, Victoriano motioned to Tom to join him out behind the cabin. He was struggling to carry the large awkward winner's ore cart trophy that weighed over one sixth of his 119 pounds. He pointed to an old length of chain wrapped around a tree. This was a rusty 12-foot length of the cheapest type of chain you could buy, and probably used in the past to tie up a dog.

Victoriano motioned that he wanted the chain. Tom quickly unwrapped the chain and gave it to Victoriano, all the while thinking that he would have bought all the Tarahumara new sections of chain if he had known they wanted those.

Victoriano then indicated that he wanted Tom to have the trophy in exchange. Tom initially motioned that he did not want to accept it. He believed Victoriano earned the trophy and should keep it, and that the trade for an old piece of chain was not fair. Victoriano kept insisting that Tom keep the trophy.

Tom finally accepted the trophy and motioned his thanks to Victoriano. He did so believing that perhaps refusing the trophy would violate some unknown Tarahumara cultural norm. He also thought about how hard it would be for Victoriano to carry the trophy the long distance over narrow trails back to his home, and how useless the trophy would be to Victoriano and his family. He thought about how he and Melissa had themselves given away hundreds of running awards they had won.

The 1993 Leadville Trail 100 trophy is one of the very few running awards the Sobals have kept. It is a reminder to them that races are not won with $250 shoes, $500 watches, high tech clothing, personal training programs or special diets. It is a reminder that age, background, race or religions are not barriers to running success. It is a reminder that one can reap big rewards from a simple hardworking lifestyle and that running success primarily comes from within.

The trophy is a reminder that in the big picture, success in running is personal, worth little more than a rusty old chain."

There is extreme prejudice against the Tarahumara in Mexico, according to Kitty Williams[3]. Gringos sitting in a restaurant in Mexico are politely served while their Tarahumara guests are ignored.

Returning home to Chihuahua from the 1993 Leadville Trail 100, the Tarahumara runners were greeted as heroes. The governor of the State of Chihuahua personally met with them and offered his congratulations. TV stations featured them in broadcasts and newspapers heralded their achievements. After the race, when the Tarahumara went into a restaurant in their homeland, patrons gave them a standing ovation.

The Tarahumara runners had the strength and wisdom to succeed at the Leadville Trail 100. Little did other runners in the race realize what life-changing impacts this race had on the lives and recognition of this remarkable culture.

While this 1993 race was incredible, an even more spectacular race was to occur the very next year at Leadville. A world champion ultrarunning woman, Ann Trason, would run against the strongest team of Tarahumara runners ever assembled, at the 1994 Leadville Trail 100.

This is a detailed report by Tony Post, who worked for the Rockport Shoe Company, about the Tarahumara's sandals, Rockport's development of a new running shoe and FiveFingers running shoes:

"Rockport Shoe Company was instrumental in getting the Tarahumara team of runners back to Leadville for this historic race.

Tony Post is a Colorado native and former vice president of Product Marketing for Rockport in 1994. Built on a reputation for comfort, Rockport's business had expanded rapidly during these years. The company entered the trail/light hiking market and was looking for an event where they could test their product and use it in their marketing.

Already familiar with the event from his running history and growing up in Colorado, Tony was put in touch with Rodney Jacobs, a filmmaker in Aspen who knew Ken and Merilee.

In the fall of 1993, Tony flew to Colorado with other members of the Rockport team, including then company president John Thorbeck. The Rockport team met Ken and Merilee, saw the course and Twin Lakes, etc. before signing up for a three-year sponsorship of the Leadville Trail 100 race. Eventually, Rodney Jacob's company, Freewheelin' Films, helped Rockport turn the event into a CBS Sports special, giving the event national exposure.

During the initial two-day meeting in 1993, while Ken was driving them around the course, Tony had the idea to add a mountain biking trail 100 to the run. Tony was an avid mountain biker and thought the altitude and terrain would make for a challenging event.

Although Ken initially wondered how he could get more willing volunteers for this new event he realized the idea made good sense. Ken was looking for a way to make the event bigger, to bring in more athletes and tourists, so they all agreed to add the bike race on the weekend preceding the run.

Then another idea came together while the Rockport team went over the course. Ken had been talking about how a tribe of Tarahumara Indians from the Copper Canyons of Mexico had previously run the race. Tony asked, "Could we get them up again? Maybe have them race against the top US ultra-runners?"

To that Ken said, "I'll bet we can get Ann Trason." Ann was easily the top female ultra-runner at the time – and many agreed the best ultra-runner of either gender.

Together with Freewheelin Films, they had the idea to stage this great race pitting top runners from the Tamahumara against Ann Trason – then film the whole thing. Ken gave Rick Fisher's phone number to Tony.

Rockport paid Fisher and the tribe to send their top runners to the race. Rockport initially agreed to pay $10,000 to bring the tribe to Leadville but the day before the race, Rick changed his mind and wanted $20,000. The demand seemed like extortion to Rockport. Everything was in place so a compromise was negotiated so the event could carry on.

Tony and his team had already developed a collection of trail shoes for Rockport called the Leadville Trail Series. As a part of the collection, Tony's team had developed one of the first mountain racing shoes called the 'Leadville Racer' for the tribe. The shoes were kind of a mix between a trail boot and a running shoe, bright red and yellow. The shoes were lightweight and featured a rugged Vibram outsole.

Tony brought a range of shoe sizes to a house where the tribe was staying a couple of days before the race. Tony took one look at the tribe's bare feet and knew instantly that the Rockport shoes would not fit them. Their feet were wide, muscular and thick, much thicker than traditional American or European feet.

Tony had the idea to have the Tarahumara start the race in Rockport shoes so the team could get a few photos, then let them change into their home made sandals for the race. Those basic sandals actually provided the inspiration for Tony and his team to make their own sandal for Rockport's Leadville collection of footwear. Rockport fittingly called it, the Tarahumara Sandal, named in honor of the tribe.

Rockport also brought in staff and a few employees who tried running the race.

Journalists were invited by Rockport to write articles about the race. These included representatives from Runner's World Magazine, Outside Magazine, and other publications to help draw attention to the race.

In the summer of 1994, Rockport held its worldwide sales meeting at the Little Nell hotel in Aspen. In order for all employees to get a feel for Leadville and the event, Rockport bussed all 200 attendees of the three-day sales meeting over Independence Pass to Leadville for a day. Tony arranged for Ken to speak to the whole group, which was very motivating. Ken gets folks fired up and believing in themselves. The group had a chance to see parts of the course and get a feel for the frontier setting of the town.

The Rockport Leadville Series of shoes ended up being quite successful. They sold well at REI and outdoor specialty stores, as well as in other countries; Japan, Australia, Canada, and throughout Europe.

The shoes were eventually phased out around 1999 mainly due to the fact that Rockport was in so many different categories of shoes, i.e., boating, hiking, running, etc. and Tony decided to leave Rockport.[5]

Tony went on to become president of Vibram USA, from 2001 through 2012, and he loved it. The company designed and produced sole platforms for various shoe companies including Merrell, TNF, Timberland, Nike, and many others.

In 2005, Vibram launched their first line of 'footwear' called Vibram FiveFingers, which many know worked as a glove for your feet with individual toe pockets that encouraged more natural movement. The idea came from the owner of the company in Italy who purchased the rights to the idea from an Italian design student. Italy and the US collaborated on the idea, eventually turning it into a business and separate division at Vibram. The Vibram FiveFingers shoes worked well for fitness training, minimalist running, and strengthening muscles in the lower legs and feet.

In 2012, Tony resigned from Vibram, but gave six-month's notice to the company so leadership could transition smoothly."

References

Chapter 8: Tarahumara – The Raramuri

1   Native Peoples Magazine, *"Return of the Tarahumara"*,
    Kitty Williams, Pages 20-27, Spring 1994
2   *Copper Canyon – Barranca del Cobre*, Fisher &
    Verplancken, 1992
3   Ultrarunning Magazine, *The Incredible Feat (or is it Feet) of
    the Tarahumara*, Kitty Williams, October 1993
4   Not only was the concept of a Tarahumara running sandal
    marketed effectively by several shoe companies, but a best-
    selling book, *"Born to Run"* by Christopher McDougall,
    inspired a new wave of runners to take up the ultrarunning
    sport. All because of the Tarahumara runners.
5   Personal correspondence, Tony Post, 2019

Chapter 9

Ann Trason: Facts vs. Myths

There has never been a more famous race in the history of ultrarunning than Ann Trason running with the Tarahumara at the 1994 Leadville Trail 100.

Sure, there have been other ultra events with strong men racing against each other and accomplished women champions competing with a stellar field of female runners. But never has there been a woman runner as accomplished and strong as Ann Trason to race against a legendary team of Tarahumara ultrarunners, at altitude and over a distance of 100 miles.

Secrets hidden by the Knights Templar, those legendary and powerful soldiers from the 12th century, have been sought for nearly 1,000 years without success. Yet the myths and legends regarding Ann Trason's record run at Leadville are more easily discovered.

Simply contacting Ann Trason revealed her story about racing the Tarahumara at Leadville and what actually took place: a story very different from the highly sensationalized, embellished and fictional accounts that have been published in numerous articles, publications and even books.

What you will read in this chapter are the events of the 1994 race, as remembered by Ann and others who were there and participated in the race.

The Leadville Trail 100 hit the really big time, finally. It only took eleven long years of shoestring budgets, donations, cajoling and convincing sponsors an ultrarunning race was something worth supporting. Free Wheelin' Films, of Aspen, was hired by CBS Television to film the event. The Leadville race organization secured a major sponsor for the race: The Rockport Company, famous shoe manufacturer from Maine.

The Rockport Company and Wilderness Expeditions sponsored the Tarahumara team that arrived in Leadville for the 1994 race. The Tarahumara team members didn't pay their own entry fees. The main sponsor Rockport paid their fees.

If you were wondering about Ann's entry into the race, "I entered Leadville on my own, paid my own entry fee and rented a place to stay." That clarifies that, unlike other fictional accounts of her entry into the race.

As mentioned previously in **Chapter 8 - Tarahumara - The Raramuri**, the Tarahumara runners spawned an entirely new running sandal industry based on their Huarache footwear and even inspired a best-selling book, *"Born to Run"* by Christopher McDougall.

McDougall's book attempts to describe the 1994 Leadville Trail 100 but for those of us at the race, the events in the book are not as accurate as the race itself. McDougall seemed to take many liberties when writing the book.[5]

For example, McDougall never contacted Ann Trason about actual race events, Ann said. The book's description of the famous competition between Ann and the Tarahumara seems to be highly sensationalized, to say the least.

Additionally, the main character in McDougall's book was Micah True, or Caballo Blanco as the renamed Micah True became in the book.

Micah True was a three-time finisher of the Leadville Trail 100 Mile race: 1986 – 25:23:56; 1987 – 22:33:27; 1993 – 24:15:14. Micah True's real name was Michael Randall Hickman but he always entered the Leadville Trail 100 as Micah True. Micah True did not race in the famous 1994 Leadville Trail 100. Instead, Micah was a pacer for a Tarahumara runner during the 1994 race after the fifty-mile point.[6]

Sadly, Micah True, aged 58, died on March 27, 2012 near Gila, New Mexico while resting during a solitary trail run. Micah died, according to Dr. James O'Keefe Jr., from "Pheidippide cardiomyopathy", essentially an enlarged, thickened heart with scar tissue.[7]

Micah was a friend of ours, racing competitor and member of the Leadville Trail 100 family. He will truly be missed.

Ann Trason: the name alone creates a vision of flawless running style, grit, determination and decisive speed in every ultrarunner's conscience. Ann's ultrarunning credentials leading up to the 1994 Leadville Trail 100 were impressive and lengthy, including a world record in 1993 at the 100 kilometer championship race in Amiens, France.

Immediately prior to the 1994 Leadville Trail 100, Ann won the women's division of the Western States 100 mile race with a time of 17:37:51. She was second overall in the race, including male runners. Ann won the women's division of the Western States 100 mile race six times prior to her appearance at the 1994 Leadville Trail 100.

Ann was not a stranger to the Leadville race either. Ann won the Leadville race in 1988 in a time of 21:40:26. Returning two years later, in 1990, she again won the women's race with a time of 20:38:51 and finished third overall.

Ann's methodology and training for ultra-distance events was legendary. Brutal long distance training runs with fleet footed California men were Ann's preferred method for her race preparation.

Additionally, Ann's husband at the time was Carl Anderson. Every now and then Carl would show up for an ultra distance race, win the race and then take his place in the ultrarunning shadows. Carl was an extremely fast runner with a 100-mile time of 14:46:05 when he won the 1983 Vermont Trail 100 Mile Endurance Run.[2] Ann Trason trained with her husband Carl as well as hardcore and fast California ultra distance runners in the California hills. But there was another side of Ann that few runners ever saw.

Ann drove to Leadville where she stayed for a month in a cabin, allowing her to train hard by herself, wanting to see what she could do, and perform her very best at the 1994 Leadville Trail 100.

Ann tried to avoid all the hoopla going on in town and simply wanted to explore, run and enjoy all that Leadville had to offer and not be bothered by the press or anyone.

Two days prior to race day, Ann heard about the Tarahumara runners who were also entered in the race and that she was being set-up to race against them. People were trying to push her into competing against the men but she gave it no thought. Ann had no knowledge of the hyped competition but started to feel a lot of stress from the mythical encounter. She felt like she was in a "pressure cooker." Along with the race pressure, driving from California to Colorado and having problems with her van didn't help either. Ann states that, "the pressure got to her."

Ann describes herself as shy and introverted, but felt she had failed everyone's expectations of her. "She was just a girl." She didn't want to disappoint or be misunderstood. Ann believed that, "people only want to bring up the negative."

What about the Tarahumara runners for the 1994 race? Seven Tarahumara runners entered the 1994 Leadville Trail 100 and were sponsored by The Rockport Company and Wilderness Expeditions.[3] The new Tarahumara team of runners only included one competitor from the 1993 Leadville race: Manuel Luna. Manuel was able to help his fellow team members by describing the course and the western cultural experience. Returning to the race with Manuel Luna were Rick Fisher and Kitty Williams, coordinators and crew for the Tarahumara team of runners.

Free Wheelin's films, the company that filmed the race, presented a picture of an ultimate confrontation between Tarahumara runners and a female runner, Ann Trason. The reality was quite different; Ann Trason simply wanted to run and do her best at the race, nothing more.

The Tarahumara were not accustomed to racing with women. Women runners in the Tarahumara culture just did not race with men. Women had their own long distance races, separate from the men, as is common in their culture.

Steve writes about the Ann and the Tarahumara:

"I ran all three of the races (1992, 1993 and 1994) with the Tarahumara (well, at least we were in the same race) and am able to give my observations about the races, including running with Ann Trason during this event. Well, I didn't really run **with** Ann Trason in the race since she was so far ahead of me. Maria, my crew, had more contact with Ann at the aid stations than I did.

The traditional shotgun blast ripped through cold air at 10,152 feet at the 4:00 am start of the 1994 Leadville Trail 100, sending 317 athletes into the dark of night.

In the darkness, crews waited anxiously at Turquoise Lake Dam, five miles into the race for the first runner to arrive.

Maria, my crew, saw Johnny Sandoval in first place, crest the Dam hill and effortlessly gain the dirt trail around Turquoise Lake. A steady stream of runners was behind Johnny including Ann Trason and a group of Tarahumara runners in their traditional colorful dress. Johnny Sandoval in first place? Who is Johnny Sandoval?

Johnny Sandoval was a runner from Gypsum, Colorado (near Vail) who finished his first Leadville Trail 100 in 1990. Johnny was a friend of Marge and me. Actually, Johnny was everyone's friend at the Leadville race. Johnny Sandoval was very personable, friendly and an excellent trail runner.

During the previous year at the Leadville race, Johnny finished in 21:45:48, good enough for ninth place overall. This year Johnny told me he was going to run harder than last year because he felt better.

Johnny was a manual laborer in the fields near Leadville. Before the 1993 race, Johnny said he wasn't feeling well because he had been sprayed by a crop duster as he was working in the fields one day. Johnny ran well in that 1993 race despite that hardship. For the race this year, Johnny had not been sprayed by a crop duster.

Maria always waits for me at the Tabor Boat Ramp, seven miles into the race. I remember running through a gauntlet of cheering and screaming well-wishers, searching for Maria near the water's edge. It was 5:00 am and really encouraging seeing all those people waiting for their runners."

May Queen aid station at the far end of the lake at 13.5 miles was the first official aid station. Johnny Sandoval arrived in first place, followed by Ann Trason in second place. The runners quickly walked through the check-in before exiting and running outside again into the first rays of the new day. It was not even 6:00 am at this point in the race for the leaders.

Tarahumara runners arrived at May Queen, changed out of the sponsor's experimental running shoes and donned their traditional Huarache sandals for the rest of the race.

Turquoise Lake shimmered in the early morning dawn as a fine mist covered the lake far below the advancing runners making their way toward Sugarloaf Pass.

With over three hundred runners in the race this year, the climb toward Hagerman Pass was not as serene or lonely as previous Leadville races. Runners were passing each other on the rutted out jeep trail, trying to gain a slight advantage on what should be a slow ascent. Saving energy during this early stage of the race might be something to think about, many Leadville race veterans thought to themselves.

Flying down from the top of Sugarloaf Pass on the Power Line Trail and into the Outward Bound aid station at mile 23.5 was Johnny Sandoval in first place. Johnny was running out of his mind and obviously enjoying his best race. Behind Johnny were two Tarahumara runners now ahead of Ann Trason.

Following Johnny into Outward Bound was Ann, looking for her crew. Maria noticed something was wrong. Ann's husband Carl was nowhere to be found.

When Ann came into the Outward Bound aid station she didn't see Carl there, she freaked out, big time. Calling and yelling, "where's Carl" and seemingly yelling at her crew was not out of anger but not knowing what might have happened to Carl. She was not upset with her crew; Ann was worried because she could not find Carl. The helicopters and the press all contributed to Ann's panicked state.

Crewmembers are the lifeblood for an ultrarunner. Every ultrarunner has at one time or another failed to connect with an essential crewmember. That eventuality is forever etched in one's consciousness and never a pleasant memory. It seems Carl was coming from Leadville a little late, having missed Ann. Ann left Outward Bound aid station without knowing where Carl was as she raced toward Halfmoon aid station, her next stop.

Race crews are not permitted to access Halfmoon aid station. The aid station is located up a long dusty rutted dirt road where vehicle traffic on the narrow road only created chaos for the runners. Hence the closest place to meet runners is four miles before the aid station at what is called Tree Line. There is a parking area adjacent to the dirt road if you decide to meet any runner at Tree Line. In prior years' races, this parking area was a party place for many of the runners' crews. Music, dancing and a jubilant air of celebration always happened at Tree Line for runners on the way BACK to Leadville.

During the first part of the race, Tree Line is a desolate place choked with dust and focused runners. Not many crews chose to meet their runner at Tree Line on the way TOWARD the Winfield turnaround.

Twin Lakes aid station is the next major point along the Leadville Trail 100 course at mile thirty-nine. There have been stories published about Ann battling two Tarahumara runners high above Twin Lakes aid station with exchanges along the way between the racers. Those accounts are purely fiction, since no pacers or anyone else was running with the leaders to witness what actually happened on that trail. Ann Trason was the first runner to arrive at Twin Lakes, ahead of the pursuing Tarahumara runners. Johnny Sandoval had slowed down and faded further back into the pack.

The climb toward definitive Hope Pass at 12,600 feet, the pinnacle of the race, is never something to joyfully anticipate. The trail is steep, slippery, and muddy and there are constant signs of bear activity. There is also very little oxygen the higher one climbs toward the Hopeless aid station and the friendly llamas grazing in the alpine meadow.

Winfield, at fifty miles, is where Ann Trason showed her dominance as an ultrarunner. Ann arrived first into Winfield, a feat no female runner had ever achieved. Seven minutes was Ann's lead over Juan Herrera, as the return trip over Hope Pass began. But now Ann had her secret weapon – her husband Carl was pacing her.

Pacers are permitted after the fifty-mile point of the Leadville Trail 100 and what could be better than having fleet-footed Carl with her? Steve recalls descending off the lower scree slope of Hope Pass when Ann passed him, going back toward Leadville. He remembers wishing Ann and Carl well as the two raced up Hope Pass together.

Ann arrived as first runner into the Twin Lakes aid station, Halfmoon aid station and even the Outward Bound aid station at seventy-two miles into the race.

Ann's lead had extended to eighteen minutes at Outward Bound over Juan Herrera in second place. Ann's elapsed time at Outward Bound aid station was 12:32. Ann was running faster than the course record at this point of the race. Ann was also eighteen minutes ahead of the closest runner with twenty-eight miles to go, or just more than a marathon distance.

Runners World Magazine sent Olympic marathon runner Don Kardong, fourth place at the Montreal Olympics in 1976 to cover the Leadville race. Don had won the LeGrizz 50 Mile Ultra Marathon race in 1987 so he was familiar with ultrarunning. Ann said she was really excited to see and meet Don at the race since he was her hero since high school.

Don wrote this about Ann when she left the Outward Bound aid station with twenty-eight miles to the finish line: "Most of us watching were ready to call it a lock. What could possibly happen in those final 28 miles?" [4]

For ultrarunners in the Leadville race, we all understand that anything can happen between Outward Bound aid station and the finish line. After all, there is the dreaded Power Line Trail and Sugarloaf Pass to contend with.

May Queen aid station at 86.5 miles saw Juan Herrera arrive six minutes ahead of Ann Trason. Juan Herrera was ahead of Ann?

Juan Herrera passed Ann on the climb up the buzzing and annoying Power Line Trail. At the summit of Sugarloaf Pass, Juan flew downward toward the distant glow of the May Queen aid station and never stopped running.

Juan Herrera crossed the finish line of the 1994 Leadville Trail 100 with a time of 17:30:42 in first place. Juan Herrera was the new champion and course record holder for the race.

Ann got sick with thirteen miles to go to the finish line. She wanted to break 18 hours, but finished in second place overall with an elapsed time of 18:06:24, the fastest a woman has ever run the race and the best finish place EVER for a woman in the Leadville Trail 100. Ann was disappointed and felt she had failed.

Six more Tarahumara runners finished the race. In fact, the entire team of Tarahumara runners finished the race. Third place overall was another Tarahumara runner, Martimano Cervantes (19:46:33). Fourth place another, Gabriel Bautista (20:26:35); Fifth place another, Rafael Holguin 20:26:35 and in seventh place was Martin Ramirez (20:51:07). The final two Tarahumara runners were: Manuel Luna, who bettered his previous finish with a time of 21:09:07 in 10th place and Corpus Quintero running 21:09:07 for 11th place.

In case you were wondering about the early race leader Johnny Sandoval, he finished the race in 34th place with an elapsed time of 24:31:28.

The second place female finisher was Barbara Dolan with a time of 24:43:11, 37th place overall. The final women's third place podium finisher was Ann Beine who ran 24:49:47.

156 runners finished the race out of 317 starters for a 49% finishing rate.

At the ceremony following the race conclusion, the Tarahumara graciously received their well-deserved recognition and awards. Ann Trason received the traditional ore cart championship trophy as the first place woman in the race.

Ann had these final thoughts about the race, as transcribed from our telephone conversation with her:

Ann didn't like being called the "white witch."[1,8] It seemed Micah True used the term "La Bruja", Spanish for witch, to describe Ann. Micah was trying to say Ann was a woman with great powers but his limited and faulty Spanish conveyed an inappropriate connotation of her.[9]

Looking back, Ann wishes she had had a better race. She always tries to do her best and does not want to be compared to men counterparts. She hopes for more opportunities for women to run their best for what women can do.

She feels there are many opportunities at Leadville to attract all women to do their best. Ann continues, "It is amazing how much the race has grown and people come out and try it. Leadville is a great little town." Ann said she had a good time in Leadville; "It's magical, affordable, good training and a tough race." The altitude was felt by Ann and for that reason she came out for a month prior to the race to train. According to Ann, the prettiest part of the run for her is Hope Pass and the worst part is climbing Sugarloaf Pass, on the way back.

Ann was diagnosed with Rheumatoid Arthritis three years ago. She cannot run any more, but hikes. She strongly hopes our book propels women to try to see what they can do and show what they are made of.

Ann states that the book, *Born to Run*, was not true as it relates to her and the Tarahumara. Ann stated that, "it broke her heart to read the book." She never talked to Christopher McDougall, author of the book, and was never given a pair of Tarahumara Huarache sandals at the awards ceremony.[10]

References

Chapter 9: Ann Trason: Facts vs. Myths

1 The Guardian, Jill Homer, February 20, 2015
2 Ultrarunning Magazine, Page 12, October 1993
3 Ultrarunning Magazine, Pages 6-9, October 1994
4 Runner's World Magazine, *The Race Across the Sky"*, Don Kardong, Page 84, March 1995
5 Personal correspondence, Tony Post, 2019
6 Running Times Magazine, *"Micah True a.k.a. Caballo Blanco"*, Brian Metzler, March 2010
7 *The Haywire Heart*. Christopher J. Case, et al. Pages 66-69. April 2018
8 The term, "White Witch" is used in voodoo tales throughout the Caribbean, Central American and Mexico. *Life At Sea Level*, Stephen J. Pavlidis
9 Sponsorthefool.blogspot.com/2011/11/in-defense-of-ann-trason-born-to-run.html. November 11, 2011
10 Personal conversation with Ann Trason, March 27, 2019

Chapter 10

The 90's

Marshall Ulrich's *LT100/PP Combo,* **Leadville Triple Crown and reflections about the Leadville Trail 100 and life:**

"Back in the 1990s, people joked about running the Leadville Trail 100 and Pikes Peak Marathon on the same weekend. What's so funny, I thought? I believed it could be done. I was very familiar with both courses; having completed – along with Scott Weber – the first ever Pikes Peak Quad (four times up and down for 104 miles total) and I had five solid Leadville Trail 100 finishes. So, in 1993, I gave it a go.

Accepting the LT 100 /PP Combo challenge, I finished in the top 10 at Leadville (21:40:18 in 8th place) in time to be driven to the Pikes Peak start.

After I finished the PP marathon (9:34), I held the dubious distinction of being the first Colorado finisher at Leadville and the last Colorado finisher on Pikes Peak. But I was able to run 126.2 miles with an average elevation above 10,000 feet and about 22,800 feet of cumulative elevation gain.

The record – although I had only done the combo to show it could be done – was finally broken in 2017 by Michael Wardian with a combined time of 26:20. In other words, he crushed it.

My thirst for adventure and new challenges continued – including adventure racing around the world, and running in Death Valley along the 146-mile route from Badwater to the summit of Mount Whitney – but Leadville was still home.

In 1999, a few weeks after I completed my Badwater Solo, I ran the Leadville Trail 100, and then biked the Leadville 100 MTB race; my results were not stellar in either one.

I was the last person into the final aid station during the bike race, temperatures were dipping, and I was ill prepared. Ken Chlouber dumped out all of the trash from one of the plastic garbage bags, tore holes in the top and sides for my head and arms, and hurriedly sent me off yelling, "pedal like hell."

If Ken Chlouber yells at you, you listen. I finished dead last with less than four minutes to spare. To my amusement, at the post-race gathering, I was awarded "the last ass over the pass" trophy. I was just glad to get it.

Still, I thought there might be a way to redeem myself.

Rumors were going around that Buzz Burell had thought up a third event: kayaking 100 miles around Turquoise Lake. I gave Buzz a call.

Yes, he had considered doing the Leadville Trail 100 run and bike, followed by 10 loops around the lake, but said he didn't think he would get around to doing it, so gave me the go.

So, fourteen days after the Leadville Trail 100 run, I dropped a wide bottomed sea kayak into Turquoise Lake at the Matchless Boat Ramp, and set out, hugging close to shore. Day turned into night and the only sound was the quiet dipping and stirring of my blades in the water.

Alone, I reflected on prior Leadville Trail 100 runs. Some years the weather made the trails more suited for skates, with runners covered in mud. I vividly recall watching Dennis Herr barreling down the Twin Lakes side of the racecourse seemingly on a collision course with a tree.

I considered how daydreaming guided me to Tim Walsh, as we both had taken a wrong turn heading up to Mt. Elbert instead of staying on the course. I thought about my connection with Mark Macy; one that can only be forged in struggle, including running the Leadville Trail 100 many times with Mace pacing me the final fifty miles. Both of us remain dear friends.

In stark contrast to my struggles, I recall coming upon one of the Tarahumara Indians sitting alongside the racecourse in 1992, the first year they came to Leadville. While none of the Tarahumara finished that year, he was looking off into the distance, seemly without a care.

The cold, along with a touch of loneliness, brought me back to the dark lake and my fear of capsizing due to sleep deprivation. I dipped my numb, gloved hands into the warmer-than-air-temperature water to keep the circulation going so I wouldn't lose purchase of the paddle.

As the steam rose from the water, the moon answered, shining through the steam, illuminating the shore as the stars shone with their own individual brilliance. In the peaceful calm, I felt small: a speck on that water, within the Rocky Mountains, encompassed by the American continent, spinning on the face of the earth, dwarfed by expanse of the universe.

Then, my aching back snapped me back to reality and the never-ending calculations of how far I still had to paddle and how long it might take.

And so it went, the state of peacefulness, then fear of falling asleep and capsizing, then loneliness; over and over and over again until finally the sun rose.

I finished late in the morning after 28 hours of paddling. There, it's done, the first Leadville Triple Crown. I had redeemed myself, not with speed, but with persistence, diversity in athleticism, and a will to prove that anything is possible if we have the desire to give it a go.

All told, I finished the Leadville Trail 100 thirteen times. It was **never** easy.

I was able to get the coveted sub-24 hour buckle the first seven finishes, and typically finished at least in the top 20, if not top 10. In 1991, I ran the course in 20:33:36 and came in third, my best time and highest place finish. As I got older, and slower, my times were over 24-hours, but I still finished – most of the time – even if it took me 29:15:00, my slowest time (in 2003).

As I write this, sitting atop my office desk is a violin. No, I don't play. But the instrument is one of my most treasured possessions. The Tarahumara came back to Leadville in 1993 and 1994, winning both years. After my finish in 1993, I approached one gentleman, and introduced myself to Patrocinio Lopez. Being a fine arts major, I was curious about their arts and crafts; he was a carver and could carve violins.

I asked Patrocinio if he would carve one for me. He was pleased, and immediately said yes. I paid him for it, and gave him my address. A few months later it arrived.

Looking at his fine piece of heartfelt craftsmanship, I am reminded that there is much more to life than running. An appreciation of the trail, of nature; the connections between people – family, friends, and fellow runners – and beautiful artistic works like my one-of-a-kind violin, are what make us whole, human, and vulnerable. We can all "dig deep and love more." In fact, it's the least we can do."

1990

The Leadville Trail 100 moved into the 1990's by maintaining a high quality, ultrarunning event. Runners were still treated as family by race management. Sponsors, while not easily lured to support a sport on the running fringe, were basically stable in their contributions.

Ken and Merilee never tired of recruiting new cash flow for the race. It was in 1990 that the shoe company from Maine, Rockport, became the title sponsor. It seemed that Rockport wanted to develop and market a running shoe. What better proving ground could there be for a new shoe than the grueling trails around Leadville? Of course the brutal Colorado Trail mystique was not lost on the bright Rockport marketing team.

The race itself went off smoothly, as Ken and Merilee had trained and honed support teams to work as clockwork-like precision organizations.

First place in this year's race was Jim O'Brien from California with a time of 17:55:57. Jim O'Brien became the first Leadville Trail 100 champion to crack the elusive 18-hour barrier. Second place was none other than Dennis "The Animal" Herr with a time of 19:57:49. Third place in the race was NOT a male. No, third place overall went to none other than Ann Trason in a time of 20:38:51 at the age of 29.

The second woman finisher was once again previous champion, Randi Bromka who ran 21:55:33 and 11th place overall. Betsy Kalmeyer placed as third woman in a time of 23:15:14.

Then there was the story of legendary ultrarunner Arthur Schwartz.

Arthur was a physician who lived "over the hill" in Aspen, Colorado. Arthur was an original finisher at the 1983 Leadville Trail 100 and an incredibly strong ultrarunner.

Something very bad happened to Arthur as he was training for the 1990 race. A car struck Arthur during one of his training runs near Aspen.

Arthur sustained contusions to his head and chest as well as compound fractures of both legs. Arthur was in and out of consciousness as he lay in the Aspen hospital following the accident.

According to another physician, Arthur's friend and original Leadville Trail 100 finisher, Barry Mink, Arthur was in serious shape following the accident. Barry related the story when Arthur regained consciousness in the hospital. Arthur's first response to the medical personnel was, *"Have I finished the race?"*

Arthur's family was at his bedside and heard Arthur's remark. Acting quickly, the response to Arthur was *"No. You are only at the first aid station and have a long way to go."* Those in Arthur's room understood how important the Leadville race was to him.

Everyone is convinced that giving Arthur, a seven time Leadville Trail 100 finisher, a goal to continue fighting and pushing toward the next race aid station was the reason he survived his trauma and continued on his long and difficult journey to recovery.

At the starting line of the 1990 Leadville Trail 100, a person with a crutch under his arm stood watching as the assembled runners milled about, waiting for the coming shotgun blast. Several runners simultaneously recognized the person with the crutch was none other than Arthur Schwartz. Those of us previously anticipating the starting gun quickly gathered around Arthur, exchanging hugs, shaking hands and pounding him affectionately on the back amidst an air of excitement. Arthur was back.

As the 1990 race unfolded, Randi Bromka, 1987 race champion and friend of Arthur, carried Arthur's official race number for the entire race. Randi finished the race in 21:55:33, ensuring Arthur finished his 8th Leadville Trail 100 in spirit if not in body. Leadville race management went as far as printing the official race long sleeve t-shirts with the number "8" emblazoned on the shoulder to honor Arthur in 1990.

I (Steve) still have my t-shirt, although it is rather tattered and faded these days but the number 8 is still oddly clear and visible. And if you were wondering, yes, I wear it when the air turns crisp and cool when going out for a run on my favorite trail to remind me of Arthur and the good times we had as he consistently raced **by** me at the Leadville Trail 100.

1991

It was a relatively dry and warm race in 1991 with sunscreen being the required substance for the racers. What a change from previous years.

The men's race was exciting as usual with 53-year-old G.E. Jensen leading almost the entire race. So much for the young bucks this year, or that was what everyone thought. However, and there is usually a word like "however" used to describe a long race like Leadville. However, 44-year-old Steve Mahieu from New Mexico overtook G.E. during the final states of the race and became the new champion, running the course in a time of 19:38:04. G.E. Jensen fought until the end and finished in second place with a time of 20:18:26. Third place went to Marshall Ulrich in a time of 20:33:36.

The women's race had a new champion as well with Alice Thurau running a very respectable time of 22:10:35, finishing in 7th place overall. Hot on Alice's heels was previous champion Marge Hickman in second place in a time of 23:40:44 with Sue Ellen Trapp rounding out the top three women with a finishing time of 24:21:22.

Other runners finishing the race included:

- Steve Fossett, world champion balloonist, sailor and adventurer who ran 29:38:12
- Crusty Lee (El Burro) Schmidt finished the race in 27:07:16
- Melissa Lee Sobal ran 29:38:43
- Last place finisher was Al Binder in 29:56:11

There was 51% of the starting field that finished the race; 286 starters and 147 finishers

1992

(Please refer to **Chapter 8: Tarahumara – The Raramuri** for a detailed report about the Tarahumara runners at the Leadville Trail 100)

Entry into the Leadville Trail 100 was still on a first come first served basis, despite the growing popularity for the race. Western States had their lottery system but Ken and Merilee decided to let the chips fall where they may regarding runners wishing to enter the race.

For this 10th edition of the Leadville Trail 100 in 1992, something historic happened that would rock the ultrarunning world to its core: Legendary Tarahumara runners from Mexico's Copper Canyon showed up at the starting line for the race.

Those of us at the race in 1992 took more than casual notice of a reticent group of strangely dressed runners standing at the starting line with what seemed to be over-sized running shoes on their feet. Word spread fast that these legendary runners from times long forgotten had come to run 100 miles amongst the high Colorado Mountains. As dawn turned into a new day after 30:00:00 hours of running, not a single Tarahumara had crossed the finish line.

With the Tarahumara nowhere to be seen, the men's race was still hotly contested. Rick Spady emerged on top with a time of 19:51:10. Second place went to Peter Downing in 20:13:30 while Bill Finkbeiner ran an excellent time of 20:30:06 to grab third place. Joe Schlereth finished immediately behind Bill in a time of 20:44:58 and Steve Mahieu rounded out the top five with a time of 21:24:49.

This year I (Steve) ran my fastest time of 22:41:17 and good enough for 12th place overall. I might have snagged 11th place but a stealth runner jumped on me coming up the Boulevard without using his lights. Geeze, I wish I had known about Theresa Daus-Weber's winning tactics of going dark at that stage of the race. The person who caught me was Raymond Bailey from Arkansas who finished less than 2 minutes ahead of me.

On the women's side, Theresa Daus-Weber became the 1992 champion with a time of 23:37:23. Right behind Theresa was Sue Ellen Trapp of Florida who ran 23:57:15 followed by Mo Bartley in 24:52:12. Perennial strong finisher and trail maintenance volunteer Margrit Howard finished in 28:02:46.

The 1992 Leadville Trail 100 women's champion was Theresa Daus-Weber who ran an excellent time of 23:37:23. Here is Theresa's account of her championship performance and strategy:

"It was one of those rare races where all the variables of an ultra just go smoothly. It was like floating in a dream climbing up the Power Line Trail inbound during the fading daylight as a volunteer on a motor bike was hanging glow sticks to mark the trail for runners who would be coming through in the dark for the next eight hours.

Crew, weather and my pace were aligned all day when I reached the May Queen aid station inbound as the first woman to come through the aid station.

Through the cheers, I was encouraged to stop and celebrate but I asked where the 2nd place woman, Sue Ellen Trapp was.

The aid station volunteers told me Sue Ellen was closing the 30-minute gap I had on her at the Halfmoon aid station to only 20 minutes behind me at the Outward Bound aid station.

With that news I promptly left the May Queen aid station. When I hit the dirt road after the Turquoise Lake Dam, I told my pacer Frank to turn off his light so Sue Ellen wouldn't be able to see us if she was closing in.

My pacer and I ran by the light of the full moon to finish in 23:37:23, still maintaining the 20-minute gap I had on Sue Ellen since the Outward Bound aid station to become the women's champion."

Then there was Arthur Schwartz running and racing for his 10th consecutive Leadville Trail 100 finisher's belt buckle.

After sustaining severe injuries before the 1990 race, Arthur recovered enough to finish the 1991 race with a battered body but an incredibly strong will to succeed. How would Arthur's quest for an unprecedented 10th finisher buckle unfold this year?

Marge and Steve both recall waiting at the finish line in downtown Leadville on Sunday morning, over twenty-nine hours after the starting rifle blast sent runners on their way onto the Leadville racecourse and into the early morning darkness.

We were not alone waiting at the finish line that Sunday morning. There was an assembled crowd of maybe 200 people standing, waiting and silently wondering in that chilling cold morning rarified air if Arthur would make it. Suddenly the finish line megaphone came alive; Arthur Schwartz had just exited the Boulevard and was on his way home.

Instantly a large pack of runners began running from the starting line, down the hill and toward a slowly moving figure in the far distance. It was Arthur and he needed encouragement. Like a wave, runners surrounded a forever-forward moving Arthur Schwartz. Cheers, laughter and an air of excitement pushed Arthur and the well wishing runners up that final hill before looking down upon the race finish line.

A huge cheer went up from those waiting at 6th and Harrison Street as Arthur appeared in the distance with his growing group of well-wishers. With thirty-eight minutes to spare, Arthur Schwartz crossed the Leadville Trail 100 finish line in a time of 29:21:57 for his 10th consecutive finish.

The race statistics showed 290 runners began the race but only 139 finished giving a finishing percentage of 48%.

1993

(Please refer to **Chapter 8: Tarahumara – The Raramuri** for a detailed report about the Tarahumara runners at the 1993 Leadville Trail 100)

There were 294 starters for this 11th edition of the Leadville Trail 100 but only 135 finished the race for a finishing percentage of 46%.

As explained in **Chapter 8**, the men's champion was Victoriano Churro with a time of 20:03:33. Second place went to Cerrildo Chacarito in 20:43:06 and third place was captured by previous champion Steve Mahieu with an elapsed time of 20:54:27.

Fourth place overall and first woman finisher was none other than Christine Gibbons in 20:55:59. Second place woman was Theresa Daus-Weber with a time of 22:50:47. Rounding out the top three women was another previous champion, our own Marge Hickman with a time of 24:33:12.

The last place finisher for the 1993 edition of the Leadville Trail 100 was Oklahoma's favorite ultrarunner Harry Deupree with a time of 29:59:45.

The race saw two other remarkable finishes: Bill Finkbeiner ran 21:40:18 for his 10th consecutive race and Al Binder, one of the original race finishers also earned his 10th belt buckle this year. Micah True (aka Caballo Blanco) finished his 3rd and final Leadville Trail 100 in a time of 24:15:14.

If you are a current reader of Ultrarunning Magazine (2019), you will notice a back page column written by Errol "Rocket" Jones. Errol finished the first of his two Leadville Trail 100s in a time of 26:55:13, a very solid time.

Ken Chlouber had his fastest race this year. I (Steve) recall Ken telling me he thought he was on pace to crack the elusive 25-hour barrier, finally.

After years of trying, Ken remembers coming strongly up the Boulevard, striding over the two sets of railroad tracks when the finishing gun sounded in the distance. That blast signified the 25:00 hour mark in the race had passed. Ken continued his race, crossing the finish line in 25:42:08. Ken was so close in his finest effort to break the twenty-five hour barrier. Cole Chlouber, Ken's son, ran 25:08:06 in 2011 to set the Chlouber family record in the race.

1994

This year at Leadville, 1994, **THE** most historic ultrarunning race in the world took place. Please see **Chapter 9; Ann Trason: Facts vs. Myths** for a complete description of the race.

Entrants for this twelfth Leadville Trail 100 were at an all-time record high due to the fact that this year's race featured a historic shootout among the world's fastest and most legendary ultrarunners: The Tarahumara of Mexico's Copper Canyon and the fastest woman ultrarunner on the planet, Ann Trason.

Other events occurring during the race included:

- Ken Chlouber finished his 10th race
- Harry Deupree finished his 10th race
- Legendary and world record balloon pilot Steve Fossett entered the race but failed to finish. Steve had previously finished the race in 1991 with a time of 29:38:12
- There were 317 starters in the race, 156 finishers and the finishing percentage was 49%
- Rockport shoes based in Maine remained the title sponsor
- CBS "Eye on Sports" televised the historic race on national TV

Race champion Marge Hickman was impressed by Rockport sponsorship. Here is her missive about getting a pair of shoes:

"Prior to this years race, Rockport via their representative, Jim Younger and others, had a great deal for those of us entered in the race. Rockport offered runners free shoes to test, try out and hopefully run the race in. Gosh, I was excited to get some new shoes to try.

We filled out a Rockport shoe form with our size preference and vital information in order to get a pair of their new model of trail running shoes. When I saw sample shoes displayed on a table, I was somewhat surprised to see not an actual running shoe but more of a low and high-top hiking boot in either black or dark brown with shoelaces. I was able to get a pair of each style and color. Hum, I thought; not what I usually wear to run in but what the heck, I'll try them and they're free.

The shoes looked heavy but well made. I was a little embarrassed to try them on "right there" as they looked kind of "dorky", especially for a running shoe. I knew I was expected to wear test them. and maybe, maybe consider wearing them on race day.

I gathered up my stuff, thanked everyone said my goodbyes to the Rockport representatives. Once outside I noticed other runners coming with their filled-out form and leaving with a Rockport shoebox, doing just what I had done. I wondered what the other runners thought about the shoes. My pairs of Rockport shoes looked quite different from David's shoes in his picture. Maybe mine were the women's version?

Finally, and to this day, I still have my two pairs of Rockport trail running shoes. They still look like new and still fit me. I think about wearing them occasionally for hiking, but after all these years I will keep them as an awesome memory and chuckle when I see them in my shoe closet."

From David Strong, who actually wore his pair of Rockport shoes in the race:

"In August 1993 I dropped out at Twin Lakes outbound having started the race limping due to a severed ACL in my right knee. I severed the ACL years before I began running, and the injury finally caught up with me.

A day did not go by that I did not think about getting back on the Leadville course and making up for the loss. I delayed ACL reconstruction until Thanksgiving because I was signed up to run the Mountain Masochist 50 in October that I miraculously completed.

Rockport was a major Leadville race sponsor in 1994. I volunteered to run the race in a pair of their street shoes. The shoes were light brown suede with crepe bottoms. I received three pairs for training and to run the race. I trained in one pair, ran the race in one pair, and saved the third for everyday use.

Nine months after ACL reconstruction I completed the Leadville Trail 100 wearing that pair of Rockport dress shoes for the entire race while finishing in 23:43:31."

David Strong's Rockport running shoes

Of special note, the inaugural Leadville Trail 100 Mile Mountain Bike race (LT100 MTB) took place on Saturday, August 13, 1994, one week before the flagship Leadville Trail 100. The LT100 MTB race covered a distance of 100 miles and was founded by Ken Chlouber and Merilee Maupin.

An initial thought for the race route was to use the same course as the 100-mile running race. However (there is that word again), upon attempting to mountain bike the proposed racecourse, it was discovered that riding Hope Pass was not a good thing for a mountain bike rider.

Tom Sobal, world champion snowshoe racer, trail expert and local resident, was asked by Ken Chlouber for advice regarding his proposed bike route.

Tom Sobal wrote this about the LT100 MTB course:

"I did not design the bike course. Ken Chlouber came up with a draft route. He knew that I mountain biked and that I had the devices and expertise to accurately measure racecourses (I am a USATF running course certifier). So I measured the bike course in exchange for a free entry. I only made one change to a route option that Ken originally suggested that was incorporated into the course.

I remember that the course I measured was over 101 miles long. I suggested some slight course changes so the distance was closer to 100 miles. Ken did not seem to care that the course was too long, and did not include my suggestions. He actually made other changes to add even more additional distance. Subsequent changes to the route in later years have made the course even longer.[3]"

The LT100 MTB high point was placed to the east of Hope Pass, at what is called Columbine Mine at nearly the same elevation as Hope Pass. Barry Mink, original Leadville Trail 100 finisher became the only person to complete the first 100-mile running race **AND** the inaugural Leadville Trail 100 Mile Mountain Bike race in a time of 12:37:40.

1995

The 13th edition of the Leadville Trail 100 turned out to be just that, unlucky.

325 runners started the race this year, a slight increase from the 1994 historic race. It was not the dramatic increase many of us expected or dreaded, based on media coverage and hype during the 1994 race.

The 1995 race proved to be notable not only for the normally competitive racing entrants but for the miserable weather; miserable weather even when judged by typical Leadville standards. Ultrarunning Magazine titled that years' race report, "Rain and Cold Batter Leadville."[1] Due to the adverse and sometimes dangerous conditions, 130 runners finished the race with a finishing percentage of only 40%.

One of the most interesting parts of the race proved to be the stream crossing at Lake Creek, located just outside the lowest point on the course at Twin Lakes at an altitude of 9,200 feet. What is usually a wide, cold and shallow stream crossing during good years turned into a dangerous, hip deep, raging torrent during the 1995 race.

Race management recognized the hazardous conditions at the Lake Creek crossing immediately. Ken and Merilee decided to string a long climbing rope across the raging stream crossing and positioned eight search and rescue divers along the rope as well as downstream from the rope. Divers positioned downstream from the rope? That did not sound good, or so runners thought when word got out about the precautions. Well, it turned out search and rescue divers were essential in saving many ultrarunners from ending their race attempt prematurely.

One notable incident at the stream crossing occurred when the women's leading runner, Theresa Daus-Weber, tried crossing Lake Creek again while running back toward the finish line.

Theresa was swept downstream after losing her grip on the safety rope. Seeing Theresa flailing in the surging water while bouncing off submerged rocks, the rescue divers went into action and successfully saved Theresa. Unfortunately Theresa was injured during her unplanned body-surfing attempt but persevered for the remainder of the race coming in as third place woman with a time of 25:24:13.

The women's champion was Linda Lee running a time of 22:59:01 followed by second place women's finisher Marge Hickman with a time of 23:44:25.

Steve vividly remembers: "I was running with Theresa Daus-Weber during the later stages of the race. As we ran together, Theresa described her near drowning and kept me occupied for several miles with her story.

Theresa and I continued to run side by side and onto the red carpet marking the race finish line in downtown Leadville. Like a bolt of lightning I remembered Ken's words about not ending the race in a tie so I literally pushed Theresa in front of me and across the finish line. Hence the one second difference in our finishing times.

The race turned out to be my 10th Leadville Trail 100 finish in 25:24:14. What a way to commemorate all those years of trail running, by pushing Theresa Daus-Weber ahead of me."

Celebrating their 10th Leadville finishes were: Martyn Greaves in 29:27:05 and Ed Williams in 29:25:25. Another finisher during the race was Gordy Ainsleigh (Western States 100 mile runner) with a time of 29:55:52. Then there was the father/son finishes of Harry Deupree 29:32:12 and his son Chisholm in 29:32:10. Note that they did not tie either.

1996

The weather Gods smiled once again on the 1996 Leadville Trail 100. Race conditions proved ideal with relatively warm temperatures and only a few scattered showers with no snow or hail.

Marti Liquori, third high school runner to break the four-minute barrier in the mile run, an Olympic runner in the 1500 meters and a running coach was at the race as part of a film crew sent by ESPN to make a documentary about the race.

Steve recalls meeting Marty Liquori:

"I called my wife Maria who was preparing to drive up to Leadville for the race. I asked her to bring my copy of Marty's running book, "Marty Liquori's Guide For The Elite Runner" so I could have him sign the book.

I still have the book with his dedication to me, "Steve, best of luck running Western States", signed Marty Liquori. Hmmm, it must have been the lack of oxygen at Leadville as he mistook Colorado for California, I thought to myself."

Patti Wixom, an entrant in the race, sang the Olympic song during the pre-race trail briefing at the 6th Street gymnasium as the crowd was whipped into the normal pre-race frenzy by Ken's stirring "pep talk." Patti failed to finish the race, despite Ken's exciting pre-race trail briefing talk.

Ken's expression, *"You are better than you think you are and you can do more than you think you can"* has become synonymous with his pre-race briefing.

Ken Chlouber has used many down-to-earth sayings to inspire gathered runners at the Friday briefing. One of our favorites is *"We'll tell you when to start and we'll tell you when to stop. In between don't think, just keep running."*[2]

The 1996 race saw 157 runners finish the race out of a starting field of 320 hopefuls. That is a finishing percentage of 49%.

Marge Hickman led the women's field from the start. Marge was shooting for her 10th Leadville finish and seemed intent on making it even more memorable by chasing the championship ore cart in the process.

Theresa Daus-Weber had other ideas and passed Marge before the Twin Lakes aid station at 40 miles. Theresa maintained her lead until between the 78-mile mark at the Fish Hatchery aid station and the final May Queen aid station when eventual women's winner Martha Swatt passed her.

Martha Swatt continued running in first place to the finish line, crossing in a time of 23:30:11. Theresa Daus-Weber came in as the second place woman with a time of 24:32:46 and Hosni Haghighian claimed the third spot on the podium with a time of 26:27:58. Marge Hickman faded during the later stages of the race to finish in 27:31:26 as 6th place woman.

Even though Marge ran slower than normal, the pain was partially offset by the fact this was Marge's 10th Leadville Trail 100 finish. Marge's finish earned her a historical place in the record books with Marge becoming the first 10-time female finisher in race history, joining only eight other runners who had achieved that desirable status.

The men's race marked a new beginning dynasty at the Leadville Trail 100. Steve Peterson and Michael Ehrlich had an intense battle throughout the race for the coveted ore cart trophy.

Michael and Steve switched the lead numerous times until the Fish Hatchery aid station. It was at the Fish Hatchery when Steve finally regained the lead and never looked back, winning the race is a time of 19:29:56. Michael finished in second place at 20:22:46. Third place went to Joe Schlereth in a time of 20:38:37. Leadville's beloved Johnny Sandoval, perennial front-runner, finished fourth in 20:53:55, followed by Stan Wingate at 21:12:07 in fifth place overall.

Steve Peterson was a member of a running group called Divine Madness Ultra Club from Boulder, Colorado. **Chapter 12 - Divine Madness** contains all you want to know and an in-depth look at the group: Divine Madness.

But before you think about skipping ahead to that chapter, you might like this story Marge and her soon-to-be husband Mike wrote about her "Turquoise Sparkly Tights":

"Oh, those turquoise sparkly tights of 1985. I (Marge) won the pair of sparkly turquoise tights at a 20-mile snowshoe race in Leadville that Tom and Melissa Sobal organized and held each year. Who knew what those bright colored tights would do or attract...?

A man, Mike Hickman, came to Vail from Lawrence, Kansas for a continuing education seminar that lasted four days."

Mike explains: "After the first day I got bored with the class and drove to Leadville to experience the real Colorado. I had just finished Ironman and was looking for a new adventure, something tougher than Ironman.

As I was walking up and down Harrison Avenue, not being able to breathe, I stopped in front of the headquarters of the Leadville Trail 100 and was gazing at the results of 1993 race that happened just the previous week. All I could see was DNF's.

Nearly half the entrants who started the race did not finish and my first thought was that this was a bike race. But suddenly I realized this was a foot race. I couldn't even breathe on Harrison Avenue at 10,152 feet and that was only the start of the race. Suddenly a virtual hand came through the front glass window, grabbed me and said, "You have to do this."

Not knowing anything about a 100-mile trail race and the fact that I could not breath at 10,152 feet, I realized this was a challenge of a lifetime. I left a message at race headquarters to send me the application and information for next year's race.

What I got in the mail following my visit was a list of things to buy from race headquarters, ever the shrewd marketers. I ordered the video of the previous race because nobody in Lawrence, Kansas knew how to train for a 100-mile race.

When the video arrived I turned it on and started watching it over, and over, and over again, enthralled by the video and realizing those might be the same people I would be competing and running with next year. As I continued to watch the video and take note of the names of people in the race, all of a sudden at the finish line I saw a pair of sparkly turquoise tights and the cutest butt I had ever seen in the world.

I had no idea it was Marge's butt in those sparkly turquoise tights but I kind of thought it might be her and in the back of my mind I knew I really wanted to meet her.

My training went well back in Kansas that winter and I decided to come out to Leadville in July to do Hope Pass, knowing full well that it was the toughest part of the race.

While training on Hope Pass I met Merilee who asked me to come out in early August to help with the inception of the 100-mile Leadville mountain bike race.

The day came for the LT100 MTB race. My friend, Ian Phillips, talked me into volunteering with him at the Columbine Mine turnaround point during the 100-mile MTB race. Ian also told me to stand at the corner of 6th Street and Harrison Avenue and someone would pick me up to go up to the Columbine Mine.

As I stood there a car pulled up and said, "Are you Mike Hickman," and I said "yes."

The person said, "We're here to pick you up and take you to Columbine." I got in the car and we headed out. As we headed down toward Stringtown, just south of Leadville on Highway 24, a big rainbow came over the highway so we stopped and pulled off the road. As everyone got out of the car and gazed at the rainbow, I said I wish I had a camera.

Well, the mayor of Leadville and his wife looked at me and said, "You don't have a camera...?"

I said "no," and they turned around and looked at me with disbelief. The mayor explained that my friend Ian said I was with the Associated Press to take pictures on the top of Columbine Mine.

I again said "no," I was not with the Associated Press. The mayor said they bumped two people out of a ride to Columbine to pick me up, thinking I was the photographer. I apologized and said, Ian is a good friend, but I was not a photographer or ever with the Associated Press. I was allowed to continue riding in the car until we reached the turnoff at Granite where I met Ian again.

Ian walked over to me and said, "I want to introduce you to Marge." My first thought was that this is the HOT woman who won the Leadville Trail 100. As I approached her, I said, "Hi, I'm Mike from Kansas", which I'm sure totally impressed her, but I didn't think so.

As we drove up to Columbine and got to the top, I was able to talk to her a little bit more and convinced her that I wasn't really a "hick" from Kansas. Knowing full well that she was going back to Denver to have Plantar Fasciitis surgery, we enjoyed the day as much as we could, came down off of Columbine, and she was gone.

I ran the 100-mile race the following weekend but dropped out at Winfield with 5 minutes to spare before the cutoff time.

I stayed in touch with Marge. On one of my follow-up trips to Leadville, Marge and I, along with another couple went to the Silver Dollar Saloon, had some drinks and danced the evening away. As Marge said, "It was Michael's dancing "dip" that won my heart."

On August 16, 1997, Marge and Mike were married on the top of Hope Pass. Their story about getting married during the race is in the next section about the 1997 event.

1997

There is a Training Run Weekend put on by race management six weeks before the actual Leadville Trail 100. The cost for that weekend's runs was set at $75 this year.

149 finishers crossed the finish line at the 15th annual Leadville Trail 100 with Rockport the title sponsor of the event.

Steve Peterson repeated as men's champion with a time of 18:10:45. Second place went to 19:30:59 and third place was 20:59:05.

First place women's champion was Julie Arter from Arizona with a time of 24:08:07, second place was Kathy White at 25:59:11 and rounding out the top three was Valerie Caldwell in 27:32:39. Former champion Martha Swatt finished in 28:18:19 and another former champion, Theresa Daus-Weber finished in 29:32:49, showing that even previous champions can have a bad day at Leadville, although those who dropped out of the race would gladly have either of the previous champion's finishing times.

Something very special happened at the top of Hope Pass during the race this year as related by Marge:

"Oh what a day filled with excitement and unexpected surprises during this year's Leadville Trail 100 (August 16th).

That's right, I was married **during** the Leadville Trail 100 race.

Why was I surprised when we planned our wedding on top of Hope Pass during the Leadville Trail 100?

Having both been married before, we wanted a very small ceremony. I mailed out a hundred or so running invitations drawn by an artist friend of mine. We knew that only a few close friends and Mike's two children could make the climb up Hope Pass. Luckily, two ministers agreed to marry us, but just in case we had one come up Hope Pass from the Winfield side and the other from the Twin Lakes side.

Whichever minister got to the summit first would get the privilege to marry us. They were acquaintances and knew their race was to get to the top of Hope Pass first.

We picked a flat area near a rock pile to the side of the racecourse for the ceremony. Runners kept running over the top of Hope Pass and would yell out congratulations to us while taking pictures.

Michael Erlich took one of the pictures, had it enlarged to poster size and gave it to us as a wedding gift.

The treasured picture hangs in our hallway for us to see everyday. Thank you, Michael.

I wore an all-white running outfit with white veiling pinned to my white hat. Mike wore a running shirt with "GET ME TO THE WEDDING ON TIME."

The unexpected surprise happened at the end of our "I do's," and a champagne toast. Heavy cloud cover came over Hope Pass and a light, cold rain started. Michael and I put on rain gear and our Leadville Trail 100 races continued.

We celebrated at the finish line with a table decorated in fine wedding fashion with a homemade cake and local flower greenery atop the cake and beverages to be shared by everyone."

1998

Steve Peterson of the Divine Madness Ultra Club made it 3-for-3 championship races, earning him the 'Triple Crown of Leadville'. Steve's time of 18:29:21 was over an hour ahead of second place Kirk Apt in 19:49:54.

Ann Trason returned to the race and ran a time of 20:58:32 to obtain yet another championship ore cart. Second place was Kathy D'Onofrio-Wood in 21:41:48.

Consistent ultrarunner Gary Curry finished his 10th race in 27:23:33, earning him a place among the elite of the elite who finished the race ten times or more.

A total of 209 runners finished the race this year under very good weather conditions as AT&T also became a title sponsor, adding to the powerhouse Rockport in supporting the race.

Ken Chlouber also finished the race in 28:39:38. Ken had been occupied with his political ambitions during the year as he was elected Colorado State Senator. Of course the Leadville Trail 100 director extraordinaire, Merilee, headed up Ken's political campaign so no wonder he was successful.

1999

The North Face became title sponsor of the Leadville Trail 100 in 1999. Price for the Training Run Weekend increased to $95.

Even though changes were in the winds, some things remained the same. Steve Peterson became a four-time champion by running 18:47:31 and dominating the race. Second place among the men was Jay Pozner in 19:22:09.

First place woman was Amanda McIntosh from Texas in a time of 22:05:22 with second place Stephanie Ehret a mere 12 minutes behind in 22:17:02. Third place woman Valerie Caldwell was close as well with a time of 23:00:00 at the tape.

Two runners joined the ten-time finisher ranks: Odin Christensen and Luther Thompson as they finished the race in 29:11:27 and 27:40:57 respectively.

References

Chapter 10: The 90's

1   Ultrarunning Magazine; October 1995, Page 7
2   Ultrarunning Magazine; October 1996, Page 4
3   Personal correspondence; January 24, 2019

Part 3

Dancing With Dragons

"If you want to win anything - a race, yourself, your life - you have to go a little berserk."

– George Sheehan

Chapter 11

Run Like a Champion

Matt Carpenter's course record run in 2005 wasn't as easy as it appeared. The previous year (2004) Matt drug himself around the course, after starting out extremely fast, and managed to finish the race in a time of 22:43:38. His time was good enough for fourteenth place overall but well off the winning time of Paul Dewitt who set a course record (17:16:19) and defeated Western States 100 mile champion Scott Jurek (18:01:46) in the process.

Lack of familiarity with the course and having never run 100 miles had a lot to do with Matt's slower performance in 2004.

Matt Carpenter was the Pikes Peak Marathon champion, having won the event twelve times. In addition, Matt won the Vail Hill Climb eight times, the Imogene Pass mountain run six times, won Sky Marathon Tibet, and held the course record for all of these events. He was also the record holder for running the fastest marathons at altitudes between 14,000 to 17,000 feet. [1,2]

The Leadville Trail 100 humbled Matt Carpenter.

Matt told the Colorado-Springs Gazette newspaper after the 2004 race, "I cried a lot. I'm not going to lie."

Matt Carpenter was the best high altitude race champion in the world and nothing was about to defeat him.

At the start of the 2005 Leadville Trail 100, Matt toed the line, once again. Matt had one goal on his mind, "redemption."

Both authors recall seeing Matt on the course, specifically at the start of the trail going up Hope Pass outside of Twin Lakes.

Unfortunately for us, Matt Carpenter was coming DOWN the trail after already returning from the Winfield turnaround as we were just starting our first climb up Hope Pass. Neither of us had never seen a front-runner this far ahead at this point in the race.

Matt had no pacers for his record race. He ran the entire race alone, and definitely in front of any other possible opponent.

Matt's use of the aid stations during the race was minimal. He merely slowed down enough to exchange empty CamelBaks with his crew, making his transitions last 30 seconds or less. Matt was running in his mental zone throughout the race.

Matt crossed the finish line in downtown Leadville as the sun was still shining.

Matt had conquered his fear and disappointment from the previous race by setting the current course record of 15:42:59. No runner had ever or has ever run that fast at the Leadville Trail 100.

In fact, no runner had even run under 16 hours until the most recent race in 2018 when Rob Krar showed up once again.

How about the most championship wins by a runner?

Steve Peterson became a five-time champion of the Leadville Trail 100.

No other champion has won the Leadville Trail 100 four consecutive years or five times total either.

Steve Peterson accomplished that remarkable goal with this winning streak:

- 1996 – 19:29:56
- 1997 – 18:10:45
- 1998 – 18:29:21
- 1999 – 18:47:31
- 2001 – 17:40:53

The missing year, 2000, Steve finished in second place with a time of 18:31:05. Chad Ricklefs beat Steve by 24 minutes, finishing in 18:07:57, ending Steve's consecutive and amazing championship performances.

Steve Peterson remains the ultimate champion of the Leadville Trail 100 race. No other person has come close to duplicating or eclipsing Steve's running achievements.

Skip Hamilton, the race's first champion has four finishes in five years.

Ian Sharman has four-first place finishes over a period of five years, equaling Skip Hamilton's performances but not Steve Peterson's record achievements.

Steve Peterson, Skip Hamilton and Ian Sharman are superior ultrarunners that anyone would hope to emulate during their running careers. It just doesn't get any better than those three men's champions if you are an ultrarunner.

What was the earlier mention of Rob Krar and the 2018 race? How was Rob's performance in the 2018 race special, besides the fact he won the race?

Rob Krar became the second man in the history of the Leadville Trail 100 to break the 16-hour barrier in the 2018 event.

Rob Krar had won the Leadville Trail 100 once before, in 2014 with a time of 16:09:32, second fastest champion in race history, following Matt Carpenter.

Rob Krar understood the Leadville course and in 2018, the week before the event, Rob decided to run the race.

Prior to the start of the 2018 Leadville Trail 100, Rob entered the 2018 LT100 MTB race and finished in fourteenth place overall with a time of 7:08:27. Remember, the LT100 MTB race is a bicycle race and it is held one week before the 100-mile race.

Rob Krar finished the 2018 Leadville Trail 100 in a time of 15:51:57. Rob's winning time was nine minutes and two seconds behind Matt Carpenter's legendary course record from the 2005 race.

Nine minutes – merely the blink of an eye in the rarified air of Leadville and over the course of a 100-mile race.

What if Rob had fresh legs for the 100-mile running race and hadn't ridden the LT100 MTB race the week before?

History is history and nothing changes the events.

How about the course difference between the 2005 running race and the 2018 event? Wasn't the 2018 course different and longer than the 2005 racecourse?

Reading Chapter 13, the 2005 course was the same length as the 2018 racecourse.

Remember, the Halfmoon Road section of the racecourse was in place for the 2005 race. The Halfmoon Road section was longer and much more difficult than the 2018 Pipeline route.

In 2018, the additional 2.3-mile trail section of Colorado Trail near Winfield remained in place for the missing Halfmoon Road section, making the course essentially equal for both races in 2005 and 2018.

How about the women?

There has only been one women's four-time champion, equaling Skip Hamilton and Ian Sharman's records. It is none-other than the famous ultrarunner and athlete Ann Trason.

Ann Trason won the Leadville Trail 100 in:

- 1988 – 21:40:26
- 1990 – 20:38:51
- 1994 – 18:06:24
- 1998 – 20:58:32

Ann's Leadville Trail 100 Mile championship races spanned a period of ten years, something unheard of in the ultrarunning world. Racing at such a high level for an entire decade is truly amazing and has not been repeated at Leadville.

Three women ultrarunners have won the Leadville Trail 100 twice in their careers:

Amanda McIntosh

- 1999 – 22:05:22
- 2000 – 22:16:17

Anthea Schmid

- 2002 – 19:44:24
- 2004 – 20:50:05

Lynette Clemens

- 2009 – 20:58:01
- 2011 – 19:59:06

There have been 1,050 women ultrarunners who have finished the Leadville Trail 100.

Compare that with the 6,187 men who have finished the Leadville Trail 100.

The women to men finishing percentage are: 17% vs. 83%. Approximately 1/6th (17%) of the finishers in a typical year's Leadville Trail 100 are women throughout the history of the race.

Perhaps in recent years the number of women finishers has changed, compared with the early years when there were fewer female ultrarunners?

The statistics for the 2017 race show female finishers at the Leadville Trail 100 comprised 19%. For 2018, female finishers comprised 18% for the race.

The finishing percentage of female runners to male runners has remained essentially consistent throughout the history of the Leadville Trail 100 at 16% – 19%.

From Marge: Comparison Men vs. Women in Ultrarunning

"Women should be encouraged to try longer distance if they want to challenge themselves more. With doing longer distances however, comes more training and commitment.

Start out with shorter mountain trail races, or pace a runner entered in a 100-miler to get a sense of what it's like, the terrain, altitude, stunning beauty, weather conditions and altitude of Leadville or wherever your first ultra may be.

I know that when I started out, I was scared to death and mostly because I feared failure. In my young growing up years in school, I had no self-esteem. That fact made me want to hide, blend into the wall and be a "wall flower," or just disappear.

It wasn't until I graduated from high school, had my first job for a few years and moved to Denver, that I came out of my shell while starting to find myself.

I always get asked by many people and some who are race directors, why more women don't participate in ultrarunning. Good question."

While the numbers of women finishing the Leadville Trail 100 has increased over time, with a jump of approximately 60% in the year 2013 vs. the year 2012, women completing the race is still fairly low compared to the men.

However, 2013 was an anomaly because the starting field increased substantially as well, resulting in more starters for the race, male and female.

Here are the numbers of finishing women in the most recent races:

- 2012: 55
- 2013: 80 (the largest increase/most entrants)
- 2014: 51
- 2015: 56
- 2016: 60
- 2017: 45
- 2018: 55
-

The figures for women's finishing percentages for two years that we have data:

- 2017: 104 women starters; 45 finishers; 43.27% finishing rate (vs. men 51.50%)
- 2018: 120 women starters; 55 finishers; 45.83% finishing rate (vs. men 50.81%)

Marge continues:

"Here are some responses I have gotten from women and others, plus a few of my own thoughts about why women do not enter the Leadville Trail 100 in larger numbers:

At least for me, the number one reason is the fear of failure and this can probably apply to any male or female runner.

We all want to be successful in all that we do in our lifetime, that's a given. Making that statement, the following can be felt by anyone, but I think these apply more to women from comments I have received:

- I don't like to run
- It's boring
- I'm self-conscious
- I have low self-esteem
- I have bad knees and/or other body part(s) issues
- It takes too much time to train
- I'm too old
- I support or crew and/or pace my spouse
- I/we need daycare for my child or children
- My husband does not support my running
- It doesn't fit into my work, home and family schedules

I'm sure there are more reasons, but those are a few I have been told.

I believe and have heard that women's pain tolerance is higher than men's because of the gift of giving birth to human life. Women also have slightly more body fat that makes women better endurance athletes. Ladies, no excuses: you can make it happen by just putting your dreams into action. Dream it, believe it and achieve it.

Hopefully in future editions of the Leadville Trail 100 more women can overcome these perceptions and obstacles to achieve successful results so many women have achieved during the history of the race."

Leadman and Leadwoman competitions began in 2003. Most entrants are seeking an ultimate challenge at the high altitude of Leadville. The Leadman and Leadwoman competitions consist of five events:

- Leadville Trail Marathon
- Silver Rush 50 MTB or Run
- LT100 MTB race
- Leadville 10K Run
- Leadville Trail 100 Run

Racers must complete each event within the allotted cut off time in order to move on and be eligible for the next. If a racer does not meet the required finish time, he or she will not be allowed to continue in the Leadman competition. However, the racer may continue racing as an individual by notifying Athlete Services.

Each event must be attempted; failing to start any of the events will disqualify the athlete from all remaining events in the series. The Leadville Race Series does not allow refunds, transfers or deferment in the midst of the Leadman competition.

(Note: Please see the Athlete Guide for the event rules[3])

First champions of the Leadman and Leadwoman competitions in 2003 were:

- Men: Jan Bear 47:38:26
- Women: Kim Bear 55:49:13

Current champions are:

- Men: Wesley Sandoval: 35:54:55 (2016)
- Women: Stephanie Wurtz: 43:18:15 (2016)

References

Chapter 11: Run Like a Champion

1 *"High-Altitude runner Matt Carpenter leaves foes gasping for breath"*, Trailrunningblog.com, Rocky Mountain News, May 29, 2007
2 *"Digging for Gold in Leadville"*, Matt Carpenter, Ultrarunning Magazine, Pages 16-18, October 2005
3 2018 Leadville Trail 100 Run Athlete Guide

Chapter 12

Divine Madness

Kenyan's world famous marathoners train at altitudes over 7,000 feet. Their training schools near Iten, Kenya are renown for producing the best runners in the world. Ethiopia is also a hotbed for elite long distance runners who compete head to head with Kenyan runners.

Kenyan's elite runners come from tribes scattered throughout the highlands of the country and make their way to running schools where they develop and hone their running skills.

The latest studies have found what makes these marathoners the fastest on the planet: chronic exposure to high altitude along with high intensity training.[1]

Throughout Europe and to a limited extent in North America, we have running clubs that bring elite runners together to train and race. One notable example in the United States is the Nike Running Club.

Yet there was another running club that many people are unfamiliar with and it was a lot closer to Leadville.

From 1996 to 2001, members of a running club based in Boulder, Colorado influenced the Leadville Trail 100 and created a legacy that has not been duplicated.

Leadville Trail 100 history would not be complete without mentioning the Divine Madness Ultra Club (Divine Madness).

Ah yes, the club. A running cult, eccentric sect, or whatever you wanted to call a community of ultrarunners who had a runner dominate the Leadville Trail 100 for six years (1996 – 2001).

Additionally, Divine Madness produced a woman's champion in the 2001 Leadville Trail 100.

Five-time Leadville Trail 100 champion, Steve Peterson, was a member of the Divine Madness Ultra Club.

The 2001 Leadville Trail 100 women's champion, Janet Runyan, was a member of the Divine Madness Ultra Club.

Divine Madness was based in Boulder, Colorado. The spiritual leader of Divine Madness was Marc Tizer or Coach or Yousamien or just Yo, as he preferred to be known.

Boulder, Colorado had and still remains one of those spiritual enclaves where certain eccentric personalities tend to call home.

In California there is Berkley, also home to an eclectic gumbo certain people migrate toward.

Yo's circle of students in Boulder, at one time numbering over 100, was comprised of sports fanatics with a very spiritual element as well. At least that was the initial attraction for joining Yo's club.

Yo's coaching consisted of extremely long training runs, fifty to seventy-five miles in high altitude areas surrounding Boulder, Colorado. Sleep deprivation along with excessive alcohol consumption were staples of Yo's training program.

Alcohol consumption merely meant a few bottles of beer chased by several shots of whiskey; something most people might consider excessive when consumed five hours before a fifty-mile training run.

Living together in a compound/house, Divine Madness runners shared an ascetic and hedonistic type of lifestyle. [1]

There were also daily sex rituals that added an additional spiritual element to Yo's normal training routine.[2]

Steve Peterson's pacers and Janet Runyans's pacers at the Leadville Trail 100 were training partners and members of the Divine Madness Club.

Yo showed up at the Leadville Trail 100 to coach his runners during the event. My crew and wife, Maria, vividly remember seeing Yo out on the Leadville course.

Maria said Yo had a scraggly beard and was short and thin. He was not easy to miss, as he gave advice to his runners, including Steve Peterson, during many parts of the race.

As shown by race results, it seems that Yo may have actually enabled his runners to become successful at the Leadville Trail 100 while they were members of his club.

During the 2001 Leadville Trail 100, Steve Peterson was behind Chad Ricklefs and Hal Koerner as the trio raced back towards Leadville.

Steve's pacer and Yo had other ideas rather than trailing two runners ahead of them. The pacer was offering inspiration in the form of New Age mantras to Steve as the pair literally flew past both Ricklefs and Koerner.[3]

Chad Ricklefs was so devastated when Steve passed him at the ninety-two mile mark of the 2001 race that Chad dropped out and failed to finish the race. Hal Koerner finished second to the champion Steve Peterson in the 2001 race.

The co-author of this book, Steve Siguaw, while not a member of Devine Madness, still had the opportunity to be paced by one of their female members.

This is the description of how Steve Siguaw (not to be confused with Steve Peterson) nearly joined a running cult:
"In the 1996 race, coming back through the Twin Lakes aid station for the second time, a woman met me as I was nearing the end of the trail adjacent to Twin Lakes aid station. I was running alone with no pacer. The woman asked me "Do you have a pacer?"

In my normal exhausted state at this point in the race I replied, "No, I didn't have a pacer." The woman forcefully said, "I'm your pacer."

Exiting the trail I crossed the highway and continued running to the aid station where Maria met me as usual. I went to the medical check and casually mentioned to Maria I had a female pacer for the next leg of the race.

Maria had seen the woman before I arrived. My new pacer was meditating alone at the edge of a stream, Maria said.

Maria helped me change my shoes, vaseline my feet, fed me, dressed me with warm clothes and strapped a fully loaded pack around my waist as she ushered me out of the aid station, wishing me good luck.

Out of the shadows my new Divine Madness pacer appeared and simply took her place next to me as we made our way from the Twin Lakes aid station and onto the trail toward the Halfmoon aid station at mile seventy-two.

I directed my new pacer to run in front of me so I could follow her on the trail. At this stage of the race my visual acuity was always pretty dim and getting worse as the miles swept by under aching legs and tired eyes.

My pacer talked with me as we ran together through the woods, offering me encouragement when I became overly quiet and depressed.

I quickly found out my pacer was part of the Divine Madness club but that had little meaning to me.

Remember, 1996 was the first year Steve Peterson entered the Leadville Trail 100 so the Divine Madness Club was not well known.

My pacer ran with me past the Halfmoon aid station and all the way to the parking area at Tree Line where my next pacer was waiting for me.

I hugged my new Divine Madness friend and thanked her for all her help as she looked for the rest of the Divine Madness group among waiting crews.

I believe my Divine Madness pacer was very effective since I finished the race with a time of 24:09:40. Yet there wasn't any beer or whiskey offered to me as she and I ran together or any spiritual chanting either.

I took that as a sign Yo didn't want me in his club. Lucky for me since communal living isn't appealing, and my crew certainly would not have been receptive to it either. Maybe the sex, drugs and rock & roll (or should I say running) might be fun but then again, maybe not."

At one Leadville Trail 100 awards ceremony, Steve Peterson was onstage receiving his championship ore cart when Yo joined him and gave a rambling speech about his elite runner as well as other nonsensical advice to the assembled crowd.

Yo was essentially talking to a group of zombies who had just ran 100 miles with no interest at all in what a very strange running coach had to say.

Whether one agrees with Yo's coaching techniques or not, Divine Madness was successful in producing two champions of the Leadville Trail 100, similar to the famous runners in far away Kenya.

From Marge who participated in a few group runs with Divine Madness Running Club:

"Founded in the 1990's by head coach, Marc Tizer, the group was based in Boulder, Colorado.

The Divine Madness Running Club was an ultrarunning club that specialized in and focused on ultramarathoning. The leader of the club was Yo Tizer, often called a teacher rather than a leader.

Yo preferred the club be referred to as a "school" or a "community." Some mainstream runners have said they liked the discipline and achievements of the club.

The top Divine Madness runners lived in a rental house in Boulder. Other runners also lived in communal groups of five or six people, whose ages ranged from the mid 20's to late 50's.

However, not everyone agreed with the beliefs and methods of the club.

During Steve Peterson's amazing 2001 championship race, Art Ives was Steve's pacer.

I met Art Ives and knew he was a member of the club. He would occasionally coach me while I was working in Boulder at a law firm. He would meet me where I worked and we would run speed workouts on the dirt cross-country track where the Boulder cross-country team trained/raced, and where Melody Fairchild competed successfully while winning collegiate cross-country meets. Melody became a top Colorado runner after college.

I also did a couple of long, eight-hour plus training runs with the Divine Madness Running Club. All my emotional fears soared with my first experience on an extremely long mountain run in Boulder: failure, not being able to keep up with them and the fear I couldn't complete the distance they had planned for that day.

However, as we headed up steep Flagstaff Mountain toward Walker Ranch and other unknown places to me, I ran in the front. I took off because I was nervous and afraid of being too slow. Art quickly was by my side and told me a memorable tip saying that they start out slow, "start out as slow as possible and then build." His comment helped me relax and settle into running with the group. We all had a great day of training together and enjoyed the beautiful scenery surrounding us.

All of the group's long runs were well planned with aid stations staffed by Divine Madness club members. After we all drank and refueled, the club volunteers would drive ahead of us for the next long stretch. I made sure to always be running with others so I wouldn't get lost or eaten alive by a bear. I also remember everyone being very friendly and it was a hot day during that first run.

References

Chapter 12: Divine Madness

1   *"Kenyan and Ethiopian distance runners: What makes them so good?"* Wilber & Pitsiladis; International Journal of Sports Physiological Performance, Page 92-102, June 7, 2012

2   Newsweek Magazine, Page 63-65, August 18, 1997

3   Sports Illustrated Magazine, Bruce Schoenfeld, August 3, 2003

Chapter 13

The Race Course and Changes

Since 1983, there have been many positive changes to the Leadville Trail 100 course. These modifications added more trail sections and eliminated paved portions of the route.

Then there was the length of the course that was taken into account.

Jim Butera made sure the original Leadville Trail 100 Mile running course was not less than 100 miles, unlike the original Western States 100 mile course.

The Western States 100 mile racecourse started out as 89 miles then lengthened to 93.5 miles. Races were run and course records were set on these shorter courses until a more accurate route of 100.2 miles was finally established for Western States. The distance of 100.2 miles is the current Western States 100 mile distance.[1]

Originally, the Leadville Trail 100 course was approximately 104 miles long, as measured by Jim Butera using a calibrated bicycle wheel.

Jim spent many long days at Leadville's high altitude jogging and walking the entire racecourse with his trusty bicycle wheel. Segments were measured and recorded to ensure an accurate distance for his race.

Even though the course was long, it was the best Jim could come up with at the time, due to topography, race access and trail configuration.

During early days of the Leadville Trail 100, participants simply ran the course because that was the described race. Sure we grumbled a little after running more than 100 miles for an advertised 100-mile race but Jim usually said, "we got our money's worth."

The first course change happened in 1986 when the aid station at Lady of the Lake Campground was moved to Printer Boy Campground at mile seven into the race.

It seemed that Lady of the Lake campers complained about runners disturbing their sleep at 5:00 am on a Saturday morning as racers dashed amongst the tents and campers near the lake.

Merilee Maupin (race director) and Ken Chlouber (race management) decided to move the aid station to Printer Boy Campground, on the paved road well before the Lady of the Lake Campground in 1986. Printer Boy Campground was more remote but easily accessed by cars and crews since it was on the main road around Turquoise Lake.

It was not until the following year, 1987, Printer Boy aid station was moved to the far end of Turquoise Lake, at May Queen Campground, mile 13 where the aid station remains today.

May Queen Campground is small but a very popular camping area for tourists. However, May Queen aid station was located at the far west end of the Campground and well away from any campsites and sleeping campers.

It was the next year, 1988, that the paved road section around Turquoise Lake was removed from the running route, finally.

Runners would now gain the Turquoise Lake trail at the Turquoise Lake Dam, instead of running up the paved road to the Tabor Boat Ramp at Lady of the Lake Campground. This change was well received by runners, even though trail congestion on the narrow Turquoise Lake Trail began much sooner during the race.

Famous nighttime pictures have been taken of runners traversing this new section of trail with only headlamps and flashlights illuminating the trail.

In 1990 there was another important change to the Leadville Trail 100 that occurred only one mile from the start/finish area: "The Boulevard" was added.

As the first verse of the song by Jackson Browne goes, *"Down on the Boulevard they make it hard."* Little did Jackson Browne know he was writing a song about the Leadville Trail 100.[2]

The Boulevard was to become the lasting memory of an epic struggle to finish a 100-mile race.

Approximately one mile from the race starting line, runners now made a LEFT TURN, ran one block and turned right onto the dirt road called "The Boulevard."

Instead of running toward the Turquois Lake Dam on pavement, as previous years, this bumpy dirt road was another approach to the Dam. Coming to the Turquoise Lake Dam with this route was an incredible success, at least from a runner's standpoint.

In 1990 something remarkable occurred on The Boulevard, one mile from the start of the race. It wasn't planned and no one had any idea who was responsible.

The lead runners passed the one-mile mark on the new Boulevard route in about eight minutes. Middle of the pack runners arrived between ten and twelve minutes, still running at course record pace so early in the race.

Steve will never forget Orion's sword shining brightly overhead in the inescapable darkness as many runners switched their flashlights off, searching for peace and solitude amongst the soft footsteps echoing through majestic pine trees. Most runners quit talking, simply enjoying themselves now that they were finally running.

Suddenly in the distance there was the sound of drums. Our ears strained to hear something out of a dream, echoes of fellow travelers perhaps, but nonetheless a rhythm from ancients who walked this way before.

Could it be the drums from the indigenous Utes or Arapahos? Most likely, but no one would ever know for sure.

The drums always beat during darkness, both at the start and finish of the race for many years. Yet no one stepped forward and admitted to helping runners on their long journey through the mountains. To this day, the drums remain a lasting symbol and mystery to an epic adventure for so many runners in the race.

The "Boulevard"

The trail section from May Queen aid station to the Fish Hatchery/Outward Bound aid station has also changed.

During the first two years of the race runners ran two miles from the trail head past May Queen Campground to the Hagerman Pass gravel road.

Once at the Hagerman Pass road, runners simply went straight across, gaining a trail that climbed to the top of Sugarloaf Pass. This trail section was to become the Colorado Trail in more recent years.

However, in 1985 the Colorado Trail segment from Hagerman Pass road to Sugarloaf Pass was eliminated.

Replacing the steep but beautiful portion of the Colorado Trail was a new route that turned west (right) once runners stepped foot on the Hagerman Pass gravel road.

Now the racecourse proceeded west on the gravel Hagerman Pass road for one mile to an intersection with a very rough jeep trail on the south side of the road.

The new course turned left onto the rough jeep road where volunteers directed runners. A little over two miles of running on this rough jeep trail takes runners to the top of Sugarloaf Pass and the start of the Power Line Trail.

Yet there is a problem at the top of Sugarloaf Pass with the new race route. The Colorado Trail crosses the jeep road at the crest of the pass creating a short cut to the racecourse up and down from the Hagerman Pass road. This shortcut eliminates nearly two miles from the race and has been used on occasion by race cheaters, as observed by the author.

In recent race years a race official has been stationed at this potential short cut eliminating any chance for cheating.

Also, remember the incident that may have occurred during the first race in 1983 when Skip Hamilton may not have followed the race route explicitly down the Power Line Trail?

The power line jeep road has always been clearly marked, rather than the shorter indistinct trail along the fall line of the power lines. That part of the course has never been changed.

Fish Hatchery/Outward Bound aid station and medical check at mile 21 has changed throughout the years. During some years the private residence just past Fish Hatchery was used as the aid station, Outward Bound was even used a couple of years while during later years the actual Fish Hatchery was finally established as the official aid station.

Halfmoon Campground aid station – that miserable cold and usually wet foreboding place on the return from Winfield was always at mile 28. Always, that is, until the 2009 race.

Just before race day for the 2009 race there was an aircraft crash causing a forest fire adjacent to Halfmoon Campground. Race management quickly rerouted the racecourse onto what is called the "Pipeline", bypassing the upper section of the Halfmoon dirt road.

The Pipeline route is used by the Leadville 100 Mile MTB race and provided a flatter and easier alternative to the rutted, dusty, narrow and unforgiving Halfmoon road. Besides making the course a little easier, the Pipeline route also shortened the course somewhat.

750 feet of elevation gain was lost along with .3 miles less distance by using the Pipeline bypass trail.

In 2012 the troublesome Halfmoon section of the course was once again rerouted, past the gravel pits near the Halfmoon dirt road. This course change added .7 miles to the course with an additional fifty feet of elevation gain.

Changing the route from Halfmoon Campground to the Pipeline route was a very positive step for the race. Some devious runners in previous races figured out the short-cut past the Halfmoon aid station, bringing them to the Mount Elbert Trail quicker than following the actual race route to the end of the Halfmoon road where the Mount Elbert Trail officially begins.

That unofficial short cut eliminated nearly a mile from the course and it was difficult to track those cheating during the race and taking that shortcut.

The race route between the Pipeline aid station and Twin Lakes aid station is one of the most runnable and enjoyable sections of the entire Leadville Trail 100. Deep dark forests, streams, quaking aspen trees and wildflower-strewn meadows typify this part of the course.

A high meadow above Twin Lakes was appropriately named "Arthur's Meadow", after ten-time Leadville Trail finisher, Arthur Schwartz. Arthur was usually observed running steeply uphill through this fantastic meadow, passing runner after runner with his strong and powerful strides.

Besides being the most enjoyable running portion of the course, the section of trail between Pipeline and Twin Lakes is the most confusing and difficult to follow for a runner. Course markings must be sighted before taking any tangents leading in another direction.

Twin Lakes aid station and medical check has always remained the same throughout race history. It is a great place to meet crew and prepare for the most difficult section of the entire race: Hope Pass at 12,600 feet. However, the race route leaving Twin Lakes has changed significantly throughout race history.

Initially, racers plodded up the dangerous paved highway; State Highway 82 leading over Independence Pass to Aspen.

Running those three miles on pavement with cars inches away from the runners provided a lot of excitement during the race, especially when darkness fell.

That paved highway led to Parry Peak Campground at mile 39.5 where runners exited the dangerous road, ran through the Campground and onto a two-mile section of beautiful trail before finding the main trail leading toward and up Hope Pass.

Finally, in 1989, running up Highway 82 to Parry Peak Campground was eliminated. No more death-defying encounters by runners with speeding sports cars racing toward Aspen.

That change meant the trail from Twin Lakes aid station toward the start of the Hope Pass trail was dramatically different.

The new racecourse exited Twin Lakes where runners crossed the dreaded Highway 82, with the help of Colorado State Patrol officers, headed into the Lake Creek Valley and headed west over small streams and along indistinct paths until encountering a jeep road that led in the direction of Hope Pass looming in the far distance.

The unused mostly indistinct jeep road crossed Lake Creek, icy and flowing rapidly forever downward from Independence Pass and the fourteen thousand foot mountains surrounding Twin Lakes. Lake Creek was not something to treat lightly, especially if you were a runner trying to cross it.

That was the reason runners previously braved traffic on Highway 82, rather than trying to cross Lake Creek.

But again, Merilee and Ken had a plan. A rope was stretched across the shallowest section of the creek with volunteers stationed at the infamous creek crossing helping runners negotiate the raging torrent.

Even more comforting was the presence of Lake County search and rescue personnel stationed downstream from the crossing area to catch any wayward runners slipping off the rope and tumbling down the swift flowing creek.

To date, no runner has drowned at the creek crossing. Theresa Daus-Weber, a champion in the Leadville Trail 100 came the closest one-year in not making it, but luckily search and rescue was able to save her. Marge also had a wet encounter with the creek during one race as well.

Once successfully crossing Lake Creek, runners wade several shallower streams and ponds before finding another unused jeep road that heads south toward tree line and the start of the Hope Pass trail.

This spectacular marshy meadow within the valley, far from the congestion and excitement of Twin Lakes and with fourteen thousand foot snowy peaks shadowing the trail was called Brendan's Meadow.

The meadow was named after Brendan Slevin, a Leadville marathon runner and pacer for the co-author (Steve) at this stage of the Leadville Trail 100. Unfortunately Brendan Slevin died in a rock climbing accident at the age of twenty-three.

Typically, runners carry extra socks and/or running shoes at this critical junction of the race, before ascending toward Hope Pass. Running in fresh socks and shoes seems to help with the agony runners are about to experience as they struggle toward 12,600 feet.

The only problem with changing shoes is that nothing can be left at the creek crossing, nothing. Unless a crewmember hauls a runner's wet shoes back to Twin Lakes, the runner must carry any additional weight up and over Hope Pass.

The trail over Hope Pass has not changed at all throughout the history of the Leadville Trail 100.

A critical aid station was established at timberline in 1984. Originally, it was simply a place to get water with a few hardy volunteers helping runners, yet the unofficial aid station became much more, beginning in 1987.

The Hopeless Aid Station officially became a true aid station in 1987, providing limited aid and even food that year. Subsequent years have seen the Hopeless aid station expand, with more llamas bringing supplies to volunteers and even a checkpoint at this high altitude point of the race. Timberline is at approximately 11,500 feet on the racecourse.

What was once a little used trail from Brendan's Meadow to the top of Hope Pass is now easily followed and well defined. The trail isn't any easier, that is certain, but at least a runner can find the trail and summit Hope Pass.

Flying down toward the Winfield road from Hope Pass a runner traverses scree slopes, abandoned mining cabins and runs past mine shafts with a magnificent valley looming far below the trail.

At the base of the trail, runners originally ran through the little-used trailhead parking area and onto the dirt road leading to Winfield. It was nearly three miles to Winfield from this point.

The Winfield dirt road was the focal point for congestion during the race. Race crews choked the road with vehicles and people. Constant traffic jams occurred where the Hope Pass trailhead encountered the Winfield dirt road.

Things became so bad that during several years, police officers were stationed at the Hope Pass trailhead termination and even along the Winfield road to maintain a semblance of order.

In 2012 there was a drastic change. It only took nearly 30 years but the change was necessary because of the dramatic increase in race entrants.

The Winfield road was finally removed from the course in 2012, after completion of the Colorado Trail into the ghost town of Winfield.

This necessary rerouting of the course added 2.2 miles to the racecourse and an additional 365 feet of elevation gain.

But this change didn't last long. One reason was complaints by runners that the course change added difficulty to the previous course and it was longer with the additional trail section.

Remember, the course had been shortened and made easier with the Pipeline segment and also shortened by using the Turquoise Lake Trail from the Turquoise Lake Dam instead of using the paved road.

So in 2013 the new portion of the Colorado Trail section was once again removed from the Leadville Trail 100, making this new course 2.3 miles shorter and ten feet less of elevation gain.

But once again in 2017, the Leadville Trail 100 course used the entire Colorado Trail section, adding back the 2.3 miles and 10 feet of elevation gain from the 2012 route.

How about the return route? How has it changed?

Once a runner arrives at the fifty-mile turnaround at Winfield, they know their way back; just run back the same way: simple, at least in theory.

Today's racecourse features an elevation gain of 18,168 feet. The lowest point on the course is 9,200 feet near Twin Lakes and the highest point is Hope Pass at an elevation of 12,600 feet.

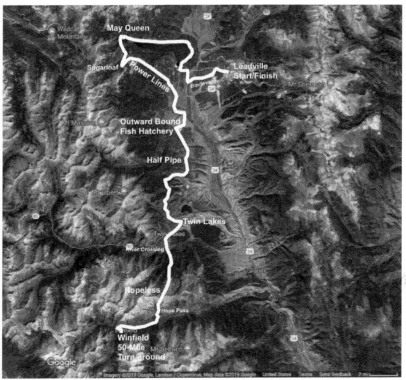

Leadville Trail 100 Course Map (2018); Courtesy Google Maps/Steve Siguaw

References

Chapter 13: The Race Course and Changes

1 *Finishing the Western States 100 Mile Endurance Run*; Dale Matson, 2011
2 *"The Boulevard";* Holdout album, written by Jackson Browne, 1980

Chapter 14

A New Millennium

2000

The beginning of a new millennium was not kind to the Leadville Trail 100, in terms of publicity.

Ultrarunning Magazine featured a small, one page summary of the race with no race results, other than the top finishers despite an incredible race that featured an epic men's duel between two outstanding ultrarunners and the crowning of a two-time Leadville Trail 100 women's champion.

The starting field for the race increased for the year 2000 as the excitement level continued just as strong among assembled ultrarunners.

Here are other highlights:

- The North Face continued as title sponsor
- Race entry fee was $175
- Training Run Weekend cost was increased to $95
- Leadville Trail Marathon cost was $40
- Leadville 10K cost $10
- 600+ volunteers assisted runners during the 100-mile race
- Ken Chlouber continued as Colorado State Senator & Assistant Majority Leader

World-class ultrarunner, Helen Klein, age 77, entered and started the race. Helen hoped to be the oldest finisher of the Leadville Trail 100 and in the process, set a world record for the oldest finisher of a 100-mile race. Unfortunately, Helen dropped out of the race at Twin Lakes aid station at mile forty and failed to finish the race.

The women's race was another one for the history books. Amanda McIntosh repeated as champion with a time of 22:16:17 and good enough for 8th place overall. Amanda became the first ever consecutive two-time Leadville Trail 100 champion. Running in second place to Amanda's incredible performance was Valerie Caldwell who finished with a time of 22:40:34 and in 10th place overall. Stephanie Ehret placed third in 23:19:29, Jill Case ran 23:53:08 to capture fourth place and Janet Runyan of the Divine Madness Ultra Club finished fifth in 24:22:28.

For the men's race there was a huge upset with Chad Ricklefs taking the championship crown away from second place finisher Steve Peterson. Chad's winning time was 18:07:57 with Steve finishing in 18:31:05.

Steve Peterson is not known to finish in second place, after winning the previous four Leadville Trail 100 races. Yet champion that Steve is, he never considered dropping out of the race when Chad took over the lead. Instead, Steve continued running for second place and a place on the podium. In third place at the finish line was Kevin Shiling who ran 20:11:41, Joe Kulak was in fourth place with a time of 20:31:37 and Kirk Apt finished in fifth place at 21:36:10.

The race had a 43% finishing percentage, which was on the lower side when compared with more recent years.

Three runners earned their ten-time finisher belt buckle this year:
- Alan Cohn
- Mike Monahan
- David Strong

2001

Where else but at the Leadville Trail 100 would one find a PACER the caliber of Mark Plaatjes, 1993 world champion and founder of the successful Boulder Running Company? Previous men's winner, Chad Ricklefs recruited Mark to pace him in his quest for a repeat win as he fought Steve Peterson.

From the start of the 2001 Leadville Trail 100, most runners knew this was a race for the record books. But it wasn't just Chad Ricklefs and Steve Peterson who were leading. No, FOUR men flew over the rocky Turquoise Lake Trail into the May Queen aid station, clocking unprecedented splits for the first 13-miles of the race while running 6:48/mile pace. Those of us behind the front pack wanted to tell those four runners it was a 100-mile race, not a marathon.

Word spread quickly during the race how the four runners were coping with the fast pace. Some inside money predicted lead runner Paul South was the next shining star on the ultrarunning horizon, only to see him crash and burn by the Twin Lakes aid station at forty-one miles. Paul was a very good 50-mile runner but had never been tested at the 100-mile distance.

Chad Ricklefs took over the lead at Twin Lakes with Hal Koerner and Steve Peterson running slightly behind.

Hal passed Steve going up Hope Pass to take over second place as he continued chasing Chad up and over the pass. Hal Koerner was a true challenger for this year's crown. Hal was a previous two-time Bear 100 mile race champion and had the speed and credentials to keep pace or even defeat Chad and Steve.

At the Winfield turnaround it was Chad in the lead followed by Hal and then Steve. Some people might like to hear the splits for these three talented runners at the Winfield aid station: [1]

- Chad 8:03
- Hal 8:15
- Steve 8:19

Steve Peterson recruited two runners to be his pacers from the 50-mile turnaround point: Russ Roberts, a 50K runner and Art Ives who was a previous finisher of the Leadville Trail 100 and a follower of the Divine Madness Ultra Club. These two pacers would alternate running with Steve. Of course Yo Tizer, the spiritual leader of Divine Madness Ultra Club was constantly giving instructions to Steve and his pacer along the course.

Chad and Hal didn't have any divine intervention, other than their quick and powerful running styles. Chad Ricklefs ran a strong race, leading the entire field on a catch-me-if-you-can style. Chad picked up his pacer, world champion marathoner Mark Plaatjes, near the final May Queen aid station and his race for the championship was within sight.

Steve just continued running and running in second place, while getting faster and faster as the finish line came ever closer. It was at mile 92 when Steve Peterson caught his prey, Chad Ricklefs. Steve accelerated past Chad with a convincing move on the narrow lake trail.

Chad never responded when Steve took over the lead. Chad dropped out of the Leadville Trail 100 with a mere five miles to the finish line, at the Turquoise Lake Dam. Chad was totally devastated when Steve passed him.

Steve Peterson won the race in a personal best time of 17:40:53 to capture his fifth Leadville Trail 100 crown. No runner in the history of the race has more championships than Steve Peterson. Second place for the men was Hal Koerner in 18:35:32 who never faltered in his quest to finish the race. Third place was Joe Kulak in 19:12:41 and coming in at fourth place was Paul Dewitt in 19:52:32. The reader may want to remember the name Paul Dewitt when they read about the 2003 race.

What was going on with the women while the men battled for race supremacy? Oh my, the women had an epic race as well but not without controversy, according to Jill Case, one of three front runners along with Janet Runyan and Amanda McIntosh.

Another Divine Madness Ultra Club member and Leadville Trail 100 finisher in the previous year, Janet Runyan, was hot on the heels of Jill Case and previous two-time champion Amanda McIntosh from the starting gun. It was a three-woman race all the way to the Winfield turn around point and even back into Twin Lakes aid station.

Janet Runyan's pacer for part of the race was Russ Roberts, the same pacer Steve Peterson was using during the race.

Divine Madness Ultra Club members were spread out over the entire racecourse, reporting runner positions to Janet and her pacer as the race progressed. Jill Case noticed observers *"hiding in bushes along the trail to radio ahead informing how their competition is doing and where they are"* [2]

It was during the stage, between Winfield and Twin Lakes aid station inbound, Jill was concerned about.

Jill said *"Things changed again at the bottom of Hope where Janet passed me. Somehow she got away from me in Twin and that point on, which bewilders me some since her ascents were significantly weak."*

Jill goes on to say, *"I was often told I was in 1st when I was not. This was especially so checking out of Twin going home. Halfmoon was also confusion, re position info."*[2]

At the finish line, Janet Runyan became women's champion with a time of 21:47:44. Second place went to Jill Case in a time of 22:10:16. Third place was Amanda McIntosh running 22:33:53. All top three women finished within 46 minutes of each other. Running in fourth place for the women was Emily Loman in a time of 23:55:36. Nothing more was mentioned about possible divine intervention for Janet Runyan.

Some interesting tidbits about the 2001 race:

- 392 ultrarunners began the race
- Trail running weekend cost $95
- The LT100 MTB cost $195
- This was the inaugural year for Ken and Merilee's Silver Rush Mountain Bike Race. This new mountain bike race was 50 miles in length. There were 56 finishers and 11 DNF's. The cost was $50 for an entry

2002

It was the 20th anniversary for the Leadville Trail 100. Cost for the race was $195 while the cost for the Training Run weekend was increased to $120. Ken and Merilee formed the Leadville Trail 100 Legacy Foundation on this anniversary date.

This foundation benefits the Leadville community by providing scholarships for the local high school, a Christmas party and many other things around Leadville including the Mineral Belt Trail, youth basketball, Community Park and SnoCat Groomer.

Prayer flags were being flown at the top of Hope Pass for the race. At the pre-race trail briefing for runners, Ken announced that a runner could purchase a prayer flag and write their name on the flag. The flags would be carried up to the top of Hope Pass where they would flutter in the wind during the race.

Proceeds from the flag sale would go to a local animal shelter organization in Leadville.

Ken went on to say something to the effect 'these flags were the only thing a runner would have in their quest to finish the race, a Hope and a prayer flag.' Now that was great sarcasm.

The men's race in 2002 saw the reappearance of Chad Ricklefs. If you remember, Chad mentally crashed and burned when Steve Peterson passed him during the previous year's Leadville Trail 100 race.

This year would be different for Chad. He ran a magnificent time of 17:23:18 to earn the championship ore cart by crossing the finish line in first place. Second place went to Paul DeWitt in a personal best time for him of 18:07:02. Third place once again was Joe Kulak who ran 18:43:13.

Anthea Schmid ran a remarkable time of 19:44:24 to capture the women's championship and finished 5th overall in the race. Second place woman was Jill Case in 22:32:02, followed by Susan Brozik in 22:41:47.

Five persistent Leadville Trail 100 runners earned their ten-time finisher awards:

- Jim Ballard
- Jeff Berino
- Mike Sadar
- Bob Stavig
- Mario Varela

2003

This was the year Bill Finkbeiner earned his 20th Leadville Trail 100 finishers buckle by running a time of 22:55:02.

Bill's streak of twenty starts without failing to cross the finish line was simply incredible. Bill's award was a belt buckle so large it was difficult to wear around his entire body. What an achievement.

This was also the year Paul Dewitt put everything together and earned the championship ore cart. Paul's winning time was 17:58:45. Once again Hal Koerner finished second with an excellent time of 19:09:46. Rounding out the top three was Hans Put in 19:36:58. The fourth place runner, Jeff Tiegs also ran under the magic 20-hour barrier in a time of 19:48:57.

Valerie Caldwell stepped up to the number one spot on the podium for the women by running 22:54:16, bettering her second place finish from the year 2000 race. The second place woman, Steph Schwartz, was nearly four hours behind Valerie in a time of 26:27:39. The third finishing woman was Helen Cospolich, who ran 27:02:32, a mere nine minutes behind Steph.

Five runners achieved their remarkable 10th finishes this year:

- Kirk Apt, a previous champion
- Bill Laster
- Eric Pence
- Johnny Sandoval
- Marshall Ulrich

A funny thing happened to me (Steve) as I was almost crawling up the Boulevard on my way to the finish line. My pacer, Bob Volzer, was keeping me alive by talking, nearly constantly. Suddenly Bob fell nearly silent as he gazed ahead.

We actually caught a runner and his pacer who were struggling, worse than me, and Bob quietly said, *"That guy only has one arm."* Sure enough, Aron Ralston, the man who cut off his own arm to save his life was pacing a runner.

Bob looked at me and said, *"That's Aron Ralston."* as we slowly jogged next to Aron and his runner.

As runners do at Leadville, we exchanged suffering stories before Aron showed us his prosthetic arm. His prosthesis was finished with a nice shiny hook, of all things.

Aron joked about his hook as only he could do and elevated everyone's spirits immensely as we struggled to finish the race before the looming 30-hour cutoff time. (Note: Aron ran and finished the 2004 Leadville Trail 100 in 29:43:41)

2004

Sierra Express runners from California once again came to the Leadville Trail 100 to prove once and for all, who was king of the mountain.

Returning to the race this year was Paul Dewitt, the previous champion along with a runner named Matt Carpenter, from Colorado Springs, just down the road a bit from Leadville. Matt Carpenter was probably the best trail runner in the world, at high altitudes and internationally. The only problem with Matt was he had never run a 100-mile race. Obviously Matt was a serious threat to the other front-runners.

Also representing the Rocky Mountain runners was Hal Koerner, second place Leadville Trail 100 finisher for two years and five-time Bear 100 mile champion. Then there were the west coast elite runners, aka the Sierra Express, lead by Scott Jurek, six-time Western States 100 mile champion and considered by many to be the best 100 mile runner, bar none.

This race was truly a duel in the mountains as a fast pace unfolded after Ken's shotgun blast into the cold dark morning air in downtown Leadville.

Matt Carpenter led the race as he left Twin Lakes aid station at mile 39.5 with Paul Dewitt going through a rough patch but hanging on to second place. Scott Jurek stayed within five minutes of the lead group, along with Jeffrey Tiegs by his side.

The climb up Hope Pass outbound was energy draining. Matt Carpenter is a mountain runner and proved how good he was by powering up and over the pass on his way to first place at the Winfield turnaround.

Scott Jurek is a notoriously great downhill runner and Paul Dewitt knew that fact as he watched Scott fly ahead of him and into second place at Winfield. Paul was still struggling in third place at the Winfield aid station.

The co-author (Steve) had seen Paul do the double-crossing of Hope Pass and understood how strong he was on that section of the course. So it came as little surprise when Steve heard Paul had passed Scott near the top of Hope Pass and even accelerated away from Jurek on the descent.

Matt Carpenter stayed in first place through the Twin Lakes aid station but was caught on the climb to the Halfmoon aid station by Paul. Jurek passed Matt on the way into Fish Hatchery aid station as Matt was struggling at this point of the race.

A record race time was possible for Paul since he was ahead of Chad Ricklefs splits at Fish Hatchery. But you never know what could happen during those final miles at Leadville.

Paul Dewitt was focused at this point of the race. He was not just running for the championship, he was running for the course record.

In a time of 17:16:19, Paul Dewitt crossed the finish line of the Leadville Trail 100, breaking the course record of Chad Ricklefs by seven minutes and becoming a two-time race champion.

Scott Jurek finished second to Paul in a time of 18:01:46. Third place was Jeffrey Tiegs in 19:30:25 followed by Joe Kulak in 19:47:47. Fourth place went to Todd Holmes who also broke the 20-hour barrier by running 19:57:06.

What about Matt Carpenter? Matt's race didn't go as planned. Again, Matt had never raced for 100 miles so this was unchartered territory for him. Matt struggled across the finish line in a slow time (well, maybe for him) of 22:43:38. But Matt didn't quit, even in the face of a poorer than normal finish for him. That in itself is admirable for a runner of his caliber.

And Hal Koerner, what happened to him? Well, Hal had a bad race and uncharacteristically for him, received a dreaded DNF.

Now for the women's race.

Anthea Schmid, the 2002 Leadville Trail 100 champion was back. Eyeing her was a fast 50-mile runner, Darcy Piceu along with Helen Cospolich who finished third in the 2003 race.

It seems that Anthea surrendered her spot on the U.S. 100 km National Team to run the Leadville Trail 100 this year. That act alone gives the reader an indication of how great a race Leadville truly is.

Throughout the entire race, Anthea ran uncontested. A second championship was hers for the taking, as long as she continued running her own race.

Coming across the finish line, Anthea was over three hours ahead of her nearest rival with a finishing time of 20:50:05 and 7th place overall.

Anthea earned her second Leadville Trail 100 championship and the spectacular ore cart trophy as her reward.

Three runners received their 10th finish at the Leadville Trail 100 this year:

- Raul Flores
- John Hobbs
- King Jordan; President of Gallaudet University

2005

This was the men's course record race year described in **Chapter 11 - Run Like a Champion.** Just to remind everyone, the men's course record set by Matt Carpenter in 2005 still stands at 15:42:59.

Finishing in second place for the men this year was Dan Vega in a time of 19:03:01, followed by Erik Solof in third place with a time of 19:15:16. Fourth place was fast closing Joe Kulak in 19:28:37.

The women's race included an amazing finish by Nikki Kimball who ran 20:28:21 to capture first place. Behind Nikki was second place Krissy Sybrowsky in a time of 22:03:03. Third place runner was Tania Pacev in 22:49:07.

There were 213 finishers in the race with 67 runners coming across the finish line during the final hour of the race.[3]

The last place finisher for the 2005 race was Giovanni Battista Torelli from Italy in a time of 29:59:59, making him the slowest official finisher in Leadville Trail 100 race history.

Three runners finished their 10th Leadville Trail 100 race this year and received the coveted huge belt buckle:

- Jay Grobeson
- Phil Kahn
- Bobby Keogh

The year 2005 also marked a milestone for Ken Chlouber. Ken was officially out of politics, but maybe not the political arena, so to speak? As Ken was quoted, *"The only way to get politics out of a man's blood is with embalming fluid."* [8]

2006

There was a shirtless champion for the race this year: Anton Krupica in a time of 17:01:56. Anton's finishing time seemed slow when compared with Matt Carpenter's course record of 15:42:59 but his time was still second fastest ever for the Leadville Trail 100. Anton's trademark running apparel consisted of running without a shirt, even in the chilly Rocky Mountains.

Steve Peterson, five-time champion of the Leadville Trail 100, chased Anton but finished in second place in a time of 18:47:13. Third place went to Jeff Beuche who also broke the 20-hour barrier in a time of 19:53:30.

The women's race featured a great run by Diana Finkel as she crossed the finish line in 7th place overall with a time of 20:43:19. Second place woman was Jamie Donaldson in 23:22:40 and third place went to Darcy Africa in 23:53:48.

Some tidbits from the 2006 race included:
- 51% finishing rate with 389 starters and 199 finishers
- 14 runners signed up for the Leadman/Leadwoman challenge. Only 8 managed to complete all five events.

Two runners received recognition for finishing Ten Leadville Trail 100 races this year:
- Joe Kulak; perennial front runner and gifted trail runner
- Stuart Nelson

Then there was Jim Butera. The genius, originator and creator of the Leadville Trail 100 decided to run his race once again. Jim had previously finished the race in 1985 in a time of 23:38:48 at the age of 37. In 2006 Jim was 58 years old, a tad older than his first finishing year.

Jim's good friend, Richard Neslund, paced Jim on the return climb over Hope Pass. During the pair's descent off the highest point of the race, back toward Twin Lakes, they came upon a suffering Ken Chlouber who was still trying to reach the top of the pass for the first crossing. Ken looked at Jim and said, "who designed this f**king course?", as everyone laughed together.

This is how Jim Butera's wife, Sheila Butera, remembers Jim's training and running in the 2006 race:

"Jim eagerly anticipated the 2006 Leadville Trail 100 as he made many trips to Leadville for his training for the race.

One of his running buddies and I went there with Jim so I would crew for them. I soon learned my way around Leadville, the back roads, where the trails were located and where the aid stations would be.

I would drive ahead of the two runners and wait for them to resupply. They were always eager to keep on running no matter what the weather was.

Many runners could eat something substantial, but Jim just had his drinks, power gel, and power bars. I was amazed that he could exert that kind of energy with so little food, but it worked for him and that's what counted.

I remember the start of the race as very early (4:00 am) and it was cold that morning. I had been to other smaller races, but this was the first major race I'd been to with Jim and it was exciting to see all the runners getting ready.

For non-runners, it is hard to understand the mindset it takes to accomplish such a feat of running 100 miles, through all kinds of weather, aches, sore feet, nausea, etc. I can see that it is the love of running and competing and pushing oneself to be the best that is at the heart of it all. I admire such grit, determination, loyalty and the camaraderie of the runners.

The race started with a bang and off they all went until I couldn't see Jim any longer in the middle of the group as it was just a sea of colors facing into the darkness.

At the first, second, and third aid stations where I met Jim, he was doing well but feeling a bit nauseated. Jim wanted to keep on going and his spirits were high.

As I waited for him to turn around at Winfield and return on the course to re-supply, I was sitting in the truck, prepared for a long night as he continued running.

Sometime between 5:00 and 6:00 pm I looked up as Jim knocked on the window and had a look of defeat and disappointment. He said, "I'm done and can't go any farther. I've ONLY finished 60 miles."

I said "only 60 miles? That is a major accomplishment. You should be proud. I know people who are much younger who work out at the gym everyday, like my daughter Heidi, and who wouldn't be able to run that far."

It was disappointing for Jim, but he gave it his all and everything he had that day on the Leadville Trail 100 racecourse."

2007

This was the 25th Anniversary edition of the Leadville Trail 100. What a race it turned out to be too, especially due to the performance by previous champion Anton Krupicka. Anton ran his personal best time of 16:14:35, second fastest time in race history and only the second person to ever run under 17-hours for the race. What a stellar performance from Anton Krupicka.

Second place men's finisher was Harry Harcrow in 19:33:17 followed in third place by Charles Corfield with a time of 19:42:30.

The women's race featured an incredible battle between four strong and fast runners: Tammy Stone, Michele Jensen, Lauren Adams and Helen Cospolich.

Dueling each other throughout the race, putting in surge after surge, one woman became the Leadville Trail 100 champion for 2007: Tammy Stone ran a time of 22:44:54 in her valiant effort for the win. Right on Tammy's heels and only four-minutes behind was second place finisher Michele Jensen in 22:49:14. Third place went to Lauren Adams in 23:31:19 while fourth place was captured by Helen Cospolich in 23:35:54 and only 4-minutes behind Lauren. What a competitive women's race this turned out to be.

Other facts from the race were:
- Entry price for the race was increased to $200
- Training Camp Weekend cost increased to $150

There were four huge belt buckle finishers this year, commemorating finishing their tenth Leadville Trail 100 race were:

- Chisolm Deupree (Harry Deupree's son. Harry earned his huge belt buckle in 1994)
- Scott Gordon
- Todd Holmes
- Neal Taylor

David Strong recalling the Last Ass Over The Pass trophy:

"Years later, in 2007, I had another memorable victory at Leadville. After battling back spasms for the last twenty miles I came across the finish line bent over sideways with my pacer nudging me like a bumper car to keep me going straight in 29:53:38 for which I earned the "Last Ass **Up** The Pass" trophy.

As I was discussing this monumental achievement with Merilee Maupin the following year, indicating how much better my finishing time was (29:53:38 in last place) compared with Harry Deupree's former 29:59:45 finish to which she replied 'but Harry looked good.' "

Last Ass **Up** The Pass trophy

2008

There were many exciting changes to the Leadville Trail 100 this year. Lifetime Fitness became the main sponsor. You can read more about this and the many changes on the horizon with this seemingly innocuous turn of events in **Chapter 15, Life Time Fitness – A New Leadville Trail 100?**

The race finally made the entry process easy with online applications available for the first time. In addition, another new race was founded by Ken and Merilee, the Silver Rush Trail Race. This addition to the group of Leadville running events was a 50-mile race and held the day after the 50-mile MTB race. Cost for this new race was $80.

Ken and Merilee now had what was to be called the *"Leadville Race Series"* of running and biking events. A half-marathon distance was also added to the Leadville Trail Marathon event, for those not up to the full marathon distance at altitude.

The Leadville Trail 100 had another course change. For years, runners and pacers, not to mention crews, lamented running the dusty, car-choked road to the turnaround point at Winfield.

Well, this year race management moved the running route off the road and onto a newly constructed trail leading from the base of Hope Pass, on the south side, all the way to Winfield and the turnaround (see **Chapter 13 – Race Course and Changes** for a full description and problems with this new route).

There was a new champion this year; Duncan Callahan ran a time of 18:02:39 to become the 2008 men's champion. Second place went to Andrew Skurka in 18:17:25 and third place was Zeke Tiernam with a time of 18:37:27.

For the women's race, Helen Cospolich finally achieved her goal and ran a solid race to capture the win in 23:21:53 and coming in 15th place overall. Second woman was Stephanie Ehret in 24:43:28 and rounding out the top three and in third place was Rhonda Claridge in 26:05:25.

There were 186 finishers in the race who braved the snowy conditions near the top of Hope Pass this year.

Four runners achieved the huge belt buckle status by finishing ten Leadville Trail 100 races:

- Julie Arter, third woman in race history to achieve this status, by following in the footsteps of Marge Hickman and Theresa Daus-Weber.
- Chuck Cofer
- Brian Manley
- Jeffrey Welsh

There was also an award presented to Gary Curry in recognition of his 20th Leadville Trail 100 race finish. Twenty finishes.

2009

This was the end of an era for the Leadville Trail 100 with some important changes.

Most importantly, Merilee O'Neal became Merilee Maupin, taking her maiden name once more. Then there was the helicopter crash.

What? You didn't see that?

Well, you probably didn't notice since the running route had to be changed due to the helicopter crash before the race and subsequent forest fire on the Halfmoon dirt road leading to the Halfmoon aid station.

Race management stepped up once again and saved the race from certain drastic consequences.

The race was re-routed to the Pipeline jeep road, avoiding Halfmoon road altogether and also moving Halfmoon aid station to the Pipeline aid station (see **Chapter 13 – Race Course and Changes** for a full description of this change and consequences).

This change in the racecourse made things easier for the runners, when compared with the original Halfmoon dirt road that rolled forever upward as runners avoided campers, hikers, dirt bikes and other assorted nasty things.

As an aside (someone you will become very familiar with in future races), Bahram Akradi finished his first Leadville Trail MTB race the week prior to the run (see **Chapter 15 – Lifetime Fitness, A New Leadville Trail 100?**)

For the first time, a *large team* (larger than the Tarahumara runners) entered the race.

Team Austin from, where else, Austin, Texas, brought a group of twelve men and three women to the event. They always do things bigger in Texas, or so we understand.

Team Austin trained together for the race in the hot Texas climate had three weekly group workouts and shared plans and resources amongst each other.[4]

Some of the team members even participated in the Training Run Weekend and reported back to the group what they thought of the course and chances of finishing.

Fourteen Team Austin members stood on the starting line for the race as the shotgun blast tore through the early morning sky.

As is normal during the race, the team's expectations were modified once pre-race enthusiasm met reality. Altitude and fatigue has a way of changing things, as we all know.

There was a great quote from one of the race members, Joseph, concerning the last fifteen miles of the race, *"I cursed at my pacers, crew and God. I wanted nothing more than a shower, a warm bed and a lower leg amputation. I was convinced I had done permanent damage to my calves and Achilles tendons."* [4]

You just have to love those words since everyone who has run the Leadville Trail 100, finishers and DNF'ers, has thought the same thing.

Team Austin was very successful because eleven group members finished the race with only three DNF's. That is remarkable for runners coming from lower altitudes to the rarified air in Leadville.

The women's race featured Lynette Clemons who ran the 9th fastest female finishing time in race history with a great 20:58:01 and taking the championship honors.

Lynette started out in third place until she passed two other women runners, including Stacy Donaldson and Darcy Africa, around the thirty-mile mark in the race. From that point on the race was decided for Lynette. Stacy Donaldson finished in second place, fifty-fifty minutes behind the winner in a time of 21:53:37. Hot on Stacy's heels and third place finisher was Darcy Africa with a 21:55:22 time.

The men's race featured a great shoot-out between Timmy Parr and Nick Lewis. Battering each other over the racecourse, it was Timmy who crossed the finish line in first place with a time of 17:27:23. Nick posted an incredibly fast second place time of 17:44:26. Third place but a little further behind was the previous year's champion, Duncan Callahan, in 18:26:40.

Two runners achieved their 10th finish and became recipients of the prized huge belt buckle:

- Tyler Curiel; Physician and excellent trail runner
- Jonathan Zeif

2010

Headline news for this edition of the Leadville Trail 100 was the entire Leadville Trail Race Series, including this flagship race, Leadville Trail 100, was sold to Lifetime Fitness and Bahram Akradi. Remember, when we wrote about paying attention to that name when writing the 2009 summary?

Avenging a 2009 third place finish in the race was Duncan Callahan who became a Leadville Trail 100 champion once again, making this his second victory in 17:43:25. Duncan ran nearly 85-miles of the race in second place before passing front-runner and two-time champion Anton Krupicka during the climb back up to Sugarloaf Pass.

Anton went out strong, and perhaps a little too quick since he wanted to better the course record of Matt Carpenter (15:42:59). Anton's blazing record-pace cost him the race and even a finishing time when he DNF'd by the final May Queen aid station.

Behind Duncan in second place was Zeke Tiernam in 18:25:30 and in third place was Dylan Bowman with a time of 18:36:16.

The women's race featured Elizabeth Howard who ran a strong 21:19:47 to capture the championship. Behind Elizabeth was second place Stephanie Jones in 22:35:05 followed by Ashley Hunter Arnold in third place with a time of 23:08:17.

Venerable Kirk Apt was still turning in impressive finishing times by running 25:56:31 for his Leadville Trail 100 finish. Just behind Kirk was another long-time Leadville finisher, Garry Curry in a time of 26:24:56.

Ted Barefoot McDonald, featured in the bestselling book *"Born to Run"* finished the race in 27:16:57. Even though Ted didn't run the race barefoot he incorporated a new middle name "Barefoot" in his race application this year.

Matt Mahoney, after a hiatus of seven years, finished the race in 29:51:56. This was Matt's fifth finish in classic style, with racing flats and no socks. Matt was the original minimalist trail runner when he crossed the Leadville Trail 100 finish line in 29:49:42 at his first finish in 1995. Some even say Matt inspired the current running trend of less is better running shoes, but that just might be a rumor.

Kristen Kern was the lone finisher who achieved his 10th finish, receiving a huge belt buckle in the process.

2011

A South African runner arrived with plans to run the 29th edition of the Leadville Trail 100 race. His name was Ryan Sandes, a fast and powerful international runner with impressive ultrarunning credentials, albeit long hot desert running races.

Ryan took four weeks to acclimatize while training in Leadville before the race, since he lives at sea level in Cape Town, South Africa.

Very much like Matt Carpenter's first attempt at Leadville, Ryan had never run a 100-mile race. What were the odds Ryan could take home the championship ore cart?

Ryan quickly silenced the doubters among us. His first place finish in 16:46:54 was an incredible effort and probably the best finish ever for a first-time 100-mile racer.

Twenty-five year old and second place Dylan Bowman wasn't very slow by any means either as he clocked in at 17:118:59. Third place went to Neal Gorman in 17:48:51 and fourth place finisher Michael Arnstein also broke the 18-hour barrier with an excellent time of 17:56:42.

There was one runner under 17 hours and another three runners under the 18:00 hour barrier to make ultrarunning history at the Leadville Trail 100 with four incredibly fast times over the course. Previous two-time champion Duncan Callahan finished in 9th place overall with a solid 19:11:15 time.

As the men flew over the racecourse, the women's race featured another incredible run from Lynette Clemons, 2009 champion. Lynette broke the finishing line tape in a time of 19:59:06 in breaking the 20-hour barrier for the first time. Second place woman was Rhonda Claridge in 21:11:24 and followed immediately by Andrea Metz in third place with a time of 21:13:14. It was a very close race for the runner-up position. In total, five women ran under the coveted 22-hour barrier for the race, a new Leadville Trail 100 record.

Three runners earned their 10th Leadville Trail 100 finishing huge belt buckle this year:

- Larry Hall
- Scott Klopfenstein
- Tom Schnitzius

Marvelous Marvin Sandoval, tough local Leadville runner, coach and future Leadman finished the race in 29:41:49.

There were 802 applicants accepted for the race but only 625 toed the starting line. Of those starters, 347 finished the Leadville Trail 100 resulting in a finishing rate of 55.5%. Runners at the Leadville race still had just a little better than 50-50 chance of finishing.

Yes, there was another controversy following the finish line cutoff time of 30:00:00 in the race.

New Leadville Trail 100 race owner, Bahran Akrad of Life Time Fitness was attempting to finish the final event of the 2011 Leadman: the Leadville Trail 100 run.

The final gun sounded at the finish line for the race at 30:00:00 and no additional runners officially finished the race. The race was over, done, caput.

Over forty-five minutes after the absolute cutoff time, a weary Bahran Akradi slowly crossed the finish line, to the sound of Ken Chlouber shooting the finishing blast once again into the morning sky.

Quite a few race finishers complained bitterly that Ken was acknowledging an unofficial finish for the race, simply because Bahran was the race owner. Racers wanted an apology from Ken or at least an explanation for his actions of shooting the finish line gun after the cutoff time. In the end, there was no resolution to the complaints.

2012

Thomas Lorblanchet from France captured the men's championship with another exceedingly fast time of 16:29:28 with second place finisher Zeke Tiernam running close behind in 16:44:20 (Zeke was also second in 2010 but in a time of 18:25:30).

Two, first and second place times under 17-hours had never been achieved at the Leadville Trail 100. The competitive field at Leadville was definitely getting much quicker. Third place went to Nick Clark in 17:11:16. In total, ten runners finished the race under 20 hours.

The first place women's runner, Tina Lewis, was included in those top ten runners by running an excellent time of 19:33:44 and 8th place overall. Second place woman was Elizabeth Howard in 20:44:04 with third place Ashley Nordell following in 20:47:51. In fourth place was Aliza Lapierre with a time of 21:14:32.

Four women ran the race under the 22-hour barrier. While this did not better the record of five women running under the 22-hour barrier in 2011, it still signified both the women and men's field at Leadville were becoming much stronger and fleet of feet over the 100-mile mountain distance.

Three finishers achieved their 10th finish at the race and received the huge belt buckle for their accomplishments:

- Bret Crock
- Paul Schoenlaub
- Paul Smith

360 runners finished the 2012 Leadville Trail 100 race resulting in only a 45% success rate.

Ken Chlouber was inducted into the class of 2012 Colorado Running Hall of Fame this year. Additionally, during this year, Ken decided he wanted to climb (not run) an 8,000-meter Himalayan mountain named Manaslu. At age 73, Ken would become the oldest American to ever reach the summit of Manaslu, if he was successful. Unfortunately, Ken developed pulmonary embolism at 19,000 feet on the ascent and his summit bid was abandoned.

2013

You probably heard about it, read about it or even participated in the race this year. The 2013 Leadville Trail 100 race was simply termed 'a disaster'. The new owner of the race, Life Time Fitness, decided to increase the starting field dramatically. The increase in number of runners toeing the start line could not be handled by neither the aid stations nor the course itself.

Chaos ensued throughout the race with aid stations running out of supplies for runners while trail trash littered the course. Congestion occurred in places unheard of on the racecourse itself.

In a town known for its Boom and Bust times, the 2013 edition of the Leadville Trail 100 was truly a Bust. Residents of Leadville complained about racers parking everywhere on city streets and creating an air of overpopulation for the small town.

The reader is advised to read **Chapter 15 - Life Time Fitness – A New Leadville Trail 100?** for all the grisly details of the debacle.

Despite all the problems, there was a stirring men and women's race happening. This year, 2013, marked the establishment of a new dynasty at the Leadville Trail 100: the rise of Ian Sharman.

A talented men's field consisting of Ryan Sandes, 2011 champion, Scott Jurek, New Zealand Olympic 5000 meter runner Michael Aish, Nick Clark and Ian Sharman had their sights set on breaking Matt Carpenter's untouchable race record of 15:42:59. It was indeed a fast men's field.

The dust was settling by the turnaround in the race with Ryan Sandes dropping out due to an injury. Nick Clark had been battling Ian Sharman in the Grand Slam of Ultrarunning races so he was not about to give up. Michael Aish was running a good race but his early fast front running pace was taking a toll on him as he ran a slower pace after the turnaround at Winfield.

At the finish line it was Ian Sharman with the championship honors and an excellent winning time of 16:30:01. Second place and Ian's challenger in the Grand Slam of Ultrarunning was Nick Clark in a time of 17:06:28. Third place went to Michael Aish who hung on for a very good 18:27:58 finish.

The women's battle for the Leadville Trail 100 champion featured Ashley Arnold running a very respectable time of 20:25:43. Second place woman, Shaheen Sattar from Texas, was further back in 22:42:41 with third place Keila Merino less than five minutes behind Shaheen in 22:47:36.

Two perennial race finishers earned their 10th huge buckle after the race:

- Fred Abramowitz
- Ken Gordon

Mario Varela was also recognized with an award for finishing his 20th Leadville Trail 100 race.

At the awards ceremony following the 31st Leadville Trail 100, Bill Finkbeiner received a standing ovation while accepting an award for his 30th race finish. This award signified running 3,000 miles at the race.

Not only did Bill finish thirty races, he finished them consecutively with fifteen of his finishes under the magical 25-hour standard as well. Bill's best finishing time was 20:30:06 in 1992. We predict Bill's magnificent record will never be broken.

Here is what Bill Finkbeiner has to say about his remarkable record:

"I remember hearing of a new 100 miler coming up in August of 1983, the inaugural Leadville Trail 100. And it was a bigger deal than the announcement of a new 100 nowadays. Back then, I was aware of only four 100s in the country: Western States, Old Dominion, Wasatch and a small 100 from Reno to Truckee and back called the Donner Trail 100,which was only a couple hours from my home in northern California.

Reletively new to ultrarunning, I had only run one 100 miler, the 1982 Donner Trail 100, after failing to be chosen in the Western States lottery. I was intrigued by the thought of a 100 miler at 10,000 feet but didn't think I could justify a trip half way across the country for a race in Colorado. And, I planned to run Donner again in '83 as well as Western States, if I were lucky enough to be chosen in the lottery.

I may have never made it to Leadville if not for meeting Ken Chlouber at the awards ceremony for the 1984 Donner Trail 100. Ken and I were two of a couple dozen participants in the Donner Trail 100 race and it turned out to be the first of my short list of race wins with a time of 16:48. At the awards ceremony, Ken suggested that I come run Leadville and told me "when you see the view from the top of Hope Pass and it isn't the prettiest view you've ever seen, you can have your entry fee back." I took him up on the suggestion and believed what he said.

After my Donner time and a sub twenty-hour finish at Western States the following month, I should be able to shoot for a sub-twenty at Leadville as well. I wasn't even close. Had I not strayed from the course, twice, I may have had a shot at twenty-four or twenty-five hours at best, but I had to settle for first among a dozen Californians with a time of 28:00:38. In 1984 that was good enough for 7th place overall of the twenty finishers. It wasn't until my 9th finish in 1992 that I ran my personal record of 20:30:06; never breaking twenty hours in any of my thirty consecutive finishes.

As I look back, two of the biggest things that stand out are that my wife, Beth, who was my girlfriend, finished the race in 1987, and my son Christian finished Leadville in 2018. Also a highlight of my years at Leadville is the many friends I made. There were many whom I only saw once a year, in Leadville, and I knew that if I quit running Leadville, I would no longer see many of them.

I was able to spend miles with many great people and great runners over the years. Some that stand out are: I was running at about mile fifteen one year with Christine Gibbons and her husband. At that point, we are running from May Queen aid station up Sugarloaf Pass to over 11,000 feet. We weren't moving fast enough for her so when she would get fifty or so feet ahead of us, rather than take a walk break, she would double back to us maintaining her running gait. She did this over and over. I remember suggesting that she race this next time and she came back to win the women's race the following year.

One year running with Marshall Ulrich and our pacers at about mile seventy, I was in a mood to just maintain and not work any harder than necessary, maybe even back off a little and make it comfortable. Marshall explained that if we kept our pace of running a little under 24 hours, he would have time to finish, take a shower, get a couple hours of sleep and make the starting line for the Pikes Peak Marathon that next morning.

I've had some great rivalries over the years as well, usually with Colorado runners with whom I became friends. And I was blessed with friends and family who made the long trip to crew and pace me many of those years. I had those friends pace me as well as people I met on race day such as Leadville Trail 100 champion Kathy D'Onofrio's 17-year-old brother as well as a collegiate runner who had placed 6th that morning at the Pikes Peak ascent. I wonder what they thought watching me falling asleep on my feet and vomiting on the Sugarloaf Pass ascent those nights?

I remember another moment during one of the very rainy years at Leadville, back in the years when I was at least attempting a top-10-finish. I was running with a younger guy approaching Twin Lakes on our way back and I think we were running in about 8th and 9th place at the time, and we wanted to stay in that position. As we crossed the river, we realized that the water level had risen significantly since our first crossing on our way out. It was now almost armpit deep. We had barely exited the water when we met a sheriff coming the other way. At the time, I thought it was likely they would close the crossing and we would remain in the top ten, and maybe the last two finishers regardless of how we ran the final forty miles. I really believed that they would not allow people to continue crossing. Fortunately, they allowed the race to continue. When I talked to Ken after the race he told me "I am not without influence around here. That won't happen again."

I'm so thankful for Ken and Merilee and all the others who have and continue to put on this great event. It has been a huge part of my life."

494 runners finished the race this year, even though for some odd reason, results reported in Ultrarunning Magazine added the unofficial finishers to the official report.[5]

There was also another course change to the Leadville Trail 100 course this year. The relatively new trail section from the base of Hope Pass to Winfield was eliminated. (Please see **Chapter 13 – Race Course and Changes** for a full description of this change and consequences)

2014

Remember we talked about a new Ian Sharman dynasty beginning with the 2013 Leadville Trail 100? Well that was short lived.

How could that be, since Ian was one of the top ultrarunners in the country? How?

Well, imagine Rob Krar and Michael Aish lining up for the 32nd running of the Leadville Trail 100. Then include Zeke Tiernam and Dave Mackey in the mix and you've got a stellar field of men ultrarunners going for the win.

Ian was prepared and favored to repeat as the champion of the race. But Rob Krar was the star of the race.

Rob, one of the best 100-mile ultrarunners in the country ran an incomprehensible 16:09:32 to take home the treasured championship ore cart.

Rob's time was faster than Anton Krupica's time of 16:14:35 run way back in 2007 and second fastest time in Leadville Trail 100 race history; second only to Matt Carpenter. Michael Aish passed a fading Ian Sharman with only five miles left in the race and captured second place with a time of 16:38:37. Ian Sharman finished in a remarkable time of 16:41:38, three minutes and one second behind Michael. Zeka Tiernam ran a superb race as well, finishing in 17:35:14 for fourth place. Dave Mackey finished in fifth place with a time of 19:10:45.

You will read an amazing story about Dave Mackey in the 2018 race report. Stay tuned for that one.

Eight men and one woman ran faster than the 20-hour barrier in the race. In fact, three runners broke the 17-hour barrier, setting yet a new record for the Leadville Trail 100.

Remember, there was one woman who ran under the 20-hour barrier with the men and her name was Emma Roca from Spain. Emma became the women's champion with a time of 19:38:04 in 8th place overall. Second place woman was Lisa Howard from Texas who ran 20:01:15. Carrie Stafford came in third place with a time of 23:56:53 and Becki Lynn Lassley rounded out the top four women by running 24:16:31.

Duncan Callahan continued his fast running by finishing in 20:27:20 for 13th place.

Four runners earned their huge buckle by finishing the race for the 10th time:

- Gene Bartzen
- Brian Costilow
- Laurie Nakauchi, became only the fourth female to achieve this remarkable status
- Todd Scott

There was not one but two runners recognized for their 20th Leadville Trail 100 finishes this year: Kirk Apt and Eric Pence. Wow.

After the disastrous 2013 Leadville Trail 100, race management reduced the number of entrants for this year's race. 350 runners crossed the Leadville Trail 100 finish line, earning their well-deserved finisher buckles.

Chuck Cofer, twelve-time race finisher, recalled an almost certain death encounter on the course:

"It was a near-perfect day for mountain running, with blue sky, no wind or afternoon thunderstorms and temperatures in the 50's.

I was pacing my friend Doug Nash through the woods on the north side of Hope pass, running inbound to Leadville.

We were running smoothly, almost effortlessly down a narrow, wooded ravine at about 11,000 feet on the north side of Hope Pass.

I was about twenty feet behind Doug, cruising through one of my favorite sections of the Leadville Trail 100: a downhill descent at a perfect gradient where minimal effort is required to make forward progress and you feel as if you could run forever. Your mind senses your body flowing down the hill, your thoughts are relaxed and free.

To our left, almost directly below us, a cascading white-water stream leapt through a jumble of downed timber and boulders. To our right the hillside rose steeply, broken by lichen-covered rock outcrops with intermingled mature blue spruces. The terrain occasionally opened up in front of us, allowing quick glimpses of the massive southern ridges of Mount Elbert plunging 4,000 feet down to Twin Lakes.

Suddenly all hell broke loose up the hill to my right. I was aware of cracking and crashing sounds, and consciously thought, "Whatever it is I can outrun it."

But before I could lift my leg the noise became much louder and much closer and I instinctively realized there was no outrunning whatever it was.

Somewhere in my mind flashed an image of a rock fall event on a cliff face almost thirty-five years earlier.

Without consciously thinking anything at all, my body threw itself headfirst toward the cut-bank side of the trail. No thoughts, no words, no reaction time.

I was stunned by the impact with the ground for perhaps five to ten seconds. "What the hell just happened?" was my first conscious thought. I really had no clue.

The ground was warm and comfortable and I didn't dare move.

Suddenly a very pale face appeared in my field of view, shouting over and over again "Are you all right?"

It was a runner from England whom we had passed a moment or two earlier, and was perhaps twenty yards behind when all this happened.

Raising up and looking around, I saw a large spruce lying across the trail about six feet behind me and began to understand the situation.

From the Englishman's angle of view it looked as if the tree had scored a direct hit.

I was a bit of a mess, covered in dirt and tree debris, but as I slowly rose to my feet it was apparent there were no major injuries. Blood oozed from multiple scrapes on my legs, arms, and hands but all were superficial.

I stood, brushing myself off as best I could.

Doug jogged back up the trail toward us, a look of concern and wonderment on his face.

Doug's hearing was affected by twenty years of flying C-130's so he was unaware of the drama that had unfolded behind him but quickly took stock of the situation.

Once he was convinced there was no damage, we resumed slowly jogging down the trail. Within a few strides I realized my shoes were full of debris and stepped to the side of the trail to clear them.

The Englishman passed us muttering "I thought you were dead, I thought you were dead…"

Looking back, had I stopped in my tracks long enough to figure out what was happening up the hillside I probably wouldn't be writing this now.

Like most people, I spend virtually my entire life practicing conceptual analysis (it's called 'thinking'). Yet in this case there was no time for conceptual analysis of the problem.

I thought perhaps something special or divine had happened, but friends have pointed out that years of mountain travel and trail running have strengthened the connection between basic perception and motor skills to the point where throwing yourself to the ground without thinking is merely an extension of the technique that allows us to jog across rough ground in the first place.

Doug eventually dropped out of the race, failing to get his fifth finisher buckle (that buckle had to wait until 2016).

I went back up the trail a couple of weeks later to re-visit the tree. It lay across the trail, smaller than I remembered and somewhat pathetic. I took a photograph. By the next year it had been cleared from the trail."

2015

Now we can get back to the Ian Sharman dynasty predicted in 2013.

Running most of the race unchallenged, Ian used his singular mental focus to finish in a remarkable 16:33:54 this year. Without anyone to push him, Ian showed what it takes to be a champion of the Leadville Trail 100.

It is one thing to finish the race under 30-hours but quite another to run 16:33:54 using one's own singular mental tenacity as competition against themself at the front of 648 other runners.

Second place finisher Kyle Pietari ran a good time of 18:16:04 while third place was captured by Juan Carlos Sagastume from Guatemala with a time of 18:29:27. Nine runners ran faster than the magic 20-hour barrier, including two women.

The first place woman was Elizabeth Howard from Texas who ran 19:34:09 and 6th place overall. Finishing close to Elizabeth was second place women Kara Henry in 9th place overall and a time of 19:54:08. Third place woman was Danielle Hilson running 22:28:00 for a podium finish.

648 runners started the race and 312 crossed the finish line for a finishing percentage of 48%. The pre-race briefing took place at the Lake County High School gym, along with the awards ceremony.

2016

Ultrarunning Magazine decided not to publish a race report for this edition of the race.

Once again, Ian Sharman ran an uncontested race, finishing in a remarkable 16:22:39 and a personal best time for him at the Leadville Trail 100. The second place finisher was Kyle Pietari for a second straight year and who ran almost the same time as his previous year's finish to cross the line in 18:16:48 (vs. 18:16:04 in 2015). Third place men's finisher was Luke Jay in a time of 18:31:22.

Eleven runners ran under the magic 20-hour barrier including one woman, Clare Gallagher in a great time of 19:00:27 and good enough for 5th place overall.

Clare claimed her women's championship ore cart with ease over second place woman's finisher Maggie Walsh with a time of 21:00:08. Rounding out the top three women was Jennifer Benna of Nevada with a time of 21:45:00.

Two runners received their huge buckles signifying ten Leadville Trail 100 finishes. These two individuals join fifty-nine other runners in history to earn this coveted buckle (Total huge buckle holders are 61; four women and fifty-seven men):

- Hollis Baugh
- Charles Bybee

The Leadville Trail 100 had become an event attracting international ultrarunners as well. This year's race included entrants from Slovenia, Germany, France, the Netherlands, Switzerland, Spain, Mexico, Japan, Chile, Sweden, Estonia, Slovakia, the Bahamas, Canada, Peru, Australia, South Africa, Latvia, Argentina, England and as Ken always says in jest, "even Arkansas."

2017

Yet another course change happened this year. The racecourse now included the new trail section from the base of Hope Pass to the Winfield turnaround at 50 miles, once again. Please see **Chapter 13 - The Race Course and Changes** to see how this course change affected the race.

Ian Sharman continued his winning ways and dynasty by running a relatively slow for him 17:34:51 to capture his fourth Leadville Trail 100 championship. In second place for the men was David Teirney running a solid 18:32:34 while Michael Hewitt captured third place in 18:54:45.

Nine runners once again broke the magic 20-hour barrier for the race but no women were among those under 20 hours.

First place woman was Devon Yanko in a good time of 20:46:29. Second place woman was Simona Morbelli in 21:16:22 followed by Christy Burns in third place with a time of 21:43:15.

284 runners finished the run this year to earn their finisher's buckle at the awards ceremony in Lake County High School's gymnasium. The finishing percentage was 46.86%.

2018

Ian Sharman's dynasty ended with the 36th edition of the Leadville Trail 100.

Once again Rob Krar, champion in 2014, came out of self-imposed ultra-racing retirement due to injuries and personal reasons to stand at the starting line.

Rob had ridden and finished the LT100 MTB race only one week before the 100-mile race and finished the bike race in a time of 7:08:27, fast enough for 14th place overall out of 1,242 finishers. One week later it was time for Rob's main event, the 100-mile run.

Racing against Rob, besides 712 other starters, was Ryan Kaiser from Oregon who ran a 21:38:20 Western States 100 in 2017, during an off year for him (he ran 16:36:49 in 2016 for the Javelina 100 miler and a 5th place at the Hardrock 100 in 27:39:16 during that same year).

Also challenging Rob was Bighorn Mountain Wild and Scenic 100 mile champion Seth Kelly who turned in an impressive time of 20:28:24 for that race in 2016.

Rob's two challengers proved to be no match for his raw speed and strength over the Leadville Trail 100 course. Rob ran a singularly focused race while gunning for the course record.

It wasn't until the dust settled at 6th and Harrison in downtown Leadville at the finish line, did the clock stop with a time of 15:51:57.

Rob Krar became the Leadville Trail 100 champion and only the second person ever to run under the magical 16-hour barrier for the race. Rob's fantastic time missed Matt Carpenter's course record by a mere nine minutes.

Second place in the men's race was Ryan Kaiser in 17:37:23. Rounding out the top three men was Seth Kelly in 18:15:29.

The women's race featured an impressive group of runners going for the championship ore cart.

Two inexperienced but fast contenders were Katie Arnold and Addie Bracy, both going for their first 100-mile finishes.

Katie had run a first place 50-mile race earlier in the season and had 100 km experience. Between raising her two children and training, Katie found time to write "Raising Rippers" for Outside Magazine as well.

Addie was having a great season with wins over the 100 km and 50-mile distances showing her trail running speed.

Gina Slaby was also in the mix of women contenders. Gina ran in the IAU 24-Hour World Championships in Ireland in 2017 covering a distance of 154.279 miles and proving she had enough endurance to finish the Leadville Trail 100.

During the race it came down to Katie and Addie battling back and forth, up and over Hope Pass while still neck and neck on their return to the Twin Lakes aid station inbound and toward the finish line.

It seemed Katie recovered nicely from a broken leg only two years ago as she pushed the pace even harder, dropping Addie on the run toward Fish Hatchery aid station.

Katie Arnold crossed the finish line to become the women's champion with her first ever 100-mile finish with a time of 19:53:40 and in 11th place overall.

Second place for the women went to Addie Bracy in her first 100-mile finish in a time of 21:17:12. Gina Slaby finished with a time of 23:13:03 for the third place podium spot.

Eclipsed by stories of the men and women's champions this year was the amazing story of an entrant named Dave Mackey, **Ultrarunner of the Year** as voted by *Ultrarunning Magazine* in 2011.

Dave Mackey finished the 2014 Leadville Trail 100 in a fast time of 19:10:45, in 5th place overall and behind Rob Krar's win. In this year's Leadville Trail 100, Dave finished the race **AND** the Leadman competition as well.

So what makes Dave's accomplishments different than others entered in both events?

In May 2015, Dave Mackey injured his leg while training on Bear Peak near Boulder, Colorado. Dave dislodged a large rock weighing nearly 400 pounds that pinned his lower left leg for hours before rescuers located him.

After thirteen separate surgeries on his lower leg, none of which seemed to help his constant pain, Dave made the decision to have his lower leg amputated in October 2016, seventeen months after the accident.[6]

Dave learned how to run again, with a prosthesis. That transition took adjustment, strength and sheer determination for this elite ultrarunner.

Dave Mackey became the first amputee ("Adaptive athlete") to finish the race AND the Leadman in the same year (2018). Dave's remarkable time for the Leadville Trail 100 was under the 25-hour barrier in 24:54:49. Simply incredible.

Side note from Marge:

"In 2018, Eric Pence finished his 24th Leadville Trail 100. Funny thing, I met Eric at Across The Years and even funnier, he has a second home in Beaver Lakes in Leadville where Michael and I live...imagine that coincidence."

There were 367 finishers out of 734 starters giving a finishing rate of 50%. (Note: the number of starters has begun increasing again when compared with 2017; 606 in 2017 vs. 734 in 2018)

2019

Record snowfall in Colorado during the winter caused massive avalanches with debris covering all the Leadville trails. Even the Hardrock 100 mile race in Silverton, Colorado was cancelled because of too much snow on that course this year.

The Forest Service and other volunteer groups worked diligently to make sure the Leadville course was runnable for the race. Only one snowfield remained near the top of Hope Pass on race day. When August 17th rolled around, the Leadville Trail 100 trails were all open with a field of 828 runners standing at the warm starting line. (NOTE: the U.S. Forest Service permit stipulates a maximum of 900 athletes)

Warm starting line? Yes, the race this year saw temperatures soar into 70's during the race, something very rare at the high altitude of Leadville in August.

Contending for the men's championship crown this year was Jared Hazen, 2nd place finisher at Western States 2019 (14:26:46) and Gediminas Grinius from Lithuania who finished in 6th place at Western States 2019. Fast Colorado runners Ryan Smith along with Devon Olson, not to mention Chad Trammell from Alaska rounded out a strong men's race.

For the women's race field, Cat Bradley, 2017 Western States women's champion in 19:31:30 and Magda Boulet, 2015 Western States champion in 19:05:21 were at the starting line. Returning champion from 2018 Leadville Train 100, Katie Arnold, was also ready for another championship attempt.

Forty-eight states and forty-one countries were represented this year, with the youngest entry twenty years old and the oldest entry seventy-three. The starting field was comprised of 78% male and 22% female runners. The cost for the 2019 Leadville Trail 100 race was set at $335 plus processing fees.

How did the race shake out this year? Well, the women's race went as expected with Magda, Katie and Cat fighting for the lead position. Magda lead the women's field through the Twin Lakes aid station, enroute to Hope Pass, with a twenty-minute lead over Katie and Cat running another fourteen minutes behind. Katie subsequently dropped out, leaving Cat in second place for the climb over Hope Pass.

Magda's lead dwindled to thirteen minutes ahead of Cat at the Winfield turnaround. Once at the Outward Bound Aid Station and twenty-three miles from the finish line, Magda had extended her lead to a little over an hour in front of Cat.

In downtown Leadville, first woman to cross the finish line was Magda Boulet, 46, from California with an official time of 20:18:07 and 11th overall (she was in 10th place overall but faded). Cat Bradley, 27 from Nederland, Colorado finished as 2nd place woman, with a time of 20:45:48. Samantha Wood, 34 from Colorado Springs, Colorado was the 3rd female, finishing in 23:52:04 and 50th overall. Samantha was also the 2018 Leadwoman champion. Rounding out the fourth place women's position was Carrie Stafford from Vail, Colorado in 51st position overall, right behind Samatha in a time of 23:55:20.

For the men, it was a close race during the initial stages. Jared was running only a minute ahead of Chad and three minutes ahead of Ryan at the Outward Bound Aid Station. Jared was on course record time at this point in the race. Jared's wicked pace took a toll on him. During the climb up Hope Pass, Jared was finished for the day, as he turned around and returned to Twin Lakes. The new leader was Chad who led Ryan and Devon to the top of Hope Pass. At the Winfield turnaround, all three men were within a few minutes of each other with Chad still in the thin lead.

Ryan then took over the lead, inbound over Hope Pass, and never looked back. Ryan picked up his new pacer with only twenty-three miles to the finish line and it was none other than 2019 Western States female champion Clare Gallagher, who ran with Ryan all the way to downtown Leadville.

Crossing the finish line and becoming the 2019 Leadville Trail 100 champion was Ryan Smith from Boulder, Colorado with a time of 16:33:2, 8th fastest time in race history. Second place was captured by Chad Trammell in 17:56:26 followed fifty-six seconds later by Devon Olson in third place with a time of 17:57:17. What a finish, with three men running under 18-hours! Rounding out fourth place was Ramon Casanovas from Chile with a time of 18:14:51. Marvelous Marvin Sandoval captured eighteenth place by running 21:06:58.

Chasing the Grand Slam of Ultrarunning record, Gediminas Grinius (Lithuania) was seventh overall in 19:22. Although Gediminas had time on Ian Sharman's record 2013 Grand Slam campaign, after the Slam's first two races, Gediminas lost a bunch in Leadville, stating afterward that the altitude was a challenge for him. Sharman ran Leadville in 16:30:03 during 2013 in setting the Grand Slam of Ultrarunning record.

David Mackey finished once again with a time of 25:54:59 in 98th place overall. Another Leadman finish for him!

Race conditions for the 2019 Leadville Trail 100 mile running race were unseasonably warm, although there was no snow, hail or rain to contend with. Yet the warm conditions resulted in a finishing percentage of only 45% with a total of 374 finishers out of 828 starters.

Also, during the race, there was a significant problem. The U.S. Forest Service closed the Winfield dirt road to vehicle traffic for all crews because of debris and damage caused by avalanches during the previous winter season. This road closure resulted in significant long delays for runners who dropped out at the fifty-mile point in Winfield. Race management arranged for a shuttle service company to ferry DNF runners from Winfield back to Twin Lakes. However, at the last minute, the contracted shuttle service company did not show up, leaving volunteers from local Arkansas River rafting companies and even race management trying to return runners to Twin Lakes in private vehicles. Long waits at Winfield were typical for many exhausted runners.

2020

There will once again be a lottery for the 2020 Leadville Trail 100 with the lottery held on January 19, 2020. There is no qualifying standard for a runner entering the Leadville Trail 100. No prior ultrarunning experience, no specific race times and no volunteer work is required to enter the race. Race date for the 2020 Leadville Trail 100 is August 22, 2020. Entry fee for the lottery is $335 plus processing fees.

There are other ways to gain entry into the 2020 Leadville Trail 100 besides the lottery process. If you sign up for the Leadville Trail 100 Running Camp plus Entry package, you are guaranteed an entry into the race at a cost of $1,000.

New for 2020 is a Coaching package called "Life Time Endurance – Premium Coaching". Subscribing for this option on the official race website, a runner will receive personalized coaching and education from a choice of four coaches to guide their training program. The package also offers discounts for other associated events like the Trail 100 Run Camp and All-Access Pass. All this can be purchased at a cost of $2,900. That price includes guaranteed entry into the race, of course.

Similarly, charity slots will again be available from the Leadville Trail 100 Legacy Foundation that provides entry into the Leadville Trail 100 race. An applicant simply makes a one-time payment to the Legacy Foundation for a minimum amount of $2,350 to get a guaranteed spot in the running race. Slots are limited.[7]

Finally, unsuccessful lottery applicants or those failing to gain entry by paying large sums of money can run one of Life Time Fitness's qualifier events to earn an entry, after paying for one of those events and running a qualifying time as explained on the website. Hmmmm.

Something remarkable and historic occurred in June, 2020. All Leadville races, including the 100-mile running race, were cancelled because of the Covid-19 virus worldwide pandemic. Runners who were already accepted into the race were given the offer to defer their entry to 2021, 2022 or 2023, receive a refund of their entry fee or permitted to donate their entry fee to charity.

References

Chapter 14: A New Millennium

1   Ultrarunning Magazine; *"Dual at 10,200 feet"* by Art Ives, Pages 20-23, November 2001
2   Personal correspondence letter from Jill Case, 2001
3   Ultrarunning Magazine, *"Rocky Mountain Wow: Carpenter's 15:42 Shatters the Leadville Record",* Pages 14-15, October 2005
4   Ultrarunning Magazine, *"Team Austin Gets Altitude"*, Page 26, October 2009.
5   Ultrarunning Magazine, Page 42, October 2013
6   Runner's World Magazine, *"Ultrarunner Dave Mackey Loses a Leg and Learns to Run Again",* May 9, 2917
7   Leadville Race Series web site, 2020. https://www.leadvilleraceseries.com/
8   Trail Runner Magazine; by Garett Braubins, September 12, 2014

Chapter 15

Life Time Fitness – A New Leadville Trail 100?

It appeared to be a simple handshake, but it was much more than just that.

There had been twenty-seven races since the first runners crossed the starting line for the Leadville Trail 100. And what a ride it had been.

Merilee Maupin and Ken Chlouber had guided the Leadville Trail 100 through some hard times for the past twenty-five years, since taking the race over from Jim Butera in the third year, 1985.

That is half a century of directing and managing the race. The renowned race director, Fred Lebow, longtime race director of the famous New York Marathon only lasted twenty-four years, before his death in 1994.

By 2010 the Leadville Trail 100 was much different than when it started in 1983. Throughout their twenty-five years of race directing and management, Merilee and Ken had formed new races in Leadville so that by 2010 there was an entire portfolio of races connected with the original Leadville Trail 100.

In 1994, Merilee and Ken came up with the remarkable idea of starting a 100-mile mountain bike race. That race became known as the Leadville Trail 100 Mile Mountain Bike race, or LT100 MTB for short.

The new bike race covered some of the same course as the legendary 100-mile running race but not exactly the same route. Mountain bike riders could not ride up to Hope Pass; that was hopeless for them.

Instead, the LT100 MTB course would go up to a point east of Hope Pass called the Columbine Mine. The elevation at the top was nearly the same as Hope Pass and the climb was equally as difficult for the mountain bike riders. World champion snowshoe racer, Tom Sobal, helped measure the grueling course so you knew it would be accurate. That mountain bike climb to Columbine Mine became the symbol for the newly formed Leadville Trail 100 Mile Mountain Bike Race. Marge and her husband Mike volunteered to be aid station captains for twenty-four years at Columbine Mine.

In addition to the 100-mile mountain bike race there was a 50-mile mountain bike race, the Silver Rush 50 MTB race and a 50-mile running race, the Silver Rush 50 run.

Two other popular events in the Leadville Race Series were the Leadville Trail Marathon and the Heavy Half Marathon.

One other fun-run was also part of the package of Leadville races, the Leadville 10K that is held on the first and last 5K of the 100-mile running course.

Merilee and Ken had eventually added six additional races since they took over the original Leadville Trail 100 in 1985 and all of the races had become synonymous as extreme ultra events for runners and mountain bikers throughout the world.

The first year of the LT100 MTB race there were 113 official finishers and the second year of the event, 228 finishers.

By the third year, 1996, the LT100 MTB race had 236 finishers and in 1997 the race had 300 finishers.

You can see the progression of the LT100 MTB race: slowly increasing in participation but nothing stellar. The number of DNF LT100 MTB racers continued to grow with the race, helping lend an aura of a very difficult challenge for every mountain bike rider.

Participation numbers in the LT100 MTB race steadily increased and in 2007 the number of finishers was 663.

Helping the popularity of the LT100 MTB race was a rider who came to the race in 2007.

A cyclist named Floyd Landis entered the 2007 LT100 MTB race, much to the chagrin of the National Off-Road Bicycle Association (NORBA). NORBA is the official sanctioning body controlling mountain bike race rules.

Floyd Landis had apparently won the 2006 Tour de France race in France, only to be stripped of his championship and disqualified due to a positive test for performance enhancing drugs.

NORBA advised Merilee and Ken that they could not allow Floyd Landis to participate in the LT100 MTB race since he was under a drug-doping suspension. Ken Chlouber thumbed his nose at NORBA and allowed Floyd to race the event. Ken's response towards NORBA helped increase the rough and tumble aura of the LT100 MTB race for many mountain bike riders.

Floyd Landis rode the 2007 LT100 MTB race and finished second to Dave Wiens, four-time champion of the event.

In the 2008 LT100 MTB race a rider named Lance Armstrong came to town to race the LT100 MTB event.

Lance Armstrong was living "over the hill" in Aspen and thought the LT100 MTB race would be something he wanted to win, especially since he knew Floyd Landis had failed the previous year. Lance had been a mountain bike rider before winning a famous race called the Tour de France seven times consecutively.

Lance Armstrong showed up for the 2008 race and was also beaten by Dave Wiens, now five-time consecutive champion of the LT100 MTB race after beating Floyd Landis the previous year.

Those two LT100 MTB races, 2007 and 2008, propelled the event into the national spotlight. The names Floyd Landis and Lance Armstrong were all that Merilee and Ken needed to boost their local mountain bike race into THE race for a mountain bike racer to complete.

Also entered in the 2008 LT100 MTB race was a rider named Bahram Akradi, CEO of Life Time Fitness. Bahram didn't finish the race in 2008 but riding in the event must have had an impact on him, as you are about to read.

What does the history of the LT100 MTB race have to do with this chapter, or even the Leadville Trail 100?

Money, money and even more money.

Following Lance's ride in the 2008 LT100 MTB race, entry requests for the mountain bike race soared to over 10,000. Merilee and Ken established a "lottery" for cyclists to enter the race.

Over 8,000 prospective entrants had to be turned away and their entries refused for entry into the race. The LT100 MTB course could only accommodate a limited number of riders, unfortunately.

Merilee and Ken had developed a package of six extreme mountain events that caught the attention of runners and mountain bike racers worldwide with an accompanying amount of entry fees as well as strong publicity.

The year 2010 changed all Leadville races forever.

It was relatively obscure thinking that an ultrarunning race or a 100-mile mountain bike race could be sold. Who would have thought of that? Obviously, Merilee and Ken had the idea.

The story goes that Ken was invited for Christmas dinner in Vail, Colorado hosted by Lifetime Fitness founder, president and CEO, Bahram Akradi. At the party, Akradi suggested that Life Time Fitness buy the Leadville race Series.[2]

Prior to the Life Time Fitness offer, other private equity companies approached Leadville race management concerning purchasing the Leadville events, now called the Leadville Race Series.[2]

The Anschutz Entertainment Group, founded by billionaire and entrepreneur Phil Anschutz, reportedly was negotiating with Ken to purchase the Leadville Race Series. The Anschutz group dropped out of bidding competition after their offer of $2.2 million was rejected.

At the Vail Christmas party, Ken shook Bahram's hand and the Leadville Race Series purchase deal was done. The details of the subsequent financial transaction have not been disclosed.

How did the sale of the Leadville Race series to Life Time Fitness affect the Leadville Trail 100, you might ask?

Merilee Maupin was no longer race director for the Leadville Trail 100. Her new title was Race Director Emeritus. Merilee still presided over race weekend as well as being the first person to welcome racers back to Leadville at the finish line of the Leadville Trail 100 with her traditional and much welcomed 'finisher hug'.

The new race director was Joshua Colley, a local mountain bike racer who took the reins for the races beginning in 2011.[3,4]

Ken Chlouber retained a financial interest in the race series and began serving as an emeritus consultant on the Life Time Fitness staff.[1]

The entry fee increased to $285 for the new edition of Leadville Trail 100.

Up to and through the completion of the 2012 race, starters and finishers for the Leadville Trail 100 basically remained status quo.

In 2011 there were 612 starters and 360 finishers for a 59% success rate. There were 360 finishers in the 2012 race, out of 788 starters for a 46% finishing ratio with the number of starters going up.

There had been a big increase in number of entrants accepted into the race, starting in 2012. The number of entrants accepted into the Leadville Trail 100 increased in 2011 to 802. In 2012, 1,100 ultrarunners were allowed entry into the race but in 2013, 1,200 ultrarunners were accepted into the race. For each additional 100 runners allowed into the race, there was an associated $28,500 more in entry fees. Yet there were storm clouds looming over the high peaks surrounding Leadville for the 2013 Leadville Trail 100.

A record 1,200 racers were allowed entry into the 2013 Leadville Trail 100, a number never seen during the history of the race. Of the 1,200 racers whose entries were accepted by race management, 946 runners showed up at the start of the 2013 Leadville Trail 100, an eighteen-percent increase over the previous year.

What was the effect of having so large a starting field poised to race the 2013 Leadville Trail 100?

How do you spell, **CHAOS**?

The Leadville Trail 100, a race dedicated to the extreme ultrarunner, had turned into exactly what Ken Chlouber wanted to avoid: an investor taking over the Leadville Race Series who wanted to "flood the community with athletes and sponsors."[2]

Life Time Fitness became exactly that type of Investment Company as evidenced by the 2013 Leadville Trail 100.

The quality and legendary persona of the Leadville Trail 100 evaporated with the 2013 ultrarunning event.

During the 2013 race, aid stations were gutted before many runners arrived for much needed food and drink; trash littered the entire course with runners tossing GU packets, cups, wrappers, etc. on the trail; and crews had a difficult time accessing their runners. Basically the 2013 Leadville Trail 100 was a total disaster.

A twenty-five-time Leadville Trail 100 finisher, Garry Curry, wrote online that he would never run the race again because of the conditions and excessive number of runners.

Life Time Fitness race director for the Leadville Trail 100, Joshua Colley, realized race management had royally screwed up after the 2013 race.

Criticism flooded magazines, online blogs, Facebook, and even came from established ultrarunning events like the Hardrock 100 race and race director Dale Garland.[1]

Yet the worst criticism of all came from much closer to home, the Leadville community. Townspeople of Leadville were highly critical of not only the Leadville Trail 100 but also of the entire Leadville Race Series in general.

Participants in all races stretched the town's resources to the limit. Parking was congested, trails were littered and the numbers of people supporting racers were choking the local roads. Remember, the population of Leadville is only 2,759 people so the massive crowds associated with the events easily double or triple the number of people in the town. That is significant.

Ken Chlouber attempted to defend the race but to little avail. Instead, Joshua Colley, race director, stepped up to the plate and admitted there were serious problems to be addressed and resolved. However, Joshua also echoed Ken's vision that "our goal is to bring money into the community, and we have been successful at that."[1]

There is always a delicate dichotomy between trail user purists and those wishing to enhance, bolster and support a local economy with the Leadville Race Series. How did Leadville Race Series management address these obvious and severe problems?

The first step was easy: limit Leadville Trail 100 entries. The number to use for race entrants in all future races was set at 750, race management decided. Race management believed that by limiting the number of entrants to 750, aid stations and crew access points would be able to handle all runners effectively and efficiently without undue over-crowding. The U.S. Forest Service was happy having 750 entrants use their trails for the race as well.

Local businesses were mixed on the number of ultrarunners and the number of LT100 MTB racers, as was expected. Some businesses loved the increase in spending while others, like the Golden Burro restaurant, were not as happy.[1]

In more recent years, Leadville residents have become tolerant of race events, following the 2013 debacle. As is usual in Colorado mountain towns, summer represents a massive increase for tourism in the state. In the case of Leadville, locals are forced to adjust their habits during peak race weekends while waiting for mountain snows to arrive again and the kiddies are back in school.

"Then it's almost like it used to be, before the circus came to town."[5]

Did Garry Curry, twenty-five-time Leadville Trail 100 finisher ever return to the race, after his criticism of the 2013 event? He never got the chance. On June 2, 2014 Garry Curry died in his sleep after a training run.

References

Chapter 15: Life Time Fitness – A New Leadville Trail 100?

1   Deadspin; *"Endurance is Booming, But Has Leadville Trail 100 Gone Too Far?"*, Sarah Baker, October 10, 2014
2   Runner's World Magazine, *"Life Time Fitness Develops National Portfolio of Events"*, Matt McCue, August 20, 2015
3   Leadville Race Series announcement, January 2017. https://www.leadvilleraceseries.com/2017/01/new-year-new-faces/
4   Ultrarunning Magazine, *"Boom and Bust"*, Donald Buraglio, October 2012
5   Jimmy Buffett lyrics, Floridays Album, *"When the Coast is Clear"*, 1986

Part 4

There is a Season

"The most difficult thing is the decision to act, the rest is merely tenacity. The fears are paper tigers. You can do anything you decide to do. You can act to change and control your life; and the procedure, the process is its own reward."

– Amelia Earhart, first woman pilot to fly across the Atlantic Ocean.

Chapter 16

In the Footsteps of Legends

Many people find it interesting knowing in whose footsteps they will be running, so to speak, along the Leadville Trail 100 Mile running course.

Here is a selection of athletes, in alphabetical order, who have completed the race or been significantly involved with the race. Are you capable of becoming one of them?

Men

Gordy Ainsleigh – 1995 (29:55:52): Twenty-three-time finisher of the Western States 100 mile race.

Otto Alppenzeller – MD and PhD Neurology and Medicine: Came along with Rick Fisher and Kitty Williams with the Tamahumara runners in 1994 to do research and study the affects of long-distance running on tribal members who came to run at Leadville.

Kirt Apt – Twenty-time finisher (Best time 19:42:53): Previous champion in 1995.

Dan Baglione – 1989 (28:33:54): Oldest person ever to compete in a six-day race at age 85 (183 miles). Ran 101 miles in 24 hours at age 84. We've known Dan since 1989 and he was one of the most wonderful, strong, determined and incredible runners in the sport. Died September 8, 2017 at age 87 from pancreatic cancer.

Al Binder – Thirteen-time finisher (Best time 24:21:17): Original finisher.

Dan Bowers – Two-time finisher (Best time 24:39:00): Micah True's training partner and friend.

Bob Burdick – 1985 (29:29:01): Persistent ultrarunner from California.

Jim Butera – 1985 (23:38:48): Leadville Trail 100 race creator and originator. The man with the genius to create a legendary race.

Trishul Cherns – 1987 (28:25:57): Multi-day ultrarunner, follower of Sri Chinmoy, finished 260 ultramarathons and still counting.

Cole Chlouber – Four-time finisher (Best time 25:08:06): LT100 MTB seven-time official finisher with 8:20:04 best time. Followed in the Tarahumara footsteps of minimalist running at Leadville. Ken Chlouber's son.

Ken Chlouber – Fourteen-time finisher (Best time 25:42:08): Leadville Race Series management, burro racer, miner, mountaineer and politician.

Chuck Cofer - Twelve-time finisher (Best time 23:14:38): Chuck and his wife Camille are long-time volunteers for the race as well.

Alan Cohn – Twelve-time finisher (Best time 25:58:19): An all-around great guy, race volunteer and local finisher.

Gary Cross – 1983 (27:36:24): Original finisher, Multi-day ultrarunner and race director.

Tyler Curiel – Eleven-time finisher (22:42:28): Strong and consistent ultrarunner, Physician.

Garry Curry – Twenty-five time finisher (Best time 24:47:59): Incomparable ultra trail runner. Died on June 2, 2014.

Dick Curtis – Three-time finisher (Best time 23:44:56): Steamboat Springs, Colorado ultrarunner. Died 2018.

Cliff Davies – Eight-time finisher (Best time 24:07:03): Great ultrarunner from Canada who entered but DNF at the first race in 1983 because he became lost, high on the slopes of Hope Pass. Cliff and his wife Mollie were always fun loving and happy, spending summers in Leadville while volunteering for pre-race support. At the pre-race dinner at the 6th Street Gym, there was always a huge birthday cake to celebrate Mollie's birthday. Mollie passed away of Parkinson's Disease, Cliff still resides in Canada.

Chisolm Deupree – Eleven-time finisher (Best time 24:24:30): Big buckle holder, Harry Deupree's son and holder of the fastest Deupree family finishing time at the Leadville Trail 100, ahead of Debbie and Harry.

Harry Deupree – Twelve-time finisher (Best time 27:34:12): Harry would always cross the finish line looking like he just stepped out of GQ Magazine: without a hair out of place and looking fresh. We still don't know how he did that.

Ted Epstein Jr. – 1988 (29:37:59): Colorado Ultra Club member, Original Leadville Trail 100 entrant - DNF, Multi-day racer. Completed Siberia 480 mile run, swam around Manhattan island, first man to swim across the Bering Strait (Russia to Alaska), first person to complete Grand Slam of Triathlons, completed Mexico's deca-Ten Ironman, climbed Mt. Vinson in Antarctica, member of Colorado Sports Hall of Fame. Died May 7, 2016 at age 81 of Alzheimer's disease.

Jim Feistner – Two-time finisher (Best time 27:16:36): Finished his first Leadville Trail 100 in 1984. Jim was a close and dear friend of Marge. She would always run into him while doing her long weekend training runs in Lodgepole Flats. He was always with his beloved dog, Honey. Jim died on April 9, 2014 and will be missed.

Cecil Fell – never finished but was a great ultrarunner, bartender in Silverthorne and friend.

Bill Finkbeiner – Thirty-time finisher (Best time 20:30:06): Mr. Leadville, holds the record for number of Leadville Trail 100 finishes (30). In June 2017 Bill was hit by a bicycle while running near Auburn, CA suffering extensive near fatal injuries that ended his daily, thirty-seven year running streak. Bill ran the 2018 race but dropped out before Winfield.

Raul Flores – Ten-time finisher (Best time 23:07:58): Perennial fast Leadville Trail 100 racer. I (Marge) remember suffering coming up the Boulevard toward the finish line when I saw a flashlight up ahead. My pacer, Michael said, "let's catch that runner." As we approached the runner we turned our lights off so he wouldn't see us coming. It worked and we passed Raul giving me 10th place overall with a sub-25 hour finish.

Steve Fossett – 1991 (29:38:12): Completed the Iditarod and Hawaii's Ironman, swam the English Channel and set a total of 115 world records including: First person to fly solo and non-stop around the world in a balloon and first solo non-stop around the world flight in an airplane, sailor who set numerous world records sailing around the world both transatlantic and Indian Ocean, completed six of the Seven Summits as a climber. Died on September 3, 2007 in an airplane accident.

Peter Gagarin – 1984 (25:42:18): Co-founder Ultrarunning Magazine.

Tom Green – Two-time finisher (best time 23:32:59): First Grand Slam finisher; finished over 280 ultramarathons, grandfather of ultrarunning. Suffered major medical problems in 2015 from a tree-trimming accident yet finished the Yeti 100-mile race in 2017 (29:46).

Martyn Greaves – Ten-time finisher (Best time 20:58:07): From England, finished the race in 1994 and 1995 after hip replacement surgery.

Skip Hamilton – Four-time finisher (Best time 18:43:50): Original finisher and four-time champion.

Gordon Hardman – Four-time finisher (Best time 24:18:56): Extremely tough endurance athlete with multiple finishes at Leadville, Hardrock, The Bear and Western States, and many more extreme ultra races.

Mike Hickman – 1996 (28:36:54): Married to Marge Hickman. Mike attributes his only finish, after several failed attempts (before meeting Marge), to Marge's coaching.

John Hobbs – Twelve-time finisher (Best time 28:26:19): Died December 2, 2018. Consistent trail runner and great person to run with because we always knew John would finish the race.

Jim Howard – Two-time finisher (Best time 19:15:57): 1985 race champion when he beat Skip Hamilton.

G.E. Jensen – Three-time finisher (Best time 20:29:52): Nearly pulled off the ultimate upset during the 1991 Leadville Trail 100 by leading the race until the home stretch when Steve Mahieu finally passed him.

Ulrich (Ulli) Kamm – Two-time finisher (Best time 29:03:54): Master race walker, walker in 250 ultra races including the Hardrock 100. When the co-author, Steve, asked Ulli during the Leadville race if it was possible to walk the entire Leadville race Ulli replied "no, because of the cut-off times."

King Jordan – Eleven-time finisher (Best time 24:41:05): Past president Gallaudet University in Washington, D.C. (University for the deaf and hard of hearing)

Scott Jureck – Two-time finisher (Best time 18:01:46): Seven-time Western States 100 mile champion, Grand Slam finisher, Badwater Ultramarathon two-time champion, Spartathlon three-time champion, Hardrock 100 mile champion, former Appalachian Trail running record holder, author.

Dean Karnazes – 2006 (23:24:29): Ran 50 marathons in 50 states in 50 days, he has run at least ten times in a 200-mile relay race while solo against teams of twelve, in 2005 he ran 350 miles in 81 hours 44 minutes, author.

Rob Krar – Two-time finisher (Best time 15:51:57): Two-time Leadville champion and second person to run under 16:00 hours at Leadville, coach at The Rob Krar Ultra Camp.

Miles Krier – Three-time finisher (Best time 26:32:07): 1997 Grand Slam finisher. Miles was a great friend, funny and a good running buddy for Marge. He liked to train in new places, like ski slopes, for more variety.

Joe Kulak – Twelve-time finisher (Best time 18:43:13): Numerous-time top 5 finisher.

Andy Lapkass – Four-time finisher (Best time 23:12:43): Original finisher, Mount Everest and Himalayan climbing guide, cyclist and ski patrol member.

John Lapkass – Three-time finisher (Best time 25:10:19): Original finisher and orthopedic surgeon.

Mark Lisak – Two-time finisher (Best time 21:41:37): Original finisher and friend of Brent Weigner, another original finisher.

Larry Mabry – Four-time finisher (Best time 27:27:50): 1989 Grand Slam finisher.

Dave Mackey – Two-time finisher (Best time 19:10:45): 2018 Leadman finisher, first amputee (Adaptive athlete) to finish the race AND the Leadman in the same year (2018).

Travis Macy – 2013 (20:15:11): Former Leadman champion, coach.

Matt Mahoney – Five-time finisher (Best time 27:24:34): First minimalist shoe runner at Leadville. "I always ran in shoes (racing flats) but no socks. I find them comfortable and they dry quickly."

Harlan (Bud) Martin – Six-time finisher (Best time 24:44:09): Perennial Leadville Trail 100 finisher.

Ted (Barefoot) McDonald – Three-time finisher (Best time 25:54:55): Minimalist shoe runner and coach.

Karl Meltzer – 2006 (20:52:20): Winningest 100-mile racer in the history of ultrarunning with thirty-eight victories, previous Appalachian Trail record holder running north to south.

Barry Mink – 1983 (28:39:22): Original finisher, Developed MAX sports drink for Skip Hamilton at the Leadville race and sold the drink to the Coca Cola Company. Barry is also a physician from Aspen. He researched why putting in the same effort changes over the years with regard to aging. For his research and studies, he was given an Aspen award.

Mike Monahan – Ten-time finisher (24:48:16): Mike and his wife Sandy were instrumental in helping Merilee and Ken during the early years of the race. Countless hours were spent not only with essential office matters but also out on the trail.

Dewitt Morris – 1995 (29:30:19): Hunter and wilderness enthusiast, took a minimalist attitude toward his training runs with Steve before finishing his one and only ultra race.

Bill Moyer – 1998 (29:42:41): Twelve-time starter and finally a finisher of the race on his 13th try with a champagne celebration at the finish line, Bill and his wife Jan became volunteers and headed up the packet stuffing for many years at the race and were great people and great friends.

Eric Pence – Twenty-four-time finisher (Best time 24:16:58):
Eric is poised to tie Garry Curry's twenty-five finishes in the 2019 race. Hopefully Marge will see more of Eric because she needs more runners to train with.

O.R. Peterson – Four-time finisher (Best time 25:07:49): Vail resident and front-runner as he always pushed the pace.

Steve Peterson – Seven-time finisher (17:40:53): Five-time Champion, Ten-time LT100 MTB finisher, coach.

Dr. John Perna – Original Leadville Trail 100 medical director and seven-time LT100 MTB finisher. Currently holds the position of geriatrician in Denver. (Kind of APROPOS since a lot of the initial ultrarunners he dealt with at Leadville have aged significantly)

Dale Perry – Four-time finisher (Best time 27:23:22): Ultrarunner supreme and also goes by the name Sasquatch. Myeloma cancer survivor and now with a heart bovine heart valve, still running ultra-distance events.

Tony Post – Never ran the race but was instrumental in getting the sponsor, Rockport, to bring the Tarahumara to the Leadville Trail 100, helped design the Tarahumara sandal, and worked on the FiveFinger running shoes. Today, Tony has his own company, *Topo Athletic*, where he developed and markets a new natural running shoe.

Aron Ralston – 2004 (29:43:41): Famous for cutting off his own right forearm as documented in the film 127 Hours, author and motivational speaker.

Craig Robertson – Six-time finisher (Best time 22:38:02): Fleet-footed ultrarunner.

Dana Roueche – Seven-time finisher (Best time 26:42:41):
Helpful coach to other Leadville ultrarunners.

Marvin Sandoval – Seven-time finisher (best time 19:44:58): Previous Leadman champion and coach.

Arthur Schwartz – Ten-time finisher (Best time 22:59:00): Original finisher and first ever ten-time finisher. Severely injured training for the race in 1990 when struck by a car in Aspen. While in and out of consciousness in the hospital, Arthur asked doctors and family at which aid station he had arrived. Arthur's doctor, family and friends said he was only at May Queen aid station and had a long way to go. Arthur fought to stay alive and eventually recovered, finishing the Leadville Trail 100 the following year.

Ian Sharman – Five-time finisher (Best time 16:30:03): Previous four-time champion in 2013, 2015, 2016 and 2017, Current record holder for the Grand Slam of Ultrarunning (69:49:38).

Bob Shaw – Two-time finisher (Best time 27:59:31): Finished his first Leadville Trail 100 in 1986.

Steve Siguaw – Eighteen-time finisher (Best time 22:41:17): Geophysicist, sailor, ultrarunner, climber and author, raced Marshall Ulrich, Stu Mittleman, Don Choi, Scott Weber and Helen Klein in the Race Across Colorado of which Marshall won.

Paul Slevin – Two-time finisher (Best time 27:36:56): Steve's training partner, friend and pacer.

Tom Sobal - World champion snowshoe racer, Colorado Running Hall of Fame and LT100 MTB course measurement official. Husband of Melissa Lee Sobal.

Rick Spady – Two-time finisher (Best time 18:04:03): Previous two-time champion, tied with Steve Warshauer in 1988 for the championship.

Keith Stegell – First person to video the race and continued his work well into the 1990's with his annual movies. The videos were captivating and favorably compared with Warren Miller's famous annual ski movies. Keith hunted shiny pieces of "fools gold" (pyrite) for the championship ore cart trophies.

Bentson Strider – Famous "stick man" DNF (See Chapter 3) and the mysterious and controversial eleventh non-finisher in 1983.

David Strong – Fourteen-time finisher (Best time 23:43:31): Ran the entire race in Rockport dress shoes when Rockport was a race sponsor.

Luther Thompson – Thirteen-time finisher (Best time 26:04:24): Three-time Grand Slam finisher. His famous quote was "You only have to decide to finish." Died October 2018, age 74.

Micah True – Three-time finisher (Best time 22:33:27): Also known as Caballo Blanco in *"Born to Run"* book. Died on March 27, 2012 near Gila, New Mexico during a solitary trail run. (See **Chapter 9**)

Marshall Ulrich – Thirteen-time finisher (Best time 20:33:36): Marshall was the first and only finisher to complete the Leadville Trail 100, LT100 MTB race, the Leadville Trail 100 AND kayak 100 miles (10 laps) around Turquoise Lake in 1999 (the kayak time was 28:32). Only runner to finish the Leadville Trail 100, drive to the Pikes Peak Marathon and finish that race the same day. Transcontinental runner and masters course recorder holder, Grand Slam finisher, Badwater Ultramarathon 18 time finisher and champion, four consecutive solo crossings of Badwater Basin self supported, Seven Summits climber (tallest summit on each continent), Race Across Colorado champion and noted author. Geeze.

Mario Varela – Twenty-time finisher (Best time 21:23:56): Eight big buckles.

Steve Warshauer – Two-time finisher (Best time 18:04:03):
Previous champion who tied with Rick Spady for the championship in 1988.

Scott Weber – Two-time finisher (Best time 29:30:24): Badwater Ultramarathon racer and solo Badwater crossing runner and coach.

Dick Webster – 1983 (27:25:42): Original finisher.

Brent Weigner – 1983 (29:31:25): Original finisher; Current World Record Holder for number of marathons and number of foreign country marathons completed. So far Brent has run marathons in 184 countries (351 total marathons and ultras), Brent is still on the hunt for new countries to run.

Hans-Dieter Weisshaar – Nine-time finisher (Best time 26:14:20): Oldest finisher at age 73 in 2013.

Reb Wickersham – Three-time finisher (Best time 26:59:03): Also known as *"The Rebel"* from racing stock cars during the 1960's in the southern circuit, World's second place record holder for 48 Hour indoor track with 148 miles, World record holder for 24 hour track race at 8,500 feet with 111 miles, Recipient of "Last Ass Over The Pass" award at 1986 Leadville Trail 100.

Ed Williams – Thirteen-time finisher (Best time 24:27:32): First 70 year old runner to ever finish the race, professor.

***

Women
Randi Bromka – Four-time finisher (Best time 21:55:33): Champion in 1987.

Lynette Clemens – Two-time finisher (Best time 19:59:06): Champion in 2011.

Cindy Corbin – Dr. John Perna's nurse for the race.

Debbie Deupree – Two-time finisher (Best time 29:03:13): Perennial front-runner, wife of Harry Deupree and mother of Chisolm Deupree.

Bobby Dixon – Two-time finisher (Best time 27:07:39): Strong ultrarunner from Montana.

Stephanie Ehret – Five-time finisher (Best time 22:17:02): Women's champion in 1998.

Essie Garrett – 1988 (29:53:08): Multi-day runner, follower of Sri Chinmoy, Colorado Hall of Fame Sportswoman and fundraiser, got lost/off course during the race and spent the night on the slopes of Hope Pass, died April 21, 2014.

Maureen Garty – 1986 (22:45:01): Women's champion. Found deceased in her pickup truck in Aspen from an apparent suicide, May 25, 2003.

Teri Gerber – 1984 (28:17:41): First women's finisher and champion. Marge met and got to know Teri prior to race day in 1984. She was quite unique, meaning that she was a lovely, confident woman with her nails done, hair in place, dressed nicely and very lady-like. Marge knew her as a competitive and strong runner.

Christine Gibbons – Four-time finisher (Best time 20:55:59): Champion in 1993. Ran with her husband Wayne and would run back along the course to find him during the race as they tried to run together.

Marge Hickman – Fourteen-time finisher (Best time 23:40:44):
Previous champion. I put the lid on any kind of ageism being in my
late 60's and still taking names (#badass). An accomplished road,
trail and ultrarunner, I think of myself as the "Pink Energizer
Bunny" that just keeps going and going, and "why not?" Because
running and exercising keeps me feeling young, strong, energetic
and healthy. I love to challenge myself. Living in Colorado, runners
should experience the adventure of Leadville's 100-mile run.
Women should be encouraged to try the race or pace a runner to get
a sense of what it's like and to experience the unexpected. Also,
volunteering and giving back to something you love to do is very
rewarding.

Pennie Hobert – Two-time finisher (Best time 28:21:54): Good
runner and training partner who was always fun to run with on the
Leadville trails.

Junko Kazukawa – Six-time finisher (Best time 26:35:18): 52, in
2015 completed the Grand Slam and the Leadwoman series in
Leadville, Colorado, becoming the first person to complete both
events in a single year. She grew up in Japan but did not want to
follow the traditional path. She did not want to be an ordinary
woman, but a woman who is not afraid to take on life-changing
challenges and to overcome obstacles. Junko was a good student but
failed in a physical education class that propelled her into motion.
She played basketball and never missed a practice. She started cross-
training, built her endurance and strength for running. She knows
adversity well being a two-time cancer survivor for which was not
going to stop her but only make her stronger, tougher and more
determined. Junko's next goal is to get certified as a cancer specialist
for exercise.

Helen Klein – 1989 (29:25:55): World-class ultrarunner and a true
legend, oldest female to finish the Leadville Trail 100 at age 66 in
1989.

Kay Lawrence-Murphy – A multi-year dedicated, hard-working volunteer and good friend. Marge was happy and tickled to have introduced Kay to her husband Mark at a house warming party at Marge's newly purchased townhome in Denver. Sadly, and far too soon, Kay passed away in her 40's of breast cancer.

Merilee (O'Neal) Maupin – Race director. Famous for giving bear hugs to finishing runners at the completion of the race, the heart and soul of the Leadville Trail 100.

Laurel Meyers – Champion of Persistence with a women's record 10 DNF's at the Leadville Trail 100. Laurel had issues making the cutoffs and/or had physical problems. Laurel died far too young of a massive heart attack. She was a close and dear friend of mine (Marge).

Laurie Nakauchi – Twelve-time finisher (Best time 24:58:03): Laurie is chasing the record of most finishes of the Leadville Trail 100 by a woman which is currently held by Marge Hickman with 14. Marge met Laurie at a Colorado Columbines Women's Running Club gathering in Washington Park in Denver. They were friends and Laurie most likely became interested in ultrarunning while listening to Marge's stories. She has done very well.

Lou Peyton – Two-time finisher (Best time 28:48:44): One of four women to complete the Grand Slam of Ultrarunning in 1989.

Pamela Reed – Six-time finisher (Best time 23:03:07): Badwater Ultramarathon overall champion 2002 & 2003, current six-day American record holder (490 miles) and author.

Monica Scholz – Five-time finisher (Best time 27:07:50): Excellent Canadian endurance athlete.

Melissa Lee Sobal – Four-time finisher (Best time 29:25:36): Very strong ultrarunner, massage therapist, married to Tom Sobal. Melissa and Tom are long-time friends, a great couple and dedicated athletes and volunteers. Melissa paced Marge one year from Winfield back into Twin Lakes.

Martha Swatt – Two-time finisher (Best time 23:30:11): 1996 champion.

Suzi Thibeault – 1989 (29:37:38): 100-mile specialist, Hardrock and Western States finisher and Grand Slam finisher, among many other endurance races.

Alice Thurau – 1991 (22:10:35): 1991 women's champion.

Sue Ellen Trapp – Three-time finisher (Best time 23:57:15): Perennial front-runner of the Leadville Trail 100 and always one to be feared by other racers.

Ann Trason – Four-time finisher (Best time 18:06:24): Four-time champion and only woman to run under 19:00 hours for the race, legendary world-class ultrarunner. World champion with twenty world records including: 50 miles (5:40:18), 100K (7:00:47), 100 miles (13:47:42) and 12-Hours (91 miles 1312 yards), writer, coach.

Liz Walker – Five-time finisher (Best time 28:05:33): Extreme endurance athlete.

Theresa Daus-Weber – Eleven-time finisher (Best time 22:50:47): 1992 race champion, persistent front-runner and never one to be counted out of a race.

Kitty Williams – Two-time finisher (Best time 29:09:39): See Chapter 8 about the Tarahumara runners.

Lynn Whittenburg – Two-time finisher (Best time 29:27:19): Finished in second place, behind champion Marge Hickman in the 1985 Leadville Trail 100.

Kathy D'Onofrio-Wood – Five-time finisher (Best time 20:50:41): Past women's champion, always a front-runner with an incredible spirit and determination.

Chapter 17

Racing and Finishing 100 Miles at Altitude

"You're better than you think you are and you can do more than you think you can." Ken Chlouber

"If you fail to prepare, you prepare to fail." Mark Spitz

"Don't dream of winning, train for it." Mo Farah

Don't stop when you're tired. Stop when you're done. Anonymous

So you want to win the Leadville Trail 100? How about just finish the race, since the event is at an altitude higher than most people ever run?

Those are two admirable goals: finishing the Leadville Trail 100 or even contending for the championship.

Your odds of finishing the race are 50-50. That's right, you have a 50% chance of finishing the Leadville Trail 100, on a good day.

Winning the race? Well you have to step it up several notches to achieve that dream.

Once your entry is chosen for the race, showing up at the pre-race briefing on Friday before the event is mandatory. At the race briefing, look at the people around you to see who is not going to cross the finish line. Every other person you cast eyes upon is going to be a dreaded DNF.

These are probably the toughest, meanest and most highly trained ultrarunners you have ever seen, and yet half of them will slink back to where they came from without success at the Leadville Trail 100.

244 | LEADVILLE TRAIL 100

The Leadville Trail 100 is 100 miles. There are no awards or trophies for dropping out, not even if you're first into the Winfield aid station at fifty-miles before calling it quits. Fifty miles is nothing at Leadville. You do not succeed by running over Hope Pass one time. The race is 100 miles, nothing less.

Speaking of awards, here is what you get for finishing the Leadville Trail 100:

- All finishers receive a finisher medal
- Under 25 hours: Large gold and silver buckle
- Under 30-Hours: Silver buckle
- Championship Ore Cart for men's and women's champion
- Women champions and finishers also receive a pendant/necklace in honor of the Unsinkable Molly Brown, long ago resident of Leadville and woman extraordinaire, along with one long-stem red rose.
- Age group awards of gold mining pan, three deep in all age categories
- Finisher sweat-shirt with name and time printed on it at the awards ceremony
- Ten-time finishers get a huge gold and silver belt buckle with their name on it
- Eleven-time finishers get a jacket with their name and Leadville Trail 100 logo on the back with eleven stars
- Twenty-time finishers get an incredibly large gold and silver belt buckle with their name on it
- Thirty-time finishers; no one except Bill Finkbeiner will ever receive this award so don't worry about it; it is gold and silver and quite large

Now that you know the rules and awards for the race, how will you get your sorry butt to the finish line of the Leadville Trail 100? The answer is simple, it really is.

There are four essential factors that determine if you can win or even finish the Leadville Trail 100.

No coach has a magic formula, a unique training program or divine insight how you should prepare for or run the race. Everything you need to know has already been said or written by those who have gone before you.

By the way, any modern day successful running coach obtains and uses information published by these authors/coaches: Arthur Lydiard and Tim Noakes. We'll discuss their effective techniques in detail throughout this chapter.

If you decide to utilize a coach for your training and racing program, always choose someone who has finished the Leadville Trail 100 – multiple finishes would be nice too. If one hasn't suffered at Leadville, there is no reason that person can understand how to run the race.

Your success at the Leadville Trail 100 depends on these four magic components:

1. VO_2max
2. Pace during a 10K, marathon or 50-mile race
3. Long training runs
4. Mental preparation and course experience

Notice that massive weekly mileage was NOT part of the components for finishing or winning the Leadville Trail 100. You will see why later in this chapter.

Let's talk about each of the four variables shown above:

1. VO_2max – This is maximum oxygen consumption or uptake.

Success at ultrarunning depends on how much oxygen your body can transport to muscles from the lungs. An increase in oxygen consumption accompanies an increase in exercise intensity.[1]

Simply explained, the amount of oxygen your lungs can supply to your muscles is critical for success at the Leadville Trail 100. The higher your VO_2max, the better chance there is of finishing the Leadville Trail 100.

As stated in Chapter 3, there is a place on the racecourse to test your VO_2max: The short two-mile trail section that leads to the Hagerman Pass gravel road. This trail portion is past the May Queen aid station and begins at about mile fourteen.

The final one-mile stretch of the VO^2max exercise, from the creek crossing at the bridge and climbing to the Hagerman Pass road will measure your VO_2max, if you can run it. Your heart rate will max out once you pant breathless onto the Hagerman Pass road.

Training increases VO_2max to some extent but that is only part of the equation regarding oxygen. Hemoglobin is necessary to transport oxygen to your aching muscles. The more hemoglobin you have to transport an abundance of oxygen the faster and longer you can exercise.

Racing at Leadville, altitude acclimatization increases the amount of hemoglobin in your system, provides better oxygen transport to muscles (from your VO_2max) and helps with your chance of success at the Leadville Trail 100.

A runner can increase their VO_2max through long training runs, interval training, threshold runs, running efficiently and participating in shorter races.

Altitude has an adverse effect on VO_2max, as does an athlete's age and gender.

Let's talk about the influence of altitude on VO_2max first.

Dr. Colin Grissom, a pulmonologist in Salt Lake City describes VO_2max decreasing 1% per 100 meters above 1,500 meters. Over 5,000 feet of altitude, for every 1,000 feet, VO_2max will decrease 2% to 3% per 1,000 feet elevation gain.[2]

Leadville's altitude is 10,152 feet. An athlete's VO_2max at the starting line of the Leadville Trail 100 will have decreased 10% to 15% from their normal VO_2max. That decrease in VO_2max assumes you are arriving and acclimated to an altitude of 5,000 feet, Denver's elevation.

Coming from sea level, an ultrarunner can expect a VO_2max 20% to 30% lower than normal.

Now you can understand why it is important to acclimate a minimum of 3-5 days in Leadville with 1-2 weeks an even better amount of time spent at Leadville's altitude.

Acclimatizing to Leadville's altitude will help increase your VO_2max for the race.

What about age and gender and their effect on VO_2max?

As you would expect, an older ultrarunner naturally loses VO_2max, but only at a rate of 10% per decade. Probably more significantly, an older ultrarunner's maximum heart rate has more of an effect on their performance than a decrease in VO_2max.[1]

Female ultrarunners have lower VO_2max values than males. Lower VO_2max values for female ultrarunners is due to their higher percentage of body fat and less powerful muscles than male ultrarunners.[1] (Ha, tell that to Ann Trason or...)

2. Pace during a 10K, marathon or 50-mile race

The faster you can run shorter distance races, the better your chance of success at the Leadville Trail 100.

The co-author, Steve, conducted a statistical analysis at the 1989 Leadville Trail 100 and it was published in Ultrarunning Magazine.[3]

Oh no, not statistics?.?

Don't worry; you don't have to know statistics or math for this magic component to achieve success at the Leadville Trail 100.

Summarizing the article, there is a statistical difference between ultrarunners who finish the Leadville Trail 100 vs. racers who finish the event under 25 hours. There were 192 participants in the statistical analysis.

Finishing the Leadville Trail 100 takes a lot of work before the actual race, a fact most of us know and expect.

Finishing vs. non-finishing (DNF) at the 1989 Leadville Trail 100 was dependent on:

- Average training pace
- Best marathon, 10K and 50-mile race time
- Training base mileage

If you want to **finish** the Leadville Trail 100 you should work on your speed and have a strong weekly base training mileage accompanied by a quicker average training pace.

A five-hour marathon runner will struggle at the Leadville Trail 100 and their chance of success will be very low.

If your 50-mile race time is in the ten-hour range, on a normal road course, you will also struggle to finish the Leadville Trail 100.

Racing success with a time under 25 hours at the 1989 Leadville Trail 100 was determined by:

- Best marathon, 10K and 50-mile race time
- Training base mileage

If you want to **race** the Leadville Trail 100 and finish under the magic 25-hour mark, increase your training base mileage and work on your pace during shorter races and during training runs.

Racing a marathon in sub three hours will help significantly with your chances of placing with the top runners at the Leadville Trail 100.

Your fifty-mile race time should be under seven hours on a road course to get that cherished podium finish at the Leadville Trail 100.

3. Long training runs

Nearly every successful Leadville Trail 100-Mile ultrarunner includes substantial, long distance runs in their base training for the race. Refer to Chapter 12 for champion Steve Peterson's long runs of up to fifty-five miles in preparation for the Leadville Trail 100.

Paul Dewitt, Leadville champion in 2003 and 2004, is a classic example of a low mileage runner who included long weekly training runs.

The co-author, Steve, trained with Paul Dewitt before the 2002 race. Paul finished in second place that year with a time of 18:07:02.

Here is Steve's story about training with Paul Dewitt:

"During a summer training run, Paul wanted me to lead him on the Leadville Trail 100 section of the course from May Queen to the top of Sugarloaf Pass. Paul did not understand the course in that area and wanted guidance.

Paul had his future pacer running with him, a 2:20 marathoner, to also learn the course.

Well, that training run didn't go well for me. Having two fast runners on my heels, pushing the entire time was quite an experience to say the least.

My training run was from Turquoise Lake Dam to the top of Sugarloaf Pass, a distance of twenty-eight miles. Because of my new running partners, the elapsed time for the run was 3:56.

No, Paul Dewitt and his friend didn't stay with me the entire run because I politely asked them to run ahead, once they were familiar with the course."

Another example of a fast training run was when Paul Dewitt and his 2:20 marathon pacer ran the course from Twin Lakes to Winfield and back, a distance of twenty-one miles.

Paul's split from Twin Lakes to the halfway point at Winfield was 2:07 and his split coming back the other way to Twin Lakes was 2:02.

I (Steve) ran the same route, on the same day but while leading and marking the course for the annual Leadville Trail training weekend. My splits were: 3:05 from Twin Lakes to Winfield and 2:39 coming back to Twin Lakes.

Comparing Paul's training splits with my splits, you can see the obvious difference between a seventeen-hour Leadville racer, Paul Dewitt, and a twenty-two hour runner, me. I claim marking the course for the training group slowed me down – not.

How about weekly training mileage for success at the Leadville Trail 100?

I (Steve) am an adherent of high mileage training. Marge thinks the same as me when it comes to training for a 100-mile race, with speed another critical factor. Training for most of my Leadville races, I ran over 100 miles for six consecutive weeks building up for the race. My highest mileage was 126 miles for one week during training. That energy-draining high mileage week included a brutal forty-five mile run from the Mount Elbert trailhead, near Halfmoon aid station, to Winfield and return in less than ten hours.

Paul Dewitt believed in running up to fifty-five miles for his highest weekly mileage while training for the Leadville race. As you noticed with Paul, he ran high quality long runs every week, instead of long slow extreme distance runs. A long run for Paul was usually less than thirty miles. There were no mega-mileage weeks for Paul Dewitt.

Tarahumara runners are renowned for their multi-day running events as well as simply running throughout their canyons for days on end.

Kenyan and Ethiopia marathon runners combine fast pace with long training runs leading to excessive weekly mileage totals.

Course record holder, Matt Carpenter, chose speed over super long runs. Five months before the Leadville Trail 100, Matt did back-to-back long runs of over two hours each. His daily run, excluding the long runs, consisted of running two hours every single day.[7]

Matt Carpenter's definition of a long run might be a little different than an ordinary ultrarunner, given his extreme speed.

Every ultrarunner and runner is *"each an experiment of one. A unique, never-to-be repeated event."* as George Sheehan said.[8]

Choose a training program that suits you and no one else.

4. Mental attitude and course experience

The Sport Competition Anxiety Test (SCAT; Martins, 1977) was used at the first Leadville Trail 100. Results from the study found a slightly lower score of 18.3 for the racers vs. a normal score of 19.7 for the general population. This difference indicates race participants are less anxious than the general population, yet the study found little difference between finishers and non-finishers. [4,5,6]

The one personality trait that was prevalent among the finishers of the first Leadville Trail 100 in 1983 was finishers developed a strategy for running the 100-mile race from previous experience at the distance, as opposed to non-finishers.[5]

Also, familiarity with the Leadville course was critical for success, as Paul and Steve and the researchers, believed.

Most research suggests the same thing – familiarity with a specific course or ability to remember the route enables a runner to mentally visualize the race, how fast they will run certain sections of the course and mentally deal with the physical and mental exhaustion during the race itself.

Arriving at Leadville prior to the actual Leadville Trail 100 not only enables an athlete to acclimate but also gives a runner the ability to experience certain sections of the course.

Another important topic in this chapter that needs to be addressed is:
Injury and Pain

The co-author of this book, Marge, injured her ankle the first time she ran the Leadville Trail 100. Marge ran over eighty-seven miles with a very painful and swollen sprained ankle and still finished the race. Darn those nasty tree roots along Turquoise Lake in the dark early morning hours of the race.

While training for an ultrarunning race, a runner is very likely to be injured at some point. An injury or extreme pain is simply part of the ultrarunning experience. Every successful ultrarunner has been injured, dealt with the injury, ran on the injury and succeeded. That is just ultrarunning.

Pain during a 100-mile ultrarunning event or training is to be expected and mentally dealt with. Ultrarunning is not a sport for the weak.

A story by first-time runner, Christopher McDermand, about being "Smitten by the Ultra Bug":

"I didn't know shit. I still don't, really.

Most of my life has been pretty aimless. For a short period of time, I found an aim, and I thought I had figured a few things out.

Ultimately, achieving a massive personal goal brings you great joy, confusion, exhaustion, and most dangerously a void that you need to be ready to fill once the accomplishment is made.

Finishing a couple of half marathons at a slightly above average pace doesn't mean anything.

That's where I was that day, running a 5-mile training run at a not great pace. Who knew that this unimportant jaunt around the neighborhood would have such a huge impact on the trajectory of my life, at least for the next few years.

Your mind wanders when you run. It doesn't matter if you are an ultramarathoner, or completing your first couch-to-5K training plan.

Another thing that is true of runners is that the long run you have planned for any given week, no matter your capabilities, feels like a long run.

If you struggle through a three-mile run because you are new to the discipline, that is a very similar feeling to struggling through the last few miles of a 25-mile run in the mountains after putting in 20+ miles the day before.

In both of those instances the mind finds little morsels for your subconscious to gnaw on. Sometimes it is great and euphoric, and other times it is a repetitive psychosis that nearly drives you insane. A lot of it depends on how well the run is going.

During that unimportant 5-mile training run my mind wandered. The weather was good. In our little part of the south that means the humidity wasn't quite to the clothes drenching level.

I was cruising along at some pace that was not helping me get any faster, but the thought occurred to me, "Just how long could I keep running at this bullshit pace." I felt so good, that I started to mull this over.

Endorphins are awesome, aren't they? They make you act like a damn fool sometimes, a happy one, but a damn fool nonetheless.

As I was getting back to the house to complete my run, I started to remember a book I had read that talked about a 100-mile race.

Remember, endorphins can bring on some weird, euphoric thoughts. I recalled reading about these athletes who would run one hundred miles all at once.

I knew I couldn't do that, but as I was walking into the house, I figured I could at least try to find out the name of the race, and see how fast these guys and gals were running that distance.

I found my copy of "Born to Run," and found the race: Leadville Trail 100.

Alright, now it was time for a quick Google search about the race. Oh, it turns out Leadville is just at 10,152 feet of elevation, above sea level.

Sitting at my computer, I was comfortably resting at about forty feet above sea level. Now how long does it take these folks to complete this race?

The good news is you have thirty hours to finish the course. That means your only have to "run" a pace of about 18 minutes per mile.

I was still buzzing from the run, so I knew that sort of pace was super easy. Maybe this 100-mile thing was more attainable than I first thought.

The winners and record holders are finishing at under a 10 minute per mile pace, but that doesn't mean that the average person in the race needs to push him or herself like that.

This ridiculous dive into the details of the race had probably gone on long enough. Why was I even wasting time looking into this?

Well I figured I'd better see when the race even takes place. Turns out that the race is in August each year; right before I would have to go back to work as a high school teacher.

The irrational thoughts start coming fast and furious again and you know what else, I would also have all summer off to train. Training at sea level on flat terrain would be pretty useless though, I thought to myself. The crazy thoughts were coming faster now.

Damn runner's high was lingering a little too long, and it was getting the best of me. Well, while we are at, when is the sign-up date for this race?

Finally, a return to sanity; the sign-up date for the race had already passed. We dodged a bullet.

More thoughts flood in, "Wait, what is this note at the bottom of the page? There are a few spots going up on the website in a just a couple of weeks.

I should definitely inquire as to how to sign up for this. What in the world am I thinking?

If I get signed up for this race, I could move there all summer since I would not have work to go to. I could get a job up there, and that would help pay for rent on some place for the summer as well.

Is this what fate feels like? Maybe I should have skipped my run that day." (Authors remark: Christopher McDermand finished the 2013 Leadville Trail 100 in a time of 28:24:49.)

Marge's perspective on training: (Steve's Note to male readers: do not miss reading Marge's perspective on training. Most guys don't train this hard.)

"Moving to Colorado in 1972 from the east coast, lucky for me, was no issue regarding altitude sickness or any altitude symptoms. I felt right at home in Denver and at 14,000+ feet.

My husband continues to say, I have lungs in my calves.

In fact, it wasn't until I got involved and addicted to sports, that I learned of many people who did suffer from altitude sickness whether it was from high altitude or dehydration.

I've never been a lush for water and always thought that I did drink plenty of water until one day when someone questioned my small fanny pack bottles and asked, Are those your only water bottles?

Yes, I said, why?

He looked at me like I was crazy and said they could never get by with that little amount of water.

I replied, "I'm okay."

My small Ultimate Direction waist pack had a small center pouch with two small mini pockets, one on each side of the pouch to hold four ounces of water or gel in plastic bottles. That used to be enough water for me during a long training run.

I did, however, learn a lesson at Western States 100 one year when I was at mile seventy-five. I started feeling nauseous and had no idea what was happening to me until I stopped at the next aid station. Medical personnel knew right away I was dehydrated. That was not fun, and put an end to my race.

Over the years, I've learned that wasn't so smart and now realize that water and energy drinks make for better performance.

Coming from a background of daily aerobic exercise classes and playing/competing in racquetball tournaments all over Colorado, transitioning and training to become an ultrarunner was easier than for most runners.

I started slowly but soon was hooked. Since Jim Butera sold me my first pair of running shoes, and we ran/trained together a lot, he always encouraged and told me that I was a "natural."

I wished I didn't have to work so that I could run and train all day long. I would run with anyone, at any time, and anywhere.

In the late '70s to late '80s, I had the hunger and passion to be the best I could be. I loved running races of any distance up to marathons. I used marathons as long, hard training runs.

My dream at this point was to attempt to qualify for the first woman's Olympic Marathon. Jim believed in me and pushed me harder and coached me to help me reach my goal. We did speed workouts on the track or tree-to-tree, hill repeats and long weekend runs with the Colorado Ultra Club. I was on top of my game.

I can remember running twice and even three times a day, once or twice a week while I was working full-time. I ran six miles before work, getting up at 4:15 am every morning and running with my neighbor, Stan Arnold, along the dirt path of the Highline Canal, which extended for miles in all directions throughout Denver.

I would run again on my lunch hour for maybe another five miles, leaving enough time to take a quick sponge bath or some times not even that.

At the time, I worked at a geothermal exploration company that was very laid back. We could wear blue jeans every day if we wanted and my bosses were very fit as well. They loved to jump rope, so we would all occasionally have a jump rope contest during the workday.

As soon as I got off of work, I drove like crazy to the athletic club in order to run as much as fifteen more miles from downtown Denver, south to a shopping mall called "Cinderella City" before I turned around and ran back to the club.

This was all on asphalt, concrete and during the height of evening traffic in Denver. I look back now and don't know how in the world I ever did that. I was young and loved running.

Once a week I would try to leave work a little early so that I could drive for an hour to get to the track for the Phidippides Running Club track speed workouts. I don't know how I didn't get stopped for speeding but the Phidippides running god and angels must have been along for the drive too.

I do believe that it was that weekly intense speed workout that gave me my fastest time at Leadville in 1991 of 23:40:44, placing me 1st in my age group and twenty-second place overall.

As one matures and ages, I also know that "speed kills." This is extremely important to understand and know what your body's limits are to avoid injury.

Back in the day, I also tried and loved taking power walking classes in Boulder taught by a man named Dave Felkley who was an orienteer/mountaineer and could power walk the Pikes Peak ascent faster than most running it.

Dave was incredible and none of us in the class could begin to keep up with him until he taught us how to do it.

A great technique he taught us was to envision ourselves as an animal, any animal, running through the jungle swiftly or chasing its prey and to think of ourselves as being that agile, swift and relaxed animal.

My favorite was, and still is, to think of myself as a graceful deer loping through the woods on trails.

Another tip that Dave told us was to hold a small rock in each of our hands as we power walked, and to swing our arms loosely back and forth to help keep our momentum moving forward, making sure not to swing our arms across in front of our body, and keep the arms moving back and forth like a pendulum or a pulley system. These great tips helped me improve my running technique and uphill power walking speed.

I remember watching other ultrarunners' technique and form as they ran: upright, straight posture, relaxed shoulders and loosely swinging arms.

I especially recall doing a long run on the east side of Leadville, up in the mining district. I was coming down from a mine site and below me running was Ann Trason striding out relaxed and graceful from the lower portion of Mosquito Pass on to the dirt road. Ann was beauty in motion.

I wanted to look like and run like Ann, and to this day still picture her image in my mind and try to emulate her running style.

I sincerely believe that if you can dream it and believe it, you can achieve it. Next you have to devote, commit and put the effort and work into anything to get results. I know because I have been there, done that.

Remember my dream of qualifying for the Olympic Marathon and training to achieve that goal?

March 1984 found me on the start line for the St. Patrick's Day Shamrock Marathon in Virginia Beach, the women's Olympic trials qualifying race.

To my surprise, my parents said that they would drive down from Pittsburgh to watch me finish. Wow, that meant the world to me, as they thought I was crazy to try to run that far. They just couldn't understand it or the thought of exercising for health.

What an experience and highlight of my life to be amongst hundreds of runners trying to accomplish the same goal that I was trying to achieve. I was a nervous wreck at the start but once the gun went off, I fell into a much faster pace than I wanted.

Breathing too heavily, I pulled back until I settled into my pace with surrounding runners at 6½ minute per mile pace.

Relax. I could definitely tell I was running at sea level, as I seemed to be gliding along effortlessly.

I was on pace to reach my qualifying time goal of 2:52:16. I felt great and only wished Jim Butera could have been there, but knowing my parents would be at the finish line made it extra special and exciting.

I vividly recall turning off an asphalt road and onto a concrete boardwalk, next to the ocean, for the final six miles to the finish.

Oh my, what just happened…strong winds coming from the north? The ocean? Whatever? This was going to be a problem if the winds continued, and they did.

A small group of a few men came up behind me and as they passed, they asked if I was trying to qualify. I said, yes.

They told me to pull in and tuck in behind them and they would help pull me along to the finish. What a kind and great thing they offered to me. As they seemed to be running faster than I was, I willed myself to stay with them.

I was starting to struggle but managed to hang at the back of them. There was no conversation, merely heart pounding, heavy breathing. Just a little farther I told myself, focusing on every step, as we got closer to the finish.

Finished, done, exhausted; but disappointment set in instantly. Looking at the clock and seeing my time of 2:56 brought me to tears. I was devastated and couldn't believe I missed the qualifying time.

The first four women to finish qualified. I was the fifth woman over the line.

The guys were equally disappointed and apologized for not getting me there in time. It wasn't their fault, and I know I could not have done as well as I did if it hadn't been for them helping to block the wind for me.

We all hugged and said our goodbyes, and I headed into the crowd to find my parents.

Back at our hotel, I found a pay phone outside near the boardwalk. I was sad but excited to call Jim and tell him the good, bad news.

That same year, I ran a marathon race every weekend in June and July (Boulder, Estes Park, Steamboat and Leadville), winning three of the four mountain marathons. The local running newspaper wrote me up as the 'Mountain Marathon Queen.'

Jim Butera told me I should try and run his 100-mile race in Leadville since I had a great training base this year. So I entered the 1984 race and finished as second woman."

Here is Marge's advice for incorporating a burro into speed training:

"I'm running 100 miles, why do I need to run fast training runs, tempo runs or even do track intervals?

Again, simple answer: Increase your VO$_2$max and an ultrarunner's chance of finishing or competing at the highest levels in the Leadville Trail 100 change significantly.

But if you absolutely dread setting foot on the local high school track and don't want to interrupt your peaceful long runs with intermittent sprints, there is another method that can be used and it is still a speed or interval workout: burro racing.

Marge is a burro racer. Ken Chlouber and Merilee Maupin are burro racers as well. Burros have a long and storied history in Leadville's mining heritage and are very much a part of Leadville Trail 100 lore where a pacer is a runner's pack mule/burro.

You might ask yourself what does burro racing and speed training have to do with ultrarunning?

Good question. I decided to include one of my secret techniques in this book as a suggestion for ultrarunners seeking speed with a unique cross-training method.

Burro racing began in 1949, the invention of local merchants in Leadville and Fairplay, Colorado as a way to bring tourists to depressed mining towns. Prize money was collected and offered to the winner of the race. In today's dollars, that would be $12,000 for a first-place finish.

Horses, mules and burros were widely used in the old west, but horses were expensive to buy and feed, while mules were also expensive to buy but they were cheaper to feed. Burros were tough, durable, strong, sure-footed, calm, patient and loyal. So, a burro became the beast of choice for prospectors, and mine owners alike.

Supplies were carried from Leadville to the surrounding mines on the backs of burros, which made them an integral part of Leadville's economy from 1860 until the early 1900's. Burros were a tremendous part of Leadville's gold and silver rushes and even today when runners recruit a pacer.

After watching Leadville's annual Boom Days Celebration, I knew I had to try running and racing with a burro.

I also asked around, talking with locals and race officials; how do I get started in this unusual race?

I was directed to Dave TenEyck who happened to be very involved in the sport. In fact, though Dave and his wife Lori lived in Golden, they also had a home in Leadville with acreage where they kept their burros.

Oh yea, for me. This was something new to try and hopefully not kill myself or get stomped to death by a beautiful yet massive, strong animal, and one of Colorado's favorite animals.

I eventually talked to Dave about running one of his burros the following year, which he said would be great as it helps to keep the burros active and "in shape."

We got to become friends and would get together, when time permitted, to take two of the burros, Peckinpah and JJ, out to Lodgepole Flats to walk/run and learn how to train a sometimes-stubborn ass, which they were for me most all the time.

Dave decided I could run next year's burro race with his well-trained male, big Jack burro, Peckinpah, who was a beauty. I remember him being huge standing next to me, really BIG. I was somewhat afraid of him but he was a "gentle giant."

Dave had run Peckinpah in many prior races at Leadville as well as in the "Triple Crown of Burro Racing" and other mountain race locations - Georgetown, Fairplay, Buena Vista, but this "smart" burro only knew the Leadville men's course, not the women's course.

Oh boy, what was I getting myself into? I remember being as nervous, worried and anxious as running a 100 miler and even a thousand times more because I didn't know what to expect and had not trained enough with Peckinpah, but it would have to do as race day was approaching.

Race day came, Sunday, August 5th, 1994. I met Dave at his home early that morning and he was already outside hooking up his trailer and loading Peckinpah. When all was ready to go, we headed into Leadville for the big event.

We parked off Main Street in a parking lot where all burro racers were staged. Each burro had to carry 35 lbs. of weight, including mining gear, a pick, a shovel, and a gold pan. We then had to take Peckinpah to be weighed and his/our information recorded for the race.

Waiting for the announcement and call to the start line, my stomach was rumbling and my nerves were a mess. There's the call and all racers with their burro head to the freshly painted white line across Main Street for the start in downtown Leadville.

Burro rules state you are not allowed to have someone help you with your burro. Also, if you drop or lose your lead and your burro takes off from you, you must fetch your burro and bring it back to where you dropped your lead and restart from that point.

There was lots of noise, calls, shouts and good luck wishes being called out to racers, which made it that much more exciting. Finally, the count down, the gun shot rang out and the racers or, should I say, the "asses" explode into full throttle down main street.

For me, Peckinpah blasted out of the gate taking me right from the get-go into a sprint start. I was so scared and afraid that I couldn't hold on to the lead or that I would do a "face plant" before making my first turn up the east side of town. My heart was pounding and my legs were going as fast as they could, and faster.

We made the turn up East 7th Street. I was hoping that the pace would slow down and that the racers would spread out, which they did…finally.

The experienced racers looked great, in control and flawless as their burro responded to their commands before disappearing ahead of us beginners who were struggling with the sprint.

Peckinpah knew what he was doing, running and keeping me "in control." I was "hupping", screaming "whoa", pulling on his lead and yelling commands.

Sometimes he seemed to do what I asked but most other times he did his own thing, taking me off the course into the bushes or trees so that he could eat. He even tried to turn me/us around and go back to the start. He was really messing with me and knew he could get away with it since I wasn't his owner.

We finally reached the split in the race where the men went one way and the women went in another direction. Dave warned me about this and to be ready when Peckinpah would try to take me down the men's course. He was right.

When we got there, I pulled with all my strength and might to keep my "ass" on the right course but "NO" he took me off my course and stopped.

I used my lead to switch him on the rump several times to no avail; harder, faster, yelling, upping, but nothing seemed to work.

He took me round and round in circles stomping on the top of my foot and toes. I yelped and screamed in pain and was afraid that he may have broken my foot or toe. "Well, can't worry about that right now, can we Peckinpah?"

Suddenly I hear someone calling me from the top of the hill. It was Dave and he figured I would need help somewhere along the course.

After much coercion from Dave and onlookers, Peckinpah decided to listen as I pulled his ass back up the trail to get back on the correct course for women. I was exhausted already and still had probably 10 miles to go. What a speed workout this was becoming.

Onward Peckinpah and we go…finally.

For the rest of the race I was constantly pulling, dragging, yelling or anything else I could do to keep him moving. He loved getting treats or a carrot along the way but that didn't seem to help too much either. All I wanted was to get to the damn finish line in one piece.

With the end in sight, we made the final turn back on to Main Street at the south end of town. The crowd of onlookers filled both sides of the street and erupted with cheers of "good job", "you're almost there."

I knew that I was not the winner but soon realized that I was the last woman to finish…fabulous, I'm done and I am a finisher.

I think my finishing time was just under five or six hours for a 15-mile burro race and that's a win in my book. I was very, very happy and pleased once the race was over.

So if you'd like to incorporate a different approach into your tempo runs or interval workouts, get yourself a burro, have some fun and race your ass off."

Nutrition and Water by Marge:

I have become a believer in these two successful tips that work for me regarding nutrition and drinking fluids during ultras or a 100 miler:

1. Fluid/Water Intake: *"If you are thirsty, drink. If you are not thirsty, don't drink."* Dr. John Hill.
2. Nutrition: *"Eat what you like and what works for your body."* Marge Hickman

Over the years I have learned it's good to try new things: sports drinks, sports bars and the many sports "shots." But try them while you are training and not on race day.

I love chocolate but not during a race. Cookies and sweets are the same for me; I love them but not on race day, I prefer "real food."

From when I started running ultras to the present, I love having macaroni with peas and some olive oil or butter. I also like the aid station peanut butter and jelly sandwiches, cantaloupe, watermelon, pretzels and some salty items.

When I start feeling hungry, I depend on my crew to have special things I really like: grapes, small chunks of cantaloupe, hard-boiled eggs, and the small six-cup packages of vanilla or tapioca puddings. They are yummy and slide down easily.

I'm a nibbler and can only eat small bites or portions at a time. It is important to know what is best for you.

Now for a topic on which everyone has a different opinion: **Equipment, by Steve:**

Many runners love the technical aspect of researching, deciding and then buying just the right gear for an extreme endeavor like the Leadville Trail 100.

Lights, packs, water bottles/hydration units, drop bags stashed at aid stations and food are some necessary items needed for a 100-mile race.

Choose a light that works for you. This is essential for the Leadville Trail 100 since the race begins in the dark and runners need a light for the first two hours of the race. Racers also need a light as they run through the night again, before approaching the finish line the next morning. Keep spare batteries in your pack as a backup too.

LED Headlamps have replaced handheld flashlights for the majority of runners. Petzl, Black Diamond, Nathan and Fenix are just a few choices waiting for a runner to pick up. Marge's new favorite is the Kogalla RA adventure light that is a lightweight, waistband running light system with rechargeable battery pack or batteries.

When choosing a light remember it will be cold and wet during the Leadville Trail 100. Shock resistance might also come in handy when you take an unexpected tumble on the trail. Chances are pretty good that will happen.

Packs, Water Bottles & Hydration Units

Most runners carry some sort of pack during the race. This can be a waist pack to carry spare gear and food or a minimalist hydration system like an amphipod for your liquids and light snacks.

The distance between aid stations during the race is about ten miles, or three to four hours of running without support throughout the event. It is essential to carry extra liquids and food for these long stretches between aid stations.

Drop Bags/Supply Bags

A runner can have resupply bags for every aid station except Hope Pass. Only clear plastic bags are allowed to contain whatever items you may want or need. Drop bags are handy when crews are not available to resupply a runner.

Then there are three main essentials:

- Running shoes
- Socks
- Clothes

Running Shoes

In certain circles, there are proponents of a minimalist approach to running shoes.

Matt Mahoney was probably the first minimalist shoe proponent at the Leadville Trail 100 in 1995.

Following in Matt's footsteps, so to speak, were Ted "Barefoot" McDonald and even Leadville's own Cole Chlouber.

However, (that word again) a minimalist shoe approach is not for every runner, as many people have discovered through injury and painful experimentation.

There are dozens of shoe choices on the market today, including training shoes, racing flats and trail shoes.

Choose what works for you and don't be lured in by creative marketing. A trail shoe is **not** required to run the Leadville Trail 100.

In the early days of the race, runners simply ran in training shoes or racing flats. Then along came trail shoes with their heavier weight and more protection, supposedly.

Trail running is about technique, not about the perfect shoe for the conditions. Again, pick a shoe you like, fits your foot well and causes a minimum number of blisters during a 100-mile race.

Socks

Don't overlook this critical piece of running equipment. Changing socks at aid stations will help your feet, not to mention your race.

Some ultrarunners prefer separate toe pouch type socks to prevent blisters. These do work but maybe they are not really necessary if you have shoes that fit properly.

Clothes

A proper wardrobe for the Leadville Trail 100 is crucial for success. No, we're not talking about a color-coordinated bling outfit, although that may make you look and feel good.

We are talking about clothing that wick sweat and rain, keeping you dry and clothing that keeps you warm during the cold nighttime running conditions and blustery cold winds when it rains. Yes, it will rain and it will be cold and it will probably snow as well.

Hats and gloves are essential gear for the Leadville Trail 100. Have at least two hats, a stocking hat for nighttime running and a daytime hat to keep the wicked high-altitude sun off your face.

References

Chapter 17: Racing and Finishing 100 Miles at Altitude

1   *Lore of Running*; Tim Noakes, 1991
2   Podcast at Stitcher.com; Dr. Colin Grissom, June 11, 2018
3   *"Finishing and Racing 100 Miles: A Statistical Analysis"*; Steve Siguaw, Pages 22-23, Ultrarunning Magazine, Page March 1990
4   Dear Ultrarunning (Letters to the Editor); Steve Siguaw reply, Ultrarunning Magazine, Pages 28-29, May 1990
5   Greenville College Report, Greenville, Illinois, November 11, 1983
6   Competitive Anxiety in Sport; Rainer Martens, 1990
7   *"Digging for Gold in Leadville"*, Matt Carpenter, Ultrarunning Magazine, Pages 8-9, October 2005
8   *"Did I Win?"*; George Sheehan essay, 1993
9   Personal correspondence from Tony Post, 2019

Chapter 18

Medical Concerns

"You're gonna kill somebody."[1]

Dr. John Perna, the first race medical director, always began his medical briefing by explaining the four major medical problems runners will encounter during the Leadville Trail 100:

- Hypoxia,
- Hydration,
- Hypernatremia and
- Hypothermia

The above are Dr. Perna's four "H's", as they were forever enshrined in Leadville lore. Make sure you are well hydrated during the race and pay heed to the four "H's."

Previously, weight checks and medical checkpoints were used at several aid stations along the racecourse. But those days are long gone, only to become part of Leadville Trail 100 race history, as you have read.

Now, each runner provides medical information online, prior to Thursday and Friday's medical check-in. A medical wristband is given each runner containing his or her provided information and the wristband must be worn throughout the race.

Medical staff members will be at aid stations to evaluate runners. They will be checking a runner's mental status and physical well-being with medical staff decisions being final.[2]

According to **100 Mile Medic** (Craig Bifano), employed by Lifetime Fitness, "We don't do weights or blood pressures etc. anymore as the science behind that has changed from years past. □"[3]

Runners requiring supplemental oxygen or IV fluids will not be allowed to continue in the race.[2]

Here are two accounts by past women's champions Theresa Daus-Weber and Marge Hickman.

Strategy from 1992 Leadville Trail 100 women's champion and eleven-time finisher Theresa Daus-Weber used during one of her races regarding hydration:

"In the early years of the Leadville Trail 100, the racecourse was on the Halfmoon Road. Halfmoon Road was slightly more than a single lane washboard rutted dirt road and runners were allowed to receive aid from their crew cars along the road as long as the crew vehicle drove slowly yielding to runners and used low beam lights to avoid blinding approaching runners with high beam headlight glare.

A rain/snow storm hit as I was running inbound to the Fish Hatchery aid station, which at that time was a small garage on private property at the intersection of the Colorado Outward Bound access road and County Road 11.

As the storm intensified and the temperature dropped, my sister Donna, who was crewing me, would stop ahead of me every couple miles and add on another layer of jacket over my drenched outer layer. By the time I got to the Fish Hatchery aid station I had about four layers of soaked clothing on and mud caked shoes.

The aid station volunteers hustled me on to the old-fashioned analog bathroom scale that had weighed every outbound and inbound runner ahead of me to determine if we were maintaining weight through hydration.

I laughed when I was praised for my increased weight at this late stage of the race. I figured my mud-caked shoes and layers of rain/snow-saturated jackets and pants contributed at least five pounds to the "precision accuracy" of the muddy scale's results.

The volunteer told me to keep up my good hydration for the next twenty-three miles to the finish. This would be easy to do as the storm continued and the racecourse was surrounded by 'hydration'."

From Marge, The Aging Process of "Addicted" Athletes:

"Oh, the "Fountain of Youth." If only we could find it. Some may still be searching. I would love to find it, but at this point in my life and aging, I don't think I'll find it any time soon.

When we are young, healthy and capable of athletic activities and competitions, we feel we can conquer the world and there are no limits to what we can do.

However (there's that word again), over my almost forty-year span of competing in various sports: racquetball, marathoning, ultrarunning and burro racing; I found it to be extremely rewarding to set goals and accomplish them.

My childhood environment was negative, unsupportive, argumentative and unstable. I was dealing with a mentally dysfunctional family setting.

I pushed myself even more to be successful in athletics, to be liked and to be a "winner", proving to my family that I was not a failure but worthy of success in life.

For myself, I have achieved much more than I ever could have dreamed. To my family, they thought I was "crazy" for getting into such extreme sports. It got so bad that I would not tell my parents what I was doing and they never asked or seemed to care.

What a blow from my family, but their unsupportive attitudes and remarks made me all the more goal oriented. I then realized that I was doing all this "crazy" stuff for ME. It made me stronger in all aspects of my life: from my legal career, massage therapy practice, friendships and relationships. It made me stronger and more capable to encourage other women to believe in themselves and to achieve whatever dream they set their minds to.

Now, as old as I am, '39' and holding like the comedian Jack Benny, the aging process is and has been rearing its head in different ways, and on no particular day, but lately seems to be on race day, of course.

My training goes great, I feel great and I'm ready to go. Mentally I'm at 100%, but during some point in the race my body tells me otherwise, whether it's knee, hip or back pain to unexpected blisters or a muscle cramp.

Sometimes it's that I get a sore throat, a cold or a sinus infection days before a race which puts me behind and under the weather on race day. It just happens more often now, yet it never happened when I was young. Why is that?

My chiropractor of thirty-four years, Clark Ruzicka of Leadville, tells me that my body has thousands of miles on it, has been beaten up for years and is wearing out. He tells me that it's like a car. You buy it new, put lots of miles on it, keep it serviced and maintained over the years but eventually the engine goes kaput. I'm not kaput yet but in the maintenance mode.

All of which brings me to reality; aging is a given and a difficult part of the human lifecycle. For some athletes who performed way outside of the normal ranges of the human lifecycle when they were young like myself, it is now hard for them to face and accept the aging process.

It is self-indulgent when aging athletes will not accept the reality of aging and try to do things the same way they did when they were young.

Adjusting to aging is more powerful, healthy and realistic than not doing things well and hurting your aging self instead of maximizing your aging self. I hope to follow that aging concept. I'm not there yet, but hope to be some day.

I was recently called a "FITOID" which means I'm old and still running. Good thing that was said to me by Arthur Schwartz, a good friend. Humans have been aging since there were humans, so that is nothing new. Shuffle on, like my husband does."

References

Chapter 18: Medical Concerns

1   Friday, August 26,1983. Dr. John Perna during the medical examination at Lake County Hospital.
2   2018 Leadville Trail 100 Run-Athlete Guide
3   Craig Bifano, **100 Mile Medic**, employed by Lifetime Fitness. Post in Facebook group "Leadville 100 MTB Participants", February 17, 2019.

Chapter 19

Pacers and Crews

Pacers are allowed after the 50-mile point, Winfield aid station. You may have as many pacers as you wish, although only one pacer at a time, until mile 99 when anything goes.

Pacing entails patience, tolerance and humor. The primary duties of a pacer include route finding, keeping the runner on pace, ensuring the runner continues to eat and drink, and making sure the runner leaves aid stations with adequate clothing and supplies to reach the next aid station.

Pacers should be aware of all significant medical conditions for their runner, and know how to respond if required. At minimum, the pacer should carry a basic medical kit, a cell phone and a space blanket.

Pacers are not allowed to push, pull, carry or tow the runner. Any special pacing situations or requests must be pre-approved by Race Management.[1]

Pacers can act as your "burro" to help carry gear, food, flashlights, etc. Pacers are also encouraged to look out for a runner's safety during the nighttime hours as well as keeping track of their runner's time, which is critical for arriving at aid stations before the cutoff time. In addition, crews for a runner are highly recommended throughout the 30-hour race.

There are few ultrarunners in the Leadville Trail 100 who do not have a crew or use pacers. If they lack pacers or crew, it is likely this is their first attempt at a 100-mile race and they probably will NOT finish. Those are just the statistics.

As the first sentence explained, pacers having a sense of humor are always appreciated. Yet runners sometimes fail to find humor in their situation during the later stages of the race, as can be expected. Still, you just have to laugh at your self-imposed misery when trying to finish a 100-mile race.

How pacers can disappoint, by Marge:

"Jim Butera once paced me inbound from Twin Lakes. Unfortunately to my surprise and disappointment, when we reached the Halfmoon aid station I missed the cutoff. I was devastated and couldn't believe Jim was not keeping track of my time. We had a great time laughing and chatting along the course but probably too much fun and not watching the clock tick. I was upset with Jim, but Jim thought I was keeping track of the time; not. Make sure your pacer knows what is expected of them. For me, this was a costly mistake on my part."

An example from Steve's pacer/son Zach Siguaw one year:

"Zach paced me from the Turquoise Lake Dam to the finish line. I was on pace to crack the 25:00 hour barrier coming up the Boulevard while trying to maintain my overall standing among the top runners in the race.

I instructed Zach to keep looking behind us, search for any lights or movement in the distance and let me know what he saw, as I was in no mood to turn around while running forward.

We crested the final hill, looked down at the finish line as I barely jogged toward the welcoming crowd and bright lights when I heard Zach say, "Dad, I see somebody behind us."

I couldn't believe someone was going to overtake me during the final quarter mile of the race. "This will not stand", I said out loud to Zach.

Summoning all my strength, my pace increased slightly to a faster jog. Zach said again, "Dad, they're gaining on us."

It was now time to run, not jog. The pain was incredible and my breathing sounded like the end of a 100-meter sprint as I hurled myself across the finish line, totally exhausted and barely able to stand up.

No one had passed us and I was thrilled not to lose to a charging runner in the final sprint. Looking behind me for the approaching runner, all I saw was darkness and an empty road.

Befuddled, I looked at Zach laughing beside me. Zach said, "Well, I had to get you running again so I kind of made up the thing about another runner."

As we said, humor is usually welcome from pacers during the race; it just takes a little while to really appreciate the laughter."

How pacers are treated at aid stations, by Steve:

"Pacers are treated just like runners at aid stations, well almost like runners, but pacers are not medically evaluated. All food and drink is available to pacers just like runners. That is a great thing too since pacers are struggling to keep their runner on the trail, prodding them to keep running and making sure their runner is eating and drinking.

Steve had one pacer named Tim Carlson who simply loved being out on the course with him. He was talkative and always had interesting stories to tell, as I struggled to listen and grunt in response to his enquiries as we ran together.

During one race Tim and I arrived together at Fish Hatchery aid station inbound, tired, cold, and wet and I was in need of encouragement from my crew. Tim was in need of food and quite a lot of food. Tim was hungry enough that he told me to go ahead and start climbing the Power Line Trail alone; he would catch up after grazing at the aid station food tables.

Yes, Tim did catch up to me a short distance up the Power Line Trail, well fed and full of fluids once again. It is great to have a refreshed pacer with you after the aid station stops."

Marge writes about crews and pacers; Mai Tai Motivation:

"One of my pacers, Linda Lee, joined me at the 63-mile Twin Lakes aid station, and we were headed home, inbound. We had a great time together and formed a forever bond and friendship.

For hours I kept telling Linda she needed to make sure I drank enough fluids. Running along and listening to Linda's stories, I thought I needed to drink while trying to run faster. Linda said she made a special Mai Tai for me and it was waiting at the next aid station, May Queen. Oh yum, I thought and couldn't wait to get there.

The funny thing was that when we arrived at May Queen, Linda gave me the promised cocktail bottle. I grabbed the new plastic bottle containing the Mai Tai and guzzled it down like I was in the desert. I then turned to her in complete surprise and said, "This is the same electrolyte crap that you've been giving me all day."

Linda said the look on my face was "priceless", and that I really thought she had made me a special cocktail. She still laughs about it today and so do I.

Ah, the magic of ultra-marathons: fatigue and friendship. Without her and our fun, I'm sure my finish time would not have been as good. I did finish well and received my 10th finisher buckle that year. Thanks Linda, my forever friend."

Another Pacer story, Chainsaw Trick by Marge:
"It is still dark and in the middle of the night when Mike, my husband, was pacing me as we made the last uphill climb up to the "Boulevard" with less than 3 miles to go.

My chainsaw pacer, Mike, said to me, "Do you know that you are in 11th place? "No", I yelled at him.

I must have been in la la land, oblivious or comatose and didn't comprehend what he said until he shouted it a couple more times. Then, I said, "What?"

As he told me one more time, I had to stop shuffling and walk to listen to what he said. I had no idea or any sense of how well I was doing but only knew that Ann Trason was in front of me and by a long way. Maybe I was so focused on Ann far ahead that it kept me pushing forward, wondering how far behind her I would finish. Once the light went on in my hollow head however, that I was in 11th place, I got it.

Ecstatic and thinking he was lying to me to get me moving faster because he knew how well I was doing, I began to shuffle faster even though there wasn't much left in my tank.

I couldn't believe it and had not one clue what time it was. Mike kept constant track of headlamps approaching behind us, but in front of us was one headlamp dimly shining so he pulled the "chainsaw trick."

This unique and cleaver trick was amazing to say the least. He pretended to start a chain saw motor and, of course, it would not start on the first several pulls. Cunningly, he kept imitating the sound of starting a saw while trying to start my engine and get me running.

Finally, the chainsaw started and we were running as we approached the dimly lighted headlamp. Mike then said to be quiet, we were sneaking up on the 10th place runner, and we were going to blow by him/her and keep running.

I was so excited and revitalized that as we caught up to him, he was down on one knee and I was sprinting. To our surprise it was Raul Flores from Kansas City, a friend who worked at Gary Gribbles Running Store. The chainsaw was at full throttle and Mike kept it going until we made the turn onto the black top that was one mile from the finish line.

I couldn't turn around but Mike must have had eyes in the back of his head because no one challenged me to the finish line.

I was the 10th place finisher overall and 2nd place woman. My best time and finish ever.

Today when I hear a chainsaw start, I have to laugh out loud and think of that memorable finish. Thanks hubby."

Marge continues about crew and pacers:

"Obviously, there are some who have completed a 100 without crew or pacers, but I do not know of any. The few who have tried Leadville totally unsupported did not finish. Those runners returned to try to get the job done but with a crew and at least one pacer on their second attempt.

For safety as well as mental and physical support, having a crew and pacers are crucial for me.

My husband has been crew for me for many years. He knows what I want and if in doubt, brings more than what I need, but that's a good thing for those "just in case" instances.

I have also experienced having no pacers lined up because I couldn't find any or they would back out shortly before race day for one reason or another. That would put me in panic mode but I knew something would always work out. Luckily, my husband came up with the idea to make a sign: "pacer needed, inquire within."

He would get to Winfield early in hopes that someone would be anxious and happy to pace. He would duct tape the sign to the front of his shirt and stand just outside the Winfield aid station where he would eventually recruit a pacer.

This turned out to be a great way to always find a pacer willing to go back over Hope Pass and even go further. I never knew these runners who helped me, but I was grateful for them. Unfortunately, I can't remember all of my pacers but do remember the many good times we shared and how they got me to where I needed to be: the finish line.

Prior to my husband crewing for me, I had a very special man who was like a dad to me for many years. His name was Sam Samuelson, a wood shop schoolteacher from Grand Junction, whom I had met at the top of the Mt. Evans Hill Climb race.

I recall race day at Mt. Evans being windy and chilly. After finishing the race, others and myself began to shiver as we waited for buses to arrive and take us back down the mountain.

Some years later, rather than wait for a bus, we would run back down the mountain to the start to get in more training mileage: marathon distance or more.

Finally at this race, a bus showed up and runners filled the bus quickly. We all squeezed and huddled together so you couldn't help but chat with the other people. I was so cold I was almost sitting on Sam's lap, and we hit it off instantly. What a character he was: funny, always talking, laughing, telling stories, volunteering for any and all things, encouraging, kind and caring. Sam's wife Debby was extra special because she put up with both of us.

Sam meant the world to me for many years until he passed away in January 1999 from symptoms of an enlarged heart.

Sam was my "Crew Chief." I had even made him his own special "Crew Chief" belt buckle similar to the Leadville Trail 100 award for an under 30-hour finishers buckle. He loved it and wore it everywhere. Sam crewed for me many, many years. He was always there for me and is still dearly missed.

I was only thirty-four when my dad passed away in 1984 of pancreatic cancer. That year was also one of my hardest and fullest racing schedules ever, including my first attempt at running the Leadville Trail 100. Having Sam as my crew during the Leadville Trail 100 and ever-present essential crew for finishing the 1989 Grand Slam were my proudest and most memorable moments in my ultrarunning career.

Debby, Sam's wife, returned his "Crew Chief" buckle to me when Sam passed away. My husband Mike still wears the buckle in honor of Sam."

References

Chapter 19: Pacers and Crews

1   2018 Leadville Trail 100 Run-Athlete Guide

Chapter 20

Cutoffs, Strategy and Trail Stories

Here are a few tips and strategies that have helped past finishers of the Leadville Trail 100.

Accommodations in Leadville

Staying in Leadville gives runners a chance to be close to the action, of course. There are hotels in Leadville that can be used, for example:

- Delaware Hotel
- Silver King Inn and Suites
- Columbine Inn and Suites
- Roadway Inn
- Alps Motel

An Internet search will turn up more accommodations as well.

Additional places to stay are also located in Twin Lakes, Buena Vista and Copper Mountain. There are campsites that runners and crews can use near Leadville, if you are looking for more basic places to stay.

Steve's pacer camping story:

"One of my pacers, Tim Carlson, camped near the racecourse for a few of my races. Tim had a new girlfriend, Deb, whom he brought up one year for the race.

Deb and Tim met me at Twin Lakes aid station on the inbound leg, where Tim's pacing duties began. Deb was appalled at my condition at the aid station.

Most of my toes were blistered along with my rain-saturated clothes hanging like rags from my sweat soaked body. I was also mumbling strange things to my wife and crew, as usual.

Tim and I left the aid station into the darkness descending upon us, only to meet Deb at Fish Hatchery aid station nearly four hours later.

At Fish Hatchery aid station, Deb saw her new boyfriend covered in mud, wet and smelling like someone who had just run four hours in the wilderness.

My new pacer, Bob, took over at Fish Hatchery while Tim and Deb went away to camp near the trail somewhere. Maria made the comment, 'She must really like him if she's sleeping next to him in the tent tonight.' "

So, campsites and Campgrounds are another viable option for places to stay for the race, if you don't mind being a little grubby. Oh, about Tim and Deb, they got married not long after the race.

Aid Stations and Cutoffs

There are ten aid stations/medical checkpoints for the Leadville Trail 100.

These aid stations and medical checkpoints have time cutoffs associated with them. You must LEAVE the aid station or medical checkpoint BEFORE the cutoff time. No exceptions. If you miss a cutoff time you are out of the race.

Here are the current, 2019, aid stations for the race, along with the cutoff times:[1]

Aid Station	Mileage	Clock Time	Cumulative Time
Start	0	4:00 AM	0
May Queen	12.6	7:30 AM	3:30
Outward Bound	23.5	10:30 AM	6:30
Half Pipe	29.3	11:30 AM	7:30
Twin Lakes	37.9	2:00 PM	10:00
Hope Pass	43.5	4:15 PM	12:15
Winfield	50.2	6:00 PM	14:00
Twin Lakes	62.5	10:00 PM	18:00
Half Pipe	71.7	1:15 AM	21:15
Outward Bound	76.9	3:00 AM	23:00
May Queen	87.8	6:30 AM	26:30
Finish	100.4	10:00 AM	30:00:00

The best strategy is to stay well ahead of any cutoff time. Easier said than done, for those running the race in the middle or back of the pack.

Write the cutoff times on your arm and keep track of where you are at all times if you are flirting with those mandatory times.

If a runner arrives in Winfield with less than 30 minutes before the cutoff time of fourteen hours, you are in serious DNF country. Very few runners at the Leadville Trail 100 have finished the race while flirting with the stringent Winfield cutoff time. Just a word to the wise, get your butt in gear, out on the trail and back up and over Hope Pass once again.

Where do runners struggle the most with missing cutoff times? Besides Winfield, every aid station on the way **back** to the finish line. Seriously.

Twin Lakes inbound to Leadville is probably the easiest of any remaining aid station. Yet darkness is fast approaching and the air is turning cool once again.

Exiting Twin Lakes aid station it is crucial to have your winter gear on or at least with your pacer during the walk/run to Pipeline. More than one runner has been surprised how cold this stretch of trail can become due to the close of day and one's increasing level of fatigue.

Tree Line inbound is a problematic place as well. Racer's crews find this stop a great place to party as runners stream past, on their way to the distant Fish Hatchery aid station. Unfortunately runners have gotten very cold and probably wet between Twin Lakes and Tree Line so their crew's warm vehicle looks very inviting to rest and warm up.

A note from Steve about his crew at Tree Line:

"Maria reluctantly let me sit in the car during the 1987 monsoon race because I told her I was slightly hypothermic. Maria said "slightly hypothermic" was kind of like "slightly pregnant" and was not happy to let me into the vehicle to warm up. Once inside the car I never came out and became a DNF.

Later I advised Maria to NEVER unlock a car to let me in, not even if I am dying. Maria has seen more than one runner enter a vehicle and never finish the race while waiting at Tree Line."

Fish Hatchery aid station inbound is brutal. The power lines are crackling in the distance, reminding runners of the one last big climb in the race. To make matters worse, it is dark and cold with only occasional moonlight showing the trail ahead, if it isn't raining or snowing by now.

How about May Queen aid station with only a half-marathon to go before the finish? Have you ever seen a medical MASH tent? It doesn't matter because you will now.

Groaning bodies are strewn about, lying on cots and mattresses with various stages of exhaustion and hypothermia.

Lucky runners streak through the aid station, well at least walk fast, and get onto the Turquoise Lake Trail as quickly as possible. Focus is critical now, so don't look around inside the tents at those lying in wait, their race most likely is finished.

Instead of taking in the sights, grab something to eat and drink, stare straight ahead and peer into the depths of your being for the strength to see that distant finish line. It's crunch time at the Leadville Trail 100.

Marge shares more memorable experiences:
River Crossing at Twin Lakes

"Approaching the river crossing, about 40 miles out, while running through the marshy, soggy meadows through the mud and ponds to the river, I'm feeling okay.

However, once I reach the river crossing, I'm concerned. The water level is very high, flowing fast, as well as being freezing cold mountain run-off water.

There is a thick, heavy rope stretched across the river and on each side of the rope is a person in a wetsuit.

I didn't give much thought to the wetsuited person, but maybe I should have. I'm standing at the river's edge contemplating what to do and becoming more and more scared.

It's time to go across, I tell myself.

I start into the river hanging onto the thick rope and knew this was going to be hard, very hard.

Not quite halfway across, my arms are fully extended away from my body and the rope. My arms start shaking.

Suddenly, I couldn't hold on any longer and was swept away down the river.

I screamed insanely thinking that I was going to drown, my worst fear ever.

It seemed like forever but thank goodness for the man in the wetsuit who rescued me and pulled me out of the river. He was my hero that day."

Volunteering and Llamas at the Hopeless aid station:

"If you have never volunteered to help at an aid station for any of the Leadville events, you shouldn't miss the chance to experience all the fun.

For example, hiking Hope Pass, pushing, pulling or dragging llamas up to the beautiful spot at timberline in the lush, green brush below the rocky summit on the north side of Hope Pass is unmatched anywhere on the Leadville Trail 100.

The Hopeless aid station is the highest aid station in the race.

Mike and I volunteered on Hope Pass in 1994 when I recently had a cast removed from my lower leg and foot from a fracture and plantar fasciitis surgery.

I was entered in the race but my podiatrist strongly suggested that I not run. For once, I listened, but was extremely disappointed. I soon realized that volunteering and giving back to the race was more important this particular year. Getting to the Hopeless aid station was half the fun.

A group of us met around noonish on the Friday before the race at a pull-off along Hwy. 82. We met, loaded up food, water, medical supplies, gear, tents, sleeping bags and more.

As we had more llamas than volunteers, some of us hiked up Hope Pass leading or following not one but two or three llamas. This was a hoot and so much fun to be next to these amazing animals and seeing their habits.

Llamas are wild or domesticated long-necked South American ruminants related to camels but smaller and without a hump. They are especially used in the Andes as a pack animal and source of wool.

Llamas can teach us many things:

- Llama messages are symbolism to remind us that only through hard work and perseverance will your dreams be realized.
- You can adapt to any situation that you find yourself in.
- Whatever loads you are carrying now, you will be able to manage and see them through.
- Also, llamas remind us that the biggest focus should be on ourself. Thus, personal growth and connections to spirit should be our highest priority at all times.
- In fact, llama symbolism insists that we follow our heart rather than our ego. This action will bring us all the rewards we are seeking.

This animal is a symbol that I have the strength and endurance to reach my goal. Alternatively, this creature could also be putting you on notice that you are worrying too much and carrying too large a load.

As with the llama, running and winning takes commitment, perseverance, mental and physical toughness, guts, grit and determination. Training is a must but having the mental strength to keep moving no matter how badly you feel or want to quit is more important. You must stay focused on your goal to finish and turn all negativity into a positive mind set, experience and result. Life should be an adventure.

Once the race was over, I was very happy that I sat this one out especially because I had such a memorable fun time at the Hopeless aid station with the llamas and was able to contribute as a volunteer."

Steve's story about Hope Pass pacers:

"You may recall Chuck Cofer's story about his near tragedy coming down Hope Pass in **Chapter 3**, the 2014 race year?

Chuck described the downhill section from Hopeless aid station to the bottom of the Hope Pass Trail, inbound, as "a downhill descent at a perfect gradient where minimal effort is required to make forward progress and you feel as if you could run forever."

My pacer, John Crawford, had a different view of that section of the course one year when his shoe became untied just past Hopeless aid station.

I told John I would continue running and he would catch up to me. Once out of John's sight I thought to myself, let's see how fast John can run, as I took off as fast as I could down the trail.

Arriving in Twin Lakes, without pacer John, my crew and John's girlfriend asked if I had seen John?

I casually replied I had not seen John since the Hopeless aid station but he would probably show up sometime soon.

Sure enough, John arrived at Twin Lakes nearly five minutes later, looking slightly haggard from trying to catch me. Sometimes a runner likes to throw in a surge or two during the race just to see how their pacer reacts."

Here is Mike Hickman's story about an incident on Hope Pass and what NOT to do:

"I left Twin Lakes, crossed the river and started up the long, never-ending Hope Pass Trail, knowing full well that the cutoff at Winfield would be difficult to make.

Barely moving up Hope, I noticed a person, let's call him Buddy (not his real name). Buddy was in front of me as he reached the point just before coming out of tree line.

I was sweating profusely, breathing harder than I ever had in my life. Buddy turned and asked if this was my first time doing the race. I said it was and unwittingly took the bait: hook, line and sinker.

Buddy also asked if it was difficult to breathe? Again I said it was. Buddy explained he could help me to breathe again in order to make the cutoff time at Winfield, if I did exactly what he said.

I was now sitting on a log sweating, heaving, panting and listening to his persuasive advice. I was willing to try anything just to breathe normally again.

Buddy told me to lie on the ground, point my feet up toward Hope Pass, and let oxygen flow into my head, allowing me to breathe normally.

Already partially delirious from the first forty-miles of the race, I quickly lay on the ground and pointed my feet toward the heavens of Hope Pass, knowing that wisdom from Buddy would only be the truth.

He told me to relax, take a few deep breaths and keep breathing. I did exactly what Buddy said, knowing this must be a secret from an experienced ultrarunner.

I slowly relaxed and began taking deep breaths.

I heard a distant sound from Buddy. It started off as a simple chuckle, yet the further Buddy got up Hope Pass the sound became even louder. Buddy was laughing so hard because I naively took his advice, lay on the ground and pointed my elevated legs toward the sky.

If you think there is a secret to climbing Hope Pass, do NOT take this advice but just keep sucking it up, moving one foot in front of the other and hoping you will catch that SOB at the pass.

If you happen to see runners with their feet pointing up toward the sky, the laughter you hear will probably help you too.

Relay this wisdom from your experience to future first-time runners on Hope Pass. Once you become a finisher, you have the ability to convey this secret training tip to many gullible, desperate, first-time Hope Pass aspirants. The moral of this story is: run your own race."

Out-of-Body Experience on the Pipeline by Marge:

"My friend was leaving Twin Lakes on the inbound run. His out-of-body experience happened as he was nearing the flatter section on the pipeline and before ascending power line, Sugarloaf Pass, in the dark of night.

This being his third attempt at the race, he was feeling good, cruising along, but the trail was a little muddy, rocky and it was cold enough to give you a chill.

All of a sudden, he came out of his body and was flying overhead watching himself glide across the trail, rocks and mud.

Several seconds went by, as he was looking down on himself, and he thought, "Wow, look at that guy glide."

It was so easy and smooth watching before reality set in as he realized that it was himself down there.

He immediately came back into his body with a ghostly uneasiness and tingle. He quickly returned to worrying about falling or tripping over the rocks in the mud.

My friend hesitated telling the story to anyone as most would not believe it, but I did, knowing that runners do have some weird experiences.

Over the years, I have had other runners tell me their strange stories with similar experiences or hallucinations.

I had an out-of-body experience during the Leadville Trail 100 years ago, when my friend and co-author, Steve, was running it too.

I knew Steve was an amazing ultrarunner and never gave it a thought that I would see him during the race, except for when we crossed paths: me still on the outbound and Steve on the inbound.

This was one of the years, however, that I had done speed work and intervals with the Pheidippides running club, as well as played games with myself pushing as hard and fast as I could on trails from tree to tree, way down yonder.

I was lucky and grateful to have a top-notch crew and pacers that year. One of my pacers was a 2:30 marathoner so I knew he would definitely push me hard. The Mt. Elbert section of the course went well with my pacer, with only a few stumbles, trips and/or potty breaks.

We were cruising down Halfmoon Road, the old course, at a comfortable but quick pace that kept getting increasingly faster. My pacer and I were in sync with not a word spoken between us as I felt lifted up off the road in a complete and effortless running stride until we caught up to a small group of runners.

That suddenly brought me back down to the road.

As we picked each runner off in succession, the last runner we passed was my co-author, Steve. I had to do a double take because I thought there was no way I could be passing Steve, as he was a faster runner than me.

I remember thinking that he saw me look over at him, and he recognized me so, of course I said, "Hi Steve, good job." He didn't respond so I figured he might not have known it was I.

My pacer and I carried on down Halfmoon to the aid station where I hooked up with my next fast marathoner pacer, Andy Dunn, who was waiting and ready to go. I can still feel the excitement and energy that was surging through my body as I was having one of my best Leadville races.

Andy, a road racer, was anxiously taking off like he was shot out of a cannon. My adrenalin was flowing, keeping my feet pumping and moving as fast as I could, but not at my pacer's lightning speed.

I tried to hang with or behind him as long as I could to try and reach the Fish Hatchery quickly, as this section was on asphalt road. We got there fine but at my pace, not his.

I don't remember anything after that, no more out-of-body experiences, but I had a great race. I must have been on a "runner's high" after floating over that portion of the course."

(Steve remembers the year as 1991 when Marge ran 23:40:44 as second woman and 22nd place overall while I ran 24:37:37, finishing in 37th place.)

One last story about the dreaded Power Line Trail, inbound to May Queen aid station, by Steve:

"It's dark, cold and the power lines are crackling and singing their electric song as you trudge slowly and relentlessly upward for nearly an hour.

During this late stage of the race, some runners suffer from stomach problems as I did one year. Yes, I tossed my cookies and everything else, four times, on the side of the road as my pacer, Bob Volzer watched.

Bob was a cross-country coach, marathoner and in addition we coached together for several years. Bob understood runners and knew he had to get me to the top of the power lines no matter what. Bob also understood I was severely dehydrated, once I lost everything on the side of the road.

Without considering his own well being, Bob fed me all the food in the pack he carried for me and gave me all the fluids as well. Even though this stretch of trail to May Queen took over three hours, Bob never complained or gave any indication he was suffering by not eating or drinking anything.

Arriving at May Queen aid station I saw Bob intensely occupied with the food tables and never gave it a second thought, until Bob told me later he didn't eat or drink anything for his entire pacer leg.

That is the kind of person every runner wants to pace them; one who will sacrifice their bodies for their runner's success. Thanks Bob."

References

Chapter 20: Cutoffs, Strategy and Trail Stories

1   2018 Leadville Trail 100 Run-Athlete Guide

Chapter 21

Economic Impact of the Race

How did the Leadville Trail 100 Mile race economically benefit the town of Leadville?

The town of Leadville was suffering from a severe economic downturn during the early 1980's due to the closing of the Climax Molybdenum Mine, their main employer.

Lake County Commissioners thought an ultra race would benefit the local economy and that was a driving force to attract Jim Butera's 100-mile race to the area.

According to a study completed during the 1989 Leadville Trail 100, it became apparent that money spent in the town of Leadville by race entrants was significant.

The results from the 1989 study showed that the minimum amount of money brought into the town of Leadville by the 100-mile runners for the race was $140,000.

Runners stayed in or near the town of Leadville for over six days, preparing, training, and acclimating for the event.

Remember, the figure of $140,000 going into local businesses and pockets was for the year 1989.[1]

As the Leadville Trail 100 grew in size, obviously the economic benefits would only increase as time went on. However, no one predicted the future for the town of Leadville.

What actually happened in the town of Leadville was simply amazing, economically speaking.

Merilee Maupin and Ken Chlouber added six additional races plus a weekend Training Camp to the town of Leadville's summer schedule:

- Leadville Trail 100 Mountain Bike Race
- Leadville Trail Marathon
- Heavy Half Marathon
- Silver Rush 50 MTB race
- Silver Rush 50-mile run

- Leadville 10K
- Leadville Training Camps

Yet it was the Leadville Trail 100 Mountain Bike Race, started in 1994, which sent the Leadville economy into the stratosphere.

The Leadville Trail 100 Mile Mountain Bike Race saw the arrival of two thousand intense, equipment driven participants, riding expensive mountain bikes, who flocked to the town of Leadville to do battle in the high-altitude.

According to a 2013 study by Colorado Mountain College, $15 million flowed into the town of Leadville from all these races.[2]

$15 million is significant for any community and that does not include the lasting benefits from the participants or their families. Economic impacts on the real estate market would be felt for future years as well.

Merilee Maupin and Ken Chlouber established the Leadville Trail 100 Legacy Foundation in 2002, specifically to benefit the Leadville community. Funding for the Foundation is obtained from donations given by racers. The Foundation is a non-profit organization.

Grants and scholarships from the Leadville Trail 100 Legacy Foundation are designated to support the needs of the Leadville community.

Additionally, every graduating Lake County high school senior who chooses to pursue any form of higher education is awarded a $2,000 scholarship.

It just goes to show that a singular spark of brilliance can transform what might have become a ghost town, Leadville, Colorado, into one of the major sporting centers in the Rocky Mountain region.

References

Chapter 21: Economic Impact of the Race

1   Ultrarunning Magazine, *"The Economic Impact of the Leadville Trail 100 Mile"*, Steve Siguaw, February 1990.
2   Deadspin; *"Endurance is Booming, But Has Leadville Trail 100 Gone Too Far?"*, Sarah Baker, October 10, 2014

Chapter 22

Remembrances of Jim Butera

By Sheila J. Butera:
"The year was 2004 and what a life-changing year it was for us.

Jim and I were both looking for a special relationship on the dating website e-Harmony. I came home from my office job on a Friday night, logged into the website, finding I had eight new matches.

Although overwhelmed a bit, I looked at each one and read their profiles. One that caught my eye was this athletic and rugged looking guy with white hair (I love white hair).

Jim was wearing running shorts and a T-shirt in an outdoor mountainous setting. He struck me as being an 'earthy kind of guy' so I read more of his profile. Soon I learned he was an 'ultra runner' and very much into athletic sports.

Honestly, I had no clue what an 'ultrarunner' was and thought he was probably too sporty for me since I was a city girl with an office job and didn't spend much time outdoors.

Long story short, we worked through the formatted e-Harmony questions and could see that there was something special we wanted to pursue.

Jim gave me his number and we talked every evening on the phone. We then met for dinner the following week. It felt so comfortable, like we'd known each other forever, and after meeting in person it was very clear that there was something magical happening.

I liked movies, fashion, interior decorating, socializing with my friends, and all things glamorous. And here was Jim, a mountain man, ultrarunner, bull riding champion, mountain biker and retired fire-fighter who obviously liked living on the edge.

It didn't take long before I traded in my high heels and beautiful clothes for running shoes (Jim bought me the first pair) and sporty casual clothes.

I never became a runner but we enjoyed hiking for hours on the weekends in the good old Rocky Mountain air.

Before long I could ALMOST keep up with him and when I got winded I'd stop and say, "Oh look how beautiful that mountain is in the distance", just to stall a bit and maybe give him a kiss or two. Then on we'd hike.

If he had a clue what I was doing, he never let on. Before too long I could go for three or four hours and it became a real bonding experience, a chance to be one with nature as we talked about everything.

Jim was much more himself when we were outdoors and that is where his heart was: doing anything outdoors.

He taught me to snowshoe and we plowed through knee-deep snow. I swear he knew almost all the trails in Winter Park where he always took me to new ones.

It was a time so warm and wonderful that will be etched in my memory forever. Every day counted and we lived it to the fullest, marrying at the end of the year in a small, intimate ceremony at the home of his good friend, a fellow runner named Richard Neslund.

Richard's wife Carol performed the ceremony, and the mood was light and full of fun. When it came time for "the kiss" part, Jim wrapped his arms around my waist, lifted me off the floor and my slip-on shoes almost fell off.

And when it came time to cut the cake and share the first bite together, I stuffed a piece in his mouth while he took a piece and stuffed it down the neckline of my dress. Anything for a laugh, so like Jim.

On the way home I asked him, "What in the world were you thinking Jim, to stuff the cake in my boobs?" He said, "I don't know, they were just sort of there and I couldn't resist." O.M.G. never a dull moment with Jim.

Being the sentimental girl that I am, the white icing stain on my beautiful plum colored wedding dress is still there. I will never wear the dress again or dry clean it, because that's a memory to cherish forever, one never to be washed away or forgotten.

On the way home Jim said to me, "This has been the happiest day of my life."

Since this wasn't his first marriage, I said, "Well, considering that you've been married before, I will take that as a compliment."

The next day we spent our honeymoon at the Winter Park home and were welcomed by a major blizzard.

After he carried the cat into the house, we shoveled and shoveled and so began our first chapter together OUTSIDE of course. Jim was invigorated and I was cold, but I soon toughened up. Life up there was not for wusses.

Life continued to be one big adventure. Many new animals to see, endless birds to feed, and we both adored all of them, although a few encounters were too close for comfort.

It was awesome taking this new journey together, and I loved Jim's rugged exterior, because underneath was a gentle, humble, down to earth, unpretentious man. Real, no games, what you see is what you get kinda guy, comfortable in his own skin, and he lived by his rules and only wanted to live up to his own standards for himself.

He was one with all of nature and never passed up an opportunity to get out and kick up some dust on the trails. He was very detail oriented, keeping notebooks full of the dates he ran, the hours and minutes it took, etc.

He was eager to participate in races whenever possible, and although he loved competition, he was mostly competing to be his best and was happy that others had the same opportunity.

To say it was a passion is an understatement, and he would plan and orchestrate smaller races and invite friends to come and participate. Often they would stay the night with us, and get up in the morning, ready to go.

It's safe to say, most of his friends were runners and some came up to run with him for the sheer joy of it.

Preparing for a race was planned down to the tiniest detail, and down to the best brand of power gel, socks, lanterns, shoes, breathable fabrics for shirts, on and on.

Jim worked out on his weight machine to stay fit, and I soon came to be more familiar with a sporting goods store than my own favorite department stores. We were always looking for the newest and best running shoes.

The Leadville Trail 100 was dear to Jim since he put so much heart and soul into the original mapping out of the trails and was there from the beginning.

He never dreamed the race would end up being one of the largest and most well known races in our country.

He loved exploring new territory and finding the best place for the trails, and relished knowing others would enjoy it as well. He was just a humble man with big dreams and willingness to work hard.

Many who knew Jim appreciated his passion for the sport. I can say that my eight years with him made me a better person, and am grateful I was able to give him love and support right down to the last day of his life in 2012.

He was a spiritual person who loved the good earth and all of nature, especially the animals. At night before we went to bed, he'd open the back door, look up at the moon and stars and say, "Come out and see how beautiful they are. "

Jim never missed a moment in life to share the simple things, the things that really matter. We had a pet raccoon we fed by hand outside the kitchen window. She loved grapes, cookies, bread, and cornbread and trusted us so much that she even brought her five adorable babies back for treats too.

We called her Roxie, and could feel her whiskers as she gently took the grapes out of our hands. Our friends couldn't believe we were doing this since she was a wild animal, but there was such a sense of trust and affection among us.

We had a fox that came for his special treat of Starbucks muffins. We called him Freddie. He was shy and waited for us to throw the treat out farther. It was quite entertaining to watch a fox with three or four muffins hanging out of his mouth.

Looking back, it was truly a magical time in our lives. We fed birds and there were new ones all the time, some looking very exotic. The raccoons loved eating the birdseed too, and so did the bears.

Late one cold winter night I awoke to the sound of clanging on the window and it was a big black bear about nine feet tall, standing on his hind feet as he bashed the metal bird feeder against the window. The bear seemed irritated that he couldn't get the feeder down.

I woke Jim and told him what was happening. As I stood watching, I couldn't believe it, Jim opened the back door, jumped up and down waving his arms, screaming at it to go away; the bear ran up the hill, stopped, and then charged towards Jim in the doorway.

I yelled, "Jim, quick, shut the door, he's charging."

Jim quickly shut the door, which sometimes caught on the throw rug, but not this time. He got it shut and we'll never know how close the bear came, but I do believe he stopped short of the door. I don't want to think of what could have happened if the bear had pushed on it.

I was mortified that this had been such a close call. Jim, however, was laughing.

Laughing of all things. I said, "Do you think this is funny? You could have been killed. Don't EVER do that again."

In true Jim fashion, he was fearless and loved a great adventure. It goes without saying that the next time the bear came at night, I did NOT wake him up to tell him. I don't think he knew the meaning of the word fear.

The things he pursued and enjoyed were adventuresome and sometimes dangerous. He was raised up in the rodeo circuit and trained at Gary Lefews Bull Riding School, going on to win the Senior Men's Bull Riding Championship in 1999 in Medicine Hat, Canada.

The buckle he won was something he worked hard for and was very proud of it, wearing it whenever possible.

There were many broken bones along the way but that never dampened his spirit. When he set out to do something, it was as good as done, and he put his all into everything he undertook.

While living in California, he became a skilled mountain bike racer, entering many competitions.

He had also been a firefighter and a HAZMAT inspector in his career. We were talking about the movie, *The Bucket List*, with Jack Nicholson and Morgan Freeman. I asked him if there was anything he hadn't accomplished that he'd like to. He said, "Yes, I would like to climb Mt. Everest." Not surprising.

One of his favorite mottos was: "Choose the path with the most heart in order to be at your best." He used this in a newsletter he sent out to runners before one of the early Leadville 100 races. Good advice for anyone.

He never let any grass grow under his feet and we would all be fortunate if we could live our lives as fully as Jim did. He had parents who always encouraged him to follow his dreams and made opportunities possible for him to do so. They believed in him and he was their only child, so he grew up believing the sky was the limit.

Those who knew Jim appreciated him for who he was: a man of integrity, honesty and loyalty. He had a keen sense of humor and loved getting a good laugh, even if at his own expense.

Only Jim would be one to laugh at such a close call with a bear in his own home. He just KNEW he was invincible. He lived to compete.

I remember one time in 2007 when he took my daughter Heidi and her best friend to Red Rocks to run up and down the stairs. Both of these girls were so fit, worked out, and yet as Heidi told me when they returned home, "Boy mom, Jim kicked my butt." Pretty funny considering she was 27 and he was more than thirty years older. I believe their love of competition and being fit was part of why they got along so well.

There was also a race in Buena Vista, Colorado where the weather was cool when the race started. By the end of the day, as runners were coming in, it had turned into a blizzard. As I sat in the truck in a coat, gloves, and the heater running, here comes Jim looking like the abominable snowman with a snow-encrusted beard, no worse for the wear.

Then there was a race in Boulder in the summer with the temperature in the high 90s with many people dropping out and becoming dehydrated. Yet Jim kept going well into the night.

I like to say he was built 'Ford Tough' because not much slowed him down. That is, until he started having some health issues – Alzheimer's, and even that diagnosis didn't slow him down.

He'd still run with a friend on the paths and trails in the Golden area. He really looked forward to his friend taking him out to run, and of course, I would walk with him on the paths around our home.

His memory may have been fading but he never forgot the people who really loved him and how much he loved being outdoors, especially to run.

My last memory with Jim was with him laughing, and getting rosy cheeks when I told him how much he meant to me. This man never wasted a minute of living life to the fullest, and we shall not soon forget him.

May the sacred grounds on which he ran still whisper his name."

By Marge Hickman:

"You may or may not have heard of the man, Jim Butera, but many of us, "old time runners" who were brave and gutsy enough to enter and participate in the Leadville Trail 100 during those initial years of the race, knew Jim well.

Jim was the man with a dream, vision and passion for wanting to organize and start an extreme challenge of running a 100-mile foot race somewhere in the high and rugged Rocky Mountains of Colorado.

Spending more than a year scouting, hiking and wheeling trail distances throughout Colorado, Jim was trying to find the perfect location to make his dream of a lifetime come true. Jim Butera did just that.

I first met Jim and Harold Strong in 1982 when they worked at Frank Shorter's running store in Cherry Creek, Denver. The three of us talked incessantly, it seemed, for hours and hours about running and shoes, of course.

We shared our stories of future running hopes and goals. The three of us instantly became friends, and Jim even sold me my first pair of trail running shoes.

After buying my shoes, I often went back to buy running gear in hopes that Jim or Harold would be there so we could talk more about running, where to find good running places/roads/trails, training schedules, tips and racing stories.

Both Jim and Harold always were in the store, or so it seemed. Though they were both great runners and very knowledgeable, Jim's love and passion for running impressed me. He reminded me of a true mountain man, like a Jeremiah Johnson of sorts with dark brown eyes, bushy curly hair and a long curly beard neatly kept. Within his somewhat "barrel chest" but well-built smaller body frame was a strong-willed and powerfully driven man.

On one of my visits to the store, Jim invited me to join his group of runners on their Saturday morning training run. I recall telling him that I was not a long distance trail runner.

I was an addicted racquetball player and competitor. I had played racquetball for a number of years working my way up from being a terrible, beginning player before evolving into a nasty, mean and aggressive player with a great "kill shot."

Along with other racquetball friends, some of us started competing in tournaments all over Colorado, traveling and carpooling together. After being beaten regularly during my initial years of playing for fun, I eventually worked my way up the ladder of success to win my first "A" class tournament putting me on top of the racquetball scene.

I had achieved my goal. Now what? I loved racquetball but it was time to find something else bigger, better and harder.

Being a member of a prestigious athletic club near downtown Denver, I started doing some indoor track running, meeting other runners who sparked my interest in running while Jim kept encouraging me to come meet his group for an early morning Saturday run.

Finally I did just that. I was afraid and scared to death to meet and run with this group of experienced runners. I didn't want to hold the group back and thought I wouldn't be able to run as far or fast as the other runners.

I was so nervous and had butterflies in my stomach at that first training run. I even thought I would puke when I arrived and wondered what I had gotten myself into.

I don't remember that run at all because I must have been too worried about it. All I do remember is that I was hooked, for sure, and had a great time with Jim, Harold and the other runners.

Soon I realized that I wasn't so bad a runner after all. I loved it. Especially when I started to lose the few extra pounds I was carrying, started toning up, getting stronger and making muscles.

I joined Jim's group of runners, the Colorado Ultra Club, in 1982. We would train every weekend somewhere, but mostly we would head to the foothills or mountains for long runs as well, all jammed into a car or two. Jim had a running and ultra-running passion that consumed him and it easily rubbed off on the group.

When it was just Jim and I running, he would tell me his hopes and dreams of becoming a race director for a 100-mile ultra running event.

The more I got to know Jim, the more I understood some of his idiosyncrasies. He was meticulous and organized in every way, even down to ironing his running T-shirts, carefully hanging them on plastic hangers and placing them in a particular order, by color and in his closet so he could rotate them.

Jim was the same way when it came to planning and organizing his running, training schedules and his dreams.

At monthly Colorado Ultra Club meetings at Jim's home, along with his wife Pat, he would have plans already made for the following weeks' training runs.

He would talk about his efforts in making his dreams come true. He would type or even hand write minutes from our group's meetings, as well as compose a monthly newsletter that was mailed out to everyone. Jim would always inspire and push everyone to believe that we could do it.

My days at the athletic club dwindled, but nearly every weekday morning I still arrived at the gym by 6 am for a one-hour exercise class, or run on the track or just play a quick game of racquetball. I'd hit the shower afterwards, get dressed for work, put on my "face" makeup, and race out of the gym, driving an hour to be at work by 8:30 or 9 am.

I was working in Golden where there were trails and a five-mile asphalt road to the top of Lookout Mountain. I would run the Lookout Mountain route on an extended lunch hour, then take a "whore" sponge bath, work past 5:00 pm to make up the time I lost from my long lunch run, and then drive another hour back home where sometimes I would do a short speed workout. By 9 or 10 pm I was dead and fell into bed with lights out, gone, until the alarm went off the following morning to do it all over again.

Weekends were always saved for Ultra Club runs or an occasional race. Tuesday evenings were reserved for Pheidippides Track Club workouts at a local track, led by Olympic marathon qualifier Creigh Kelly.

Jim was creative in coming up with great ideas, events and places to hold races that included:

- The A.E. Packer 50 Mile Endurance Run held at Chatfield Reservoir south of Denver
- The Bowl of Tears 24-Hour Track Run in downtown Denver at the Auraria Junior College campus outdoor track and
- A weekend 24-hour loop fun run/get together near where he lived in the mountains at an area known as Tabernash (near Winter Park)

At the 24-hour loop fun run, Jim and his wife provided food and beverages but everything else was "bring your own" stuff including tent and sleeping bag.

Jim would make a bon-fire that we all used to warm up when we came in after finishing a loop, sometimes spending too much time enjoying the company of other runners as well as the warmth and yummy food and munchies.

During those long night hours, some of us were tempted to throw in the towel because we were getting too comfortable, but Jim would urge and push us back out on the trail.

After twenty-four hours went by, those of us remaining crashed with fatigue but what a great, fun memory we were left with. We gathered together, packed up all of our gear and hiked out of the area to our vehicles.

But we were not done. Everyone had to make numerous trips back and forth, helping Jim and his wife load up all of their stuff too. It was a long hard day and night but well worth it.

You could always count on Jim to come up with new ideas.

Having someone like Jim Butera jump-start my ultrarunning career certainly helped me immensely.

Jim made me understand I had to figure things out for *me* and *my* body mechanics, training, speed work, hill repeats and recovery, etc.

Jim was possessed to run every day and kept a daily running/training logbook that detailed long runs every weekend, somewhere, but mostly in the mountains.

Of course, we were much younger back then and could push ourselves to extremes.

Jim inspired me, coached me and always told me that I could do anything if I put my mind to it, and he was so right. Jim will always be with me and in my heart."

By Corky Watts:
"I first met Jim Butera in 1982, at Frank Shorter's running store in Denver. I had recently run a 50-mile ultramarathon at Chatfield Reservoir near Denver in preparation for the Western States 100 Mile Endurance Run and was in the store to buy shoes.

As Jim was helping me, I found out he was instrumental in the Chatfield 50 and he was also planning to run Western States 100. We exchanged contact information and that began a long-term friendship.

In June that year, we met at Lake Tahoe to participate in Western States 100. We did a few runs before the event and talked about strategies about how to finish under 24 hours.

At the start of the run, Jim bolted up the face of Squaw Valley; I walked the first four miles and never saw Jim the rest of the race.

It was a challenging year. Runners had to deal with 35 miles of intermittent snow in the higher elevations. As the trail descended to Auburn, daytime temperatures rose to 100 degrees. Jim finished the race in just over 24 hours; unfortunately I did not, quitting at eighty-six miles.

We continued our correspondence and met up when I was in Denver. My wife and I lived and worked in Aspen in the early 80's and visited Denver often.

I got a call from Jim in early 1983 about his vision of holding a 100-mile endurance running race in Leadville. He had discussions with folks in Leadville about a proposed event. During this period, there was some economic distress in the town and folks were looking to help stimulate the local economy. The thought was that an endurance race in Leadville would help bring folks to town and increase local revenues.

I recall there was a trail that started near the town that ran along the mountains to the west that crossed Highway 82 at Twin Lakes and headed over Hope Pass, elevation of 12,600 feet.

Jim organized a group of runners, myself included, running the trail over a couple of days. We ran the first part of it one day to Twin Lakes and then ascended and descended Hope Pass the following day. As I was running up Hope Pass, I thought to myself that no one could do this at forty miles and then turn around to do it again at sixty miles.

I told Jim I was not interested in participating in the actual race, but wanted to help by sponsoring the first official race. The mortgage company I managed, Aspen Home Mortgage, was one of the sponsors for that first race.

Jim was passionate about the Leadville run and was instrumental in getting it on ultra-marathoner's radar screen. He was intimately involved with the local group in helping pull off a great first event. All the aid stations were well stocked with enthusiastic volunteers. My wife and I helped out at the Twin Lakes aid station.

There was a lively and enthusiastic group of runners for the first race with a local Aspen runner, Skip Hamilton, placing first.

Over the course of our friendship, I paced Jim at another Western States 100, and he helped me on a couple of 50-mile runs. He finished Western States under 24 hours and earned his silver buckle.

Jim eventually moved out to California and worked for a mortgage company I managed in the San Francisco Bay area. We ran together many times in the Santa Cruz Mountains and the Diablo Range.

I lost track of Jim when he moved back to Colorado. We both became busy with family, work and personal interests. I thought about Jim often. I reminisced about our runs together and time we spent working on the first Leadville race.

In 2015, my wife and I were visiting friends near Aspen and decided to visit Leadville on our way. As we drove through Leadville, we noticed the Leadville race retail store on the main street. We stopped to see what it was all about. We inquired about Jim and were told he had recently passed away. I was shocked. Jim was only 64.

They did not share with me the cause, but gave me Marge Hickman's phone number. I called Marge and had a conversation about Jim's illness.

Jim was a very special friend and I regret I did not keep in touch. We all need to make sure we keep in touch with special friends we meet over our lifetime.

Jim Butera should always be remembered as a key individual that helped grow the ultrarunning sport. He was the key driver in launching the first Leadville Trail 100."

By Steve Siguaw

"This book represents my many fond memories of Jim Butera and his race. Writing it was truly a labor of passion, combined with immersing myself in past race events, long hidden away in the deep recesses of an ultrarunner's very being.

Jim was my inspiration for running, and his creation of the Leadville Trail 100 essentially shaped and molded what I have become as a person and runner. As each sunrise greets my daily run, thoughts of Jim and this 100-mile race he created are never far away.

How apropos are these lyrics, when I run up Hope Pass, gazing into the distance and feeling Jim Butera's spirit with me?

"He climbed cathedral mountains, he saw silver clouds below
He saw everything as far as you can see
And they say that he got crazy once and he tried to touch the sun
And he lost a friend but kept his memory."

– "Rocky Mountain High" by John Denver was adopted as the State Song of Colorado in 2007

Epilogue

There is no other 100-mile race on the planet having a more storied legacy as rich and vivid as the Leadville Trail 100.

Sure, these days, more difficult 100-mile races exist; such as the graduate level Hardrock 100 in Colorado.

The original 100-mile race, the Western States 100 mile endurance run is still alive and well. That race is a fine goal for any ultrarunner if they get lucky enough to win a lottery entry.

Yet no 100-mile race except the Leadville Trail 100 had the creative genius of Jim Butera as its originator. And what an event Jim's race has become over the past thirty-seven years.

If any runner believes they have the guts, strength and mental fortitude to finish or race over 100 high altitude miles, then the Leadville Trail 100 is for you.

You too can become part of the Leadville Trail 100 Family by racing and finishing this legendary race, running on the high altitude trails and discovering what your future holds. You never know who may show up at the starting line in any given year.

***

On Friday, November 22, 2019, Marge received an email from the new race director for the Leadville Trail 100, Timothy Brosious. Marge deferred her entry from the 2019 race until the 2020 race because of an injury. Deferrals to the next race year are allowed by race rules, as explained on the Life Time Fitness Race Series website.

This is the response Marge received when she was banned from the race: "Unfortunately at this time the Leadville Race Series will not be able to grant entry into the race. I know you'll understand why we've come to this decision after the differences between you, your husband, the Race Series and Ken and Merilee. I know we have not met in the past and trust me this is not the way I wanted to have an introduction.
Tim Brosious | Event Director – Leadville Race Series"

With those three short and cowardly sentences, Marge was denied the opportunity to become the oldest woman finisher in the history of this once great race. All the hype and hyperbole about being part of the "Leadville family" seems to have gone by the wayside. At least the majestic mountains and enticing forest trails in the Colorado Rockies remain timeless.

'Now on the day that great race died
I found myself on the Continental Divide
Tell me where do I go from here
Think I'll run into Leadville and have a few beers
Think of Hope Pass or climbing Power Line
Can't believe the old race has gone'
(With apologies to Jimmy Buffett's "Incommunicado")

Acknowledgements and Contributors

So many people have helped us with the facts and stories contained in this book. We would like to acknowledge these great friends and fellow ultrarunners:

Randi Bromka, Sheila Butera, Jill Case, Chuck Cofer, Bill Finkbeiner, Michael Hickman, Sarah Hoover, Matt Mahoney, Christopher McDermand, Barry Mink, Richard Neslund, Tony Post, Patrick Rooney, Arthur Schwartz, Frank Shorter, Maria Siguaw, Melissa Sobal, Tom Sobal, David Strong, Justin Talbot, Dave and Lori TenEyck, Ann Trason, Marshall and Heather Ulrich, Corky Watts, Bent Weigner, and Reb Wickersham. Also, thank you to Dawn and Laurie Corbett for providing editorial help from the prospective of non-runners. Google Maps was used to create the image showing the Leadville Trail 100 racecourse.

Marge Hickman and Steve Siguaw, co-authors for this book, would like to describe how they got together to become running and racing competitors, friends and eventually joined forces to write this comprehensive and amazing history of the Leadville Trail 100.

Marge's memories about Steve:
"He is one fantastic man, and his wife Maria is special too. They are an incredibly wonderful and perfect couple who share the same interests, as well as being first-class sailors. Steve has also written a book about one of their sailing adventures, *"Voyage Into Hell."*

Steve has so many talents I can't list them all. I do know however that he is extremely gifted when it comes to ultrarunning, writing, sailing and much more.

But, and there's always a "but," for the life of me I do not remember when I first met Steve. It's funny how the years can dull one's memory or totally disappear which is apparently what happened for me.

So, having to rely on Steve's memory, here's how he says we met. In 1982 we met at a Colorado Ultra Club meeting at Jim Butera's home in Denver. Steve recalls Jim introducing us at the monthly Club meeting. Though this was my first time meeting Steve, he says that he had heard about my running prior to our meeting. Thereafter, we began running together at the Club's weekly long training runs usually in the mountains somewhere harder, higher, steeper, rockier and always a good challenge.

I especially remember an eight-hour training run in Leadville from the Turquoise Lake Dam to Twin Lakes and back, mercy. What made it even more special was the cloudy, cool and thunderstorming day with power lines crackling and buzzing directly above our heads on top of Sugarloaf Pass. The thunderclaps scared me and I recall shrieking several times and ducking down on the trail.

Steve yelled, "Just keep running." Shit, running I did, as fast as possible. Not only did this get the heart pumping and the legs moving faster, it turned out to be a great day for our long run as we all survived and had fun."

Steve's memories about Marge:

"It should have been the "turquoise sparkly tights" as my first memories about Marge, but I don't really recall ever seeing those tights.

Marge's perspective on ultrarunning and life has brought an incredible depth and passion to this book, something my scientific training cannot easily permit me to express. I'm the fact and numbers guy while Marge is the touchy-feely, people oriented person that brings out a much more complete history of the Leadville Trail 100 than mere black and white finishing results, oxygen uptake analysis and statistics represent."

Selected Bibliography

Adams, Douglas. *Hitch Hikers Guide to the Galaxy*. Del Rey Trade, Random House, Inc. New York. 2009

Case, Christopher J., Dr. John Mandrola and Lennard Zinn. *The Haywire Heart: How too much exercise can kill you, and what you can do to protect your heart*. Velo Press, Boulder, CO. April 2018

Liquori, Marty. *Marty Liquori's Guide For The Elite Runner*. Playboy Press. 1980

Lydiard, Arthur. *Running with Lydiard*. Mayer and Mayer Sport (UK) Ltd. 2017

Marshall, Nick. *Ultradistance Summary*. Various years; 1982 - 1986

McDougall, Christopher. *Born to Run*. Vintage Books, Random House, Inc. New York. 2009

Noakes, Timothy. *Lore of Running*. Oxford University Press South Africa. 2002

Pavlidis, Stephen. *Life At Sea Level*. Seaworthy Publications, Cocoa Beach, Florida. 2012

Shorter, Frank and John Brant. *My Marathon: Reflections on a Gold Medal Life*. Rodale Inc. 2016

Ulrich, Marshall. *Running on Empty: An Ultrarunner's Story of Love, Loss and a Record Setting Run Across America*. Penguin Group. 2011

Ultrarunning. Monthly magazine. Bend, Oregon. Various editions as noted in chapters (1982-2018).

Part 5
Addendum

Leadville Trail 100
Race Results

"Don't be afraid," the cat told Alice. *"Everybody here is mad."*
– Alice in Wonderland

Leadville Trail 100 Race Results

Records (1983 thru 2019)

"The pain is nothing compared to what it feels like to quit."

—Anonymous

Fastest Times Men:
1. Matt Carpenter, 15:42:59 (2005)
2. Rob Krar, 15:51:57 (2018)
3. Rob Krar, 16:09:32 (2014)
4. Anton Krupicka, 16:14:35 (2007)
5. Ian Sharman, 16:22:39 (2016)
6. Thomas Lorblanchet, 16:29:28 (2012)
7. Ian Sharman, 16:30:03 (2013)
8. Ryan Smith, 16:33:24 (2019)
9. Ian Sharman, 16:33:54 (2015)
10. Michael Aish, 16:38:37 (2014)

Fastest Times Women:
1. Ann Trason, 18:06:24 (1994)
2. Clare Gallagher, 19:00:27 (2016)
3. Tina Lewis, 19:33:44 (2012)
4. Elizabeth Howard, 19:34:09 (2015)
5. Emma Roca, 19:38:04 (2014)
6. Anthea Schmid, 19:44:24 (2002)
7. Katie Arnold, 19:53:40 (2018)
8. Kara Henry, 19:54:08 (2015)
9. Lynete Clemons, 19:59:06 (2011)
10. Liza Howard, 20:01:15 (2014)

Oldest Finishers Men:
1. Hans Dieter Weisshaar, 73; 29:34:48 (2013)
2. Irvin McGreachy, 71; 29:39:58 (2017)
3. Stuart Nelson, 70; 28:17:36 (2010)
4. Ed Williams, 70; 29:21:49 (1999)

Oldest Finishers Women:
1. Helen Klein, 66; 29:25:55 (1995)
2. Marge Hickman, 60; 28:53:58 (2010)
3. Karen Bonnet, 59; 29:20:06 (2015)
4. Jeanne McCurnin, 58; 28:17:39 (2014)

Runners with the most finishes:
Bill Finkbeiner - 30 finishes
Gary Curry - 25 finishes
Eric Pence - 25 finishes
Kirk Apt - 20 finishes
Mario Varela - 20 finishes
Steve Siguaw - 18 finishes
Ken Chlouber - 14 finishes
Marge Hickman - 14 finishes
Bill Laster - 14 finishes
Stuart Nelson - 14 finishes
David Strong - 14 finishes

Leadman and Leadwoman Records:
Wesley Sandoval: 35:54:55 (2016) - Male
Stephanie Wurtz: 43:18:15 (2016) – Female

Sixty-four runners have earned the coveted Leadville Trail 1,000 mile belt buckle:

Name	(State)	Year Earned
Arthur Schwartz	(CO)	1992
Al Binder	(CO)	1993
Bill Finkbeiner	(CA)	1993
Ken Chlouber	(CO)	1994
Harry Deupree	(OK)	1994
Martyn Greaves	(ENG)	1995
Steve Siguaw	(CO)	1995
Ed Williams	(MO)	1995
Marge Adelman	(KS)	1996
Garry Curry	(CO)	1998
Odin Christensen	(CO)	1999
Luther Thompson	(MN)	1999
Alan Cohn	(CO)	2000

Mike Monahan (CA)	2000
David Strong (CO)	2000
Theresa Daus-Weber (CO)	2001
Daniel Munoz (CO)	2001
Wendell Robison (WY)	2001
Jim Ballard (OR)	2002
Jeff Berino (CO)	2002
Mike Sadar (CO)	2002
Bob Stavig (MN)	2002
Mario Varela (CO)	2002
Kirk Apt (CO)	2003
Bill Laster (CO)	2003
Eric Pence (CO)	2003
Johnny Sandoval (CO)	2003
Marshall Ulrich (CO)	2003
Raul Flores (KS)	2004
John Hobbs (CO)	2004
King Jordan (DC)	2004
Jay Grobeson (CA)	2005
Phil Kahn (CO)	2005
Bobby Keogh (NM)	2005
Joe Kulak (CO)	2006
Stuart Nelson (MI)	2006
Chisolm Deupree (OK)	2007
Scott Gordon (NM)	2007
Todd Holmes (CO)	2007
Neal Taylor (CO)	2007
Julie Arter (AZ)	2008
Chuck Cofer (CO)	2008
Brian Manley (CO)	2008
Jeffrey Welsh (NC)	2008
Tyler Curiel (TX)	2009
Jonathan Zeif (CO)	2009
Kristen Kern (NM)	2010
Larry Hall (Il)	2011
Scott Klopfenstein (CO)	2011
Tom Schnitzius (CO)	2011
Bret Crock (CO)	2012
Paul Schoenlaub (MO)	2012

Paul Smith (CO)	2012
Fred Abramowitz (CO)	2013
Ken Gordon (NM)	2013
Gene Bartzen (CO)	2014
Brian Costilow (CO)	2014
Laurie Nakauchi (CO)	2014
Todd Scott (MI)	2014
Hollis Baugh (CO)	2016
Charles Bybee (CO)	2016
Wade Jarvis (Canada)	2019
Chuck Stone (CO)	2019
Shawn R. Churchill (WI)	2019

Five runners have achieved the extremely rare 2,000 mile buckle:

Bill Finkbeiner (CA)	2003
Gary Curry (CO)	2008
Mario Varela (CO)	2013
Kirk Apt (CO)	2014
Eric Pence (CO)	2014

One runner has earned the unheard of 3,000 mile buckle:
Bill Finkbeiner (CA)   2013

***

Finishers Lists (1983 thru 2019)

"Come dance with the west wind and touch on the mountain tops
Sail o'er the canyons and up to the stars
And reach for the heavens and hope for the future
And all that we can be and not what we are."
–The Eagle and the Hawk; John Denver

Everyone who finishes the Leadville Trail 100 under the cut-off time of 30:00:00 will have their name included within these lists. Congratulations, you are a Leadville Trail 100 finisher!

1983

Name	Finish Time	State	Year	Age	Sex	#Finished
Hamilton, Skip**	20:11:18	CO	1983	38	M	4
Lapkass, John**	25:10:19	CO	1983	26	M	3
Lapkass, Andy**	25:16:24	CO	1983	25	M	4
Lisak, Mark**	26:24:13	WY	1983	26	M	2
Schwartz, Arthur**	27:23:16	CO	1983	37	M	10
Webster, Dick**	27:25:42	CO	1983	45	M	1
Cross, Gary**	27:36:24	CO	1983	23	M	1
Binder, Al**	27:56:26	CO	1983	38	M	13
Mink, Barry**	28:39:22	CO	1983	42	M	1
Weigner, Brent**	29:31:25	WY	1983	33	M	1

** Denotes original finisher

1984

Name	Finish Time	State	Year	Age	Sex	#Finished
Hamilton, Skip**	18:43:50	CO	1984	39	M	4
Lapkass, Andy**	23:45:44	CO	1984	26	M	4
Petersen, O.R.	25:07:49	CO	1984	46	M	4
Gagarin, Peter	25:42:18	MA	1984	39	M	1
Martin, Harlan (Bud)	25:57:50	IL	1984	42	M	6
Schwartz, Arthur**	27:27:54	CO	1984	38	M	10
Finkbeiner, Bill	28:00:38	CA	1984	28	M	30

Wickersham, Reb	28:00:59	CO	1984	50	M	3
Deupree, Harry	28:08:54	OK	1984	46	M	12
Gerber, Teri	28:17:41	CA	1984	35	F	1
Feistner, Jim	28:29:41	CO	1984	46	M	2
Davies, Cliff	28:52:11	Canada	1984	50	M	8
Humphrey, Mark	28:52:11	NM	1984	31	M	1
Chlouber, Ken	28:55:29	CO	1984	45	M	14
Siguaw, Steve	28:59:22	CO	1984	35	M	18
Jackson, Tommie	29:01:40	CA	1984	36	M	1
Hickman, Marge	29:13:13	CO	1984	34	F	14
Baughman, Wayne	29:28:29	CO	1984	43	M	2
Christopherson, D.	29:35:02	MT	1984	42	M	2
Willison, Bob	29:36:51	CO	1984	47	M	1

1985

Name	Finish Time	State	Year	Age	Sex	#Finished
Howard, Jim	19:15:57	CA	1985	30	M	2
Dewell, Ben	22:35:43	CA	1985	30	M	1
Portelance, Rolly	23:03:35	Canada	1985	42	M	2
Lapkass, Andy**	23:12:43	CO	1985	27	M	4
Butera, Jim	23:38:48	CO	1985	37	M	1
Martin, Harlan (Bud)	24:44:09	IL	1985	43	M	6
Brotherton, Mark	24:51:41	CA	1985	28	M	2
Finkbeiner, Bill	24:51:41	CA	1985	29	M	30
Ferguson, Charles	26:20:45	ID	1985	45	M	1
Sutton, Dale	26:43:38	CA	1985	45	M	2
Hickman, Marge	26:57:50	CO	1985	35	F	14
Feistner, Jim	27:16:36	CO	1985	47	M	2
Schwartz, Arthur**	27:20:34	CO	1985	39	M	10
Carr, Mike	27:24:41	CO	1985	32	M	3
Binder, Al**	27:41:19	CO	1985	40	M	13
Williams, Ed	27:55:45	NC	1985	56	M	13
Barber, Luke	28:02:08	TX	1985	40	M	1
Deupree, Harry	28:10:57	OK	1985	47	M	12
Chlouber, Ken	28:28:44	CO	1985	46	M	14
Olson, Mark	28:42:16	CA	1985	38	M	1
Holder, Kent	28:50:25	CA	1985	46	M	2

Demaree, Scott	28:57:19	TX	1985	34	M	4
Burdick, Robert	29:29:01	CA	1985	53	M	1
Lee, Paul	29:29:01	OK	1985	46	M	1
Robinson, E.B. Jr. (Bud)	29:29:45	MS	1985	43	M	2
Whittenburg, Lynne	29:46:07	CO	1985	39	F	2
Graber, Ray	29:49:37	NV	1985	42	M	1

1986

Name	Finish Time	State	Year	Age	Sex	#Finished
Hamilton, Skip**	19:26:09	CO	1986	41	M	4
Jones, Chuck	20:48:37	CA	1986	27	M	2
Larsen, Dane	22:24:57	CA	1986	35	M	1
Finkbeiner, Bill	22:38:59	CA	1986	30	M	30
Garty, Maureen	22:45:01	CO	1986	36	F	1
Greaves, Martyn	23:01:24	England	1986	27	M	10
Carr, Mike	23:13:39	CO	1986	33	M	3
Campbell, Joe	23:36:19	OR	1986	40	M	5
Bandur, John	23:43:09	WA	1986	48	M	2
Lapkass, Andy**	23:49:01	CO	1986	28	M	4
Starbuck, Don	24:10:06	CO	1986	40	M	1
Gates, Richard	24:15:15	UT	1986	29	M	7
Binder, Al**	24:21:17	CO	1986	41	M	13
Demorest, John	24:23:46	CA	1986	35	M	3
Williams, Ed	24:27:32	MO	1986	57	M	13
Hickman, Marge	24:37:53	CO	1986	36	F	14
Green, Tom	25:00:39	MD	1986	35	M	2
Oberheide, Jim	25:07:23	CO	1986	41	M	5
True, Micah	25:23:56	CO	1986	32	M	3
Lutton, Lyle	25:50:41	CA	1986	40	M	1
Davies, Cliff	26:36:16	Canada	1986	52	M	8
Hagen, Jeff	26:46:32	SD	1986	39	M	2
Schwartz, Arthur**	26:48:49	CO	1986	40	M	10
Lapkass, John**	26:57:36	VA	1986	29	M	3
Siguaw, Steve	26:57:45	CO	1986	37	M	18
Wickersham, Reb	26:59:03	CO	1986	52	M	3
Carr, Tom	27:23:46	CO	1986	33	M	2

Makris, Pete	27:30:08	CO	1986	37	M	4
Deupree, Harry	27:34:12	OK	1986	48	M	12
Putnam, Ted	27:40:35	MT	1986	42	M	1
Shaw, Bob	28:07:39	CO	1986	43	M	2
Beach, Bob	28:09:29	CA	1986	42	M	2
Ferguson, David	28:10:35	ID	1986	47	M	1
McComish, John H.	28:13:07	CA	1986	49	M	1
Werth, Dennis	28:13:12	CO	1986	44	M	2
Chlouber, Ken	28:20:42	CO	1986	47	M	14
Evans, Ken	28:27:20	WA	1986	40	M	1
Kaufman, Charlie	28:53:04	CO	1986	46	M	2
Foster, Ron	28:55:16	CO	1986	41	M	2
Spenceley, Bill	29:13:39	CA	1986	36	M	3
Demaree, Scott	29:14:10	TX	1986	35	M	4
Klaich, Nick	29:19:28	NV	1986	41	M	2
Christopherson, D.	29:34:55	MT	1986	44	M	2
Robbins, Larry	29:42:19	GA	1986	42	M	2
Murphy, Mike	29:44:37	MD	1986	40	M	3

1987

Name	Finish Time	State	Year	Age	Sex	#Finished
Hamilton, Skip**	18:44:55	CO	1987	42	M	4
Warshawer, Steve	18:54:05	GA	1987	29	M	2
Herr, Dennis	21:04:12	VA	1987	40	M	5
Greaves, Martyn	21:09:26	England	1987	28	M	10
Hayes, Joe	22:23:28	UT	1987	38	M	1
Evers, Eric	22:26:49	CA	1987	38	M	1
Whyte, Pat	22:26:49	CA	1987	39	M	1
Carr, Mike	22:28:56	CO	1987	34	M	3
Carr, Tom	22:28:57	CO	1987	34	M	2
True, Micah	22:33:27	CO	1987	33	M	3
Finkbeiner, Bill	22:55:24	CA	1987	31	M	30
Peffer, Dennis	22:56:42	CO	1987	34	M	2
Demorest, John	22:58:54	CA	1987	36	M	3
Howard, Jim	23:15:47	CA	1987	32	M	2
Schwartz, Arthur**	23:22:21	CO	1987	41	M	10
Bogenhuber, Alfred	23:30:29	CA	1987	47	M	1

Snow, Sabin	23:34:33	AZ	1987	45	M	1
King, Jim	23:40:22	CA	1987	30	M	1
Gates, Richard	23:45:34	UT	1987	30	M	7
Christensen, Odin	23:47:00	NV	1987	39	M	10
Pomroy, Jim	24:07:15	MT	1987	40	M	2
Schubert, Guy	24:07:45	CO	1987	36	M	1
Bromka, Randi	24:12:57	CO	1987	35	F	4
Curry, Garry	24:22:21	CA	1987	33	M	25
Bandur, John	24:30:43	WA	1987	49	M	2
O'Neil, Thomas	24:33:32	MT	1987	38	M	1
Mills, Scott	24:41:16	VA	1987	36	M	4
Makris, Pete	24:44:45	CO	1987	38	M	4
Robbins, Larry	24:50:50	GA	1987	43	M	2
D'Onofrio, Kathy	25:07:25	CA	1987	23	F	5
Norman, Jay	26:56:53	TX	1987	49	M	1
Murphy, Mike	26:57:54	NY	1987	41	M	3
Gardner, Bill	27:07:47	CA	1987	44	M	1
Eidenschink, Chuck	27:24:18	OR	1987	34	M	2
Dixon, Bobbie	27:28:54	MT	1987	40	F	2
Hawley, Barry	27:34:10	CA	1987	45	M	2
Davies, Cliff	27:36:27	Canada	1987	53	M	8
Miller, Geoff	27:37:40	CO	1987	29	M	4
Robison, Wendell	27:44:14	WY	1987	35	M	10
Kelk, Chris	27:56:24	Canada	1987	44	M	3
Cappis, John	27:56:40	NM	1987	45	M	1
Nale, John	27:58:43	CO	1987	41	M	2
Montgomery, Greg	28:14:45	CA	1987	37	M	1
Lee, Skip	28:14:46	CA	1987	42	M	1
Edmonds, Eric Jr.	28:21:51	CA	1987	34	M	1
Martin, Roland	28:23:17	NV	1987	32	M	3
Lujan, Edward	28:23:23	CA	1987	48	M	1
Brainard, Dick	28:25:57	MA	1987	41	M	2
Cherns, Trishul	28:25:57	CO	1987	30	M	1
Chlouber, Ken	28:26:20	CO	1987	48	M	14
Gibbons, Christine	28:30:06	NJ	1987	25	F	4
Gibbons, Wayne	28:30:06	NJ	1987	28	M	3
Foster, Ron	28:32:42	CO	1987	42	M	2

Ellis, Randy	28:33:10	OK	1987	35	M	6
Christopherson, W.	28:35:32	MI	1987	39	M	1
Clery, Brian	28:36:17	NY	1987	47	M	2
Kendall, John	28:39:19	Canada	1987	53	M	1
Donoff, Mick	28:41:42	CA	1987	43	M	3
Haley, Roy	28:42:24	TX	1987	51	M	3
Patenaude, Norm	28:43:00	Canada	1987	42	M	1
Kneuer, Bruce	28:45:28	CO	1987	29	M	2
Winton, Hal	28:46:11	CA	1987	56	M	2
Kaufman, Charlie	28:48:23	CO	1987	47	M	2
Randall, Richard	28:52:35	UT	1987	43	M	1
Dewalt, John	28:53:41	PA	1987	51	M	2
Deupree, Harry	29:00:44	OK	1987	49	M	12
Crone, Dave	29:08:07	WI	1987	49	M	4
Binder, Al**	29:11:37	CO	1987	42	M	13
Bailinson, Jay	29:11:41	CA	1987	40	M	1
Tanimoto, Herb	29:15:19	CA	1987	39	M	1
Williams, Kitty	29:16:00	NM	1987	29	F	2
Williams, Ed	29:16:01	MO	1987	58	M	13
Kehn, Keith	29:18:19	MN	1987	35	M	2
Gillis, James	29:18:56	FL	1987	52	M	1
Russell, Jeff	29:21:00	LA	1987	33	M	1
McGie, Michael	29:24:37	CA	1987	52	M	2
Thompson, Don	29:24:37	CO	1987	49	M	3
Walsh, Tim	29:25:43	NM	1987	40	M	4
Cox, Bob	29:27:07	NV	1987	45	M	2
Bowen, Wayne	29:29:21	CO	1987	41	M	3
Smith, Terry	29:29:40	SD	1987	33	M	3
O'Grady, Kevin	29:31:14	OH	1987	28	M	2
Rossmann, Tony	29:44:30	CA	1987	46	M	2
Ingalls, Frank (Jim)	29:48:25	TX	1987	42	M	6
Matteson, Beth	29:51:00	CA	1987	27	F	1
Brown, Mark	29:53:28	CO	1987	28	M	1

1988

Name	Finish Time	State	Year	Age	Sex	#Finished
Spady, Rick	18:04:03	MT	1988	36	M	2

321

Warshawer, Steve	18:04:03	GA	1988	30	M	2
Herr, Dennis	19:54:30	VA	1988	41	M	5
Tweitmeyer, Tim	20:19:59	CO	1988	29	M	1
Peffer, Dennis	20:42:29	CO	1988	35	M	2
Greaves, Martyn	20:58:07	England	1988	29	M	10
Trason, Ann	21:40:26	CA	1988	27	F	4
Oberheide, Jim	21:48:48	CO	1988	43	M	5
Von Borstel, Bruce	22:03:51	CO	1988	42	M	1
Horton, David	22:04:59	VA	1988	38	M	1
Pelechaty, Mike	22:09:20	OH	1988	34	M	2
Demarre, Scott	22:22:07	CO	1988	37	M	4
Jensen, G.E.	22:26:51	WI	1988	50	M	3
Barger, Dan	22:36:48	CA	1988	23	M	3
Anderson, Andy	22:46:51	NM	1988	40	M	1
Kelk, Chris	22:49:23	Canada	1988	45	M	3
Ulrich, Marshall	22:58:14	CO	1988	37	M	13
Christensen, Odin	23:11:43	NV	1988	40	M	10
Beach, Bob	23:17:02	CA	1988	44	M	2
Schwartz, Arthur**	23:18:34	CO	1988	42	M	10
Campbell, Joe	23:23:50	OR	1988	42	M	5
West, Dick	23:24:18	MI	1988	46	M	1
Gibbons, Christine	23:25:05	NJ	1988	26	F	4
Gibbons, Wayne	23:25:06	NJ	1988	29	M	3
Garland, Dale	23:26:38	CO	1988	31	M	4
Curry, Garry	23:28:23	CA	1988	34	M	25
Portelance, Rolly	23:48:07	Canada	1988	45	M	2
Finkbeiner, Bill	23:51:23	CA	1988	32	M	30
Matteson, Tim	23:51:23	MN	1988	30	M	1
Jensen, Jeff	23:57:05	CA	1988	26	M	4
Zalokar, Fred Jr.	23:58:30	NV	1988	28	M	1
Martin, Roland	24:04:44	NV	1988	39	M	3
Davies, Cliff	24:07:03	Canada	1988	54	M	8
Adamski, Ted	24:10:13	NC	1988	40	M	2
Lygre, David	24:14:35	WA	1988	46	M	1
Weber, Niklaus	24:24:49	NM	1988	45	M	1
McKeever, Doug	24:27:37	WA	1988	40	M	2
Ciolfi, Dante	24:35:07	AZ	1988	33	M	1

Day, John	24:43:35	CO	1988	26	M	1
Bell, Raymond	24:44:44	FL	1988	41	M	1
Kingston, George	24:45:09	Canada	1988	49	M	1
Robison, Wendell	24:47:21	WY	1988	36	M	10
Walsh, Tim	24:48:52	NM	1988	41	M	4
Develice, Robert	24:53:50	OR	1988	34	M	1
McGie, Michael	24:56:33	CA	1988	53	M	2
Miller, Geoff	25:18:12	CO	1988	30	M	4
Harmer, Burgess	25:28:55	NV	1988	46	M	7
Siguaw, Steve	25:42:11	CO	1988	39	M	18
Webster, Larry	25:47:31	WA	1988	55	M	1
Kahn, Phillip	26:04:28	CO	1988	35	M	11
Laster, Bill	26:07:54	AR	1988	35	M	14
Petersen, O.R.	26:18:48	CO	1988	50	M	4
Mensching, Jim	26:26:28	NM	1988	41	M	1
Bromka, Randi	26:28:09	CO	1988	36	F	4
Jensen, Jim	26:37:06	CO	1988	41	M	2
Bogenhuber, Edith	26:40:37	CA	1988	44	F	1
Maloney, Steve	26:42:43	CO	1988	42	M	1
Blinn, Jerry	26:51:48	CA	1988	41	M	1
Kneuer, Bruce	27:04:25	CO	1988	30	M	2
Spears, Randy	27:08:10	TX	1988	28	M	3
Wickersham, Reb	27:09:15	CO	1988	54	M	3
Samons, Dick	27:11:16	MI	1988	51	M	1
Walter, Hal	27:11:34	CO	1988	28	M	1
De Souza, Ferdinand	27:12:50	UT	1988	35	M	2
Ensslen, Dick	27:23:19	Canada	1988	45	M	1
Binder, Al**	27:36:00	CO	1988	43	M	13
Castano, Larry	27:38:31	CA	1988	35	M	2
Hawley, Barry	27:48:57	CA	1988	46	M	2
Johnson, Bill	27:49:23	CT	1988	43	M	1
Hubbard, Gordon	27:57:17	CA	1988	49	M	1
McKim, Kenneth	27:58:00	NV	1988	46	M	1
Shaw, Bob	27:59:31	CO	1988	45	M	2
Harvey, Steve	28:04:28	CA	1988	44	M	1
Heroux, Jess	28:07:28	Canada	1988	42	M	1
Mader, Jack	28:13:06	CO	1988	43	M	4

Westland-Litus, Julie	28:14:51	CO	1988	30	F	2
Deupree, Harry	28:19:04	OK	1988	50	M	12
Coffey, Marty	28:21:46	CA	1988	38	M	1
Baughman, Wayne	28:25:27	CO	1988	47	M	2
Murphy, Mike	28:28:13	NY	1988	42	M	3
Hagele, Denny	28:29:09	IL	1988	44	M	1
Kroeger, Al	28:30:28	CO	1988	28	M	2
Curry, Mike	28:31:23	CO	1988	47	M	1
Williams, Nick	28:31:37	AR	1988	45	M	1
Hooper, Max	28:31:40	AR	1988	41	M	2
Thomas, Bob	28:34:55	WA	1988	53	M	1
Sloniger, Ronald	28:35:07	PA	1988	45	M	1
Doucett, Bret	28:35:35	MT	1988	29	M	1
Mabry, Larry	28:37:24	AR	1988	41	M	4
Combs, David	28:38:20	CA	1988	30	M	1
Lapkass, John**	28:43:13	VA	1988	31	M	3
Spenceley, Bill	28:47:52	CA	1988	38	M	3
Givens, Bob	28:48:06	TX	1988	44	M	1
Peyton, Lou	28:48:44	AR	1988	44	F	2
Williams, Ed	28:49:54	MO	1988	59	M	13
Thalmann, Fred	28:50:09	UT	1988	31	M	1
Remner, Craig	28:52:36	CO	1988	37	M	3
Slaughter, Bill	28:53:01	CO	1988	45	M	2
Michel, J. (Mo)	28:53:15	CO	1988	50	M	1
Munding, Peter	28:53:26	CO	1988	37	M	4
Simonson, Larry	28:55:35	SD	1988	41	M	3
Gordon, Dave	29:01:20	CO	1988	30	M	1
Brown, Tim	29:02:15	MN	1988	49	M	1
Judd, Mike	29:03:34	UT	1988	42	M	1
Kamm, Ulrich	29:03:54	Germany	1988	41	M	2
Howard, Ken	29:07:26	CO	1988	42	M	1
Imrie, Curtis	29:08:45	CO	1988	41	M	2
Mrozek, Don	29:08:53	KS	1988	43	M	2
Chlouber, Ken	29:12:23	CO	1988	49	M	14
Smith, Harrison	29:13:03	CA	1988	61	M	1
Krull, Steve	29:13:44	CO	1988	30	M	2
Cameron, Tim	29:15:33	CO	1988	38	M	1

Hornbruch, Fred III	29:17:13	CA	1988	46	M	1
Ingalls, Frank (Jim)	29:17:56	TX	1988	43	M	6
Werth, Dennis	29:20:16	CO	1988	46	M	2
Kirkland, Robert	29:22:06	IL	1988	29	M	1
Kalmeyer, Betsy	29:22:48	CO	1988	27	F	4
Rossmann, Tony	29:23:29	CA	1988	47	M	2
Krueger, Don	29:23:53	CO	1988	31	M	1
Lash, Dorothy	29:26:43	AZ	1988	45	F	1
Whittenburg, Lynne	29:27:19	CO	1988	42	F	2
Hooks, Bill	29:29:17	TX	1988	59	M	1
Weber, Scott	29:30:24	CO	1988	35	M	2
Deupree, Debbie	29:30:43	OK	1988	34	F	2
Glasscock, Mike	29:34:43	TX	1988	40	M	4
Lowe, Pat	29:37:15	TX	1988	39	M	7
Epstein, Ted Jr.	29:37:59	CO	1988	53	M	1
Ostrowski, Daniel	29:39:28	CO	1988	28	M	1
Abt, Jim	29:43:57	TX	1988	41	M	1
Clark, Suzi	29:44:47	CA	1988	40	F	1
Clery, Brian	29:45:05	NY	1988	48	M	2
McDonnell, Jim	29:45:11	CO	1988	31	M	1
Wholey, Jim	29:49:56	CA	1988	41	M	1
Garrett, Essie	29:53:08	CO	1988	41	F	1
Macy, Mark	29:54:13	CO	1988	34	M	5

1989

Name	Finish Time	State	Year	Age	Sex	#Finished
Crom, Sean	18:56:40	NV	1989	33	M	1
Brotherton, Mark	19:24:51	CA	1989	32	M	2
Brainard, Dick	20:02:47	MA	1989	43	M	2
Jensen, G.E.	20:29:52	WI	1989	51	M	3
D'Onofrio-Wood, Kathy	20:50:41	CA	1989	25	F	5
Ulrich, Marshall	21:20:21	CO	1989	38	M	13
Bogenhuber, Max	21:31:50	Australia	1989	47	M	1
Tucker, Stephen	21:32:45	AR	1989	36	M	1
Makris, Pete	22:01:04	CO	1989	40	M	4
Arguello, Marcello	22:05:11	CO	1989	42	M	3
Gibbons, Christine	22:11:39	NJ	1989	28	F	4

Gibbons, Wayne	22:11:40	NJ	1989	30	M	3
Christian, Jack	22:20:36	OK	1989	36	M	6
Greaves, Martyn	22:22:50	England	1989	29	M	10
McCarthy, Willis	22:48:13	CA	1989	33	M	2
Mills, Scott	22:53:57	CA	1989	38	M	4
Sandlin, Michael	22:55:05	TX	1989	34	M	1
Schwartz, Arthur**	22:59:00	CO	1989	43	M	10
Spears, Randy	22:59:14	TX	1989	29	M	3
Bromka, Randi	23:02:56	CO	1989	37	F	4
Adamski, Ted	23:10:34	SWE	1989	41	M	2
Garland, Dale	23:17:52	CO	1989	32	M	4
Demaree, Scott	23:18:36	CO	1989	38	M	4
Marchand, Joseph	23:19:47	Canada	1989	48	M	6
Bussy, Jack	23:24:45	CO	1989	28	M	2
Van Willigen, Hans	23:25:37	MA	1989	51	M	2
Beech, George III	23:43:33	CO	1989	39	M	1
Simonson, Larry	23:47:40	SD	1989	42	M	3
Robison, Wendell	23:51:24	WY	1989	37	M	10
Day, Conn	23:55:07	IN	1989	30	M	2
Frome, Jeff	23:57:01	CA	1989	38	M	1
Modzelewski, Scott	24:07:57	AZ	1989	26	M	1
Hagen, Jeff	24:12:20	SD	1989	42	M	2
Hardman, Gordon	24:18:56	CO	1989	38	M	4
Norris, Brad	24:20:19	CA	1989	35	M	1
Schlereth, Joe	24:25:31	CA	1989	39	M	7
Greene, Charles	24:37:17	CA	1989	54	M	1
Finkbeiner, Bill	24:38:49	CA	1989	33	M	30
Nephew, Terry	24:38:49	CA	1989	38	M	3
Savage, Charles	24:43:12	CA	1989	41	M	1
Smith, Terry	24:44:46	SD	1989	35	M	3
Spenceley, Bill	24:47:04	CA	1989	39	M	3
Campbell, Joe	24:47:06	CO	1989	43	M	5
Pazaski, Kevin	24:48:07	WA	1989	27	M	1
Monahan, Mike	24:48:16	CA	1989	43	M	10
Kahn, Phillip	24:48:48	CO	1989	36	M	11
Petersen, O.R.	25:13:24	CO	1989	51	M	4
Kalmeyer, Betsy	25:15:10	CO	1989	28	F	4

Jensen, Jim	25:17:02	CO	1989	42	M	2
Trapp, Sue Ellen	25:19:57	FL	1989	43	F	3
Meyer, Bert	25:49:29	CT	1989	44	M	1
Field, Harold	25:57:35	NM	1989	40	M	1
Herten, Jeff	25:57:36	CA	1989	42	M	1
Degner, Michael	25:59:36	CO	1989	40	M	1
Williams, Ed	26:05:05	MO	1989	60	M	13
Staton-Carter, Laurie	26:08:05	UT	1989	36	F	1
Siguaw, Steve	26:26:22	CO	1989	40	M	18
Casteran, Rene	26:40:44	OR	1989	41	M	1
Volkenand, Rob	26:40:47	OR	1989	58	M	2
Price, Mike	27:04:49	GA	1989	39	M	1
Elam, Linda	27:12:58	CA	1989	43	F	2
Remner, Craig	27:13:38	CO	1989	38	M	3
Gray, David	27:19:09	WI	1989	35	M	2
Crone, Dave	27:24:33	WI	1989	51	M	4
Eidenschink, Chuck	27:26:19	OR	1989	36	M	2
Ellis, Randy	27:26:51	OK	1989	37	M	6
Hook, Geoff	27:27:37	AUS	1989	44	M	1
McAward, John Jr.	27:28:58	CO	1989	29	M	1
Curiel, Michael	27:32:02	CO	1989	37	M	2
Schalkham, Gus	27:38:05	CO	1989	40	M	1
Scribner, John	27:44:42	CA	1989	41	M	1
Goss, Lance	27:46:34	CA	1989	44	M	2
Klein, Howard	27:47:13	CA	1989	37	M	2
Moore, Arthur	27:52:31	OH	1989	52	M	1
Deupree, Harry	27:52:42	OK	1989	51	M	12
Scott, Ronald	27:53:56	AZ	1989	39	M	1
Walsh, Tim	27:55:09	NM	1989	42	M	4
Bellante, Richard	27:58:16	CA	1989	37	M	1
Slaughter, Bill	28:05:22	CO	1989	46	M	2
Daus-Weber, Theresa	28:09:58	CO	1989	34	F	11
Olney, Dave	28:10:55	CA	1989	47	M	1
Thompson, Don	28:11:25	CO	1989	51	M	3
Dickson, Rod	28:15:45	CA	1989	43	M	1
McKenna, Michael	28:15:45	CA	1989	36	M	1
Pintane, Terence	28:15:45	CA	1989	38	M	1

Bergman, Marc	28:21:32	CO	1989	37	M	4
Sabatine, Charlie	28:24:20	NY	1989	56	M	2
Markl, John	28:25:56	CA	1989	41	M	1
Ellis, Bob	28:26:36	CO	1989	43	M	3
Castano, Larry	28:27:34	CA	1989	36	M	2
Grindley, Jim	28:30:33	MT	1989	54	M	1
Young, Charlie	28:30:45	NM	1989	39	M	3
Baglione, Dan	28:33:54	CA	1989	58	M	1
Doolittle, Mike	28:35:34	CA	1989	50	M	1
De Souza, Ferdinand	28:36:07	UT	1989	36	M	2
Chlouber, Ken	28:37:29	CO	1989	50	M	14
Holder, Kent	28:42:19	CA	1989	50	M	2
Strauss, Randy	28:44:41	CO	1989	34	M	1
Russ, Dale	28:45:02	OK	1989	42	M	1
Krull, Steve	28:45:33	CO	1989	31	M	2
Mabry, Larry	28:47:38	AR	1989	42	M	4
Griffiths, Donald	28:47:57	CO	1989	39	M	1
Waldron, Joseph	28:48:25	CO	1989	30	M	1
Moshier, Stan Jr.	28:48:44	WA	1989	45	M	1
Silver, Steven	28:49:07	TX	1989	41	M	4
McReynolds, Mark	28:49:34	CO	1989	33	M	1
Johnson, Jack	28:51:46	TX	1989	48	M	3
Binder, Al**	28:54:06	CO	1989	44	M	13
Bowers, Dan	28:57:56	CO	1989	43	M	2
Hobert, Pennie	28:58:03	CO	1989	42	F	2
Peyton, Lou	28:58:34	AR	1989	45	F	2
Gross, Carl	29:00:59	TX	1989	50	M	3
Davies, Cliff	29:06:00	Canada	1989	55	M	8
Collins, Shane	29:08:42	Canada	1989	39	M	1
Bowen, Wayne	29:10:49	CO	1989	43	M	3
Hooper, Max	29:11:34	AR	1989	42	M	2
Rehorn, Mike	29:14:28	CA	1989	48	M	1
Gilbert, Bob	29:14:51	CA	1989	40	M	2
Haynes, Daniel	29:16:45	CO	1989	38	M	1
Soileau, Billy	29:18:44	TX	1989	48	M	1
Slevin, Paul	29:21:47	CO	1989	42	M	2
Thomas, Robert	29:21:47	CA	1989	33	M	2

Berryman-Shafer, Claudia	29:21:55	NV	1989	40	F	2
Lowe, Pat	29:22:18	NM	1989	40	M	7
Perry, Rollin	29:22:49	IA	1989	50	M	1
MacPherson, Hugh	29:23:58	OK	1989	50	M	1
Cox, Bob	29:24:28	NV	1989	47	M	2
Sobal, Melissa Lee	29:25:36	CO	1989	33	F	4
Klein, Helen	29:25:55	CA	1989	66	F	1
Dunlap, Ron	29:30:45	CA	1989	50	M	4
Chastain, Rick	29:34:19	CO	1989	25	M	2
Robinson, E.B. Jr. (Bud)	29:36:50	MS	1989	47	M	2
Bassett, Nick	29:37:29	CA	1989	44	M	4
Jorgensen, Fred	29:37:29	CO	1989	41	M	3
Thibeault, Suzi	29:37:38	CA	1989	41	F	1
Leigh, Todd	29:38:20	CA	1989	47	M	3
Johnson, Gary	29:45:09	NM	1989	36	M	1
Hickman, Marge	29:52:39	CO	1989	39	F	14
Haraway, Chuck	29:54:45	CO	1989	41	M	1

1990

Name	Finish Time	State	Year	Age	Sex	#Finished
O'Brien, Jim	17:55:57	CA	1990	37	M	1
Herr, Dennis	19:57:49	VA	1990	43	M	5
Trason, Ann	20:38:51	CA	1990	29	F	4
Crompton, Terry	21:04:06	IA	1990	28	M	1
Finkbeiner, Bill	21:08:37	CA	1990	34	M	30
Arguello, Marcello	21:10:12	CO	1990	43	M	3
Garland, Dale	21:22:35	CO	1990	33	M	4
Clements, Bill	21:27:04	WA	1990	32	M	2
Thibeault, Gene	21:54:44	CA	1990	44	M	1
Winter, Thomas	21:54:44	CA	1990	41	M	1
Bromka, Randi	21:55:33	CO	1990	38	F	4
Atlas, Dave	21:57:47	ID	1990	31	M	1
Ulrich, Marshall	22:01:21	CO	1990	39	M	13
Fricker, Harald	22:28:36	CO	1990	30	M	3
Laster, Bill	22:43:35	AR	1990	41	M	14
Wrolstad, David	22:51:51	ND	1990	31	M	3
Robison, Wendell	22:54:44	WY	1990	38	M	10

Kahn, Philip	22:56:15	CO	1990	37	M	11
Greaves, Martyn	23:04:55	England	1990	30	M	10
Drach, David	23:10:04	NC	1990	34	M	1
Kalmeyer, Betsy	23:15:14	CO	1990	29	F	4
Kelk, Chris	23:24:57	Canada	1990	47	M	3
Adams, David	23:27:02	WY	1990	38	M	1
Lee, Chip	23:30:19	CO	1990	35	M	5
Vorster, Johan	23:48:21	South Africa	1990	34	M	1
Harmer, Burgess	23:51:49	NV	1990	48	M	7
Siguaw, Steve	23:58:59	CO	1990	41	M	18
Britcliff-Thome, Kathy	24:16:38	CA	1990	35	F	1
Gates, Richard	24:22:53	UT	1990	33	M	7
Meyers, Dan	24:34:56	CA	1990	33	M	4
Coffelt, Bill	24:43:11	AR	1990	30	M	1
Briggs, Bill	24:45:40	CO	1990	41	M	2
Curtis, Dick	24:50:00	CO	1990	45	M	3
Flores, Raul	24:51:32	KS	1990	34	M	10
Campbell, Joe	24:52:57	CO	1990	44	M	5
Mader, Jack	24:53:55	CO	1990	45	M	4
Heaps, Steve	24:54:02	WA	1990	46	M	1
Seymour, Dag	24:58:07	CO	1990	31	M	2
Strong, David	25:22:26	CO	1990	45	M	14
Johnson, Jack	25:30:35	TX	1990	49	M	3
Young, Charlie	26:24:01	NM	1990	40	M	3
Petersen, O.R.	26:27:50	CO	1990	52	M	4
Demorest, Lisa	26:34:42	CA	1990	37	M	2
Williams, Bob	26:58:34	TX	1990	47	M	1
Berryman-Shafer, Jim	27:19:39	NV	1990	36	M	2
Davies, Cliff	27:26:43	Canada	1990	56	M	8
Trimboli, Lil	27:28:23	CO	1990	31	F	2
Munding, Peter	27:29:03	CO	1990	39	M	4
Christensen, Odin	27:29:50	NV	1990	42	M	10
Martin, Harlan (Bud)	27:34:34	IL	1990	48	M	6
Slevin, Paul	27:36:56	CO	1990	43	M	2
Archuleta, Wayne	27:49:56	CO	1990	27	M	2
LaSala, John	27:50:47	CO	1990	31	M	1
Sutton, Dale	27:50:47	CA	1990	50	M	2

Gilbert, Bob	27:53:37	CA	1990	41	M	2
Schmidt, Lee (El Burro)	27:54:07	CA	1990	50	M	8
Nale, John	27:55:17	CO	1990	44	M	2
Scott, Dennis	27:55:52	CA	1990	42	M	1
Monahan, Mike	27:59:13	CA	1990	44	M	10
Baer, Ernst	28:02:18	CO	1990	47	M	4
Westland-Litus, Julie	28:02:57	CO	1990	32	F	2
Ritchie, Gary	28:03:16	CA	1990	49	M	2
Morgan, Brian	28:14:30	CA	1990	32	M	1
Collins, Dick	28:15:12	CA	1990	56	M	1
Howard, Margrit	28:16:03	CO	1990	46	F	4
Mundy, Sandra	28:18:10	CO	1990	51	F	2
Moore, Russell	28:18:15	CA	1990	50	M	1
Peterson, Wayne	28:24:45	NV	1990	35	M	2
Kehn, Keith	28:26:01	MN	1990	38	M	2
Kramer, Tony	28:29:03	MO	1990	44	M	1
Covert, Ron	28:29:56	CA	1990	55	M	1
Steckbeck, Mike	28:32:08	NM	1990	29	M	2
Lowe, Pat	28:37:51	NM	1990	41	M	7
Sauser, James	28:38:26	IL	1990	35	M	1
DeSouza, Diane	28:40:05	UT	1990	33	F	1
Chlouber, Ken	28:42:06	CO	1990	51	M	14
Nelson, David	28:43:50	MN	1990	49	M	3
Thompson, Luther	28:43:50	MN	1990	45	M	13
Whyte, Sandy	28:44:13	CA	1990	42	F	1
Orr, Duncan	28:44:41	UT	1990	39	M	1
Sandoval, Johnny	28:48:39	CO	1990	32	M	12
Ellis, Bob	28:51:02	CO	1990	44	M	3
Johansing, Bruce	28:55:11	CO	1990	38	M	1
Walsh, Tim	28:55:37	NM	1990	43	M	4
Humphrey, Jack	28:56:32	CO	1990	33	M	1
Wickman, Tom	28:56:32	CO	1990	37	M	1
Blanchard, Michael	28:57:19	CO	1990	29	M	1
Rowe, Thomas	28:59:47	MT	1990	42	M	2
Simms-Masters, Jerri	29:01:42	UT	1990	33	F	1
Deupree, Debbie	29:03:13	OK	1990	36	F	2
Deupree, Harry	29:03:13	OK	1990	52	M	12

Williams, Kitty	29:09:39	TX	1990	32	F	2
Williams, Ed	29:09:40	MO	1990	61	M	13
Wright, Phil	29:12:08	CA	1990	46	M	1
Mowen, Mike	29:13:33	CA	1990	30	M	1
Lassiter, Tony	29:14:22	TX	1990	27	M	1
Macy, Mark	29:20:44	CO	1990	36	M	5
Binder, Al**	29:20:45	CO	1990	45	M	13
Adolf, Don	29:20:55	IL	1990	53	M	3
Smith, Michael	29:23:46	CO	1990	45	M	1
Ooley, John	29:26:58	OK	1990	35	M	6
Creighton, Bridget	29:28:08	CO	1990	24	F	1
Curry, Garry	29:28:08	CA	1990	36	M	25
Day, Conn	29:28:08	CO	1990	31	M	2
Sabatine, Charlie	29:28:40	NY	1990	57	M	2
Sisley, Steve	29:30:29	OK	1990	42	M	1
Castle, Scott	29:33:38	OK	1990	35	M	2
Chastain, Rick	29:33:52	CO	1990	26	M	2
Black, David	29:39:48	MN	1990	39	M	1
Mrozek, Don	29:41:55	CO	1990	45	M	2
Weber, Scott	29:42:22	CO	1990	37	M	2
Archuleta, Clyde	29:45:10	CO	1990	35	M	1
Stephenson, Thomas	29:46:46	MN	1990	41	M	1
Eldridge, William	29:47:34	CO	1990	58	M	2
Hickman, Marge	29:48:46	CO	1990	40	F	14
Werth, Kenneth	29:51:37	CO	1990	59	M	1
Thompson, Jim	29:54:20	KS	1990	40	M	1
Ballard, Jim	29:54:21	CO	1990	40	M	11
Haley, Roy	29:56:52	TX	1990	53	M	3
Schwartz, Arthur**	**:**:**	CO	1990	44	M	10

1991

Name	Finish Time	State	Year	Age	Sex	#Finished
Mahieu, Steve	19:38:04	NM	1991	44	M	3
Jensen, G.E.	20:18:26	WI	1991	53	M	3
Ulrich, Marshall	20:33:36	CO	1991	40	M	13
Downing, Peter	20:40:19	CO	1991	36	M	2
Herr, Dennis	21:02:30	VA	1991	44	M	5

Nephew, Terry	21:28:38	CA	1991	40	M	3
Thurau, Alice	22:10:35	PA	1991	35	F	1
Hileman, Keith	22:17:52	PA	1991	42	M	1
Schlereth, Joe	22:22:39	CA	1991	41	M	7
Johnson, Jack	22:28:11	TX	1991	50	M	3
Masters, Ed	22:40:53	UT	1991	39	M	1
Briggs, Bill	22:42:00	CO	1991	42	M	2
Lee, Chip	22:49:14	CO	1991	36	M	5
Oberheide, Jim	22:51:30	CO	1991	46	M	5
Laster, Bill	22:55:45	AR	1991	42	M	14
Finkbeiner, Bill	22:56:38	CA	1991	35	M	30
Arguello, Marcello	23:13:03	CO	1991	44	M	3
Seymour, Dag	23:16:03	CO	1991	32	M	2
Garland, Dale	23:26:41	CO	1991	34	M	4
Carr, Derrick	23:28:38	VA	1991	30	M	3
Green, Tom	23:32:59	MD	1991	40	M	2
Hickman, Marge	23:40:44	CO	1991	41	F	14
Harmer, Burgess	23:42:50	NV	1991	49	M	7
Curtis, Dick	23:44:56	CO	1991	46	M	3
Bohlmann, Wayne	23:51:21	WI	1991	44	M	1
Greaves, Martyn	23:58:01	England	1991	31	M	10
Curry, Garry	23:59:19	CA	1991	37	M	25
Nelson, Stuart	24:03:42	IA	1991	51	M	14
Landry, Dan	24:08:45	FL	1991	39	M	2
Braninburg, Joe	24:19:12	NV	1991	47	M	1
Trapp, Sue Ellen	24:21:22	FL	1991	45	F	3
Apt, Kirk	24:21:53	CO	1991	29	M	20
Spears, Randy	24:25:42	TX	1991	31	M	3
Kahn, Philip	24:28:55	CO	1991	38	M	11
Federico, Enzo	24:36:07	Canada	1991	34	M	2
Sandoval, Johnny	24:37:14	CO	1991	33	M	12
Siguaw, Steve	24:37:37	CO	1991	42	M	18
Davies, Cliff	24:37:49	Canada	1991	57	M	8
Godville, James	24:41:41	MD	1991	41	M	1
Alire, Larry	24:42:25	CO	1991	44	M	1
Christensen, Odin	24:46:09	NV	1991	43	M	10
Bassett, Nick	24:50:48	CA	1991	46	M	4

Robison, Wendell	24:56:41	WY	1991	39	M	10
Bergman, Marc	25:15:07	CO	1991	39	M	4
Baer, Ernst	25:18:56	CO	1991	47	M	4
Strong, David	25:49:01	CO	1991	46	M	14
Blakely, Gary	26:02:10	NM	1991	35	M	1
Trimboli, Lil	26:35:44	CO	1991	32	F	2
White, Eric	26:44:54	MA	1991	50	M	5
Klein, Howard	26:52:10	CA	1991	39	M	2
Boyer, Harry	26:57:59	PA	1991	40	M	1
Strange, John	27:00:07	CO	1991	38	M	1
Leighton, John	27:04:50	MN	1991	47	M	1
Schmidt, Lee (El Burro)	27:07:16	CA	1991	51	M	8
Miller, Geoff	27:17:48	CO	1991	33	M	4
Meyers, Dan	27:25:56	CA	1991	34	M	4
Martin, Harlan (Bud)	27:26:21	IL	1991	49	M	6
Mabry, Larry	27:27:50	AR	1991	44	M	4
Sadar, Mike	27:31:25	CO	1991	27	M	10
Huntzicker, Anne	27:33:46	MI	1991	47	F	2
Frame, Chuck	27:35:47	MI	1991	48	M	2
Harrell, Willie	27:38:34	TX	1991	51	M	1
Fisher, Jim	27:41:12	NM	1991	40	M	5
Thompson, Don	27:42:35	CO	1991	53	M	3
Hamilton, Nancy	27:43:46	MD	1991	42	F	1
Hamilton, Rick	27:43:46	MD	1991	42	M	1
Crom, Christopher	27:46:33	NV	1991	37	M	1
Bowen, Wayne	27:46:55	CO	1991	45	M	3
Mundy, Sandra	27:49:28	CO	1991	52	F	2
Petersen, Wayne	27:49:39	NV	1991	36	M	2
Lowe, Pat	27:52:27	NM	1991	42	M	7
Soltanovich, Esaak	27:53:04	CO	1991	32	M	1
Williams, Ed	27:53:51	MO	1991	62	M	13
Rombough, Charles	27:54:04	TX	1991	43	M	2
Holmes, John	27:55:15	FL	1991	49	M	1
Moore, Richard	27:56:09	TX	1991	33	M	1
Eliot, Eileen	27:56:26	FL	1991	47	F	1
Weaver, Cort	28:02:02	CO	1991	40	M	3
Silver, Steven	28:03:40	NY	1991	43	M	4

Thompson, Luther	28:03:46	MN	1991	46	M	13
Young, Charlie	28:04:44	NM	1991	41	M	3
Laine, Richard	28:07:15	CA	1991	61	M	2
McCone, Steve	28:09:12	CO	1991	29	M	1
Welker, Max	28:14:58	WA	1991	49	M	4
Burge, Ken	28:16:10	OH	1991	40	M	3
Rusch, Robert	28:18:14	WI	1991	49	M	1
Curiel, Michael	28:20:30	CO	1991	39	M	2
Hobert, Pennie	28:21:54	CO	1991	44	F	2
Linkhart, Bennie	28:27:41	AZ	1991	60	M	1
Jones, Jay	28:36:17	CO	1991	38	M	3
Dahl, Joel	28:39:04	CO	1991	33	M	3
Nutting, Chris	28:40:08	CO	1991	31	F	1
Lambrechts, James	28:41:33	CO	1991	43	M	1
Gross, Carl	28:42:15	TX	1991	52	M	3
Biggers, Ron	28:44:13	CA	1991	45	M	3
Purcell, Bill	28:44:36	TX	1991	55	M	1
Romesberg, Ephraim	28:45:51	CA	1991	60	M	3
Elam, Linda	28:47:22	CA	1991	45	F	2
Dunlap, Ron	28:48:33	CA	1991	52	M	4
Williams, Larry	28:48:43	AZ	1991	42	M	1
Imrie, Curtis	28:50:59	CO	1991	44	M	2
Crone, Dave	28:53:07	WI	1991	53	M	4
Frawley, Bob	28:54:35	MN	1991	35	M	2
Solorio, Robert	28:55:41	CA	1991	44	M	3
Lee, Bill	28:56:35	CO	1991	42	M	2
Leigh, Todd	28:59:46	CA	1991	49	M	3
Fricker, Harald	29:00:51	CO	1991	31	M	3
Ballard, Jim	29:01:18	MT	1991	41	M	11
Cohn, Alan	29:01:35	CO	1991	36	M	12
Ellison, Steve	29:01:52	CO	1991	31	M	1
Thomas, Robert	29:03:04	CA	1991	35	M	2
Deason, Edward	29:05:44	CO	1991	40	M	1
Blomquist, Bob	29:06:05	TX	1991	39	M	1
Heath, Kelly	29:06:05	TX	1991	30	M	1
Murphy, Timothy	29:10:19	MN	1991	37	M	1
Vulgarian, John	29:13:23	MA	1991	39	M	1

Name	Finish Time	State	Year	Age	Sex	#Finished
Vulgarian, Rick	29:13:23	MA	1991	36	M	1
Phillips, Ian	29:13:24	CA	1991	39	M	6
Martoglio, Chris	29:13:58	CO	1991	31	M	1
Everett, Larry	29:14:26	CO	1991	49	M	1
Snyder, Gail	29:14:53	CO	1991	32	F	4
Wunder, Armin	29:21:38	Germany	1991	23	M	1
Glasscock, Mike	29:22:00	TX	1991	43	M	4
Wilkins, Charlie	29:23:20	GA	1991	46	M	1
Berkshire, Walker	29:26:05	CO	1991	48	M	2
Jarvis, Wade	29:29:30	Canada	1991	29	M	9
Deupree, Harry	29:29:42	OK	1991	53	M	12
Sallis, Jimmy	29:29:55	OK	1991	45	M	1
Klaich, Nick	29:30:05	NV	1991	46	M	2
Bailey, Skip	29:31:05	CA	1991	39	M	4
Platt, Don	29:34:05	CO	1991	37	M	3
Ellis, Bob	29:34:50	CO	1991	45	M	3
Simonson, Larry	29:36:30	SD	1991	44	M	3
Fossett, Steve	29:38:12	IL	1991	47	M	1
Sobal, Melissa Lee	29:38:43	CO	1991	35	F	4
DeWalt, John	29:40:50	PA	1991	55	M	2
Vance, Fred	29:41:46	CO	1991	38	M	2
O'Grady, Kevin	29:42:16	OH	1991	32	M	2
Farley, Tim	29:43:35	OR	1991	49	M	1
Witek, Andy	29:44:32	CA	1991	37	M	1
Ooley, John	29:45:09	OK	1991	36	M	6
Schwartz, Arthur**	29:46:49	CO	1991	45	M	10
Haley, Roy	29:47:58	TX	1991	55	M	3
Ward, Bruce	29:48:31	CO	1991	46	M	1
Yates, Carl	29:50:31	CA	1991	63	M	2
Quiggle, Louis	29:50:35	CA	1991	50	M	1
Binder, Al**	29:56:11	CO	1991	46	M	13

1992

Name	Finish Time	State	Year	Age	Sex	#Finished
Spady, Rick	19:51:10	MT	1992	40	M	2
Downing, Peter	20:13:30	CO	1992	37	M	2
Finkbeiner, Bill	20:30:06	CA	1992	36	M	30

Schlereth, Joe	20:44:58	CA	1992	42	M	7
Mahieu, Steve	21:24:49	NM	1992	45	M	3
Marchand, Joseph	21:48:27	Canada	1992	51	M	6
Ulrich, Marshall	22:11:56	CO	1992	41	M	13
Lee, Chip	22:28:05	CO	1992	37	M	5
Fricker, Harald	22:32:20	CO	1992	32	M	3
Carr, Derrick	22:34:21	VA	1992	31	M	3
Bailey, Raymond	22:39:29	AR	1992	35	M	3
Siguaw, Steve	22:41:17	CO	1992	43	M	18
Albrecht, Randy	22:54:48	KS	1992	36	M	3
McCormick, Steve	23:15:40	CO	1992	47	M	1
Sandoval, Johnny	23:16:56	CO	1992	34	M	12
Pelechaty, Mike	23:33:20	OH	1992	38	M	2
Baer, Ernst	23:36:45	CO	1992	48	M	4
Daus-Weber, Theresa	23:37:23	CO	1992	37	F	11
Gates, Richard	23:43:10	UT	1992	35	M	7
Nephew, Terry	23:47:37	CA	1992	41	M	3
Trapp, Sue Ellen	23:57:15	FL	1992	46	F	3
DiNapoli, Lee	23:59:21	CA	1992	35	M	1
Trapp, Ron	24:08:53	FL	1992	48	M	2
Knutson, Thomas	24:10:00	MN	1992	42	M	6
Sadar, Mike	24:11:54	CO	1992	28	M	10
Rombough, Charles	24:18:03	TX	1992	44	M	2
Strong, David	24:21:07	CO	1992	47	M	14
McGrew, John	24:24:31	CO	1992	34	M	2
Amies, John	24:25:01	Canada	1992	50	M	1
Dahl, Joel	24:25:20	CO	1992	34	M	3
Berino, Jeff	24:25:30	CO	1992	34	M	10
Harmer, Burgess	24:26:55	NV	1992	50	M	7
Campbell, Joe	24:31:38	CO	1992	46	M	5
Hardman, Grodon	24:37:58	CO	1992	41	M	4
Ochsendorf, Larry	24:46:32	MN	1992	47	M	3
Pomroy, Jim	24:46:33	MT	1992	45	M	2
Newton, Jeff	24:47:49	VA	1992	40	M	1
Greaves, Martyn	24:49:01	England	1992	32	M	10
Bartley, Mo	24:52:12	CA	1992	37	F	1
Laster, Bill	25:22:15	AR	1992	43	M	14

Sheehan, Kellie	25:25:21	CA	1992	39	F	1
Pierce, Philip	25:40:02	ME	1992	50	M	1
Federico, Enzo	25:44:12	Canada	1992	35	M	2
Allison, Dean	26:05:33	CO	1992	28	M	1
McHugh, Melanie A	26:24:32	CO	1992	27	F	1
Trahern, Eugene	26:25:36	WA	1992	29	M	1
Franks, Ray	26:28:04	CO	1992	57	M	1
Munoz, Daniel	26:29:48	CO	1992	27	M	11
Konen, Jim	26:33:01	MT	1992	57	M	1
Atchley, Rachel	26:44:45	NV	1992	28	F	1
Thompson, Luther	26:45:44	MN	1992	47	M	13
Platt, Don	26:48:15	CO	1992	38	M	3
Johnson, Douglas	26:57:56	CO	1992	34	M	3
Mader, Jack	26:59:04	CO	1992	47	M	4
Dickey, Bill	27:00:38	CA	1992	52	M	3
Burge, Ken	27:05:01	OH	1992	41	M	3
Monahan, Mike	27:05:51	CA	1992	46	M	10
Dixon, Bobbie	27:07:39	MT	1992	45	F	2
Christensen, Odin	27:12:41	CO	1992	44	M	10
Macy, Mark	27:25:31	CO	1992	38	M	5
Englemann, Eb	27:34:18	OR	1992	50	M	2
Binienda, Patrick	27:39:42	GA	1992	37	M	1
Steckbeck, Mike	27:41:16	NM	1992	31	M	2
Gunzelman, Eric	27:43:49	CA	1992	30	M	1
Wyns, Julie Ann	27:44:14	CO	1992	37	F	1
Cole, Chris	27:52:58	CA	1992	29	M	2
Meyers, Dan	27:55:04	CA	1992	35	M	1
Miller, Ellen	27:56:19	CO	1992	33	F	1
White, Eric	27:56:26	MA	1992	51	M	5
Whiting, Floyd	27:57:26	NV	1992	51	M	1
Watson, William	27:57:56	SD	1992	46	M	2
Howard, Margrit	28:02:46	CO	1992	48	F	4
Duffy, Murray	28:05:09	MT	1992	62	M	2
Kinman, Bill	28:10:39	TX	1992	42	M	1
McDermott, Mark	28:12:02	CO	1992	30	M	1
Golding, Keith	28:12:10	CO	1992	31	M	6
Shear, Richard	28:17:22	NY	1992	44	M	3

Hypio, Richard	28:18:32	CO	1992	36	M	2
Winton, Hal	28:18:50	CA	1992	61	M	2
Hickman, Marge	28:19:07	CO	1992	42	F	14
Junger, Ron	28:20:20	CO	1992	50	M	1
Chlouber, Ken	28:22:52	CO	1992	53	M	14
Hermann, Fredric	28:25:04	CA	1992	53	M	1
Solomos, Nico	28:26:08	CO	1992	53	M	4
Frawley, Bob	28:27:00	MN	1992	36	M	2
Smith, Margaret	28:29:26	MT	1992	36	F	3
Pedroia, Vince	28:31:00	CA	1992	45	M	1
Heard, Jim	28:32:18	CA	1992	48	M	1
Blattel, Larry	28:32:19	CA	1992	40	M	2
Rastall, Patrick	28:33:07	CO	1992	40	M	1
Welker, Max	28:34:44	WA	1992	50	M	4
Garrison, David	28:35:53	CO	1992	36	M	2
Morgan, Mary Lou	28:39:32	CO	1992	38	F	2
Mabry, Larry	28:40:12	AR	1992	44	M	4
Heald, Michael	28:40:13	AR	1992	32	M	1
Schmidt, Lee (El Burro)	28:41:28	CA	1992	52	M	8
Mighell, Edwin	28:44:24	CO	1992	62	M	2
Williams, Suzanne	28:45:29	CA	1992	38	F	1
Bassett, Nick	28:45:30	WY	1992	47	M	4
Green, Terry	28:46:08	NM	1992	47	M	1
Wenmark, Bill	28:49:06	MN	1992	44	M	1
Booker Bill	28:51:23	CO	1992	47	M	2
Dupey, Roger	28:51:26	MN	1992	41	M	1
Ballard, Jim	28:54:56	MT	1992	42	M	11
Moore, Matthew	28:55:58	CA	1992	35	M	3
Lang, Dave	28:57:37	NY	1992	38	M	1
Munding, Peter	29:02:17	NV	1992	41	M	4
Wright, Gary	29:05:37	WA	1992	41	M	1
Archuleta, Wayne	29:07:13	CO	1992	29	M	2
Null, Steven	29:08:20	CO	1992	52	M	2
Grant, Rob	29:10:22	Canada	1992	47	M	2
Stevenson, Jim	29:12:04	Canada	1992	45	M	1
Leigh, Todd	29:12:42	CA	1992	50	M	3
Mauldin, Tonya	29:14:07	CA	1992	45	F	1

Name	Finish Time	State	Year	Age	Sex	#Finished
Mauldin, Bruce	29:14:08	CA	1992	44	M	1
Jordan, King	29:15:23	DC	1992	49	M	11
Cohn, Alan	29:15:43	CO	1992	37	M	12
Wilkie, Jose	29:16:49	KY	1992	29	M	5
O'Grady, Janice	29:20:20	CA	1992	43	F	1
Schwartz, Arthur**	29:21:57	CO	1992	46	M	10
Ingalls, Frank (Jim)	29:24:58	IN	1992	47	M	6
Jorgensen, Fred	29:27:13	CO	1992	44	M	3
Lowe, Pat	29:28:08	NM	1992	43	M	7
Turner, David	29:29:54	CA	1992	31	M	2
Bergman, Marc	29:30:35	CO	1992	40	M	4
Glinn, James	29:30:35	CA	1992	47	M	1
Luptowitz, Josef	29:32:50	CA	1992	49	M	1
Prugh, Wallace	29:33:20	CO	1992	39	M	2
Binder, Al**	29:33:37	CO	1992	47	M	13
Hill, Al	29:34:55	CA	1992	55	M	1
Honstad, Les	29:35:33	MN	1992	47	M	1
Vance, Fred	29:37:05	CO	1992	39	M	2
Eldridge, William	29:40:25	CO	1992	60	M	2
Nitzky, Alene	29:40:26	CO	1992	28	F	4
Karlin, Leo	29:42:38	TX	1992	55	M	1
Glasscock, Mike	29:42:43	TX	1992	44	M	4
Louth, Steve	29:44:08	CO	1992	32	M	3
Zicker, Gary	29:47:31	NV	1992	41	M	3
Riemer, Fred	29:49:36	UT	1992	44	M	1

1993

Name	Finish Time	State	Year	Age	Sex	#Finished
Churro, Victoriano	20:03:33	Mexico	1993	55	M	1
Chacarito, Cerrildo	20:43:06	Mexico	1993	38	M	1
Mahieu, Steve	20:54:27	NM	1993	46	M	3
Gibbons, Christine	20:55:59	NJ	1993	31	F	4
Luna, Manuel	21:26:09	Mexico	1993	30	M	2
Schlereth, Joe	21:32:42	CA	1993	43	M	7
Finkbeiner, Bill	21:40:18	CA	1993	37	M	30
Ulrich, Marshall	21:40:18	CO	1993	42	M	13
Sandoval, Johnny	21:45:48	CO	1993	35	M	12

Ingstrom, Heikki	21:59:35	UT	1993	35	M	1
Cave, John	22:01:35	WA	1993	33	M	1
Marchand, Joseph	22:05:00	Canada	1993	52	M	6
Daus-Weber, Theresa	22:50:47	CO	1993	38	F	11
Bussy, Jack	22:54:58	CO	1993	33	M	2
Graves, Tom	23:06:22	CO	1993	50	M	1
Golding, Keith	23:10:30	CO	1993	32	M	6
Makris, Pete	23:18:56	CO	1993	44	M	4
Huffman, Dennis	23:25:03	CA	1993	44	M	1
Scharberg, Rodney	23:33:08	NM	1993	33	M	2
Siguaw, Steve	23:35:19	CO	1993	44	M	18
Berino, Jeff	23:41:41	CO	1993	35	M	10
McGrew, John	23:44:50	CO	1993	35	M	2
Kahn, Philip	23:49:44	CO	1993	40	M	11
Greenlaw, Raymond	23:53:48	NH	1993	32	M	1
Turner, Kevin	23:56:47	England	1993	36	M	1
Flores, Raul	23:59:35	KS	1993	37	M	10
Seminoff, Tim	24:01:54	UT	1993	35	M	3
Thorn, Charles	24:12:00	NM	1993	47	M	1
True, Micah	24:15:14	CO	1993	39	M	3
Pence, Eric	24:22:19	CO	1993	27	M	24
Platt, Don	24:31:40	CO	1993	39	M	3
Hickman, Marge	24:33:12	CO	1993	43	F	14
O'Malley, Lynn	24:38:16	WA	1993	43	F	2
Bowers, Dan	24:39:00	CO	1993	47	M	2
Donoff, Mick	24:41:27	CA	1993	49	M	3
Perkins, Murray	24:42:14	WA	1993	29	M	1
Honeycutt, Chuck	24:47:28	CA	1993	45	M	1
Curry, Garry	24:48:01	CO	1993	39	M	25
Greaves, Martyn	25:15:26	England	1993	33	M	10
Munoz, Daniel	25:36:37	CO	1993	28	M	11
Chlouber, Ken	25:42:08	CO	1993	54	M	14
Van Dam, Jim	25:58:39	CO	1993	49	M	1
Macy, Mark	26:08:14	CO	1993	39	M	5
Demorest, Lisa	26:11:14	CA	1993	40	F	2
Lees-McGeough, Lorraine	26:23:00	Canada	1993	34	F	1
Grant, Rob	26:23:00	Canada	1993	48	M	2

Cohn, Alan	26:24:16	CO	1993	38	M	12
Sadar, Mike	26:27:02	CO	1993	29	M	10
Palma, Antonio	26:40:19	Mexico	1993	29	M	1
Lowe, Pat	26:50:29	NM	1993	44	M	7
Jones, Errol	26:55:13	CA	1993	43	M	2
Johnson, Stuart	26:59:22	KS	1993	34	M	2
Remner, Craig	27:02:59	CO	1993	42	M	3
Monahan, Mike	27:07:20	CA	1993	47	M	10
Taylor, Neal	27:08:14	CO	1993	30	M	12
Simpson, Peter	27:13:04	England	1993	45	M	1
Juknys, Peter	27:24:17	Canada	1993	41	M	2
Davies, Cliff	27:30:15	Canada	1993	59	M	8
Meyers, Dan	27:30:18	CA	1993	36	M	4
Nava, Benjamin	27:45:49	Mexico	1993	21	M	2
Stemsrud, Arne	27:48:25	OR	1993	35	M	1
Coonrod, Kurt	27:52:35	NM	1993	33	M	8
Roueche, Dana	27:54:53	CO	1993	36	M	7
Molleck, William	28:00:42	NM	1993	35	M	3
Booker, Bill	28:06:20	CO	1993	48	M	1
Kahn, Valerie	28:09:11	CO	1993	32	F	1
White, Eric	28:10:20	MA	1993	52	M	5
Solomos, Nico	28:11:20	CO	1993	54	M	4
Chesbro, Clark	28:12:57	CO	1993	32	M	1
Garrison, David	28:13:29	CO	1993	37	M	2
Thompson, Luther	28:14:33	MN	1993	49	M	13
McDearmon, Jack	28:17:49	TX	1993	52	M	1
Hypio, Richard	28:17:52	CO	1993	37	M	2
Eaton, Bob	28:19:15	NM	1993	39	M	2
Miller, Barbara	28:23:24	CA	1993	48	F	1
Ward, Arne	28:27:05	CO	1993	61	M	1
Rickards, Jim	28:27:15	MN	1993	46	M	1
Christensen, Odin	28:27:27	CO	1993	45	M	10
Anderson, Bryan	28:28:43	CO	1993	30	M	1
Bailey, Skip	28:30:40	CA	1993	41	M	4
Dickey, Bill	28:30:40	CA	1993	53	M	3
Fisher, Jim	28:33:56	NM	1993	42	M	5
Frye-Krier, Miles	28:35:35	CA	1993	41	M	7

Garrison, Rich	28:37:10	WY	1993	50	M	1
Solorio, Robert	28:39:33	CA	1993	46	M	3
Hornung, Matt	28:40:39	CO	1993	36	M	2
Stavig, Bob	28:41:47	MN	1993	44	M	13
Steinacker, Greg	28:42:54	MN	1993	36	M	3
Prochno, Walt	28:44:25	IN	1993	39	M	1
Miville, Ed	28:45:55	NH	1993	46	M	2
Schmidt, Lee (El Burro)	28:48:08	CA	1993	53	M	8
Cole, Conrad	28:49:58	CO	1993	42	M	1
Martin, Harlan (Bud)	28:53:22	NC	1993	51	M	6
Williams, Ed	28:54:18	MO	1993	64	M	13
Lustic, Chris	28:55:00	CA	1993	45	M	1
Rencoret, Ben	28:55:25	CO	1993	41	M	3
Booker, Chris	28:56:14	CO	1993	36	F	2
Wilcox, David	28:59:49	CO	1993	31	M	8
Boeder, Bob	29:04:44	NC	1993	51	M	2
Ellsworth, Jack	29:04:44	CO	1993	41	M	1
Ooley, John	29:07:41	OK	1993	38	M	6
Stafford, Margaret	29:09:45	WI	1993	45	F	1
Daus, Donna	29:10:23	CO	1993	33	F	5
Perkins, Ron	29:10:48	CA	1993	53	M	2
Mason, Margaret	29:20:01	Canada	1993	47	F	2
Frame, Chuck	29:20:01	MI	1993	50	M	2
Nitzky, Alene	29:23:04	CO	1993	29	F	4
Hacker, Rob	29:23:40	CO	1993	33	M	2
Robison, Wendell	29:23:55	WY	1993	41	M	10
Crone, Dave	29:25:37	WI	1993	55	M	4
Berkshire, Walker	29:26:05	CO	1993	50	M	2
Null, Steven	29:26:05	CO	1993	53	M	2
Kapke, Dan	29:26:32	NE	1993	42	M	6
Martell, Gregg	29:27:31	WY	1993	35	M	6
Williams, Ricky	29:28:09	WA	1993	44	M	1
Varela, Mario	29:28:15	CO	1993	32	M	20
Soupios, Michael	29:29:01	NY	1993	44	M	1
Schultz, David	29:32:32	CO	1993	40	M	1
Volkenand, Rob	29:34:59	OR	1993	62	M	2
Binder, Al**	29:35:32	CO	1993	48	M	13

Day, Bridget	29:36:15	CO	1993	27	F	1
Duran, Ramon	29:36:17	CO	1993	25	M	1
Zicker, Gary	29:38:21	NV	1993	42	M	3
Nelson, David	29:39:29	MN	1993	52	M	3
Gray, David	29:39:43	WI	1993	39	M	2
Reed, Jim	29:40:32	AZ	1993	32	M	2
Enboden, Tim	29:41:01	CO	1993	33	M	4
Jones, Jay	29:42:25	CO	1993	40	M	3
Greer, John	29:44:46	AZ	1993	34	M	8
Holland, Tom	29:44:46	AZ	1993	44	M	1
Burt, Steven	29:46:07	WA	1993	42	M	3
Jester, Bobbie	29:52:09	TX	1993	39	F	2
Glasscock, Mike	29:52:10	TX	1993	45	M	4
Muller, Craig	29:53:50	NJ	1993	26	M	1
Kellogg, Robert	29:58:22	MN	1993	52	M	1
Deupree, Harry	29:59:45	OK	1993	55	M	12

1994

Name	Finish Time	State	Year	Age	Sex	#Finished
Herrera, Juan	17:30:42	Mexico	1994	25	M	1
Trason, Ann	18:06:24	CA	1994	33	F	4
Cervantes, Martimano	19:46:33	Mexico	1994	42	M	1
Bautista, Gabriel	20:26:35	Mexico	1994	24	M	1
Holguin, Rafael	20:26:35	Mexico	1994	25	M	1
Madden, Kurt	20:36:57	CA	1994	38	M	4
Ramirez, Martin	20:51:07	Mexico	1994	31	M	1
Taylor, Thomas	20:51:26	MI	1994	39	M	1
Schlereth, Joe	20:59:36	CA	1994	44	M	7
Luna, Manuel	21:09:07	Mexico	1994	31	M	2
Quintero, Corpus	21:09:07	Mexico	1994	22	M	1
Demorest, John	21:36:25	CA	1994	43	M	3
Mills, Scott	22:21:38	VA	1994	43	M	4
Tarr, Mark	22:25:03	MT	1994	32	M	1
Johnson III, Harry	22:26:40	AK	1994	38	M	1
Scharberg, Rodney	22:35:06	NM	1994	34	M	2
Bailey, Raymond	22:37:34	AR	1994	37	M	3
Flores, Raul	23:07:58	KS	1994	38	M	10

Golding, Keith	23:18:43	CO	1994	33	M	6
Strong, David	23:43:31	CO	1994	49	M	14
Smith, Terry	23:45:57	SD	1994	40	M	3
Pals, Lou	23:53:04	Canada	1994	52	M	1
Mackey, Monte	23:57:17	CA	1994	38	M	1
Curry, Garry	23:57:39	CO	1994	40	M	25
Wojno, Randy	23:57:39	CO	1994	34	M	2
Atchley, Greg	24:03:59	NV	1994	27	M	1
Siguaw, Steve	24:08:16	CO	1994	45	M	18
Finkbeiner, Bill	24:17:46	CA	1994	38	M	30
Isler, Randy	24:18:18	NM	1994	37	M	2
Stark, Ed	24:22:37	MA	1994	48	M	2
Coonrod, Kurt	24:23:47	NM	1994	34	M	8
Pozner, Jay	24:23:58	CO	1994	23	M	2
Culp, Howard	24:30:07	TX	1994	46	M	1
Sandoval, Johnny	24:31:28	CO	1994	36	M	12
Ochsendorf, Larry	24:36:22	MN	1994	49	M	3
Kahn, Philip	24:40:14	CO	1994	41	M	11
Dolan, Barbara	24:43:11	CO	1994	38	F	1
Seminoff, Tim	24:44:38	UT	1994	36	M	3
Knutson, Thomas	24:49:37	MN	1994	44	M	6
Beine, Jo Ann	24:49:47	CO	1994	38	F	3
Rhodes, Randy	24:51:02	CO	1994	44	M	2
Solomos, Nico	24:53:12	CO	1994	56	M	4
Reed, Pamela	25:05:52	AZ	1994	33	F	6
Stavig, Bob	25:06:15	MN	1994	45	M	13
Baer, Ernst	25:13:30	CO	1994	50	M	4
Howard, Ron	25:18:02	CA	1994	42	M	2
Dahl, Robert	25:23:54	MN	1994	48	M	1
Munoz, Daniel	25:31:53	CO	1994	29	M	11
Sadar, Mike	26:04:11	CO	1994	30	M	10
Howard, Margrit	26:10:54	CO	1994	50	F	4
Furnish, James	26:13:16	CA	1994	52	M	1
Dickey, Bill	26:18:49	CA	1994	54	M	3
Berino, Jeff	26:29:34	CO	1994	36	M	10
Gassan, Larry	26:33:18	CA	1994	38	M	2
Roueche, Dana	26:42:41	CO	1994	37	M	7

Hunter, Joe	26:49:40	CO	1994	49	M	1
Boothman, Stephen	26:51:08	Canada	1994	34	M	1
Hopkins, Jennifer	26:54:31	CO	1994	33	F	2
Pence, Eric	26:55:14	UT	1994	28	M	24
Bodamer, Mark	27:07:29	WA	1994	35	M	1
McKeever, Doug	27:07:29	WA	1994	46	M	2
Thompson, Luther	27:12:09	MN	1994	50	M	13
Benjamin, Steve	27:13:33	VA	1994	39	M	1
Monahan, Mike	27:15:56	CA	1994	48	M	10
Fisher, Jim	27:17:30	NM	1994	43	M	5
Booker, Bill	27:19:11	CO	1994	49	M	2
Ehrlich, Michael	27:20:25	CO	1994	31	M	9
Chlouber, Ken	27:21:30	CO	1994	55	M	14
Harmer, Burgess	27:24:57	NV	1994	52	M	7
Nelson, David	27:25:27	MN	1994	53	M	3
Morgan, Mary Lou	27:26:18	CO	1994	40	F	2
Gates, Gordon	27:27:17	CO	1994	44	M	2
Tilley, Steve	27:28:25	AR	1994	47	M	2
Eaton, Bob	27:28:35	NM	1994	40	M	2
Christensen, Odin	27:32:16	CO	1994	46	M	10
Johnson, Douglas	27:32:16	CO	1994	36	M	3
Hughes, Jill	27:35:41	CO	1994	29	F	2
Robbins, Brick	27:38:21	CA	1994	35	M	2
Nicholson, Ken	27:39:40	Canada	1994	38	M	1
Miville, Ed	27:42:03	NH	1994	47	M	2
Woodworth, Bob	27:42:33	FL	1994	35	M	1
Thomas, Michael	27:44:04	CO	1994	32	M	2
Thouvenelle, Jon	27:45:33	CO	1994	38	M	3
Petschar, Perry	27:45:49	CA	1994	40	M	1
Black, Carson	27:46:46	CO	1994	53	M	2
Burge, Ken	27:50:38	OH	1994	43	M	3
Ooley, John	27:53:57	OK	1994	39	M	6
Phillips, Ian	27:54:52	CA	1994	42	M	6
Watson, Mark	27:59:09	England	1994	29	M	1
Espinoza, Joe	27:59:42	CO	1994	50	M	1
Beaulieu, Moe	28:04:15	Canada	1994	49	M	1
Biggers, Ron	28:07:27	CO	1994	48	M	3

Pence, Brian	28:13:19	UT	1994	34	M	4
Wright, Ronald	28:13:33	CO	1994	47	M	9
Goodman, Steve	28:14:18	CO	1994	22	M	1
Grunt, Cindie	28:14:40	OR	1994	44	F	1
Jester, Bobbie	28:15:02	TX	1994	40	F	2
Molleck, William	28:16:20	NM	1994	36	M	3
Trapp, Ron	28:17:54	FL	1994	50	M	2
Arter, Julie	28:18:41	AZ	1994	33	F	10
Cohn, Alan	28:20:45	CO	1994	39	M	12
Deupree, Harry	28:21:45	OK	1994	56	M	12
Williams, Ed	28:22:02	MO	1994	65	M	13
Blattel, Larry	28:27:39	CA	1994	42	M	2
Juknys, Peter	28:31:45	Canada	1994	42	M	2
Klingbeil, James	28:34:01	WY	1994	44	M	2
Lepley, R. Herb	28:38:47	UT	1994	42	M	1
Cole, Chris	28:40:24	CA	1994	31	M	2
Powers, Karen	28:46:09	WY	1994	44	F	1
Schmidt, Lee (El Burro)	28:46:53	CA	1994	54	M	8
Weaver, Cort	28:47:29	CO	1994	43	M	3
Heaphy, Mark	28:47:55	MT	1994	31	M	1
Miller, Martin	28:48:27	MT	1994	42	M	1
Boisseree, Kirk	28:49:02	CA	1994	36	M	1
Vaassen, Glen	28:53:21	CO	1994	35	M	3
Newton, Jim	28:55:14	TX	1994	47	M	3
Wilson, Bob	28:55:52	NM	1994	48	M	1
Martin, Harlan (Bud)	28:56:37	NC	1994	52	M	6
Helling, Dot	28:58:20	VT	1994	44	F	1
Martin, Roland	28:59:38	NV	1994	45	M	3
King, Harley	29:02:54	UT	1994	48	M	1
Mighell, Edwin	29:03:34	CO	1994	64	M	2
Wagner, Clayton	29:04:04	CO	1994	53	M	1
Greaves, Martyn	29:04:44	England	1994	34	M	10
Steinacker, Greg	29:06:21	MN	1994	37	M	3
Varela, Mario	29:08:34	CO	1994	34	M	20
Fernandez, Luis	29:08:56	CO	1994	27	M	4
Sharp, Greg	29:09:13	MT	1994	42	M	1
Allen, Lisa	29:10:53	CO	1994	30	F	3

Name	Finish Time	State	Year	Age	Sex	#Finished
Newsom, Claudia	29:15:34	CA	1994	44	F	1
Binder, Al**	29:15:35	CO	1994	49	M	13
Shear, Richard	29:17:03	NY	1994	46	M	3
Keirn, Kevin	29:19:01	CO	1994	32	M	2
Zicker, Gary	29:19:57	NV	1994	43	M	3
Boeder, Bob	29:20:38	NC	1994	52	M	2
Kapke, Dan	29:22:15	NE	1994	43	M	6
O'Connell, Tom	29:23:37	CA	1994	43	M	2
Homelvig, Pat	29:24:45	CO	1994	35	M	5
Hoffman, Paul	29:26:25	MO	1994	39	M	1
Stahl, Bill	29:28:13	CO	1994	35	M	4
Hargrove, John	29:28:47	OK	1994	49	M	1
Keogh, Bobby	29:28:49	NM	1994	45	M	12
Akiyama, Paul	29:29:20	NV	1994	50	M	1
Hornung, Matt	29:34:39	CO	1994	37	M	2
Wiegand, Sylvia	29:34:48	NE	1994	49	F	1
Smith, Margaret	29:36:22	MT	1994	38	F	3
Daus, Donna	29:36:44	CO	1994	34	F	5
Burns, Steve	29:36:57	MO	1994	41	M	1
Jorgensen, Fred	29:40:02	CO	1994	46	M	3
Sobal, Melissa Lee	29:41:54	CO	1994	38	F	4
Prugh, Wallace	29:42:58	CO	1994	41	M	2
Mercil, Bob	29:43:13	CO	1994	54	M	3
Valenta, Joe	29:47:17	IL	1994	39	M	1
Jones, Jay	29:53:02	CO	1994	41	M	3
Baugh, Hollis	29:53:47	TX	1994	25	M	11
Yates, Carl	29:57:26	CA	1994	66	M	2

1995

Name	Finish Time	State	Year	Age	Sex	#Finished
Apt, Kirk	20:33:05	CO	1995	33	M	20
Samuelson, Mark	21:03:35	CA	1995	41	M	1
Wojno, Randy	22:17:46	CO	1995	35	M	2
Albrecht, Randy	22:31:45	KS	1995	39	M	3
Lee, Linda	22:59:01	CA	1995	39	F	1
Park, David	23:08:10	CA	1995	39	M	1
Holmes, Todd	23:08:45	CO	1995	39	M	12

Schlereth, Joe	23:19:13	CA	1995	45	M	7
Wilcox, David	23:22:18	CO	1995	33	M	8
Hickman, Marge	23:44:25	CO	1995	45	F	14
Munoz, Daniel	23:46:39	CO	1995	30	M	11
Hughes, Bryan	23:46:52	CO	1995	29	M	3
Thompson, Robert	23:55:13	CO	1995	42	M	1
Flores, Raul	23:58:43	MO	1995	39	M	10
Finkbeiner, Bill	24:13:38	CA	1995	39	M	30
Benike, James	24:14:03	MN	1995	45	M	3
Mills, Scott	24:21:22	VA	1995	44	M	4
Macy, Mark	24:23:25	CO	1995	41	M	5
Curry, Garry	24:28:14	CO	1995	41	M	25
Marchand, Joseph	24:32:52	Canada	1995	54	M	6
Knutson, Thomas	24:43:10	MN	1995	45	M	6
Ochsendorf, Larry	24:43:11	MN	1995	50	M	3
Molleck, William	24:45:43	NM	1995	37	M	3
Benet, Reed	24:55:13	CA	1995	33	M	1
Buehler, Gregg	25:00:49	CO	1995	24	M	1
Ehrlich, Michael	25:21:57	CO	1995	32	M	9
Daus-Weber, Theresa	25:24:13	CO	1995	40	F	11
Siguaw, Steve	25:24:14	CO	1995	46	M	18
Beaman, Timothy	25:26:55	VT	1995	44	M	1
Nelson, Stuart	26:05:04	IA	1995	55	M	14
Schlichter, Beth	26:08:16	CO	1995	46	F	1
Ritchie, Gary	26:10:56	CA	1995	54	M	2
Gates, Richard	26:16:18	UT	1995	38	M	7
Bennett, Debbie	26:19:08	MN	1995	36	F	1
Stavig, Bob	26:22:06	MN	1995	46	M	13
Palermo, George	26:36:50	CA	1995	43	M	2
Hildebrand, Joe	26:50:48	IL	1995	38	M	1
Johnson, Douglas	26:51:28	CO	1995	37	M	3
Ash, Kevin	27:01:04	MN	1995	22	M	1
Roueche, Dana	27:05:59	CO	1995	38	M	7
Welker, Max	27:18:00	WA	1995	53	M	4
Varela, Mario	27:20:18	CO	1995	35	M	20
Ridgway, Diane	27:27:35	CO	1995	46	F	2
McInturff, Douglas	27:27:48	CO	1995	35	M	2

Phillips, Ian	27:29:52	CA	1995	43	M	6
Duffy, Murray	27:36:13	MT	1995	65	M	2
Martell, Gregg	27:39:01	WY	1995	38	M	6
Gates, Gordon	27:43:25	CO	1995	45	M	2
Golding, Keith	27:47:51	CO	1995	34	M	6
Rencoret, Ben	27:51:26	CO	1995	43	M	3
Gillespie, Richard	27:53:43	CA	1995	49	M	2
Thompson, Luther	27:53:52	MN	1995	51	M	13
Thouvenelle, Jon	28:00:55	CO	1995	39	M	3
Monahan, Mike	28:01:00	CA	1995	49	M	10
Gains, John	28:06:45	CO	1995	32	M	2
Braden, Jim	28:06:52	TX	1995	59	M	1
Christensen, Odin	28:09:09	CO	1995	47	M	10
Berryman-Shafer, Claudia	28:13:39	NV	1995	46	F	2
Berryman-Shafer, Jim	28:13:39	NV	1995	41	M	2
Christian, Jack	28:14:36	OK	1995	42	M	6
Strong, David	28:15:30	CO	1995	50	M	14
Whitehead, David	28:17:12	England	1995	47	M	1
Bailey, Skip	28:18:29	CA	1995	43	M	4
Freedman, Gary	28:19:39	MA	1995	35	M	1
Evans, Jack	28:24:57	AR	1995	48	M	1
Alvarez, Rudy	28:26:51	TX	1995	40	M	1
Saffery, Clive	28:29:19	Thailand	1995	40	M	1
Stimac, Larry	28:30:25	MN	1995	46	M	3
Coudurier, Bernard	28:38:38	CA	1995	43	M	1
Wilkie, Jose	28:40:34	KY	1995	32	M	5
Pence, Eric	28:41:43	CO	1995	29	M	24
Greiner, Dale	28:42:53	MA	1995	43	M	2
Foraker, Greg	28:49:13	CO	1995	36	M	2
Booker, Chris	28:49:17	CO	1995	38	F	2
Gardner, Renne	28:51:11	CA	1995	37	M	2
Janney, Matt	28:53:29	OR	1995	40	M	1
Miller, Sandee	28:54:54	CO	1995	42	F	2
Jordan, King	28:56:32	DC	1995	52	M	11
Klingbeil, James	28:57:06	WY	1995	45	M	2
Silver, Steven	29:02:55	TX	1995	47	M	4
Schmidt, Lee (El Burro)	29:04:56	CA	1995	55	M	8

Homelvig, Pat	29:05:50	CO	1995	36	M	5
Abshire, Danny	29:06:57	CO	1995	37	M	2
Jensen, Jeff	29:07:50	CO	1995	33	M	4
Gerkits, Marty	29:08:51	CO	1995	37	M	1
Ballard, Jim	29:10:55	MT	1995	45	M	11
Anderson, Bob	29:12:16	VA	1995	51	M	1
Reedy, Robert	29:13:43	NM	1995	53	M	1
Kapke, Dan	29:14:16	NE	1995	44	M	6
Chlouber, Ken	29:14:37	CO	1995	56	M	14
Ellis, Randy	29:16:24	OK	1995	43	M	6
Gnass, Jon	29:17:52	OR	1995	40	M	1
Adolf, Don	29:17:57	IL	1995	58	M	3
Mork, Joanie	29:20:44	CA	1995	41	F	2
Welch, Kathy	29:20:44	CA	1995	42	F	1
Hornung, Eva	29:21:32	CO	1995	29	F	1
Braden, Paul	29:24:08	Canada	1995	31	M	2
Keogh, Bobby	29:25:00	NM	1995	46	M	12
Williams, Ed	29:25:25	MO	1995	66	M	13
Greaves, Martyn	29:27:05	England	1995	35	M	10
Creel, Norman	29:27:17	CO	1995	46	M	3
Fields, Todd	29:28:08	CO	1995	33	M	1
Readio, Stu	29:29:52	CO	1995	44	M	1
Howard, Ron	29:29:54	CA	1995	43	M	2
Pence, Brain	29:30:05	UT	1995	35	M	4
Morris, DeWitt	29:30:19	CO	1995	43	M	1
Castle, Scott	29:32:09	OK	1995	40	M	2
Deupree, Chisholm	29:32:10	OK	1995	29	M	11
Deupree, Harry	29:32:12	OK	1995	57	M	12
Fernandez, Luis	29:34:47	CO	1995	29	M	4
Schmidt, Paul	29:35:30	CA	1995	43	M	3
Spencer, Doug	29:36:52	CA	1995	37	M	1
Cohn, Alan	29:37:26	CO	1995	40	M	12
Lowe, Pat	29:37:58	NM	1995	46	M	7
Munding, Peter	29:38:05	NV	1995	44	M	4
Ooley, John	29:38:40	OK	1995	40	M	6
Schlueter, Jan	29:39:12	MN	1995	35	F	1
Keirn, Kevin	29:41:39	CO	1995	33	M	2

Turner, David	29:41:48	CA	1995	34	M	2
Laub, Jane	29:42:56	MN	1995	45	F	1
Nakauchi-Hawn, Laurie	29:42:59	CO	1995	25	F	12
Mishler, Robert	29:43:53	CO	1995	45	M	1
Fabrizio, Dominic	29:44:34	IL	1995	27	M	2
Harding, Bill	29:46:26	TX	1995	56	M	1
Mahoney, Matt	29:49:42	FL	1995	40	M	5
Hobbs, John	29:50:22	CO	1995	50	M	12
Louth, Steve	29:52:36	CO	1995	35	M	3
Hought, Roman	29:53:53	CO	1995	47	M	1
Ainsleigh, Gordy	29:55:52	CA	1995	48	M	1
Buck, Kip	29:56:52	OR	1995	43	M	1

1996

Name	Finish Time	State	Year	Age	Sex	#Finished
Peterson, Steve	19:29:56	CO	1996	34	M	7
Ehrlich, Michael	20:22:46	CO	1996	33	M	9
Schlereth, Joe	20:38:37	CA	1996	46	M	7
Sandoval, Johnny	20:53:55	CO	1996	38	M	12
Wingate, Stan	21:12:07	CA	1996	36	M	2
Towner, Earl	21:18:33	CA	1996	46	M	1
Varela, Mario	21:48:12	CO	1996	36	M	20
Dreyer, Daniel	22:23:44	CO	1996	46	M	1
Apt, Kirk	22:24:53	CO	1996	34	M	20
Taverner, Kevin	22:25:14	CO	1996	33	M	1
Hughes, Bryan	23:12:07	CO	1996	30	M	3
Phillips, Ian	23:20:43	FL	1996	44	M	6
Nelson, Stuart	23:26:56	IA	1996	56	M	14
Swatt, Martha	23:30:11	WY	1996	34	F	2
Heinemann, Mark	23:46:04	CO	1996	39	M	7
Grobeson, Jay	23:51:08	CA	1996	35	M	11
Stavig, Bob	23:53:41	MN	1996	47	M	13
Cofer, Chuck	23:56:07	TX	1996	45	M	12
Petersen, Dale	24:03:58	CO	1996	39	M	2
Siguaw, Steve	24:09:40	CO	1996	47	M	18
Munoz, Daniel	24:12:05	CO	1996	31	M	11
Banderas, Carlos	24:16:12	CA	1996	46	M	1

Koch, Paul	24:18:23	CO	1996	28	M	1
Van Oene, Brian	24:19:02	Canada	1996	40	M	2
Curiel, Tyler	24:25:08	CO	1996	40	M	11
Taylor, Neal	24:28:18	CO	1996	33	M	12
Daus-Weber, Theresa	24:32:46	CO	1996	41	F	11
Hinte, Jeff	24:34:17	MD	1996	41	M	1
Rosenthal, Aaron	24:36:10	CO	1996	36	M	1
Berino, Jeff	24:41:14	CO	1996	38	M	10
Marchand, Joseph	24:42:18	Canada	1996	55	M	6
Feeney, Bob	24:43:40	Canada	1996	44	M	1
Wisoff, Douglas	24:44:36	CO	1996	48	M	6
Curry, Garry	24:47:59	CO	1996	42	M	25
Finkbeiner, Bill	24:52:08	CA	1996	40	M	30
Welker, Max	24:53:10	WA	1996	54	M	4
Robbins, Brick	25:39:20	CA	1996	37	M	2
Strong, David	25:48:18	CO	1996	51	M	14
Golding, Keith	25:59:13	CO	1996	35	M	6
Gordon, Scott	26:03:40	NM	1996	35	M	11
Hatfull, Rod	26:05:04	Canada	1996	36	M	1
Solomos, Nico	26:05:04	CO	1996	58	M	4
Muttke, Klaus-Dieter	26:16:04	Germany	1996	42	M	1
Haghighian, Hosni	26:27:58	TX	1996	38	F	1
Palermo, George	26:31:09	CA	1996	44	M	2
Arter, Julie	26:32:27	AZ	1996	35	F	10
Sadar, Mike	26:35:22	CO	1996	32	M	10
Khajavi, Jamshid	26:36:18	WA	1996	43	M	7
Jordan, King	26:38:00	DC	1996	53	M	11
Vaassen, Glen	26:38:40	CO	1996	37	M	3
Pence, Eric	26:40:55	CO	1996	30	M	24
Fleetham, Frank Jr.	26:45:16	WA	1996	53	M	1
Howard, Margrit	26:45:32	CO	1996	52	F	4
Barton, Michael	26:47:09	CO	1996	27	M	1
Rencoret, Ben	26:47:09	CO	1996	44	M	3
Mark, John	26:54:34	CA	1996	43	M	1
Ryan, Kelly	27:20:23	CO	1996	27	F	1
Pittenger, Will	27:27:04	CO	1996	45	M	1
Rebstock, Hans Dieter	27:27:30	Germany	1996	56	M	1

Hickman, Marge	27:31:26	KS	1996	46	F	14
Lincoln, Charlie	27:32:56	CA	1996	45	M	2
Solof, Erik	27:34:19	CO	1996	29	M	4
Ridgway, Diane	27:37:41	CO	1996	47	F	2
Fernandez, Luis	27:39:27	CO	1996	29	M	4
O'Malley, Lynn	27:40:54	WA	1996	46	F	2
Keogh, Bobby	27:42:06	NM	1996	47	M	12
Wells, Damian	27:43:46	CO	1996	26	M	1
Vargas, Eddie	27:52:33	CO	1996	33	M	1
Kocher, Wayne	27:54:20	NV	1996	59	M	1
Moha, John	28:01:18	CO	1996	52	M	2
Fisher, Jim	28:05:14	NV	1996	45	M	5
Cohn, Alan	28:06:32	CO	1996	41	M	12
Ooley, John	28:14:22	OK	1996	41	M	6
Herrera, Louie	28:14:44	CO	1996	35	M	1
Huysmar-Morris, June	28:16:29	NM	1996	40	F	1
Holloway, Gary	28:16:44	ID	1996	34	M	2
Drake, Bud	28:18:31	WY	1996	49	M	1
Tilley, Steve	28:19:29	AR	1996	49	M	2
Greiner, Dale	28:20:20	MA	1996	44	M	2
Gillespie, Richard	28:21:10	CA	1996	50	M	2
Johnson, Stuart	28:22:26	KS	1996	37	M	2
Jensen, Jeff	28:23:35	CO	1996	34	M	4
Smith, Sean	28:24:15	NM	1996	31	M	1
Bennett, Thomas	28:24:26	KY	1996	50	M	1
Hobbs, John	28:26:19	CO	1996	51	M	12
Perkins, Ron	28:27:26	CA	1996	56	M	2
Braden, Paul	28:32:09	Canada	1996	32	M	2
Mason, Margaret	28:33:58	NV	1996	50	F	2
Chlouber, Ken	28:34:53	CO	1996	57	M	14
Hickman, Mike	28:36:54	KS	1996	48	M	1
Solorio, Robert	28:38:03	CA	1996	49	M	3
Robison, Wendell	28:38:51	WY	1996	44	M	10
Morstein-Marx, Tom	28:39:38	CA	1996	44	M	1
Swenson, Alex	28:41:03	IL	1996	32	M	1
Curtis, Dick	28:44:02	CO	1996	51	M	3
Johnston, Susan	28:44:32	VT	1996	30	F	1

Daus, Donna	28:45:03	CO	1996	36	F	5
Reed, Jim	28:51:33	AZ	1996	35	M	2
Probst, Frank	28:51:37	VA	1996	53	M	2
Lucas, Phyllis	28:51:53	CO	1996	37	F	1
Christensen, Odin	28:51:53	CO	1996	48	M	10
Roueche, Dana	28:51:59	CO	1996	39	M	7
Whittemore, Dan	28:52:46	NH	1996	44	M	1
Stump, Dek	28:53:21	NY	1996	53	M	1
Snyder, Gail	28:53:24	CO	1996	37	F	4
Ballard, Jim	28:54:05	MT	1996	46	M	11
Cassidy, Kevin	28:56:05	AZ	1996	36	M	1
Creel, Norman	28:57:07	CO	1996	47	M	3
Lee, Bill	28:58:39	CO	1996	47	M	2
McLean, Amy	28:59:07	ND	1996	27	F	1
Daley, Andy	28:59:09	Canada	1996	50	M	1
Rembolt, Michael	29:03:56	WA	1996	46	M	1
Georges, Jean-Pierre	29:06:15	CO	1996	50	M	1
Doman, Wendell	29:08:03	WI	1996	37	M	1
Berdis, David	29:09:49	TX	1996	38	M	2
Ashworth, John	29:11:35	TX	1996	50	M	1
Just, David	29:14:23	MN	1996	36	M	1
Strohm, Christopher	29:15:40	CA	1996	49	M	1
Duncan, Rob	29:16:25	NM	1996	36	M	2
Rebstock, Christa	29:17:14	Germany	1996	53	F	1
Thompson, Luther	29:18:50	MN	1996	52	M	13
Boston, Rich	29:20:48	AZ	1996	48	M	1
Abramowitz, Fred	29:21:03	NM	1996	44	M	10
Kristof, Gabor	29:22:25	CO	1996	48	M	3
Crofton, Michael	29:25:20	MN	1996	46	M	2
Huntzicker, Anne	29:26:22	CO	1996	52	F	2
Curley, Dan	29:27:57	CA	1996	40	M	1
Monahan, Mike	29:31:05	CA	1996	50	M	10
Allen, Mark	29:32:19	CO	1996	33	M	2
Kaplan, Allan	29:32:53	CA	1996	40	M	1
Magill, Jim	29:33:48	CA	1996	49	M	1
Schmidt, Lee (El Burro)	29:34:44	CA	1996	56	M	8
Gathmann, Tom	29:36:10	CO	1996	44	M	1

Burgess, Todd	29:37:03	CO	1996	27	M	4
Mader, Jack	29:37:19	CO	1996	51	M	4
Dierkes, Richard	29:37:55	TX	1996	33	M	1
Louth, Steve	29:38:20	CO	1996	36	M	3
Friend, Rex	29:39:09	OK	1996	41	M	1
Martisko, Les	29:39:39	MN	1996	52	M	3
Nitzky, Alene	29:40:10	CO	1996	32	F	4
Ingalls, Frank (Jim)	29:41:08	MI	1996	51	M	6
Lindblom, John	29:41:40	UT	1996	39	M	1
Kapke, Dan	29:44:40	NE	1996	45	M	6
Enboden, Tim	29:46:04	CO	1996	36	M	4
Allen, Lisa	29:46:26	CO	1996	32	F	3
Spencer, Caroline	29:46:54	WI	1996	34	F	1
Wood, Mark	29:46:54	WI	1996	40	M	1
Mahoney, Matt	29:47:36	FL	1996	41	M	5
Laine, Richard	29:47:43	CA	1996	66	M	2
Goldman, Aaron	29:47:54	NM	1996	64	M	2
Romesberg, Ephraim	29:48:06	CA	1996	65	M	3
Morin, Tom	29:49:04	CO	1996	41	M	2
Williams, Ed	29:49:04	MO	1996	67	M	13
Burton, Lee	29:49:12	CO	1996	35	M	9
Shear, Richard	29:52:52	NY	1996	48	M	3
Nagata, Kiyoto	29:54:59	ID	1996	59	M	1
Wilkins, Kenneth	29:55:14	OK	1996	37	M	1

1997

Name	Finish Time	State	Year	Age	Sex	#Finished
Peterson, Steve	18:10:45	CO	1997	35	M	7
Madden, Kurt	19:30:59	CA	1997	41	M	4
Leck, Dennis	20:59:05	CO	1997	36	M	1
Varela, Mario	21:23:56	CO	1997	37	M	20
Apt, Kirk	21:28:15	CO	1997	35	M	20
Kulak, Joseph	21:35:55	CO	1997	29	M	12
Lisak, Mark**	21:41:37	CO	1997	40	M	2
Wilcox, David	21:54:18	CO	1997	35	M	8
Lundy, Kevin	21:58:09	CA	1997	42	M	1
Heinemann, Mark	22:07:02	CO	1997	40	M	7

Holmes, Todd	22:26:54	CO	1997	41	M	12
Ives, Art	22:36:57	CO	1997	42	M	3
Curiel, Tyler	22:42:28	CO	1997	41	M	11
Golding, Keith	22:47:13	CO	1997	36	M	6
Grobeson, Jay	22:50:52	CA	1997	36	M	11
Mattingly, Dow	22:53:42	CA	1997	46	M	1
Gordon, Scott	22:54:59	NM	1997	36	M	11
Boggess, Edward	23:07:10	CO	1997	39	M	2
Wingate, Stan	23:22:33	CA	1997	37	M	2
Wisoff, Douglas	23:31:50	CO	1997	49	M	6
Munoz, Daniel	23:51:28	AR	1997	32	M	11
Stavig, Bob	23:59:44	MN	1997	48	M	13
Taylor, Neal	24:01:45	CO	1997	33	M	12
Solof, Erik	24:06:50	CO	1997	30	M	4
Crompton, Charles	24:07:46	CA	1997	49	M	1
Arter, Julie	24:08:07	AZ	1997	36	F	10
Gasson, Larry	24:21:20	CA	1997	41	M	2
Phillips, Ian	24:23:54	FL	1997	45	M	6
Deupree, Chisholm	24:24:30	OK	1997	31	M	11
Berino, Jeff	24:29:23	CO	1997	39	M	10
Sadar, Mike	24:32:17	CO	1997	33	M	10
Jordan, King	24:41:05	DC	1997	54	M	11
Kadlecek, John	24:48:13	CO	1997	40	M	5
Perkins, Bill	24:52:36	CO	1997	37	M	1
Frye-Krier, Miles	24:52:59	FL	1997	45	M	7
Curry, Garry	24:55:19	CO	1997	43	M	25
Hampton, Don	24:57:37	MI	1997	57	M	1
Crofton, Michael	25:07:47	MN	1997	47	M	2
Kesend, Othon	25:13:59	CO	1997	52	M	2
Laster, Bill	25:36:29	AR	1997	48	M	14
Schreiber, Craig	25:51:45	CO	1997	38	M	1
Cohn, Alan	25:58:19	CO	1997	42	M	12
White, Kathy	25:59:11	CO	1997	46	F	1
Shivers, Regis	25:59:30	OH	1997	48	M	2
Brunson, Greg	26:05:06	CO	1997	37	M	1
Clarke, Chris	26:06:05	CO	1997	40	M	7
Fiala, Jan	26:08:22	NM	1997	44	M	1

Rhodes, Randy	26:10:31	CO	1997	47	M	2
Mazaud, Jean Paul	26:41:21	CA	1997	45	M	1
Johnson, Jeff	26:43:35	UT	1997	27	M	1
Strong, David	26:44:30	CO	1997	52	M	14
Dorgan, Jason	26:46:59	WI	1997	31	M	4
Robison, Wendell	26:52:30	WY	1997	45	M	10
Cofer, Chuck	26:52:31	TX	1997	46	M	12
Thompson, Luther	26:52:45	MN	1997	52	M	13
Siguaw, Steve	26:56:40	CO	1997	48	M	18
Wright, Ron	27:05:56	CO	1997	50	M	9
Blumberg, Kurt	27:06:34	CO	1997	51	M	2
Noll, Tom	27:11:00	ID	1997	42	M	2
Stevenson, Jeff	27:17:40	CA	1997	51	M	6
Litus, Greg	27:18:12	CO	1997	37	M	1
Finkbeiner, Bill	27:20:21	CA	1997	41	M	30
Gains, John	27:23:30	CO	1997	34	M	2
Goss, Lance	27:29:29	CA	1997	52	M	2
Caldwell, Valerie	27:32:39	NM	1997	33	F	4
Scheefer, David	27:37:50	CO	1997	46	M	2
Ross, Ronald	27:38:09	OH	1997	39	M	1
Hutcheson, Ian	27:42:38	Canada	1997	41	M	1
Jensen, Jeff	27:43:36	CO	1997	35	M	4
LaVelle, Michael	27:43:56	CA	1997	41	M	1
Schicktanz, Klaus	27:45:30	Germany	1997	45	M	1
Sayers, Kevin	27:55:23	MD	1997	38	M	2
Ballard, Jim	28:10:18	MT	1997	47	M	11
Sommerfeldt, Drew	28:11:14	Canada	1997	45	M	1
Lincoln, Charlie	28:12:40	CA	1997	47	M	2
Reese, Steve	28:14:27	CO	1997	47	M	1
Wightman, Rick	28:16:22	AZ	1997	41	M	1
McBride, Myrrl	28:18:07	NM	1997	44	M	3
Swatt, Martha	28:18:19	WY	1997	35	F	2
Black, Carson	28:18:38	CO	1997	56	M	2
Johnson, Gregg	28:26:08	IL	1997	50	M	1
Brueland, Harold	28:26:44	NY	1997	54	M	1
Roberts, Seth	28:30:37	MA	1997	45	M	1
Sunderland, Mike	28:33:13	MN	1997	38	M	1

Whorton, Randy	28:35:22	CO	1997	36	M	1
Grosvenor, Paul	28:36:06	NM	1997	40	M	1
Scholl, Todd	28:39:10	CO	1997	38	M	1
Farkas, Harry	28:40:32	CA	1997	35	M	1
Lederer, Adam	28:41:05	CO	1997	32	M	1
Probst, Frank	28:41:12	VA	1997	54	M	2
Hickman, Jason	28:43:15	CO	1997	25	M	1
Stimac, Larry	28:44:14	MN	1997	48	M	3
Horadam, Donny	28:47:45	TX	1997	42	M	2
Sorensen, Lorraine	28:48:03	UT	1997	47	F	1
Greer, John	28:50:05	AZ	1997	38	M	8
Gallegos, Donald	28:51:10	CO	1997	37	M	1
Foraker, Greg	28:51:35	CO	1997	38	M	2
Pedretti, Robert	28:53:07	CO	1997	33	M	1
Witwer, John	28:55:27	CO	1997	39	M	1
Dunn, Randall	28:56:11	CO	1997	42	M	5
Horton, Roch	28:58:51	CO	1997	39	M	2
Shott, Ann	28:58:55	CO	1997	38	F	1
Cunningham, Ronald	29:00:27	OR	1997	48	M	2
Sigley, Guy	29:04:54	CO	1997	39	M	1
Chlouber, Ken	29:07:17	CO	1997	58	M	14
Hausdoerffer, William	29:08:57	CA	1997	27	M	1
Gaul, Larry	29:10:44	CO	1997	42	M	1
Snyder, Scott	29:11:32	CO	1997	42	M	9
Jacolenne, Michael	29:12:33	OH	1997	45	M	1
Harmer, Burgess	29:13:06	OR	1997	55	M	7
Vigus, Dale	29:14:15	CA	1997	51	M	1
Bradham, Art	29:18:15	SC	1997	40	M	1
Homelvig, Pat	29:19:20	CO	1997	38	M	5
Garcia, Frank	29:20:52	TX	1997	40	M	1
Donoff, Mick	29:22:03	CA	1997	53	M	3
Michels, Danna	29:23:29	CO	1997	35	F	1
Dwyer, Robert Jr.	29:23:40	CA	1997	33	M	1
Steinacker, Greg	29:24:08	MN	1997	40	M	3
Hodde, Jason	29:24:50	IN	1997	27	M	1
Roueche, Dana	29:25:27	CO	1997	40	M	7
Holloway, Gary	29:25:47	ID	1997	35	M	2

Williams, Ed	29:27:31	MO	1997	68	M	13
Lister, Bevin	29:28:28	Canada	1997	47	M	1
Deupree, Harry	29:31:03	OK	1997	59	M	12
Honzak, Ingrid	29:31:57	OH	1997	48	F	1
Daus-Weber, Theresa	29:32:49	CO	1997	42	F	11
Romesberg, Ephraim	29:32:57	CA	1997	66	M	3
Monahan, Mike	29:33:34	CA	1997	51	M	10
Hobbs, John	29:33:56	CO	1997	52	M	12
Smith, James	29:34:16	CO	1997	42	M	1
Hurley, Jamie	29:35:43	OH	1997	29	M	2
McElligott, Tony	29:35:43	IL	1997	44	M	1
Rochelle, Rick	29:37:00	CO	1997	33	M	1
Fowler, John	29:38:02	NM	1997	55	M	1
Bollig, Jerry	29:39:06	WI	1997	48	M	1
Moser, Jane	29:39:06	WI	1997	38	M	1
Fernandez, Luis	29:39:40	CO	1997	30	M	4
Marston, Bob	29:40:14	MO	1997	46	M	1
Krall, Teresa	29:42:37	CO	1997	35	F	2
Wilkins, Rebecca	29:44:20	CO	1997	39	F	1
Dahl, Joel	29:45:27	CO	1997	39	M	3
Close, Bill	29:47:31	WA	1997	37	M	1
Martisko, Les	29:48:23	MN	1997	53	M	3
Kroeger, Al	29:49:00	CO	1997	37	M	2
Burgess, Todd	29:49:25	CO	1997	28	M	4
Draxler, Leon	29:49:33	WA	1997	55	M	2
Ingalls, Frank (Jim)	29:52:59	AZ	1997	52	M	6
Woestehoff, Keith	29:56:27	CO	1997	48	M	1
Parker, Ian	29:56:51	CA	1997	46	M	2

1998

Name	Finish Time	State	Year	Age	Sex	#Finished
Peterson, Steve	18:29:21	CO	1998	36	M	7
Apt, Kirk	19:42:53	CO	1998	36	M	20
Carlson, John	19:49:54	AK	1998	41	M	1
Seminoff, Tim	20:09:26	UT	1998	40	M	3
Barger, Dan	20:23:37	CA	1998	33	M	3
Kulak, Joseph	20:23:50	England	1998	30	M	12

Holmes, Todd	20:27:50	CO	1998	42	M	12
Clarke, Chris	20:44:47	CO	1998	41	M	7
Trason, Ann	20:58:32	CA	1998	37	F	4
Simonsen, Rick	21:10:54	CA	1998	37	M	1
Anderson, Nate	21:25:48	CO	1998	40	M	2
Kadlecek, John	21:35:43	CO	1998	41	M	5
Hewitt, Tim	21:37:21	PA	1998	43	M	2
D'Onofrio-Wood, Kathy	21:41:48	CA	1998	34	F	5
Turner, Glen	21:50:03	CO	1998	38	M	4
Petersen, Dale	22:06:35	CO	1998	41	M	2
Albrecht, Randy	22:20:51	KS	1998	42	M	3
Jensen, Ken	22:20:51	UT	1998	30	M	1
Grobeson, Jay	22:23:13	CA	1998	37	M	11
Hughes, Bryan	22:27:50	CO	1998	32	M	3
Heinemann, Mark	22:59:31	CO	1998	41	M	7
Reed, Pam	23:03:07	WY	1998	37	F	6
Sandoval, Johnny	23:18:03	CO	1998	40	M	12
Byrne, Rob	23:24:20	CA	1998	40	M	1
Youngren, Robert	23:28:16	CA	1998	24	M	1
GoonPan, Peter	23:28:42	AUS	1998	39	M	1
Noll, Tom	23:29:04	ID	1998	43	M	2
Wisoff, Douglas	23:33:41	CO	1998	50	M	6
Shelafo, Steve	23:35:05	CO	1998	36	M	3
Curiel, Tyler	23:43:34	TX	1998	42	M	11
Scheefer, David	23:48:00	CO	1998	47	M	2
Ulrich, Marshall	23:48:42	CO	1998	47	M	13
Munoz, Daniel	23:51:41	CO	1998	33	M	11
Gaylord, Topher	23:52:00	CA	1998	26	M	1
Ehret, Stephanie	24:06:30	CO	1998	35	F	5
Cofer, Chuck	24:07:30	TX	1998	47	M	12
Berino, Jeff	24:08:26	CO	1998	40	M	10
Ives, Art	24:11:09	CO	1998	43	M	3
Siguaw, Steve	24:18:10	CO	1998	49	M	18
Blumberg, Kurt	24:23:35	CO	1998	52	M	2
Manning, Christopher	24:28:21	CO	1998	31	M	1
Freim, Jim	24:29:27	CO	1998	52	M	1
Landry, Dan	24:34:36	NM	1998	46	M	2

Boak, Roger	24:35:15	TX	1998	49	M	3
Mitchell, Michael	24:35:41	UT	1998	39	M	1
Arter, Julie	24:38:24	AZ	1998	37	F	10
Dorgan, Jason	24:44:09	WI	1998	32	M	4
Manley, Brian	24:45:19	CO	1998	34	M	13
Meyers, Dan	24:45:57	CA	1998	41	M	4
Romalia, Mark	24:46:44	CO	1998	39	M	1
Lee, Chip	24:48:54	CO	1998	43	M	5
Smith, Steven	24:51:20	IL	1998	35	M	1
Scott, Geoffrey	24:51:54	CT	1998	49	M	1
Coonrod, Kurt	24:52:02	NM	1998	38	M	8
Manning, Ryan	24:57:12	CA	1998	27	M	2
Varela, Mario	25:11:26	CO	1998	38	M	20
Gillis, Shawn	25:14:29	AZ	1998	33	M	1
Hobbins, Gordon	25:25:32	Canada	1998	36	M	1
Jordan, King	25:35:15	DC	1998	55	M	11
DuPlessis, Janine	25:38:15	WA	1998	43	F	2
Steward, Dan	25:53:26	CO	1998	37	M	8
Thompson, Luther	26:04:24	MN	1998	54	M	13
Finkbeiner, Bill	26:05:48	CA	1998	42	M	30
Abramowitz, Fred	26:07:41	NM	1998	46	M	10
Stephon, Michael	26:26:27	CO	1998	32	M	4
Strong, David	26:26:46	CO	1998	53	M	14
Vernon, Jim	26:30:56	CA	1998	33	M	2
Cooper, Rick	26:32:56	MT	1998	40	M	1
Hardman, Gordon	26:38:55	CO	1998	47	M	4
Knutson, Tom	26:38:55	MN	1998	48	M	6
Taylor, Neal	26:39:02	CO	1998	35	M	12
Marquer, Barbara	26:43:28	WY	1998	42	F	2
Farris, Michael	26:44:39	MN	1998	42	M	1
Van Oene, Brian	26:47:27	Canada	1998	43	M	2
Dallmann, Ed	26:49:13	MN	1998	53	M	1
Trenker, Margrit	26:58:55	CO	1998	54	F	3
Hayes, Amy	27:04:05	NM	1998	37	F	1
Cohn, Alan	27:10:43	CO	1998	43	M	12
Dunn, Randall	27:14:34	CO	1998	43	M	5
Kutcipal, David	27:17:13	CO	1998	29	M	1

Curry, Garry	27:23:33	CO	1998	44	M	25
Hughes, Jill	27:25:38	CO	1998	33	F	2
Ramsey, Philip	27:25:53	CA	1998	32	M	1
Berdis, David	27:26:34	TX	1998	40	M	2
Horadam, Donny	27:28:06	TX	1998	43	M	2
Khajavi, Jamshid	27:31:47	WA	1998	45	M	7
Lindquist, Rick	27:32:41	MN	1998	42	M	1
Sadar, Mike	27:34:39	CO	1998	34	M	10
Eppelman, Scott	27:36:07	TX	1998	31	M	1
Huber, David	27:36:39	CO	1998	47	M	3
Wagner, John	27:37:03	WI	1998	49	M	2
James III, Ellis	27:38:02	AR	1998	41	M	1
McBride, Myrrl	27:38:53	NM	1998	45	M	3
Frye, Barbara	27:54:12	FL	1998	43	F	2
Wright, Ron	27:55:05	CO	1998	51	M	9
Graubins, Garett	27:56:00	CO	1998	25	M	5
Urbana, John	27:56:00	CO	1998	33	M	1
Kristof, Gabor	27:56:54	CO	1998	50	M	3
Keogh, Bobby	27:58:49	NM	1998	49	M	12
Dulin, Colleen	28:02:33	VA	1998	29	F	1
Cruse, Pam	28:05:50	CO	1998	39	F	1
Hewitt, Neil	28:07:26	TX	1998	37	M	1
Laster, Bill	28:08:24	AR	1998	49	M	14
McEllhiney, Loretta	28:11:33	CO	1998	34	F	2
Urbanek, Terri	28:14:38	CO	1998	41	F	1
Christian, Jack	28:16:40	OK	1998	45	M	6
Fisher, Jim	28:20:29	NM	1998	47	M	5
Gebhart, Susan	28:23:34	CO	1998	43	F	5
Daus-Weber, Theresa	28:25:16	CO	1998	43	F	11
Kraut, Thane	28:26:45	CO	1998	35	M	1
Hughes, Richard	28:28:30	NM	1998	44	M	1
Snyder, Scott	28:29:10	CO	1998	43	M	9
Beine, Jo Ann	28:31:47	CO	1998	42	F	3
Dudley, Peter	28:32:47	CO	1998	43	M	3
Silver, Steven	28:32:47	TX	1998	50	M	4
Krall, Teresa	28:34:58	CO	1998	37	F	2
Brunetto, Thomas	28:35:30	NJ	1998	38	M	1

Fisher, Doug	28:36:03	TX	1998	36	M	2
Henslee, Gary	28:37:25	CA	1998	47	M	1
Kapke, Robert	28:37:36	NE	1998	51	M	5
Harmer, Burgess	28:38:51	NV	1998	56	M	7
Wilkie, Jose	28:39:08	KY	1998	34	M	5
Chlouber, Ken	28:39:38	CO	1998	59	M	14
Andrews, Bill	28:40:48	CA	1998	46	M	1
Scott, Douglas	28:41:49	WI	1998	46	M	1
Marchand, Joseph	28:43:56	Canada	1998	57	M	6
Rossman, Mitchell	28:44:51	MN	1998	42	M	1
Bradley, Marv	28:44:58	CO	1998	59	M	2
Ballard, Jim	28:47:55	MT	1998	48	M	11
Bashor, Cheri	28:48:10	MT	1998	44	F	1
Robertson, Craig	28:48:44	TX	1998	38	M	6
Barnes, Christopher	28:49:45	CO	1998	30	M	1
Pann, Terry	28:50:20	WI	1998	38	M	1
Lillie, Annette	28:50:42	CO	1998	30	F	2
Burrell, Buzz	28:50:53	CO	1998	46	M	1
Fortune, Gary	28:51:26	MI	1998	48	M	1
Trammell, Kerry	28:51:37	TN	1998	42	M	1
Kesend, Othon	28:52:01	CO	1998	53	M	2
Barnes, Molly	28:52:07	CO	1998	29	F	6
Mettler, Jack	28:54:48	WY	1998	51	M	1
Burton, Lee	28:55:36	CO	1998	37	M	9
Linzbichler, Helmut	28:56:52	Aus	1998	56	M	1
Stavig, Bob	28:58:33	MN	1998	49	M	13
Stark, Ed	29:01:33	MA	1998	52	M	2
Mignery, Edward	29:02:22	WY	1998	52	M	1
Moore, Matthew	29:03:15	CA	1998	41	M	3
Czecholinski, Al	29:04:05	WI	1998	51	M	1
Pence, Eric	29:04:54	CO	1998	32	M	24
Montgomery, Allen	29:06:10	SC	1998	59	M	1
Maples, W.C.	29:07:36	CA	1998	34	M	1
Weber, Jonathan	29:09:44	UT	1998	45	M	1
Mastin, Kevin	29:10:30	CO	1998	33	M	3
Miller, Geoff	29:10:45	CO	1998	40	M	4
From, James	29:11:41	GA	1998	27	M	1

Bainbridge, Richard	29:14:46	CO	1998	35	M	1
Esser, Walt	29:16:13	NC	1998	59	M	1
Abram, Jeff	29:18:04	CO	1998	44	M	1
Roueche, Dana	29:18:33	CO	1998	41	M	7
Gleman, Michael	29:19:03	FL	1998	50	M	1
Greer, John	29:19:44	AZ	1998	39	M	8
Kurth, Todd	29:19:58	NM	1998	35	M	1
Kahn, Phil	29:20:04	CO	1998	45	M	11
Nitzky, Alene	29:20:21	CO	1998	34	F	4
Stevenson, Jeff	29:21:11	CA	1998	52	M	6
Platko, Donald	29:21:20	CT	1998	56	M	1
Robertson, Joy	29:22:53	CO	1998	40	F	4
Halvorson, Steven	29:22:58	CO	1998	41	M	2
Hobbs, John	29:23:35	CO	1998	53	M	12
Daus, Donna	29:24:27	CO	1998	38	F	5
Zeif, Jonathan	29:25:42	CO	1998	45	M	11
Thomas, Michael	29:26:35	CO	1998	36	M	2
Richmeier, Debra	29:26:42	CO	1998	38	F	2
Orr, Roberta	29:27:34	AR	1998	31	F	1
Adolf, Don	29:28:43	CA	1998	61	M	3
Purdy, Bruce	29:28:44	MI	1998	42	M	1
Palazzo, Nicholas	29:28:57	NY	1998	51	M	1
Opsahl, Richard	29:29:14	NY	1998	66	M	1
Rafferty, Scott	29:31:42	DC	1998	42	M	1
Kaufman, Jacqui	29:32:33	CO	1998	46	F	1
Weix, Kathy	29:33:19	WI	1998	49	F	1
Romero, Jim	29:35:33	CO	1998	58	M	2
Keough, Ian	29:36:16	MI	1998	21	M	1
Burt, Steven	29:37:18	WA	1998	47	M	3
Kapke, Dan	29:38:28	NE	1998	47	M	6
Binder, Al**	29:38:56	CO	1998	53	M	13
Dana, Joe	29:39:29	OR	1998	62	M	1
Limacher, Rich	29:40:14	IL	1998	48	M	1
Jones, Errol	29:40:27	CA	1998	48	M	2
Sayers, Kevin	29:40:50	MD	1998	39	M	2
Yanacheck, Tim	29:41:46	WI	1998	50	M	1
Olson, Noelle	29:42:19	MN	1998	39	F	1

Moyer, Bill	29:42:41	MI	1998	49	M	1
Martisko, Les	29:43:11	MN	1998	54	M	3
Pike, Tyler	29:43:34	China	1998	26	M	1
Calvert, Randy	29:44:22	NV	1998	45	M	1
Perry, Dale	29:45:47	CO	1998	41	M	4
Morin, Tom	29:45:56	CO	1998	43	M	2
Spranger, Kurt	29:46:03	CO	1998	35	M	1
Schlett, Stefan	29:46:06	Germany	1998	36	M	1
Lavicky, Candy	29:46:45	CO	1998	38	F	1
Masters, Anthony	29:47:21	KS	1998	42	M	1
Burgess, Todd	29:47:44	CO	1998	29	M	4
Korngold, Jamie	29:49:28	OH	1998	32	F	1
Martinez, Mario	29:49:28	TX	1998	46	M	1
Ransom, Angie	29:50:11	AR	1998	48	F	1
Simmons, Stephen	29:53:55	WV	1998	32	M	1
Bear, Jan	29:56:30	NM	1998	42	M	4
Dean, Jeffrey	29:59:12	CO	1998	41	M	1
Hughes, Roy	29:59:52	CO	1998	46	M	1

1999

Name	Finish Time	State	Year	Age	Sex	#Finished
Peterson, Steve	18:47:31	CO	1999	37	M	7
Pozner, Jay	19:22:09	CO	1999	M2	M	2
Boggess, Edward	19:55:05	CO	1999	M4	M	2
Kulak, Joseph	20:05:02	England	1999	31	M	12
Poolheco, Dennis	20:34:28	AZ	1999	38	M	3
Garcia, James	21:11:57	MA	1999	M4	M	1
Apt, Kirk	21:32:18	CO	1999	M3	M	20
Hirst, Scott	21:35:40	CO	1999	M3	M	1
Clarke, Chris	21:41:38	CO	1999	M4	M	7
Kadlecek, John	21:54:59	CO	1999	42	M	5
Gordon, Scott	22:00:00	NM	1999	38	M	11
McIntosh, Amanda	22:05:22	TX	1999	34	F	3
Rumon, Kevin	22:12:57	CA	1999	M3	M	1
Ehret, Stephanie	22:17:02	CO	1999	F3	F	5
Matthys, Ignace	22:41:40	Belgium	1999	M4	M	1
Caldwell, Valerie	23:00:00	NM	1999	F3	F	4

Anderson, Nate	23:00:11	CO	1999	M4	M	2
Holmes, Todd	23:18:14	CO	1999	40	M	12
Heinemann, Mark	23:35:26	CO	1999	42	M	7
Wisoff, Douglas	23:35:26	CO	1999	51	M	6
Sandoval, Johnny	23:39:15	CO	1999	41	M	12
Sheridan, Phil	23:47:14	KS	1999	M4	M	2
Berino, Jeff	23:47:41	CO	1999	M4	M	10
Coonrod, Kurt	23:50:49	NM	1999	M3	M	8
Edwards, Mark	23:56:12	TX	1999	M4	M	1
Varela, Mario	23:57:24	CO	1999	39	M	20
Munoz, Daniel	23:58:00	CO	1999	34	M	11
Flores, Raul	24:10:27	KS	1999	M4	M	10
Grobeson, Jay	24:12:14	CA	1999	38	M	11
Fulkerson, Robert	24:13:39	CO	1999	M4	M	1
Stephon, Michael	24:17:18	CO	1999	M3	M	4
Mastin, Kevin	24:22:46	CO	1999	M3	M	3
Thedinga, Todd	24:22:59	NY	1999	M2	M	1
Taylor, Neal	24:24:30	CO	1999	M3	M	12
Nelson, Stuart	24:26:25	CO	1999	59	M	14
Chapman, Marcus	24:28:35	NH	1999	M2	M	1
Rosenfeld, Daniel	24:29:02	CO	1999	M3	M	1
Murray, Todd	24:33:43	CO	1999	M3	M	2
Bear, Jan	24:35:25	NM	1999	M4	M	4
Benike, Jim	24:39:32	MN	1999	M4	M	3
Steward, Dan	24:39:35	CO	1999	M3	M	8
Skaden, Erik	24:40:47	NE	1999	M2	M	2
Ringstad, Curtis	24:40:49	OR	1999	M4	M	1
Welsh, Jeffrey	24:41:36	NC	1999	44	M	13
Vaassen, Glen	24:45:02	CO	1999	M4	M	3
Horton, Roch	24:46:47	CO	1999	M4	M	2
Vernon, Jim	24:47:41	CO	1999	M3	M	2
Turner, Glen	24:53:59	CO	1999	M3	M	4
Dunn, Randall	24:54:43	CO	1999	M4	M	5
Perry, Lyman	24:59:18	HI	1999	M3	M	1
Blewett, Earl	25:01:53	OK	1999	M3	M	1
Case, Jill	25:19:22	CO	1999	F4	F	4
Phillips, Ian	25:23:07	SC	1999	M4	M	6

Garrison, Tom	25:23:17	NM	1999	40	M	9
Megaffin, J. Kim	25:35:28	Canada	1999	M4	M	1
Laster, Bill	25:35:33	AR	1999	50	M	14
Pence, Eric	25:37:17	CO	1999	33	M	24
Snyder, Scott	25:37:43	CO	1999	44	M	9
Wagner, John	25:54:27	WI	1999	M5	M	2
Hoffman, Kathleen	25:54:52	CO	1999	F3	F	1
Jensen, Karl	25:55:22	Canada	1999	49	M	3
Moha, John	25:55:29	CO	1999	55	M	2
Martell, Gregg	25:57:15	WY	1999	42	M	6
Keogh, Bobby	26:01:34	NM	1999	50	M	12
Dodge, Ben	26:13:15	CO	1999	M3	M	1
Moore, Travis	26:13:15	CO	1999	M3	M	1
Wilkey, William	26:38:07	WI	1999	M4	M	1
McEllhieny, Loretta	26:41:23	CO	1999	F3	F	2
Finkbeiner, Bill	26:47:13	CA	1999	M4	M	30
Gebhart, Susan	26:49:40	CO	1999	44	F	5
Hawk, Terence	26:51:26	OH	1999	M4	M	1
Knutson, Tom	26:51:47	MN	1999	M4	M	6
Moyer, Jason	27:00:01	OR	1999	M2	M	1
Mahr, Paul	27:12:41	NM	1999	M3	M	1
Pirogowicz, David	27:14:15	CA	1999	M4	M	1
DuPlessis, Janine	27:16:40	WA	1999	F4	F	2
Little, Jerry	27:17:16	CO	1999	M3	M	1
Frank, Glen	27:19:04	OH	1999	M3	M	1
Jarvis, Wade	27:21:31	Canada	1999	M3	M	9
Perry, Dale	27:23:22	CO	1999	M4	M	4
Morelock, John	27:23:41	OR	1999	M5	M	1
Ehrlich, Michael	27:23:42	CO	1999	M3	M	9
Robertson, Craig	27:34:25	TX	1999	M3	M	6
Fortune, David	27:34:49	CO	1999	M3	M	1
Taylor, Dana	27:37:58	CA	1999	M3	M	2
Thompson, Luther	27:40:57	MN	1999	M5	M	13
Staley, Marcus	27:41:08	FL	1999	M2	M	2
Hammons, Rodney	27:42:43	LA	1999	M4	M	1
Daus-Weber, Theresa	27:44:00	CO	1999	F4	F	11
McCarthy, Willis	27:44:34	CA	1999	M4	M	2

Cohn, Alan	27:47:12	CO	1999	M4	M	12
Hodges, Eric	27:47:51	CA	1999	50	M	2
Herr, Dennis	27:51:56	VA	1999	M5	M	5
Siguaw, Steve	27:53:03	CO	1999	50	M	18
Strong, David	27:55:39	CO	1999	M5	M	14
Kelley, Rick	27:57:03	AZ	1999	M4	M	1
Deupree, Chisholm	28:00:29	OK	1999	M3	M	11
Ulrich, Marshall	28:04:31	CO	1999	M4	M	13
Zeif, Jonathan	28:04:57	CO	1999	46	M	11
Dudley, Peter	28:06:24	CO	1999	44	M	3
Martin, Robert	28:06:54	MA	1999	M3	M	1
Hersey, David	28:07:21	CO	1999	M4	M	2
Montoya, David	28:08:34	CO	1999	M3	M	1
Jordan, King	28:09:56	DC	1999	56	M	11
Jensen, Stan	28:17:03	CA	1999	M4	M	1
Manley, Brian	28:17:33	CO	1999	35	M	13
Kutcipal, Carin	28:19:20	CO	1999	F2	F	1
Daus, Donna	28:19:46	CO	1999	F3	F	5
Frith, Stuart	28:21:03	CO	1999	M4	M	1
Dailey, Bruce	28:21:48	CT	1999	M2	M	7
Curry, Garry	28:22:26	CO	1999	45	M	25
Schancer, Gary	28:23:18	NM	1999	M4	M	1
Allen, Jackie	28:26:00	CO	1999	F3	F	1
Allen, Mark	28:27:01	CO	1999	M3	M	2
Jess, Carl	28:29:14	NM	1999	40	M	4
Guthrie, Mike	28:31:16	WA	1999	M3	M	1
Wilkie, Jose	28:34:35	KY	1999	M3	M	5
Redland, Rickie	28:36:14	WY	1999	45	F	6
Morris, Mark	28:37:30	TX	1999	M4	M	3
Matulionis, Andrew	28:37:57	MT	1999	M3	M	1
Pugsley, Steve	28:38:35	CO	1999	M3	M	1
Carpenter, Bob	28:38:56	CA	1999	M6	M	1
Conover, Lisa	28:39:37	WI	1999	F4	F	1
Hickman, Marge	28:40:56	KS	1999	M4	F	14
Lagace, Maynard	28:41:08	MN	1999	M5	M	1
Miller, Sandee	28:41:41	CO	1999	F4	F	2
Manning, Ryan	28:42:08	SD	1999	M2	M	2

Engel, Jay	28:43:17	CO	1999	M3	M	1
Escobar, Luis	28:43:27	CA	1999	M3	M	1
Wunsch, Andy	28:44:15	CO	1999	M3	M	1
Halpin, Nancy	28:45:50	NM	1999	38	F	4
Tavernini, Robert	28:49:15	TX	1999	31	M	5
Greco, Kenneth	28:49:23	AZ	1999	32	M	2
Pettigrew, Jeff	28:50:35	CA	1999	M3	M	1
Weaver, Cort	28:54:15	CO	1999	M4	M	3
Rideg, William	28:55:29	MT	1999	M3	M	2
Stimac, Larry	28:57:32	MN	1999	M5	M	3
Griffith, Scott	28:59:33	IL	1999	M3	M	1
Gardner, Susan	29:00:19	NM	1999	F3	F	1
Dorband, Wayne	29:02:32	CO	1999	M4	M	1
Dunlap, Ron	29:02:37	CA	1999	M6	M	4
Burrows, Steve	29:05:01	Canada	1999	M4	M	1
Collins, Jeff	29:05:54	CA	1999	M4	M	2
Stavig, Bob	29:05:59	MN	1999	50	M	13
Grooms, Jeanie	29:08:07	CO	1999	43	F	6
Burt, Steven	29:11:13	WA	1999	M4	M	3
Christensen, Odin	29:11:27	CO	1999	M5	M	10
Chapman, Tom	29:12:32	OR	1999	M4	M	1
Robison, Wendell	29:13:56	WY	1999	M4	M	10
Quinlan, Andrea	29:14:22	Canada	1999	F3	F	1
LeBoeuf, Richard	29:14:23	MA	1999	M4	M	1
McInturff, Douglas	29:14:50	CO	1999	M3	M	2
Roueche, Dana	29:14:50	CO	1999	M4	M	7
Trenker, Margrit	29:15:08	CO	1999	F5	F	3
Walsh, Buck	29:15:27	WV	1999	M5	M	1
Cantu, Ruben	29:16:02	CA	1999	M5	M	1
Burton, Lee	29:20:02	CO	1999	M3	M	9
Williams, Ed	29:21:49	MO	1999	70	M	13
Bailey, Skip	29:22:14	CO	1999	M4	M	4
Schmidt, Lee (El Burro)	29:24:13	CA	1999	59	M	8
Hobbs, John	29:25:10	CO	1999	54	M	12
Justin, Mick	29:25:27	MN	1999	M5	M	1
Newton, Jim	29:25:55	TX	1999	52	M	3
Michler, Ruth	29:26:03	TX	1999	F3	F	1

Allmon, Butch	29:26:07	TX	1999	M4	M	5
Craven, Brent	29:26:29	UT	1999	M4	M	3
Monahan, Mike	29:30:16	CA	1999	53	M	10
Buller, Kurt	29:31:20	NV	1999	M3	M	1
Enboden, Tim	29:32:29	CO	1999	M3	M	4
Huber, David "Bruce"	29:32:34	CO	1999	48	M	3
Ballard, Jim	29:33:13	MT	1999	M4	M	11
Catalano, Al	29:33:36	MA	1999	M4	M	2
Lester, Jere	29:34:54	CO	1999	F3	F	1
Valenta, Mike	29:35:54	CO	1999	M4	M	2
Barnes, Molly	29:36:11	CO	1999	F3	F	6
Rayburn, Bob	29:38:56	CO	1999	M4	M	1
Nowlin, Melvin	29:39:39	CO	1999	M3	M	1
Duncan, Rob	29:40:07	NM	1999	M3	M	2
Abshire, Danny	29:40:42	CO	1999	M4	M	2
Sharp, Kevin	29:40:49	OH	1999	M3	M	1
Kapke, Dan	29:41:06	NE	1999	M4	M	6
Schnitzius, Thomas	29:41:44	IL	1999	46	M	11
Parker, Scott	29:42:22	AL	1999	M3	M	1
Nakauchi-Hawn, Laurie	29:42:35	CO	1999	F2	F	12
Magee, Peter-Michael	29:43:05	FL	1999	M5	M	1
Benson, Katie	29:43:15	CO	1999	F2	F	3
Felton, Rick	29:43:22	CO	1999	M4	M	1
O'Neil, Jim	29:43:58	MT	1999	M5	M	1
Ingalls, Jim	29:45:54	IN	1999	M5	M	6
Tuller, Jr., Robert	29:46:06	NY	1999	M3	M	1
Sheehan, Greg	29:46:10	CA	1999	M4	M	1
Lillie, Annette	29:47:20	CO	1999	F3	F	2
Denove, Peter	29:47:50	TX	1999	M3	M	1
Steele, Eric	29:48:19	KS	1999	M3	M	1
Horung, Matt	29:50:36	CO	1999	M4	M	1
Joline, Louis	29:50:45	MO	1999	M6	M	1
Jackson, Jr., George	29:50:50	CO	1999	M4	M	1
Nelson, Scott	29:51:52	UT	1999	M3	M	1
Goldman, Aaron	29:52:26	NM	1999	67	M	2
Kamm, Ulrich	29:52:37	CO	1999	M5	M	2
Draxler, Leon	29:52:38	WA	1999	57	M	2

Salhelm, Karsten	29:53:16	AZ	1999	M6	M	1
Thouvenelle, Jon	29:54:47	CO	1999	M4	M	3
Washburn, Jeff	29:54:54	MA	1999	M4	M	1
Sobal, Melissa Lee	29:55:01	CO	1999	F4	F	4
Caldwell, Elizabeth	29:55:13	CO	1999	F4	F	1
Siff, Barry	29:55:13	CO	1999	M4	M	1
Parker, Ian	29:58:00	CA	1999	M4	M	2
Peebles, Debbie	29:58:47	TX	1999	F4	F	1
Miller, Morris	29:58:47	AR	1999	M4	M	1

2000

Name	Finish Time	State	Year	Age	Sex	#Finished
Ricklefs, Chad	18:07:57	CO	2000	33	M	2
Peterson, Steve	18:31:05	CO	2000	38	M	7
Shilling, Kevin	20:11:41	CO	2000	32	M	2
Kulak, Joe	20:31:37	England	2000	32	M	12
Apt, Kirk	21:36:10	CO	2000	38	M	20
Ives, Art	21:36:10	CO	2000	45	M	3
Clarke, Chris	22:08:06	CO	2000	43	M	7
McIntosh, Amanda	22:16:17	TX	2000	35	F	3
Gordon, Scott	22:26:31	NM	2000	39	M	11
Caldwell, Valerie	22:40:34	NM	2000	36	F	4
Coonrod, Kurt	22:49:02	NM	2000	40	M	8
Kadlecek, John	23:14:31	CO	2000	43	M	5
Blaugrund, Benjamin	23:17:56	NY	2000	27	M	1
Ehret, Stephanie	23:19:29	CO	2000	37	F	5
Wisoff, Douglas	23:24:56	CO	2000	52	M	6
Mitchell, Stephen	23:34:07	CO	2000	44	M	3
Jones, Chuck	23:35:39	CA	2000	41	M	2
Wilcox, David	23:36:01	CO	2000	38	M	8
Smith, Jeffrey	23:36:35	NM	2000	35	M	1
Welsh, Jeffrey	23:42:27	NC	2000	45	M	13
Hayes, Tom	23:51:27	MT	2000	49	M	1
Case, Jill	23:53:08	CO	2000	41	F	4
Frye-Krier, Miles	23:53:43	FL	2000	48	M	7
Garrison, Tom	24:00:57	NM	2000	41	M	9
Flores, Raul	24:08:48	KS	2000	44	M	10

Pence, Eric	24:16:58	CO	2000	34	M	24
Berino, Jeff	24:18:53	CO	2000	42	M	10
Barlow, Stephen	24:19:51	TX	2000	39	M	2
Runyan, Janet	24:22:28	CO	2000	41	F	2
Varela, Mario	24:28:15	CO	2000	40	M	20
Nelson, Stuart	24:31:43	CO	2000	60	M	14
Desort, George	24:39:25	CO	2000	30	M	1
Petroni, Bruno	24:49:07	Switzerland	2000	38	M	1
Heinemann, Mark	24:54:49	CO	2000	43	M	7
Bond, Bert	24:56:50	CO	2000	46	M	2
Kern, Kristen	24:57:49	NM	2000	35	M	10
Moroney, Elizabeth	25:12:06	MT	2000	40	F	1
Laster, Bill	25:24:23	CO	2000	51	M	14
Martell, Gregg	25:33:44	WY	2000	43	M	6
Isler, Randy	25:47:32	NM	2000	43	M	2
Oberheide, Jim	25:55:51	CO	2000	55	M	5
Loman, Emily	26:03:23	CO	2000	24	F	2
Deupree, Chisholm	26:05:50	OK	2000	34	M	11
Thiry, George	26:07:54	Belgium	2000	44	M	1
Grobeson, Jay	26:14:32	CA	2000	39	M	11
Bailey, Raymond	26:20:30	AR	2000	43	M	3
Curiel, Tyler	26:22:53	TX	2000	44	M	11
Van Tiel, Jill	26:30:15	CO	2000	36	F	2
Ackerman, Robin	26:33:42	CO	2000	31	F	1
Dewey, Torin	26:35:48	CO	2000	36	M	1
Baker*, Keith	26:39:45	NM	2000	45	M	1
Gebhart, Susan	26:44:16	CO	2000	45	F	5
Cohn, Alan	26:49:32	CO	2000	45	M	12
Scott, Todd	26:51:33	MT	2000	36	M	11
Biggers, Ron	26:52:42	CO	2000	54	M	3
Odell, Dan	26:55:48	CO	2000	39	M	1
Adams, Tim	26:58:42	MT	2000	48	M	2
Bartzen, Gene	26:59:25	WI	2000	46	M	10
Fisher, Barry	27:00:35	CA	2000	56	M	1
Christian, Jack	27:01:40	OK	2000	47	M	6
Marsh, Scott	27:02:18	MN	2000	31	M	2
Salzer, Todd	27:03:30	CO	2000	26	M	2

Marquer, Barbara	27:04:50	WY	2000	44	F	2
Malone, Susan	27:09:21	PA	2000	43	F	1
Munoz, Daniel	27:18:43	CO	2000	35	M	11
Sandoval, Johnny	27:18:45	CO	2000	42	M	12
Jess, Carl	27:19:18	NM	2000	41	M	4
Grimes, Keith	27:24:51	CO	2000	41	M	9
Menzies, Ray	27:26:21	Canada	2000	33	M	3
Hodges, Eric	27:34:39	CA	2000	51	M	2
Zeif, Jonathan	27:35:47	CO	2000	47	M	11
Ehrlich, Mike	27:36:42	CO	2000	37	M	9
Scholz, Monica	27:37:39	Canada	2000	33	F	5
Shadowlight, Simon	27:38:01	CO	2000	35	M	1
Sadar, Mike	27:43:49	CO	2000	36	M	10
Barnes, Molly	27:47:08	CO	2000	31	F	6
Stevenson, Jeff	27:48:34	CA	2000	54	M	6
Keogh, Bobby	27:50:46	NM	2000	51	M	12
Bear, Jan	27:51:18	NM	2000	44	M	4
Redland, Rickie	27:52:17	WY	2000	46	F	6
Kristof, Gabor	27:53:58	CO	2000	52	M	3
McClung, Steve	27:54:24	CO	2000	38	M	1
Keefe, Dan	27:55:44	OK	2000	35	M	7
Jensen, Karl	27:56:17	Canada	2000	50	M	3
Scott, Pat	27:59:19	NM	2000	47	M	8
Pick, Dan	27:59:20	NM	2000	38	M	1
Burke, Mike	28:01:18	OR	2000	49	M	1
Allmon, Butch	28:04:43	TX	2000	45	M	5
DeVita, Vicki	28:04:48	CA	2000	47	F	1
Finkbeiner, Bill	28:06:25	CA	2000	44	M	30
Zaeppel, Stephanie	28:07:53	CO	2000	30	F	1
Rowe, Tom	28:10:16	MT	2000	52	M	2
Stalion, Tony	28:10:39	CO	2000	35	M	1
Millar, Douglas	28:15:12	UT	2000	42	M	1
Garden, Bill	28:18:12	CO	2000	29	M	1
Haukkala, Edward	28:20:06	VA	2000	32	M	1
Manley, Brian	28:21:00	CO	2000	36	M	13
Olson, Steve	28:22:32	AZ	2000	38	M	1
Boyd, Bruce	28:22:51	CT	2000	61	M	2

Richmeier, Debra	28:23:15	CO	2000	40	F	2
Halpin, Nancy	28:24:54	NM	2000	39	F	4
Eielson, Ken	28:25:07	CO	2000	51	M	2
Meeks, Kenneth	28:25:37	NM	2000	35	M	1
Jordan, King	28:30:32	DC	2000	57	M	11
Bachani, Bob	28:31:11	AZ	2000	44	M	2
King, David	28:31:21	NC	2000	54	M	1
Montanez, Ryan	28:33:45	CO	2000	22	M	1
Benson, Katie	28:35:40	CO	2000	25	F	3
Kapke, Robert	28:38:43	NE	2000	53	M	5
McCobb, Jr., Douglas	28:41:41	CO	2000	31	M	1
LeRoy, Don	28:41:42	CA	2000	50	M	1
Pence, Brian	28:41:43	CO	2000	40	M	4
McMullen, Amy	28:42:40	CO	2000	30	F	1
Hayes, Richard	28:42:59	CA	2000	49	M	1
Thompson, Jared	28:43:08	UT	2000	23	M	1
Medina, Laura	28:43:14	CO	2000	36	F	1
Kartes, Jodi Lynn	28:45:36	OR	2000	30	F	1
Grooms, Jeanie	28:46:28	CO	2000	44	F	6
Stavig, Bob	28:48:04	MN	2000	51	M	13
Wright, Ron	28:49:28	CO	2000	53	M	9
Baugh, Hollis	28:50:36	CO	2000	31	M	11
Muramatsu, Tatsuya	28:51:21	Japan	2000	44	M	2
Wells, Douglas	28:51:58	CO	2000	37	M	1
Weisshaar, Hans-Dieter	28:54:37	Germany	2000	60	M	9
Africa, Bob	28:56:05	CO	2000	27	M	4
Kelecy, Thomas	28:58:31	CO	2000	44	M	1
Irvin, Kristina	28:59:01	CA	2000	42	F	2
Daus-Weber, Theresa	28:59:17	CO	2000	45	F	11
Boulbol, Scott	29:00:38	CO	2000	35	M	1
Miller, Dan	29:00:38	CO	2000	37	M	1
Greco, Ken	29:02:43	AZ	2000	33	M	2
Lynes, Robert	29:03:22	WA	2000	61	M	1
McFadden, Linda	29:03:38	CA	2000	37	F	1
White, Trevor	29:04:31	CA	2000	31	M	2
Schilf, Laura	29:05:58	CO	2000	38	F	1
Fassett, Katy	29:07:02	CO	2000	33	F	1

Tavernini, Robert	29:07:38	TX	2000	32	M	5
Cuffin, Gary	29:08:06	CO	2000	49	M	2
Hunter, Scott	29:09:24	MA	2000	55	M	1
Baues, Reinhold	29:10:00	OR	2000	49	M	1
Ritzman, Michael	29:11:22	CO	2000	28	M	1
Siguaw, Steve	29:12:30	CO	2000	51	M	18
Hobbs, John	29:14:47	CO	2000	55	M	12
Monahan, Mike	29:16:55	CA	2000	54	M	10
Larson, Michael	29:17:04	ID	2000	45	M	1
Bourque, Arthur	29:18:00	AZ	2000	38	M	1
Newton, Jim	29:18:49	TX	2000	53	M	3
Rushing, William	29:19:14	CO	2000	29	M	1
Hawks, Brents	29:19:23	WY	2000	40	M	1
Carlson, Jeanine	29:20:17	MA	2000	46	F	2
Blake, Neil	29:20:38	NM	2000	35	M	7
Strong, David	29:23:55	CO	2000	55	M	14
Collins, Sean	29:25:12	KY	2000	30	M	1
Storrow, Alan	29:25:12	KY	2000	37	M	1
Philip, Bill	29:29:19	CO	2000	54	M	2
Leenaerts, Sean	29:31:44	CO	2000	36	M	2
Burton, Lee	29:31:59	CO	2000	39	M	9
Stodghill, Mark	29:32:06	MN	2000	52	M	1
Jackson, David	29:35:43	KY	2000	41	M	1
Tessler, Keri	29:36:35	NJ	2000	24	F	1
Sullivan, Dennis	29:36:35	NJ	2000	26	M	2
Byrnes, Al	29:37:21	NJ	2000	45	M	1
Curry, Garry	29:37:39	CO	2000	46	M	25
Lindsay, Steve	29:38:04	SC	2000	50	M	1
McCloy, Rush	29:40:44	NY	2000	26	M	1
Walsh, Michael	29:41:04	VA	2000	44	M	1
Decker, Joe	29:43:11	MD	2000	30	M	1
Van Tiel, Wouter	29:45:12	CO	2000	39	M	1
Allen, Lisa	29:47:10	CO	2000	36	F	3
Ackerman, Roger	29:47:25	GA	2000	54	M	3
Dunlap, Ron	29:47:46	CA	2000	61	M	4
Youde, Jeffrey	29:48:12	AZ	2000	31	M	1
Bear, Kim	29:51:55	NM	2000	37	F	2

Stockwell, Chris	29:53:10	ID	2000	37	M	1
Mercil, Robert	29:55:49	CO	2000	60	M	3
Lucido, Sam	29:59:44	MN	2000	41	M	1

2001

Name	Finish Time	State	Year	Age	Sex	#Finished
Peterson, Steve	17:40:53	CO	2001	39	M	7
Koerner, Hal	18:35:32	CO	2001	25	M	2
Kulak, Joe	19:12:41	England	2001	33	M	12
Dewitt, Paul	19:52:32	CO	2001	33	M	5
Bakwin, Peter	20:20:30	CO	2001	39	M	1
Poolheco, Dennis	20:34:40	AZ	2001	40	M	3
Oberle, Christian	20:42:23	MA	2001	25	M	1
Skaden, Erik	21:22:38	CA	2001	29	M	2
Heinemann, Mark	21:41:31	CO	2001	44	M	7
Runyan, Janet	21:47:44	CO	2001	42	F	2
Grimes, Keith	22:08:05	CO	2001	42	M	9
Case, Jill	22:10:16	CO	2001	42	F	4
Clarke, Chris	22:26:42	CO	2001	44	M	7
Kerby, James	22:29:53	WA	2001	38	M	1
McIntosh, Amanda	22:33:53	TX	2001	36	F	3
Grobeson, Jay	22:43:44	CA	2001	40	M	11
Graubins, Garett	22:45:22	CO	2001	25	M	5
Berino, Jeff	22:52:52	CO	2001	43	M	10
Garrison, Tom	22:56:39	NM	2001	42	M	9
Miller, James	23:29:28	CO	2001	46	M	1
Loman, Emily	23:35:19	CO	2001	25	F	2
Rambach, Whit	23:40:11	CA	2001	34	M	1
Flores, Raul	23:55:36	KS	2001	45	M	10
Kadlecek, John	23:57:08	CO	2001	44	M	5
Munoz, Daniel	23:58:06	CO	2001	36	M	11
Thomas, Bill	24:10:01	WA	2001	45	M	2
Varela, Mario	24:10:09	CO	2001	40	M	20
Van Tiel, Jill	24:14:10	CO	2001	37	F	2
Scott, Karen	24:22:42	CO	2001	34	F	2
Stenzel, William	24:29:51	CA	2001	26	M	1
Andrews, Kevin	24:35:52	CO	2001	36	M	2

Cofer, Chuck	24:40:27	TX	2001	50	M	12
Tavernini, Robert	24:44:17	TX	2001	33	M	5
Apt, Kirk	24:44:32	CO	2001	39	M	20
Jess, Carl	24:44:44	NM	2001	42	M	4
Taylor, Neal	24:51:09	CO	2001	38	M	12
Wisoff, Douglas	24:51:31	CO	2001	53	M	6
Robertson, Craig	24:55:53	TX	2001	41	M	6
Welsh, Jeffrey	24:58:08	NC	2001	46	M	13
Smith, Paul	25:00:42	CO	2001	27	M	10
Keogh, Bobby	25:00:54	NM	2001	52	M	12
Frye, Barbara	25:04:14	FL	2001	46	F	2
Ehrlich, Mike	25:10:30	CO	2001	38	M	9
Gerard, Prasad	25:38:24	MD	2001	42	M	1
Stern, Howie	25:48:09	CA	2001	31	M	1
Shults, Joseph	26:01:38	CO	2001	40	M	1
Scott, Pat	26:02:07	NM	2001	48	M	8
Eckert, Eric	26:04:33	WI	2001	35	M	1
Bond, Bert	26:20:35	CO	2001	47	M	2
Travis, Richard	26:24:50	Canada	2001	46	M	1
Barlow, Stephen	26:33:08	TX	2001	40	M	2
Drey, Dennis	26:35:33	NM	2001	49	M	6
Dorgan, Jason	26:36:46	WI	2001	33	M	4
Nakauchi-Hawn, Laurie	26:38:19	CO	2001	31	F	12
Fleagle, Glenn	26:39:05	CO	2001	51	M	1
Borne, Jeff	26:40:36	CO	2001	32	M	1
Jensen, Karl	26:43:58	Canada	2001	51	M	3
Zeif, Jonathan	26:45:27	CO	2001	48	M	11
Menzies, Ray	26:46:31	Canada	2001	34	M	3
Laster, Bill	26:50:57	CO	2001	52	M	14
Hasse, Paul	26:52:58	MN	2001	40	M	1
Morris, Mark	26:52:58	TX	2001	43	M	3
Bergman, Julie Ann	26:55:31	CO	2001	49	F	3
Nagel, Dale	27:00:35	AZ	2001	43	M	1
Barnes, Molly	27:02:38	CO	2001	32	F	6
Kalmeyer, Betsy	27:07:39	CO	2001	40	F	4
Scholz, Monica	27:07:50	Canada	2001	34	F	5
Swanson, Grant	27:08:12	CA	2001	49	M	2

Gerber, Carol	27:12:30	CO	2001	35	F	3
Snyder, Gail	27:16:41	OR	2001	42	F	4
Takahashi, Kaoru	27:23:26	NY	2001	34	M	1
Ledesma, Vincente	27:26:14	TX	2001	53	M	3
Benson, Katie	27:29:04	CO	2001	26	F	3
Johnson, Lance	27:29:09	NM	2001	35	M	1
Miller, Tim	27:29:19	CO	2001	31	M	2
Pence, Eric	27:29:21	CO	2001	35	M	24
Siguaw, Steve	27:34:04	CO	2001	52	M	18
Christian, Jack	27:38:04	OK	2001	48	M	6
Deupree, Chisholm	27:38:04	OK	2001	35	M	11
Melendy, Byron	27:41:45	CA	2001	60	M	1
Libsch, Karen	27:47:03	MN	2001	31	F	1
Benegas, Willie	27:49:56	CA	2001	35	M	1
Ehret, Stephanie	27:56:08	CO	2001	38	F	5
Young, Dale	27:56:32	MI	2001	48	M	1
Allmon, Butch	28:00:48	TX	2001	46	M	5
Jordan, King	28:04:19	DC	2001	58	M	11
Finkbeiner, Bill	28:11:24	CA	2001	45	M	30
Wick, David	28:12:04	CO	2001	40	M	1
Steward, Dan	28:16:04	CO	2001	40	M	8
Simpson, Billy	28:18:39	TN	2001	46	M	2
Sadar, Mike	28:21:34	CO	2001	37	M	10
Eason, Greg	28:26:13	AR	2001	31	M	2
Crawford, Jim	28:28:24	GA	2001	23	M	3
Berkshire, Skip	28:31:25	CO	2001	58	M	1
Davis, Tim	28:31:51	CO	2001	34	M	1
Daus-Weber, Theresa	28:32:50	CO	2001	46	F	11
Marcellus, Sally	28:35:54	Canada	2001	47	F	1
Lang, Rob	28:35:54	Canada	2001	45	M	1
Strong, David	28:37:41	AZ	2001	56	M	14
Goransson, Paul	28:40:01	ME	2001	47	M	1
Pidcock, Kathy	28:41:09	CO	2001	47	F	2
Trenker, Margrit	28:43:17	CO	2001	57	F	3
Kapke, Robert	28:46:13	NE	2001	54	M	5
Boyd, Bruce	28:47:44	CT	2001	62	M	2
Kent, Michael	28:47:44	MA	2001	38	M	1

Stahl, Thomas	28:50:15	NM	2001	37	M	2
Stavig, Bob	28:51:58	MN	2001	52	M	13
Ernst, Christopher	28:53:14	CO	2001	39	M	1
Quiggle, Dee Dee	28:53:30	CO	2001	48	M	1
Eielson, Ken	28:53:54	CO	2001	52	M	2
Hanson, Wendy	28:54:51	MN	2001	29	F	1
Burchenal, Jeb	28:54:54	CO	2001	39	M	3
Wilkie, Jose	29:02:12	KY	2001	38	M	5
Robison, Wendell	29:04:09	WY	2001	49	M	10
Wolfe, Alexander	29:04:10	CO	2001	35	M	1
Hurley, Jamie	29:04:26	CO	2001	35	M	2
Clark, Kim	29:04:54	CO	2001	34	F	1
Thieme, John	29:05:32	CO	2001	39	M	1
Turner, Joy	29:05:55	CO	2001	43	M	4
Johnson, Rebecca	29:07:10	CO	2001	32	F	1
Wright, Ron	29:08:43	CO	2001	54	M	9
Bailey, Howard	29:12:54	GA	2001	45	M	1
Rainey, John	29:14:22	CA	2001	52	M	4
Thompson, Luther	29:14:49	MN	2001	56	M	13
Busse, Dan	29:15:30	MA	2001	32	M	5
Romero, Jim	29:17:38	CO	2001	61	M	2
Curry, Garry	29:19:02	CO	2001	47	M	25
Baker, Jim	29:20:05	OK	2001	51	M	2
Gothard, Terry	29:21:23	CO	2001	36	M	1
Schnitzius, Thomas	29:22:18	IL	2001	48	M	11
Leenaerts, Sean	29:23:15	CO	2001	37	M	2
Halpin, Nancy	29:23:48	NM	2001	40	F	4
Hansel, Doug	29:24:25	OH	2001	41	M	1
Craven, Brent	29:24:27	UT	2001	51	M	3
Mercil, Bob	29:24:52	CO	2001	61	M	3
Hobbs, John	29:25:47	CO	2001	56	M	12
O'Connell, Laura	29:26:14	CO	2001	32	F	1
Calabria, Robert	29:26:35	NC	2001	60	M	3
Van Willigen, Rona	29:26:47	NC	2001	33	F	1
Van Willigan, Hans	29:26:47	ME	2001	63	M	2
Enboden, Tim	29:28:43	CO	2001	41	M	4
Stradley, Doug	29:28:55	CO	2001	35	M	1

Covey, Dave	29:29:16	CA	2001	40	M	1
Schwartz, Steph	29:29:54	CO	2001	38	F	2
Philip, Bill	29:31:17	CO	2001	55	M	2
Lundell, Don	29:32:32	CA	2001	39	M	1
Crouse, Don	29:35:41	TX	2001	44	M	1
Treptow, Thorsten	29:35:41	Germany	2001	43	M	1
Ballard, Jim	29:35:45	OR	2001	51	M	11
Kerwin, Sarah	29:38:22	CO	2001	30	F	1
Bergman, Marc	29:39:27	CO	2001	46	F	4
Abramowitz, Fred	29:40:55	NM	2001	49	M	10
McBride, Myrrl	29:40:55	NM	2001	48	M	3
Pence, Brian	29:41:02	CO	2001	41	M	4
Holovnia, Paul	29:41:19	MN	2001	39	M	3
Sprague, Denise	29:42:50	CA	2001	41	M	1
Smith, James C.	29:44:41	CO	2001	38	M	1
Benjamin, Ben	29:46:31	OR	2001	54	M	4
Huntsman, Beach	29:47:29	CO	2001	25	M	1
Binder, Al**	29:50:20	CO	2001	56	M	13
Cohn, Alan	29:51:44	CO	2001	46	M	12
Pichlmaier, Axel	29:54:33	NM	2001	32	M	1
Elkins, Jake	29:54:40	WY	2001	50	M	3
Martin, M. Shane	29:54:50	UT	2001	34	M	1
Dudley, Peter	29:55:25	CO	2001	46	M	3
McGuire, John	29:55:45	CO	2001	46	M	2

2002

Name	Finish Time	State	Year	Age	Sex	#Finished
Ricklefs, Chad	17:23:18	CO	2002	35	M	2
DeWitt, Paul	18:07:02	CO	2002	34	M	5
Kulak, Joe	18:43:13	CO	2002	34	M	12
Shilling, Kevin	19:33:43	UT	2002	34	M	2
Schmid, Anthea	19:44:24	CO	2002	30	F	2
Torrence, Ian	20:38:42	UT	2002	29	M	1
Solof, Erik	20:42:10	CO	2002	35	M	4
Holmes, Todd	21:09:51	CO	2002	46	M	12
Heinemann, Mark	21:21:35	CO	2002	41	M	7
Pomeroy, Paul	21:36:34	CO	2002	41	M	1

Adamowski, Andrew	21:47:16	CO	2002	28	M	1
Wilcox, David	22:04:36	CO	2002	40	M	8
Farrett, William	22:10:40	CO	2002	32	M	1
Morris, Mark	22:19:03	TX	2002	44	M	3
Poolheco, Dennis	22:31:02	AZ	2002	41	M	3
Case, Jill	22:32:02	CO	2002	43	F	4
Guerrero, Luis	22:38:04	Mexico	2002	39	M	9
Hessek, Rick	22:39:53	CO	2002	36	M	4
Brozik, Susan	22:41:47	NM	2002	35	F	5
Feerst, Adam	22:53:51	CO	2002	42	M	2
Apt, Kirk	22:55:01	CO	2002	40	M	20
Welsh, Jeffrey	23:00:03	NC	2002	47	M	13
Askew, Deborah	23:04:36	CA	2002	44	F	1
Peak, David	23:08:18	CO	2002	31	M	1
Finkbeiner, Bill	23:30:11	CA	2002	46	M	30
Ripka, Danny	23:33:35	MN	2002	45	M	1
Hallsten, John	23:38:58	MT	2002	45	M	1
Cofer, Chuck	23:46:09	TX	2002	51	M	12
Curiel, Tyler	23:47:55	LA	2002	46	M	11
Andrews, Kevin	23:50:53	CO	2002	37	M	1
Manley, Brian	23:54:22	CO	2002	38	M	13
Seremet, Eric	23:58:52	CO	2002	31	M	7
Pollock, Steven	24:05:45	CO	2002	42	M	1
Scott, Pat	24:06:26	NM	2002	49	M	8
Long, Art	24:12:29	CO	2002	33	M	4
Smith, Paul	24:15:55	CO	2002	46	M	10
Frye-Krier, Miles	24:17:10	CO	2002	50	M	7
Koehler, Robert	24:23:21	CO	2002	39	M	3
Constantino, Joe	24:24:44	TX	2002	33	M	3
Piceu, Darcy	24:29:55	CO	2002	27	F	2
Scott, Todd	24:34:13	MI	2002	38	M	11
Riley, Peter	24:35:50	UT	2002	41	M	1
Gordon, Scott	24:39:44	NM	2002	41	M	11
Gordon, Ken	24:42:40	NM	2002	37	M	10
Crawford, Jim	24:42:42	GA	2002	54	M	3
Stone, Tammy	24:42:43	CO	2002	40	F	4
Reed, Pamela	24:45:32	AZ	2002	41	F	6

Crock, Bret	24:48:47	CO	2002	44	M	11
Varela, Mario	24:51:26	CO	2002	41	M	20
Tavernini, Robert	24:53:29	TX	2002	34	M	5
Ham, Jason	24:58:10	CA	2002	31	M	1
Genet, John	25:05:55	CO	2002	44	M	6
Laney, Tim	25:07:13	UK	2002	43	M	2
Gabe, Eric	25:33:41	CO	2002	33	M	3
Flores, Raul	25:37:26	KS	2002	46	M	10
Berino, Jeff	25:38:55	CO	2002	44	M	10
Williams, Mark	25:39:16	MO	2002	44	M	1
Roycroft, Max	25:50:44	TX	2002	38	M	1
Hamilton, Glenn	25:58:22	TX	2002	46	M	1
Mayer, Bob	26:02:13	CO	2002	40	M	1
Anderson, Janice	26:08:15	GA	2002	36	F	2
Grobeson, Jay	26:13:59	CA	2002	41	M	11
Ulrich, Marshall	26:21:05	CO	2002	51	M	13
Turner, Joy	26:35:11	CO	2002	44	F	4
Turner, Glen	26:35:12	CO	2002	42	M	4
Allmon, Butch	26:39:39	TX	2002	47	M	5
Ostrom, Jason	26:40:39	CO	2002	26	M	1
Taylor, Neal	26:41:41	CO	2002	39	M	12
Nelson, Stuart	26:42:44	CO	2002	62	M	14
Turzynski, Michael	26:44:25	Germany	2002	34	M	1
Mahieu, Sherry Kae	26:49:37	NM	2002	47	F	1
Knutson, Tom	26:52:19	MN	2002	52	M	6
Addink, Sylvan	26:56:41	IA	2002	60	M	2
Smith Batchen, Lisa	26:56:58	ID	2002	41	F	1
Bartzen, Gene	27:01:31	WI	2002	48	M	10
Gerber, Carol	27:05:40	CO	2002	39	F	3
Pence, Eric	27:07:48	CO	2002	36	M	24
Mays, Jason	27:07:49	TX	2002	25	M	1
Deupree, Chisholm	27:11:10	OK	2002	36	M	11
Bur, Michael	27:18:52	MD	2002	37	M	2
Weisshaar, Hans-Dieter	27:24:23	Germany	2002	62	M	9
Jess, Carl	27:26:15	NM	2002	43	M	4
Menzies, Ray	27:28:10	Canada	2002	35	M	3
May, Emily	27:30:39	CO	2002	34	F	3

Drey, Dennis	27:31:36	NM	2002	50	M	6
Elliott, Travis	27:37:13	CO	2002	21	M	1
Traxler, Michael	27:40:08	OR	2002	33	M	1
Munoz, Daniel	27:45:02	CO	2002	37	M	11
Rayburn, James	27:45:11	PA	2002	40	M	1
Chicksen, Malvern	27:45:12	Hong Kong	2002	38	M	1
Decker, Ian	27:47:23	CO	2002	33	M	2
Sykes, Greg	27:48:52	CO	2002	41	M	1
Garrison, Tom	27:49:21	NM	2002	43	M	9
Pierce, Brett	27:49:40	CO	2002	30	M	1
Euler, Peter	27:51:42	CO	2002	21	M	1
Klippenstein, Brian	27:57:20	DC	2002	38	M	1
Mahon, Ted	28:00:13	CO	2002	30	M	1
Rideg, William	28:02:45	MT	2002	36	M	2
Bennett, Bradley	28:05:04	MT	2002	46	M	5
Suminski, Mike	28:05:52	Canada	2002	50	M	2
Hall, Larry	28:14:21	IL	2002	48	M	10
Boak, Roger	28:16:39	TX	2002	53	M	3
Jordan, King	28:17:47	DC	2002	59	M	11
Rainey, John	28:18:31	CO	2002	53	M	4
Lange, Bob	28:19:14	SD	2002	39	M	1
Siguaw, Steve	28:19:52	CO	2002	53	M	18
Curry, Garry	28:20:53	CO	2002	48	M	25
Van Horn, Luke	28:22:42	CO	2002	26	M	1
Schmidt, Paul	28:22:51	CA	2002	50	M	3
Greer, John	28:26:19	AZ	2002	43	M	8
Scholz, Monica	28:29:04	Canada	2002	35	F	5
Musclow, Sherry	28:35:09	WY	2002	28	F	1
Franz, Daniel	28:35:56	CO	2002	21	M	2
Halvorson, Steven	28:36:15	CO	2002	45	M	2
Wielgat, Doug	28:37:53	WI	2002	46	M	2
Kern, Stuart	28:38:04	DC	2002	40	M	4
Lee, Chip	28:40:04	CO	2002	47	M	5
Schubert-Akin, Jennifer	28:40:18	CO	2002	45	F	3
Phillips, Bud	28:42:38	CA	2002	55	M	1
Jones, Les	28:43:27	TN	2002	43	M	9
Nelson, Jeff	28:46:25	NM	2002	36	M	2

Cosentino, Michael	28:47:27	GA	2002	31	M	1
Brockmeier, Scott	28:48:49	NC	2002	40	M	2
Salzer, Todd	28:51:48	CO	2002	28	M	2
Daus-Weber, Theresa	28:52:17	CO	2002	47	F	11
Fernandez, Monica	28:52:29	Guatamala	2002	36	F	1
Hartnett, Kevin	28:52:30	CO	2002	40	M	3
Taylor, Greg	28:52:48	MN	2002	55	M	5
Ledesma, Vincente	28:54:31	TX	2002	51	M	3
Stavig, Bob	28:54:44	MN	2002	53	M	13
Wright, Ron	28:56:43	CO	2002	55	M	9
Huber, Bruce	28:59:18	CO	2002	51	M	3
Ackerman, Roger	29:00:39	GA	2002	55	M	3
Loomis, Gregory	29:00:40	VA	2002	28	M	1
Voltaggio, Sam	29:00:46	TX	2002	51	M	1
Meendering, Nancy	29:01:33	IA	2002	27	F	1
Kirstein, Sam	29:01:33	MN	2002	32	M	1
Klingman, Kyle	29:01:43	IA	2002	26	M	1
Busse, Daniel	29:01:54	MA	2002	33	M	5
Tibbetts, Cathy	29:04:59	NM	2002	47	F	2
Mitchell, Stephen	29:05:32	CO	2002	42	M	3
Cuffin, Gary	29:06:27	CO	2002	51	M	2
Klopfenstein, Scott	29:07:32	CO	2002	31	M	12
Wildeboer, Travis	29:08:57	IA	2002	23	M	1
Cogar, Rockford	29:14:20	CO	2002	47	M	2
Rochelle, James	29:14:20	TN	2002	38	M	1
Strong, David	29:15:09	AZ	2002	57	M	14
Carlson, Jeanine	29:15:58	MA	2002	48	F	2
Watson, William	29:18:29	CO	2002	56	M	2
Ostor, Pierre	29:20:16	MN	2002	45	M	3
Shwartz, Steph	29:21:28	CO	2002	29	F	1
Arellano, Joel	29:22:15	CO	2002	30	M	2
Clute, Dennis	29:23:04	WA	2002	49	M	1
Valenta, Mike	29:23:15	CO	2002	48	M	2
Weaver, Kevin	29:25:17	CO	2002	21	M	1
Mahoney, Matt	29:26:10	FL	2002	47	M	5
Hobbs, John	29:26:21	CO	2002	57	M	12
Marrs, Clinton	29:26:27	NM	2002	45	M	1

Pressler, Greg	29:26:34	OR	2002	34	M	1
Thompson, Bill	29:27:56	AUS	2002	59	M	1
Ward, Craig	29:29:02	CO	2002	38	M	1
Schulz, Robert	29:29:12	NY	2002	44	M	1
Despres, Renee	29:29:17	NM	2002	38	F	3
DeMoss, Jean	29:30:36	CO	2002	30	F	6
Kern, Kristen	29:30:54	NM	2002	37	M	10
Sadar, Mike	29:32:23	CO	2002	38	M	10
Sauter, Jeff	29:32:36	CA	2002	45	M	1
Taylor, Alexander	29:32:52	WI	2002	40	M	1
Heidmous, Jeff	29:33:20	CO	2002	47	M	1
Moore, Matthew	29:34:02	CA	2002	45	M	3
Snyder, Scott	29:34:08	CO	2002	47	M	9
Ballard, Jim	29:37:04	OR	2002	52	M	11
Elkins, Jake	29:39:29	WY	2002	51	M	3
Halpin, Nancy	29:40:02	NM	2002	41	F	4
Hickman, Marge	29:40:34	CO	2002	52	F	14
Kimm, Ed	29:41:36	CO	2002	42	M	1
Cruthirds, Letha	29:41:39	TX	2002	49	F	2
George, Craig	29:41:46	CO	2002	41	M	1
D'Onofrio, Kathy	29:41:52	CA	2002	38	F	5
Thompson, Luther	29:42:54	MN	2002	57	M	13
Bunts, Daniel	29:43:50	AZ	2002	30	M	1
Benjamin, Ben	29:46:20	OR	2002	55	M	4
Herrera, Al	29:48:49	TX	2002	46	M	1
Baugh, Hollis	29:49:33	CO	2002	33	M	11
Pearcy, Rick	29:50:01	CO	2002	49	M	2
Gutierrez, Mona	29:52:10	CA	2002	40	F	1
Ehrlich, Michael	29:54:55	CO	2002	39	M	9
Burgess, Todd	29:55:52	CO	2002	33	M	4
Whitworth, Elroy	29:58:06	TX	2002	50	M	1

2003

Name	Finish Time	State	Year	Age	Sex	#Finished
Dewitt, Paul	17:58:45	CO	2003	M3	M	5
Koerner, Hal	19:09:46	CO	2003	M2	M	2
Put, Hans	19:36:58	NY	2003	M4	M	1

Tiegs, Jeff	19:48:57	CO	2003	M3	M	3
Kulak, Joe	20:03:25	CO	2003	M3	M	12
Carr, Derrick	20:10:14	VA	2003	M4	M	3
Hessek, Rick	20:38:17	CO	2003	M3	M	4
Barker, Leland	21:16:35	UT	2003	M4	M	1
Guerrero, Luis	22:32:47	Mexico	2003	M4	M	9
Long, Art	22:37:06	CO	2003	M3	M	4
Apt, Kirk	22:42:00	CO	2003	M4	M	20
Welsh, Jeffrey	22:45:54	NC	2003	M4	M	13
Clarke, Chris	22:50:11	CO	2003	M4	M	7
Caldwell, Valerie	22:54:16	NM	2003	F3	F	4
Finkbeiner, Bill	22:55:02	CA	2003	M4	M	30
Hamlin, Nick	22:57:24	CO	2003	M2	M	1
Shelafo, Steve	23:13:11	CO	2003	M4	M	3
Wilcox, David	23:31:55	CO	2003	M4	M	8
Grobeson, Jay	23:33:02	CA	2003	M4	M	11
Flores, Raul	23:36:13	KS	2003	M4	M	10
Simpson, Billy	23:41:49	TN	2003	M4	M	2
Curiel, Tyler	23:42:59	LA	2003	M4	M	11
Schmidt, Daniel	23:59:21	CO	2003	M4	M	6
Manley, Brian	24:13:31	CO	2003	M3	M	13
Holmes, Todd	24:17:13	CO	2003	M4	M	12
Scott, Pat	24:17:40	NM	2003	M5	M	8
Gordon, Scott	24:20:01	NM	2003	M4	M	11
Tidmore, Paul	24:21:06	TX	2003	M3	M	1
Bidwell, Ted	24:23:42	CO	2003	M5	M	3
Crock, Bret	24:24:01	CO	2003	M4	M	11
Marsh, Scott	24:28:38	MN	2003	M3	M	2
Boyd, David	24:30:30	TX	2003	M4	M	1
Decker, Ian	24:35:04	CO	2003	M3	M	2
Gabe, Eric	24:42:49	CO	2003	M3	M	3
Orr, Robert	24:43:34	AR	2003	M4	M	1
Frye-Krier, Miles	24:46:40	CO	2003	M5	M	7
Jones, Jake	24:51:20	CO	2003	M3	M	2
Vandenburg, Larry	24:55:22	WA	2003	M4	M	1
Kern, Kristen	24:55:49	NM	2003	M3	M	10
Taylor, Neal	25:20:31	CO	2003	M4	M	12

McBee, Steve	25:26:57	AR	2003	M3	M	1
Heller, Edwin	25:38:08	NM	2003	M4	M	4
Tavernini, Robert	25:42:57	TX	2003	M3	M	5
Varela, Mario	25:44:21	CO	2003	M4	M	20
Bachani, Bob	25:44:41	AZ	2003	M4	M	2
Pence, Eric	25:47:27	CO	2003	M3	M	24
Baugh, Hollis	25:53:01	CO	2003	M3	M	11
Jones, Les	26:06:47	TN	2003	M4	M	9
Schryburt, Patrick	26:06:58	Canada	2003	M3	M	1
Dobbins, Chris	26:07:30	CO	2003	M3	M	3
Kennedy, Todd	26:09:13	CO	2003	M2	M	1
Reimer, Rick	26:11:15	CO	2003	M5	M	6
Zeif, Jonathan	26:14:41	CO	2003	M5	M	11
Baker, Keith	26:16:26	NM	2003	M4	M	1
Keogh, Bobby	26:19:44	NM	2003	M5	M	12
Schwartz, Steph	26:27:39	CO	2003	F3	F	2
Hewitt, Tim	26:33:00	PA	2003	M4	M	2
Nelson, Stuart	26:38:33	MI	2003	63	M	14
Biles, Bobby	26:40:24	NC	2003	M3	M	1
Wrolstad, David	26:44:23	ND	2003	M4	M	3
Schoenlaub, Paul	26:55:37	MO	2003	M4	M	12
Bloom, Jerry	26:56:06	CA	2003	M5	M	1
Genet, John	26:57:54	CO	2003	M4	M	6
Campbell, Michael	26:58:35	VA	2003	M5	M	1
Laster, Bill	26:58:37	CO	2003	M5	M	14
Bear, Jan	27:00:04	NM	2003	M4	M	4
Cofer, Chuck	27:02:25	TX	2003	M5	M	12
Cospolich, Helen	27:02:32	CO	2003	F2	F	4
Klopfenstein, Scott	27:05:46	CO	2003	M3	M	12
Gimenez, Kim	27:10:09	CA	2003	F3	F	1
Steward, Dan	27:10:44	CO	2003	M4	M	8
Martin, Christopher	27:13:40	NH	2003	M3	M	1
Reed, Pamela	27:14:46	AZ	2003	F4	F	6
Stephon, Michael	27:18:44	CO	2003	M3	M	4
Mahoney, Matt	27:24:34	FL	2003	M4	M	5
Graim, Timothy	27:27:41	CO	2003	M5	M	1
Bur, Michael	27:28:01	MD	2003	M3	M	2

Watts, Matthew	27:29:38	CO	2003	M4	M	5
Meyers, Scott	27:31:00	WI	2003	M3	M	4
DeMoss, Jean	27:31:35	CO	2003	F3	F	6
Trefenanko, Charlene	27:31:54	Canada	2003	F2	F	1
Deupree, Chisholm	27:32:24	OK	2003	M3	M	11
Cawthon, Lawrence	27:33:08	NM	2003	M5	M	1
Balsley, David	27:35:16	NY	2003	M5	M	1
Turner, Joy	27:36:13	CO	2003	F4	F	4
May, Emily	27:36:47	CO	2003	F3	F	3
Schnitzius, Thomas	27:37:09	IL	2003	M5	M	11
Bursler, David	27:46:03	Denmark	2003	M3	M	1
Nowakowski, Stan	27:46:55	MN	2003	M4	M	1
Kosek, Jon	27:50:59	CA	2003	M3	M	1
Boak, Roger	27:53:07	TX	2003	M5	M	3
Skrien, Orlyn	27:54:37	CO	2003	M6	M	1
Wielgat, Douglas	27:56:07	WI	2003	M4	M	2
Bosard, Bradley	27:56:08	CO	2003	M5	M	1
Fall, Christopher	27:56:49	AZ	2003	M4	M	1
Anderson, Kirk	27:57:39	IL	2003	M3	M	4
Sandoval, Johnny	27:58:39	CO	2003	M4	M	12
Woodbeck, Ben	28:00:36	CO	2003	M3	M	2
Kahn, Phil	28:01:53	CO	2003	M5	M	11
Hurd, Steven	28:06:40	CO	2003	M2	M	1
Busse, Dan	28:06:41	MA	2003	M3	M	5
Vinci, Paul	28:11:56	MA	2003	M5	M	1
Johnson, Marco	28:13:02	WY	2003	M4	M	1
McCarville, Kirk	28:13:11	AZ	2003	M4	M	2
Bennett, Bradley	28:14:29	MT	2003	M4	M	5
Loehding, Ryan	28:15:40	TX	2003	M3	M	1
Bartzen, Gene	28:17:43	WI	2003	M4	M	10
Geisler, Brenda	28:20:44	CO	2003	F4	F	2
Galvan, Juan	28:26:19	TX	2003	M3	M	1
Johnson, Randy	28:26:41	NM	2003	M4	M	1
Wallace, Ryan	28:28:30	CO	2003	M2	M	1
Lewis, Bobby	28:28:31	CO	2003	M3	M	1
Curry, Garry	28:29:15	CO	2003	49	M	25
Collins, Jeff	28:30:11	CA	2003	M4	M	2

Sauld, Alfred	28:31:29	WI	2003	M5	M	1
Arter, Julie	28:33:55	AZ	2003	F4	F	10
Garrison, Tom	28:33:57	NM	2003	M4	M	9
Hagen, Chris	28:34:31	CO	2003	M2	M	1
Schloss, Henry	28:36:56	CO	2003	M2	M	5
Andrews, Steven	28:37:36	MD	2003	M2	M	1
Zucker, Zeke	28:38:28	VT	2003	M5	M	1
Crawford, Jim	28:38:39	GA	2003	M5	M	3
Lichtenfels, Christine	28:44:10	WY	2003	F4	F	1
Grooms, Jeanie	28:45:08	CO	2003	F4	F	6
Perry, Dale	28:47:34	CO	2003	M4	M	4
Gomez-Rosas, Camilo	28:48:24	Mexico	2003	M3	M	1
Kern, Leland	28:48:32	MT	2003	M4	M	1
Gordon, Ken	28:48:39	NM	2003	M3	M	10
Rainey, John	28:49:52	CO	2003	M5	M	4
Despres, Renee	28:50:08	NM	2003	F3	F	3
Thompson, David	28:50:16	CO	2003	M4	M	1
Pidcock, Kathy	28:51:23	CO	2003	F4	F	2
Shay, Timothy	28:52:16	NJ	2003	M5	M	1
Minnehan, Brian	28:52:23	NY	2003	M3	M	1
Ledesma, Vincente	28:52:28	TX	2003	M5	M	3
VanDeren, Diane	28:53:00	CO	2003	F4	F	1
Burchenal, Jeb	28:56:41	CO	2003	M4	M	3
Olmer, Scott	28:56:48	CO	2003	M3	M	2
Losey, Bill	28:57:28	OH	2003	M3	M	1
Thompson, Dennis	28:57:42	TX	2003	M5	M	2
Burton, Lee	28:57:47	CO	2003	M4	M	9
Schwartz, Michelle	28:58:27	CO	2003	F3	F	7
Hall, Larry	28:59:11	IL	2003	M4	M	10
Allmon, Butch	28:59:22	TX	2003	M4	M	5
Teodoru, Daniel	28:59:24	CO	2003	M3	M	1
Turner, Glen	29:00:21	CO	2003	M4	M	4
Rahmer, Mike	29:01:10	NM	2003	M3	M	1
Priestley, Terry	29:01:25	NM	2003	M3	M	1
Anaya-Acevedo, Mario	29:02:01	Mexico	2003	M5	M	1
Wright, Ron	29:02:08	CO	2003	M5	M	9
Cruthirds, Letha	29:03:10	TX	2003	F5	F	2

Brozik, Susan	29:03:54	NM	2003	F3	F	5
Knapp, Richard	29:04:04	NM	2003	M5	M	1
Perrault, Mark	29:04:48	VT	2003	M4	M	1
Olexa, Raymond	29:05:01	CO	2003	M3	M	1
Smith-Batchen, Lisa	29:05:22	ID	2003	F4	F	1
Martell, Gregg	29:05:49	WY	2003	M4	M	6
Rieland, Dan	29:07:51	MT	2003	M3	M	4
Johnson, Dennis	29:08:09	IA	2003	M5	M	2
Nakauchi-Hawn, Laurie	29:08:18	CO	2003	F3	F	12
Telles, David	29:08:19	NM	2003	M4	M	1
Penna, Phil	29:08:28	CA	2003	M5	M	1
Ripol, Cosme	29:08:55	NM	2003	M4	M	1
Walker, Liz	29:11:43	GA	2003	F4	F	5
Dee, Dee	29:11:50	CO	2003	F5	F	1
Kreb, Kim	29:14:01	CO	2003	F3	F	4
Ostor, Pierre	29:14:15	MN	2003	M4	M	3
Ulrich, Marshall	29:15:00	CO	2003	M5	M	13
Haefele, Rich	29:15:01	CO	2003	M3	M	1
Sage, Gregory	29:15:05	CA	2003	M5	M	1
Franz, Daniel	29:16:43	AZ	2003	M2	M	2
Murri, Morgan	29:17:20	CO	2003	M3	M	4
McHugh, Brendan	29:18:12	CO	2003	M5	M	1
Hartnett, Kevin	29:18:13	CO	2003	M4	M	3
Siguaw, Steve	29:18:55	CO	2003	M5	M	18
Muller, Chris	29:20:11	CA	2003	M3	M	1
Ackerman, Roger	29:20:30	GA	2003	M5	M	3
Hardwick, David	29:20:40	NC	2003	M6	M	1
Dieter, Hans	29:21:21	Germany	2003	M6	M	1
Cunningham, Dave	29:21:40	CO	2003	M3	M	6
Giampa, Nick	29:22:25	CA	2003	M4	M	1
Hill, Jon	29:23:25	TX	2003	M3	M	2
Ballard, Jim	29:26:37	OR	2003	M5	M	11
Donnelly, Susan	29:26:47	TN	2003	F4	F	1
Neupauer, Wendy	29:29:35	MN	2003	F3	F	1
Burchat, Paula	29:30:57	Canada	2003	F3	F	1
Bierman, Tony	29:31:55	IL	2003	M4	M	1
Hinsey, Kent	29:33:25	CO	2003	M4	M	2

Name	Finish Time	State	Year	Age	Sex	#Finished
Coonrod, Kurt	29:34:09	NM	2003	M4	M	8
Drey, Dennis	29:34:10	NM	2003	M5	M	6
Homelvig, Pat	29:34:45	CO	2003	M4	M	5
Jensen, David	29:34:47	OK	2003	M4	M	1
Hobbs, John	29:38:26	CO	2003	M5	M	12
Parks, Terry	29:39:41	CA	2003	M4	M	1
Snyder, Scott	29:40:33	CO	2003	M4	M	9
Cohn, Alan	29:41:05	CO	2003	M4	M	12
Gutmann, Brenda	29:41:29	KY	2003	F4	F	1
De, Chris	29:41:43	CO	2003	M3	M	1
Mork, Joanie	29:41:45	CA	2003	F4	F	2
Elkins, Jake	29:44:03	WY	2003	M5	M	3
Calabria, Robert	29:47:16	NC	2003	M6	M	3
Wallace, Mark	29:49:12	CO	2003	M4	M	3
Pearcy, Rick	29:50:01	CO	2003	M5	M	2
Werner, Lynne	29:51:55	WA	2003	F5	F	1
Craven, Brent	29:52:41	UT	2003	M5	M	3
Bear, Kim	29:53:29	NM	2003	F4	F	2

2004

Name	Finish Time	State	Year	Age	Sex	#Finished
DeWitt, Paul	17:16:19	CO	2004	M3	M	5
Jurek, Scott	18:01:46	WA	2004	M3	M	2
Tiegs, Jeffrey	19:30:25	CO	2004	M3	M	3
Kulak, Joe	19:47:47	CO	2004	M3	M	12
Holmes, Todd	19:57:06	CO	2004	M4	M	12
Marron, Luis Guerrero	20:41:18	Mexico	2004	M4	M	1
Schmid, Anthea	20:50:05	CO	2004	F3	F	2
Graubins, Garett	21:20:58	CO	2004	M3	M	5
Eisman, Darrin	21:23:29	CO	2004	M3	M	2
Shelafo, Steve	22:04:05	CO	2004	M4	M	3
Cooper, Ryan	22:27:53	CO	2004	M3	M	4
Feerst, Adam	22:31:47	CO	2004	M4	M	2
Hessek, Rick	22:34:02	CO	2004	M3	M	4
Carpenter, Matt	22:43:38	CO	2004	M4	M	2
Fisher, Brian	22:53:05	CO	2004	M3	M	7
Snow, Justin	22:54:31	CO	2004	M3	M	2

Welsh, Jeffrey	22:59:13	NC	2004	M4	M	13
Apt, Kirk	23:00:28	CO	2004	M4	M	20
Schmidt, Daniel	23:10:08	CO	2004	M4	M	6
Boese, Jamie	23:24:50	CO	2004	M4	M	1
Brozik, Susan	23:30:43	NM	2004	F3	F	5
Holak, Andy	23:36:43	MN	2004	M3	M	1
Laney, Tim	23:38:22	England	2004	M4	M	2
Piceu, Darcy	23:44:11	CO	2004	F2	F	2
Clarke, Chris	23:45:08	CO	2004	M4	M	7
Winch, Joe	23:47:28	IA	2004	M4	M	1
Cospolich, Helen	23:51:44	CO	2004	F2	F	4
Genet, John	24:06:34	CO	2004	M4	M	6
Wiegand, Andrea	24:07:27	CO	2004	F2	F	1
Zeif, Jonathan	24:13:46	CO	2004	M5	M	11
Taylor, Neal	24:24:18	CO	2004	M4	M	12
Scott, Karen	24:25:46	CO	2004	F3	F	2
Smith, Tony	24:26:01	NC	2004	M5	M	1
Bidwell, Ted	24:31:05	CO	2004	M5	M	3
Ishikawa, Hiroki	24:34:02	Japan	2004	M2	M	2
Grobeson, Jay	24:35:34	CA	2004	M4	M	11
Kreb, Kim	24:36:33	CO	2004	F3	F	4
Reimer, Rick	24:36:58	CO	2004	M5	M	6
Luckey, Stephen	24:38:30	CO	2004	M3	M	1
Hughes, John	24:40:07	AR	2004	M3	M	1
Coblentz, David	24:46:47	NM	2004	M4	M	2
Kern, Kristen	24:50:48	NM	2004	M3	M	10
Varela, Mario	24:57:33	CO	2004	M4	M	20
Cote, Gilles	25:02:31	CO	2004	M4	M	6
Garrison, Tom	25:14:33	NM	2004	M4	M	9
Cooper, Lori	25:33:33	CO	2004	F2	F	1
Earnest, Frank	25:45:00	CA	2004	M5	M	1
Finkbeiner, Bill	25:45:00	CA	2004	M4	M	30
Manley, Brian	25:45:00	CO	2004	M4	M	13
Nelson, Stuart	25:56:01	MI	2004	64	M	14
Meyers, Scott	25:56:17	WI	2004	M3	M	4
Bennett, Brad	25:58:14	MT	2004	M4	M	5
Klopfenstein, Scott	25:59:40	CO	2004	M3	M	12

Harcrow, Gina	26:08:13	CO	2004	F3	F	3
Holovnia, Paul	26:27:00	MN	2004	M4	M	3
Heller, Edwin	26:31:09	NM	2004	M4	M	4
Edinger, Perry	26:39:26	AZ	2004	M4	M	2
Teodoru, Danny	26:43:27	CO	2004	M3	M	1
Davenport, Michael	26:44:51	IL	2004	M4	M	1
Arter, Julie	26:47:23	AZ	2004	F4	F	10
Flores, Raul	26:48:06	KS	2004	M4	M	10
Schoenlaub, Paul	26:48:07	MO	2004	M4	M	12
Keogh, Bobby	26:56:27	NM	2004	M5	M	12
Kern, Stuart	26:56:27	DC	2004	M4	M	4
Sanderson, Marc	27:05:57	UT	2004	M3	M	4
Smith, Paul	27:13:49	CO	2004	M4	M	10
Bandy, Dana	27:25:38	OR	2004	M5	M	1
Pence, Eric	27:34:42	CO	2004	M3	M	24
Weisshaar, Hans-Dieter	27:37:47	Germany	2004	64	M	9
Szekeresh, Richard	27:38:11	OH	2004	M4	M	1
Bassham, Brett	27:38:55	TX	2004	M4	M	1
Frye-Krier, Miles	27:39:39	CO	2004	M5	M	7
Gordon, Scott	27:44:08	NM	2004	M4	M	11
Guzman, Henry	27:45:37	CO	2004	M4	M	2
Tucker, Dean	27:53:24	CO	2004	M4	M	1
Brenden, Dan	28:02:12	AZ	2004	M5	M	8
Mitchell, Laura	28:02:46	CO	2004	F4	F	1
Goldberg, David	28:02:46	AZ	2004	M4	M	3
Mitchell, Stephen	28:02:46	CO	2004	M4	M	3
Robertson, Craig	28:03:23	TX	2004	M4	M	6
May, Emily	28:03:52	CO	2004	F3	F	3
DeBoer, Amber	28:06:37	CO	2004	F2	F	3
Laster, Bill	28:06:37	CO	2004	M5	M	14
Grimes, Keith	28:07:10	CO	2004	M4	M	9
Chaffee, Steve	28:07:58	CO	2004	M3	M	1
Muzzy, Richard	28:08:09	CO	2004	M3	M	1
Deupree, Chisholm	28:08:16	OK	2004	M3	M	11
Arellano, Joel	28:09:09	CO	2004	M3	M	2
Khajavi, Jamshid	28:11:15	WA	2004	M5	M	7
Hall, Larry	28:12:07	IL	2004	M5	M	10

Keefe, Dan	28:12:58	OK	2004	M3	M	7
Seremet, Eric	28:21:49	CO	2004	M3	M	7
Richardson, Norman	28:23:46	MA	2004	M4	M	2
Watts, Matthew	28:24:01	CO	2004	M4	M	5
Hartnett, Kevin	28:24:17	CO	2004	M4	M	3
Aslett, Jody	28:30:05	ID	2004	F3	F	1
Hansberry, Charles	28:30:30	MT	2004	M3	M	1
Cunningham, Ron	28:32:37	OR	2004	M5	M	2
Hinsey, Kent	28:33:21	CO	2004	M4	M	2
Monken, Bill	28:34:40	Canada	2004	M4	M	1
Sandoval, Johnny	28:34:47	CO	2004	M4	M	12
Teaster, Buddy	28:36:45	TX	2004	M4	M	1
Leitch, William	28:36:46	Canada	2004	M6	M	1
Crownover, R.Matthew	28:36:47	TX	2004	M3	M	1
Redland, Rickie	28:37:08	CO	2004	F5	F	6
Wrublik, Rodger	28:37:30	AZ	2004	M4	M	1
McGuire, John	28:38:32	CO	2004	M4	M	2
Steward, Dan	28:41:07	CO	2004	M4	M	8
Wagers, Barb	28:42:30	CO	2004	F4	F	1
Snyder, Scott	28:48:27	CO	2004	M4	M	9
Ulrich, Marshall	28:48:27	CO	2004	M5	M	13
Drey, Dennis	28:49:21	NM	2004	M5	M	6
Cogar, Rockford	28:51:19	CO	2004	M4	M	2
Wright, Ron	28:51:24	CO	2004	M5	M	9
Dobbins, Chris	28:52:03	CO	2004	M3	M	3
Dodd, Gary	28:52:35	NM	2004	M4	M	2
Ostor, Pierre	28:52:42	MN	2004	M4	M	3
Hill, Calvin	28:52:50	TN	2004	M3	M	1
Geisler, Brenda	28:53:12	CO	2004	F4	F	2
Burton, Lee	28:54:37	CO	2004	M4	M	9
Gnass, Karen	28:55:31	OR	2004	F4	F	1
Schnitzius, Tom	28:56:15	IL	2004	M5	M	11
Jordan, King	28:58:07	DC	2004	M6	M	11
Tiernan, Sean	29:00:24	MA	2004	M3	M	1
McKinney, Mark	29:01:15	CA	2004	M3	M	1
Gerber, Carol	29:02:00	CO	2004	F4	F	3
Homelvig, Pat	29:02:15	CO	2004	M4	M	5

Sullivan, Paul	29:02:40	CO	2004	M3	M	1
Apple, Rob	29:07:32	TN	2004	M4	M	2
Aslett, Dennis	29:07:33	ID	2004	M5	M	1
Dudney, Gary	29:08:26	CA	2004	M5	M	1
Vogt, Lonney	29:09:37	CO	2004	M5	M	1
Roark, Steve	29:10:01	NV	2004	M3	M	1
Taylor, Greg	29:10:20	MN	2004	M5	M	5
Bearden, Quent	29:11:00	TX	2004	M2	M	2
Hersey, David	29:13:02	CO	2004	M4	M	2
Creamer, Fred	29:15:58	CO	2004	M4	M	1
Karwowski, Natalie	29:18:15	CO	2004	F3	F	1
Jewell, Jack	29:18:25	CO	2004	M5	M	2
Hobbs, John	29:19:35	CO	2004	M5	M	12
Dunn, Randall	29:19:46	CO	2004	M4	M	5
Curry, Garry	29:20:14	CO	2004	50	M	25
Addink, Sylvan	29:21:46	IA	2004	M6	M	2
Bostow, Jeff	29:21:53	MN	2004	M4	M	4
Walker, Liz	29:24:01	GA	2004	F4	F	5
Tibbetts, Cathy	29:24:30	NM	2004	F4	F	2
Ingebrigtsen, J.P.	29:24:35	CO	2004	M4	M	1
Constantino, Joe	29:25:10	TX	2004	M3	M	3
Koutani, Pierre	29:25:10	TX	2004	M3	M	1
Gimenez, Doug	29:26:15	TX	2004	M5	M	1
Crock, Bret	29:27:28	CO	2004	M4	M	11
Dutrow, Barb	29:29:26	LA	2004	F4	F	1
Gross, Paul	29:30:44	CO	2004	M3	M	3
Monroney, Steven	29:31:20	CO	2004	M4	M	1
Thompson, Luther	29:31:34	MN	2004	M6	M	13
Martinez, Hector	29:31:41	CO	2004	M2	M	2
DuBois, Thaddeus	29:32:00	AK	2004	M3	M	1
Stavig, Bob	29:32:13	MN	2004	M5	M	13
Hickman, Marge	29:32:59	CO	2004	F5	F	14
Abramowitz, Fred	29:33:57	CO	2004	M5	M	10
Perry, Doug	29:34:30	CO	2004	M4	M	1
Clark, Doug	29:34:58	Canada	2004	M5	M	1
Gardner, Renne	29:35:17	CA	2004	M4	M	2
Witt, Chris	29:35:34	CO	2004	M4	M	1

Name	Finish Time	State	Year	Age	Sex	#Finished
Catalano, Al	29:35:47	MA	2004	M5	M	2
Mahan, Dave	29:35:47	MA	2004	M4	M	1
Mount, Ray	29:35:47	MA	2004	M5	M	1
Marchant, Timothy	29:36:40	MT	2004	M4	M	1
Baugh, Hollis	29:36:59	CO	2004	M3	M	11
Porter, John	29:37:34	CO	2004	M3	M	1
Wrolstad, David	29:37:50	ND	2004	M4	M	3
Findlay, Bob	29:38:29	CO	2004	M5	M	1
Thompson, Dennis	29:40:05	TX	2004	M5	M	2
Haugh, Bob	29:40:30	KY	2004	M5	M	1
Hudgens, Stephen	29:40:38	TX	2004	M4	M	1
Muriel, Thomi	29:42:01	Switzerland	2004	F4	F	1
Fraser, Mark	29:42:21	TX	2004	M4	M	1
Ralston, Aron	29:43:41	CO	2004	M2	M	1
Braga-Levaggi, Ana	29:44:04	CA	2004	F4	F	1
Gallagher, Tommy	29:44:50	NV	2004	M4	M	3
Barbour, Lisa	29:45:00	CO	2004	F4	F	1
Twiggs, Chris	29:45:01	FL	2004	M3	M	1
Kahn, Phil	29:45:14	CO	2004	M5	M	11
Kreiling, Steve	29:45:15	CA	2004	M5	M	1
Tankovich, Bill	29:45:25	CO	2004	M3	M	1
Schwartz, Michelle	29:45:31	CO	2004	F3	F	7
Benjamin, Ben	29:46:29	OR	2004	M5	M	4
Walters, Fred	29:49:22	MI	2004	M5	M	1
Wieneke, Brian	29:49:36	AZ	2004	M4	M	1
Weissman, Joshua	29:50:44	CO	2004	M3	M	3
Calabria, Robert	29:51:19	NC	2004	M6	M	3
Gable, Carl	29:53:28	NM	2004	M4	M	1
Stahl, Tom	29:54:10	NM	2004	M4	M	2
Johnson, Dennis	29:54:48	IA	2004	M5	M	2

2005

Name	Finish Time	State	Year	Age	Sex	#Finished
Carpenter, Matt	15:42:59	CO	2005	M4	M	2
Vega, Dan	19:03:01	CO	2005	M3	M	2
Solof, Eric	19:15:16	CO	2005	M3	M	4
Kulak, Joe	19:28:37	CO	2005	M3	M	12

Hartell, Mark	19:35:19	England	2005	M4	M	1
Fisher, Brian	19:51:10	CO	2005	M3	M	7
Kimball, Nikki	20:28:21	MT	2005	F3	F	1
Tiegs, Jeffrey	20:37:55	CO	2005	M3	M	3
Schmidt, Daniel	20:40:04	CO	2005	M4	M	6
Harcrow, Harry	21:07:54	CO	2005	M3	M	7
Cooper, Ryan	21:45:25	CO	2005	M3	M	4
Beuche, Jeffrey	21:46:31	CO	2005	M3	M	3
Sybrowsky, Kristin Moehl	22:03:03	WA	2005	F2	F	1
Adams, Paul	22:15:04	CO	2005	M4	M	3
Lefever, John	22:22:25	NE	2005	M3	M	3
Klopfenstein, Scott	22:37:50	CO	2005	M3	M	12
Coblentz, David	22:41:16	NM	2005	M4	M	2
Poole, Jason	22:42:34	CO	2005	M3	M	1
Pacev, Tania	22:49:07	CO	2005	F4	F	2
Gala, Scott	22:49:08	MI	2005	M3	M	1
Meyers, Scott	22:57:24	WI	2005	M3	M	4
Hadley, Allen	23:05:08	CO	2005	M4	M	1
Kiddoo, Phill	23:05:46	CA	2005	M3	M	1
Zeif, Jonathan	23:10:11	CO	2005	M5	M	11
Goodman, Russ	23:17:55	IN	2005	M3	M	1
Rice, John	23:18:11	CO	2005	M2	M	1
Wilcox, David	23:23:45	CO	2005	M4	M	8
Welsh, Jeffrey	23:27:31	NC	2005	M5	M	13
Donaldson, Jamie	23:37:40	CO	2005	F3	F	3
Handelsman, Corey	23:38:37	MD	2005	M2	M	1
Finkbeiner, Bill	23:42:34	CA	2005	M4	M	30
Long, Art	23:47:50	CO	2005	M3	M	4
Seremet, Eric	23:49:50	CO	2005	M3	M	7
Guerrero, Luis	23:53:10	CO	2005	M4	M	9
Kelly, Chad	23:53:20	MN	2005	M3	M	1
Robbins, Christian	23:57:16	CO	2005	M3	M	2
Stuht, Jennifer	23:57:43	CO	2005	F3	F	1
Staley, Marc	23:58:05	CO	2005	M2	M	2
Bartzen, Gene	24:02:27	CO	2005	M5	M	10
Stofko, Paul	24:04:36	IN	2005	M2	M	6
Apt, Kirk	24:04:50	CO	2005	M4	M	20

Woodbeck, Benjamin	24:16:37	CO	2005	M3	M	2
Cote, Gilles	24:25:54	CO	2005	M4	M	6
Gordon, Scott	24:28:06	NM	2005	M4	M	11
Geer, John	24:31:02	AZ	2005	M4	M	1
Snow, Justin	24:32:06	CO	2005	M3	M	2
Dobbins, Chris	24:32:07	CO	2005	M3	M	3
Grimes, Keith	24:32:50	CO	2005	M4	M	9
Swaney, Scott	24:33:52	CO	2005	M3	M	2
Stone, Tammy	24:35:09	CO	2005	F4	F	4
Nash, Doug	24:35:12	CO	2005	M5	M	5
Bennett, Brad	24:35:17	MT	2005	M4	M	5
Ehredt, Michael	24:36:06	CO	2005	M4	M	1
Keogh, Bobby	24:36:48	NM	2005	M5	M	12
Wasson, Mike	24:48:27	CO	2005	M3	M	1
Frye-Krier, Miles	24:52:02	CO	2005	M5	M	7
Martinez, Hector	25:04:10	CO	2005	M2	M	2
Afanador, Rudy	25:06:02	NY	2005	M4	M	1
Varela, Mario	25:06:26	CO	2005	M4	M	20
Garrison, Tom	25:11:39	NM	2005	M4	M	9
Meyer, Drew	25:11:50	TX	2005	M5	M	2
Brenden, Dan	25:41:58	AZ	2005	M5	M	8
Cofer, Chuck	25:44:09	CO	2005	M5	M	12
Holmes, Todd	25:49:16	CO	2005	M4	M	12
DeBoer, Amber	25:50:40	CO	2005	F2	F	3
Gill, J. Russell III	25:53:49	VA	2005	M4	M	1
Stickland, Rex	25:56:37	England	2005	M6	M	1
Smith, Paul	26:10:29	CO	2005	M4	M	10
Ellerbruch, Robert	26:15:25	SD	2005	M3	M	1
Baugh, Hollis	26:18:30	CO	2005	M3	M	11
Nelson, Stuart	26:19:54	MI	2005	65	M	14
Grobeson, Jay	26:22:33	CA	2005	M4	M	11
Manley, Brian	26:27:36	CO	2005	M4	M	13
Pence, Eric	26:31:47	CO	2005	M3	M	24
Krautmann, Charlie	26:38:58	CO	2005	M2	M	1
Servilla, Michael	26:39:37	NM	2005	M4	M	1
Schoenlaub, Paul	26:41:32	MO	2005	M4	M	12
Kern, Kristen	26:45:10	NM	2005	M4	M	10

Bohn, Eric	26:46:43	CA	2005	M3	M	2
Hill, Jon	26:50:50	TX	2005	M3	M	2
Bodington, Tia	26:54:30	CO	2005	F4	F	2
Goldberg, Dave	26:56:05	AZ	2005	M4	M	3
Mackie, Glenn	26:56:37	TX	2005	M4	M	1
Blom, Keith	26:58:48	CA	2005	M4	M	1
Miller, Larry	27:06:39	AZ	2005	M3	M	2
Brown, James	27:08:24	WI	2005	M4	M	1
Matticks, Kerry	27:20:38	CO	2005	M3	M	3
Hall, Larry	27:21:57	IL	2005	M5	M	10
Redland, Rickie	27:24:34	CO	2005	F5	F	6
Arter, Julie	27:26:55	AZ	2005	F4	F	10
Benner, Patrick	27:29:57	CO	2005	M4	M	4
Ruiz, George	27:35:32	NV	2005	M4	M	2
Laster, Bill	27:40:54	CO	2005	M5	M	14
Turner, Joy	27:45:27	CO	2005	F4	F	4
Curiel, Tyler	27:45:56	LA	2005	M4	M	11
Ulrich, Marshall	27:45:56	CO	2005	M5	M	13
Freeman, Richard	27:48:08	PA	2005	M4	M	2
Costilow, Brian	27:49:15	CO	2005	M3	M	10
Schwartz, Michelle	27:49:30	CO	2005	F3	F	7
Van Deren, Diane	27:49:51	CO	2005	F4	F	1
Anthony, Annette	27:49:52	CO	2005	F5	F	1
Truhe, Eric	27:52:20	CO	2005	M3	M	9
Massoud, Michael	27:52:22	CA	2005	M2	M	1
DeWitt, Larry	27:54:28	CO	2005	M4	M	3
Perry, Dale	27:56:23	CO	2005	M4	M	4
Jones, Les	27:56:41	TN	2005	M4	M	9
Heist, Gwen	27:58:16	MO	2005	F3	F	1
Drey, Dennis	28:02:07	NM	2005	M5	M	6
Muthig, Alec	28:03:06	WY	2005	M3	M	1
Gebhart, Susan	28:04:44	CO	2005	F5	F	5
Scholz, Monica	28:05:10	Canada	2005	M3	M	5
Lamb, Gordon	28:07:42	England	2005	M4	M	1
Carlson, Bill	28:09:39	CA	2005	M4	M	1
Gabe, Eric	28:10:19	CO	2005	M3	M	3
Weisshaar, Hans-Dieter	28:17:12	Germany	2005	65	M	9

Oberheide, Jim	28:19:49	CO	2005	M6	M	5
Trapp, Gregory	28:20:06	OHH	2005	M4	M	2
Goodrich, Sara	28:20:33	CO	2005	F2	F	1
Fox, Jason	28:21:09	AZ	2005	M3	M	1
Allison, Russell	28:21:24	OK	2005	M4	M	1
Busse, Dan	28:23:27	VT	2005	M3	M	5
Griffin, George	28:27:22	CO	2005	M6	M	1
McCarville, Kirk	28:27:45	AZ	2005	M5	M	2
Murphy, Natalie	28:28:26	CO	2005	F3	F	1
Stoll, Barbara	28:30:08	CO	2005	F4	F	4
Kelleher, Jim	28:30:59	CO	2005	M4	M	1
Reimer, Rick	28:31:08	CO	2005	M5	M	6
Kahn, Phil	28:34:32	CO	2005	M5	M	11
Schubert-Akin, Jennifer	28:44:19	CO	2005	F4	F	3
Gebger, Vince	28:46:28	CO	2005	M5	M	3
Crock, Bret	28:47:23	CO	2005	M4	M	11
Dodd, Gary	28:47:28	NM	2005	M4	M	2
Simpson, Beth	28:49:01	WI	2005	F4	F	3
Burton, Lee	28:49:18	CO	2005	M4	M	9
Cunningham, David	28:49:55	CO	2005	M4	M	6
Walker, Liz	28:50:59	GA	2005	F4	F	5
Fiet, Richard	28:52:28	UT	2005	M3	M	1
Bergman, Julie Ann	28:53:31	CO	2005	F5	F	3
Young, Alexander	28:54:33	Canada	2005	M2	M	1
Taylor, Greg	28:55:18	MN	2005	M5	M	5
Shwer, Steven	28:56:37	FL	2005	M4	M	2
Grooms, Jeanie	28:58:09	CO	2005	F4	F	6
Willis, Jeanne	28:58:40	CO	2005	F4	F	1
Gessner, June	28:59:47	CA	2005	F5	F	1
James, Michael	29:01:45	CO	2005	M3	M	2
Hopkins, Jennifer	29:02:42	CO	2005	F4	F	2
Bunk, Tom	29:03:40	WI	2005	M6	M	1
Mason, Scott	29:04:03	UT	2005	M4	M	1
Schloss, Henry	29:07:32	CO	2005	M3	M	5
Richardson, Norm	29:08:22	MA	2005	M5	M	2
Hobbs, John	29:08:44	CO	2005	M6	M	12
Striker, Douglas	29:09:47	CO	2005	M3	M	1

Murphy, Terry	29:10:47	GA	2005	M5	M	1
Bostow, Jeff	29:11:07	MN	2005	M4	M	4
Wright, Ron	29:12:17	CO	2005	M5	M	9
Baker, James	29:13:24	OK	2005	55	M	2
Curry, Garry	29:13:24	CO	2005	51	M	25
Jordan, King	29:13:43	DC	2005	M6	M	11
Fitzpatrick, Ben	29:13:52	CA	2005	M3	M	1
Jewell, Jack	29:14:09	CO	2005	M5	M	2
Kessler, Steven	29:14:28	CO	2005	M2	M	1
Steward, Dan	29:14:55	CO	2005	M4	M	8
Sullivan, Dennis	29:15:13	OR	2005	M3	M	2
Kerse, Jim	29:15:44	NZ	2005	M5	M	1
Villar, John	29:16:22	MT	2005	M4	M	1
Lambert, Willie	29:17:19	KS	2005	M4	M	1
Kapke, Robert	29:17:54	New Zealand	2005	M5	M	5
Yackley, Stephen Jr.	29:19:40	CO	2005	M2	M	1
Rainey, John	29:20:19	CO	2005	M5	M	4
Watanabe, Michio	29:21:27	CO	2005	M3	M	1
Stavig, Bob	29:22:38	MN	2005	M5	M	13
Williamson, Jim	29:23:17	UT	2005	45	M	1
Schnitzius, Tom	29:23:24	CO	2005	M5	M	11
Horan, Mark	29:23:29	CO	2005	M4	M	1
MacDonald, Geoff	29:23:55	Canada	2005	M3	M	1
Seebohar, Bob	29:24:08	CO	2005	M3	M	2
Otto, Jerome	29:24:49	New Zealand	2005	M4	M	1
Tate, Brian	29:25:48	SC	2005	M3	M	1
Julier, Michael	29:28:52	OR	2005	M3	M	1
Blenden, Mark	29:29:52	TX	2005	M5	M	1
Grauch, Chris	29:31:27	CO	2005	M3	M	2
Powell, Sandra	29:31:29	NM	2005	F4	F	1
Geist, William	29:32:20	NM	2005	M3	M	3
Halladay, Jason	29:32:20	NM	2005	M3	M	2
Cross, Stephen	29:33:20	CA	2005	M5	M	1
Miller, Greg	29:34:26	IL	2005	M4	M	1
Stevenson, Jeff	29:35:15	CA	2005	M5	M	6
Snyder, Gail	29:36:55	OR	2005	F4	F	4
Johnson, Kirk	29:37:18	CO	2005	M4	M	1

Name	Finish Time	State	Year	Age	Sex	#Finished
Bright, Shay	29:38:52	CO	2005	F3	F	1
Green, Ed	29:39:59	CO	2005	M5	M	1
Delman, Reid	29:41:29	CO	2005	M3	M	1
Rhodes, Terry	29:42:12	NV	2005	F4	F	1
Gallagher, Tommy	29:42:12	NV	2005	M4	M	3
Apple, Ron	29:42:28	TN	2005	M4	M	2
Benjamin, Ben	29:43:14	OR	2005	M5	M	4
Stahl, Bill	29:43:19	CO	2005	M4	M	4
Ferguson, Chrissy	29:43:42	AR	2005	F4	F	2
Brown, Thomas	29:43:59	CA	2005	M3	M	1
Gersitz, Lorraine	29:44:27	CA	2005	F5	F	1
Stringer, Pete	29:44:54	MD	2005	M6	M	2
Horne, Damian	29:46:51	NM	2005	M4	M	1
Mena, Ray	29:48:59	CA	2005	M4	M	1
Burchenal, Jeb	29:49:26	CO	2005	M4	M	3
Hulett, Jeffrey	29:49:28	CO	2005	M4	M	1
Fortunas, Daniel	29:50:57	FL	2005	M4	M	1
Joy, Ben	29:52:20	CO	2005	M3	M	1
Kumeda, Andy	29:52:43	CA	2005	M3	M	2
Scholl, Randolph	29:53:10	CA	2005	M4	M	1
Nemet, Alex	29:54:52	OH	2005	M3	M	1
Kinross-Wright, Cary	29:55:36	CO	2005	F3	F	1
Byrne, John	29:57:43	IA	2005	M4	M	3
Torelli, Giovanni Battista	29:59:59	Italy	2005	M5	M	1

2006

Name	Finish Time	State	Year	Age	Sex	#Finished
Krupicka, Anton	17:01:56	CO	2006	M2	M	3
Peterson, Steve	18:47:13	CO	2006	M4	M	7
Beuche, Jeff	19:53:30	CO	2006	M3	M	3
Harcrow, Harry	20:17:42	CO	2006	M3	M	7
Adams, Paul	20:19:22	CO	2006	M4	M	3
Powell, Bryon	20:42:26	VA	2006	M2	M	1
Finkel, Diana	20:43:19	CO	2006	F3	F	1
Meltzer, Karl	20:52:20	UT	2006	M3	M	1
Schmidt, Daniel	21:17:50	CO	2006	M4	M	6
Jamie, Scott	21:27:28	CO	2006	M3	M	1

Draney, Ty	21:33:07	WY	2006	M3	M	1
Hemsky, John	21:44:20	CO	2006	M3	M	2
Holmes, Todd	22:04:12	CO	2006	M5	M	12
Anderson, John	22:14:48	CO	2006	M2	M	2
Blaugrund, Daniel	22:16:59	NM	2006	M3	M	1
Meyers, Scott	22:19:39	WI	2006	M3	M	4
Bindner, Eric	22:23:58	CO	2006	M4	M	2
Allen, Michael	22:36:13	AL	2006	M4	M	1
Klopfenstein, Scott	22:40:50	CO	2006	M3	M	12
Kulak, Joe	22:47:26	PA	2006	M3	M	12
Clay, Matt	22:56:03	CO	2006	M2	M	1
Welsh, Jeffrey	22:57:35	NC	2006	M5	M	13
Frost, Paul	23:00:43	TX	2006	M3	M	1
Farrett, Bill	23:11:01	CO	2006	M3	M	1
Kochik, Phil	23:12:36	WA	2006	M2	M	1
Donaldson, Jamie	23:22:49	CO	2006	F3	F	3
Karnazes, Dean	23:24:29	CA	2006	M4	M	1
Grant, Bruce	23:35:22	Canada	2006	M4	M	1
Farris, Mike	23:38:48	CO	2006	M3	M	1
Seremet, Eric	23:39:04	CO	2006	M3	M	7
Stofko, Paul	23:39:17	IN	2006	M3	M	6
Hendrickson, Christian	23:41:28	CO	2006	M3	M	4
Walker, Justin	23:43:18	CO	2006	M2	M	1
Africa, Darcy	23:53:48	CO	2006	F3	F	2
Myers, Jeff	24:05:07	CO	2006	M4	M	4
Adams, Lauren	24:15:25	UT	2006	F2	F	2
Bidwell, William	24:19:52	CO	2006	M5	M	1
Truhe, Eric	24:23:25	CO	2006	M3	M	9
Schoenlaub, Paul	24:33:13	MO	2006	M4	M	12
Campbell, Jared	24:41:28	UT	2006	M2	M	1
Crock, Bret	24:43:22	CO	2006	M4	M	11
Hutchison, Lorie	24:45:25	UT	2006	F4	F	1
Gingerich, Zach	24:46:32	IL	2006	M2	M	1
Cofer, Chuck	24:47:42	TX	2006	M5	M	12
Brozk, Susan	24:49:32	NM	2006	F3	F	5
Genet, John	24:51:00	CO	2006	M4	M	6
Kern, Kristen	24:51:47	NM	2006	M4	M	10

Gordon, Ken	24:59:51	NM	2006	M4	M	10
Varela, Mario	25:24:45	CO	2006	M4	M	20
Smith, Paul	25:49:20	CO	2006	M5	M	10
Meyer, Jack	25:55:21	CA	2006	M4	M	1
Sheridan, Phil	25:56:52	KS	2006	M4	M	2
Robbins, Christian	25:57:34	CO	2006	M3	M	1
Brenden, Dan	26:00:15	AZ	2006	M5	M	8
Rodriguez, Andy	26:00:37	CO	2006	M2	M	2
Reimer, Rick	26:10:07	CO	2006	M5	M	6
Grauch, Chris	26:13:51	CO	2006	M3	M	2
Gordon, Scott	26:14:11	NM	2006	M4	M	11
Englund, Tim	26:14:38	WA	2006	M4	M	1
Ehrlich, Mike	26:16:01	CO	2006	M4	M	9
Neadeau, Kevin	26:16:56	CO	2006	M3	M	2
Courtney, Michael	26:18:53	NM	2006	M5	M	4
Garrison, Tom	26:19:50	NM	2006	M4	M	9
Apt, Kirk	26:31:35	CO	2006	M4	M	20
Nelson, Stuart	26:33:22	CO	2006	M6	M	14
Schurr, David	26:36:30	CA	2006	M4	M	1
Goldberg, David	26:37:10	AZ	2006	M4	M	3
Curry, Garry	26:40:48	CO	2006	M5	M	25
Deupree, Chisholm	26:40:48	OK	2006	M4	M	11
Robertson, Craig	26:44:04	CO	2006	M4	M	6
Khajavi, Jamshid	26:44:59	WA	2006	M5	M	7
Labbe, Chris	26:47:07	CO	2006	M3	M	3
Dewitt, Larry	26:55:43	CO	2006	M4	M	3
Cosmas, Mark	26:58:55	AZ	2006	M3	M	1
Olson, Joshua	27:01:41	ID	2006	M3	M	1
Laster, Bill	27:07:23	CO	2006	M5	M	14
Costilow, Brian	27:08:31	CO	2006	M3	M	10
Arter, Julie	27:12:01	AZ	2006	F4	F	10
Fancett, Ken	27:15:14	England	2006	M5	M	1
McHargue, Mike	27:15:58	CO	2006	M4	M	4
DeWitt, Judy	27:20:30	CO	2006	F4	F	1
Kent, Brian	27:24:53	CO	2006	M4	M	2
Weisshaar, Hans-Dieter	27:29:16	Germany	2006	M6	M	9
Petrisko, Kevin	27:29:38	WA	2006	M3	M	1

Zeif, Jonathan	27:30:59	CO	2006	M5	M	11
Schwartz, Michelle	27:34:00	CO	2006	F3	F	7
Watts, Matthew	27:35:54	CO	2006	M4	M	5
Jones, Les	27:46:19	TN	2006	M4	M	9
Geist, Bill	27:47:41	NM	2006	M3	M	3
Riddick, Jerry	27:50:01	AZ	2006	M5	M	1
Pence, Eric	27:50:36	CO	2006	M4	M	24
Kern, Stuart	27:52:16	MD	2006	M4	M	4
Wzientek, Nick	27:54:26	MO	2006	M2	M	3
Knipling, Keith	27:59:34	IL	2006	M3	M	1
Allemang, Jason	28:00:07	MO	2006	M3	M	2
Lang, Chris	28:00:09	CO	2006	M4	M	1
Robertson, Joy	28:04:24	CO	2006	F4	F	4
Walker, Liz	28:05:33	GA	2006	F4	F	5
Ferrari, Guido	28:05:53	NC	2006	M4	M	2
Gebhart, Susan	28:06:51	CO	2006	F5	F	5
Diak, Peter	28:08:27	NM	2006	M2	M	1
Bartzen, Gene	28:08:50	CO	2006	M5	M	10
Finkbeiner, Bill	28:10:34	CA	2006	M5	M	30
Van, Dave	28:10:44	CA	2006	M5	M	1
Blake, Neil	28:10:57	NM	2006	M4	M	7
Keogh, Bobby	28:11:18	NM	2006	M4	M	12
Scott, Geoff	28:12:09	NC	2006	M5	M	1
Busse, Dan	28:12:43	CO	2006	M3	M	5
Sandoval, Johnny	28:13:00	CO	2006	M4	M	12
Manley, Brian	28:13:45	CO	2006	M4	M	13
Fromm, Anita	28:13:55	CO	2006	F3	F	2
Nilsen, Amanda	28:14:30	CO	2006	F2	F	1
Weissman, Joshua	28:16:46	CO	2006	M3	M	3
Kreb, Kim	28:20:22	CO	2006	F3	F	4
Brown, Mathieu	28:21:59	AZ	2006	M3	M	2
Quivey, David	28:22:22	VA	2006	M4	M	1
Engelmann, Eb	28:27:05	OR	2006	M6	M	2
Knight, Andy	28:27:27	UT	2006	M2	M	1
Geiss, Jean-Francois	28:27:56	France	2006	M5	M	1
James, Michael	28:28:30	CO	2006	M3	M	2
Thom, Bill	28:32:17	IL	2006	M4	M	2

Benner, Pat	28:34:47	CO	2006	M4	M	4
Hoger, Steve	28:34:56	NE	2006	M4	M	1
Steward, Dan	28:38:35	CO	2006	M4	M	8
Bergeron, John	28:42:44	CO	2006	M4	M	1
Piala, Chad	28:44:34	CO	2006	M3	M	3
Eason, Greg	28:46:11	AR	2006	M3	M	2
Boddy, Ted	28:47:04	CO	2006	M2	M	1
Lynch, Mike	28:48:56	NJ	2006	M4	M	1
Cunningham, Dave	28:49:07	CO	2006	M4	M	6
Bryant, Patty	28:49:43	CA	2006	F4	F	2
Saraniero, Robert	28:50:27	VA	2006	M3	M	1
Dove, John	28:50:40	GA	2006	M4	M	1
Abramowitz, Fred	28:50:50	CO	2006	M5	M	10
Simmons, Keith	28:51:25	TX	2006	M4	M	1
Cassady, Robert	28:52:04	CO	2006	M4	M	1
Douglas, Steven	28:54:16	CA	2006	M4	M	1
Nelson, Jeff	28:56:39	UT	2006	M4	M	2
Gordon, David	29:04:22	CA	2006	M6	M	1
Reed, Pam	29:05:24	AZ	2006	F4	F	6
Andrews, Kevin	29:05:58	CO	2006	M4	M	2
Simpson, Beth	29:06:53	WI	2006	F4	F	3
Hall, Larry	29:06:53	IL	2006	M5	M	10
Swanson, Grant	29:10:13	CA	2006	M5	M	2
Leahy, Patrick	29:10:42	CO	2006	M3	M	1
Nichols, Stephen	29:10:52	CO	2006	M4	M	1
Delman, Glen	29:12:11	CO	2006	M4	M	1
Barnes, Molly	29:12:13	CO	2006	F3	F	6
Breyfogle, James	29:12:52	NM	2006	M2	M	1
Stavig, Bob	29:14:59	MN	2006	M5	M	13
Mease, Luke	29:15:21	CO	2006	M2	M	1
Stum, Richard	29:15:35	UT	2006	M5	M	1
Henry, Gary	29:18:59	KS	2006	M5	M	2
Dorsey, Kevin	29:19:46	TN	2006	M3	M	1
Samuelson, Mike	29:19:46	TN	2006	M4	M	1
Barnett, Gordon	29:20:32	CO	2006	M5	M	1
Lloyd, John	29:20:50	CO	2006	M3	M	1
Cuyler, Collins	29:21:00	CO	2006	M2	M	2

Kapke, Robert	29:21:06	NE	2006	M5	M	5
Kennedy, Matt	29:21:49	CO	2006	M3	M	1
Miller, Larry	29:21:56	AZ	2006	M3	M	2
Houck, Eric Sr.	29:22:15	CO	2006	M4	M	1
Ruiz, George	29:22:19	NV	2006	M4	M	2
Schneider, Richard	29:22:21	CO	2006	M5	M	1
Fessick, Michael	29:23:28	CO	2006	M3	M	1
Knipling, Gary	29:23:51	VA	2006	M6	M	1
Taylor, Greg	29:26:40	MN	2006	M5	M	5
Gruenewald, Ray	29:27:45	WA	2006	M4	M	1
Carty, Sean	29:28:18	NY	2006	M2	M	1
Seglie, Scott	29:28:18	CO	2006	M2	M	1
Thompson, Keith	29:31:04	ID	2006	M4	M	1
Rikoon, Robert	29:32:25	NC	2006	M5	M	1
Benhammon, Daniel	29:32:58	CO	2006	M2	M	5
Bostow, Jeff	29:34:42	MN	2006	M5	M	4
Creel, Norm	29:36:20	SD	2006	M5	M	3
Leedy, Gail	29:36:40	WY	2006	F5	F	3
Swanson, Bruce	29:37:44	NY	2006	M4	M	1
Schnitzius, Tom	29:39:49	CO	2006	M5	M	11
Guevara, Augustin	29:40:45	WI	2006	M4	M	1
Rastall, Jan	29:40:51	CO	2006	F4	F	1
Rastall, Pat	29:40:51	CO	2006	M5	M	1
Shwer, Steven	29:41:16	FL	2006	M4	M	2
Bogenrief, Angela	29:41:41	CO	2006	F2	F	1
Mueller, Marcus	29:45:36	CO	2006	M4	M	4
DePuy, Timothy	29:46:30	CO	2006	M4	M	1
Gebhardt, Terry	29:46:51	CO	2006	M3	M	1
Grimm, Paul	29:46:54	CO	2006	M3	M	2
Stone, Kyle	29:47:04	CO	2006	M3	M	1
Welch, Daniel	29:47:15	CO	2006	M2	M	2
McDonald, Ryan	29:47:57	MO	2006	M3	M	2
D'Onofrio, Kathy	29:48:20	CA	2006	F4	F	5
Mathis, John	29:48:51	CO	2006	M4	M	1
Faurie, Marie-Helene	29:50:27	CO	2006	F3	F	1
Anderson, Joey	29:50:40	NC	2006	M5	M	1
Lederer, Eric	29:52:10	AZ	2006	M2	M	2

Stoll, Barbara	29:55:08	TX	2006	F4	F	4
Alexander, Robert	29:55:08	TX	2006	M5	M	2
Bianciotto, Erick	29:57:31	CO	2006	M4	M	1
Peters, Gregory	29:58:44	CO	2006	M4	M	2

2007

Name	Finish Time	State	Year	Age	Sex	#Finished
Krupicka, Anton	16:14:35	CO	2007	M2	M	3
Harcrow, Harry	19:33:17	CO	2007	M4	M	7
Corfield, Charles	19:42:30	CA	2007	M4	M	5
Bearden, Quent	19:58:57	CA	2007	M3	M	2
Schmidt, Daniel	20:17:52	CO	2007	M4	M	6
Holmes, Todd	20:26:10	CO	2007	M5	M	12
Callahan, Duncan	20:35:55	CO	2007	M2	M	7
Bindner, Eric	21:05:19	CO	2007	M5	M	2
Adams, Paul	21:08:39	CO	2007	M4	M	3
Hendrickson, Christian	21:15:33	CO	2007	M3	M	4
Redpath, Glen	21:33:41	NY	2007	M4	M	1
Shaw, Phil	21:40:48	WA	2007	M2	M	1
Welsh, Jeffrey	21:53:55	NC	2007	M5	M	13
Goggins, David	22:15:36	CA	2007	M3	M	1
Hemsky, John	22:15:36	CO	2007	M3	M	2
Seremet, Eric	22:39:05	CO	2007	M3	M	7
Wolf, Joe	22:40:03	CO	2007	M3	M	1
Ishikawa, Hiroki	22:41:56	Japan	2007	M3	M	2
Stone, Tammy	22:44:54	CO	2007	F4	F	4
Jensen, Michele	22:49:14	CO	2007	F3	F	1
Stofko, Paul	22:56:32	CO	2007	M3	M	6
Cofer, Chuck	23:14:38	CO	2007	M5	M	12
Courtney, Michael	23:18:57	NM	2007	M5	M	4
Stott, Gary	23:24:15	ID	2007	M4	M	1
Adams, Lauren	23:31:19	UT	2007	F2	F	2
Thomas, Bill	23:34:37	WA	2007	M5	M	2
Cospolich, Helen	23:35:54	CO	2007	F3	F	4
Kulak, Joe	23:41:49	PA	2007	M3	M	12
Klopfenstein, Scott	23:42:47	CO	2007	M3	M	12
Robbins, Christian	23:47:15	CO	2007	M3	M	2

Guerrero, Luis	23:50:25	Mexico	2007	M4	M	9
Jolley, Kenneth	23:52:18	CO	2007	M2	M	2
Fisher, Brian	23:54:22	CO	2007	M4	M	7
Brozik, Susan	23:59:33	NM	2007	F4	F	5
Baugh, Hollis	24:01:38	CO	2007	M3	M	11
Dalton, Greg	24:01:54	CO	2007	M3	M	1
Holscher, Jake	24:06:09	CO	2007	M3	M	2
Carner, David	24:07:38	CO	2007	M4	M	4
Bidwell, Ted	24:09:13	CO	2007	M5	M	3
Koehler, Robert	24:13:16	CO	2007	M4	M	3
Truhe, Eric	24:15:22	CO	2007	M3	M	9
Miller, Marc	24:16:03	WY	2007	M2	M	1
Sundermeier, Ronda	24:16:26	OR	2007	F4	F	2
Nuttelman, Charlie	24:28:51	CO	2007	M3	M	1
Myers, Jeff	24:32:15	CO	2007	M4	M	4
Pacev, Tania	24:40:08	CO	2007	F4	F	2
Goding, Bryan	24:44:52	CO	2007	M3	M	2
Crock, Bret	24:46:35	CO	2007	M4	M	11
Varela, Mario	24:47:33	CO	2007	M4	M	20
Meyer, Darrel	24:47:37	TX	2007	M6	M	1
Scott, Pat	24:49:06	NM	2007	M5	M	8
Labbe, Gregory	24:51:49	CO	2007	M3	M	1
Genet, John	24:56:48	CO	2007	M4	M	6
Heller, Edwin	25:10:30	NM	2007	M4	M	4
Heard, Andrew	25:12:05	AZ	2007	M4	M	1
Kern, Kristen	25:19:21	NM	2007	M4	M	10
Taylor, Neal	26:03:13	CO	2007	M4	M	12
Kral, Steven	26:03:36	KY	2007	M4	M	1
Laster, Bill	26:06:00	CO	2007	M5	M	14
Crockett, David	26:15:46	UT	2007	M4	M	1
Struble, Robert	26:18:22	PA	2007	M5	M	2
Guerard, Ben	26:20:16	Canada	2007	M3	M	1
DeBoer, Amber	26:24:11	CO	2007	F2	F	3
Curiel, Tyler	26:25:17	TX	2007	M5	M	11
Costilow, Brian W.	26:25:21	CO	2007	M3	M	10
Wzientek, Nick	26:26:57	MD	2007	M2	M	3
Deitlaf, Leon	26:34:26	UT	2007	M4	M	1

Sanderson, Marc	26:34:27	UT	2007	M3	M	4
Neadeau, Kevin	26:35:58	CO	2007	M3	M	2
Leppert, Cory	26:36:45	CO	2007	M3	M	2
McHargue, Mike	26:40:58	CO	2007	M4	M	4
Moden, Don	26:43:05	AZ	2007	M4	M	1
Robertson, Joy	26:46:35	CO	2007	F4	F	4
Murri, Morgan	26:47:13	CO	2007	M4	M	4
Siljander, Brian	26:51:18	CA	2007	M3	M	1
Delfausse, Aaron	26:56:14	CO	2007	M3	M	1
King, Robert	27:00:24	TX	2007	M4	M	2
Pence, Eric	27:03:50	CO	2007	M4	M	24
Nelson, Stuart	27:04:06	CO	2007	M6	M	14
Smith, Paul	27:04:46	CO	2007	M5	M	10
Coogan, Fred	27:08:38	TX	2007	M4	M	1
Brenden, Dan	27:12:08	AZ	2007	M5	M	8
Deupree, Chisholm	27:13:28	OK	2007	M4	M	11
Schoenlaub, Paul	27:13:29	MO	2007	M4	M	12
Bybee, Charles	27:19:25	CO	2007	M4	M	12
Owen, Elwyn	27:22:54	CO	2007	M4	M	3
Khajavi, Jamshid	27:22:55	WA	2007	M4	M	7
Krier, Miles	27:24:26	CO	2007	M5	M	3
Curry, Garry	27:25:13	CO	2007	M5	M	25
Vargas, Erwin	27:26:44	CO	2007	M3	M	1
Garcia, Chris	27:30:17	CA	2007	M4	M	1
Garrison, Tom	27:32:32	NM	2007	M4	M	9
Gordon, Ken	27:32:33	NM	2007	M4	M	10
Finkbeiner, Bill	27:34:35	CA	2007	M5	M	30
Apt, Kirk	27:34:36	CO	2007	M4	M	20
Teeples, John	27:34:36	GA	2007	M4	M	1
Guzman, Henry	27:35:39	CO	2007	M4	M	2
Hagen, Julie	27:37:51	CO	2007	F3	F	1
Sowers, Thomas	27:39:46	CO	2007	M3	M	3
Trapp, Gregory	27:42:20	OH	2007	M4	M	2
Appleman, Donald	27:43:48	CO	2007	M3	M	1
Collins, Nick	27:44:07	OR	2007	M4	M	1
Glojek, William	27:45:20	CO	2007	M2	M	1
Townsend, Kevin	27:54:39	VA	2007	M3	M	2

Geist, Bill	27:55:28	NM	2007	M3	M	3
Halladay, Jason	27:55:28	NM	2007	M3	M	2
Miller, Jill	27:57:15	NC	2007	F3	F	1
Salasovich, James	27:59:24	CO	2007	M3	M	1
Staron, Jeff	27:59:29	CO	2007	M3	M	1
Miller, John	27:59:32	NM	2007	M3	M	1
Lebel, Lori	28:00:52	MA	2007	F3	F	1
Bauer, Thomas	28:02:13	OH	2007	M5	M	1
Wiley, Philip	28:04:08	CO	2007	M4	M	2
Arter, Julie	28:06:15	AZ	2007	F4	F	10
Benhammou, Daniel	28:08:58	CO	2007	M2	M	5
Weisshaar, Hans-Dieter	28:11:59	Germany	2007	M6	M	9
Ross, Joe	28:12:25	TX	2007	M3	M	1
Lederer, Eric	28:14:33	AZ	2007	M2	M	2
Zea, Donn	28:15:32	CA	2007	M4	M	1
Jarvis, Wade	28:15:53	Canada	2007	M4	M	9
Beine, Jo Ann	28:16:35	CO	2007	F5	F	3
Kline, Russell	28:17:28	AZ	2007	M4	M	1
Burch, Ryan	28:18:18	CO	2007	M2	M	4
Weissman, Joshua	28:20:15	CO	2007	M3	M	3
Piper, Daniel	28:21:49	CA	2007	M5	M	1
Long, Art	28:22:30	CO	2007	M3	M	4
Manley, Brian	28:23:09	CO	2007	M4	M	13
Hoffman, Karyn	28:24:49	CA	2007	F4	F	1
Redland-MacManus, Rickie	28:26:00	CO	2007	F5	F	6
Scott, Todd	28:27:29	MI	2007	M4	M	11
Fisher, Doug	28:29:11	TX	2007	M4	M	2
Eaton, Lyle	28:31:30	CO	2007	M4	M	1
Nash, Doug	28:31:32	CO	2007	M5	M	5
Mueller, Markus	28:33:09	CO	2007	M4	M	4
Gordon, Scott	28:33:29	NM	2007	M4	M	11
Gerber, Vince	28:34:04	CO	2007	M5	M	3
Bergman, Julie Ann	28:35:47	CO	2007	F5	F	3
Teisher, Jon	28:37:32	CO	2007	M3	M	4
Yeakel, Jr., Dave	28:38:17	VA	2007	M4	M	1
Johnson, Cory T.	28:40:34	UT	2007	M4	M	2
Bruno, Benjamin	28:41:02	CO	2007	M2	M	1

Simpson, Beth	28:41:12	WI	2007	F4	F	3
Hall, Larry	28:41:12	IL	2007	M5	M	10
DeWitt, Jim	28:42:02	NC	2007	M5	M	1
DeWitt, Paul	28:42:02	CO	2007	M3	M	5
Oliver, Gerald	28:44:07	CO	2007	M3	M	1
Martin, Ryan	28:47:27	CO	2007	M3	M	2
Gates, Rick	28:50:39	UT	2007	M5	M	7
Welch, Daniel	28:52:55	CO	2007	M2	M	2
Walker, Liz	28:54:19	GA	2007	F4	F	5
Bryant, Patty	28:54:35	CA	2007	F4	F	2
Abramowitz, Fred	28:54:52	CO	2007	M5	M	10
Lee, Eric	28:55:57	CO	2007	M2	M	1
Freeman, Richard	28:56:05	PA	2007	M4	M	2
Harrington, John	28:56:14	NM	2007	M4	M	1
Pfeil, Terri	28:56:39	CO	2007	F4	F	2
Suminski, Mike	28:57:19	Canada	2007	M5	M	2
Reichelt, Richard	28:57:27	NM	2007	M4	M	1
Kahn, Philip	28:58:39	CO	2007	M5	M	11
Lee, Euihwa	29:02:03	PA	2007	M4	M	1
Grooms, Jeanie	29:03:54	CO	2007	F5	F	6
Willigen, Hans van	29:04:08	ME	2007	M6	M	1
Stockton, Thomas	29:04:51	NM	2007	M4	M	1
Jones, Les	29:06:17	TN	2007	M4	M	9
Blake, Neil	29:07:02	NM	2007	M4	M	7
Martell, Gregg	29:07:53	ID	2007	M5	M	6
Jessen, David	29:08:44	IA	2007	M4	M	1
Kirstein, Nancy	29:11:10	SD	2007	F3	F	1
Burton, Lee	29:12:41	CO	2007	M4	M	9
Ehasz, James	29:13:51	WI	2007	M5	M	1
Rosenstein, Phil	29:15:34	WI	2007	M3	M	1
Hacker, Rob	29:15:48	CO	2007	M4	M	2
Benner, Pat	29:15:57	CO	2007	M4	M	4
Hicks, Tim	29:16:03	CA	2007	M6	M	1
Ehrlich, Mike	29:17:37	CO	2007	M4	M	9
Foley, Lucas	29:18:00	CA	2007	M2	M	1
Pennington, Luke	29:18:09	CO	2007	M2	M	1
Millar, Jed	29:19:00	UT	2007	M2	M	1

Smith, Mike	29:19:54	IN	2007	M4	M	3
Bennett, Heidi	29:20:59	UT	2007	F3	F	1
Reimer, Rick	29:21:16	CO	2007	M5	M	6
Park, Janet	29:21:35	CO	2007	F4	F	2
Sanders, Peter	29:21:39	CO	2007	M3	M	1
Gallagher, Tommy	29:22:03	NV	2007	M5	M	3
Steward, Dan	29:22:08	CO	2007	M4	M	8
Picon, Chris	29:22:28	CO	2007	M3	M	3
Hoffman, Michael	29:22:38	CA	2007	M4	M	1
Schnitzius, Tom	29:22:54	CO	2007	M5	M	11
Holtz, Allan	29:25:43	MN	2007	M5	M	3
Bodington, Tia	29:27:06	CO	2007	F5	F	2
Karzen, Matt	29:28:19	GA	2007	M4	M	1
Hobbs, John	29:30:11	CO	2007	M6	M	12
Bradley, Marv	29:33:00	CO	2007	M6	M	2
Basford, Chris	29:34:05	VA	2007	M4	M	1
Handy, Terri	29:34:50	CO	2007	F4	F	1
Read, Robert	29:35:53	CO	2007	M4	M	1
Branch, Tracey	29:36:06	CO	2007	F3	F	1
Huskie, Will	29:37:04	CO	2007	M4	M	5
Schmidt, Paul	29:38:01	IA	2007	M4	M	3
Stringer, Peter	29:38:57	MA	2007	M6	M	2
Ketchell, Bob	29:39:32	NY	2007	M5	M	1
Wieneke, Mark	29:39:55	CA	2007	M5	M	1
Pastorello, Joseph	29:40:23	CO	2007	M3	M	1
Amadori, Jason	29:40:36	FL	2007	M3	M	1
Francisco, Charles	29:44:04	ID	2007	M5	M	1
Bostow, Jeff	29:46:45	MN	2007	M5	M	4
Halloran, Robin	29:49:38	CO	2007	F3	F	1
Drey, Dennis	29:51:36	NM	2007	M5	M	6
Nelson, Jamen	29:52:38	UT	2007	M2	M	8
Strong, David	29:53:38	AZ	2007	M6	M	14

2008

Name	Finish Time	State	Year	Age	Sex	#Finished
Callahan, Duncan	18:02:39	CO	2008	25	M	7
Skurka, Andrew	18:17:25	MA	2008	27	M	1

Tiernan, Zeke	18:37:27	CO	2008	32	M	4
Hessek, Rick	19:18:22	CO	2008	42	M	4
Jaime, Scott	20:29:59	CO	2008	38	M	2
Corfield, Charles	21:18:33	CO	2008	49	M	5
Kane, Robin	21:19:40	VA	2008	45	M	1
Ciaramitaro, Shawn	21:27:12	CO	2008	36	M	2
Schmidt, Daniel	21:43:03	CO	2008	50	M	6
Goding, Bryan	21:46:07	CO	2008	36	M	2
Stofko, Paul	21:54:16	CO	2008	32	M	6
Fisher, Brian	22:10:26	CO	2008	42	M	7
Koop, Jason	22:37:08	CO	2008	29	M	5
Rodriguez, Andy	23:17:43	CO	2008	30	M	2
Cospolich, Helen	23:21:53	CO	2008	31	F	4
Murri, Morgan	23:24:57	CO	2008	43	M	4
Steckler, Glenn	23:28:04	CO	2008	43	M	2
Cofer, Chuck	23:31:51	CO	2008	57	M	12
Welsh, Jeffrey	23:34:18	NC	2008	53	M	13
Sarnquist, Bret	23:38:27	VT	2008	29	M	1
Garner, Trevor	23:44:02	ID	2008	30	M	1
Klopfenstein, Scott	23:48:43	CO	2008	37	M	12
Courtney, Michael	23:56:17	NM	2008	52	M	4
Bertot, Jeff	23:59:43	UT	2008	35	M	1
Truhe, Eric	24:04:07	CO	2008	33	M	9
Kulak, Joseph	24:21:32	PA	2008	40	M	12
Brackelsberg, Chad	24:23:24	UT	2008	35	M	2
Curiel, Tyler	24:31:29	TX	2008	52	M	11
Gaudet, David Wayne	24:32:08	Canada	2008	51	M	1
Seremet, Eric	24:35:46	CO	2008	37	M	7
Baugh, Hollis	24:36:48	CO	2008	39	M	11
Jarvis, Wade	24:40:27	Canada	2008	46	M	9
Ehret, Stephanie	24:43:28	CO	2008	45	F	5
Zurstadt, Caleb	24:46:21	ID	2008	36	M	1
Bawn, Robert	24:53:42	CO	2008	46	M	2
Labbe, Chris	25:15:55	CO	2008	39	M	3
Kirk, Steve	25:16:05	AR	2008	47	M	1
Black, Andy	25:39:14	CA	2008	50	M	2
Genet, John	25:59:02	CO	2008	50	M	6

Royse, Robert	26:03:22	WY	2008	35	M	2
Smith, Paul	26:03:44	CO	2008	52	M	10
Varela, Mario	26:04:15	CO	2008	49	M	20
Claridge, Rhonda	26:05:25	CO	2008	41	F	2
Ferguson, Stan	26:20:45	AR	2008	44	M	2
Gerber, Christopher	26:22:20	CO	2008	34	M	1
Townsend, Kevin	26:24:01	VA	2008	35	M	2
Longcope, David	26:26:49	CO	2008	41	M	4
Curry, Garry	26:29:02	CO	2008	54	M	25
Crock, Bret	26:35:13	CO	2008	50	M	11
Wheeler, Theresa	26:43:07	KS	2008	41	F	1
Struble, Robert	26:44:05	PA	2008	57	M	2
Beck, Christian	26:51:46	OR	2008	36	M	1
Burch, Ryan	26:58:36	CO	2008	28	M	4
Bybee, Charles	26:59:19	CO	2008	46	M	12
Olmer, Scott	27:01:46	CO	2008	37	M	2
Muzzy, Rich	27:04:45	CO	2008	42	M	1
Schoenlaub, Paul	27:04:46	MO	2008	49	M	12
Ramsay, John	27:04:47	TN	2008	24	M	3
Hanson, Geoff	27:14:47	WI	2008	33	M	1
Costilow, Brian	27:15:31	CO	2008	34	M	10
Bennett, Brad	27:17:42	MT	2008	52	M	5
Weisshaar, Hans-Dieter	27:18:48	Germany	2008	68	M	9
Nelson, Stuart	27:19:54	CO	2008	68	M	14
Jameson, Joseph	27:21:08	MI	2008	49	M	1
Prater, John	27:21:52	CO	2008	37	M	1
Kent, Brian	27:23:07	CO	2008	51	M	2
Holscher, Jake	27:24:36	CO	2008	31	M	2
Becker, Shane	27:24:50	CO	2008	42	M	1
Brenden, Dan	27:25:55	AZ	2008	57	M	8
Roman, Christopher	27:30:18	FL	2008	38	M	1
King, Robert	27:31:58	TX	2008	47	M	2
Hyson, Chad	27:32:42	Canada	2008	37	M	2
May, Mike	27:32:53	CO	2008	39	M	2
Swenson, Kristin	27:33:54	UT	2008	38	F	1
Jones, Les	27:36:31	TN	2008	49	M	9
Gordon, Ken	27:38:06	NM	2008	43	M	10

Manley, Brian	27:39:50	CO	2008	44	M	13
Jensen, Roger	27:40:10	CO	2008	58	M	1
Mueller, Markus	27:40:16	CO	2008	44	M	4
Taft, Kim	27:42:20	WY	2008	37	F	1
Kern, Kristen	27:43:04	NM	2008	43	M	10
Park, Janet	27:43:38	CO	2008	45	F	2
Kepple, Rich	27:49:25	NC	2008	36	M	1
Kelpe, Bryan	27:50:04	MO	2008	30	M	1
Sowers, Thomas	27:50:11	CO	2008	37	M	3
Fumich, Frank	27:54:34	VA	2008	40	M	1
Barloga, Scott	27:55:06	FL	2008	40	M	1
Humphrey, Jeremy	27:58:05	CO	2008	29	M	1
Arter, Julie	27:59:40	AZ	2008	47	F	10
Clark, Tony	28:00:46	KS	2008	30	M	1
Bauer-Walker, Liz	28:04:34	GA	2008	49	F	5
Halk, Matthew	28:07:03	CO	2008	30	M	1
Ulrich, Marshall	28:09:03	CO	2008	57	M	13
Khajavi, Jamshid	28:11:24	WA	2008	55	M	7
Weiner, John	28:12:45	WY	2008	43	M	2
Herbert, Jean	28:14:10	NM	2008	51	F	2
Jorgensen, Will	28:15:21	TN	2008	49	M	2
Wright, Bill	28:18:11	CO	2008	46	M	1
Churchill, Sean R.	28:18:54	WI	2008	42	M	9
Vaughn, Will	28:21:05	CO	2008	36	M	1
Murray, Brian	28:23:03	NM	2008	35	M	3
Hedlund, Roger	28:24:54	CO	2008	49	M	2
Grant, Todd	28:27:45	CO	2008	44	M	3
Maylin, Russell	28:29:09	New Zealand	2008	45	M	2
O'Hear, Carol	28:31:31	MA	2008	33	F	1
Labo, Todd	28:32:29	CO	2008	38	M	1
Harry, Chris	28:33:07	CO	2008	39	M	1
Irvin, Kristina	28:33:22	CA	2008	50	F	2
Hedges, Jeremy	28:33:37	CO	2008	33	M	1
McDonald, Ted	28:33:51	CA	2008	44	M	3
Lucas, Sue	28:35:47	Canada	2008	44	F	1
Rispolie, Denise	28:36:52	Canada	2008	36	F	1
Owen, Elwyn	28:38:13	CO	2008	46	M	3

Zerbe, John	28:38:41	CA	2008	40	M	1
Canning, Phil	28:40:17	GA	2008	44	M	1
Greer, John	28:41:16	AZ	2008	49	M	8
Blake, Neil	28:42:18	NM	2008	43	M	7
Coonrod, Kurt	28:42:18	NM	2008	48	M	8
Harcrow, Gina	28:49:12	CO	2008	36	F	3
Scott, Todd	28:50:48	MI	2008	44	M	11
Keogh, Bobby	28:51:36	NM	2008	59	M	12
Do, Theresa	28:52:28	CO	2008	45	F	1
Wilcox, David	28:54:00	CO	2008	46	M	8
Quinn, Tim	28:55:29	CA	2008	61	M	1
Geraldi, Alan	28:57:35	CA	2008	43	M	1
McBee, Natalie	28:58:04	AR	2008	35	F	1
Smith, Alan	28:59:15	CO	2008	39	M	8
Hall, Larry	28:59:43	IL	2008	54	M	10
Jones, Stephanie	29:00:36	CO	2008	38	F	4
Wang, Gary	29:01:38	CA	2008	40	M	1
Leedy, Gail	29:02:07	WY	2008	54	F	3
Kreb, Kim	29:05:37	CO	2008	39	F	4
Wiaderek, Markus	29:08:24	Canada	2008	40	M	1
Burleson, Joe	29:10:37	CO	2008	58	M	2
Finkbeiner, Bill	29:14:29	CA	2008	52	M	30
Deugan, Jessica	29:14:35	CO	2008	32	F	3
Stone, Chuck	29:15:51	CO	2008	45	M	8
Nakauchi-Hawn, Laurie	29:16:08	CO	2008	38	F	12
McKenzie, Gavin	29:17:44	CO	2008	24	M	1
Weller, Clyde	29:17:44	CO	2008	45	M	1
Edinger, Perry	29:18:33	AZ	2008	47	M	2
Bales, James	29:18:47	TX	2008	28	M	1
Burton, Lee	29:19:01	CO	2008	47	M	9
Guest, Kevin	29:19:51	MO	2008	39	M	1
Sterner, Nicholas	29:20:37	CO	2008	46	M	1
Gates, Rick	29:23:37	UT	2008	51	M	7
Goldberg, David	29:23:46	AZ	2008	48	M	1
Snyder, Jeffrey	29:24:46	TX	2008	31	M	1
Norquist, Craig	29:26:18	AZ	2008	41	M	2
Slagel, Craig	29:28:43	CA	2008	35	M	1

Janssens, Frank	29:29:37	Canada	2008	48	M	1
Earle, Lieko	29:29:52	CO	2008	33	F	2
Lettovsky, Ladislav	29:30:30	CO	2008	47	M	2
Fortney, Darren	29:32:10	WI	2008	40	M	1
Zeif, Jonathan	29:32:52	CO	2008	55	M	11
Talbot, Justin	29:33:04	CO	2008	31	M	1
Keefe, Daniel	29:33:12	OK	2008	43	M	7
Appert, John	29:35:03	NV	2008	29	M	3
Schnitzius, Thomas	29:35:39	CO	2008	55	M	11
Stegner, Benjamin	29:36:51	CA	2008	36	M	1
Resa, Brandi	29:37:25	CO	2008	35	F	1
Baker, Jay	29:38:06	SC	2008	47	M	5
Peters, Marcia	29:38:16	PA	2008	51	F	1
Brown, Michael	29:38:40	OH	2008	45	M	2
Cunningham, Dave	29:39:01	CO	2008	44	M	6
Holtz, Allan	29:39:11	MN	2008	58	M	3
Malone, Kristin	29:39:41	CO	2008	33	F	1
Ficke, James	29:40:42	TX	2008	47	M	1
McDonald, Ryan	29:40:59	CA	2008	34	M	2
Westerhoff, Bruce	29:41:06	IL	2008	47	M	1
Kane, Roger	29:41:30	CO	2008	50	M	1
Churgovich, Raymond	29:44:06	CO	2008	42	M	4
Letendre, Jerry	29:44:39	OR	2008	46	M	1
Parish, Ryan	29:45:24	CO	2008	22	M	1
Houlette, Ronald	29:45:53	CO	2008	55	M	1
Stevenson, Jeff	29:46:22	CA	2008	62	M	6
Schloss, Henry	29:46:40	CO	2008	34	M	5
Harrington, Justin	29:47:00	CO	2008	21	M	1
Telles, Louis	29:47:23	NM	2008	48	M	2
Schubert-Akin, Jennifer	29:49:02	CO	2008	51	F	3
Harrington, Matt	29:51:09	TX	2008	40	M	1
Colonnieves, Felix	29:52:00	CO	2008	47	M	1
Martin, Brian	29:52:17	CA	2008	30	M	1
Redland, Rickie	29:53:21	CO	2008	54	F	6
Kruger, Kyle	29:55:20	AR	2008	26	M	1
Parsons, Tammy	29:59:30	NM	2008	45	F	2

2009

Name	Finish Time	State	Year	Age	Sex	#Finished
Parr, Timmy	17:27:23	CO	2009	27	M	3
Lewis, Nick	17:44:26	TN	2009	23	M	1
Callahan, Duncan	18:26:40	CO	2009	26	M	7
Henshaw, Andrew	18:56:41	NY	2009	23	M	1
Beuche, Jeff	18:58:40	CO	2009	34	M	3
Pedatella, Nick	19:29:36	CO	2009	23	M	1
Graubins, Garett	19:38:57	CO	2009	36	M	5
Koop, Jason	19:43:08	CO	2009	30	M	5
Jones-Wilkins, Andy	19:49:42	ID	2009	41	M	1
Powell, Bryon	19:54:26	VA	2009	31	M	1
Schwartzbard, Aaron	20:17:36	VA	2009	32	M	1
Guerrero, Luis	20:47:33	Mexico	2009	46	M	9
Burch, Ryan	20:51:32	CO	2009	29	M	4
Wacker, Marty	20:52:12	CO	2009	38	M	3
Clemons, Lynette	20:58:01	CO	2009	35	F	2
Kocanda, Tony	21:05:27	MN	2009	36	M	1
Ziegenfuss, Joe	21:08:12	MN	2009	35	M	2
Truhe, Eric	21:17:51	CO	2009	34	M	9
Steckler, Glenn	21:29:42	CO	2009	44	M	2
Cooper, Ryan	21:33:11	CO	2009	35	M	4
Donaldson, Jamie	21:53:37	CO	2009	34	F	3
Africa, Darcy	21:55:22	CO	2009	34	F	2
Bawn, Bob	22:37:23	CO	2009	47	M	2
Mietz, Josh	22:59:39	NE	2009	30	M	1
Welsh, Jeffrey	23:04:09	NC	2009	54	M	13
Fisher, Brian	23:07:19	CO	2009	43	M	7
Harcrow, Harry	23:10:49	CO	2009	42	M	7
Coury, Nick	23:12:03	AZ	2009	21	M	1
Poland, Mike	23:16:02	CO	2009	42	M	1
Williams, Brooks	23:21:27	CO	2009	26	M	4
Walick, Dave	23:24:11	TX	2009	38	M	2
Smith, Alan	23:29:07	CO	2009	40	M	8
Murri, Morgan	23:33:32	CO	2009	44	M	4
Grant, Todd	23:35:25	CO	2009	45	M	3
Pashley, Drew	23:45:11	CO	2009	26	M	2

Rancourt, Wayne	23:52:09	ID	2009	46	M	1
Price, John	23:53:15	OR	2009	51	M	2
Royse, Robert	23:54:49	WY	2009	36	M	2
Klopfenstein, Scott	23:56:11	CO	2009	38	M	12
Wheeler, Rebecca	23:58:24	WY	2009	35	F	1
Traylor, Peter	24:08:14	AZ	2009	32	M	1
Myers, Jeff	24:10:22	CO	2009	50	M	4
DeWitt, Larry	24:10:35	CO	2009	51	M	3
Cronin, Kelly	24:14:22	CA	2009	32	F	1
Brozik, Sus	24:18:47	NM	2009	42	F	1
Smith, Paul	24:22:26	CO	2009	53	M	10
Defty, Peter	24:26:23	CA	2009	49	M	1
LaBelle, Bruce	24:26:23	CA	2009	53	M	1
Cardwell, Nick	24:26:57	IA	2009	22	M	1
Teisher, Jon	24:29:20	CO	2009	33	M	4
Hanson, Corey	24:32:29	CO	2009	32	M	1
Holmes, Todd	24:33:41	CO	2009	53	M	12
Ferguson, Stan	24:43:55	AR	2009	45	M	2
Cofer, Chuck	24:44:25	CO	2009	58	M	12
Boyack, Chris	24:44:37	CO	2009	39	M	6
Beard, John	24:45:40	TX	2009	45	M	1
Snow, Justin	24:47:01	CO	2009	35	M	1
Burton, Tara	24:54:42	CO	2009	36	F	1
Holovnia, Paul	24:58:57	MN	2009	47	M	3
Hunt, Jay	25:19:18	CO	2009	30	M	4
Costilow, Brian	25:19:46	CO	2009	35	M	10
Curiel, Tyler	25:26:29	TX	2009	53	M	11
Wright, Chris	25:38:46	CO	2009	37	M	7
Turk, Jerry	25:38:58	CT	2009	51	M	1
Gordon, Ken	25:39:53	NM	2009	44	M	10
Sauer, Christy	25:41:52	CO	2009	34	F	1
Jarvis, Wade	25:43:23	Canada	2009	47	M	9
Willis, Benjamin	25:47:13	IL	2009	33	M	1
Schoenlaub, Paul	25:49:08	MO	2009	50	M	12
Heller, Edwin	25:54:42	NM	2009	47	M	4
McDonald, Ted	25:54:55	WA	2009	45	M	3
Kin Law, Chor	25:59:30	Hong Kong	2009	32	M	1

Kwok Keung, Chan	25:59:30	Hong Kong	2009	48	M	1
Remkes, Tom	26:10:44	UT	2009	47	M	1
Reich, Paul	26:12:56	CO	2009	50	M	1
Weisshaar, Hans-Dieter	26:14:20	Germany	2009	69	M	9
Dunn, Benjamin	26:15:02	CO	2009	36	M	1
Fraser, Kari	26:18:23	CO	2009	43	F	1
Apt, Kirk	26:21:06	CO	2009	47	M	20
Coogan III, Fred	26:25:18	TX	2009	45	M	1
Mueller, Markus	26:26:01	CO	2009	45	M	4
Erbele, Matt	26:31:23	CO	2009	36	M	1
Krier, Miles	26:32:07	CA	2009	57	M	3
Jones, Les	26:33:21	TN	2009	50	M	9
Williams, Richard	26:33:21	TN	2009	42	M	4
Glogovac, Scott	26:34:00	NV	2009	55	M	1
Peterman, Timothy	26:34:22	MO	2009	34	M	1
Beard, Marcy	26:38:56	TX	2009	40	F	1
Norberg, Paul	26:39:13	AZ	2009	57	M	1
Sissman, Matthew	26:39:19	WY	2009	35	M	1
Greer, John	26:39:47	AZ	2009	50	M	8
Gordon, Scott	26:42:00	NM	2009	48	M	11
Madden, Lisa	26:44:28	NY	2009	36	F	1
Picon, Chris	26:44:36	CO	2009	36	M	3
Smith, Christopher	26:46:19	TN	2009	25	M	1
Zeif, Jonathan	26:49:46	CO	2009	56	M	11
Lee, Terry	26:50:48	CA	2009	40	M	1
Morrissey, Megan	26:53:31	CO	2009	40	F	3
Holden, Carolyn	26:53:34	CO	2009	36	F	1
Norcia, Christopher	26:53:44	CO	2009	41	M	3
Stoll, Barbara	26:53:54	TX	2009	47	F	4
Bartzen, Gene	27:01:27	CO	2009	55	M	10
Lippman, Jason	27:04:09	TX	2009	37	M	5
Young, Olan	27:04:54	CO	2009	41	M	1
Wetzel, Lori	27:09:41	MA	2009	36	F	1
Kelly, Stewart	27:10:33	AZ	2009	31	M	2
Guerard, Debbie	27:12:22	Canada	2009	33	F	1
Christian, Jack	27:14:07	OK	2009	56	M	6
Battaglia, Veronica	27:16:10	AR	2009	36	F	1

Abram, Clare	27:17:54	CA	2009	38	F	1
LaBerge, Scott	27:17:54	CA	2009	52	M	1
Brenden, Dan	27:18:03	AZ	2009	58	M	8
Miller, Tim	27:25:23	CO	2009	39	M	2
Haubert, Donnie	27:28:11	CO	2009	31	M	3
Longcope, David	27:30:18	CO	2009	42	M	4
Copeland, Milada	27:31:01	UT	2009	45	F	1
Black, Andy	27:32:29	CA	2009	51	M	2
Grimm, Paul	27:34:03	CO	2009	40	M	2
Fullem, Jeffrey	27:35:43	PA	2009	32	M	1
Fein, Leah	27:38:03	CO	2009	29	F	1
Corrales, Ben	27:38:16	UT	2009	35	M	1
Bauer, Tom	27:40:34	OH	2009	58	M	3
Scott, Pat	27:41:23	NM	2009	56	M	8
Taylor, Dana	27:42:26	CA	2009	48	M	2
Varela, Mario	27:42:56	CO	2009	49	M	20
Telles, Louie	27:43:04	NM	2009	49	M	2
Stone, Tammy	27:45:30	CO	2009	47	F	4
Vogan, Lonnie	27:45:30	AL	2009	53	M	1
Kelly, Richard	27:46:11	MA	2009	48	M	1
Franklin, Martin	27:47:24	CO	2009	44	M	1
Owens, Kerry	27:51:42	DC	2009	46	F	1
Duncan, Randy	27:51:43	Canada	2009	47	M	1
Coulter, Bruce	27:52:25	UT	2009	50	M	1
Roberts, Stephen	27:53:43	CO	2009	43	M	1
Pence, Eric	27:54:30	CO	2009	43	M	24
Bauer, Liz	27:55:10	GA	2009	50	F	5
Peltonen, Garrett	27:55:30	CO	2009	27	M	2
Weiner, John	27:57:12	WY	2009	44	M	2
Decker, Kurt	27:58:06	MN	2009	38	M	1
Denys, Douglas	28:00:42	UT	2009	40	M	1
Lund, Trace	28:00:42	UT	2009	39	M	1
Preston, Peter	28:04:37	CT	2009	57	M	1
Odle, John	28:05:36	ID	2009	40	M	1
Curry, Garry	28:06:09	CO	2009	55	M	25
Finkbeiner, Bill	28:06:09	CA	2009	53	M	30
Moore, Joseph	28:07:09	TX	2009	31	M	1

Schwartz, Michelle	28:07:16	CO	2009	40	F	7
Seebohar, Bob	28:10:14	CO	2009	37	M	2
Piala, Chad	28:10:55	CO	2009	33	M	3
Coonrod, Kurt	28:11:49	NM	2009	49	M	8
Owen, Elwyn	28:12:52	CO	2009	47	M	3
Foster, Jen	28:15:32	AR	2009	37	F	1
Nagel, Mark	28:18:38	CO	2009	42	M	1
Schlotterback, Bryan	28:19:03	IA	2009	38	M	1
Martinez, Julian	28:21:25	CO	2009	47	M	1
Thrasher, Matt	28:21:54	CO	2009	26	M	1
Smith, Jason	28:23:54	OK	2009	37	M	1
Abramowitz, Fred	28:24:17	CO	2009	57	M	10
Neadeau, Kevin	28:24:43	CO	2009	38	M	2
Morgan, Jael	28:30:24	CO	2009	34	F	1
Masterson, Tom	28:30:40	CO	2009	64	M	1
Waterman, Tom	28:31:35	IA	2009	50	M	1
Hartman, Scot	28:32:51	CO	2009	40	M	2
Bybee, Charles	28:34:01	CO	2009	47	M	12
Keefe, Daniel	28:35:10	OK	2009	44	M	7
Nash, Doug	28:35:38	CO	2009	55	M	5
Nelson, Stuart	28:39:09	CO	2009	69	M	14
Parsons, Sharon	28:40:01	CO	2009	49	F	1
Grobeson, Jay	28:40:29	CA	2009	48	M	11
Hardwicke, Chanadra	28:40:39	CO	2009	37	F	1
Andresen, Will	28:41:16	MI	2009	48	M	1
Ellis, Randy	28:41:36	CO	2009	57	M	6
Basich, Crystal	28:42:22	OH	2009	26	F	1
Burleson, Joe	28:43:27	CO	2009	60	M	2
Couture, Troy	28:43:30	FL	2009	38	M	1
Sowers, Thomas	28:43:41	CO	2009	38	M	3
Stephens, Abigail	28:48:29	TX	2009	24	F	1
Grimes, Keith	28:49:11	CO	2009	50	M	9
Burger, Greg	28:51:21	KS	2009	42	M	1
Lang, Nicholas	28:51:32	KS	2009	27	M	1
Corley, David	28:53:57	TX	2009	47	M	1
Stone IV , Chuck	28:54:12	CO	2009	46	M	8
Tetsuro, Ogata	28:54:22	Japan	2009	27	M	1

Hampton, Dustin	28:56:47	CO	2009	32	M	1
Gallicchio, Luigi	28:56:50	TX	2009	28	M	1
Freedman, Aaron	28:57:24	FL	2009	44	M	1
Martin, Ryan	28:58:37	CO	2009	39	M	2
Henry, Gary	28:59:45	KS	2009	53	M	2
Kurisky, Jack	29:00:40	VA	2009	42	M	2
Kern, Kristen	29:02:43	NM	2009	44	M	10
Hall, Larry	29:03:18	IL	2009	55	M	10
Cassidy, John	29:04:12	CO	2009	44	M	1
Fries, Ken	29:05:24	TX	2009	42	M	3
Bright, Adam	29:05:40	FL	2009	43	M	1
Baker, Jay	29:06:06	SC	2009	48	M	5
Hall, Brian	29:06:09	MN	2009	32	M	1
Wescott, Scott	29:07:04	CO	2009	34	M	1
Carner, David	29:07:27	CO	2009	42	M	4
Walch, David	29:07:31	MO	2009	31	M	2
Cunningham, Dave	29:07:34	CO	2009	45	M	6
Homan, Paul	29:07:38	CO	2009	30	M	1
Grooms, Jeanie	29:08:17	CO	2009	53	F	6
Jones, Ryan	29:09:09	PA	2009	30	M	3
Bishop, Timothy	29:09:39	CO	2009	33	M	3
Churgovich, Raymond	29:12:26	CO	2009	43	M	4
Fegyveresi, John	29:13:11	PA	2009	33	M	4
Plumb, Steve	29:13:27	KS	2009	38	M	1
Hedlund, Roger	29:13:53	CO	2009	50	M	2
Sandhaas, Lawrence	29:15:08	IL	2009	41	M	1
Lowe, Greg	29:16:09	MA	2009	45	M	5
Reimer, Rick	29:17:16	CO	2009	60	M	6
Vincent, Charles	29:17:45	UT	2009	49	M	1
Godfrey, Paul	29:19:33	OR	2009	39	M	4
Herrera Cuadra, Mauricio	29:19:57	Mexico	2009	31	M	1
Thom, Bill	29:20:11	IL	2009	49	M	2
Chu, Ling-ru	29:20:15	CA	2009	35	F	1
Heinz, Jonathan	29:20:37	Canada	2009	22	M	1
Waggoner, Nancy	29:21:21	CO	2009	44	F	1
Timmermans, Lambert	29:22:16	CA	2009	42	M	1
Henges, Cynthia	29:22:35	TX	2009	31	F	2

425

Hadlich, Daniel	29:23:16	NM	2009	39	M	1
Mickelberry, Shad	29:23:27	NV	2009	33	M	1
Blake, Brendan	29:23:36	CO	2009	31	M	1
Stark III, Joseph	29:23:36	CA	2009	28	M	1
Simpson-Hall, Beth	29:24:19	WI	2009	50	F	1
Valdez, Russell	29:24:27	CO	2009	49	M	2
Middleton-Davis, Ashley	29:25:23	CO	2009	44	M	1
Newton, Doug	29:26:31	CO	2009	32	M	5
Huskie, Will	29:27:54	CO	2009	49	M	5
Taylor, Greg	29:28:00	MN	2009	62	M	5
Tilp, Jon	29:28:21	CO	2009	52	M	1
Bone, Theresa	29:28:44	CO	2009	37	F	1
Robertson, Joy	29:28:58	CO	2009	51	F	4
Wallace, Bill	29:30:22	CO	2009	46	M	1
Marquette, Andre	29:31:50	Canada	2009	44	M	1
Fargo, Bob	29:33:06	PA	2009	50	M	1
Henrikson, Scott	29:33:54	KS	2009	45	M	1
Mueller, Jasper	29:34:20	UT	2009	42	M	1
Tosch, David	29:34:31	AL	2009	59	M	1
Garcia, David	29:34:42	CO	2009	36	M	1
McHargue, Mike	29:35:22	CO	2009	49	M	4
Ferguson, Chrissy	29:36:04	AR	2009	48	F	2
Micklo, David	29:36:07	PA	2009	40	M	1
Gossman, Mike	29:36:13	IN	2009	49	M	1
Smith, Mike	29:36:14	IN	2009	51	M	3
Ruby, Abby	29:36:37	CO	2009	30	F	1
Dickson, Seth	29:37:08	CO	2009	23	M	1
Scott, Todd	29:37:16	MI	2009	45	M	11
Alexander, Robert	29:37:20	TX	2009	55	M	2
Abdo, Antonio	29:37:24	Mexico	2009	36	M	1
Renee Dessler, Jill	29:37:29	MN	2009	40	F	1
Fromm, Anita	29:40:16	NM	2009	38	F	2
Bassett, Nick	29:41:24	AZ	2009	64	M	4
Holtz, Allan	29:41:30	MN	2009	59	M	3
Martin, Claire	29:45:41	NH	2009	45	F	1
Banker, Bob	29:46:08	MO	2009	56	M	1
Kjellsen, Trygve	29:46:28	CO	2009	38	M	1

Brown, Michael	29:46:52	OH	2009	46	M	2
Pilcher, Kimberly	29:47:20	TX	2009	46	F	2
Crandall, Tom	29:47:46	TX	2009	44	M	1
Vasquez, Alberto	29:47:50	MD	2009	40	M	1
Broomfield, Robert	29:47:58	CO	2009	33	M	2
Voeks, Coleen	29:48:07	KS	2009	36	F	1
McCartney, Patrick	29:48:59	IN	2009	37	M	1
Dawson, Dave	29:50:29	TX	2009	42	M	2
Chapman, Donna	29:50:30	TX	2009	41	F	3
Hodges, Jerry	29:50:48	TX	2009	39	M	1
Godin, Tammy	29:50:55	MA	2009	46	F	1
Godin, Jeffrey	29:50:55	MA	2009	41	M	1
Baker, Geoffrey	29:51:55	MD	2009	51	M	1
O'Connell, Tom	29:52:37	CO	2009	58	M	2
Wiley, Philip	29:53:16	CO	2009	47	M	2
Hagin, John	29:55:11	CO	2009	66	M	1
Luckett, Carolyn	29:58:08	UT	2009	42	F	1

2010

Name	Finish Time	State	Year	Age	Sex	#Finished
Callahan, Duncan	17:43:25	CO	2010	27	M	7
Tiernan, Zeke	18:25:30	CO	2010	34	M	4
Bowman, Dylan	18:36:16	CO	2010	24	M	2
Gorman, Neal	18:47:54	DC	2010	33	M	1
Beuche, Jeff	18:58:37	CO	2010	35	M	1
Waggoner, Tim	19:19:35	CO	2010	38	M	2
Harcrow, Harry	19:23:56	CO	2010	43	M	7
Koop, Jason	19:40:11	CO	2010	31	M	5
Bien, Rod	19:46:03	OR	2010	38	M	2
Scott, W. Jared	19:47:49	CO	2010	39	M	1
Williams, Brooks	19:57:52	CO	2010	27	M	4
Truhe, Eric	20:56:59	CO	2010	35	M	9
Lewis, Sean	21:11:48	TX	2010	43	M	1
Lantz, Jason	21:18:30	PA	2010	29	M	1
Howard, Elizabeth	21:19:47	TX	2010	38	F	3
KIRCHER, Ryan	21:23:41	CO	2010	31	M	1
Reiss, Thomas	21:29:20	CA	2010	42	M	1

Moore, Steven	21:31:18	TX	2010	42	M	1
Schoenlaub, Paul	21:38:15	MO	2010	51	M	12
Hardel, Fabrice	21:43:45	CA	2010	36	M	1
Carrara, Joe	21:50:34	VT	2010	47	M	1
Doniec, Jacek	22:04:59	CA	2010	33	M	1
Larsen, David	22:12:58	OR	2010	39	M	1
Hendrickson, Christian	22:16:20	CO	2010	34	M	4
Willis, Matt	22:28:01	NC	2010	34	M	1
Lindermueller, Kurt	22:31:55	Spain	2010	50	M	1
Jones, Stephanie	22:35:05	CO	2010	40	F	4
Robertson, Craig	22:38:02	CO	2010	50	M	6
McCarthy, Micheal	22:39:46	OR	2010	46	M	1
Teirney, David	22:42:10	CO	2010	31	M	3
Arnstein, Michael	22:48:45	NY	2010	33	M	3
Dehlin, Daniel	22:49:28	MI	2010	29	M	1
McBride, Peter	22:51:30	CT	2010	24	M	1
Klopfenstein, Scott	22:53:53	CO	2010	39	M	12
Wolfrum, Ryan	22:54:31	CO	2010	33	M	1
MUSAL, Rasim	22:55:15	TX	2010	34	M	1
Van de Water, Joe	23:05:07	CA	2010	42	M	1
Sanel, Nathan	23:06:30	NH	2010	41	M	2
Pilla, Jack	23:07:28	VT	2010	52	M	1
Arnold, Ashley Hunter	23:08:17	CO	2010	23	F	2
Hoopes, Rick	23:16:38	NE	2010	55	M	1
Brozik, Sus	23:23:50	NM	2010	43	F	1
Hoover, Todd	23:24:41	UT	2010	43	M	1
Montero, Javier	23:28:11	Spain	2010	47	M	3
Postle, Mark	23:28:18	OR	2010	41	M	1
Constantino, Joe	23:29:56	TX	2010	41	M	3
Crock, Bret	23:30:01	CO	2010	52	M	11
Metz, Andrea	23:34:35	WI	2010	24	F	2
Young, Stephen	23:35:35	CO	2010	27	M	2
Hunt, Jay	23:38:39	CO	2010	31	M	4
Mulder, Aaron	23:39:46	PA	2010	35	M	1
Fisher, Chris	23:39:47	CO	2010	35	M	1
Liles, Travis	23:41:49	IL	2010	31	M	1
Teisher, Jon	23:42:16	CO	2010	35	M	4

Patrizi, Michael	23:44:56	CO	2010	27	M	2
Abramson, Lloyd	23:53:13	CO	2010	34	M	1
ONEILL, Patrick	23:54:28	CO	2010	46	M	1
Gordon, Ken	23:56:20	NM	2010	45	M	10
Passenti, Brian	23:57:22	CO	2010	36	M	5
Grant, Todd	23:58:44	CO	2010	46	M	3
Mobley, Mark	24:00:49	CO	2010	39	M	4
Hlavacek, Michael	24:03:13	CO	2010	38	M	2
HICKLE, Jay	24:07:56	CA	2010	45	M	1
Courtney, Michael	24:08:53	NM	2010	54	M	4
VOGLER, PoDog	24:11:14	AR	2010	44	M	1
Wacker, Marty	24:12:16	CO	2010	39	M	3
DALLEY, Josh	24:15:41	CO	2010	27	M	1
Bechtel, Adam	24:18:20	CO	2010	35	M	2
Jolley, Kenny	24:18:42	CO	2010	30	M	2
WORTS, Darren	24:19:41	NJ	2010	39	M	1
MASON, Mike	24:20:48	NC	2010	39	M	1
GAINES, Patrick	24:21:26	CO	2010	43	M	1
Welsh, Jeffrey	24:23:09	NC	2010	55	M	13
SWIGART, Jayson	24:24:43	CO	2010	30	M	1
COWAN, Charles	24:24:54	NY	2010	58	M	1
PATTON, Jason	24:30:21	NM	2010	31	M	1
Pashley, Drew	24:31:29	CO	2010	27	M	2
CHAN, Kwok-keung	24:31:46	Hong Kong	2010	50	M	1
DUNKELBERG, Kevin	24:32:01	CO	2010	39	M	1
Degrave, Leila	24:36:20	CO	2010	32	F	2
STEVENSON, Pete	24:36:46	CO	2010	37	M	1
Bradford, Jeremy	24:37:04	CO	2010	32	M	5
SALAZAR, Paul	24:37:23	TX	2010	47	M	1
HERMSEN, Zach	24:38:22	CO	2010	33	M	1
Maylin, Russell	24:38:37	New Zealand	2010	48	M	2
SISLER, Grant	24:39:53	CA	2010	33	M	1
DROUT, Jonathan	24:41:21	CO	2010	38	M	1
CRONE, Brian	24:41:27	NM	2010	44	M	1
SWINEFORD, Stuart	24:42:41	CO	2010	41	M	1
Wallace, Mark	24:44:01	CO	2010	48	M	3
DOMINGUEZ, Sebastian	24:44:24	Chile	2010	36	M	1

Longcope, David	24:46:44	CO	2010	43	M	4
Hornsby, Wyatt	24:47:54	CO	2010	37	M	5
MANNING, Andrew	24:48:24	CO	2010	44	M	1
PETERSON, Eric	24:48:34	AZ	2010	35	M	1
Scott, Pat	24:56:18	NM	2010	57	M	8
HAWKINS, Dale	24:57:07	CO	2010	36	M	1
Nakauchi-Hawn, Laurie	24:58:03	CO	2010	40	F	12
BROWN, Ryan	24:58:42	England	2010	36	M	1
FRIES, Ken	25:04:36	TX	2010	43	M	3
Churgovich, Raymond	25:07:30	CO	2010	44	M	4
SCHNEIDEWIND, Darin	25:11:00	KS	2010	41	M	1
LACHOWSKY, Jason	25:22:15	MN	2010	30	M	1
DOWSON, Katherine	25:22:19	ID	2010	44	F	1
Garber, Anthony	25:26:34	WY	2010	47	M	2
Mccurnin, Jeanne	25:33:27	IA	2010	54	F	4
Smith, Paul	25:40:43	CO	2010	54	M	10
Stofko, Paul	25:41:58	IN	2010	34	M	6
Morrissey, Megan	25:45:01	CO	2010	41	F	3
BASFORD, Chris	25:50:26	VA	2010	48	M	1
Apt, Kirk	25:56:31	CO	2010	48	M	20
BARRERA, Ruben	26:02:09	ME	2010	36	M	1
Veltman, Michael	26:03:32	NV	2010	27	M	2
SUNDAHL, Clark	26:04:31	CO	2010	40	M	2
Lippman, Jason	26:06:30	TX	2010	37	M	5
Ramsay, John	26:09:18	TN	2010	26	M	3
Costilow, Brian	26:09:28	CO	2010	36	M	10
BAKER, Steven	26:11:46	VA	2010	25	M	1
Constan, John	26:15:40	CO	2010	42	M	2
Holland, James	26:21:28	TN	2010	34	M	3
Curry, Garry	26:24:56	CO	2010	56	M	25
Bybee, Charles	26:26:05	CO	2010	48	M	12
SANCHEZ, Ray	26:29:00	CA	2010	43	M	1
COOK, William	26:29:05	CA	2010	41	M	1
Koehler, Robert	26:41:39	CO	2010	47	M	3
KUHN, Scott	26:44:48	CO	2010	40	M	1
Wzientek, Nick	26:49:05	MD	2010	29	M	3
Newton, Doug	26:50:12	CO	2010	33	M	5

SCHAMBERGER, Michelle	26:50:34	CO	2010	42	F	1
Benhammon, Daniel	26:56:44	CA	2010	29	M	5
HOUSE, David	26:57:50	FL	2010	28	M	1
KISTNER, Brian	26:59:11	SC	2010	39	M	1
LUPTON, Pat	27:01:07	CO	2010	37	M	1
Pence, Eric	27:05:39	CO	2010	44	M	24
RITA, Jason	27:06:18	MD	2010	44	M	1
Blake, Neil	27:11:13	NM	2010	45	M	7
Jones, Les	27:14:49	TN	2010	51	M	9
Lowe, Gregory	27:15:50	MA	2010	46	M	5
PETERS, Jamie	27:16:00	CO	2010	31	M	1
MAYO, Rick	27:16:25	MO	2010	34	M	1
McDonald, Ted Barefoot	27:16:57	WA	2010	46	M	3
SIMONSEN, Paal	27:18:46	Norway	2010	50	M	1
WELK, Margaret	27:19:16	NM	2010	35	F	1
STURGES, Frank	27:22:09	IN	2010	31	M	1
Herbert, Jean	27:24:36	NM	2010	53	F	2
Whitehead, Adam	27:26:26	CO	2010	42	M	3
Watts, Matthew	27:28:05	CO	2010	53	M	5
Koenig, Brad	27:30:54	NJ	2010	34	M	2
HOUDE, Patrick	27:31:13	CA	2010	43	M	1
FOUTS, Keith	27:31:47	CO	2010	32	M	1
MIKULA, Ty	27:33:32	CA	2010	34	F	1
Shivers, Regis	27:33:32	CO	2010	40	M	2
Janssen, Todd	27:35:08	OR	2010	42	M	2
Pilgrim, Brian	27:35:31	NM	2010	43	M	2
WEIGAND, Michael	27:36:19	VT	2010	36	M	1
Deupree, Chisholm	27:37:41	OK	2010	44	M	11
MAGIERA, Jay	27:38:13	NY	2010	42	M	1
Manley, Brian	27:39:29	CO	2010	46	M	13
Finkbeiner, Bill	27:39:29	CA	2010	54	M	30
OBERHEIDE, Tom	27:40:15	CO	2010	35	M	1
MARTIN, Brian	27:40:27	CA	2010	32	M	1
Churchill, Sean R.	27:40:39	WI	2010	44	M	9
BRACKELSBERG, Emily Mitzel	27:41:29	UT	2010	37	F	1
FERREIRA, Danny	27:43:23	NH	2010	27	M	1
Beuke, Donald	27:45:36	CO	2010	34	M	3

Name	Time	State	Year	Age	Sex	#
SANTOS, Rick	27:45:46	CA	2010	46	M	1
Rettig, Brad	27:46:12	NE	2010	30	M	2
SHANAHAN, Jason	27:46:21	NE	2010	35	M	1
Kelly, Stewart	27:46:33	AZ	2010	32	M	2
Curtis, Matthew	27:46:46	CO	2010	34	M	7
Scholz, Monica	27:46:59	CA	2010	43	F	5
HOLDAWAY, Dale	27:47:11	MI	2010	43	M	1
SWEENEY, Steven	27:48:40	NY	2010	55	M	1
WOLFF, Chris	27:49:16	CA	2010	38	M	1
STAFFORD, Rob	27:50:07	UT	2010	36	M	1
COBURN, Kirk Brand	27:50:44	TX	2010	38	M	1
HOOGE, Paul	27:51:14	CO	2010	47	M	2
MAHONEY, Mary	27:51:21	CO	2010	34	F	1
Ownbey, Garrett	27:51:30	CO	2010	21	M	3
Boyack, Chris	27:52:07	CO	2010	40	M	6
Scott, Todd	27:55:13	MI	2010	46	M	11
WORTMANN, Phillip	27:56:20	CO	2010	32	M	1
Bauer, Liz	27:56:26	GA	2010	51	F	5
STRATTON, Michael	28:00:07	VA	2010	26	M	1
CABILES, Nelinia	28:01:21	CO	2010	45	F	1
PLETTNER, Stefan	28:02:16	CA	2010	31	M	1
Mastin, Kevin	28:03:23	CO	2010	45	M	3
JONES, Daniel	28:03:55	CO	2010	36	M	1
Greer, John	28:06:00	AZ	2010	51	M	8
ASBELL, Robbie	28:06:39	UT	2010	35	M	1
Sanderson, Marc	28:06:42	UT	2010	39	M	4
BROWN, Karen	28:07:27	CO	2010	47	F	1
GOODMAN, Harris	28:07:45	CA	2010	45	M	1
Dawson, Dave	28:09:19	CO	2010	43	M	2
Schloss, Henry	28:09:38	CO	2010	36	M	5
Hartman, Scot	28:10:32	CO	2010	41	M	2
BENANZIN, Giuseppe	28:11:43	Italy	2010	43	M	1
Stephon, Michael	28:12:20	CO	2010	44	M	4
Jarvis, Wade	28:12:52	CA	2010	48	M	9
WACHT, Lynda	28:15:00	CO	2010	41	F	2
HAMRICK, Ruthanne	28:16:54	NM	2010	45	F	1
Nelson, Stuart	28:17:36	CO	2010	70	M	14

DeMoss, Jean	28:18:04	CO	2010	38	F	6
DAVIS, John	28:18:09	WV	2010	26	M	1
TANKOVICH, Bill	28:20:14	CO	2010	43	M	1
Piala, Chad	28:20:51	CO	2010	34	M	3
Bishop, Timothy	28:21:06	CO	2010	34	M	3
Clark, David	28:21:36	CO	2010	39	M	6
DUNMORE, Geoffrey	28:21:49	IL	2010	37	M	1
Godfrey, Paul	28:21:54	AZ	2010	40	M	4
Dehne, Aaron	28:22:38	CO	2010	37	M	2
GNOJEK, Tim	28:23:02	CO	2010	36	M	1
GNOJEK, Danny	28:23:03	CO	2010	43	M	1
FLOYD, Ernie	28:24:18	UT	2010	56	M	1
Parsons, Tammy	28:25:32	NM	2010	47	F	2
GARASA, Sergio	28:26:01	Spain	2010	43	M	1
KLEVETER, Jim	28:26:57	NE	2010	38	M	1
Ellis, Randy	28:27:30	OK	2010	58	M	6
HOLBROOK, Gerald	28:28:00	TX	2010	49	M	1
STEVENSON, Jeff	28:28:21	CA	2010	64	M	1
BOUEY, Stephen	28:28:32	CO	2010	32	M	1
SPEIGHTS, Catharine	28:29:08	CO	2010	46	F	1
PYLE, Holly	28:29:31	CO	2010	36	F	1
Huss, Sheila	28:29:53	CO	2010	34	F	3
SCHENCK, Amy	28:30:51	WY	2010	25	F	1
Lynde, Robert	28:31:45	CO	2010	46	M	2
KUHN, Brian	28:31:49	IL	2010	36	M	1
THOMAS, Tracy	28:31:50	IL	2010	48	F	1
COOK, Denis	28:32:00	DC	2010	27	M	1
SMYTHE, Brad	28:33:16	NC	2010	32	M	1
GILBERT, Ben	28:35:34	NE	2010	37	M	2
NORTON, Kevin	28:36:23	NE	2010	43	M	1
POOL, Joshua	28:36:30	KS	2010	30	M	1
WEISMILLER, Rick	28:38:23	CO	2010	30	M	1
MIKA, Shad	28:39:04	CO	2010	34	M	2
Gerber, Vince	28:39:07	CO	2010	55	M	3
WILSON, Daniel	28:39:37	CO	2010	52	M	1
TOWN, David	28:39:56	OR	2010	32	M	1
FISH, Elinor	28:40:35	CO	2010	35	F	1

NICHOLS, Joshua	28:40:49	CO	2010	37	M	1
NATION, Michael	28:41:13	WA	2010	43	M	1
Hartman, Andy	28:41:55	CO	2010	36	M	2
TIGHE, Jarett	28:42:41	VA	2010	43	M	1
PECK, John	28:43:58	TX	2010	38	M	3
BECKER, Bill	28:46:35	CO	2010	46	M	1
SPERRY, Bryan	28:47:14	CO	2010	47	M	1
OVESON, Mark	28:48:29	CO	2010	42	M	1
CUMMINGS, Shawn	28:50:52	NM	2010	31	M	1
LLOYD, Chris	28:51:44	CO	2010	48	M	1
Moncada, Jordi	28:52:00	CA	2010	34	M	2
WYMORE, Adam	28:53:06	AZ	2010	33	M	1
Fuller, Brandon	28:53:11	CO	2010	35	M	2
Keefe, Dan	28:53:15	OK	2010	45	M	7
Hickman, Marge	28:53:58	CO	2010	60	F	14
PASSMAN, Scott	28:54:08	IL	2010	23	M	1
SURAN, Kamil	28:54:23	IL	2010	35	M	1
CHALITA ABDO, Antonio	28:54:52	ME	2010	37	M	1
FREIDMAN, Jeff	28:54:57	IA	2010	27	M	1
Macdonald, Steve	28:55:06	TX	2010	43	M	3
TUMMINELLO, Doug	28:56:42	CO	2010	44	M	1
GREEN, Stephanie	28:58:17	CO	2010	41	F	1
Stacy, John	28:58:50	VA	2010	53	M	3
Meyer, Drew	28:59:38	TX	2010	63	M	2
PELLEGRINO, Charlie	29:00:17	CO	2010	50	M	1
ESPINOSA, Cinthia	29:00:38	ME	2010	26	F	1
KRAUSE, Shawn	29:01:27	MD	2010	30	M	1
Clover, Geoff	29:01:35	CO	2010	42	M	2
SCHEELER, Rob	29:01:47	CO	2010	24	M	1
Hardman, Grodon	29:02:07	CO	2010	59	M	4
May, Mike	29:02:25	CO	2010	41	M	2
RADEL, Kevin	29:02:31	WI	2010	51	M	1
SWARTWOUT, Craig	29:02:31	WI	2010	52	M	1
Varela, Mario	29:03:25	CO	2010	50	M	20
SHAFAI, Michael	29:03:26	CO	2010	40	M	1
HARDING, Andrew	29:04:14	MI	2010	50	M	1
LABBE, Chris	29:05:29	CO	2010	41	M	3

TUCKER, Mark	29:06:19	IL	2010	47	M	1
Stone, Chuck	29:09:18	CO	2010	47	M	8
DONOSKY, Jay	29:10:10	AZ	2010	40	M	3
Nelson, Jamen	29:10:44	UT	2010	26	M	8
Hall, Larry	29:11:57	IL	2010	56	M	10
GALT, Jesse	29:13:33	CO	2010	21	M	1
STOVALL, Mark	29:14:37	MO	2010	43	M	1
DOMINGUEZ, Bernardo	29:16:58	Chile	2010	40	M	1
GUGLIELMETTI, Giancarlo	29:16:59	Chile	2010	42	M	1
Baker, Jay	29:17:04	SC	2010	49	M	5
FOUST, Terry	29:17:22	UT	2010	48	M	1
Kern, Stuart	29:17:35	MD	2010	48	M	4
Kern, Kristen	29:17:35	NM	2010	45	M	10
HALE-CASE, Genevieve	29:18:50	CO	2010	25	F	1
KENNEDY, John	29:19:01	OH	2010	43	M	1
Abramowitz, Fred	29:19:08	CO	2010	58	M	10
Chapman Dawson, Donna	29:19:32	CO	2010	42	F	3
HEDGPETH, Teri	29:20:28	CO	2010	45	F	1
DOI, Paul	29:20:49	AZ	2010	39	M	1
Benike, Jim	29:20:57	MN	2010	60	M	3
Bedard, Andy	29:21:05	CO	2010	39	M	2
EBEL, Jeremy	29:21:44	CO	2010	25	M	2
SPRINGER, David	29:22:00	TX	2010	41	M	1
Seremet, Eric	29:22:37	CO	2010	39	M	7
BLAND, Brenda	29:25:41	WI	2010	50	F	1
KUTE, Sean	29:26:00	CO	2010	37	M	1
JAMBOR, Kathy	29:26:39	MN	2010	44	F	1
WRAY, Peter	29:26:45	MD	2010	53	M	1
DUNN, William	29:27:13	FL	2010	52	M	1
SILSBY, Kevin	29:27:16	CO	2010	43	M	1
Peters, Gregory	29:27:20	CO	2010	49	M	2
LOPEZ, Casey	29:27:26	WI	2010	34	M	1
Schnitzius, Thomas	29:27:39	CO	2010	57	M	11
BRIGHT, Charles	29:27:42	WY	2010	39	M	1
KRAJEWSKI, Dustin	29:28:17	CO	2010	31	M	1
DELMAN, Michele	29:28:44	CO	2010	40	F	1
BURFORD, Levi	29:28:50	CO	2010	29	M	1

435

Krier, Miles	29:28:58	CA	2010	58	M	3
SOLIS, Ray	29:29:57	CO	2010	41	M	2
Dougherty, Lisa	29:31:57	NM	2010	39	F	2
BALL, Dennis	29:32:13	NY	2010	32	M	1
SALETTE, Joe	29:32:22	CO	2010	60	M	1
TOMLINSON, Brett	29:32:44	CO	2010	38	M	1
HILL, John	29:34:02	CO	2010	54	M	1
Wooten, Andy	29:34:11	CO	2010	42	M	6
REISSNECKER, Axel	29:34:49	TX	2010	57	M	1
Leedy, Gail	29:34:53	NC	2010	56	F	3
CALDWELL, Gregory	29:35:51	CA	2010	36	M	1
Khajavi, Jamshid	29:36:08	WA	2010	57	M	7
CULVER, Charles	29:36:09	CO	2010	30	M	1
SELMER JR, Michael	29:36:17	MD	2010	53	M	1
Williams, John	29:36:19	CO	2010	48	M	3
Reiff, Andrew	29:36:20	CO	2010	37	M	7
Wickham, Juston	29:36:29	OH	2010	34	M	1
Schwartz, Michelle	29:36:55	CO	2010	42	F	7
Stahl, Bill	29:37:37	CO	2010	51	M	4
HODGES, Jerry	29:37:59	TX	2010	40	M	1
SILTMAN, Michael	29:38:06	IL	2010	41	M	1
Anderson, Shane	29:38:19	CO	2010	34	M	2
SHAW, Vanessa	29:38:42	MT	2010	29	F	1
KITZIG, Mary	29:39:12	OH	2010	53	F	1
Bartz, Matt	29:40:19	WI	2010	35	M	3
GAHBAUER, Barbara	29:40:33	CO	2010	34	F	1
DEWEES, Linda	29:42:02	CA	2010	53	F	1
WATTERS, Adam	29:43:05	NM	2010	38	M	1
OCONNOR, Stephen	29:43:53	IN	2010	51	M	1
SMITH, Julian	29:44:07	CO	2010	44	M	1
Maslowski-Yerges, Cathy	29:44:38	CO	2010	43	F	1
Lewis, Tina	29:45:38	CO	2010	37	F	3
Lettovsky, Ladislav	29:45:51	CO	2010	49	M	2
Labbe, Andrew	29:46:59	CO	2010	35	M	3
PENCE, Anne	29:47:39	CO	2010	43	F	1
Dunn, Randall	29:49:03	CO	2010	55	M	5
MOLL, Aaron	29:49:21	CA	2010	29	M	1

DENNIS, Cary	29:49:31	MO	2010	46	M	1
MCCOIN, Thomas	29:49:35	CA	2010	44	M	1
MARSAK, Lucas	29:49:50	PA	2010	31	M	1
PIERCE, Jasmine	29:51:15	CO	2010	31	F	1
FROST, Mercedes	29:51:20	TX	2010	30	F	1
Mahoney, Matt	29:51:56	FL	2010	55	M	5
LEONARD, Charles	29:52:10	NY	2010	55	M	1
Strong, David	29:52:16	AZ	2010	65	M	14
Straw, Keith	29:52:21	PA	2010	55	M	3
RAMIREZ, Jaime	29:55:25	FL	2010	41	M	1
Henges, Cynthia	29:57:00	TX	2010	32	F	2
DAVENPORT, Michael	29:58:09	IL	2010	51	M	1
BIELAK, Ross	29:59:13	CO	2010	39	M	1

2011

Name	Finish Time	State	Year	Age	Sex	#Finished
Sandes, Ryan	16:46:54	South Africa	2011	M2	M	1
Bowman, Dylan	17:18:59	CO	2011	M2	M	2
Gorman, Neal	17:48:51	DC	2011	M3	M	1
Arnstein, Michael	17:56:42	NY	2011	M3	M	3
Browning, Jeff	18:27:03	OR	2011	M4	M	1
Burch, Ryan	18:35:42	CO	2011	M3	M	4
Parr, Timmy	19:02:04	CO	2011	M3	M	3
Corfield, Charles	19:09:32	CA	2011	M5	M	5
Callahan, Duncan	19:11:15	CO	2011	M3	M	7
Clemons, Lynette	19:59:06	CO	2011	F3	F	2
Trimboli, Brendan	20:08:17	CO	2011	M2	M	1
Fisher, Brian	20:28:23	CO	2011	M4	M	7
Garcia, Patrick	20:56:36	CO	2011	M2	M	1
Stewart, Patrick	20:59:33	CO	2011	M2	M	1
Long, Tim	21:04:04	CO	2011	M4	M	1
Mobley, Mark	21:07:06	CO	2011	M4	M	4
Claridge, Rhonda	21:11:24	CO	2011	F4	F	2
Metz, Andrea	21:13:14	WI	2011	F2	F	2
Williams, Brooks	21:21:31	CO	2011	M2	M	4
Brown, Mathieu	21:32:42	AZ	2011	M3	M	2
Africa, Bob	21:33:07	CO	2011	M3	M	4

437

Oliva, Michael	21:33:59	Canada	2011	M3	M	2
Wildeboer, Alyssa	21:35:01	CO	2011	F3	F	1
TURK, Philip	21:36:39	WV	2011	M4	M	1
Lewis, Tina	21:53:05	CO	2011	F3	F	3
Denesik, Ricky	22:07:54	CO	2011	M5	M	1
Pearlman, Oz	22:18:32	NY	2011	M2	M	1
Benhammon, Daniel	22:30:20	CO	2011	M3	M	5
Hornsby, Wyatt	22:35:01	CO	2011	M3	M	5
Sundahl, Clark	22:40:48	CO	2011	M4	M	2
Hlavacek, Michael	22:45:35	CO	2011	M3	M	2
Hunt, James	22:57:42	CO	2011	M3	M	1
Warnke, Andrew	23:10:38	CO	2011	M3	M	1
Truhe, Eric	23:21:13	CO	2011	M3	M	9
Ramsay, John	23:25:20	TN	2011	M2	M	3
Mackstaller, Adam	23:32:05	CO	2011	M4	M	1
Guerrero, Luis	23:33:49	Mexico	2011	M4	M	9
O'Connor, Michael	23:35:26	MA	2011	M3	M	1
Curtis, Matthew	23:39:23	CO	2011	M3	M	7
Lowe, Bob	23:40:45	CO	2011	M3	M	1
Remkes, Thomas	23:42:27	UT	2011	M5	M	1
Froehlich, Robert	23:43:22	MA	2011	M3	M	1
Benner, Pat	23:43:48	CO	2011	M4	M	4
Faul, Justin	23:44:07	AZ	2011	M3	M	1
Koenig, Brad	23:44:27	NJ	2011	M3	M	2
Carson, Chad	23:46:46	UT	2011	M5	M	3
Belshaw, Allen	23:46:55	CO	2011	M4	M	1
Degrave, Leila	23:47:33	CO	2011	F3	F	2
Anderson, Woody	23:48:27	CO	2011	M3	M	5
MADDY, Doug	23:48:49	CO	2011	M2	M	1
DUDA, John	23:49:44	CO	2011	M3	M	1
Clark, David	23:50:20	CO	2011	M4	M	6
Klopfenstein, Scott	23:52:45	CO	2011	M4	M	12
GAY, Lance	23:53:32	TX	2011	M4	M	1
Koch, Kevin	23:54:10	CO	2011	M3	M	2
ST. PIERRE, Adam	23:56:15	CO	2011	M3	M	1
Johnson, Cory	23:56:55	UT	2011	M4	M	2
Jarvis, Wade	23:57:41	Canada	2011	M4	M	9

Taylor, Neal	23:58:44	CO	2011	M4	M	12
Bradford, Jeremy	24:03:06	CO	2011	M3	M	5
Doyle, Paul	24:07:42	CO	2011	M4	M	2
Murray, Todd	24:08:19	CO	2011	M4	M	2
CRANDALL, Zach	24:09:43	CO	2011	M3	M	1
HINTERBERG, Michael	24:11:03	CO	2011	M3	M	1
MCKEARIN, Tobin	24:12:32	CO	2011	M3	M	1
Brockmeier, Scott	24:13:00	GA	2011	M4	M	2
Adams, Tim	24:17:22	England	2011	M3	M	2
SMITH, Chris	24:19:20	CO	2011	M2	M	1
QUARANTO, Michael	24:19:32	IL	2011	M3	M	1
Costilow, Brian	24:22:23	CO	2011	M3	M	10
Jones, Stephanie	24:27:29	CO	2011	F4	F	4
Schoenlaub, Paul	24:27:32	MO	2011	M5	M	12
DONOSKY, Jay	24:31:24	AZ	2011	M4	M	3
Sanel, Nathan	24:34:14	NH	2011	M4	M	2
Lippman, Jason	24:35:40	TX	2011	M3	M	5
Janssen, Todd	24:36:55	OR	2011	M4	M	2
Scotton, Matt	24:37:59	IA	2011	M4	M	2
PHILIP, Ted	24:38:20	MA	2011	M4	M	1
Cofer, Chuck	24:38:47	TX	2011	M6	M	12
STONESMITH, Cindy	24:39:23	CO	2011	F4	F	1
Churgovich, Raymond	24:40:30	CO	2011	M4	M	4
Constan, John	24:41:08	CO	2011	M4	M	2
Sundermeier, Ronda	24:41:37	OR	2011	F4	F	2
CARDWELL, Roy	24:44:21	CO	2011	M3	M	1
BROWN, David	24:46:35	TX	2011	M3	M	1
NELSON, Jeremiah	24:46:47	CO	2011	M3	M	1
HORNE, Ben	24:47:10	CA	2011	M3	M	1
SHEFFIELD, Drew	24:47:18	England	2011	M3	M	1
Pence, Eric	24:48:14	CO	2011	M4	M	24
PREST, Simon	24:49:11	England	2011	M3	M	1
BRATKA, Aaron	24:53:58	OH	2011	M3	M	1
Carner, David	24:54:55	CO	2011	M4	M	4
Myers, Jeff	25:04:33	CO	2011	M5	M	4
Chlouber, Cole	25:08:06	MN	2011	M3	M	4
Hattan, Gregory	25:21:24	NE	2011	M4	M	2

BUTLER, Todd	25:26:23	CO	2011	M4	M	1
Murray, Brian	25:32:17	NM	2011	M3	M	3
Fegyveresi, John	25:36:21	PA	2011	M3	M	4
Bundrock, Danny	25:40:32	CO	2011	M3	M	5
CARUSO, Scott	25:43:52	CO	2011	M4	M	1
GOODMAN, James	25:44:46	IN	2011	M3	M	1
JONES, Caitlin	25:50:04	CO	2011	F2	F	1
Agnew, Kelly	25:55:14	FL	2011	M3	M	6
Haubert, Donnie	25:57:36	CO	2011	M3	M	3
XU, Weihao	26:00:45	NY	2011	M2	M	1
Miller, Michael	26:07:06	AZ	2011	M4	M	2
LEWELLEN, Robert	26:13:57	GA	2011	M4	M	1
KLEIN, Mark	26:16:55	CA	2011	M2	M	2
Newton, Doug	26:18:51	CO	2011	M3	M	5
Whitehead, Adam	26:19:08	CO	2011	M4	M	3
Dailey, Bruce	26:26:26	FL	2011	M4	M	7
SMITH, Zane	26:27:10	TN	2011	M3	M	1
Picon, Chris	26:27:14	CO	2011	M3	M	3
ELSON, James	26:29:30	England	2011	M2	M	1
LAVIN, Helen	26:30:36	MN	2011	F3	F	1
Scott, Todd	26:32:40	MI	2011	M4	M	11
Lowe, Gregory	26:33:05	MA	2011	M4	M	5
Crock, Bret	26:39:31	CO	2011	M5	M	11
Smith, Paul	26:40:24	CO	2011	M5	M	10
SOOTER, Randy	26:40:33	AZ	2011	M3	M	1
GORMAN, Paul	26:40:50	CA	2011	M4	M	1
CAPEL, Jenny	26:43:10	NV	2011	F3	F	1
THOMPSON, Morgan	26:46:03	NY	2011	M3	M	1
Bybee, Charles	26:49:03	CO	2011	M5	M	12
ROBERTS, Frederic	26:51:43	AZ	2011	M5	M	1
WRIGHT, Jeff	26:52:36	WA	2011	M5	M	1
Nielsen, Pam	26:52:55	MN	2011	F3	F	2
Miller, Gregory	26:57:35	OH	2011	M4	M	1
LOWE, Matt	27:00:44	VA	2011	M3	M	1
Churchill, Sean R.	27:04:10	WI	2011	M4	M	9
Vaughn, Josh	27:04:45	CO	2011	M3	M	2
Welsh, Jeffrey	27:05:25	NC	2011	M5	M	13

Smith, Alan	27:06:58	CO	2011	M4	M	8
SMUIN, Bookis	27:10:53	WA	2011	M2	M	1
WILLIAMS, Ray	27:13:24	NS	2011	M5	M	1
Canowitz, Liza	27:15:53	OH	2011	F3	F	2
LINCKE, Paul	27:15:54	OH	2011	M4	M	1
COX, Jesse	27:18:03	OR	2011	M3	M	1
Edmondson, Marshall	27:18:16	TN	2011	M3	M	2
FERGUSON, Ben	27:21:43	OH	2011	M3	M	1
BENNETT, Jeff	27:24:43	TX	2011	M4	M	1
Miller, Jeff	27:25:12	CO	2011	M3	M	2
Humphrey, Dale	27:25:30	MN	2011	M5	M	2
Gordon, Ken	27:25:45	NM	2011	M4	M	10
Scott, Pat	27:25:46	NM	2011	M5	M	8
MANTHEY, David	27:26:43	CO	2011	M3	M	1
PETERSEN, Harald	27:26:51	Peru	2011	M4	M	1
POLLIHAN, Steve	27:28:05	MO	2011	M3	M	1
ROZMARIN, Christopher	27:28:16	CO	2011	M4	M	1
LYNE, Timothy	27:28:54	CA	2011	M3	M	1
KEMPF, Brooke	27:29:20	ID	2011	F5	F	1
HEMPFLING, Lesley	27:29:25	TX	2011	F3	F	1
FRIES, Ken	27:29:27	TX	2011	M4	M	3
Huss, Sheila	27:29:32	CO	2011	F3	F	3
Urbine, Tim	27:32:16	MN	2011	M3	M	3
Greer, John	27:33:02	AZ	2011	M5	M	8
Bauer, Liz	27:33:22	GA	2011	F5	F	5
Anderson, Jill	27:33:23	NV	2011	F3	F	1
Bartzen, Gene	27:33:56	CO	2011	M5	M	10
Bauer, Tom	27:34:57	OH	2011	M6	M	3
NASSIF, Jon	27:36:46	CO	2011	M4	M	1
PECK, John	27:40:45	TX	2011	M3	M	3
MARTIN, Jp	27:40:53	CO	2011	M4	M	1
Bechtel, Adam	27:41:18	CO	2011	M3	M	2
Ownbey, Garrett	27:41:40	CO	2011	M2	M	3
Loughney, Scott	27:41:53	OR	2011	M4	M	2
Curry, Garry	27:42:38	CA	2011	M5	M	25
APT, Kirk	27:42:40	CO	2011	M4	M	20
DOELLMAN, Matthew	27:43:57	IL	2011	M2	M	1

THURMAN, Wes	27:44:20	CO	2011	M4	M	1
Hyson, Chad	27:48:48	Canada	2011	M4	M	2
DICROCE, Chris	27:49:06	CO	2011	M4	M	1
BRIER, Travis	27:49:14	AZ	2011	M2	M	1
Mcqueeney Penamonte, Abby	27:50:50	CO	2011	F2	F	2
HUNTER, Tammy	27:51:05	WI	2011	F4	F	1
WRINKLE, Allen	27:52:46	TX	2011	M4	M	1
HANNULA, Rebekka	27:53:22	CO	2011	F4	F	1
SHANKS, Daimeon	27:57:00	CO	2011	M3	M	1
THIESSEN, Patrick	27:58:52	CO	2011	M3	M	1
Wooten, Andy	27:59:11	CO	2011	M4	M	6
PHILLIPS, John	28:01:20	TN	2011	M5	M	1
BURGESS, Mark	28:01:21	CO	2011	M3	M	1
MEDICA, Nicholas II	28:02:18	GA	2011	M2	M	1
Bishop, Brad	28:02:42	MO	2011	M2	M	2
Nelson, Jamen	28:02:58	UT	2011	M2	M	8
Watts, Matthew	28:06:01	CO	2011	M5	M	5
BATTILLA, Mitchell	28:07:06	CO	2011	M3	M	1
FRIEDMAN, Jason	28:08:02	NJ	2011	M3	M	1
GRUTERS, Kurtis	28:09:11	NC	2011	M2	M	1
PACE, Rex	28:12:04	OK	2011	M3	M	1
Finkbeiner, Bill	28:13:07	CA	2011	M5	M	30
ROSE, Steven	28:13:46	MI	2011	M3	M	1
SKAGGS, Jim	28:20:22	UT	2011	M5	M	1
Yin, Xi	28:20:47	MA	2011	M2	M	1
YOUNG, Dan	28:21:15	CO	2011	M3	M	1
REZNIK, Eduard	28:22:30	NY	2011	M2	M	1
Gartside, Stephen	28:22:43	CO	2011	M4	M	2
Boyack, Chris	28:23:16	CO	2011	M4	M	6
Longcope, David	28:23:43	CO	2011	M4	M	4
Stacy, John	28:23:55	VA	2011	M5	M	3
DANAHY, Stephanie	28:23:59	VA	2011	F5	F	1
DeDoncker, John	28:25:38	IA	2011	M4	M	5
HUSTED, Dave	28:26:57	CA	2011	M4	M	1
POWELL, Scott	28:27:50	NY	2011	M4	M	1
HANSEN, Jens	28:27:51	WA	2011	M4	M	1
Kaminski, James	28:30:17	CO	2011	M3	M	5

APPERT, John	28:31:56	OK	2011	M3	M	3
KROEGER, Rocky	28:32:05	MO	2011	M4	M	1
Delbecq, Carrie	28:32:34	TX	2011	F3	F	2
Williams, John	28:33:16	CO	2011	M4	M	3
FIELD, Ben	28:33:25	CA	2011	M4	M	1
PYLE, Laura	28:34:42	CO	2011	F4	F	1
Baker, Jay	28:35:02	SC	2011	M5	M	5
Adami, Deanna	28:35:05	CO	2011	M3	M	1
MARTIN, Theodore	28:35:08	MI	2011	M4	M	1
Kazukawa, Junko	28:35:14	CO	2011	F4	F	6
ZEIF, Jonathan	28:36:21	CO	2011	M5	M	11
Schloss, Henry	28:36:35	CO	2011	M3	M	5
Schneider, Amy	28:38:44	CO	2011	F3	F	2
DOUGLAS, Karen	28:39:11	NE	2011	F4	F	1
NIELSEN, Bard	28:39:15	CO	2011	M3	M	1
HILMER, Mike	28:39:19	CO	2011	M4	M	1
MCLAUGHLIN, Christy	28:39:27	CO	2011	F3	F	1
HUGHES, Iain	28:39:28	OH	2011	M4	M	2
POINTER, Lauren	28:39:33	CO	2011	F3	F	1
Dehne, Aaron	28:40:02	CO	2011	M3	M	2
Keefe, Dan	28:40:06	OK	2011	M4	M	7
KELLER, James	28:42:45	CO	2011	M4	M	1
BEATY, Pat	28:43:02	UT	2011	M4	M	1
HEININGER, Matthew	28:43:15	TX	2011	M3	M	1
EULER, Laurie	28:44:58	KS	2011	F2	F	1
McHargue, Mike	28:45:15	CO	2011	M5	M	4
STELLER, Terry	28:45:30	MI	2011	M2	M	1
SCRIMAGER, Aaron	28:46:42	FL	2011	M3	M	1
MIX, Bryan	28:47:11	NY	2011	M4	M	2
WOLFE, Dan	28:47:58	WA	2011	M4	M	1
Marks, Aaron	28:48:31	IL	2011	M2	M	1
Sanderson, Marc	28:48:48	UT	2011	M4	M	4
SMITH, Rodger	28:48:49	UT	2011	M4	M	1
GANGER, Rob	28:49:46	CO	2011	M4	M	1
POSNER, Kenneth	28:49:49	NY	2011	M4	M	1
STUBBE, Cale	28:50:04	CA	2011	M2	M	1
Lamond, Michael	28:50:21	CO	2011	M3	M	3

Varela, Mario	28:50:36	CO	2011	M5	M	20
ORRICO, Tony	28:51:25	IL	2011	M4	M	1
DILL, Franz	28:51:36	CA	2011	M3	M	1
VAUGHAN, Eric	28:51:36	CA	2011	M5	M	1
SNIPES, David	28:53:50	VA	2011	M4	M	1
Torres, Michelle	28:54:44	CO	2011	F4	F	3
NEVITT, Dave	28:55:06	Canada	2011	M5	M	1
Hartman, Andrew	28:55:33	CO	2011	M3	M	2
Labbe, Andrew	28:56:33	CO	2011	M3	M	3
Atkinson, Phil	28:57:21	WY	2011	M3	M	7
ARBLE, Kenneth	28:59:43	MI	2011	M5	M	1
ERSKINE, Stuart	29:01:31	Canada	2011	M4	M	1
Metsky, Jeff	29:02:20	MT	2011	M3	M	1
Antoniou, Matthew	29:02:23	MI	2011	M3	M	1
ENGEL, Tim	29:02:27	CO	2011	M3	M	1
CALCATERA, Mark	29:02:42	OH	2011	M6	M	1
Nakauchi, Laurie	29:03:07	CO	2011	F4	F	12
CARPENTER, Jason	29:03:39	CA	2011	M3	M	1
Schnitzius, Thomas	29:04:12	CO	2011	M5	M	11
WACHT, Lynda	29:04:52	CO	2011	F4	F	2
Booth, Emily	29:06:23	CO	2011	F3	F	2
Williams, Richard	29:06:32	TN	2011	M4	M	4
SMITH, Geoff	29:06:40	CO	2011	M3	M	1
EINSWEILER, Brian	29:08:01	CO	2011	M3	M	1
BETCHER, Nathan	29:08:19	CO	2011	M2	M	1
WALSWORTH, Stuart	29:08:58	CO	2011	M4	M	1
TUELL, Zsuzsanna	29:11:55	CO	2011	F4	F	1
Hall, Larry	29:16:22	IL	2011	M5	M	10
FUESS, Kim	29:16:44	CA	2011	F5	F	2
SCOGGINS, Michael	29:17:23	OK	2011	M3	M	1
SHEPPARD, Norman	29:17:29	NH	2011	M5	M	1
Schwartz, Michelle	29:17:37	CO	2011	F4	F	7
Harrison, Christine	29:18:07	CA	2011	F5	F	2
Muramatsu, Tatsuya	29:18:52	Japan	2011	M5	M	2
Kottke, Cassie	29:20:13	WI	2011	F2	F	2
BYERS, Jonathan	29:21:06	CO	2011	M2	M	1
MORENO, Francisco	29:21:21	TX	2011	M4	M	1

Theodore, Phillip	29:21:22	TN	2011	M4	M	3
EDER, Eric	29:21:54	MI	2011	M4	M	1
Reiff, Andrew	29:22:47	CO	2011	M3	M	7
GLEASON, Jeff	29:22:57	PA	2011	M5	M	1
PARMAIN, Charles	29:23:59	OK	2011	M2	M	1
DECOU, Robert	29:24:35	WA	2011	M3	M	1
FRITZ, Chuck	29:25:04	IA	2011	M4	M	1
MARTIN, Kim	29:25:46	MN	2011	F4	F	1
Stevenson, Jeff	29:26:09	CO	2011	M6	M	6
LOUNSBERY, Anthony	29:26:20	MO	2011	M3	M	1
FORSHEE, Maurice	29:26:31	TX	2011	M3	M	1
VILLANI, Robert	29:30:45	NY	2011	M5	M	1
Peck, Henry	29:31:29	MD	2011	M5	M	2
BAR, Daniel	29:32:18	CO	2011	M2	M	1
SHAMASH, Micah	29:33:13	CO	2011	M3	M	1
WALCH, Edward	29:33:26	MO	2011	M3	M	1
CHRISTIE, Peter JR	29:34:14	MA	2011	M4	M	1
BOW, Chris	29:34:51	CO	2011	M4	M	1
THOMAS, Mark	29:34:51	CO	2011	M4	M	1
MORELAND, Jason	29:35:16	UT	2011	M3	M	1
Romero, Jason	29:36:41	CO	2011	M4	M	4
DUNHAM, Darin	29:37:07	VA	2011	M4	M	1
ROBERTSON, Alex	29:37:33	CO	2011	M3	M	1
CLOUTIER, Jeff	29:37:53	CO	2011	M4	M	1
Walch, David	29:38:02	MO	2011	M3	M	2
MURASE, Yosuke	29:38:14	DC	2011	M3	M	1
LACROIX, John	29:38:41	NH	2011	M3	M	1
KEPLER, Kristopher	29:39:08	TX	2011	M3	M	1
SHARK, Jonathan	29:39:26	WA	2011	M3	M	1
BURRY, Debbie	29:39:31	CO	2011	F5	F	2
White, Eric	29:39:32	TX	2011	M4	M	5
FARRELL, Devin	29:39:35	NM	2011	M4	M	1
BURMAN, Kevin	29:40:07	WA	2011	M3	M	1
OWENS, Adria	29:40:12	CO	2011	F4	F	1
HUSKIE, Will	29:40:43	CO	2011	M5	M	5
GOODRICH, Thomas	29:41:00	CO	2011	M3	M	1
Howarth, Charles	29:41:11	CO	2011	M3	M	2

MELDRUM, Tom	29:41:16	England	2011	M4	M	1
GREEN, Kevin	29:41:30	MI	2011	M3	M	1
Sandoval, Marvin	29:41:49	CO	2011	M3	M	7
OGLESBY, Katie	29:41:58	CO	2011	F4	F	1
Levasseur, Keith	29:42:08	MD	2011	M3	M	2
DECAMP, Alexander	29:43:01	CO	2011	M3	M	1
YARBROUGH, Christina	29:43:23	CO	2011	F3	F	1
Harfst, Gregory	29:43:33	NY	2011	M3	M	2
CULLIGAN, Patrick	29:44:07	CO	2011	M3	M	1
Dougherty, Lisa	29:44:31	NM	2011	F4	F	2
WHITT, Bryan	29:44:52	CO	2011	M3	M	1
ARNOLD, Mary	29:45:46	NY	2011	F3	F	1
PITT, Sydney	29:45:51	TX	2011	F2	F	1
HALE, Joseph	29:46:00	TN	2011	M3	M	1
OROSHIBA, Shellie	29:46:04	TX	2011	F4	F	1
Bleakley, Laura	29:46:10	NH	2011	F4	F	2
STYPULA, Elaine	29:47:38	MI	2011	F4	F	1
MACKENZIE, Mark	29:47:55	NM	2011	M4	M	1
Rieland, Dan	29:48:37	MT	2011	M4	M	4
SAINT-AMOUR, Jim	29:48:39	NY	2011	M3	M	1
Franklin, James	29:48:59	CO	2011	M4	M	2
DICKERSON, Julie	29:49:14	NJ	2011	F2	F	1
KEEFE, Ryan	29:49:19	Canada	2011	M3	M	1
LEE, Nick	29:50:33	CO	2011	M3	M	1
SWANSON, Larry	29:50:34	IL	2011	M6	M	1
HALEY, William	29:53:25	IA	2011	M3	M	1
Abramowitz, Fred	29:53:36	CO	2011	M6	M	10
SCHRAMM, Taylor	29:53:39	IA	2011	M3	M	1
CARNAHAN, Kevin	29:53:52	GA	2011	M4	M	1
Comstock, Amy	29:57:19	IL	2011	F4	F	2

2012

Name	Finish Time	State	Year	Age	Sex	#Finished
Lorblanchet, Thomas	16:29:28	France	2012	32	M	1
Tiernan, Zeke	16:44:20	CO	2012	36	M	4
Clark, Nick	17:11:16	CO	2012	38	M	2
Krupicka, Anton	17:21:09	CO	2012	29	M	3

Aldous, Jay	18:42:42	UT	2012	51	M	1
Catalano, Andrew	19:28:35	NJ	2012	25	M	2
Stapanowich, Brandon	19:32:02	CO	2012	27	M	1
Lewis, Tina	19:33:44	CO	2012	39	F	3
Arnstein, Michael	19:37:14	NY	2012	35	M	3
Howie, Craig	19:50:11	CO	2012	35	M	3
Waggoner, Tim	20:12:36	CO	2012	40	M	2
Curtis, Matthew	20:17:15	CO	2012	36	M	7
Howard, Troy	20:32:00	CO	2012	39	M	1
Howard, Elizabeth	20:44:06	TX	2012	40	F	3
Nordell, Ashley	20:47:51	OR	2012	32	F	1
Corfield, Charles	20:57:10	CO	2012	54	M	5
Terranova, Paul	21:04:45	TX	2012	38	M	1
Lapierre, Aliza	21:14:32	VT	2012	32	F	1
Harem, Robert	21:26:47	TN	2012	28	M	1
Gangelhoff, Todd	21:32:09	CO	2012	40	M	1
Tinder, Brian	21:36:03	AZ	2012	32	M	1
Coury, Jamil	21:45:42	AZ	2012	27	M	1
Cooper, Ryan	22:06:45	CO	2012	38	M	4
Berg, Joseph	22:14:37	CO	2012	34	M	1
Koop, Jason	22:17:44	CO	2012	33	M	5
Williams, Bryan	22:19:21	CO	2012	37	M	3
Leblanc, Michel	22:35:06	Canada	2012	33	M	1
Pietari, Kyle	22:40:22	CO	2012	25	M	4
Montero, Javier	22:40:24	Mexico	2012	49	M	3
Long, Ken	22:43:09	CO	2012	34	M	2
Truhe, Eric	22:47:07	CO	2012	37	M	9
Thompson, Ryan	22:52:15	SC	2012	31	M	1
Nagaraj, Harsha	22:58:14	CO	2012	38	M	3
Cappellini, Christopher	23:07:41	MA	2012	46	M	2
Suwinski, Jeremy	23:08:19	UT	2012	33	M	1
Mueller, Robert	23:08:31	UT	2012	25	M	1
Lazar Adler, Adrian	23:09:46	VI	2012	32	M	1
Mccarthy, Kieran	23:13:10	CO	2012	34	M	1
Pope, Eric	23:15:08	NM	2012	49	M	2
Anderson, Woody	23:18:03	CO	2012	37	M	5
Piceu Africa, Darcy	23:20:06	CO	2012	37	F	1

Segger, Jen	23:26:01	Canada	2012	31	F	1
Benke, Blake	23:28:25	CT	2012	35	M	1
Harcrow, Harry	23:29:06	CO	2012	45	M	7
Le Roux, Mike	23:37:11	Australia	2012	36	M	1
Herget, Ted	23:38:12	AR	2012	38	M	1
Bohn, Eric	23:46:41	AZ	2012	31	M	2
Meckenstock, Matt	23:47:09	WA	2012	26	M	1
Spencer, Jeffrey	23:47:57	CO	2012	30	M	1
Graubins, Garett	23:49:33	CO	2012	39	M	5
Brennan, Tom	23:51:45	OK	2012	41	M	1
Neal, Mike	23:51:54	CO	2012	36	M	1
Klopfenstein, Scott	23:53:19	CO	2012	41	M	12
Ayers Jr., Bob	23:54:09	VT	2012	52	M	2
Urbanski, Matt	23:54:37	WA	2012	31	M	1
Gerenz, Bob	23:55:47	MN	2012	44	M	4
Wildeboer, Alyssa	24:03:05	CO	2012	33	F	1
Wacker, Marty	24:05:17	CO	2012	41	M	3
Frost, Troy	24:06:06	MT	2012	46	M	1
Greenhill, Jaclyn	24:10:56	CO	2012	35	F	1
Wetstine, Sean	24:15:26	CO	2012	36	M	6
Fegyveresi, John	24:17:25	PA	2012	35	M	4
Mcintosh, Travis	24:21:52	CO	2012	36	M	1
Pennington, Jeremy	24:22:26	IL	2012	36	M	2
Koch, Kevin	24:23:12	CO	2012	37	M	2
Westerman, Christopher	24:25:50	CO	2012	32	M	2
Gilbert, Micky	24:32:40	CO	2012	41	M	2
Vogel, Lane	24:34:56	FL	2012	35	M	1
Bajer, Scott	24:35:05	AZ	2012	37	M	1
Zeiger, Ben	24:37:48	CO	2012	29	M	1
Lippman, Jason	24:41:18	TX	2012	40	M	5
Mattern, Travis	24:43:10	CO	2012	38	M	1
Beuke, Donald	24:43:17	CO	2012	36	M	3
Silsby, Kevin	24:44:02	CO	2012	45	M	1
Levasseur, Keith	24:44:59	MD	2012	34	M	2
Wallace, Mark	24:49:21	CO	2012	50	M	3
Stafford, Carrie	24:49:24	CO	2012	33	F	5
Wrenholt, Valerie	24:49:47	NC	2012	37	F	2

Newton, Doug	24:50:13	CO	2012	35	M	5
Dalley, Josh	24:51:29	CO	2012	29	M	3
Ebel, Jeremy	25:03:07	CO	2012	27	M	2
Hamilton, Harry	25:08:20	NJ	2012	52	M	2
Wright, Chris	25:12:37	CO	2012	40	M	7
Hunt, Jay	25:26:27	CO	2012	32	M	4
Smithberger, Jay	25:29:39	OH	2012	43	M	1
Ownbey, Garrett	25:36:34	CO	2012	23	M	3
Trocha, Francois	25:39:10	CO	2012	46	M	1
Whittle, Brad	25:42:06	CO	2012	46	M	1
Lopez Reyes, Alejandro	25:42:30	Mexico	2012	43	M	1
Richards, Emily	25:45:26	CA	2012	32	F	1
Scotton, Matt	25:52:39	IA	2012	43	M	2
Pacitto, Tim	25:53:08	MI	2012	33	M	1
Wheeler, Craig	26:01:32	KY	2012	50	M	1
Haase, David	26:03:36	WI	2012	44	M	1
Wooten, Andy	26:05:15	CO	2012	44	M	6
Szablewski, Zachary	26:05:48	OH	2012	22	M	2
Brackelsberg, Chad	26:12:08	UT	2012	39	M	2
Sattar, Shaheen	26:15:39	TX	2012	28	F	2
Schoenlaub, Paul	26:16:48	MO	2012	53	M	12
Wirfs-Brock, Jordan	26:19:42	CO	2012	28	F	1
Crock, Bret	26:27:40	CO	2012	54	M	11
Swaney, Scott	26:28:24	CO	2012	43	M	2
Antin, Jason	26:31:43	CO	2012	29	M	2
Petterson, Jim	26:33:36	CO	2012	45	M	1
Korosec, Adrian	26:34:31	AZ	2012	41	M	1
Madden, Kurt	26:37:26	CA	2012	56	M	4
Campanelli, Joseph	26:38:49	UT	2012	26	M	1
Kracaw, Dana	26:38:55	CO	2012	27	F	2
Burgess, Smokey	26:42:02	CO	2012	40	M	2
Wellman, Andrew	26:44:12	CO	2012	35	M	1
Ochs, Margaret	26:45:50	NM	2012	37	F	1
Behunin, Molly	26:46:08	UT	2012	48	F	1
Peterman, David	26:47:04	OH	2012	49	M	1
Hooge, Paul	26:49:05	CO	2012	49	M	2
Clark, Erin	26:49:55	UT	2012	35	F	1

Name	Time	Location	Year	Age	Sex	Count
Silva, Katrin	26:50:10	NM	2012	42	F	6
Bolls, Rod	26:50:56	CO	2012	37	M	3
Cecill, Matt	26:51:01	Canada	2012	30	M	1
Norcia, Christopher	26:52:12	CO	2012	44	M	3
Passenti, Brian	26:52:17	CO	2012	38	M	5
Jason, Morgan	26:57:46	CO	2012	37	M	1
Anderson, Shane	27:06:51	CO	2012	36	M	2
Apt, Kirk	27:07:17	CO	2012	50	M	20
Piepgrass, Ammon	27:07:19	Canada	2012	35	M	1
Jones, Ryan	27:09:00	PA	2012	33	M	3
Lall, Mike	27:10:27	England	2012	31	M	1
Smith, Paul	27:12:59	CO	2012	56	M	10
Davis, Elizabeth	27:14:57	AZ	2012	32	F	1
Jones, Jake	27:17:01	CO	2012	39	M	2
Holland, James	27:18:28	TN	2012	36	M	3
Fountain, Rick	27:22:16	IA	2012	42	M	2
Byrne, John	27:22:17	IA	2012	47	M	3
Boyle, Dan	27:23:20	CA	2012	48	M	2
Tucker, Paul	27:23:37	CO	2012	39	M	2
Howard, Robert	27:25:47	CO	2012	25	M	1
Sahni, Vishal	27:27:47	DC	2012	32	M	1
Tovey, Michael	27:28:42	CT	2012	42	M	1
Halsne, Michelle	27:28:55	WA	2012	43	F	1
Zuniga, Victor	27:29:15	Puerto Rico	2012	33	M	1
Fuller, Brandon	27:29:17	CO	2012	37	M	2
Hellman, Joan	27:31:54	AZ	2012	41	F	2
Bianco, Peter	27:34:20	NY	2012	30	M	1
Lamond, Michael	27:34:22	CO	2012	38	M	3
Gilbert, Ben	27:35:57	NE	2012	39	M	2
Davis, Nicholas	27:37:43	CO	2012	23	M	1
Vieth, Jason	27:41:23	CO	2012	39	M	1
Costilow, Brian	27:41:24	TN	2012	38	M	10
Henry, Kara	27:41:48	CO	2012	27	F	3
Dale, Christopher	27:41:59	CO	2012	34	M	1
Fisher, Marta	27:42:14	OR	2012	37	F	1
Gilliam, Thaddeus	27:43:04	GA	2012	27	M	1
Henzl, Vlad	27:43:40	NM	2012	33	M	1

Vogler, Podog	27:44:43	AR	2012	46	M	1
Delbecq, Carrie	27:46:40	TX	2012	40	F	2
Duncan, Todd	27:48:25	CO	2012	42	M	1
Evans, Daniel	27:50:08	CO	2012	34	M	1
Straw, Keith	27:52:27	PA	2012	57	M	3
Gordon, Ken	27:52:40	NM	2012	47	M	10
Charnecki, Tim	27:53:41	UT	2012	37	M	1
Atkinson, Phil	27:53:54	WY	2012	40	M	7
Sweeney, Megan	27:54:56	CO	2012	31	F	5
Worthington, Brandon	27:55:25	CO	2012	27	M	1
Turner, Paul	27:57:17	AR	2012	49	M	1
Parish, Rob	27:57:53	CO	2012	35	M	1
Labrecque, Daniel	27:58:44	NC	2012	56	M	1
Kaminski, James	28:00:35	CO	2012	30	M	5
Foster, Sheri	28:01:34	Canada	2012	39	F	2
Valdez, Russell	28:01:43	CO	2012	52	M	2
England, Stephen	28:02:16	NY	2012	32	M	1
Maloney, Tr	28:02:42	CO	2012	44	M	1
Hamos, Brian	28:04:56	UT	2012	49	M	1
Gerasopoulos, Vasilios	28:06:51	CO	2012	38	M	1
Gates, Trevor	28:07:48	CO	2012	33	M	1
Pearson, Larry	28:08:39	TX	2012	51	M	2
O'Connell, Dan	28:10:16	CO	2012	34	M	2
Pence, Eric	28:12:30	CO	2012	46	M	24
Moreland, Ross	28:12:36	Finland	2012	29	M	1
Webster, Richard	28:12:37	England	2012	45	M	1
Weiman, Drew	28:12:43	CO	2012	28	M	1
Gartside, Stephen	28:14:43	CO	2012	47	M	2
Aberger, Johann	28:16:21	CO	2012	34	M	1
Gant, Matt	28:16:38	CO	2012	25	M	2
Reiff, Andrew	28:18:47	CO	2012	39	M	7
Dekanich, Joel	28:19:31	CO	2012	41	M	1
Kazukawa, Junko	28:20:06	CO	2012	49	F	6
Hauschulz, Benjamin	28:20:18	CO	2012	27	M	1
Watkins, Matthew	28:20:30	CO	2012	33	M	1
Guldan, Ryan	28:20:47	CO	2012	28	M	4
Seracuse, Joe	28:21:01	CO	2012	50	M	1

Deneen, Mathew	28:22:39	CO	2012	35	M	1
Humphrey, Dale	28:22:45	MN	2012	53	M	2
Nelson, Jamen	28:23:44	UT	2012	28	M	8
Blake, Neil	28:25:40	NM	2012	47	M	7
Aguirre, Andreas	28:27:07	CA	2012	33	M	1
McRoberts, Adam	28:27:10	WI	2012	37	M	2
Zakaras, Jason	28:30:08	NE	2012	29	M	1
Baker, Jay	28:30:11	SC	2012	51	M	5
Solis, Ray	28:30:26	CO	2012	43	M	2
Buraglio, Donald	28:32:49	CA	2012	41	M	1
Meyer, Thaddeus	28:33:15	MD	2012	33	M	1
Agnew, Kelly	28:33:26	FL	2012	39	M	6
Boelen, Filip	28:33:47	CO	2012	35	M	3
Spieker, Meghan	28:34:10	CO	2012	27	F	1
Zelaya, Humberto	28:34:41	CO	2012	37	M	1
Rapinz, Paul	28:35:16	CO	2012	42	M	1
Maldonado, Enrique	28:35:21	CO	2012	44	M	2
Manley, Brian	28:35:30	CO	2012	48	M	13
Grund, Matthew	28:36:27	GA	2012	35	M	1
Miller, Jessica	28:37:38	CO	2012	34	F	1
Urbine, Tim	28:37:55	CO	2012	32	M	3
Nakauchi, Laurie	28:38:18	CO	2012	42	F	12
Thieme, Jaeson	28:38:41	CO	2012	34	M	1
Allen, Zach	28:39:19	CO	2012	33	M	1
Churchill, Sean	28:40:52	WI	2012	46	M	9
Winter, Joshua	28:41:20	CO	2012	38	M	1
Schultz, Todd	28:41:36	AZ	2012	43	M	1
Oestrike, Brian	28:42:29	NY	2012	33	M	2
Barnes, Molly	28:42:30	CO	2012	43	F	6
Anfang, Matt	28:42:58	WI	2012	28	M	2
Mccurnin, Jeanne	28:43:00	IA	2012	56	F	4
Wilson, Kurt	28:43:03	NC	2012	33	M	2
Berdine, Matthew	28:43:13	CO	2012	33	M	1
Bishop, Timothy	28:43:41	CO	2012	36	M	3
Ragainis, Ivars	28:44:25	OH	2012	32	M	1
Boyack, Chris	28:44:41	CO	2012	42	M	6
Richardson, Erik	28:44:45	MI	2012	34	M	4

Tanttila, Amelia	28:45:18	CO	2012	45	F	1
Enlow, Lori	28:45:26	OK	2012	39	F	2
Brown, Richard	28:45:32	LA	2012	43	M	1
Howarth, Charles	28:46:00	CO	2012	35	M	2
Barry, Timothy	28:46:40	CO	2012	51	M	1
Wroblewski, Tom	28:47:36	CA	2012	53	M	1
Smith, Scooter	28:47:52	CO	2012	22	M	1
Carroll, Everett	28:48:28	AZ	2012	19	M	1
Perry, Tom	28:49:12	UT	2012	57	M	2
Hubert, Beck	28:49:40	Germany	2012	54	M	1
Waggett, Samantha	28:50:03	CO	2012	46	F	1
Wharton, Sophia	28:50:46	KS	2012	42	F	1
Friedman, Jeff	28:50:56	IA	2012	29	M	2
Romero, Jason	28:52:08	CO	2012	42	M	4
Costello, Aiden	28:52:12	CO	2012	32	M	1
Martin, Joel	28:53:00	CO	2012	32	M	1
Parillo, Anthony	28:53:24	MA	2012	28	M	1
Hammett, Ron	28:53:38	NV	2012	42	M	1
Scott, Todd	28:54:00	MI	2012	48	M	11
Coleman, Jason	28:54:54	MO	2012	34	M	1
Fortin, Will	28:55:16	WY	2012	27	M	1
Vork, Jesse	28:55:37	TX	2012	29	M	1
Mchugh, Dan	28:56:29	NY	2012	41	M	1
Walsh, Brian	28:57:15	MI	2012	29	M	2
Vicens, Carlos	28:58:00	ON	2012	38	M	1
Wheeler, Mark	28:58:18	ID	2012	47	M	1
Thresher, Al	28:59:34	NV	2012	44	M	1
Howard, Fritz	28:59:34	CO	2012	44	M	1
Bartzen, Gene	29:00:35	CO	2012	58	M	10
Young, Daniel	29:00:41	PA	2012	52	M	1
Bauer, Tom	29:01:53	OH	2012	61	M	3
Stclaire, Rachael	29:02:04	CO	2012	54	F	1
Sides, Vernon	29:02:07	NC	2012	40	M	4
Gould, Stephen	29:02:40	Canada	2012	54	M	1
Lightburn, Janet	29:03:02	CO	2012	46	F	2
Salvesen, Greg	29:03:08	CO	2012	25	M	2
Tonsmeire, Julian	29:03:47	CO	2012	36	M	1

Martin, Michael	29:05:01	IL	2012	31	M	1
Juskiewicz, Nicholas	29:05:10	NM	2012	51	M	1
Emmert, Steve	29:05:14	IL	2012	44	M	1
Caldwell, Jim	29:05:53	OR	2012	41	M	1
Ponak, David	29:06:20	MO	2012	32	M	2
Courogen, Peter	29:06:28	OR	2012	45	M	1
Ferrer, Christopher	29:06:29	IL	2012	31	M	1
Kurisky, Jack	29:06:53	VA	2012	45	M	2
Dicke, Ben	29:07:34	CO	2012	32	M	2
Armstrong, Jerry	29:07:40	CO	2012	35	M	1
Martinez, Edgar	29:07:53	TX	2012	34	M	2
Campbell, Matt	29:07:57	WA	2012	29	M	2
Krol, Ryan	29:08:46	CO	2012	27	M	4
Leppert, Jenni	29:09:17	CO	2012	38	F	1
Curry, Garry	29:10:35	CA	2012	58	M	25
Kroeger, Rocky	29:11:43	CO	2012	42	M	1
Seiler, Peter	29:11:56	MN	2012	37	M	1
Facchino, Carlo	29:12:18	CA	2012	37	M	1
Keefe, Dan	29:12:28	OK	2012	47	M	7
Brenden, Dan	29:12:45	AZ	2012	61	M	8
Debize, Jerome	29:12:49	TO	2012	35	M	1
Boyd, Terry	29:12:50	CO	2012	45	M	3
Bybee, Charles	29:13:16	CO	2012	50	M	12
Pilgrim, Brian	29:13:26	NM	2012	45	M	2
Zon, Ludwik	29:13:29	NC	2012	57	M	2
Strand, Eric	29:13:46	MO	2012	51	M	7
Oakes, Tony	29:13:52	CO	2012	42	M	1
Peterka, George	29:15:22	AR	2012	52	M	1
Oliver, Dave	29:16:30	CO	2012	46	M	2
Hughes, Iain	29:16:51	OH	2012	49	M	2
Finkbeiner, Bill	29:16:52	CA	2012	56	M	30
Parish, Mark	29:17:43	CO	2012	29	M	2
Hoffmann, Brian	29:17:44	CO	2012	46	M	1
Holman, Steve	29:17:48	CA	2012	55	M	1
Riegert, Ed	29:18:52	CO	2012	34	M	1
King, John	29:21:08	MO	2012	39	M	1
Gauden, Carrie	29:21:29	CO	2012	37	F	1

Gaskins, Aaron	29:22:03	CO	2012	28	M	1
Meador, Jen	29:22:08	CO	2012	28	F	1
Cromwell, Jonathan	29:22:37	OR	2012	22	M	1
Mcphaul, Christopher	29:23:23	MD	2012	46	M	1
Snyder, Philip	29:23:59	CO	2012	43	M	2
Swedenborg, Chris	29:24:27	CO	2012	39	M	1
Bondurant, Robert	29:24:31	WA	2012	39	M	1
Allie, Adam	29:24:58	SC	2012	32	M	1
Nash, Doug	29:24:59	CO	2012	58	M	5
Szoradi, Stephen	29:25:27	CO	2012	43	M	2
Venner, Laura	29:25:59	CO	2012	30	F	2
Ferrell, Tim	29:27:07	MN	2012	41	M	1
Welch, Ryan	29:28:36	CO	2012	39	M	1
Desantis, Kt	29:28:51	CO	2012	49	F	3
Kriewaldt, Marc	29:28:53	CO	2012	48	M	3
Williams, Brian	29:28:56	TN	2012	31	M	1
Betz, Matthew	29:29:03	TX	2012	26	M	2
Hutton, Shane	29:29:49	VI	2012	30	M	1
Ross, David	29:30:16	England	2012	44	M	1
Langlais, Bethany	29:30:51	WA	2012	29	F	1
Bauer, Liz	29:31:14	GA	2012	53	F	5
Roberts, Jarod	29:31:54	CO	2012	28	M	1
Egner, Mark	29:32:49	MI	2012	55	M	1
Aker, Clyde the Glide	29:33:43	CA	2012	60	M	1
Durbin, Elizabeth	29:33:47	CO	2012	43	F	2
Bartz, Matt	29:35:34	WI	2012	37	M	3
Hornbaker, Charles	29:35:50	CO	2012	30	M	3
Scott, Jesse	29:36:06	MI	2012	25	M	1
Martinek, John	29:36:11	TX	2012	25	M	1
Poirier, Jessica	29:36:36	CO	2012	32	F	1
Miller, Corky	29:36:42	MO	2012	40	M	1
Vanderwaal, Aaron	29:37:36	WA	2012	37	M	1
Smith, Alan	29:38:08	CO	2012	43	M	8
Dessler, Jill-Renee	29:39:29	MN	2012	43	F	1
Koehler, Kelley	29:39:46	NM	2012	46	F	1
Peck, John	29:40:45	TX	2012	40	M	3
Milligan, Jake	29:40:55	IL	2012	29	M	1

Stone, Chuck	29:41:06	CO	2012	49	M	8
Bigard, Nicolas	29:41:14	MO	2012	38	M	1
Lundy, Diana	29:41:35	CA	2012	58	F	1
White, Trevor	29:41:48	OR	2012	43	M	2
Kottke, Cassie	29:42:00	WI	2012	29	F	2
May, Alex	29:42:05	CO	2012	38	M	1
Stones, Roger	29:42:12	CO	2012	39	M	1
Vyhlidal, Michele	29:42:22	CO	2012	41	F	1
Hill, David	29:42:46	IL	2012	42	M	1
Kirk, John	29:43:07	CO	2012	36	M	1
Kreutzer, Alyson	29:43:12	CO	2012	29	F	1
Olsen, Walter	29:44:06	CO	2012	35	M	1
Hardester, Kurt	29:44:26	CO	2012	44	M	1
Galioto, Joe	29:44:54	NJ	2012	48	M	1
Forshee, Maurice	29:45:36	TX	2012	38	M	1
Harfst, Greg	29:47:10	NY	2012	34	M	2
Schnitzius, Tom	29:48:07	CO	2012	59	M	11
Hellenthal, Mark	29:48:58	AZ	2012	40	M	1
Halajian, Paul	29:50:25	CO	2012	41	M	1
Smith, Emily	29:50:44	CO	2012	38	F	1
Fisher, Jared	29:52:26	NV	2012	42	M	1
Gonzalez, Edgardo	29:52:31	TX	2012	35	M	1
Fuess, Kim Ann	29:53:33	CA	2012	53	F	2

2013

Name	Finish Time	State	Year	Age	Sex	#Finished
Sharman, Ian	16:30:03	England	2013	M3	M	5
Clark, Nick	17:06:29	England	2013	M3	M	2
Aish, Michael	18:27:59	CO	2013	M3	M	3
Pietari, Kyle	18:37:21	CO	2013	M2	M	4
Catalano, Andrew	18:43:26	NJ	2013	M2	M	2
Meyer, Timo	19:04:19	Germany	2013	M3	M	1
Sullivan, Eric	19:17:33	CO	2013	M3	M	1
Jurek, Scott	19:21:54	CO	2013	M3	M	2
Africa, Bob	19:38:41	CO	2013	M4	M	4
Montero, Javier	19:45:46	Costa Rica	2013	M5	M	3
Kelly, Seth	19:46:15	CO	2013	M2	M	2

Vaughn, Joshua	19:50:45	CO	2013	M3	M	2
Curtis, Matthew	20:02:01	CO	2013	M3	M	7
Jay, Luke	20:14:12	CO	2013	M3	M	2
Macy, Travis	20:15:11	CO	2013	M3	M	1
Arnold, Ashley	20:25:43	CO	2013	F2	F	2
Hewitt, Michael	20:44:33	CO	2013	M4	M	3
Matticks, Kerry	20:46:34	CO	2013	M4	M	3
Rome, Jeff	20:58:21	MT	2013	M2	M	1
Bradley, Owen	21:06:31	AL	2013	M3	M	1
Corfield, Charles	21:18:44	CO	2013	M5	M	5
Patrizi, Michael	21:27:59	CO	2013	M3	M	2
Peinado, Marco	21:32:22	CO	2013	M2	M	1
Reed, Andy	21:33:37	Canada	2013	M4	M	1
Ciaramitaro, Shawn	21:37:28	CO	2013	M4	M	2
Leehman, Nathan	21:40:56	NC	2013	M3	M	2
Kilcoyne, Jamie	21:44:41	CO	2013	M4	M	3
Campos, Igor	21:45:48	CA	2013	M2	M	1
Smith, Garrett	21:47:51	AZ	2013	M3	M	1
Meyers, Kyle	22:07:52	KS	2013	M3	M	1
Graglia, Michele	22:10:25	CA	2013	M2	M	1
Oestrike, Brian	22:17:53	NY	2013	M3	M	2
Palmer, Andy	22:22:29	CO	2013	M4	M	1
Anderson, Woody	22:27:43	CO	2013	M3	M	5
Sweeney, Bob	22:30:18	CO	2013	M4	M	4
Gulvan, Ryan	22:33:05	CA	2013	M2	M	4
Hunt, Jay	22:36:29	CO	2013	M3	M	4
Truhe, Eric	22:37:04	CO	2013	M3	M	9
Hornsby, Wyatt	22:40:21	CO	2013	M4	M	5
Sweeney, Patrick	22:41:19	CA	2013	M3	M	5
Sattar, Shaheen	22:42:41	TX	2013	F2	F	2
Ambrose, Mike	22:43:43	CO	2013	M2	M	2
Haubert, Donnie	22:44:40	CO	2013	M3	M	3
Merino, Keila	22:47:36	NY	2013	F3	F	2
Ziegenfuss, Joe	22:49:14	CO	2013	M3	M	2
Bohr, Adam	22:54:23	CO	2013	M2	M	1
Pennington, Jeremy	22:55:57	IN	2013	M3	M	2
Lefever, John	22:56:21	NE	2013	M4	M	3

Marion, Zac	22:56:26	UT	2013	M2	M	1
Steene, Johan	22:56:49	SWE	2013	M3	M	1
Clements, Bill	22:57:17	CA	2013	M3	M	2
Stephenson, Luke	22:58:27	CO	2013	M2	M	2
Rabb, Scott	23:06:24	TX	2013	M4	M	1
Wetstine, Sean	23:08:19	CO	2013	M3	M	6
Peltonen, Garrett	23:11:37	WI	2013	M3	M	2
Mobley, Mark	23:13:16	CO	2013	M4	M	4
Sherwood, Stephen	23:13:56	CO	2013	M3	M	1
Madden, Kurt	23:15:33	CA	2013	M5	M	4
Silva, Katrin	23:16:25	NM	2013	F4	F	6
Wooten, Andy	23:18:29	CO	2013	M4	M	6
Peterson, Stefan	23:18:35	CO	2013	M4	M	1
Gerenz, Bob	23:21:32	MN	2013	M4	M	4
Benson, Gregory	23:24:49	CA	2013	M3	M	1
Seymour, Nick	23:28:32	OK	2013	M3	M	2
Sandoval, Marvin	23:28:48	CO	2013	M3	M	7
Lind, Paul	23:33:10	ID	2013	M4	M	2
Bradford, Jeremy	23:34:37	CO	2013	M3	M	5
Breinan, Howard	23:35:53	CT	2013	M4	M	1
Howie, Craig	23:39:07	CO	2013	M3	M	3
Courkamp, Kirt	23:40:24	CO	2013	M5	M	3
Szablewski, Zach	23:41:43	OH	2013	M2	M	2
Lingg, Ryan	23:43:02	CO	2013	M2	M	1
Hall, Rebecca	23:43:13	CO	2013	F3	F	1
Cooper, Will	23:43:28	CA	2013	M5	M	2
Rossi, Alberto	23:44:39	CO	2013	M3	M	1
Haaland, Judd	23:44:56	NM	2013	M4	M	1
Sanchez, Lorenzo	23:46:51	TX	2013	M3	M	1
Walick, Dave	23:48:04	CO	2013	M4	M	2
Henry, Kara	23:50:20	CO	2013	F2	F	3
Bigelow, Michael	23:51:04	CO	2013	M4	M	1
Ponak, David	23:51:32	CO	2013	M3	M	2
Ayers Jr., Bob	23:54:03	VT	2013	M5	M	2
Hoberg, Scott	23:54:56	MN	2013	M3	M	1
Hamann, Hendrik	23:57:15	NY	2013	M4	M	1
Carson, Mark	23:57:59	CO	2013	M3	M	1

Kjerengtroen, Lars	24:06:06	CO	2013	M3	M	2
Mcqueeney Penamonte, Abby	24:06:21	CO	2013	F3	F	2
Graham, Dave	24:07:50	AUS	2013	M4	M	1
Arnold, Mathew	24:08:07	CO	2013	M3	M	1
Burgess, Smokey	24:11:08	CO	2013	M4	M	2
Young, Brandon	24:11:24	GA	2013	M3	M	1
Dario Barrera Muñoz, Rubén	24:11:45	Mexico	2013	M3	M	1
Hammonds, Samuel	24:11:52	TN	2013	M3	M	1
Lund, Ryan	24:12:29	ID	2013	M3	M	2
Del Conte, Joe	24:13:20	NY	2013	M3	M	1
Krol, Ryan	24:13:27	CO	2013	M2	M	4
Ferrara, Nick	24:14:25	PA	2013	M4	M	1
Johnson, Josh	24:15:43	CO	2013	M3	M	1
Boruta, Mirek	24:16:56	CO	2013	M3	M	1
Hamilton, Harry	24:17:20	NJ	2013	M5	M	2
Lamond, Michael	24:18:40	CO	2013	M4	M	3
Brennan, James	24:19:27	CO	2013	M3	M	1
Caughlan, Thomas	24:20:21	CO	2013	M3	M	1
Curiel, Tyler	24:21:38	TX	2013	M5	M	11
Hribar, Maddy	24:24:21	MA	2013	F2	F	1
Chamoun, Michael	24:24:51	CO	2013	M3	M	1
Studer, Nicole Kalogeropoulos	24:25:43	TX	2013	F3	F	1
Young, Stephen	24:25:59	CO	2013	M3	M	2
Rickey, Carson	24:26:01	CO	2013	M2	M	1
Dedoncker, John	24:26:27	IA	2013	M4	M	5
Fletes, Sinuhe	24:27:16	Mexico	2013	M2	M	1
Reiff, Andrew	24:28:55	CO	2013	M4	M	7
Brown, Edward	24:30:00	TX	2013	M2	M	1
Loughney, Scott	24:31:17	OR	2013	M4	M	2
Oliva, Michael	24:31:28	CO	2013	M3	M	2
Cote, Gilles	24:34:05	CO	2013	M5	M	6
Hornbaker, Charles	24:34:59	VA	2013	M3	M	3
Fober, Matthew	24:35:53	HI	2013	M3	M	1
Stepanovic, Adam	24:36:27	MA	2013	M2	M	1
Nelsen, Margaret	24:37:45	Canada	2013	F3	F	1
Flynn, Patrick	24:40:55	CO	2013	M3	M	1
Guerrero, Luis	24:41:26	Mexico	2013	M5	M	9

Lippman, Jason	24:42:08	TX	2013	M4	M	5
Knight, Chad	24:42:35	CO	2013	M4	M	1
Garvey, Timothy	24:43:11	MO	2013	M4	M	1
Sentinella, Terry	24:44:09	WA	2013	M4	M	1
Rodes, Chris	24:45:11	ID	2013	M4	M	1
Duplak, Michael	24:45:53	FL	2013	M2	M	1
Fegyveresi, John	24:47:28	PA	2013	M3	M	4
Durbin, Elizabeth	24:47:46	CO	2013	F4	F	2
Miller, Jeff	24:47:56	TX	2013	M3	M	2
Pless, Mitchel	24:48:56	GA	2013	M3	M	1
Kroeger, Daniel	24:49:06	AUS	2013	M3	M	1
Corky, Dean	24:50:13	CA	2013	M5	M	1
Svatek, Robert	24:51:17	TX	2013	M3	M	1
Sahibi, Noureddine	24:51:56	Germany	2013	M3	M	1
Jones, Chris	24:54:33	CA	2013	M4	M	2
Willis, James	25:04:54		2013	M2	M	1
Chapman, Donnie	25:06:58	MD	2013	M5	M	1
Brackley, Ryan	25:08:27	CO	2013	M4	M	1
Schafer, Rick	25:16:54	CO	2013	M4	M	1
Dowell, Derek	25:19:02	LA	2013	M3	M	3
Bourassa, Denise	25:20:33	OR	2013	F4	F	2
Kracaw, Dana	25:20:36	CO	2013	F2	F	2
Walker, Lee	25:31:14	MD	2013	M3	M	1
Pashley, Alex	25:36:45	CO	2013	M3	M	1
Clover, Geoffery	25:47:43	CO	2013	M4	M	2
Boelen, Filip	25:49:14	CO	2013	M3	M	3
Moncada, Jordi	25:50:27	CA	2013	M3	M	2
Stores, Chris	25:53:15	SD	2013	M3	M	1
Lindh, Christy	25:54:01	CO	2013	F3	F	2
Nishina, Soken	25:54:35	Japan	2013	M3	M	1
Thompson, Mark	25:56:42	CO	2013	M4	M	3
Liberatore, Ray	25:56:47	TX	2013	M2	M	1
Plant, Jeff	25:59:11	Canada	2013	M4	M	1
Pomeroy, Richard	26:06:56	England	2013	M4	M	1
Dessy, Luigi	26:10:24	Puerto Rico	2013	M3	M	1
Allemang, Jason	26:12:16	MO	2013	M4	M	2
Ritchie, Sam	26:15:42	VA	2013	M2	M	2

Silva, Ryan	26:16:57	OK	2013	M3	M	1
Jumper, Alison	26:17:12	AR	2013	F3	F	1
Lingerfield, Dan	26:18:41	CO	2013	M4	M	4
Agnew, Kelly	26:19:24	UT	2013	M4	M	6
Spencer, Eddie	26:19:50	OK	2013	M4	M	1
Crockett, Jason	26:22:38	TX	2013	M3	M	1
Wetstine, Laura	26:22:57	CO	2013	F3	F	2
Pardoe, Niki	26:23:44	CO	2013	F3	F	1
Hattan, Gregory	26:25:27	NE	2013	M5	M	2
Tobin, Andrew	26:26:45	NH	2013	M3	M	1
Jones, Stephanie	26:29:05	CO	2013	F4	F	4
Edmondson, Marshall	26:29:15	TN	2013	M3	M	2
Meredith, Shannon	26:30:42	CO	2013	F4	F	1
Miller, Michael	26:31:18	AZ	2013	M5	M	2
Lindner, Erno	26:31:54	TN	2013	M3	M	1
Lassley, Becki Lynn	26:32:38	CO	2013	F3	F	2
Urbine, Tim	26:37:16	CO	2013	M3	M	3
Echizenya, Daigo	26:38:06	CA	2013	M4	M	1
Bybee, Charles	26:38:57	CO	2013	M5	M	12
Sweeney, Megan	26:39:07	CO	2013	F3	F	5
Tomasello, Tyler	26:39:39	CO	2013	M2	M	1
Kabanuck, Chas	26:41:06	ND	2013	M2	M	1
Woody, Jeff	26:43:20	TN	2013	M4	M	1
Reeves, Ben	26:43:50	CO	2013	M3	M	1
Vella, Victor	26:45:16	Italy	2013	M6	M	1
Thornton, Colin	26:46:00	England	2013	M3	M	1
Mcgargill, Tim	26:47:37	NE	2013	M3	M	1
Spivey, David	26:47:59	IN	2013	M4	M	1
Noll, Jon	26:48:39	WI	2013	M2	M	1
Nielsen, Pamela	26:49:05	MN	2013	F3	F	2
Morton, Tom	26:53:27	MA	2013	M3	M	1
Donosky, Jay	26:54:34	AZ	2013	M4	M	3
Schneider, Amy	26:54:35	CO	2013	F3	F	2
Lightburn, Janet	26:55:13	CO	2013	F4	F	2
Westerman, Chris	26:56:58	CO	2013	M3	M	2
Canowitz, Liza	26:57:09	OH	2013	F3	F	2
Cecere, Matthew	26:57:17	CO	2013	M3	M	1

Emerson, Andy	26:57:37	MO	2013	M4	M	1
Plante, Edward	27:00:48	NJ	2013	M3	M	1
Larsen, Matthew	27:01:46	CO	2013	M4	M	1
Rittenberry, Jordan	27:04:38	IL	2013	M3	M	1
Ritner, Wes	27:06:36	SC	2013	M4	M	2
Vasquez, Rolando	27:06:55	TX	2013	M3	M	1
Gould, Jeffrey	27:07:11	CA	2013	M4	M	1
Seman, Milan	27:07:33	Netherlands	2013	M3	M	1
Woodsmall, David	27:09:04	DC	2013	M2	M	1
Johnson, Molly	27:10:49	UT	2013	F4	F	2
Passenti, Brian	27:14:05	CO	2013	M3	M	5
Sanders, Clayton	27:15:26	NC	2013	M5	M	1
Speirs, Steve	27:16:18	VA	2013	M4	M	1
Pence, Eric	27:17:07	CO	2013	M4	M	24
Churchill, R. Sean	27:20:16	WI	2013	M4	M	9
Gregory, Richard	27:20:50	CO	2013	M3	M	1
Yedlinsky, Ryan	27:22:51	WA	2013	M3	M	1
Cales, Ken	27:27:35	CO	2013	M4	M	1
Boyack, Chris	27:28:46	CO	2013	M4	M	6
Chlouber, Cole	27:29:34	CO	2013	M3	M	4
Snyder, Philip	27:32:36	CO	2013	M4	M	2
Deaven, Jerome	27:33:20	MI	2013	M4	M	3
Gordon, Ken	27:33:55	NM	2013	M4	M	10
Sides, Vernon	27:35:00	NC	2013	M4	M	4
Cleveland, Carl	27:35:09	KS	2013	M4	M	1
Maughan, Grant	27:35:32	AUS	2013	M4	M	2
Westphal, Brian	27:37:02	ID	2013	M4	M	1
Chapman, Donna	27:37:38	CO	2013	F4	F	3
Freed, Jason	27:37:47	WY	2013	M4	M	1
Schulof, Daniel	27:39:11	UT	2013	M3	M	1
Enger, Mike	27:39:17	CO	2013	M3	M	1
Bielik, Michael	27:39:38	NY	2013	M3	M	2
Garber, Anthony	27:40:34	WY	2013	M5	M	2
van Knotsenburg, Trevor	27:41:08		2013	M2	M	1
Freeman, Jimmy Dean	27:41:24	CA	2013	M3	M	2
Stone, Chuck	27:42:06	CO	2013	M5	M	8
Duncan, Ian	27:42:29	AUS	2013	M3	M	1

Costilow, Brian	27:42:43	TN	2013	M3	M	10
Booth, Emily	27:43:49	CO	2013	F3	F	2
Atkinson, Phil	27:44:52	WY	2013	M4	M	7
Nelson, Jamen	27:45:01	UT	2013	M2	M	8
Gant, Matt	27:45:07	CO	2013	M2	M	2
Kunkel, Kenneth	27:45:17	CO	2013	M5	M	1
Dougherty, Dutch	27:45:57	CO	2013	M4	M	1
Richardson, Erik	27:46:02	MI	2013	M3	M	4
Donner, Brian	27:46:33	WY	2013	M3	M	1
Toillion, Charlie	27:46:41	WA	2013	M4	M	1
Dalley, Josh	27:46:47	CO	2013	M3	M	3
Davison, Ted	27:47:22	TX	2013	M4	M	1
Sticksel, Jennifer	27:49:29	TX	2013	F4	F	1
Maldonado, Enrique	27:49:46	CO	2013	M4	M	2
Olmer, Barbara	27:52:42	CO	2013	F3	F	1
Hovenga, Bard	27:53:03	NY	2013	M2	M	4
Scott, Todd	27:53:10	MI	2013	M4	M	11
Beard, Ryan	27:53:38	TX	2013	M3	M	1
Sandor, Edward	27:55:53	MN	2013	M3	M	1
Goicoechea, Brittany	27:57:20	ID	2013	F2	F	1
Gartside, Stephen	27:57:50	CO	2013	M4	M	1
Keeling, Charles	27:58:10	CO	2013	M2	M	1
Wells, Glenn	27:58:21	NC	2013	M5	M	1
Mayer, Adam	27:59:56	NJ	2013	M3	M	2
Zaylor, Kyle	28:00:52	MO	2013	M2	M	1
Mccurnin, Jeanne	28:01:04	IA	2013	F5	F	4
Strand, Eric	28:01:59	MO	2013	M5	M	7
Butler, Sean	28:02:34	NC	2013	M4	M	1
Finkbeiner, Bill	28:06:08	CA	2013	M5	M	30
Nowak, Sean	28:06:22	Rwanda	2013	M3	M	1
Beachler, Cory	28:07:04	CO	2013	M4	M	1
Asmussen, Jess	28:08:10	CO	2013	M3	M	1
Kysar-Carey, Jeanne	28:08:52	CA	2013	F4	F	1
Bartzen, Gene	28:09:04	CO	2013	M5	M	10
Rubino, Vito	28:10:33	CA	2013	M3	M	1
Alexander, William (Big Willie)	28:11:30	CO	2013	M5	M	2
Thomas, Christophe	28:11:46	Germany	2013	M3	M	1

463

Falbo, Traci	28:11:57	IN	2013	F4	F	1
Barrera, Walter	28:14:03	DC	2013	M3	M	3
Urbanski, Jeffrey	28:14:55	WI	2013	M2	M	1
Braeger, Greg	28:14:58	CO	2013	M4	M	1
Stafford, Carrie	28:15:24	CO	2013	F3	F	5
Lassen, Ryan	28:15:30	CO	2013	M2	M	1
Ellis, Randy	28:15:51	OK	2013	M6	M	6
Eide, Chris	28:16:06	CA	2013	M3	M	1
Schulz, Flynn	28:16:23	IA	2013	M3	M	1
Mead, Chris	28:16:27	CA	2013	M4	M	2
Erikson, Lisa	28:17:09	CO	2013	F3	F	1
Whitehead, Adam	28:18:34	CO	2013	M4	M	3
Chananie, Andrew	28:19:32	South Africa	2013	M4	M	1
Horn, Gary	28:20:51	TX	2013	M5	M	1
Hagen, Mike	28:21:19	NE	2013	M3	M	1
Clark, David	28:21:31	CO	2013	M4	M	6
Randall, Mike	28:22:05	CO	2013	M3	M	1
Lundy, Jonathan	28:22:41	KY	2013	M3	M	3
Hernandez, Oscar	28:23:07	Italy	2013	M3	M	1
Carpenter, Sandra	28:23:24	CO	2013	F4	F	1
Lucas, Daniel	28:23:41	TN	2013	M3	M	1
Crump, Robin	28:23:41	TN	2013	F4	F	1
Priebe, Iris	28:23:48	Canada	2013	F4	F	1
Mcdermand, Chris	28:24:49	TX	2013	M3	M	1
White, Timothy	28:25:19	NM	2013	M5	M	1
Zon, Ludwik	28:25:41	NC	2013	M5	M	2
Dempsey, Christopher	28:25:57	VA	2013	M3	M	2
Mcmeans, Keri	28:26:04	WY	2013	F3	F	1
Jorgensen, Will	28:27:28	TN	2013	M5	M	2
Dumars, Jason	28:28:53	CA	2013	M4	M	1
Kaminski, James	28:29:31	CO	2013	M3	M	5
Erdman, Phoebe	28:30:02	CO	2013	F2	F	2
Gardner, Alexander	28:31:00	England	2013	M2	M	1
Demoss, Jean	28:31:55	CO	2013	F4	F	6
Crock, Bret	28:32:52	CO	2013	M5	M	11
Reed, Pam	28:33:22	WY	2013	F5	F	6
Mastin, Marvin	28:34:04	KS	2013	M4	M	1

Murphy, Alan	28:34:28	MI	2013	M2	M	1
Straw, Keith	28:34:29	PA	2013	M5	M	3
Boyd, Terry	28:34:49	CO	2013	M4	M	3
Pfister, Brian	28:34:53	IL	2013	M4	M	1
Solomon, Brandon	28:34:54	CA	2013	M3	M	1
Thier, Liam	28:35:01	CA	2013	M3	M	1
Edmundson, Chris	28:35:16	CO	2013	M3	M	1
Solberg, Jamie	28:36:09	CO	2013	F2	F	1
Pritchard, Siobhan	28:36:22	CO	2013	F3	F	2
Hackworth, Steve	28:36:30	CO	2013	M3	M	1
Carter, Josh	28:36:31	CO	2013	M4	M	1
Thomas, Edward	28:36:52	SD	2013	M5	M	2
Kazukawa, Junko	28:37:06	CO	2013	F5	F	6
Buffington, Marc	28:37:21	CO	2013	M3	M	1
Richburg, Jimmy	28:37:23	NY	2013	M2	M	1
Eccles, Allan	28:38:23	South Africa	2013	M5	M	1
Murray, Brian	28:39:22	CO	2013	M3	M	3
Curry, Garry	28:39:52	CA	2013	M5	M	25
Apt, Kirk	28:39:52	CO	2013	M5	M	20
Utke, Shane	28:40:20	CA	2013	M3	M	1
Enlow, Lori	28:40:23	OK	2013	F4	F	2
Nakauchi, Laurie	28:40:37	CO	2013	F4	F	12
Schardein, Tim	28:41:21	CO	2013	M4	M	4
Quick, Geoff	28:42:26	CA	2013	M5	M	1
Hiller, Stephany	28:42:58	CA	2013	F4	M	1
Grimes, Keith	28:43:28	CO	2013	M5	M	9
Richard, Steven	28:43:30	TX	2013	M3	M	1
Benhammou, Daniel	28:43:33	CO	2013	M3	M	5
Martin, Shane	28:43:34	UT	2013	M4	M	1
Moll, David	28:44:11	CO	2013	M4	M	2
Stamp, Natalie	28:44:42	SD	2013	F3	F	2
Stavig Just, Christina	28:44:54	MN	2013	F3	F	1
Ringler, Daniel	28:45:05	CO	2013	M3	M	2
Ahern, Dennis	28:47:31	ID	2013	M5	M	1
Layman, Jay	28:48:09	CO	2013	M5	M	1
Schliff, Henry	28:48:15	CO	2013	M3	M	2
Bross, Ted	28:49:08	OH	2013	M2	M	1

Name	Time	Location	Year	Div	Sex	
Brotman, William	28:49:13	CO	2013	M3	M	1
Klover, Sherrie	28:49:16	KS	2013	F4	F	1
Bordeleau, Jp	28:49:35	IL	2013	M3	M	1
Frost, Jerry	28:51:34	MO	2013	M5	M	1
Rezac, Jason	28:52:38	MN	2013	M4	M	1
Yoneji, Jerald	28:53:33	MT	2013	M6	M	1
Sturdivant, Heather	28:53:33	CO	2013	F3	F	1
Eastwood, Robert	28:54:20	England	2013	M2	M	2
Duarte, Chase	28:55:52	AZ	2013	M4	M	1
Fenninger, Joanne	28:55:53	VA	2013	F4	F	1
Gates, Jay	28:56:01	IA	2013	M2	M	1
Shaffer, Daniel J.	28:56:25	TN	2013	M3	M	1
Trent, John	28:56:28	NV	2013	M5	M	1
Terry, Parker	28:56:55	VA	2013	M2	M	1
Moller, Stacy	28:57:22	CO	2013	F4	F	1
Priolo, Peter	28:57:41	NY	2013	M4	M	1
Buchanan, Douglas	28:57:51	CO	2013	M4	M	1
Lang, Nick	28:58:16	CO	2013	M3	M	1
Hoefen, Kimberley	28:58:33	CO	2013	F3	F	3
Damrow, Alisha	28:59:18	WI	2013	F2	F	1
Bovaird, Ray	28:59:36	OH	2013	M4	M	1
Cardenas, Raul	29:00:30	TX	2013	M3	M	1
Hewitt, Greg	29:01:05	CO	2013	M5	M	1
Kriewaldt, Marc	29:02:05	CO	2013	M5	M	3
Desantis, Kt	29:02:05	CO	2013	F5	F	3
Crawford, Lindsay	29:02:38	TN	2013	M4	M	1
Anfang, Matt	29:04:28	WI	2013	M2	M	2
Wainhouse, Owen	29:05:20	England	2013	M3	M	1
Skog, Daniel	29:05:25	SWE	2013	M3	M	2
Friedman, Jason	29:06:38	NJ	2013	M3	M	1
Grimmer, Geoff	29:06:53	CO	2013	M3	M	1
Crady, Troy	29:07:02	IL	2013	M4	M	1
Noble, Dewey	29:07:13	CO	2013	M3	M	1
Keyes, Christopher	29:07:31	CO	2013	M2	M	1
Maisel, Paul	29:07:40	CO	2013	M4	M	1
Cales, Nancy	29:08:08	CO	2013	F4	F	1
Marritt, Kirsty	29:09:14	CA	2013	F4	F	1

Robinson, Will	29:09:16	CO	2013	M2	M	2
Curreri, Justin	29:09:30	CT	2013	M2	M	1
Harrison, Chris	29:11:11	CA	2013	F5	F	2
Kitamura, Makoto	29:11:19	NY	2013	M4	M	1
Salvesen, Greg	29:11:19	CO	2013	M2	M	2
Adamson, Cameron	29:11:50	UT	2013	M2	M	1
Bland, Bo	29:12:10	ME	2013	M3	M	1
Sasseman, Elizabeth	29:12:24	IN	2013	F2	F	1
Sapp, Brian	29:13:06	CO	2013	M2	M	1
Matys, Michelle	29:14:41	FL	2013	F3	F	1
Law, Eric	29:15:16	FL	2013	M2	M	1
Morse, Toby	29:16:04	CO	2013	M5	M	1
Barney, Andrew	29:16:12	UT	2013	M4	M	1
Seydel, Julie	29:16:54	CO	2013	F4	F	1
Tomas, Brian	29:17:27	CO	2013	M5	M	1
Macsas, Allison	29:18:31	TX	2013	F2	F	1
Matthews, Clifford	29:18:32	NM	2013	M5	M	1
Feign, Cory	29:18:46	IL	2013	M3	M	2
Comstock, Amy	29:19:01	IL	2013	F4	F	2
Ferrari, Guido	29:19:39	NC	2013	M5	M	2
Torres, Michelle	29:19:54	CO	2013	F4	F	3
Brenden, Dan	29:20:00	AZ	2013	M6	M	8
Schoenlaub, Paul	29:20:00	MO	2013	M5	M	12
Jourdain, Benoit	29:20:04	France	2013	M4	M	1
Schnepp, Michael	29:20:08	CT	2013	M2	M	1
Battey, Hoyt	29:20:23	DC	2013	M3	M	1
Romero, Jason	29:20:58	CO	2013	M4	M	4
Macdonald, Steve	29:21:52	TX	2013	M4	M	3
Cuyler, Collins	29:22:21	HI	2013	M2	M	2
Wolf, Chad	29:23:04	OH	2013	M2	M	1
Carvill, Anna	29:23:22	CO	2013	F3	F	1
Castello, Patrick	29:23:56	HI	2013	M3	M	1
Mohr, Stephen	29:24:06	VA	2013	M3	M	1
Hill, Brian	29:24:29	TX	2013	M3	M	1
Brooks, Curtis	29:24:45	MO	2013	M5	M	1
Klanjsek, Oza	29:24:56	CO	2013	F4	F	1
Stofel, James	29:25:23	CO	2013	M2	M	1

Persolja, Pete	29:25:33	TN	2013	M3	M	1
Portman, Mark	29:25:45	England	2013	M4	M	1
Barber, Bill	29:25:51	SD	2013	M5	M	1
Bargo, Greg	29:26:10	TX	2013	M3	M	1
Kent, Craig	29:26:19	OH	2013	M3	M	1
Wilburn, Jessie	29:26:31	CO	2013	F2	F	1
Whitis, Matt	29:26:35		2013	M5	M	1
Chado, Robert	29:26:49	CO	2013	M1	M	1
Ramsey, Alexander	29:27:00	HI	2013	M2	M	1
Hanousek, Jan	29:27:22	Czech Republic	2013	M4	M	1
Winn, Yitka	29:27:24	CO	2013	F2	F	1
Ray, Mike	29:27:31	SC	2013	M4	M	1
Baker, Billy	29:27:37	CT	2013	M3	M	1
Anderson, Janice	29:27:57	GA	2013	F4	F	2
Greene, Nick	29:28:09	England	2013	M4	M	1
Barnwell, Christopher	29:28:10	TX	2013	M4	M	1
Driscoll, Jeff	29:28:14	CO	2013	M4	M	4
Najjar, Steven	29:28:39	FL	2013	M4	M	1
Hopper, Orlin	29:28:40	CO	2013	M4	M	3
Blumberg, Andre	29:28:56	Hong Kong	2013	M4	M	1
Sooter, David	29:29:27	OK	2013	M4	M	1
Decker, Sonya	29:30:12	MN	2013	F4	F	1
Chandler, Jonathan	29:30:25	WA	2013	M2	M	1
Snyder, Scott	29:30:57	CO	2013	M5	M	9
Brundage, Cory	29:31:15	IN	2013	M6	M	1
Huskie, Will	29:31:32	CO	2013	M5	M	5
Cooper, Kevin	29:31:51	CO	2013	M3	M	1
Steiner, Randy	29:31:57	WI	2013	M5	M	1
Steffenson, Dustin	29:32:17	CO	2013	M3	M	1
Cartier, Gregory	29:32:29	MA	2013	M3	M	1
Ham, Robert	29:32:42	TX	2013	M4	M	2
Wong, Thomas	29:32:51	NY	2013	M4	M	1
Ornelas, Eduardo	29:32:58	Italy	2013	M4	M	1
Kreaden, Mike	29:33:23	CA	2013	M5	M	1
Southern, Chip	29:33:56	CO	2013	M4	M	3
Weisshaar, Hans-Dieter	29:34:48	Germany	2013	73	M	9
Grimes, Amanda	29:35:03	CO	2013	F3	F	1

Aardal, Jon	29:35:25	CO	2013	M4	M	1
Jozefczyk, Stephen	29:36:46	CO	2013	M3	M	1
Bullock, Ethan	29:37:50	CO	2013	M3	M	1
Zigich, Matthew	29:38:08	MI	2013	M3	M	1
Spivey, Craig	29:38:34	CO	2013	M4	M	1
Friedman, Jeff	29:38:41	CO	2013	M3	M	2
Martinez, Edgar	29:39:03	TX	2013	M3	M	2
Cougot, Dale	29:39:13	TX	2013	M4	M	1
Murdock, Jennifer	29:39:29	CO	2013	F2	F	1
Cody, Brent	29:40:19	CO	2013	M3	M	1
Abramowitz, Fred	29:41:46	CO	2013	M6	M	10
Broomfield, Robert	29:42:10	CO	2013	M3	M	2
Fu, Chihping	29:42:15	CA	2013	M4	M	1
Shah, Sandeep	29:42:19	TX	2013	M3	M	1
Frank, Jeremy	29:42:50	CO	2013	M3	M	2
Morton, Lisa	29:43:20	CO	2013	F3	F	1
Theodore, Phillip	29:43:26	TN	2013	M4	M	3
Hall, Tony	29:43:46	IN	2013	M5	M	1
Smith, Alan	29:44:14	CO	2013	M4	M	8
Biden, Ed	29:44:17	Germany	2013	M3	M	1
Malone, Brett	29:45:10	VA	2013	M4	M	1
Zdon, William	29:45:10	NY	2013	M2	M	1
Odebunmi, Emmanuel	29:45:52	NY	2013	M3	M	2
Wamack, Chad	29:45:55	TN	2013	M4	M	1
Carson, Chad	29:46:01	UT	2013	M5	M	3
Rolnick, Wesley	29:46:17	NY	2013	M2	M	1
Ormond, Scott	29:46:46	CO	2013	M4	M	1
Ravenscraft, Megan	29:47:32	MD	2013	F2	F	1
Cook, Kate	29:48:01	MA	2013	F3	F	1
Mccreight, Scott	29:48:07	KS	2013	M4	M	1
Bass, Cara	29:48:46	TX	2013	F2	F	1
Parnell, Edwin	29:49:13		2013	M3	M	1
Bartel, Jennifer	29:50:28	WY	2013	F3	F	2
Varela, Mario	29:51:58	CO	2013	M5	M	20
Gutierrez, Kody	29:52:09	CO	2013	M3	M	2
Shark, Jonathan	29:53:38	WA	2013	M3	M	2
Shark, Linh	29:53:48	WA	2013	F3	F	1

| Ratliff, Douglas | 29:54:24 | TX | 2013 | M4 | M | 1 |
| Parham, Terry | 29:57:40 | AZ | 2013 | M3 | M | 1 |

2014

Name	Finish Time	State	Year	Age	Sex	#Finished
Krar, Rob	16:09:32	AZ	2014	37	M	2
Aish, Michael	16:38:37	CO	2014	38	M	3
Sharman, Ian	16:41:38	CA	2014	33	M	5
Tiernan, Zeke	17:35:14	CO	2014	38	M	4
Mackey, Dave	19:10:45	CO	2014	44	M	2
Kjerengtroen, Lars	19:19:43	UT	2014	35	M	2
Airey, Richard	19:27:16	NJ	2014	38	M	3
Roca, Emma	19:38:04	Spain	2014	41	F	1
Howie, Craig	19:43:31	CO	2014	37	M	3
Howard, Liza	20:01:15	TX	2014	42	F	1
Wros, John	20:17:48	OR	2014	25	M	1
Africa, Bob	20:25:11	CO	2014	41	M	4
Callahan, Duncan	20:27:20	CO	2014	31	M	7
Verdi, Daniel	20:30:27	CO	2014	32	M	2
Curtis, Matthew	20:38:37	CO	2014	38	M	7
Ambrose, Michael	20:41:17	CO	2014	26	M	2
Radford, Chuck	20:46:35	CO	2014	43	M	2
Sweeney, Bob	20:51:12	CO	2014	47	M	4
Sandoval, Marvin	21:20:00	CO	2014	36	M	7
Diaz, Fernando Gonzalez	21:40:52	Spain	2014	40	M	1
Williams, Bryan	21:45:09	CO	2014	39	M	3
Landry, Paul	21:50:18	CO	2014	44	M	1
Papathanasopoulos, Argyrios	21:52:25	Greece	2014	42	M	1
Smith, Matt	21:53:23	TX	2014	35	M	1
Bundrock, Danny	21:57:20	CO	2014	35	M	5
Parr, Timmy	21:58:14	CO	2014	32	M	3
Green, Jared	22:09:23	Canada	2014	38	M	1
Hooper, Chris	22:12:16	Canada	2014	36	M	1
Gerenz, Bob	22:16:40	MN	2014	46	M	4
Kinner, Jon	22:27:34	CO	2014	34	M	2
Mobley, Mark	22:33:53	CO	2014	43	M	4
Anderson, Joel	22:37:20	MN	2014	32	M	3

Stanciu, Adrian	22:38:29	CO	2014	45	M	4
Ritchie, Sam	22:38:36	VA	2014	27	M	2
Antin, Jason	22:41:48	CO	2014	31	M	2
Wetstine, Sean	22:42:51	CO	2014	38	M	6
Jump, Jay	22:44:06	CO	2014	33	M	2
Backes, Mark	22:51:48	CA	2014	50	M	1
Bradford, Jeremy	22:57:50	CO	2014	36	M	5
Blumentritt, David	23:06:28	CO	2014	31	M	1
Courkamp, Kirt	23:08:20	CO	2014	52	M	3
McGlade, Patrick	23:10:00	CO	2014	25	M	1
Jimenez, Rodrigo	23:13:26	CO	2014	38	M	5
Fulton, Max	23:15:28	CO	2014	37	M	5
Bolls, Rod	23:19:45	CO	2014	39	M	3
Wegscheider, Erich	23:23:29	CA	2014	28	M	2
Nagaraj, Harsha	23:26:05	CO	2014	40	M	3
Smith, Aaron	23:27:11	CO	2014	27	M	3
Lehmann, John	23:28:29	PA	2014	39	M	1
Sweeney, Patrick	23:32:22	CA	2014	35	M	5
Spatt, Nicolas	23:35:22	AZ	2014	26	M	1
Dobson, Corey	23:39:26	CO	2014	30	M	1
Cooper, Will	23:43:19	CA	2014	51	M	2
Harcrow, Harry	23:50:50	CO	2014	47	M	7
Stafford, Carrie	23:56:53	CO	2014	35	F	5
Nunn, Tyson	24:00:41	CO	2014	41	M	1
Smith, Darian	24:04:06	NC	2014	33	M	1
Hornsby, Wyatt	24:09:08	CO	2014	41	M	5
O'Brien, Michael	24:13:17	CO	2014	31	M	2
Clark, David	24:14:35	CO	2014	43	M	6
Lassley, Becki Lynn	24:16:31	CO	2014	36	F	2
Schrader, Scott	24:17:41	CO	2014	29	M	1
Sandoval, Wesley	24:19:31	CO	2014	37	M	4
Alex, Barefoot	24:22:07	HI	2014	29	M	1
Finocchio, Tim	24:22:57	MA	2014	36	M	1
Walsh, Brian	24:23:02	MI	2014	31	M	2
Freeman, Jimmy Dean	24:23:44	CA	2014	37	M	2
Bailey, Jack	24:25:04	MA	2014	35	M	1
Blakeley, Mark	24:26:08	MA	2014	50	M	1

Cappellini, Christopher	24:26:08	MA	2014	48	M	2
Larsen, Timothy	24:26:52	NE	2014	45	M	1
Lass, Barry	24:28:23	NJ	2014	50	M	1
Sides, Vernon	24:28:45	NC	2014	42	M	4
Tucker, Paul	24:28:59	CO	2014	41	M	2
Merino, Keila	24:30:56	NY	2014	33	F	2
Ritner, Wes	24:34:55	SC	2014	46	M	2
Howell, Scott	24:35:34	CO	2014	36	M	1
Moll, Jeff	24:40:06	CO	2014	44	M	1
Earnshaw, Jack	24:40:32	PA	2014	33	M	1
Davis, Jerry	24:41:22	CO	2014	41	M	2
Thomas, Edward	24:41:29	SD	2014	55	M	2
Gillespie, Joseph	24:41:34	CO	2014	33	M	1
Youngblom, Justin	24:42:14	MN	2014	29	M	1
Agnew, Kelly	24:44:40	UT	2014	41	M	6
Lundy, Jonathan	24:45:07	KY	2014	37	M	3
Wooten, Andy	24:51:25	CO	2014	46	M	6
Young, Kyle	24:52:08	CO	2014	28	M	2
McRoberts, Adam	24:53:45	CO	2014	39	M	2
O'Connell, Dan	25:21:40	CO	2014	36	M	2
Sim, Jason	25:26:22	American Samoa	2014	37	M	1
Boelen, Filip	25:41:55	CO	2014	37	M	3
Earle, Lieko	25:42:45	CO	2014	39	F	2
De Vrieze, Martin	25:43:55	WA	2014	44	M	1
Mulligan, David	25:49:51	CO	2014	53	M	1
Romero, Ted	25:51:13	CO	2014	33	M	1
Stafford, Tony	25:53:33	CO	2014	35	M	1
Atkinson, Phil	25:54:45	WY	2014	42	M	7
Perez, Angel G	26:02:00	CA	2014	43	M	2
Barrera, Walter	26:05:31	DC	2014	33	M	3
Ewing, Amanda	26:10:23	CO	2014	33	F	1
LaTourette, Dave	26:10:45	WA	2014	52	M	1
Kaminski, James	26:14:50	CO	2014	32	M	5
Lingerfield, Dan	26:16:14	CO	2014	41	M	4
Brittenham, Sarah	26:17:06	CO	2014	31	F	1
Mollenhour, John	26:17:41	GA	2014	58	M	2
Norcia, Christopher	26:17:47	CO	2014	46	M	3

Bourassa, Denise	26:23:25	OR	2014	44	F	2
Sims, Don	26:27:21	CO	2014	48	M	2
Dowell, Derek	26:29:11	LA	2014	32	M	3
Johnson, Molly	26:29:50	US	2014	49	F	2
Smith, Nick	26:29:58	CO	2014	41	M	1
Wright, Chris	26:30:03	CO	2014	42	M	7
Honert, Jeff	26:30:51	CO	2014	52	M	1
Kazukawa, Junko	26:35:18	CO	2014	51	F	6
Hultquist, Daryl	26:41:46	MD	2014	44	M	1
Skog, Daniel	26:45:36	Sweden	2014	34	M	2
Collins, Steven	26:48:09	England	2014	40	M	1
Long, David	26:48:53	CO	2014	48	M	1
DeDoncker, John	26:50:26	IA	2014	50	M	5
McNeill, Justin	26:51:21	VA	2014	40	M	1
Seymour, Nick	26:54:30	OK	2014	33	M	2
Anderson, Matthew	26:56:20	CO	2014	36	M	1
Baier, Daniel	27:00:26	WA	2014	39	M	1
Kumeda, Andy	27:01:56	CA	2014	46	M	2
Dysert, David	27:05:21	MI	2014	48	M	1
Trzcienski, Edward	27:09:02	NM	2014	52	M	1
Bedard, Andy	27:09:58	CO	2014	43	M	2
Hauser, Michael	27:10:29	WA	2014	24	M	1
Burmaster, Travis	27:11:58	CO	2014	40	M	2
Bauermeister, Andrew	27:14:30	IN	2014	32	M	1
Jones, Jeffrey	27:14:46	MO	2014	34	M	1
Snape, Steven	27:15:32		2014	24	M	1
Martinez, Miguel Gunturiz	27:15:38	Spain	2014	40	M	1
Kunkle, Jeff	27:19:05	CO	2014	40	M	1
Coulter, Jean	27:20:01	CO	2014	42	F	1
Bartzen, Gene	27:21:23	CO	2014	60	M	10
Harmon, Adam	27:22:10	CO	2014	25	M	2
Pack, Steven	27:27:48	NY	2014	33	M	1
Teisher, Jon	27:27:55	CO	2014	39	M	4
Chlouber, Cole	27:29:08	MN	2014	40	M	4
Turosak, Jim	27:30:58	CO	2014	52	M	1
Carson, Chad	27:32:26	UT	2014	55	M	3
Malcolm, Dave	27:39:21	Australia	2014	38	M	1

Hobbs, Nicholas	27:44:50	IN	2014	30	M	1
Churchill, Sean R.	27:45:39	WI	2014	48	M	9
Geyser, Reinier	27:46:03	NV	2014	38	M	1
Ouaalla, Abdessamad	27:47:06	Canada	2014	30	M	1
Goulden, Matthew	27:47:07	Canada	2014	33	M	1
Pence, Eric	27:49:06	CO	2014	48	M	24
Yocum, Aaron	27:49:40	WV	2014	49	M	1
Oliver, Dave	27:50:22	CO	2014	48	M	2
Dalley, Josh	27:50:38	CO	2014	31	M	3
North, Keeler	27:51:45	CO	2014	34	M	1
Anderson, Shane	27:54:29	CO	2014	38	M	1
Hauptman, Barry	27:54:43	MD	2014	51	M	1
Searfoss, Jason	27:55:35	IL	2014	42	M	1
Campbell, Matt	27:55:52	WA	2014	31	M	2
Hardin, Joseph	27:57:55	WA	2014	32	M	1
Barringer, Chris	27:58:41	CO	2014	40	M	2
Kobayashi, Satoshi	27:59:26	Japan	2014	33	M	1
Mazurkiewicz, Robert	27:59:33	IL	2014	43	M	2
Wetstine, Laura	28:01:32	CO	2014	32	F	2
Munch, Aaron	28:02:19	CO	2014	35	M	1
Hovenga, Bard	28:03:11	NY	2014	26	M	4
Munari, Dana	28:03:58	TX	2014	49	M	1
Schwarz, Haley	28:06:46	MO	2014	34	F	1
Rettig, Brad	28:07:34	NE	2014	34	M	2
Mix, Bryan	28:07:47	CO	2014	49	M	2
Featherstone, Andrew	28:12:14	WI	2014	42	M	1
Harelson, Cory	28:13:34	ID	2014	33	M	1
Dorgan, Jason	28:14:28	WI	2014	48	M	4
Wilken, Aaron	28:15:36	CO	2014	39	M	1
Goundry, Jim	28:15:53	NJ	2014	35	M	1
Mitchell, Rex	28:16:26	CO	2014	48	M	1
Irby, Joel	28:17:04	CO	2014	30	M	1
Welch, Jenny	28:17:11	CA	2014	32	F	1
Corsten, Dave	28:17:14	CO	2014	46	M	1
McCurnin, Jeanne	28:17:39	IA	2014	58	F	4
Tiffany, Kevin	28:18:02	IA	2014	38	M	1
Garcia, Diego	28:19:28	Chile	2014	34	M	3

Strand, Eric	28:20:31	MO	2014	53	M	7
Torres, Michelle	28:21:05	CO	2014	48	F	3
Ringler, Daniel	28:21:06	CO	2014	40	M	2
Apt, Kirk	28:22:31	CO	2014	52	M	20
Williams, Gary	28:24:41	Canada	2014	46	M	1
Cole, Gracie	28:25:40	CO	2014	31	F	1
Parker, Travis	28:25:43	HI	2014	40	M	1
Hoven, David	28:26:19	CO	2014	30	M	1
Ryan, Joey	28:27:04	SC	2014	35	M	1
Camann, Doug	28:27:42	NJ	2014	47	M	1
Ostler, Marta	28:28:28	WY	2014	46	F	1
Costilow, Brian	28:31:37	TN	2014	40	M	10
Nadon, Norman	28:32:13	Canada	2014	45	M	1
Williams, Bryce	28:32:28	CA	2014	34	M	1
Greenberg, Rebecca	28:32:55	NY	2014	25	F	1
Godfrey, Paul	28:33:24	OR	2014	44	M	4
Conner, Lee	28:33:26	OH	2014	41	F	1
McMillan, David	28:33:51	CO	2014	37	M	1
Zajac, Valerie	28:34:16	CO	2014	29	F	2
McKenna, Martin	28:34:30	PA	2014	42	M	1
Carroll, Jeff	28:37:09	CO	2014	33	M	1
Smith, Mike	28:37:31	IN	2014	56	M	3
Reiff, Andrew	28:38:15	CO	2014	41	M	7
Fredenburg, Denver	28:38:31	TX	2014	38	M	1
Williams, John	28:40:00	CO	2014	52	M	3
Boyack, Chris	28:40:36	CO	2014	44	M	6
Hansen, Nolan	28:41:50	CA	2014	32	M	1
Anderson, Katy	28:43:14	Australia	2014	37	F	5
Dailey, Bruce	28:43:16	ME	2014	43	M	7
Grimes, Keith	28:47:33	CO	2014	55	M	9
Clarke, John	28:47:57	CO	2014	49	M	1
Richards, T. Scott	28:48:55	CO	2014	49	M	1
Robinson, William	28:50:04	CO	2014	30	M	2
Kaupas, Daniel	28:52:00	MI	2014	32	M	1
Lynde, Robert	28:52:21	CO	2014	50	M	2
Luther, Joey	28:53:15	CO	2014	35	M	1
Pardue, Jason	28:54:29	VA	2014	39	M	2

Gagnon, Joseph	28:54:46	NY	2014	53	M	1
Herzog, Ryan	28:54:53	CO	2014	34	M	2
Nakauchi, Laurie	28:55:08	CO	2014	44	F	12
Dunnigan, Tony	28:55:11	CA	2014	42	M	1
Errecart, Christopher	28:55:15	CA	2014	39	M	1
Hoffman-Schmittou, Sammi	28:55:35	TN	2014	41	F	1
Nicholls, Steve	28:55:45	CO	2014	48	M	2
Nichols, Russel	28:56:14	OR	2014	41	M	2
Beeman, Bowman	28:56:43	CO	2014	37	M	1
McNulty, Brendan	28:56:58	CO	2014	26	M	1
Fey, Sean	28:57:00	CO	2014	48	M	1
Schoenlaub, Paul	28:57:31	MO	2014	55	M	12
Chahl, Tara	28:58:07	Canada	2014	37	F	1
White, Bret	28:58:51	CO	2014	45	M	1
Miller, Shaun	28:59:00	MA	2014	36	M	2
Miller, Barry	28:59:26	England	2014	34	M	1
Busche, Lester	29:00:34	CO	2014	42	M	1
Ray, Ashby	29:00:37	NC	2014	41	M	1
Gunderson, Jonathan	29:01:20	CA	2014	36	M	1
Lebreton, Sylvain	29:01:24	AZ	2014	40	M	1
Bybee, Charles	29:03:03	CO	2014	52	M	12
Skeels, Jennifer	29:05:22	CO	2014	40	F	1
Taylor, Jed	29:05:27	MO	2014	35	M	2
Flinn, Andrew	29:06:15	CO	2014	31	M	1
Nicholson, Leah	29:07:13	CO	2014	27	F	1
Lawrence, Jeremey	29:08:02	CO	2014	37	M	1
Graham, Nick	29:08:30	MN	2014	41	M	1
Healey, Jason	29:08:47	CA	2014	43	M	1
Beachy, Trent	29:09:13	CO	2014	31	M	1
Spencer, Eric	29:09:21	FL	2014	35	M	1
Cassidy, Donnacha	29:10:26	Ireland	2014	25	M	2
Larson, Ryan	29:10:35	CO	2014	36	M	1
James, Sharon	29:10:47	OK	2014	47	F	1
Rogers, Jessica	29:10:49	TN	2014	37	F	1
Bennett, David	29:11:25	KS	2014	54	M	1
Hendrix, David	29:12:43	CO	2014	50	M	1
Rivera, Lucas	29:12:54	CO	2014	27	M	2

Betty, Eugene L.	29:13:49	CO	2014	42	M	1
Blank, Gil	29:14:17	CA	2014	50	M	1
Dacar, Michael	29:15:00	NC	2014	37	M	1
Frank, Jeremy	29:15:16	CO	2014	35	M	2
Brenkus, Lizzie	29:16:03	CA	2014	37	F	1
Heavey, James	29:16:10	Canada	2014	41	M	1
Harvie, Dean	29:17:35	TX	2014	38	M	1
DeYoung, Lisa	29:18:27	NC	2014	46	F	1
Carrier, Alyssa	29:18:46	CO	2014	31	F	1
Bermudez, Conrado	29:19:11	NJ	2014	41	M	2
Lane, Tom	29:19:15	AZ	2014	43	M	1
Dailey, Edward	29:19:57	IL	2014	44	M	1
Malec, Ryan	29:21:38	GA	2014	38	M	1
Chambers, Stephen	29:21:51	CO	2014	34	M	2
Wharton, Julia	29:22:28	KS	2014	44	F	1
Watson, Charles	29:22:33	NY	2014	34	M	1
Furrer, Toni	29:22:52	CO	2014	38	M	2
Amaya, Maria	29:23:33	WA	2014	40	F	1
Lefferts, Stephanie	29:23:38	CO	2014	25	F	1
Parkison, Jenny	29:23:50	CO	2014	30	F	1
DeRose, Jordan	29:24:05	MO	2014	37	F	2
Randle, Chris	29:24:12	CO	2014	40	M	2
Vickers, William	29:24:42	CO	2014	35	M	1
Pellegrino, Dean	29:25:41	CO	2014	42	M	1
Donovan, Marie	29:25:55	NV	2014	36	F	1
Donovan, Douglas	29:25:58	NV	2014	44	M	1
Goeckermann, Rob	29:25:58	WI	2014	35	M	1
Lyon, Barry	29:26:20	CO	2014	35	M	1
Martin, Kyle	29:26:42	CO	2014	32	M	2
Nekouei, Tom	29:26:53	CO	2014	41	M	1
Sarkar, Arun	29:27:51	WI	2014	36	M	1
Bucalo, Jeremy	29:27:52	PA	2014	34	M	1
Dymmel, Kristen	29:28:10	CA	2014	37	F	1
Martinez, Gabriel	29:28:18	CO	2014	22	M	3
Pigott, Tricia	29:29:08	CO	2014	34	F	1
Thill, Mark	29:29:29	IN	2014	39	M	1
Colwell, Brent	29:29:30	IN	2014	37	M	1

Wilkinson, Mike	29:30:06	CO	2014	42	M	1
Ward, Amy	29:30:13	CO	2014	47	F	1
Brown, Nathan	29:30:27	CO	2014	35	M	1
Hofmann, Anthony	29:30:42	KS	2014	48	M	1
Forkas, Len	29:32:13	VA	2014	54	M	1
Hanlon, Jordan	29:32:31	MN	2014	30	M	1
Hayen, Lisa	29:32:40	CO	2014	39	F	1
Mangrum, Ryan	29:33:03	CO	2014	40	M	1
Klein, Mark	29:33:05	CA	2014	31	M	2
Marquez, Kristina	29:33:31	NY	2014	35	F	1
Bishop, Brad	29:33:34	CO	2014	29	M	2
Greenleaf, Brian	29:34:01	CO	2014	34	M	1
Macdonald, Steve	29:34:04	TX	2014	47	M	3
Griffin, Dina L	29:34:39	CO	2014	44	F	1
Scott, John	29:34:42	CO	2014	49	M	2
Samuel, Heidi	29:34:50	CO	2014	44	F	1
Ford, Mimi	29:34:54	AZ	2014	54	F	1
Blakemore, Conan	29:34:54	CO	2014	31	M	1
Blakemore, Ashley	29:34:58	CO	2014	29	F	1
McGarry, Jack	29:36:10	CO	2014	55	M	1
DeMoss, Jean	29:36:12	CO	2014	42	F	6
Bauer, Mark	29:36:16	CO	2014	38	M	1
Karczynski, Daniel	29:36:20	CO	2014	29	M	1
Cockman, Dave	29:36:26	CO	2014	57	M	1
Pritchard, Daniel	29:36:53	CO	2014	35	M	1
Hansen, Mads Holm	29:38:01	Denmark	2014	32	M	1
Cohen, Jonathan	29:38:05	CO	2014	33	M	1
Hanley, Erik	29:41:54	TX	2014	33	M	1
Ervin, Daley	29:42:20	WA	2014	28	M	2
Theodore, Phillip	29:42:27	TN	2014	47	M	3
Kraxner, Joe	29:42:39	CO	2014	36	M	1
Urban, Joe	29:42:40	GA	2014	40	M	1
Aronhalt, Gary	29:42:44	CO	2014	45	M	1
Ayers, Matthew	29:42:46	CO	2014	38	M	1
Bearss, Joseph	29:42:47	CO	2014	44	M	2
Feign, Cory	29:42:58	IL	2014	37	M	2
Leary, Douglas	29:42:59	CO	2014	51	M	2

Betz, Matthew	29:43:06	CO	2014	28	M	2
Wester, Trent	29:43:06	NM	2014	30	M	2
Kriewaldt, Marc	29:43:28	CO	2014	51	M	3
DeSantis, KT	29:43:34	CO	2014	51	F	3
Thompson, Mark	29:44:03	TX	2014	31	M	3
Redinger, Phil	29:44:11	CO	2014	43	M	1
Fuller, Brandon	29:44:43	CO	2014	39	M	1
Rose, Michael	29:45:07	CO	2014	49	M	1
Scott, Todd	29:45:08	MI	2014	50	M	11
Li, Guannan	29:45:56	CA	2014	32	M	1
Wu, Di	29:45:56	CA	2014	31	M	1
Roberg, Jason	29:47:08	CA	2014	35	M	1
Theiss, Mark	29:47:19	CO	2014	38	M	1
Hanley, Josh	29:47:59	NY	2014	26	M	1
Currens, Joe	29:48:01	TX	2014	48	M	1
Fabrizio, Dominic	29:48:51	OH	2014	46	M	2
Shark, Jonathan	29:48:52	WA	2014	35	M	2
Bailey, Joe	29:49:19	CO	2014	49	M	1
Song, KiSuk	29:49:20	South Korea	2014	48	M	1
Hodge, Angie	29:51:35	NE	2014	34	F	4
Gutierrez, Kody	29:53:55	CO	2014	38	M	2
Green, Thomas	29:55:49	MD	2014	63	M	1
Teeselink, Trevor	29:56:17	AZ	2014	42	M	1

2015

Name	Finish Time	State	Year	Age	Sex	#Finished
Sharman, Ian	16:33:54	OR	2015	34	M	5
Pietari, Kyle	18:16:04	CO	2015	28	M	4
Sagastume, Juan Carlos	18:29:27	Guatemala	2015	43	M	1
Radford, Chuck	18:43:18	CO	2015	44	M	2
Hewitt, Michael	19:28:32	CO	2015	45	M	3
Howard, Elizabeth	19:34:09	TX	2015	43	F	3
Verdi, Daniel	19:36:09	CO	2015	33	M	2
Sandoval, Marvin	19:44:58	CO	2015	37	M	7
Henry, Kara	19:54:08	CO	2015	30	F	3
Anderson, Joel	20:09:33	CO	2015	33	M	3
Teirney, David	20:23:43	CO	2015	36	M	3

Rusiecki, Brian	20:31:19	MA	2015	36	M	1
Jump, Jay	20:32:55	CO	2015	34	M	2
Reyes, Gustavo	20:50:32	Argentina	2015	36	M	1
Murphy, Jeason	21:18:43	CO	2015	35	M	1
Desjardins, Amos	21:26:04	VA	2015	34	M	1
Matticks, Kerry	21:29:37	CO	2015	49	M	3
Young, Kyle	21:37:03	CO	2015	29	M	2
Sweeney, Bob	21:44:58	CO	2015	48	M	4
Broomhall, Pete	21:49:16	CA	2015	37	M	1
Kinner, Jon	21:53:00	CO	2015	35	M	2
Stanciu, Adrian	21:54:41	CO	2015	46	M	4
Sandoval, Wesley	22:13:29	CO	2015	38	M	4
Jimenez, Rodrigo	22:19:34	CO	2015	39	M	5
Crespin, Lucas	22:21:53	CO	2015	31	M	1
Hilson, Danielle	22:28:00	CO	2015	27	F	1
Herzog, Ryan	22:35:45	CO	2015	35	M	2
King, Zach	22:36:48	CO	2015	29	M	1
Marshall, Jeff	22:49:38	CO	2015	32	M	1
Anderson, Woody	23:06:58	CO	2015	40	M	5
Kilcoyne, Jamie	23:14:40	CO	2015	45	M	3
Zack, George	23:23:49	CO	2015	45	M	1
Prentice, Michael	23:23:54	NZ	2015	29	M	1
Kelly, Charles	23:25:00	CO	2015	38	M	1
Kaminski, James	23:26:03	CO	2015	33	M	5
Silva, Katrin	23:34:39	NM	2015	45	F	6
Fulton, Max	23:34:53	CO	2015	38	M	5
Lingerfield, Dan	23:36:01	CO	2015	42	M	4
Sweeney, Patrick	23:38:26	CA	2015	36	M	5
Atkins, Benjamin	23:39:59	CA	2015	42	M	1
Bundrock, Danny	23:43:33	CO	2015	36	M	5
Fennon, Myles	23:46:49	NY	2015	36	M	1
Morgan, Micah	23:49:22	CO	2015	31	M	1
Perry, Tom	23:52:15	UT	2015	60	M	2
Staley, Marc	23:53:12	CO	2015	39	M	1
Lassley, Becki Lynn	23:56:35	CO	2015	37	F	1
Decker, Nate	23:58:38	HI	2015	37	M	1
Mika, Shad	24:00:58	CO	2015	39	M	2

Giblin, JP	24:02:30	CO	2015	21	M	1
Davis, Jerry	24:04:28	CO	2015	42	M	2
Haans, Mildred	24:11:46	Belgium	2015	43	F	1
Lloyd, Ben	24:13:58	NY	2015	44	M	1
Bradford, Jeremy	24:18:32	CO	2015	37	M	5
Krol, Ryan	24:21:44	CO	2015	30	M	4
Palmison, Ryan	24:26:54	MA	2015	30	M	1
Raivo, Erik	24:28:58	MN	2015	31	M	1
Burnett, Adam	24:29:12	Canada	2015	42	M	1
Hastings, Jon	24:29:40	OH	2015	40	M	2
Curtis, Matthew	24:31:03	CO	2015	39	M	7
Smith, Aaron	24:34:12	CO	2015	28	M	3
Wieczorek, Aaron	24:35:01	VA	2015	32	M	1
Biddle, Richard	24:35:13	CO	2015	32	M	1
Garcia, Diego	24:36:29	Chile	2015	35	M	3
Hovenga, Bard	24:37:07	NY	2015	27	M	4
Ragona, Rachel	24:40:06	CA	2015	32	F	1
Pearson, Anabel	24:41:55	TX	2015	45	F	2
Scherz, Alexander	24:41:57	Switzerland	2015	42	M	1
Reiff, Andrew	24:42:19	CO	2015	42	M	7
Bucklin, Tyler	24:45:24	MT	2015	39	M	1
Emery, Trevor	24:48:01	CO	2015	44	M	1
Hunt, Wesley	24:49:43	AR	2015	32	M	1
Gzybowski, Andrew	24:52:11	CO	2015	33	M	2
Mullett, Sean	24:55:39	GA	2015	47	M	3
Beaumont, Jean	24:57:15	NZ	2015	50	F	1
West, Jason	24:57:34	Australia	2015	43	M	1
Bowman, Sean	24:59:27	CA	2015	39	M	2
Leppert, Cory	25:00:36	CO	2015	40	M	2
Law, Chor Kin	25:02:41	Hong Kong	2015	38	M	1
Martinez, Gabriel	25:08:24	CO	2015	23	M	3
Hronik, Laura	25:22:41	CO	2015	36	F	2
Cassidy, Donnacha	25:31:46	KY	2015	26	M	2
Sweeney, Megan	25:34:13	CO	2015	34	F	5
Bolls, Rod	25:39:31	CO	2015	40	M	3
Dickason, Benjamin	25:40:55	CO	2015	26	M	1
Zurn, Molly	25:42:55	NV	2015	44	F	1

Heuze, Franck	25:51:15	France	2015	49	M	2
Newton, Peter	25:57:30	CO	2015	34	M	1
Azuaje, Jaime	25:58:46	CO	2015	28	M	1
Persson, Johan	25:59:13	Sweden	2015	47	M	1
Bantle, Collin	26:03:08	CO	2015	23	M	1
Gregory, Rick	26:05:56	CO	2015	40	M	1
Niemimaa, Ken	26:07:03	Canada	2015	44	M	1
Wester, Trent	26:13:36	NM	2015	31	M	2
Fisher, Brian	26:15:02	CO	2015	49	M	7
Jarvis, Wade	26:17:54	Canada	2015	53	M	9
Scott, Todd	26:20:58	MI	2015	51	M	11
Thurnhoffer, Dan	26:25:47	CO	2015	28	M	1
Case, Ryan	26:28:37	CO	2015	34	M	1
Grimes, Keith	26:29:11	CO	2015	56	M	9
Salisbury, Brandon	26:30:34	CO	2015	32	M	1
Barrera, Walter	26:30:54	DC	2015	34	M	3
Agnew, Kelly	26:31:07	UT	2015	42	M	6
Lambert, Bree	26:32:01	CA	2015	47	F	1
Eakin, Laura	26:34:48	CO	2015	33	F	1
Bielik, Michael	26:45:14	NY	2015	36	M	2
Smith, Alan	26:45:30	CO	2015	46	M	8
Churchill, R. Sean	26:45:50	WI	2015	49	M	9
Labbe, Andrew	26:47:19	CO	2015	40	M	3
Deer, Timothy	26:48:31	WV	2015	51	M	3
Evans, LeAnne	26:52:31	CO	2015	33	F	1
Howery, Susie	26:54:10	CO	2015	45	F	1
Barnes, Trey	27:02:50	CO	2015	31	M	1
Miller, Andrew	27:03:19	CO	2015	46	M	1
Dailey, Bruce	27:05:43	ME	2015	44	M	7
Short, Alden	27:07:59	CO	2015	39	M	2
Gibbs, DeDe	27:12:59	WI	2015	51	F	1
Duval, Sara	27:18:28	CT	2015	37	F	1
Foltz, Nolan	27:18:49	CO	2015	43	M	2
Bitters, Matthew	27:18:55	CO	2015	23	M	1
Long, Ken	27:19:20	MI	2015	37	M	2
Deaven, Jerome	27:20:21	MI	2015	51	M	3
Hopper, Orlin	27:21:26	CO	2015	44	M	3

Nichols, Russel	27:22:33	OR	2015	42	M	2
Wight, Jordan	27:23:52	CO	2015	33	M	1
Reichler, Jamie	27:25:26	CO	2015	46	M	2
Carner, David	27:26:17	CO	2015	49	M	4
Fisher, Will	27:27:02	CO	2015	44	M	1
Holland, Nathan	27:28:10	TN	2015	31	M	1
Pribramsky, Mark	27:28:30	CO	2015	46	M	1
Russell, Chelsey	27:31:01	CO	2015	34	F	1
McCabe, John	27:39:21	CT	2015	43	M	2
Kazukawa, Junko	27:40:39	CO	2015	52	F	6
Davis, Jack	27:45:42	South Africa	2015	38	M	2
Pence, Eric	27:46:46	CO	2015	49	M	24
Pierson, Aaron	27:46:51	CO	2015	39	M	1
English, Michael	27:47:20	CO	2015	48	M	2
Herne, David	27:51:03	Russia	2015	44	M	1
Wright, Chris	27:53:19	CO	2015	43	M	7
Dicke, Ben	27:54:07	NY	2015	35	M	2
Mayer, Adam	27:56:10	NJ	2015	36	M	2
Bowen, Joshua	27:56:46	CO	2015	27	M	1
Friedl, William	27:57:15	AZ	2015	26	M	1
Kabanuck, Richard	27:57:16	FL	2015	31	M	1
Clark, David	27:57:39	CO	2015	44	M	6
Lindh, Christy	27:58:16	CO	2015	32	F	2
Moll, David	28:00:58	CO	2015	50	M	2
Obregon, Alma	28:06:24	Spain	2015	31	F	1
Bennett, Jonathan	28:12:42	MI	2015	46	M	1
Moore, Paula	28:12:52	CO	2015	40	F	1
Feldman, Neil	28:14:41	MA	2015	45	M	1
Fernandez, Jose Manuel Domenech	28:16:14	Spain	2015	39	M	1
Gaul, Davis	28:18:03	CO	2015	28	M	2
Hall, Julian	28:18:19	England	2015	40	M	1
Forno, Cristobal	28:20:22	Chile	2015	33	M	3
Boyd, Terry	28:21:20	CO	2015	48	M	3
Gibbons, Garrett	28:21:34	CO	2015	37	M	1
Gear, Jonathan	28:23:05	CO	2015	44	M	1
Willson, Scott	28:27:07	KS	2015	50	M	1
Stukuls, Jeffrey	28:27:25	TX	2015	45	M	1

Jacobs, Kimberly	28:27:50	CO	2015	39	F	2
Corley, William	28:29:05	FL	2015	53	M	1
Lund, Magnus	28:30:20	Sweden	2015	43	M	1
Truan, Ashley	28:30:52	MI	2015	32	F	1
Deighan, Joseph	28:34:19	MI	2015	44	M	1
Reedy, Matthew	28:34:35	FL	2015	41	M	1
Chupka, Gina	28:35:42	CO	2015	38	F	1
Marshall, Ed	28:36:25	SC	2015	47	M	1
Norquist, Craig	28:36:45	AZ	2015	48	M	2
Iaconis, Chris	28:37:05	CO	2015	44	M	1
McGovern, MaryClaire	28:37:15	CO	2015	29	F	1
Rieland, Dan	28:38:29	MT	2015	48	M	4
Vilchis, Javier	28:38:30	TX	2015	39	M	1
Hronik, Brian	28:41:07	CO	2015	38	M	3
Velez, Ezra	28:41:19	CO	2015	37	M	1
Bartz, Matt	28:41:23	WI	2015	40	M	3
Zangerle, David	28:41:41	IA	2015	46	M	1
Curley, Matt	28:42:26	IL	2015	48	M	3
Legat, Joseph	28:42:49	NV	2015	49	M	2
Combs, Kendall	28:43:11	NH	2015	35	M	1
Meinhardt, Stephen	28:43:21	CO	2015	36	M	1
Curran, Tom	28:44:40	CO	2015	40	M	1
Hawks, Nikolas	28:45:46	CA	2015	37	M	1
Lofts, William	28:46:51	CO	2015	41	M	1
Baugh, Hollis	28:46:54	CO	2015	46	M	11
Gruener, Ted	28:47:24	MO	2015	46	M	1
Calimano, Chris	28:50:19	NY	2015	34	M	2
Churgovich, Hawaiian Shirt Ray	28:51:35	CO	2015	49	M	3
Hetherington, Kirk	28:51:42	CO	2015	33	M	1
Parish, Mark	28:51:56	CO	2015	33	M	2
Carfaro, Frank	28:52:38	NJ	2015	45	M	1
Menke, Sean	28:52:43	HI	2015	46	M	1
Heller, David	28:53:06	CO	2015	46	M	1
Tevault, James	28:53:28	AZ	2015	42	M	1
Connors, Dan	28:53:38	CO	2015	42	M	1
Bainbridge, Andrew	28:54:05	CO	2015	22	M	1
Obsitos, Monica	28:54:52	CO	2015	28	F	1

Taylor, Hannah	28:55:01	CO	2015	36	F	1
Donchey, Steven	28:55:12	FL	2015	52	M	1
Kerschbaum, Michael	28:55:25	CO	2015	33	M	1
Ballard, Rachel	28:56:17	IL	2015	50	F	1
Junkans, Mark	28:57:14	TX	2015	43	M	1
Reichelt, Don	28:58:43	CO	2015	29	M	1
Hebert, Eric	28:58:53	MT	2015	42	M	1
Benhammou, David	28:59:04	WI	2015	31	M	1
Ekstrom, Heather	28:59:18	NC	2015	25	F	2
Luhrs, Emily	28:59:29	CO	2015	25	F	1
Kraxner, Jennifer	29:01:52	CO	2015	37	F	1
Kraxner, Joe	29:01:53	CO	2015	37	M	1
Nalezny, Gerard	29:02:02	CO	2015	52	M	1
Talbott, Shawn	29:02:36	UT	2015	48	M	1
Brown, Monica	29:02:59	CA	2015	37	F	1
Balentine, Michelle	29:03:38	CO	2015	46	F	1
Strickland, Jeffrey	29:03:38	CO	2015	26	M	1
Bartel, Jennifer	29:04:12	WY	2015	33	F	2
Daily, Ashley	29:05:06	CT	2015	28	F	1
Barnett, John	29:05:17	CO	2015	58	M	1
Pruitt, Kristopher	29:05:52	CA	2015	30	M	1
Belz, Rob	29:07:04	MN	2015	50	M	1
Schardein, Timothy	29:07:04	CO	2015	47	M	4
Hicks, Stephan	29:07:15	GA	2015	36	M	1
O'Toole, Brian	29:07:32	TX	2015	51	M	1
Christiansen, Darren	29:07:54	TX	2015	44	M	1
LeNeveu, Shana	29:08:27	CO	2015	45	F	3
Wahlstrom, Erik	29:08:48	WA	2015	42	M	1
Barron, Daniel	29:08:51	CO	2015	20	M	1
Freeman, Corbin	29:10:05	TX	2015	28	M	2
Anderson, Katy	29:10:20	Australia	2015	38	F	5
Heineman, John	29:10:34	IA	2015	30	M	1
Hall, James	29:10:43	PA	2015	51	M	1
Pardo, Francis	29:11:03	DC	2015	33	M	1
DeLozier, Ron	29:11:49	OH	2015	37	M	1
Mason, Jason	29:11:50	IA	2015	34	M	1
Szoradi, Stephen	29:12:01	CO	2015	46	M	2

Sandoval, Greg	29:12:33	CO	2015	40	M	2
Griffis, Anna	29:14:19	CO	2015	30	F	1
Leary, Douglas	29:14:37	CO	2015	52	M	2
Leighton, Mike	29:14:52	CO	2015	28	M	1
Pfeil, Terri	29:15:04	CO	2015	49	F	2
Wilson, Kurt	29:16:12	NC	2015	36	M	2
Stone, Chuck	29:16:22	CO	2015	52	M	8
Stoll, Barbara	29:16:36	TX	2015	53	F	4
Spirito, Andrew	29:16:58	MA	2015	27	M	1
Menacher, Matthew	29:17:04	IL	2015	38	M	1
Sakiewicz, Paul	29:17:31	CO	2015	49	M	1
Bybee, Charles	29:18:00	CO	2015	53	M	12
Snyder, Scott	29:18:07	CO	2015	60	M	9
Stowell, Jeff	29:19:03	UT	2015	53	M	1
Seaman, John	29:19:05	TX	2015	28	M	1
Shuey, Gretchen	29:19:50	MD	2015	45	F	1
Bonnett, Karen	29:20:06	CA	2015	59	F	1
Grafnetterova, Nikola	29:20:37	TX	2015	27	F	1
Eshleman, Katie	29:21:10	PA	2015	40	F	1
Bilou, Travis	29:21:21	Canada	2015	33	M	1
Dougherty, Lee	29:21:37	IL	2015	65	M	1
Danahey, James	29:23:35	CO	2015	20	M	1
Edwards, Huw	29:23:54	CO	2015	34	M	2
Mawn, Sheryl	29:24:15	CO	2015	50	F	1
Simpson, Cliff	29:24:23	NC	2015	48	M	1
Reich, Marc	29:25:20	CO	2015	30	M	1
Hess, Eric	29:25:48	CO	2015	45	M	1
Franklin, Jim	29:26:18	CO	2015	49	M	2
Welk, Michael	29:26:34	CO	2015	42	M	1
Chambers, Stephen	29:26:42	CO	2015	35	M	2
Tate, Dallas	29:26:57	OR	2015	28	M	1
Larson, Nathan	29:27:00	CO	2015	48	M	1
Gane, William	29:27:14	IL	2015	40	M	1
Gore, Timothy	29:27:17	CO	2015	48	M	1
Nelson, Jamen	29:27:51	UT	2015	31	M	8
Conlin, Jared	29:28:18	CO	2015	34	M	3
Rasor, Amy	29:28:22	AZ	2015	36	F	1

Baldwin, Raymond	29:28:47	MD	2015	52	M	1
Batterman, Ryan	29:29:28	NM	2015	29	M	1
Perkins, Mark	29:29:32	CO	2015	62	M	3
Boggs, Timothy	29:29:57	OH	2015	53	M	1
Galligan, Christopher	29:30:34	CO	2015	37	M	3
Nossaman, Sean	29:30:44	CO	2015	33	M	1
Mullins, Thomas	29:31:13	TX	2015	41	M	1
Adams, Zach	29:31:19	KS	2015	38	M	1
Strand, Eric	29:31:24	MO	2015	55	M	7
Huskie, Will	29:31:25	CO	2015	55	M	5
Stamp, Natalie Kaufman	29:31:44	SD	2015	41	F	2
Driscoll, Jeff	29:32:12	CO	2015	43	M	4
Huss, Sheila	29:32:56	CO	2015	39	F	3
Thorne, Eric	29:33:08	PA	2015	43	M	1
Lowe, Gregory	29:33:16	MA	2015	51	M	5
Pauka, Luis	29:33:38	CO	2015	49	M	1
DeMoss, Jean	29:34:22	CO	2015	43	F	6
Young, Jarred	29:34:34	KS	2015	40	M	1
Hodge, Angie	29:34:39	NE	2015	35	F	4
Nakauchi, Laurie	29:34:57	CO	2015	45	F	12
Negoro, Yuki	29:35:27	NJ	2015	54	M	1
Brown, Tony	29:36:24	NC	2015	54	M	1
McKernan, David	29:36:37	CO	2015	39	M	1
Davis, Chad	29:37:15	CO	2015	33	M	2
Pardue, Jason	29:38:05	VA	2015	40	M	2
Vergara, Mike	29:38:15	TX	2015	38	M	4
Smith, Timothy	29:38:33	MN	2015	47	M	1
Burry, Debbie	29:38:53	CO	2015	53	F	2
LeBlanc, Dane	29:39:04	MA	2015	57	M	1
DeRose, Jordan	29:40:06	MO	2015	38	F	2
Cook, Sean	29:40:55	CO	2015	43	M	4
Morgan, Eric	29:41:27	CO	2015	49	M	2
Bailey, Kristen	29:44:56	CO	2015	36	F	1
Pedras, Rui	29:46:56	Peru	2015	56	M	1
Bauer, F. Scott	29:49:35	TX	2015	48	M	1
Jackson, David W.	29:51:34	MS	2015	50	M	1
Holmes, Joshua	29:56:19	CA	2015	37	M	1

Name	Finish Time	State	Year	Age	Sex	#Finished
Kromeich, Mark	29:57:18	UT	2015	44	M	1
Stahl, Bill	29:57:54	CO	2015	56	M	4

2016

Name	Finish Time	State	Year	Age	Sex	#Finished
Sharman, Ian	16:22:39	OR	2016	35	M	5
Pietari, Kyle	18:16:48	CO	2016	29	M	4
Jay, Luke	18:31:22	CO	2016	36	M	2
Sandoval, Wesley	18:40:01	CO	2016	39	M	4
Gallagher, Clare	19:00:27	CO	2016	24	F	1
Cordova, Lee	19:16:47	CO	2016	29	M	1
Tiernan, Alex	19:31:55	CO	2016	29	M	1
Bien, Rod	19:39:09	OR	2016	44	M	2
King, Max	19:50:54	OR	2016	36	M	1
Stanciu, Adrian	19:51:47	CO	2016	47	M	4
Kuehler, Jon	19:57:14	CO	2016	28	M	3
Sandoval, Marvin	20:23:37	CO	2016	38	M	7
Wegscheider, Erich	20:25:27	CO	2016	30	M	2
Revenis, Bradley	20:27:46	MD	2016	30	M	1
Guldan, Ryan	20:45:28	CO	2016	32	M	4
Walsh, Maggie	21:00:08	CO	2016	34	F	1
Bybliw, Adam	21:03:48	CO	2016	35	M	3
Abbott, Brent	21:42:11	CO	2016	33	M	1
Benna, Jennifer	21:45:00	NV	2016	36	F	1
Olson, Timothy	21:47:23	CO	2016	32	M	1
Lefever, John	21:47:53	NE	2016	46	M	3
Aish, Michael	21:56:26	CO	2016	40	M	3
Doyle, Paul	21:56:30	CO	2016	46	M	2
Bundrock, Danny	21:56:49	CO	2016	37	M	5
Volcansek, Mitja	22:11:24	Slovenia	2016	36	M	1
Gaul, Davis	22:11:59	CO	2016	29	M	2
Baker, Joshua	22:23:06	CO	2016	35	M	1
Stanley, Sabrina	22:30:30	CO	2016	26	F	1
Wooten, Andy	22:43:21	CO	2016	48	M	6
Martinez, Jadd	22:43:49	CA	2016	34	M	1
Schliff, Henry	22:44:44	CO	2016	36	M	2
Fulton, Max	22:47:22	CO	2016	39	M	5

Schmidt, Michael	22:50:22	Germany	2016	45	M	1
Stephenson, Luke	22:54:39	CO	2016	29	M	2
Nee, Darin	22:55:01	CA	2016	34	M	1
Krol, Ryan	22:55:40	CO	2016	31	M	4
Strickland, Jeff	22:57:55	CO	2016	27	M	1
Linck, Ethan	22:58:05	WA	2016	25	M	1
Jimenez, Rodrigo	23:01:04	CO	2016	40	M	5
Moreno, Tomas	23:04:56	TX	2016	33	M	1
Hornbaker, Charles	23:08:00	MA	2016	34	M	3
Wurtz, Stephanie	23:21:11	CO	2016	34	F	1
Dougherty, Mike (Dutch)	23:23:12	CO	2016	44	M	1
Stafford, Carrie	23:24:38	CO	2016	37	F	5
Jaime, Scott	23:28:53	CO	2016	46	M	2
Curtis, Matthew	23:31:35	CO	2016	40	M	7
Vega, Dan	23:35:07	CO	2016	48	M	2
Smith, Aaron	23:37:05	CO	2016	29	M	3
Cogswell, Nathan	23:37:38	HI	2016	34	M	1
Barlow, Tommy	23:40:01	UT	2016	36	M	1
Pritchard, Siobhan	23:41:17	CO	2016	38	F	2
Pope, Eric	23:42:48	NM	2016	53	M	2
Hronik, Laura	23:43:23	CO	2016	37	F	2
Maughan, Grant	23:44:03	Australia	2016	52	M	2
Richard, Steve	23:45:49	CO	2016	28	M	1
Darnell, Max	23:50:02	MA	2016	27	M	1
Thompson, Mark	23:51:39	CO	2016	51	M	3
Mollenhour, John	23:51:50	AZ	2016	60	M	2
Orders, Nathaniel	23:57:00	WV	2016	38	M	2
Wright, Chris	23:58:00	CO	2016	44	M	7
Perry, Laura	23:59:35	Canada	2016	34	F	1
Heuze, Franck	24:01:17	France	2016	50	M	2
Brenes, Chris	24:01:36	WA	2016	41	M	1
Dailey, Bruce	24:03:54	Australia	2016	45	M	7
Steinkamp, Barry	24:06:15	IN	2016	35	M	1
King, Kate	24:08:45	CO	2016	29	F	1
Ramirez, Austin	24:10:10	WI	2016	38	M	1
Brenner, Louis	24:10:27	MT	2016	32	M	1
Silva, Katrin	24:14:39	NM	2016	46	F	6

Lindahl, Adam	24:15:18	MN	2016	35	M	1
Bastings, Maartje	24:15:50	MA	2016	32	F	1
Halko, Nathan	24:15:59	CO	2016	34	M	1
Smith, Neil	24:21:17	TX	2016	45	M	3
Hornsby, Wyatt	24:25:49	CO	2016	43	M	5
Harkey, Brett	24:30:37	CO	2016	45	M	1
Passenti, Brian	24:32:32	CO	2016	42	M	5
Wolf, Kevin	24:32:36	CO	2016	31	M	1
Hoelscher, Josef	24:33:04	CO	2016	34	M	1
Riff, Joshua	24:33:20	MN	2016	41	M	1
Rood, Adam	24:33:48	NE	2016	36	M	1
Poppele, Brad	24:37:49	CO	2016	45	M	1
Hovenga, Bard	24:41:51	NY	2016	28	M	4
Lee, Andrew	24:46:51	Australia	2016	46	M	1
Rubesch, Chris	24:56:06	MN	2016	30	M	1
Weening, Marc	24:56:37	Netherlands	2016	39	M	1
Bowman, Sean	24:57:42	CA	2016	40	M	2
DeOliva, Juan	25:01:14	NV	2016	32	M	1
Yasinski, Michael	25:12:48	Canada	2016	45	M	2
Denney, Jeff	25:22:46	MN	2016	58	M	1
Nicholson, Natalie	25:23:06	CO	2016	34	F	1
Hardy, Jeremy	25:25:24	CA	2016	43	M	1
Barr, Tim	25:33:37	CO	2016	40	M	1
Deaven, Jerome	25:42:44	MI	2016	52	M	3
Chlouber, Cole	25:47:21	MN	2016	42	M	4
Hale, Muriel	25:51:01	CO	2016	32	F	1
Coats, Andrew	25:54:12	CO	2016	45	M	2
Mead, Chris	25:54:58	CA	2016	45	M	2
Curley, Matt	25:56:37	IL	2016	49	M	3
Schiff, Daniel	25:56:50	Switzerland	2016	33	M	1
Esterby, Travis	25:57:22	TN	2016	37	M	1
Husmann, Brian	25:57:37	CO	2016	44	M	2
Weiss, Annie	25:58:22	WI	2016	31	F	2
Romero, Ramon Sanchez	25:59:12	Spain	2016	39	M	1
Tischer, Jason	26:12:01	NC	2016	41	M	2
Wiskowski, David	26:13:25	IL	2016	39	M	1
Karol, Johnathan	26:14:06	SD	2016	35	M	1

Thwaites, Thomas	26:15:31	CO	2016	40	M	1
Mankus, Michael	26:20:10	Germany	2016	46	M	1
Langevin, Beau	26:21:42	ME	2016	36	M	1
Nakamura, Kentaro	26:32:08	--	2016	30	M	1
Dempsey, Christopher	26:33:37	VA	2016	39	M	2
Cote, Gilles	26:41:09	CO	2016	59	M	6
Mullenax, Raymond	26:45:07	ID	2016	49	M	1
English, Mike	26:48:37	CO	2016	49	M	2
Holmes, Todd	26:49:58	AZ	2016	60	M	12
Guerrero, Luis	26:50:26	Mexico	2016	53	M	9
Sutter, Ryan	26:50:38	CO	2016	41	M	1
Taska, Woody	26:58:24	AZ	2016	27	M	1
Smith, Alan	27:00:48	CO	2016	47	M	8
Pence, Eric	27:02:43	CO	2016	50	M	24
Southern, Chip	27:04:00	CO	2016	48	M	3
Hebert, Jennifer	27:15:12	MT	2016	37	F	1
Novak, John	27:17:09	CO	2016	51	M	3
Lam, Otto	27:17:22	NJ	2016	42	M	1
Schulz, Ry	27:17:25	CO	2016	32	M	1
Tulloch, Ken	27:17:45	CT	2016	50	M	1
Smith, Margaret	27:18:22	MD	2016	36	F	3
Lowe, Gregory	27:18:38	MA	2016	52	M	5
Churchill, R. Shawn	27:18:46	WI	2016	50	M	9
Bath, Alec	27:20:42	IL	2016	46	M	2
Tally, Steven	27:24:14	CA	2016	55	M	1
Clark, David	27:25:34	CO	2016	45	M	6
Saiz, Carlos Prieto	27:27:35	Spain	2016	35	M	1
Saiz, Lorenzo Prieto	27:27:35	Spain	2016	36	M	1
Lambert, Jonathan	27:27:59	OK	2016	37	M	2
Agnew, Kelly	27:29:18	UT	2016	43	M	6
Sweeney, Patrick	27:29:18	CA	2016	37	M	5
Miller, Brian	27:33:36	TX	2016	43	M	1
Miller, Alison	27:33:37	TX	2016	37	F	1
Sweeney, Megan	27:36:28	CO	2016	35	F	5
Barringer, Chris	27:36:45	CO	2016	42	M	2
Stout, Mike	27:37:56	IA	2016	29	M	1
Schulte, Drew	27:37:57	CO	2016	26	M	2

Cenkl, Pavel	27:40:23	VT	2016	45	M	1
Forno, Cristobal	27:41:17	Chile	2016	34	M	3
Garcia, Diego	27:41:17	Chile	2016	36	M	3
Hahn, Chris	27:41:57	MO	2016	47	M	1
Chapman, Vernon	27:43:53	CO	2016	42	M	1
Wickless, Andrew	27:44:14	CO	2016	42	M	1
Glover, Will	27:45:20	FL	2016	45	M	1
Broering, Christopher	27:46:57	VA	2016	42	M	1
Schuster, Charles	27:48:45	WY	2016	47	M	1
Kingrey, Kyle	27:49:00	CO	2016	43	M	1
Deer, Timothy	27:50:26	WV	2016	52	M	3
Richardson, Erik	27:51:00	MI	2016	38	M	4
Anderson, Katy	27:51:24	Australia	2016	39	F	5
Hooper, Tom	27:53:13	NH	2016	37	M	1
Conlin, Jared	27:53:45	CO	2016	35	M	3
Wetstine, Sean	27:53:45	CO	2016	40	M	6
Goetz, Brenden	27:55:00	CO	2016	31	M	1
Veltman, Michael	27:58:14	AL	2016	33	M	2
Ehlers, Aaron	27:59:54	MN	2016	28	M	1
Schrauben, Tracy	28:00:58	CO	2016	29	F	1
Keske, Mark	28:01:58	NC	2016	29	M	1
Redl, Nicky	28:03:34	Australia	2016	37	F	1
Zani, Paul	28:04:46	TN	2016	48	M	1
Hawes, Ben	28:04:51	OH	2016	30	M	1
Jarvis, Wade	28:05:38	Canada	2016	54	M	9
Manley, Brian	28:06:28	CO	2016	52	M	13
Hodge, Angie	28:07:09	NE	2016	36	F	4
Wood, Samantha	28:13:32	CO	2016	31	F	2
Fortner, Eric	28:13:35	TX	2016	42	M	1
Shapiro, Clayton	28:13:35	TX	2016	40	M	1
Flanagan, Will	28:19:20	TX	2016	28	M	1
Weeter, Bryce	28:20:09	TN	2016	31	M	2
Sanderson, Philip	28:20:28	CA	2016	48	M	2
Strand, Eric	28:22:51	MO	2016	56	M	7
Nelson, Jamen	28:23:14	UT	2016	32	M	8
Calimano, Chris	28:24:13	NY	2016	35	M	2
Sandoval, Greg	28:25:57	CO	2016	41	M	2

Geiger, Greg	28:26:07	MN	2016	37	M	1
Heinila, Marko	28:27:54	NM	2016	46	M	1
Pearson, Anabel	28:28:35	TX	2016	46	F	2
Lundy, Jonathan	28:28:47	KY	2016	39	M	3
Reiff, Andrew	28:28:52	CO	2016	43	M	7
Miller, Shaun	28:31:03	MA	2016	38	M	2
Smidt, Karen	28:32:58	CO	2016	49	F	1
West-Hoover, Sarah	28:34:06	CO	2016	45	F	3
Rieland, Dan	28:34:14	MT	2016	49	M	4
Russell, William	28:34:27	TX	2016	33	M	1
McCune, Justin	28:36:18	OK	2016	40	M	1
Seeberger, Bobby	28:38:23	UT	2016	52	M	2
Olsson, Jan	28:38:51	Sweden	2016	59	M	1
Ekstrom, Heather	28:39:11	AZ	2016	26	F	2
Garnier, Killian Duncan	28:39:41	CO	2016	35	M	1
Hoefen, Kimberley	28:39:59	CO	2016	42	F	3
Marasse, John	28:40:47	Canada	2016	42	M	1
Grimes, W Jay	28:41:28	CO	2016	32	M	1
OBrien, John	28:42:08	IA	2016	48	M	1
Denicke, Rik	28:42:45	MO	2016	44	M	2
Valk, Priit	28:42:53	Estonia	2016	42	M	2
Gomez, Miguel	28:43:22	CO	2016	36	M	1
Csmereka, Joseph	28:45:18	IN	2016	40	M	1
Appert, John	28:45:32	NV	2016	37	M	3
Dundervill, Robert	28:45:53	WV	2016	52	M	1
Martin, Kyle	28:46:28	CO	2016	34	M	2
Boozan, Rebecca	28:46:41	CO	2016	34	F	1
Trujillo, Jeff	28:47:20	CO	2016	47	M	1
Price, Jill	28:47:53	TX	2016	42	F	2
Newton, Doug	28:48:44	CO	2016	39	M	5
Young, Christopher	28:49:11	CO	2016	39	M	1
Davis, Michelle	28:51:20	South Africa	2016	37	F	1
Cheetham, Gregg	28:51:20	South Africa	2016	40	M	1
Davis, Jack	28:51:21	South Africa	2016	39	M	2
Hurm, Jeremy	28:52:05	KY	2016	39	M	1
Fountain, Rick	28:52:39	IA	2016	46	M	2
Lind, JP	28:53:15	CO	2016	44	M	2

Moorhouse, Anthony	28:53:33	CO	2016	38	M	1
Speirs, Chad	28:53:56	MI	2016	35	M	1
Fields, Andrew	28:54:38	CO	2016	37	M	2
Holland, James	28:54:44	TN	2016	40	M	3
Breslin, Chavet	28:55:36	CO	2016	34	F	1
Bird, Nora	28:55:56	WI	2016	32	F	1
Polonsky, Joe	28:59:04	CO	2016	39	M	2
Oster, John	28:59:40	CO	2016	51	M	1
Foster, Sheri	28:59:50	Canada	2016	43	F	2
Baugh, Hollis	28:59:50	CO	2016	47	M	11
Taylor, Neal	29:01:07	CO	2016	53	M	12
Bafaro, Joseph Jr.	29:01:26	MA	2016	46	M	1
Skadins, Laimonis	29:01:37	Latvia	2016	48	M	1
Aponte, Jean	29:03:14	LA	2016	32	M	1
Nash, Doug	29:04:11	CO	2016	62	M	5
Morrissey, Megan	29:04:28	CO	2016	47	F	3
Pearson, Larry	29:05:29	TX	2016	55	M	2
Mitchell, Cal	29:06:24	Canada	2016	55	M	1
Ziemski, Nate	29:08:03	MN	2016	38	M	1
Keith, Berton	29:08:15	TX	2016	55	M	1
Alexander, William (Big Willie)	29:08:16	CO	2016	61	M	2
Mehta, Rupin	29:08:42	South Africa	2016	35	M	1
Bauer, Andrea	29:09:29	CO	2016	54	F	1
Bolze, Alexandre	29:09:50	CA	2016	32	M	1
Reed, Craig	29:10:34	MA	2016	49	M	1
Moore, Michael	29:11:43	FL	2016	47	M	2
Dick, Britt	29:11:48	CO	2016	30	F	1
Hamilton, Brian	29:12:04	CA	2016	46	M	1
Cook, Sean	29:12:20	CO	2016	44	M	4
DeDoncker, John	29:13:45	IA	2016	52	M	5
Hanson, Keith	29:14:13	SC	2016	30	M	1
Klassen, Allan	29:14:14	Canada	2016	57	M	1
Lauters, Nick	29:15:23	CO	2016	33	M	1
Smith, Kevin	29:15:29	CO	2016	60	M	1
Simpson, Shane	29:15:58	Australia	2016	44	M	1
Thompson, Greg	29:16:03	CO	2016	46	M	1
Urschel, Casey	29:16:16	LA	2016	37	M	2

Peck, Henry	29:16:20	MD	2016	59	M	2
Stanley, Cole	29:16:27	CO	2016	43	M	1
Jacobs, Kimberly	29:16:31	CO	2016	40	F	2
MacBeath, Gavin	29:16:51	MA	2016	46	M	1
Layton, Melanie	29:16:56	CO	2016	43	F	1
Provenzano, Donnamarie	29:17:03	CO	2016	40	F	1
Steele, Aaron	29:17:41	CA	2016	39	M	1
Rhodes, Bryce	29:17:54	NV	2016	39	M	1
Cunningham, Dave	29:18:03	CO	2016	52	M	6
Crockett, Claudette	29:18:06	TX	2016	34	F	1
Churgovich, Ray Hawaiian Shirt	29:18:29	CO	2016	50	M	3
Erdman, Phoebe	29:19:00	CO	2016	27	F	2
Witherell, Colton	29:19:36	CO	2016	21	M	1
Bush, David	29:19:50	OH	2016	36	M	1
Mediate, Phillip	29:19:54	MT	2016	29	M	1
LeDuc, Courtney	29:20:02	CO	2016	33	F	1
Hoberg, Rick	29:20:03	CO	2016	27	M	1
Boyle, Dan	29:20:10	CA	2016	52	M	2
Pittard, Noah	29:20:55	CO	2016	43	M	1
Mougin, Christine	29:21:21	CO	2016	49	F	1
Kleiner, Ty	29:21:33	IA	2016	44	M	1
Hronik, Brian	29:21:46	CO	2016	39	M	3
Randle, Chris	29:21:53	CO	2016	42	M	2
Jones, Les	29:21:57	TN	2016	57	M	9
McCracken, John	29:22:16	IL	2016	46	M	1
Heady, Cynthia	29:23:04	KY	2016	55	F	1
Newberg, Nason	29:23:12	CO	2016	42	M	1
Fitzler, Joe	29:23:32	CO	2016	34	M	1
Becker, Jill	29:24:01	IA	2016	29	F	1
Peterson, Patience Baldwin	29:24:07	CO	2016	35	F	1
Goulandris, Basil	29:24:24	Bahamas	2016	49	M	1
Wisdom, Bryan	29:24:26	CO	2016	26	M	1
Pasley, Lauren	29:25:16	TN	2016	50	F	1
Snyder, Steve	29:25:27	MO	2016	50	M	1
Rivarola, Rodrigo Morey	29:25:41	Peru	2016	36	M	1
Ham, Robert	29:26:58	TX	2016	48	M	2
Prouty, Aaron	29:27:07	CO	2016	38	M	1

Karak, Stefan	29:27:14	Slovakia	2016	64	M	1
McAfee, Ryan	29:27:18	CO	2016	35	M	1
Atkinson, Phil	29:27:21	WY	2016	44	M	7
Yamamoto, Hirofumi	29:28:11	TX	2016	46	M	1
Scott, John	29:28:18	CO	2016	51	M	2
Orthwein, Clark	29:29:02	FL	2016	26	M	1
Kumasaka, Deby	29:29:51	WA	2016	52	F	1
McNamara, Tim	29:29:56	CO	2016	50	M	1
Bivins, Mark	29:30:16	CO	2016	31	M	2
Yamashita, Shuhei	29:30:21	NY	2016	28	M	1
Humble, Jeffrey	29:31:10	Canada	2016	44	M	1
Schwender, James	29:32:07	MN	2016	49	M	1
Stacy, John	29:32:55	VA	2016	59	M	3
Bleakley, Laura	29:35:20	NH	2016	46	F	2
Driscoll, Jeff	29:36:16	CO	2016	44	M	4
Shulman, Ben	29:36:42	CO	2016	31	M	1
Stone, Chuck	29:38:37	CO	2016	53	M	8
Parpart, Andrew	29:39:09	OH	2016	28	M	1
Seekamp, Jessica	29:40:18	TX	2016	34	F	2
Sisengrath, Greg	29:40:18	TX	2016	40	M	1
Krekeler, Paige	29:40:27	TX	2016	45	F	1
Roberts, Karen	29:41:51	TX	2016	53	F	1
Hellman, Joan	29:42:08	AZ	2016	45	F	2
Cyphers, Jane	29:42:10	CO	2016	37	F	1
Rodgers, Stephen	29:42:21	CO	2016	48	M	2
Blobel, Norbert	29:42:42	Australia	2016	44	M	1
Isola, Leonardo	29:43:29	Argentina	2016	41	M	1
Kooiman, Andrea	29:45:16	CA	2016	41	F	1
Koehler, Jody	29:46:12	TX	2016	45	F	1
Vergara, Mike	29:47:48	TX	2016	39	M	4
Brennand, Michael	29:47:57	NM	2016	49	M	2
Studebaker, John	29:48:28	TX	2016	55	M	1
Bybee, Charles	29:48:48	CO	2016	54	M	12
Noret, Jeremy	29:49:03	TX	2016	30	M	2
Blackard, Michelle	29:49:12	TX	2016	37	F	1
English, Steve	29:50:06	MN	2016	49	M	1
Rivera, Lucas	29:50:53	CO	2016	29	M	2

Name	Finish Time	State	Year	Age	Sex	#Finished
Hveding, Fred	29:51:55	AK	2016	42	M	1
Eastwood, Robert	29:52:03	England	2016	29	M	2
Conner, Dave	29:53:50	CO	2016	54	M	1
Boyle, Bryan	29:53:54	CO	2016	45	M	1
Andrews, Liz	29:55:28	CO	2016	25	F	1
Marvan, Clarence	29:57:27	CO	2016	48	M	1

2017

Name	Finish Time	State	Year	Age	Sex	#Finished
Sharman, Ian	17:34:51	OR	2017	36	M	5
Teirney, David	18:32:34	CO	2017	38	M	3
Hewitt, Michael	18:59:45	CO	2017	47	M	3
Moran, Juan	19:16:36	WI	2017	35	M	1
Jimenez, Rodrigo	19:23:30	CO	2017	41	M	5
Rivers, Brett	19:25:55	CA	2017	36	M	1
Sweeney, Bob	19:33:14	CO	2017	50	M	4
Bybliw, Adam	19:35:21	CO	2017	36	M	3
Sandoval, Wesley	19:57:12	CO	2017	40	M	4
Wardian, Michael	20:18:57	VA	2017	43	M	1
Guldan, Ryan	20:37:38	CO	2017	33	M	4
Sandoval, Marvin	20:45:53	CO	2017	39	M	7
Yanko, Devon	20:46:29	CA	2017	35	F	1
Airey, Richard	21:08:22	OK	2017	41	M	3
Morbelli, Simona	21:16:22	CO	2017	45	F	1
Burns, Christy	21:43:15	CO	2017	40	F	1
Green, Tyler	21:51:51	OR	2017	33	M	1
Venzor, Alejandro	21:51:51	CO	2017	33	M	2
Kuehler, Jon	22:02:59	CO	2017	29	M	3
Seabury, Ian	22:12:49	CA	2017	27	M	1
Wang, Xiaolin	22:22:09	China	2017	41	M	1
Liechty, Steve	22:34:52	MT	2017	47	M	2
Robinson, Jason	22:41:19	Malaysia	2017	50	M	1
Kimber, Evan	22:51:23	CO	2017	40	M	1
Malcolm, Corrine	22:52:25	WA	2017	27	F	1
Courkamp, Kirt	22:53:22	CO	2017	55	M	3
Ellison, Aaron	23:06:18	MD	2017	41	M	1

Slauson, Stephen	23:07:37	CO	2017	42	M	1
Barger, Dan	23:10:53	CA	2017	52	M	3
Teger, Mike	23:13:08	CO	2017	48	M	1
Fagan, Brian	23:16:46	TX	2017	39	M	1
Lieber, Elan	23:23:57	CA	2017	27	M	1
Ernst, Justin	23:26:01	NY	2017	29	M	1
Fulton, Max	23:30:10	CO	2017	40	M	5
Hendrickson, Christian	23:31:26	CO	2017	41	M	4
Bunting Lamos, Sarah	23:39:20	CO	2017	42	F	1
Springborn, Dan	23:48:58	CO	2017	39	M	1
Muir, John	24:03:51	MT	2017	39	M	1
Hill, Casey	24:06:01	CO	2017	38	M	1
Wright, Chris	24:06:41	CO	2017	45	M	7
Grimes, Billy	24:12:54	CO	2017	40	M	1
Sulhanek, Roman	24:14:51	Slovakia	2017	33	M	1
Short, Alden	24:16:44	CO	2017	40	M	2
Curley, Matt	24:21:50	IL	2017	50	M	3
Jones, Ryan	24:23:17	PA	2017	38	M	3
Enderlin, Matt	24:25:56	CO	2017	40	M	1
Drummond, Grant	24:27:48	CO	2017	40	M	1
Cole, Patrick	24:31:08	CO	2017	36	M	1
Sanderson, Phil	24:31:15	CA	2017	49	M	2
Barber, Kelly	24:33:37	CA	2017	47	M	1
Novak, John	24:34:56	CO	2017	52	M	3
Trotter, Blake	24:35:57	AL	2017	39	M	1
Hauschulz, Ben	24:36:18	CO	2017	32	M	1
Gzybowski, Andrew	24:36:25	CO	2017	35	M	2
Chad, Prichard	24:45:01	CO	2017	39	M	1
Norman, Todd	24:45:06	CO	2017	49	M	1
Fellows, Brandon	24:50:23	IL	2017	30	M	1
Rivera, Will	24:50:45	KY	2017	46	M	1
Yucra, Iso	24:53:35	Bolivia	2017	49	M	1
Morgan, Kaitlyn	24:54:15	CO	2017	27	F	1
Wetstine, Sean	25:03:04	CO	2017	41	M	6
Holmes, Frank	25:07:05	CO	2017	47	M	1
Earthman, Ben	25:20:33	CO	2017	40	M	1
Harmon, Adam	25:21:47	CO	2017	28	M	2

Hagen, Lindsey	25:24:43	OR	2017	33	F	1
Perez, Angel G	25:27:37	CA	2017	46	M	2
DeVreese, Joseph	25:28:37	CA	2017	50	M	1
Weiss, Annie	25:39:16	WI	2017	32	F	2
Lucrezi, Gina	25:41:38	CO	2017	34	F	1
Silva, Katrin	25:51:48	NM	2017	47	F	6
Dankel, Justin	25:52:19	CA	2017	41	M	1
Schulte, Drew	25:57:02	OH	2017	27	M	2
Ahern, Jon	25:57:38	CO	2017	47	M	1
Williams, Richard	26:12:42	CO	2017	48	M	4
Klopfenstein, Scott	26:13:30	CO	2017	46	M	12
Callahan, Duncan	26:13:47	CO	2017	34	M	7
Pentler, Steven	26:16:21	CO	2017	25	M	2
Sweeney, Patrick	26:20:33	CA	2017	38	M	5
Harper, Raquel	26:21:14	CO	2017	38	F	2
Schneiderman, James	26:21:18	NC	2017	42	M	2
Hunt, Lee	26:35:39	NM	2017	42	M	1
Nothem, Michael	26:36:44	CO	2017	23	M	1
Lingerfield, Dan	26:39:49	CO	2017	44	M	4
Edwards, Huw	26:42:08	TX	2017	35	M	2
Brosseau, Jason	26:57:10	CO	2017	31	M	1
Abrahamson, Greg	27:00:23	CO	2017	36	M	2
Pandiscio, Sarah	27:00:33	CT	2017	27	F	1
Hodge, Angie	27:03:03	NE	2017	36	F	4
Nelson, Jamen	27:05:23	UT	2017	33	M	8
Lambert, Jonathan	27:09:38	OK	2017	38	M	2
Meconis, Todd	27:10:42	GA	2017	42	M	1
Veltri, Caroline	27:12:21	NJ	2017	27	F	1
Ortiz, Roberto	27:13:41	Costa Rica	2017	28	M	1
Glover, Erik	27:16:03	NY	2017	37	M	1
Stofko, Paul	27:17:54	IN	2017	41	M	6
Cote, Gilles	27:22:32	CO	2017	60	M	6
Laird, Billy	27:24:38	CO	2017	40	M	1
Sheetz-Willard, Jacob	27:27:46	CO	2017	27	M	2
Tronoski, William	27:30:47	NJ	2017	46	M	1
McLaughlin, Sean	27:33:28	CO	2017	32	M	1
McLean, Robb	27:33:59	NM	2017	43	M	1

Anderson, Katy	27:34:14	Australia	2017	40	F	5
Dailey, Bruce	27:34:47	Australia	2017	46	M	7
Shockley, Cannon	27:35:06	CO	2017	40	M	1
Odell, David	27:35:58	CA	2017	50	M	1
Nastrom, Austin	27:40:53	MN	2017	22	M	1
Shepherd, Brian	27:41:17	IN	2017	41	M	1
Gobert, Yann	27:41:43	France	2017	40	M	1
Daane, Lisa	27:44:14	NV	2017	46	F	1
Tweed, Geoffrey	27:44:48	TX	2017	33	M	1
Bradley, John	27:45:00	MO	2017	50	M	1
Bradley, Jacob	27:45:04	MO	2017	29	M	1
Reichler, Jamie	27:46:27	CO	2017	48	M	2
Smith, Bryson	27:50:27	VA	2017	28	M	1
Becker, Colton	27:52:18	WA	2017	25	M	1
Jordan, Jeffrey	27:53:37	TN	2017	54	M	2
Geldeard, Ben	27:55:26	England	2017	30	M	1
Bisese, Jimmy	27:55:27	CO	2017	55	M	1
Wooten, Mark	27:56:25	TX	2017	37	M	2
Layer, Jeremy	27:57:19	CO	2017	45	M	1
Mather, Carl	27:58:17	CO	2017	53	M	1
Coats, Andrew	27:59:21	CO	2017	46	M	2
Sides, Vernon	28:01:01	NC	2017	45	M	4
Walmsley, Konstantin	28:03:24	NJ	2017	47	M	1
Nicholls, Steve	28:05:11	CO	2017	51	M	2
McGilvery, Wayne	28:08:54	CA	2017	49	M	1
Bybee, Charles	28:12:30	CO	2017	55	M	12
LaBranche, Steven	28:13:22	CT	2017	44	M	1
Byrne, John	28:13:31	IA	2017	52	M	3
Soukup, David	28:14:27	MN	2017	45	M	1
Gerhard, Veronica	28:14:29	CO	2017	27	F	1
Forman, Scott	28:14:36	NM	2017	46	M	1
Janay, Barry	28:16:26	NJ	2017	39	M	1
Ewing, Andrew	28:18:56	CA	2017	39	M	1
Ballard, Jason	28:21:36	TX	2017	35	M	1
Johansen, Thor	28:27:05	AZ	2017	41	M	1
Rowthorn, Jeff	28:27:32	MA	2017	39	M	1
Gerenz, Bob	28:28:31	CO	2017	49	M	4

Fields, Andrew	28:28:50	CO	2017	38	M	2
Guerrero, Luis	28:29:22	Mexico	2017	54	M	9
Driscoll, Jeff	28:29:46	CO	2017	45	M	4
Kuksin, Nikita	28:30:11	NY	2017	36	M	2
Hutchins, Andrea	28:30:19	MI	2017	40	F	1
Kazukawa, Junko	28:30:42	CO	2017	54	F	6
Yang, Billy	28:31:14	CA	2017	40	M	1
Kubes, Dan	28:32:01	CO	2017	33	M	1
Whatley, Stephen	28:33:34	MS	2017	33	M	1
Smith, Neil	28:35:22	TX	2017	46	M	3
Schardein, Tim	28:36:03	CO	2017	49	M	4
Smith, Dave	28:36:23	WI	2017	36	M	1
Bellucci, Justin	28:37:17	CO	2017	38	M	1
Talevi, Christopher	28:37:29	CT	2017	28	M	1
Wrenholt, Valerie	28:37:41	CO	2017	42	F	2
Smotherman, Fred	28:37:47	WI	2017	37	M	1
Martin, Nicholas	28:37:57	WA	2017	35	M	1
Harp, Clint	28:38:28	TX	2017	32	M	1
Efta, Caleb	28:38:33	CO	2017	27	M	1
Strand, Randi	28:38:50	CO	2017	38	F	1
DeLaney, Evan	28:39:58	CO	2017	46	M	1
Meeth, David	28:41:12	KS	2017	54	M	1
O'Reilly, Martin	28:41:54	Ireland	2017	44	M	1
Barnard, Joe	28:42:18	KS	2017	37	M	2
Wise, Andrew	28:42:32	CO	2017	37	M	1
Swetlishnoff, Kyle	28:42:53	TX	2017	24	M	1
McCaffrey, Kevin	28:43:04	NE	2017	48	M	1
Murphy, Tim	28:44:22	OR	2017	35	M	1
McHargue, Nicholas	28:44:27	CO	2017	26	M	1
Sinn, Jacob	28:45:30	VA	2017	38	M	1
Harrison, Genevieve	28:46:19	CO	2017	30	F	1
Maloney, David	28:48:09	RI	2017	31	M	1
Wielkoszewski, Beau	28:49:01	MT	2017	35	M	1
Smits, Bobby	28:49:36	VA	2017	43	M	1
Mullett, Sean	28:50:52	OH	2017	48	M	3
Taylor, Brandy	28:52:26	MO	2017	34	F	1
Trundley, Tony	28:54:57	England	2017	51	M	1

Noret, Jeremy	28:56:15	TX	2017	31	M	2
Foltz, Nolan	28:57:41	CO	2017	45	M	2
Chavez, Michael	29:00:27	CO	2017	37	M	1
Moors, Stephen	29:00:56	IN	2017	21	M	1
Perkins, Mark	29:01:30	CO	2017	64	M	3
Roche, Jim	29:01:39	NC	2017	48	M	1
West-Hoover, Sarah	29:01:48	CO	2017	46	F	3
Rittgers, Mary	29:02:16	CO	2017	36	F	1
Andrews, Bobby	29:02:35	WA	2017	36	M	2
Bonkowsky, Josh	29:02:45	UT	2017	47	M	1
Lee, Eliot	29:02:58	CO	2017	44	M	1
Atkinson, Phil	29:03:40	WY	2017	45	M	7
Drasler, Erin	29:03:45	CO	2017	36	F	1
Knoll, David	29:04:03	TX	2017	47	M	1
Gonzalez, Lelis	29:04:54	TX	2017	33	M	1
Whipple, James	29:05:32	CT	2017	39	M	1
Downing, Matt	29:05:50	OH	2017	41	M	1
Beltz, Jimmy	29:05:58	MN	2017	41	M	1
Hoefen, Kimberley	29:06:42	CO	2017	43	F	3
Provenzano, Donna	29:07:18	CO	2017	40	F	1
McDowell-Larsen, Sharon	29:07:41	CO	2017	57	F	1
Vickers, Esteban	29:07:54	MD	2017	41	M	1
Stahl, Craig	29:08:35	UT	2017	49	M	2
Bivins, Mark	29:09:03	CO	2017	32	M	2
Spencer, Paul	29:09:17	CO	2017	36	M	1
Lund, Ryan	29:10:12	ID	2017	42	M	2
Anderson, Brad	29:11:00	CO	2017	37	M	1
Ruse, Melissa	29:12:55	AZ	2017	40	F	1
Ruse, Deron	29:12:55	AZ	2017	40	M	1
Price, John	29:15:00	CO	2017	46	M	2
Ketchell, Robby	29:15:03	NH	2017	34	M	1
Hayes, Danny	29:16:47	DC	2017	41	M	1
Brower, Chad	29:16:49	SD	2017	45	M	2
Strand, Eric	29:17:32	MO	2017	57	M	7
Strand, Zachary	29:17:34	MI	2017	28	M	1
O'Connell, Amy	29:17:35	CO	2017	39	F	1
Jokano, Urko	29:17:35	Spain	2017	45	M	1

Craigo, Chris	29:17:41	TX	2017	46	M	1
Goeckermann, Daniel	29:17:46	WI	2017	36	M	1
Bennett, Andie	29:17:49	SD	2017	38	F	1
Haler, Alex	29:18:09	CO	2017	31	M	1
Montano, Bryce	29:18:19	NM	2017	26	M	1
Heyne, Alicia	29:18:39	KY	2017	36	F	1
Pence, Ethan	29:18:43	CO	2017	19	M	2
LEON, LUIS	29:19:41	AZ	2017	48	M	1
Runyan, Dennis	29:19:44	TX	2017	40	M	1
Cook, Sean	29:19:47	NC	2017	45	M	4
Burmaster, Travis	29:19:53	CO	2017	43	M	2
Stewart, Willie	29:20:28	ID	2017	55	M	1
Zarif, Farhad	29:20:46	KS	2017	41	M	1
Mengers, James	29:21:22	OK	2017	33	M	1
Wunderlich, Dennis Scott	29:21:28	KY	2017	55	M	1
Cox, Stuart	29:21:34	Australia	2017	38	M	1
Callaghan, Anna	29:21:37	NM	2017	27	F	1
Polonsky, Joe	29:22:11	CO	2017	40	M	2
Vergara, Mike	29:22:16	TX	2017	39	M	4
Rasmussen, Thor	29:22:30	WY	2017	40	M	1
Alas, Monica	29:22:46	TX	2017	39	F	1
Galligan, Christopher	29:23:11	CO	2017	38	M	3
Iannello, Amanda	29:23:15	NC	2017	32	F	1
Williams, Jeffrey	29:25:06	CO	2017	44	M	1
Frizzo, Marcelo	29:25:36	TX	2017	41	M	1
Freeman, Corbin	29:26:18	TX	2017	30	F	2
Arellano, Miguel	29:27:19	KS	2017	36	M	1
Honey, Ashley	29:27:45	CO	2017	37	M	1
DeDoncker, John	29:28:01	IA	2017	53	M	5
Rankinen, Jake	29:28:21	VA	2017	32	M	1
Morton, Jeremy	29:28:23	IN	2017	35	M	1
Jones, Chris	29:28:24	CA	2017	45	M	2
Nordeen, Andy	29:28:28	WI	2017	59	M	1
Conley, Heather	29:31:23	IL	2017	30	F	1
Lockhart, Jessamyn	29:31:24	CO	2017	34	F	1
Bell, Mike	29:31:39	CO	2017	36	M	1
Graham, Aiji	29:31:52	NJ	2017	41	M	1

Thompson, Christina	29:32:23	FL	2017	27	F	1
Pilcher, Kimberly	29:33:28	TX	2017	53	F	2
LeNeveu, Shana	29:33:44	CO	2017	47	F	3
Horan, Pete	29:34:04	FL	2017	47	M	1
Morgan, Eric	29:35:44	CO	2017	50	M	2
Martinez, Camilo	29:36:03	NY	2017	35	M	2
Pence, Eric	29:36:11	CO	2017	51	M	24
Amato, Josh	29:36:15	MO	2017	43	M	1
Stone, Chuck	29:38:03	CO	2017	54	M	8
Pope, Jonathan	29:38:46	CO	2017	25	M	1
Snyder, Scott	29:39:10	CO	2017	62	M	9
Mortensen, Soren Hadsund	29:39:44	Denmark	2017	50	M	1
Lynch, Dylan	29:39:56	FL	2017	26	M	1
McGeachy, Irvin	29:39:58	ID	2017	71	M	1
Sellers, B.J.	29:40:50	FL	2017	39	M	1
Brennand, Michael	29:41:32	NM	2017	50	M	2
Simonsen, Bryan	29:41:33	GA	2017	31	M	1
Schaunaman, Scott	29:42:14	TX	2017	40	M	1
Merz, Shane	29:42:25	TX	2017	50	M	1
Dines, Tim	29:43:15	TN	2017	38	M	1
White, Eric	29:43:20	TX	2017	50	M	5
Beach, Keith	29:43:45	IL	2017	40	M	1
Mitchell, Abby	29:43:54	CO	2017	27	F	1
Neeley, Jarrod	29:44:36	CT	2017	44	M	1
Bousliman, Jason	29:45:40	NM	2017	41	M	1
Hallnan, Rachel	29:46:28	NV	2017	24	F	1
Wong, Misty	29:48:41	TN	2017	39	F	1
Bailey, Brian	29:49:22	AR	2017	40	M	1
Lloyd, Chris	29:49:27	CO	2017	55	M	1
Carlson, Alex	29:51:00	CO	2017	31	M	2
Cascante, Pablo	29:52:03	Costa Rica	2017	31	M	1
Bruno, John	29:52:21	SC	2017	31	M	1
Hashimoto, Kenta	29:54:36	Japan	2017	32	M	1
Grote, Henner	29:55:11	Germany	2017	39	M	1
Brand, Skip	29:55:46	CA	2017	51	M	1

2018

Name	Finish Time	State	Year	Age	Sex	#Finished
Krar, Rob	15:51:57	AZ	2018	41	M	2
Kaiser, Ryan	17:37:23	OR	2018	39	M	1
Kelly, Seth	18:15:29	CO	2018	34	M	2
Ruibal, Carlos	18:22:11	CO	2018	31	M	1
Wesolowski, Jesse	18:32:00	CO	2018	27	M	1
Kuehler, Jon	18:48:04	CO	2018	30	M	3
Anderson, Joel	19:21:55	CO	2018	36	M	3
Koop, Jason	19:26:33	CO	2018	39	M	5
Logdson, Cory	19:39:44	NE	2018	30	M	1
Delgado Gil, Ruben	19:53:26	Spain	2018	40	M	1
Arnold, Katie	19:53:40	NM	2018	46	F	1
Jimenez, Rodrigo	20:12:34	CO	2018	42	M	5
Stanciu, Adrian	20:17:59	CO	2018	49	M	4
Slauson, Steve	20:25:44	CO	2018	44	M	1
Bien, Rodney	20:31:19	OR	2018	46	M	1
Airey, Richard	20:44:37	CO	2018	42	M	3
Bybliw, Adam	20:47:59	CO	2018	37	M	3
Bracy, Addie	21:17:12	CO	2018	32	F	1
Sivanich, Andy	21:20:10	CO	2018	33	M	1
Darrigrand, Roger	21:23:14	Brazil	2018	36	M	1
Keyworth, Tyler	21:26:16	CO	2018	33	M	1
Letherby, Andrew	21:38:12	CO	2018	44	M	1
Kilcoyne, Jamie	21:42:03	CO	2018	48	M	3
Bundrock, Danny	21:42:57	CO	2018	39	M	5
Sandoval, Marvin	21:58:23	CO'	2018	40	M	7
Scott, Jared	22:15:22	CO	2018	47	M	1
Martinez, Michael	22:15:43	CO	2018	32	M	1
Wright, Chris	22:20:57	CO	2018	46	M	7
Williams, Bryan	22:22:50	CO	2018	43	M	3
Venzor, Alejandro	22:25:30	CO	2018	34	M	2
Robertson, Josh	22:28:59	CO	2018	30	M	1
Moore, Dustin	22:29:51	CO	2018	31	M	1
Husmann, Brian	22:34:05	CO	2018	46	M	2

Friedman, Jason	22:40:20	NY	2018	42	M	1
Chrysler, Andy	22:42:35	AZ	2018	30	M	1
Williams, Richard	22:45:29	CO	2018	49	M	4
Lanciaux, James	22:49:23	CO	2018	28	M	1
Mazzarese, Mike	22:49:40	CO	2018	42	M	1
Oakes, Duncan	22:53:31	England	2018	53	M	1
Dayton, Bryan	22:54:01	CO	2018	45	M	1
LiPuma, Eric	22:55:57	CO	2018	25	M	1
Williams, Brooks	22:56:27	CO	2018	35	M	4
Jenkins, Timbo	22:59:32	KY	2018	37	M	1
Banta, Jacob	23:07:51	CO	2018	24	M	1
Slaby, Steve	23:12:38	WA	2018	37	M	1
Slaby, Gina	23:13:03	WA	2018	37	F	1
Primault, Cedric	23:14:01	France	2018	35	M	1
O'Brien, Michael	23:14:22	CO	2018	35	M	2
Samples, Justin	23:17:11	OR	2018	35	M	1
Fulton, Max	23:21:54	CO	2018	42	M	5
Betouret, Sebastien	23:22:31	England	2018	41	M	1
Ommen, Andy	23:28:38	WY	2018	37	M	1
Mills, Joe	23:30:18	CO	2018	33	M	1
Moreno, Tomas	23:37:05	TX	2018	35	M	1
Riehle, Carmen	23:37:15	CO	2018	44	M	1
Greening, Muriel	23:39:25	CO	2018	34	F	1
Pretak, Stephen	23:40:23	CO	2018	33	M	1
Pemsel, Dennis	23:41:35	Germany	2018	31	M	1
Kepes, Ben	23:42:45	New Zealand	2018	46	M	1
Dailey, Bruce	23:43:40	CO	2018	47	M	7
Schneiderman, James	23:44:10	NC	2018	43	M	2
Hampshire, Christian	23:44:14	UT	2018	41	M	1
Sheetz-Willard, Jacob	23:44:57	CO	2018	28	M	2
Wasteney, Duke	23:47:06	OR	2018	31	M	1
Hastings, Jonathan	23:50:54	OH	2018	43	M	2
Novak, John	23:57:32	CO	2018	53	M	3
Liechty, Steve	23:59:45	MT	2018	48	M	2
Hanks, Jamie	23:59:59	OH	2018	22	M	1
Martinez, Gabriel	24:01:12	CO	2018	26	M	3
Ranken, David	24:02:42	Australia	2018	34	M	1

Lobb, Tyler	24:04:40	CO	2018	33	M	1
Wood, Samantha	24:05:43	CO	2018	33	F	2
Harper, Raquel	24:19:26	CO	2018	39	F	2
Tomek, Ondrej	24:21:07	WI	2018	48	M	1
Wait, Isaac	24:23:27	WV	2018	41	M	1
Braunlich, David	24:26:25	CO	2018	28	M	1
Mariash, Jax	24:30:34	UT	2018	38	F	1
Sims, Don	24:34:12	CO	2018	52	M	2
Robinson, Max	24:34:16	CO	2018	25	M	1
Scanlan, Jeremy	24:35:28	CO	2018	35	M	1
Robertshaw, Thomas	24:35:51	Hong Kong	2018	35	M	1
Antinori, Christopher	24:42:05	UT	2018	43	M	1
Wagner, Jason	24:42:14	MO	2018	48	M	1
Valk, Priit	24:43:08	Estonia	2018	44	M	2
Ryder, John	24:44:27	MD	2018	41	M	1
Gray, Sho	24:47:57	TN	2018	30	M	1
Leehman, Nathan	24:51:47	NC	2018	44	M	2
Zimmerman, Ronnie	24:52:05	WY	2018	38	M	1
Van Zanten, Hans	24:52:28	MO	2018	44	M	1
Lashley, Kevin	24:52:43	KY	2018	39	M	1
Barry, Jeremy	24:52:57	CO	2018	38	M	1
Hopper, Orlin	24:53:06	CO	2018	47	M	3
Tiislar, Kaupo	24:53:22	Estonia	2018	39	M	1
Eisman, Darrin	24:53:47	CO	2018	53	M	2
Mackey, Dave	24:54:49	CO	2018	48	M	2
Dicke, Benjamin	25:00:37	IL	2018	39	M	1
Leon, Javier	25:12:25	Chile	2018	26	M	1
Kirchhoff, Ryan	25:19:58	CO	2018	37	M	1
Seeberger, Robert	25:38:33	UT	2018	54	M	2
Pantoja, Eddie	25:42:20	PA	2018	32	M	1
St. Sauveur, Shawn	25:43:21	CO	2018	40	M	1
Stafford, Carrie	25:47:29	CO	2018	39	F	5
Andrews, Bobby	25:54:24	WA	2018	37	M	2
Pizarro, Rachelle	26:01:22	CO	2018	36	F	1
Balan, Robert	26:12:29	Romania	2018	42	M	1
Price, Rob	26:16:23	CO	2018	42	M	1
Wetstine, Sean	26:18:26	CO	2018	42	M	6

507

Gilbert, Micky	26:22:12	CO	2018	47	M	2
Hoffman, Bill	26:22:28	NY	2018	51	M	1
Ortiz Seas, Jose Carlos	26:23:25	Costa Rica	2018	27	M	1
Moore, Scott	26:23:37	CO	2018	47	M	1
Silva, Katrin	26:24:37	NM	2018	48	F	6
Cote, Gilles	26:26:48	CO	2018	61	M	6
Nagaraj, Harsha	26:27:55	CO	2018	44	M	3
Hidaka, Yuichiro	26:28:46	NM	2018	39	M	1
Kacsmar, Paul	26:32:20	CO	2018	27	M	1
Kunz, Ryan	26:35:29	FL	2018	36	M	1
Dobson, Aaron	26:38:28	CO	2018	29	M	1
Wooten, Mark	26:39:20	TX	2018	38	M	2
Anderson, Woody	26:41:25	CO	2018	43	M	5
Castan Peralta, Jose Antonio	26:44:35	CA	2018	40	M	1
Denicke, Rik	26:45:58	MO	2018	46	M	2
Pentler, Steve	26:56:00	CO	2018	27	M	2
Warren, Mack	26:56:20	CO	2018	40	M	1
Beuke, Donald	26:58:24	CO	2018	42	M	3
Gao, Bibo	26:59:38	IL	2018	40	F	1
Anderson, Katy	27:07:24	CO	2018	41	F	5
Finkbeiner, Christian	27:07:26	NV	2018	24	M	1
Hodulich, Marc	27:07:34	GA	2018	38	M	1
Palles, Neal	27:07:45	CO	2018	50	M	1
Onan, Lucas	27:11:58	CO	2018	28	M	1
Fannin, Tyler	27:12:15	UT	2018	32	M	1
Sobol, Tomasz	27:15:31	Poland	2018	41	M	1
Edgar, Jeff	27:20:58	NM	2018	52	M	1
Dowell, Derek	27:22:14	LA	2018	36	M	3
Hunter, Robert	27:22:24	OH	2018	59	M	1
Ray, Karen	27:23:04	NM	2018	40	F	1
Duncan, Matt	27:23:56	CO	2018	30	M	1
Kelman, Erin	27:24:16	MD	2018	41	M	1
Grotenhuis, John	27:27:10	CO	2018	25	M	1
Venner, Laura	27:33:31	CO	2018	36	F	2
Buckley, Stacey	27:35:27	NE	2018	42	F	1
Sweeney, Megan	27:36:32	CO	2018	37	F	5
Poland, Andrew	27:37:45	CO	2018	32	M	1

Vine, Zachary	27:41:07	CO	2018	37	M	1
Churchill, R. Sean	27:43:12	WI	2018	52	M	9
Orders, Nathaniel	27:47:19	WV	2018	40	M	2
Miller, Brent	27:47:37	CO	2018	38	M	1
Cadotte, Travis	27:48:39	CO	2018	33	M	1
Whelchel, Christopher	27:49:57	CO	2018	43	M	1
Morrissey, Shane	27:50:23	MT	2018	36	M	1
Pennington, Jason	27:53:55	CO	2018	37	M	1
Polski, Daniel	27:57:57	MN	2018	40	M	1
Schardein, Tim	27:58:20	CO	2018	50	M	4
Gagliardi, Michael	28:04:25	PA	2018	42	M	1
Smith, Alan	28:05:02	CO	2018	49	M	8
Price, Jill	28:05:47	TX	2018	44	F	2
Resutek, Brian	28:08:21	GA	2018	38	M	1
Mitchell, Abby	28:11:27	CO	2018	28	F	1
Hall, Jim	28:11:53	NC	2018	43	M	1
Mendes, Katy	28:12:23	CO	2018	45	F	1
Bianco, Peter	28:12:33	NY	2018	36	M	1
Moore, Michael	28:13:13	FL	2018	49	M	2
Furrer, Bruno	28:13:44	CO	2018	41	M	1
Jackson, Ben	28:15:50	CO	2018	32	M	1
Bermudez, Conrado	28:17:06	SC	2018	45	M	2
Barton, Timothy	28:18:23	Mexico	2018	54	M	1
Newman, Greg	28:18:26	CO	2018	43	M	1
Ingvardsen, David	28:19:59	TN	2018	49	M	1
Nelson, Chad	28:20:51	CO	2018	37	M	1
Richardson, Erik	28:21:09	MI	2018	40	M	4
Roederer, Alex	28:22:53	WA	2018	21	M	1
Covey, Kate	28:22:55	OR	2018	35	F	1
Murrell, Casey	28:23:00	TX	2018	44	M	1
Atkinson, Phil	28:23:54	WY	2018	46	M	7
Johnston, Curt	28:24:30	IA	2018	42	M	1
Spence, Steve	28:25:54	CO	2018	57	M	1
Jamrogiewicz, Amanda	28:26:03	CO	2018	32	F	1
Cook, Art	28:27:00	TX	2018	52	M	1
Peirano, Marcelo	28:27:16	Peru	2018	41	M	1
Taylor, Jed	28:28:14	MO	2018	39	M	2

Harrison, Jeremy	28:28:19	OK	2018	40	M	1
Edwards, Walter	28:28:47	CO	2018	43	M	1
Wheat, Kevin	28:29:18	CO	2018	33	M	1
West-Hoover, Sarah	28:29:36	CO	2018	48	F	3
Barr, Andrew	28:30:36	CO	2018	30	M	1
Deer, Timothy	28:30:53	WV	2018	54	M	3
Smith, Neil	28:31:07	TX	2018	47	M	3
Cook, Sean	28:31:10	VA	2018	46	M	4
Sodia, Patrick	28:31:13	CO	2018	55	M	1
Campbell, David	28:31:37	TX	2018	39	M	1
Martinez, Camilo	28:31:41	NY	2018	37	M	2
Brower, Chad	28:31:55	SD	2018	46	M	2
Shanahan, Francis	28:32:36	NJ	2018	43	M	1
Nuber, Toby	28:32:56	CO	2018	44	M	1
Vargo, Andrew	28:33:07	CO	2018	40	M	1
Schaaf, Andrew	28:33:17	VA	2018	50	M	1
Craig, Caleb	28:33:28	CO	2018	32	M	1
Lynch, Robert	28:34:30	IN	2018	46	M	1
Selonick, Emily	28:35:33	CO	2018	31	F	1
Buck, Teri	28:36:17	AK	2018	56	F	1
McCoy, Sean	28:36:51	CO	2018	42	M	1
Roersma, Jake	28:37:14	MI	2018	35	M	1
Legat, Joseph	28:38:09	NV	2018	52	M	2
Leasure, Julie	28:38:33	OR	2018	47	F	1
Ceccanti, Brian	28:38:47	CO	2018	40	M	1
Bokoski, Kevin	28:39:39	CO	2018	29	M	1
Wynn, Joshua	28:40:37	VA	2018	42	M	1
Ervin, Daley	28:40:47	GA	2018	32	M	2
Diamond-Husmann, Kara	28:40:58	CO	2018	41	F	1
Talley, Suzie	28:41:19	NC	2018	56	F	1
Hoogenboom, Shane	28:41:19	Canada	2018	46	M	1
McCabe, John	28:41:30	CT	2018	46	M	2
Seekamp, Jessica	28:41:41	TX	2018	36	F	2
O'Brien, Tracy	28:44:10	CO	2018	31	F	1
Harcrow, Gina	28:44:42	CO	2018	46	F	3
Metzler, Brian	28:44:43	CO	2018	49	M	1
Trubow, Adam	28:46:07	NM	2018	37	M	1

Torrens Marin, Guillem	28:47:30	Panama	2018	37	M	1
O'Connor, Ryan	28:47:53	PA	2018	32	M	1
Farr, Nicholas	28:48:02	NC	2018	43	M	1
Tischer, Jason	28:48:02	NJ	2018	28	M	2
Compagnone, Brian	28:48:58	VA	2018	44	M	1
Weeter, Bryce	28:49:59	TN	2018	33	M	2
Curtin, David	28:50:53	IN	2018	44	M	1
Katalin, Katie	28:51:55	CO	2018	48	F	1
Brooks, Melissa	28:54:01	UT	2018	41	F	1
Vergara, Mike	28:54:05	TX	2018	41	M	4
Harvey, Matt	28:54:23	IN	2018	27	M	1
Galligan, Christopher	28:56:43	CO	2018	40	M	3
Yasinski, Michael	28:57:04	Canada	2018	47	M	2
Sutherland, Benjamin	28:58:17	New Zealand	2018	39	M	1
Thomas, Edwin	28:58:48	AL	2018	48	M	1
Barnard, Joe	28:59:47	KS	2018	38	M	2
Chaves, Andre	28:59:49	CO	2018	32	M	1
Muir, Lauren	29:00:34	CO	2018	35	F	1
Frizzo, Marcelo	29:00:47	TX	2018	42	M	1
Feehrer, David	29:03:28	CA	2018	43	M	1
Odebunmi, Emmanuel	29:04:05	NY	2018	35	M	2
Ferguson, Andrew	29:04:34	England	2018	52	M	1
Reinholt, Abby	29:04:48	CO	2018	37	F	1
Badershall, Jodi	29:05:29	ME	2018	40	F	1
Perez Colon, Francisco	29:05:30	Puerto Rico	2018	39	M	1
Schmidt, Charlie	29:05:48	MI	2018	38	M	1
Scarlett, Matthew	29:06:17	WY	2018	21	M	1
Meaney, John	29:07:49	TX	2018	44	M	1
Leonard, Lucja	29:07:55	England	2018	39	F	1
Stotler, Gary	29:08:10	WY	2018	34	M	1
Saenz Gutierrez, Sergio	29:08:12	CO	2018	49	M	1
Bronson, Melissa	29:08:13	CO	2018	37	F	1
Hronik, Brian	29:08:49	CO	2018	41	M	3
Lennert, Eric	29:09:17	CO	2018	47	M	1
Davis, Chad	29:09:46	CO	2018	36	M	2
Bruce, Doug	29:09:53	Canada	2018	44	M	1
Baugh, Hollis	29:10:09	CA	2018	29	M	11

Gileau, Ross	29:10:09	CO	2018	49	M	1
Kuksin, Nikita	29:10:13	NY	2018	37	M	2
Sicher, Nathan	29:10:16	MO	2018	37	M	1
Grimes, Keith	29:10:20	CO	2018	59	M	9
Bennett, Justin	29:11:26	NJ	2018	36	M	1
Antonio, Rogelio	29:11:30	NV	2018	41	M	1
Welker, Erik	29:12:07	CO	2018	36	M	1
Stevens, Johnathon	29:12:11	AL	2018	35	M	1
Brodlieb, Stuart	29:13:01	CA	2018	46	M	1
Bath, Alec	29:13:33	IL	2018	48	M	2
Kohler, Keith	29:13:49	MI	2018	46	M	1
Bonnett, Paul	29:14:01	AZ	2018	56	M	1
DuBois, Matthew	29:14:08	CA	2018	36	M	1
Skalla, Marc	29:14:32	GA	2018	40	M	1
Pospisil, Luke	29:15:25	CO	2018	39	M	1
Perkins, Mark	29:15:39	CO	2018	65	M	3
Wanless, Ryan	29:15:53	SD	2018	40	M	1
Lampe, Jeff	29:16:37	PA	2018	49	M	1
Fiorelli, Christian	29:16:40	NY	2018	38	M	1
Pence, Eric	29:16:52	CO	2018	52	M	24
Pence, Ethan	29:16:54	CO	2018	20	M	2
Jimenez, Gonzo	29:16:59	CO	2018	34	M	1
Wells, Donald	29:17:09	FL	2018	50	M	1
Jordan, Jeffrey	29:17:23	TN	2018	55	M	2
Porter, Mike	29:17:24	CO	2018	45	M	1
Passenti, Brian	29:17:33	CO	2018	44	M	5
Conlin, Jared	29:17:35	CO	2018	37	M	3
Marley, Patrick	29:17:38	AK	2018	37	M	1
Amo, Joe	29:18:06	SD	2018	52	M	1
Murray, Emma	29:18:30	CO	2018	23	F	1
Wahlstrom, Erik	29:18:33	WA	2018	45	M	1
Smith, Larry	29:18:35	CO	2018	43	M	1
Lepikhina, Marina	29:19:05	CO	2018	46	F	1
Laurence, Doug	29:19:54	MI	2018	55	M	1
Strand, Eric	29:19:56	MO	2018	58	M	7
Mullett, Sean	29:21:24	TN	2018	50	M	3
Schwaller, Sam	29:22:19	TN	2018	31	M	1

Bayona, Ines	29:22:24	Colombia	2018	55	F	1
Sasamoto, Wataru	29:22:47	Japan	2018	55	M	1
Nakauchi, Laurie	29:23:21	CO	2018	48	F	12
Zajac, Val	29:23:22	CO	2018	33	F	2
Murphy, Chad	29:23:43	Canada	2018	44	M	1
Stasiowski, Mike	29:23:50	MD	2018	53	M	1
Smith, Dean	29:24:05	England	2018	28	M	1
Schmidt, Todd	29:24:22	CO	2018	51	M	1
Mecheri, Jasmine	29:24:27	CT	2018	27	F	1
England, Tiffany	29:24:51	NY	2018	34	F	1
Becker, Jill	29:25:25	CO	2018	31	F	1
Cohen, Jason	29:25:52	LA	2018	34	M	1
Nicholson, Bradley	29:26:04	CO	2018	30	M	1
Farmiga, Victor	29:26:31	CO	2018	46	M	1
Bybee, Charles	29:26:42	CO	2018	56	M	12
Kilpatrick, John (Muck)	29:27:00	CO	2018	36	M	1
Ripmaster, Peter	29:27:38	NC	2018	41	M	1
Stahl, Craig	29:29:05	UT	2018	50	M	2
Warner, Ash	29:29:07	CO	2018	32	F	1
Holowesko, Stephen	29:29:31	Bahamas	2018	50	M	1
Forno, Cristobal	29:30:01	CO	2018	36	M	3
Bosch, Tanner	29:30:19	NC	2018	28	M	1
Banel, Paul	29:30:35	CO	2018	29	M	1
Lammert, Kelly	29:32:19	CO	2018	32	F	1
Kabra, Aashish	29:33:02	CO	2018	31	M	1
White, Andrew	29:33:05	CO	2018	33	M	1
Johnson, Corey	29:33:34	OH	2018	29	M	1
Mazurkiewicz, Robert	29:33:43	CO	2018	47	M	2
Smith, Mark	29:33:50	MN	2018	39	M	1
Godfrey, Paul	29:34:11	NC	2018	48	M	4
Alexakis, Adam	29:34:35	Greece	2018	49	M	1
Feinberg, Benjamin	29:34:38	VA	2018	36	M	1
Lewman, Jeff	29:35:04	OK	2018	48	M	1
Blake, Neil	29:35:11	NM	2018	53	M	7
Jakubiuk, Victor	29:36:17	CA	2018	28	M	1
Blinn, Brenda	29:36:18	CA	2018	51	F	1
Sterling, Amanda	29:36:20	NY	2018	49	F	1

513

Hollister, Brian	29:36:49	CO	2018	51	M	1
Calder, Phil	29:36:52	New Zealand	2018	44	M	1
White, Jim	29:36:55	KY	2018	53	M	1
Wing, Jeremy	29:37:42	GA	2018	44	M	1
Furrer, Toni	29:38:07	CO	2018	43	M	2
Leung, Solomon	29:38:45	CA	2018	29	M	1
Dec, Eric	29:38:55	CO	2018	46	M	1
Urschel, Casey	29:39:09	LA	2018	39	M	2
Southern, Chip	29:39:47	CO	2018	50	M	3
Vincent, Andrea	29:39:48	Costa Rica	2018	37	F	1
Romero, Jason	29:40:15	CO	2018	48	M	4
Shibazaki, Junya	29:41:16	Japan	2018	47	M	1
Scozzaro, Sarah	29:41:35	ND	2018	39	F	1
Politte, Ted	29:41:48	CO	2018	39	M	1
Stokes, Mike	29:42:19	OH	2018	51	M	1
Stemberger, Andreas	29:42:56	Austria	2018	47	M	1
Krause, Jeffrey	29:43:53	CO	2018	50	M	1
LeNeveu, Shana	29:43:54	CO	2018	48	F	3
Anderson, John	29:44:19	IA	2018	35	M	2
Mills, Chuck	29:45:18	AZ	2018	59	M	1
Durkin, Mike	29:45:59	WA	2018	36	M	1
Lehman, Scott	29:46:04	IL	2018	36	M	1
Gottshall, Alyssa	29:46:18	CO	2018	28	F	1
Hathcock, Alan	29:46:40	CO	2018	37	M	1
Stone, Chuck	29:48:21	CO	2018	55	M	8
Rodgers, Stephen	29:48:48	CO	2018	50	M	2
Churgovich, Hawaiian Shirt Ray	29:49:27	CO	2018	52	M	3
Friedman, Jason	29:49:33	NJ	2018	37	M	1
Porter, Matthew	29:49:39	VA	2018	57	M	1
Woods, Doug	29:49:39	MO	2018	41	M	1
Carlson, Alex	29:50:05	CO	2018	32	M	2
McDonnell, Richard	29:51:23	NC	2018	36	M	1
Drake, Brent	29:51:27	NY	2018	41	M	1
Vicera, Christian Joseph	29:52:47	Philippines	2018	34	M	1
Nielsen, Paul	29:52:53	CO	2018	57	M	1
Seher, Kari	29:52:58	TX	2018	34	F	1
Bearss, Joseph	29:53:18	CO	2018	48	M	2

| Rotte, Shelly | 29:54:49 | CO | 2018 | 44 | F | 1 |

2019

Name	Finish Time	State	Year	Age	Sex	# Finished
Smith, Ryan	16:33:24	CO	2019	40	M	1
Trammell, Chad	17:56:26	AK	2019	35	M	1
Olson, Devon	17:57:17	CO	2019	31	M	1
Casanovas, Ramon	18:14:51	Switzerland	2019	39	M	1
Knight, Tate	18:51:47	CT	2019	23	M	1
Marzen, Mark	19:10:29	CO	2019	33	M	1
Grinius, Gediminas	19:22:13	Lithuania	2019	40	M	1
Green, Jock	19:33:10	South Africa	2019	45	M	1
Joyes, Gabe	19:37:23	WY	2019	33	M	1
Urbanski, Matthew	19:51:14	CO	2019	38	M	2
Boulet, Magdalena	20:18:06	CA	2019	46	F	1
DeNucci, Christopher	20:41:11	CA	2019	39	M	1
Jimenez, Rodrigo	20:45:14	CO	2019	43	M	6
Bradley, Cat	20:45:48	CO	2019	27	F	1
Robinson, Max	20:51:47	CO	2019	26	M	2
Delgado Gil, Ruben	21:00:20	Spain	2019	41	M	2
Ladner, Justin	21:04:42	PA	2019	39	M	1
Sandoval, Marvin	21:06:58	CO	2019	41	M	8
Urbanski, Jeffrey	21:12:28	CO	2019	34	M	2
Messman, Clark	21:15:31	CO	2019	23	M	1
Milea, Radu	21:28:03	Romania	2019	30	M	1
Slauson, Steve	21:35:52	CO	2019	44	M	3
Frank, Daniel	21:58:23	MD	2019	36	M	1
Samokhvalov, Anton	22:01:29	Russia	2019	32	M	1
Bradford, Jeremy	22:10:51	CO	2019	41	M	6
Banta, Jacob	22:13:02	CO	2019	25	M	2
Anderson, Lance	22:14:20	UT	2019	41	M	1
Harrison, Jon	22:16:18	CO	2019	29	M	1
Mortimer, Peter	22:23:13	AZ	2019	38	M	1
Cade, Pat	22:28:38	CO	2019	35	M	1
Harrison, Matthew	22:32:07	PA	2019	36	M	1
Sandoval, Wesley	22:48:52	CO	2019	42	M	5
Mau, Mackenzie	22:48:53	CO	2019	33	M	1
Kilcoyne, Jamie	22:51:06	CO	2019	48	M	4
Goggins, David	22:55:44	TN	2019	44	M	2

Van Ness, Ryan	22:58:28	CO	2019	43	M	1
Braun, Chad	23:00:05	CO	2019	39	M	1
Lantz, Jonathan	23:02:21	CO	2019	34	M	1
Dill, Todd	23:09:14	CO	2019	37	M	1
Kerl, Bryan	23:11:07	CO	2019	27	M	1
Monke, Adam	23:15:27	NE	2019	32	M	1
Orders, Nathaniel	23:15:29	WV	2019	41	M	3
Nazar, Tito	23:19:37	Chile	2019	37	M	1
Becker, Ezra	23:25:08	CA	2019	34	M	1
Allen, Zachary	23:27:40	CO	2019	25	M	1
Korth, Kilian	23:29:19	CO	2019	24	M	1
Williams, Brooks	23:38:15	CO	2019	36	M	5
Olar, John	23:42:07	CO	2019	45	M	1
Worthington, Brandon	23:50:06	CO	2019	34	M	2
Wood, Samantha	23:52:04	CO	2019	34	F	3
Stafford, Carrie	23:55:20	CO	2019	40	F	6
Schneiderman, James	23:57:14	NC	2019	44	M	3
Dailey, Bruce	24:01:46	CO	2019	48	M	8
Ricks, Jordan	24:04:33	UT	2019	36	M	1
Barr, Timothy	24:06:15	CO	2019	43	M	2
Finocchio, Tim	24:08:39	MA	2019	41	M	2
Devillaz, Sacha	24:12:39	France	2019	30	M	1
Reutlinger, Phil	24:15:36	CO	2019	40	M	1
Adams, Drew	24:15:39	ID	2019	31	M	1
Muir, John	24:16:29	MT	2019	41	M	2
Fulton, Max	24:18:03	CO	2019	42	M	6
Zani, Paul	24:18:19	TN	2019	51	M	2
Gonzalez, Lelis	24:19:54	CO	2019	35	M	2
Ray, Brandon	24:24:18	TX	2019	36	M	1
Orellana, Steve	24:28:54	NY	2019	32	M	1
Sperlich, Jens	24:29:14	Germany	2019	46	M	1
Cummings, Alex	24:29:56	CO	2019	32	M	1
Harvey, Matt	24:31:48	IN	2019	28	M	2
Pentler, Steve	24:32:23	CO	2019	28	M	3
Vogt, Howard	24:32:31	CO	2019	28	M	1
Arnold, Daniel	24:33:24	AR	2019	34	M	1
Schwaller, Sam	24:34:37	TN	2019	32	M	2
Acuna, Aaron	24:37:59	CO	2019	33	M	1
Leite, Leonardo	24:39:46	Brazil	2019	37	M	1

Cronk, Tim	24:40:36	NH	2019	57	M	1
Robbert, Michael	24:42:24	CO	2019	44	M	1
Stowe, Robert	24:43:34	MI	2019	42	M	1
Daniels, Travis	24:44:59	CO	2019	41	M	1
Pardoe, Niki	24:45:12	CO	2019	38	F	2
Wickless, Andrew	24:47:25	CO	2019	45	M	2
Vieth, Jason	24:47:56	CO	2019	46	M	2
Alfred, Michael	24:50:25	CO	2019	38	M	1
Morgan, Kaitlyn	24:51:05	CO	2019	29	F	2
Ulrich, George	24:51:18	NV	2019	48	M	1
King, Michael	24:53:11	ME	2019	30	M	1
Leonard, Dion	24:57:15	France	2019	44	M	1
Ellison, Aaron	24:57:53	MD	2019	43	M	2
Stevens, Joshua	25:01:08	CO	2019	48	M	1
Howell, Shannon	25:17:45	SC	2019	40	F	1
Wright, Chris	25:22:24	CO	2019	47	M	8
Ebener, Kenneth	25:35:11	SC	2019	49	M	1
Mast, Randy	25:36:57	CO	2019	49	M	1
Baker, Shaun	25:43:40	DE	2019	39	M	1
Stotler, Gary	25:46:20	WY	2019	35	M	2
Fearing, Aaron	25:46:46	WI	2019	40	M	1
Levchenko, Nikita	25:47:26	Russia	2019	31	M	1
Diamond-Husmann, Kara	25:54:02	CO	2019	42	F	2
Mackey, David	25:54:59	CO	2019	49	M	3
Joslyn, Jonathan	25:55:22	CO	2019	37	M	1
Tucker, Paul	25:55:43	CO	2019	46	M	3
Grills, Mat	25:57:02	Australia	2019	36	M	1
Marion, Stacey	25:59:03	WI	2019	30	F	1
Grenney, Peter	26:02:18	CO	2019	39	M	1
Romero, Jason	26:02:22	CO	2019	49	M	5
Basacoma, Francesc	26:05:07	Spain	2019	45	M	1
Hunsucker, Matthew	26:06:03	CO	2019	39	M	1
Tomek, Ondrej	26:19:22	WI	2019	49	M	2
Snepste, Janis	26:19:22	Latvia	2019	45	M	1
Dart, Richie	26:21:18	CO	2019	31	M	1
Feldman, Neil	26:30:30	MA	2019	49	M	2
Hauschulz, Benjamin	26:31:53	CO	2019	34	M	2
Mead, Chris	26:35:44	CA	2019	48	M	3
Bolls, Rod	26:40:16	CO	2019	44	M	4

Messegee, Emily	26:42:37	CO	2019	41	F	1
Dickson, Joshua	26:46:20	CO	2019	35	M	1
Jochem, Hannah	26:50:08	CO	2019	27	F	1
Silva, Katrin	26:51:07	NM	2019	49	F	7
White, Melanie	26:53:01	CO	2019	30	F	1
Erichsen, Kenneth	26:55:02	Guatemala	2019	46	M	1
Hedley, Giles	27:01:38	South Africa	2019	30	M	1
Mollenhour, John	27:03:31	AZ	2019	63	M	3
Seyler, Daniela	27:06:17	FL	2019	44	F	1
Handloser, Walter	27:07:41	CA	2019	37	M	1
Hoffman, Bill	27:08:51	NY	2019	52	M	2
Smith, Alan	27:10:45	CO	2019	50	M	9
Forno, Cristobal	27:13:58	Chile	2019	37	M	4
Kerr III, David	27:15:29	CA	2019	35	M	1
Shapiro, Clayton	27:15:35	TX	2019	43	M	2
Zolnikov, Dan	27:16:57	CO	2019	36	M	1
O'Gorman, Christine	27:20:54	CO	2019	30	F	1
Howard, Jeremy	27:21:39	RI	2019	48	M	1
Bain, Hope	27:25:07	CO	2019	53	F	1
O'Brien, Tracy	27:30:42	CO	2019	32	F	2
Wood, Anders	27:34:02	CO	2019	34	M	1
Goble, John	27:40:45	MO	2019	48	M	1
Semrau, Randy	27:41:56	PA	2019	31	M	1
Hagan, Jay	27:43:47	NV	2019	38	M	1
Luhrs, Emily	27:45:08	IL	2019	29	F	2
Vargas, Cristian	27:45:29	England	2019	39	M	1
Lawler, Max	27:45:39	CO	2019	41	M	1
De Beer, Nic	27:49:01	South Africa	2019	46	M	1
Mohrmann, Jeff	27:49:15	CO	2019	37	M	1
McLaughlin, Sean	27:50:21	CO	2019	34	M	2
Wright, Rob	27:54:40	CO	2019	45	M	1
Anderson, Katy	27:55:27	Australia	2019	42	F	6
Kuchinad, Amar	27:57:32	NY	2019	45	M	1
Leppert, Cory	27:58:13	CO	2019	44	M	3
Kirkendall, Matthew	28:01:09	CO	2019	39	M	1
Walton, Dreama	28:01:22	CO	2019	38	F	1
Jarvis, Wade	28:01:47	Canada	2019	57	M	10
Forgensi, Max	28:02:36	CO	2019	45	M	1
Welker, Tom	28:04:10	ID	2019	52	M	1

Flinn, Andrew	28:05:15	CO	2019	36	M	2
McManus, Drew	28:07:25	CO	2019	37	M	1
Bourke, Andy	28:08:16	Singapore	2019	44	M	1
Zenger, Jeff	28:09:54	IN	2019	26	M	1
Schneekloth, Martin	28:10:49	AL	2019	48	M	1
Churchill, R. Sean	28:15:00	WI	2019	53	M	10
Nothem, Michael	28:16:40	CO	2019	25	M	2
Sylvester, Michael	28:16:42	ID	2019	48	M	1
Hendry, Gabriel	28:16:44	MN	2019	37	M	1
Park, Erin	28:18:35	CO	2019	30	F	1
Romeiser, Lillie	28:18:42	WY	2019	34	F	1
Allen, Zach	28:19:38	TX	2019	38	M	2
Onan, Lucas	28:20:18	CO	2019	29	M	2
Coleman, Andrew	28:20:21	CO	2019	37	M	1
Pospisil, Luke	28:20:31	CO	2019	40	M	2
Nelson, Eric	28:21:57	UT	2019	44	M	1
Wright, Robert	28:22:49	CA	2019	53	M	1
Wilmoth, Brandon	28:23:29	TN	2019	42	M	1
McHale, Denise	28:23:50	Canada	2019	45	F	1
Vilchis, Javier	28:24:02	TX	2019	43	M	2
Mitchell, Clark	28:26:01	PA	2019	53	M	1
Barr, Caitlin	28:26:27	CO	2019	31	F	1
Palles, Neal	28:26:57	CO	2019	51	M	2
Kenyon, April	28:28:57	CO	2019	33	F	1
Grabowski, Marc	28:33:42	IL	2019	42	M	1
Kassahun, Jemil	28:33:43	CO	2019	20	M	1
Biddison, Kenneth	28:33:53	CO	2019	26	M	1
Drasler, Erin	28:34:20	CO	2019	38	F	2
Kilpatrick, John (Muck)	28:35:10	CO	2019	37	M	2
Maloney, TR	28:35:29	NC	2019	51	M	2
Willson, Carey	28:36:24	TX	2019	36	M	1
Jost, LaMar	28:36:41	CO	2019	42	M	1
Ogden, John Paul	28:36:56	CO	2019	52	M	1
Pearce, Lance	28:37:57	CO	2019	38	M	1
Kardasis, Pete	28:38:40	CO	2019	45	M	1
Atkinson, Phil	28:39:25	WY	2019	47	M	8
Richardson, Ted	28:39:28	NC	2019	49	M	1
Music, John	28:39:54	NV	2019	34	M	1
Brester, Sonja	28:40:06	UT	2019	36	F	1

Koch, Robert J.	28:41:07	MO	2019	54	M	1
Wasson, Mike	28:41:20	CO	2019	53	M	2
Hanley, Geoff	28:41:52	OK	2019	43	M	1
Harte, Canice	28:42:20	UT	2019	52	M	1
McDonald, Ted Barefoot	28:42:30	CA	2019	55	M	4
Sundahl, Scott	28:44:19	CO	2019	40	M	1
Koch, James	28:44:55	CO	2019	40	M	1
Taylor, Brandy	28:46:05	MO	2019	37	F	2
Goss, Jason	28:46:23	TN	2019	36	M	1
Miller, Joe	28:46:50	CO	2019	46	M	1
Dube, Paul	28:48:11	Canada	2019	37	M	1
McCollum, Newton	28:48:39	MD	2019	24	M	1
Quinn, Tyler	28:49:35	PA	2019	27	M	1
Anderson, Kayde	28:49:36	CO	2019	36	F	1
Nelson, Lisa	28:51:01	UT	2019	51	F	1
Erickson, Andrew	28:51:04	NV	2019	33	M	1
Serban, Mihai	28:52:03	Romania	2019	40	M	1
Mazurkiewicz, Robert	28:53:39	CO	2019	48	M	3
Degennaro, Helen	28:53:39	CO	2019	52	F	1
Sprungli, Caspar	28:54:04	Argentina	2019	49	M	1
Burton, Brian	28:56:50	WA	2019	42	M	1
McAfee, Ryan	28:57:30	CO	2019	38	M	2
Simcik, Trey	28:57:40	TX	2019	31	M	1
Grebosky, Becky	28:58:26	OR	2019	52	F	1
Provenzano, Donna	28:58:56	CO	2019	43	F	2
Jennings, Denzil	28:59:04	OR	2019	37	M	1
Mittelman, Alexandra	28:59:38	CO	2019	42	F	1
Jenson, Jeremiah	29:00:31	CO	2019	43	M	1
Stephenson, Sam	29:01:27	CO	2019	29	M	1
Furrer, Bruno	29:02:07	CO	2019	42	M	2
Webb, Amanda	29:02:29	PA	2019	39	F	1
Smith, Neil	29:02:49	TX	2019	48	M	4
Mentz, Colleen	29:04:07	CO	2019	40	F	1
Kumm, Chris	29:04:19	CO	2019	34	M	1
Carey, Jason	29:04:22	CO	2019	37	M	1
Anderson, Brad	29:04:44	CO	2019	39	M	2
Ortega, Ciro	29:05:35	KS	2019	49	M	1
Gzybowski, Andrew	29:05:46	CO	2019	37	M	3
Hirschfeld, Madeline	29:06:00	MI	2019	26	F	1

Nemechek, Jeremiah	29:07:16	MO	2019	32	M	1
Nielsen, Erik	29:08:53	CO	2019	34	M	1
Leung, Moon-Ka	29:09:35	Hong Kong	2019	43	M	1
Repasky, Jack	29:10:00	CO	2019	33	M	1
Hull, Erik	29:10:21	MN	2019	49	M	1
Merseal, Brian	29:10:27	MT	2019	30	M	1
Ballard, Dave	29:11:54	NE	2019	50	M	1
Moore, Kevin	29:12:20	CA	2019	33	M	1
Laplander, Erin	29:12:35	MI	2019	27	F	1
Bybee, Charles	29:12:36	CO	2019	57	M	13
Edwards, Walter	29:12:36	CO	2019	44	M	2
Koncilja, Kevin	29:13:32	MA	2019	30	M	1
Daly, Jimmy	29:14:28	CO	2019	33	M	1
Passenti, Brian	29:14:36	CO	2019	45	M	6
Reinholt, Abby	29:14:37	CO	2019	38	F	2
Weisel, Evan	29:14:41	VA	2019	48	M	1
Kazukawa, Junko	29:15:11	CO	2019	56	F	7
Wisdom, Bryan	29:15:50	CO	2019	29	M	2
Kinsler, Allen	29:15:51	OH	2019	41	M	1
Holbel, Trish	29:15:54	MI	2019	29	F	1
Saenz, Sergio	29:16:03	CO	2019	50	M	2
McLean, Robb	29:16:04	NM	2019	46	M	2
Colomo, Ramiro Hector Calderon	29:16:05	Mexico	2019	43	M	1
Nielsen, Paul	29:16:27	CO	2019	58	M	2
Tam, Chung-Man	29:16:30	CA	2019	43	M	1
Patterson, Tyler	29:16:47	KS	2019	35	M	1
Politte, Ted	29:17:36	CO	2019	40	M	2
Pence, Ethan	29:17:52	CO	2019	21	M	3
Pizzi, Todd	29:17:56	CA	2019	45	M	1
Doran, Sean	29:20:09	CO	2019	55	M	1
Obsitos, Monica	29:21:42	CO	2019	32	F	2
Anderson, Jacey	29:21:51	MT	2019	27	F	1
Zavisiute, Karolina	29:22:22	MO	2019	28	F	1
Ploof, Jim	29:22:41	VT	2019	50	M	1
Rawls, Jack	29:22:52	AL	2019	58	M	1
Cook, Aaron	29:23:52	CO	2019	51	M	1
Corwin, Benjamin	29:24:05	CO	2019	26	M	1
Finken, Luke	29:24:41	CO	2019	43	M	1
Roop, Alexa	29:25:20	CO	2019	35	F	1

Brown, Stephen	29:25:42	WA	2019	57	M	1
Heady, Brent	29:26:21	TX	2019	46	M	1
Walls, Kristin	29:27:09	MO	2019	44	F	1
Madalena, Daniel	29:27:12	NM	2019	34	M	1
Churgovich, Ray Hawaiian Shirt	29:27:18	CO	2019	53	M	4
Pierce, Nathan	29:27:30	CO	2019	40	M	1
Santerre, Ben	29:27:47	AZ	2019	31	M	1
Hornung, Harrison	29:28:00	CO	2019	21	M	1
Miller, Lexi	29:28:07	CO	2019	29	F	1
Klinghagen, Chris	29:28:16	WY	2019	43	M	1
Minton, Chris	29:28:21	WA	2019	43	M	1
Steinberg, Jason	29:29:14	CO	2019	41	M	1
Yasinski, Mike	29:29:39	Canada	2019	48	M	3
Baum, Casey	29:29:53	VA	2019	41	M	1
Stone, Chuck	29:29:54	CO	2019	56	M	10
Watkins, Garren	29:30:10	CO	2019	44	M	1
Vergara, Mike	29:30:31	CO	2019	42	M	5
Carter, Emily	29:30:34	NC	2019	39	F	1
Ederle, Nicole	29:30:54	TX	2019	48	F	1
Jønsson, Maj-Britt	29:30:56	Denmark	2019	53	F	1
Constabel, Jonathan	29:30:57	PA	2019	24	M	1
Lepikhina, Marina	29:31:03	CO	2019	47	F	2
Nakamura, Sean	29:32:06	CA	2019	40	M	1
Wilson, Tom	29:32:25	IL	2019	52	M	1
Skocaj, Eric	29:32:26	WA	2019	33	M	1
Reily, Matthew	29:33:10	OK	2019	44	M	1
Ewing, Amy	29:33:27	TX	2019	50	F	1
Keller, Lauren	29:33:33	CO	2019	34	F	1
Smith, Geoff	29:34:01	CO	2019	38	M	2
Weller, Clyde	29:34:08	CO	2019	55	M	2
Keyes, Tyler	29:34:37	CO	2019	29	M	1
Sandoval, Greg	29:35:15	CO	2019	44	M	3
Warburg, Shannon Hogan	29:35:20	WA	2019	49	F	1
Kubes, Daniel	29:35:29	CO	2019	35	M	2
Harris, Gabrielle	29:35:46	CO	2019	38	F	1
Heinemann, Eric	29:35:49	OR	2019	45	M	1
Sleeman, Ben	29:35:54	CO	2019	30	M	1
Delgado, Joey	29:37:18	AZ	2019	49	M	1
Woods, Rachael	29:37:24	CO	2019	45	F	1

Rolls, Ian	29:37:27	TX	2019	41	M	1
Dughi, Coco	29:37:31	CO	2019	56	F	1
Braun, Rhonda	29:37:43	NY	2019	35	F	1
Kratzer, Marshall	29:37:46	WA	2019	29	M	1
Smith, Isaac	29:37:59	CO	2019	41	M	1
Beard, Ryan	29:38:05	TX	2019	44	M	2
Grogan, Kyle	29:38:06	CO	2019	27	M	1
Rinkenberger, Matt	29:38:07	NE	2019	44	M	1
Pence, Eric	29:38:13	CO	2019	53	M	25
Sommerdorf, Craig	29:38:19	CO	2019	56	M	1
Coon, Kelsey	29:38:20	CO	2019	26	F	1
Hall, Julian	29:38:23	England	2019	44	M	2
Davis, Brian	29:38:40	GA	2019	39	M	1
Clarke, John	29:38:43	CO	2019	54	M	2
Aminzade, Daniel	29:39:00	CA	2019	39	M	1
Wilson, David	29:39:04	WA	2019	49	M	1
Peterson, Gabe	29:39:25	UT	2019	45	M	1
Orme, Graham	29:39:35	CA	2019	38	M	1
Carey, Brian	29:39:36	CO	2019	50	M	1
Kuhta, Mo	29:39:52	MI	2019	33	F	1
Bradfield, Kristin	29:40:42	NY	2019	44	F	1
Bjes, Michael	29:40:49	CO	2019	35	M	1
Mlynarczyk, Ernest	29:41:33	Poland	2019	48	M	1
Lam, Bryan	29:41:56	DC	2019	37	M	1
George, Jeremy	29:42:05	CO	2019	30	M	1
Lucarelli, Charles	29:42:05	CO	2019	37	M	1
Robbins, Amy	29:42:05	IN	2019	49	F	1
Welsh, Shane	29:42:19	CO	2019	30	M	1
Strand, Eric	29:42:39	MO	2019	58	M	8
Soriano, Franco	29:43:01	CA	2019	48	M	1
Witman, Matthew	29:43:25	CO	2019	33	M	1
Bennett, Andrea	29:43:52	SD	2019	40	F	2
Pulver, Joe	29:44:08	MI	2019	60	M	1
Gray, Wesley	29:44:13	PA	2019	39	M	1
Steiner, Brian	29:44:23	OK	2019	30	M	1
Acosta, Alina	29:45:00	IL	2019	24	F	1
England, Tiffany	29:46:29	NY	2019	35	F	2
Blakemore, Conan	29:46:41	CO	2019	36	M	2
Service, Patrick	29:46:59	CA	2019	35	M	1

Ellers, Forrest	29:47:19	NM	2019	27	M	1
Guardia, Felipe	29:47:30	Costa Rica	2019	43	M	1
Sakiewicz, Paul	29:48:07	CO	2019	53	M	2
Newell, Jim	29:48:26	CO	2019	65	M	1
Cedergren, Ola	29:48:28	Sweden	2019	46	M	1
Hurelbrink, Michael	29:49:09	CO	2019	44	M	1
Crouse, Casey	29:49:20	IN	2019	31	M	1
Drake, Brent	29:49:29	TX	2019	42	M	2
Kelly, Erin	29:49:30	CO	2019	34	F	1
Bartzen, Gene	29:49:39	CO	2019	65	M	11
Allen, Brandon	29:49:51	AR	2019	37	M	1
Gagnon, Joseph	29:49:54	NY	2019	58	M	2
Waggoner, Josiah	29:49:55	CO	2019	32	M	1
Scott, John	29:50:01	CO	2019	54	M	3
Lyhne, Jacob	29:50:20	CO	2019	44	M	1
Garcia, Paul	29:50:50	IL	2019	45	M	1
Nazarewicz, Rafal	29:51:37	CA	2019	45	M	1
Gray, Amy	29:52:14	CO	2019	35	F	1
Smith, Jenny	29:52:32	CO	2019	36	F	1
Straw, Keith	29:53:04	PA	2019	64	M	4
Martin, Kyle	29:53:28	AR	2019	37	M	3
Siebold, Carl John	29:53:29	Guatemala	2019	42	M	1
D'Angelo, Heather	29:55:15	CO	2019	27	F	1
Hanousek, Jan	29:56:08	Czech Republic	2019	55	M	2
Gates, Jason	29:56:35	TX	2019	38	M	1
Bawden, Toosie	29:56:45	England	2019	39	F	1
Gooden, Armin	29:56:51	CO	2019	40	M	1

** Denotes original finisher

***

Printed in Great Britain
by Amazon